D1570569

The Cartulary of Chatteris Abbey

The fifteenth-century cartulary of the Benedictine nunnery of Chatteris abbey in Cambridgeshire (founded in the early eleventh century) has important implications for the study of women religious, especially in the light of the small number of surviving cartularies from English nunneries. The manuscript contains copies of documents dating from the mid-twelfth to the fifteenth centuries; this critical edition comprises a full transcription, together with historical notes and apparatus. The introduction draws on the cartulary itself, as well as manorial and episcopal records, to analyse the nunnery's relationship with its patron, the bishop of Ely, and the development and management of its estates; it also examines the location and layout of the abbey, the social and geographical origins of the nuns, and the production and organisation of the cartulary. The edition is accompanied by an annotated list of all known abbesses, prioresses and nuns.

CLAIRE BREAY gained her Ph.D. at the Institute of Historical Research in the University of London; she is currently a curator of medieval manuscripts at the British Library.

The Cartulary of Chatteris Abbey

EDITED BY

Claire Breay

THE BOYDELL PRESS

First published 1999

Published by The Boydell Press
an imprint of Boydell & Brewer Ltd
PO Box 9, Woodbridge, Suffolk IP12 3DF, UK
and of Boydell & Brewer Inc.
PO Box 41026, Rochester, NY 14604–4126, USA
website: http://www.boydell.co.uk

ISBN 0 85115 750 5

A catalogue record for this book is available
from the British Library

Library of Congress Cataloging-in-Publication Data
applied for

This publication is printed on acid-free paper

Printed in Great Britain by
St Edmundsbury Press Ltd, Bury St Edmunds, Suffolk

Contents

List of Illustrations   vii

Abbreviated References   viii

Abbreviations   xi

Acknowledgements   xiii

I   **The Cartulary of Chatteris Abbey and the History of English Nunneries**   1

II   **The Foundation and Patronage of Chatteris Abbey**   8

III   **The Endowment**   25

The development and extent of the abbey's endowment   25
    Temporalities   25
    Spiritualities   33

The value of the abbey's temporalities and spiritualities   37

The chronology, type and size of donations made to the abbey   41

The abbey's benefactors   45

Donations to the abbey for purposes specified by the benefactors   49

Dowry-grants   51

Bequests to Chatteris abbey   54

IV   **The Management of the Estate**   58

Purchases, sales and exchanges made by the abbey   58

The abbey's methods of exploiting its estates   62

The sale and consumption of agricultural produce   70

Mills   71

Manorial courts   74

The abbey's officials   76

vi   *Contents*

V   **The Abbey**   79

      The site, plan and seal of the abbey   79

      The nuns   96

      Chaplains, servants and lay-sisters   104

VI   **The Production and Arrangement of the Cartulary**   107

VII   **Editorial Method**   132

VIII **The Cartulary of Chatteris Abbey and an Original Charter** 138

      Appendix 1: The Known Abbesses, Prioresses, Nuns and Lay-
           sister of Chatteris   391

           Chronological list of the known abbesses   391

           Chronological list of the known prioresses   402

           Alphabetical list of the known abbesses, prioresses, nuns
                and lay-sister   403

      Appendix 2: The Inventory of Chatteris Abbey, 1538   415

      Bibliography   423

      Index   435

List of Illustrations

1   Map showing the location of the estates of Chatteris abbey   28

2   Ordnance Surveyors' Drawings, 2 inch, Cambs., Hunts. and Norf.:
    sheet 250 (1810)   81

3   Ordnance Survey, 25 inch, 1st edn, Cambs.: sheet 20. 16 (1888)   83

4   Watercolour of Park House from the east   90

5   Watercolour of Park House from the south-west   90

6   The seal attached to no. 281, the early thirteenth-century gift by
    abbess Agnes and the convent of Chatteris to Geoffrey son of
    Eustace of half an acre of land in Madingley (Cambridge, St
    John's College Archive, D 25. 22)   94

7   The signatures of the abbess, prioress and nuns of Chatteris
    abbey in the margin of the surrender of the abbey, 3 September
    1538 (PRO E 322/53)   97

8   Examples of the main hand of the cartulary (details of fos. 126r   109
    and 175r)

Abbreviated References

Ault ed. *Ramsey Court Rolls*   W. O. Ault ed. *Court Rolls of the Abbey of Ramsey and of the Honour of Clare* (New Haven, 1928).

Book of Fees   *Liber Feodorum. The Book of Fees Commonly Called Testa de Nevill* 2 vols in 3 (PRO Texts and Calendars, 1920, 1923, 1931).

Cal. IPM   *Calendar of Inquisitions Post Mortem and Other* Analogous *Documents Preserved in the Public Record Office* (PRO Texts and Calendars, 1904–).

CCR   *Calendar of the Close Rolls Preserved in the Public Record Office* (PRO Texts and Calendars, 1892–1963).

CPR   *Calendar of the Patent Rolls Preserved in the Public Record Office* (PRO Texts and Calendars, 1891–).

CRR   *Curia Regis Rolls Preserved in the Public Record Office* (PRO Texts and Calendars, 1922–).

Cambs. Fines   *Pedes Finium: or Fines, Relating to the County of Cambridge, Levied in the King's Court from the Seventh Year of Richard I to the End of the Reign of Richard III* ed. W. Rye (Cambridge Antiquarian Society, octavo ser. xxvi, 1891).

Cur. Reg. R.   *Curia Regis Rolls* (PRO Texts and Calendars, 1922–).

Domesday Book   *Domesday Book, seu Liber Censualis Willelmi Primi* 2 vols (London, 1783).

Mon. Ang.   *W. Dugdale Monasticon Anglicanum* ed. J. Caley, H. Ellis and B. Bandinel, 6 vols in 8 (London, 1817–30).

Farrer *Honors*   W. Farrer *Honors and Knights' Fees* 3 vols (London, 1923–5).

Fasti 1066–1300 i   J. le Neve *Fasti Ecclesiae Anglicanae 1066–1300* i *St Paul's, London* comp. D. E. Greenway (London, 1968).

Fasti 1066–1300 ii   J. le Neve *Fasti Ecclesiae Anglicanae 1066–1300* ii *Monastic Cathedrals* comp. D. E. Greenway (London, 1971).

Fasti 1066–1300 iii	J. le Neve *Fasti Ecclesiae Anglicanae 1066–1300* iii *Lincoln* comp. D. E. Greenway (London, 1977).
Fasti 1300–1541 iv	*Fasti Ecclesiae Anglicanae 1300–1541* iv *Monastic Cathedrals* (Southern Province) comp. B. Jones (London, 1963).
Fasti 1300–1541 v	J. le Neve *Fasti Ecclesiae Anglicanae 1300–1541* v *St Paul's, London* comp. J. M. Horn (London, 1963).
Feudal Aids	*Inquisitions and Assessments Relating to Feudal Aids; with Other Analagous Documents Preserved in the Public Record Office A.D. 1284–1431* 6 vols (PRO Texts and Calendars, 1899–1920).
Hunts. Fines	*A Calendar of the Feet of Fines Relating to the County of Huntingdon Levied in the King's Court from the Fifth Year of Richard I to the End of the Reign of Elizabeth 1194–1603* ed. G. J. Turner (Cambridge Antiquarian Society, octavo ser. xxxvii, 1913).
Liber Eliensis ed. Blake	*Liber Eliensis* ed. E.O. Blake (Camden 3rd ser. xcii, 1962).
Liber de Bernewelle ed. Clark	*Liber Memorandorum Ecclesie de Bernewelle* ed. J. W. Clark (Cambridge, 1907).
Norf. Fines 1198–1202	*Feet of Fines for the County of Norfolk for the Tenth Year of the Reign of King Richard the First 1189–1199 and for the First Four Years of the Reign of King John 1199–1202* ed. B. Dodwell (Pipe Roll Society, new ser. xxvii, 1950).
Norf. and Suff. Fines	*Feet of Fines for the County of Norfolk for the Reign of King John 1201–1215, for the County of Suffolk for the Reign of King John 1199–1214* ed. B. Dodwell (Pipe Roll Society, new ser. xxxii, 1956).
Palmer 'The Clerical Poll Tax of 1379 in Cambridge-shire'	W. M. Palmer 'A List of Cambridgeshire Subsidy Rolls: The Clerical Poll Tax of 1379 in Cambridge-shire' *The East Anglian* new ser. xiii (1909–10) pp. 121–2.
Papsturkunden in England	*Papsturkunden in England* ed. W. Holtzmann, 3 vols (Abhandlungen der Gesellschaft der Wissenschaften zu Göttingen, Phil.-Hist. Klasse, new series xxv, 3rd series xiv–xv, xxxiii; Berlin, 1930, 1935–6, Göttingen, 1952).

Pipe R.	*The Great Roll of the Pipe* (Pipe Roll Society, 1884–).
R. Cur. Reg.	*Rotuli Curiae Regis. Rolls and Records of the Court Held Before the King's Justiciars or Justices* ed. F. Palgrave, 2 vols (Record Commission, 1835).
Reg. Gravesend	*Registrum Radulphi Baldock, Gilberti Segrave, Ricardi Newport et Stephani Gravesend, Episcoporum Londoniensium 1304–1338* ed. R.C. Fowler (Canterbury and York Society vii, 1911).
Rot. Hund.	*Rotuli Hundredorum Temp. Hen. III et Edw. I in Turr' Lond' et in Curia Receptae Scaccarii West. Asservati* eds W. Illingworth and J. Caley, 2 vols (Record Commission, 1812–18).
Rot. Litt. Pat.	*Rotuli Litterarum Patentium in Turri Londinensi Asservati* ed. T. D. Hardy, i, part i (Record Commission, 1835).
VCH Cambs.	*The Victoria History of the Counties of England. Cambridge and the Isle of Ely* 9 vols, ii ed. L. F. Saltzman, iv ed. R. B. Pugh, v ed. C. R. Elrington, viii ed. A. P. M. Wright, ix eds A. P. M. Wright and C.P. Lewis (London, 1948–89).
VCH Herts.	*The Victoria History of the Counties of England. Hertfordshire* 4 vols, iii–iv ed. W. Page (London, 1912–14).
VCH Hunts.	*The Victoria History of the Counties of England. Huntingdonshire* 3 vols, ii eds W. Page, G. Proby and S. I. Ladds (London, 1932).
VCH Shrops.	*The Victoria History of the Counties of England. Shropshire* 11 vols, i ed. W. Page, ii ed. A. T. Gaydon (London, 1908, 1973).
VCH Wilts.	*The Victoria History of the Counties of England. Wiltshire* 15 vols, iii eds R. B. Pugh and E. Crittall (London, 1956).
Visitations of Religious Houses ed. Thompson	*Visitations of Religious Houses in the Diocese of Lincoln* ed. A. H. Thompson, 3 vols (Canterbury and York Society xvii, xxiv, xxxiii; 1915, 1919, 1927).

Abbreviations

CCRO	Cambridgeshire County Record Office
corr. marg.	corrected in margin
EDC	Ely Dean and Chapter
EDR	Ely Diocesan Registry
ins. marg.	inserted in margin
par.	parish
PRO	Public Record Office
UL	University Library

Note

All places are in Cambridgeshire unless otherwise stated.

Publication of this volume was aided by a grant from the Scouloudi Foundation, in association with the Institute of Historical Research. It was further assisted by a grant from the Isobel Thornley Bequest Fund of the University of London.

In memory of
John Breay
and
Annie Procter

Acknowledgements

This book is based on my University of London doctoral thesis and I am grateful to the British Academy for awarding a three-year postgraduate studentship to me.

I wish to thank the staff of: the Institute of Historical Research; the Manuscripts Students' Room in the British Library; Lambeth Palace Library; the Public Record Office; Cambridge University Library Manuscripts Room; Cambridge County Record Office; the Library of Trinity College Cambridge; and the Bodleian Library. Figures 2, 3 and 8 are published by permission of the British Library and figure 7 by permission of the Public Record Office. I am indebted to the Master, Fellows and Scholars of St John's College Cambridge for allowing me to publish one of their charters (D 25. 22) and to reproduce a photograph of its seal (figure 6), and I am grateful to Malcolm Underwood, the college's archivist, for all his help. I also wish to thank Andrew Spooner and Helen Pope for allowing me to see and photograph the nineteenth-century watercolours of Park House in Chatteris which incorporated some of the remains of the abbey.

I am grateful for the help, advice and references I received from Dr Janet Burton, Professor Barrie Dobson, Dr Joan Greatrex, Dr Rosemary Horrox, who first encouraged me to embark on research in medieval history, Professor Jane Sayers, Professor David Smith, who suggested that I should edit this cartulary, and Pru Harrison at Boydell & Brewer.

I received much moral as well as academic support during the years I spent working on the cartulary of Chatteris abbey. For this I thank my parents, Jane Ellis and Terry Breay, and also Jane Breay, Stephen Lovell, Irena Nicoll, Mared Owen, Emma Soares and Aidan Timlin. Most especially, I thank Martin Norris for helping to convert my text into camera-ready copy, for producing the map showing the location of the abbey's estates, and for his unfailing kindness and forbearance.

Finally, I owe the greatest debt to Professor Diana Greenway, my supervisor, for all her advice and encouragement, and for taking me to Chatteris and to the sites of the abbey's other estates in Cambridgeshire, Hertfordshire and Suffolk. I am very grateful for all her help and for her friendship.

I

The Cartulary of Chatteris Abbey and the History of English Nunneries

After Eileen Power published *Medieval English Nunneries c. 1275–1535* in 1922, English nunneries attracted little attention for more than 50 years.[1] Power studied only later medieval nunneries and used a limited range of printed sources. She believed that most nuns were drawn from the upper levels of society but that most nunneries were beset with poverty. She also emphasized what she perceived to be the financial mismanagement and the declining religious and moral standards in English nunneries in the later medieval period. Although the 50 years after the publication of *Medieval English Nunneries* saw several works on individual houses for women, Power's arguments went largely unchallenged until the 1970s.[2]

It is only in the last two decades that medieval nunneries have attracted far more research. Much of this work has concentrated on the foundation and early history of nunneries in the twelfth and thirteenth centuries, a period largely ignored by Power.[3] In their work on this period, Sharon Elkins and Sally Thompson have emphasized the links between religious women and the men

---

[1] E. Power *Medieval English Nunneries c. 1275–1535* (Cambridge, 1922).

[2] Work on nunneries before the 1970s includes: *Cartulary of St Mary Clerkenwell* ed. W. O. Hassall (Camden 3rd ser. lxxi, 1949); W. M. Sturman 'The History of the Nunnery of St Mary and St Michael Outside Stamford', M.A. thesis (University of London, 1946); W. M. Sturman 'Barking Abbey. A Study in its Internal and External Administration from the Conquest to the Dissolution', Ph.D. thesis (University of London, 1961); J. Wake and W. A. Pantin 'Delapré Abbey, its History and Architecture' *Northamptonshire Past and Present* ii (1958) pp. 225–41.

[3] J. Burton *The Yorkshire Nunneries in the Twelfth and Thirteenth Centuries* (Borthwick Paper no. 56; York, 1979); S. K. Elkins *Holy Women of Twelfth-Century England* (Chapel Hill, North Carolina, 1988); B. Golding *Gilbert of Sempringham and the Gilbertine Order c. 1130–c. 1300* (Oxford, 1995); C. V. Graves 'Stixwould in the Market-Place' in *Distant Echoes. Medieval Religious Women* i, eds J. A. Nichols and L. T. Shank (Kalamazoo, Michigan, 1984) pp. 213–35; S. Thompson *Women Religious: the Founding of English Nunneries after the Norman Conquest* (Oxford, 1991).

who were their patrons, their priests and their fellow-members of double houses. They have also integrated the history of female hermits and anchoresses into their work on women religious, showing the variety of origins from which houses for women could develop. Other research, which has focused on later medieval nunneries, has largely repudiated Power's conclusions. For example, John Tillotson's study of Marrick priory (Yorks. N.) showed that this remote nunnery drew its recruits mainly from the local lesser landholding families and that, though undoubtedly poor, it was able to attract local support for its religious and charitable activities.[1] Marilyn Oliva and Catherine Paxton found that most of the nunneries in East Anglia and London were not aristocratic institutions but that, like Marrick, they drew the majority of their recruits and donations from local families of middling status. Oliva and Paxton also showed that benefactors and testators actively supported these nunneries throughout the later medieval period.[2] Similarly, Clementhorpe priory – which lay just outside the city of York – attracted numerous bequests in the century and a half before its dissolution. Some of these bequests came from the Yorkshire gentry and from local clerics, but most came from the wealthier members of the local laity.[3]

Jackie Mountain examined Power's assertion that the poverty faced by so many nunneries was rooted in financial incompetence. She found that the problem of debt faced by many late medieval nunneries had more to do with inadequate endowments than incompetent administration.[4] In addition, Tillotson concluded in his study of Yorkshire nunneries that, although the behaviour of certain nuns continued to cause scandal, none of the houses had persistent difficulty in remaining reasonably reputable in the two centuries before the Dissolution.[5] Given the cumulative weight of the arguments in opposition to Power's work, it is striking how long-lived her influence has been. Nevertheless a new consensus seems to have emerged that most nunneries were moderately

1 J. H. Tillotson *Marrick Priory: a Nunnery in Late Medieval Yorkshire* (Borthwick Paper no. 75; York, 1989).
2 M. Oliva *The Convent and the Community in Late Medieval England: Female Monasteries in the Diocese of Norwich, 1350–1540* (Woodbridge, 1998); C. Paxton 'The Nunneries of London and its Environs in the Later Middle Ages', D.Phil. thesis (University of Oxford, 1992).
3 R. B. Dobson and S. Donaghey *The History of Clementhorpe Nunnery* (The Archaeology of York ii, fasc. i, 1984) pp. 22–5.
4 J. Mountain 'Nunnery Finances in the Early Fifteenth Century' in *Monastic Studies* ii *The Continuity of Tradition* ed. J. Loades (Bangor, 1991) pp. 263–72.
5 J. H. Tillotson 'Visitation and Reform of the Yorkshire Nunneries in the Fourteenth Century' *Northern History* xxx (1994) pp. 1–21.

or poorly-endowed local institutions which were supported by local people whose needs they met.

In spite of the increased interest in nunneries in recent years, the cartulary of Chatteris abbey (Cambs.) has been used little by historians. One reason for the neglect of the cartulary (BL Cotton MS Julius A. i, fos. 72–188) is probably that it was damaged by the fire which broke out in 1731 in Ashburnham House, Little Dean's Yard, Westminster, where the Cotton library was then housed. Many folios, particularly towards the end of the cartulary, have been badly distorted by the fire. A substantial proportion of the folios contain holes, many suffer from the offsetting of the ink on to the opposite folio and some have dark patches caused by damp. Nineteenth-century repairs have further impaired the legibility of the manuscript since the repair-tissue, which is attached to the parchment around the holes, makes the text underneath difficult or impossible to read. However most of the cartulary is legible and many difficult passages may be read with the help of an optical fibre light-cable or under ultra-violet light. The light-cable is especially useful for reading text hidden underneath repair-tissue, whilst ultra-violet light makes it possible to read some words and passages where the ink has faded or been offset. Although the latter part of the manuscript does present difficulties, the Chatteris cartulary was far less badly damaged in the Cotton fire than many other manuscripts such as the cartulary of Nunkeeling priory, a Benedictine nunnery in the East Riding of Yorkshire.[1]

The neglect of the Chatteris cartulary as a source for the history of medieval nuns probably stems less from the illegibility of a small proportion of the manuscript than from the abbey's status as a poor and late Anglo-Saxon foundation. Chatteris was by far the poorest of the eight nunneries which occur in Domesday Book.[2] It was also the last Anglo-Saxon nunnery to be established: it was founded in the early eleven th century – *c.* 1007 × 1016 – whereas all the other Anglo-Saxon nunneries had been founded before the end of the tenth century. As well as being poor and a late foundation, Chatteris abbey was geographically isolated from the other nunneries in the country. Six of the nine nunneries which survived after 1066 – Shaftesbury, Romsey, Winchester, Wherwell, Amesbury and Wilton – lay in the three adjoining southern counties of Dorset, Hampshire and Wiltshire within a radius of 20 miles; the nearest pre-Conquest nunneries to Chatteris were Barking abbey in south-west Essex and

---

1 BL Cotton MS Otho C. viii, fos. 65–95.
2 D. Knowles *The Monastic Order in England. A History of its Development from the Times of St Dunstan to the Fourth Lateran Council 940–1216* 2nd edn (Cambridge, 1963) pp. 702–3.

Polesworth abbey in north Warwickshire. Chatteris abbey was also different from the other Anglo-Saxon nunneries because it alone was founded by a bishop – Eadnoth, bishop of Dorchester – rather than by a king or queen. As a result Chatteris did not attract the substantial royal and aristocratic patronage which allowed the nunneries at Shaftesbury (Dorset), Wilton (Wilts.), Barking (Essex) and Romsey (Hants.) to accumulate extensive estates.[1]

As a poor Anglo-Saxon house without royal connections, Chatteris abbey seems to have fallen between two stools. Historians working on pre-Conquest houses have concentrated on the richer, aristocratic, Anglo-Saxon foundations in the south and have given little attention to Chatteris.[2] On the other hand, historians working on nunneries in the post-Conquest period have focused either on those same, rich, Anglo-Saxon houses or, more especially, on the nunneries founded after 1066.[3] In addition to the emphasis given to post-Conquest foundations, much recent work on nunneries has concentrated on the new orders, again excluding the pre-Conquest, Benedictine abbey at Chatteris.[4]

Despite the difficulties of the manuscript and the fact that Chatteris was a poor Anglo-Saxon foundation, the lack of attention which the cartulary has received is surprising. The amount of research on medieval English nunneries has increased enormously in the last 20 years but historians of women's religious houses have faced the problem that most nunneries are less well recorded than many monasteries. Previously the relative scarcity of sources for nunneries was used to justify the scant attention given to women religious. In his preface to the second volume of *The Religious Orders in England*, Knowles defended his neglect of nunneries by stating that, 'immediate or detailed records of the nun-

---

1 D. Knowles and R. N. Hadcock *Medieval Religious Houses: England and Wales* 2nd edn (London, 1971) pp. 253–68.

2 D. K. Coldicott *Hampshire Nunneries* (Chichester, 1989); M. A. Meyer 'Patronage of the West Saxon Royal Nunneries in Late Anglo-Saxon England' in *Revue Bénédictine* xci (1981) pp. 332–58; B. Yorke '"Sisters Under the Skin?" Anglo-Saxon Nuns and Nunneries in Southern England' in *Medieval Women in Southern England* (Reading Medieval Studies xv, 1989) pp. 95–117.

3 K. Cooke 'Donors and Daughters: Shaftesbury Abbey's Benefactors, Endowments and Nuns c. 1086–1130' in *Anglo-Norman Studies* xii *Proceedings of the Battle Conference 1989* (Woodbridge, 1990) pp. 29–45; Burton *Yorkshire Nunneries*; Elkins *Holy Women*; Thompson *Women Religious*.

4 Golding *Gilbert of Sempringham*; S. K. Elkins 'The Emergence of a Gilbertine Identity' in *Distant Echoes* eds Nichols and Shank, pp. 131–50; Elkins *Holy Women*; J. A. Nichols 'Medieval Cistercian Nunneries and English Bishops' in *Distant Echoes* eds Nichols and Shank, pp. 237–49; J. A. Nichols 'The Internal Organization of English Cistercian Nunneries' *Cîteaux* xxx (1979) pp. 23–40; Thompson *Women Religious*.

neries are almost entirely wanting from the whole period between *c.* 1200 and the Dissolution'.[1] More recently historians of nunneries have challenged this assumption. They have shown that even though many nunneries left few surviving records, much information about these houses can be found in other local records, in the archives of bishops and in the records of central government. As Oliva points out, these records are the very same sources which historians of monasteries have always used.[2]

Although nunneries tend to have fewer of their own surviving records compared with monasteries, Chatteris abbey is one of the small minority whose endowments are recorded in a cartulary. The number of houses for women peaked at 146 in the century and a half before the Black Death.[3] However, there are only 19 extant cartularies from nunneries, one of which is the burnt manuscript from Nunkeeling priory (Yorks. E.), whilst two more – the cartularies of the priory of St Sepulchre in Canterbury (Kent) and of Westwood priory (Worcs.) – consist only of a few folios from the original manuscripts. It is impossible to say how many other houses once had a cartulary but 14 more cartularies are known to have existed at one time. Although they no longer survive, antiquarian copies preserve excerpts from nine of these lost manuscripts.[4] The charters and other documents copied into cartularies provide much information about the endowments and benefactors of religious houses. Since so few original nunnery cartularies still exist, the Chatteris manuscript is all the more significant for the history of medieval religious women.

Chatteris abbey has not previously been the subject of detailed study, but it provides important insights into the economic and social history of medieval nunneries. This is partly because its cartulary survives, but also because of its moderate size and wealth. As the poorest of the Anglo-Saxon nunneries, Chatteris has been overlooked. However, the foundation of many very poor nunneries after the Conquest meant that by the end of the twelfth century Chatteris was no longer exceptionally poor in comparison with other houses for women. Instead the profusion of new, under-endowed nunneries made the estates of Chatteris seem quite reasonable. For example, of the 11 houses for women in Norfolk and Suffolk, all of which were founded after the Conquest, only the Augustinian priory at Campsey Ash (Suff.) and the Gilbertine priory at Should-

[1] D. Knowles *The Religious Orders in England* ii (Cambridge, 1955) p. viii.

[2] Oliva *Convent and Community*, pp. 3–4.

[3] Knowles and Hadcock *Medieval Religious Houses* 2nd edn, p. 494.

[4] G. R. C. Davis *Medieval Cartularies of Great Britain. A Short Catalogue* (London, 1958); Thompson *Women Religious*, p. 8.

ham (Norf.) were worth more than Chatteris abbey at the Dissolution.[1] In 1535, when Chatteris abbey was valued at £97 3s. 4d., Campsey Ash was valued at £182 9s. 5d. and Shouldham at £138 18s. 1d.[2] Although Chatteris had received the core of its estates in the eleventh century, the cartulary shows that it continued to attract many donations in the twelfth and thirteenth centuries. It is possible to analyse the size and type of donation made to the abbey as well as the social status of benefactors. The conclusions drawn from these analyses may well be applicable to the many other houses for women of a similar size.

The new patterns in the foundation of nunneries after the Conquest made Chatteris abbey less exceptional in another respect. Whereas in 1066 Chatteris was the only nunnery which had been founded by a bishop rather than by a king or queen, by 1130 it was one of eight nunneries which had been founded or refounded by a bishop. The other seven were Malling abbey (Kent), the priory of St Sepulchre at Canterbury (Kent), Stratford-at-Bow priory (Middx), St Margaret's priory (Herts.), Brewood Black Ladies priory (Staffs.), Minster priory (Kent) and Clementhorpe priory outside York.[3] Elkins points out that the enthusiasm of the Norman episcopate for the foundation of houses for women was in contrast to the behaviour of the Norman barons. Whilst the barons were active patrons of nunneries in Normandy, they founded at most three nunneries in England in the six decades after 1066. During the same period the kings and queens of England founded none.[4]

Chatteris abbey's size and its episcopal patron mean that the abbey's cartulary is an important source for the history of moderately-sized nunneries and for nunneries whose patron was a bishop, but it is of course most useful for the history of Chatteris abbey itself. It is a particularly important source for the history of the abbey since so few other documents produced by the abbey still exist and since all the original charters once kept there have been lost. The loss of the muniments is unfortunate because the scribe who copied the cartulary omitted most of the witness-lists, making it difficult in many cases to date charters accurately.

---

1 R. Gilchrist and M. Oliva *Religious Women in Medieval East Anglia: History and Archaeology c. 1100–1540* (Studies in East Anglian History i; Norwich, 1993) p. 24.
2 *Valor Ecclesiasticus Temp. Henr. VIII Auctoritate Regia Institutus* ed. J. Caley, iii (Record Commission, 1817) pp. 499, 416, 378.
3 Elkins *Holy Women*, pp. 14–18.
4 Ibid. pp. 13–14.

Apart from the cartulary and a single original charter preserved at St John's College Cambridge,[1] the only other extant documents produced by the nunnery are manorial court rolls. Most of the rolls which survive are from the abbey's south Cambridgeshire manor of Foxton with members; one group dates from the late thirteenth and early fourteenth centuries and another from the late fifteenth and early sixteenth centuries.[2] There are also a few court rolls from the abbey's manor at Barley (Herts.) which date from the 1460s and the early sixteenth century.[3] As well as the documents produced by the nunnery itself, the hundred rolls for 1279 contain detailed information about the abbey's lands in southern Cambridgeshire.[4] The hundred rolls shed much light on the way in which the abbey was administering its estate in 1279, but the absence of account rolls and rentals from the nunnery makes it impossible to investigate the economy of the abbey in detail. Although there is not a wide range of surviving material from the abbey itself, the records of the bishops of Ely provide more information about the nunnery. The bishops' registers show the bishops exercising their spiritual authority over the nunnery by overseeing the election of abbesses, professing nuns and visiting the abbey.[5] In addition central government records contain much detail about the abbey at the end of its life. These records include an inventory of the abbey, a list of the nuns at the surrender of the abbey in 1538 and the post-Dissolution minister's accounts for the former abbey's lands.[6]

The introduction looks next at the foundation of the nunnery and the nature of its relationship with its patron, the bishop of Ely. The third chapter analyses the endowment of the abbey, examining how it developed, how much its temporalities and spiritualities were worth, who the benefactors were and what they gave. Chapter four investigates the ways in which the abbey exploited and administered its estates. The fifth chapter examines the location of the abbey, the layout of its buildings and the social and geographical origins of the nuns. The introduction concludes with a chapter on the production and arrangement of the manuscript, followed by a description of the editorial method used in the transcription.

---

[1] Cambridge, St John's College Archives, D 25. 22.
[2] Cambridge, Trinity College Archives, Foxton 1–6; CCRO L 63/17–18.
[3] PRO SC 2/177/1; CCRO L 63/18, rot. 12d.
[4] *Rot. Hund.* ii, pp. 446, 448, 465–6, 478, 514, 543–4, 548, 559, 560–2.
[5] Cambridge UL, EDR G/1/1–7.
[6] PRO E 117/11/13; E 322/53; SC 6 Hen VIII/266–74.

II

The Foundation and Patronage of Chatteris Abbey

The first document copied into the cartulary, after the opening request for prayers, is a narrative taken from the *Liber Eliensis*.[1] The narrative describes the discovery of the body of St Ivo at St Ives and its translation to Ramsey abbey (Hunts.) by the abbot, Eadnoth. This is followed by a brief reference to the foundation of Chatteris abbey by Eadnoth, who had become bishop of Dorchester and whose sister, Ælfwen, became the first abbess:

> circa condendas ecclesias et augendas congregationes assiduus insistebat quarum unam apud Chatriz ob amorem sancte Dei genetricis Marie et Alfwenne, sororis sue cognomento domine, ad ponendas ibi cum ipsa sanctimoniales construxit et rebus necessariis ampliavit.[2]

The accuracy of this statement is hard to judge. If the narrative in the cartulary reflects the true origins of the abbey, it must have been founded in 1007 × 1016 since Eadnoth became bishop of Dorchester in 1007 × 1009 and died at the battle of *Assandun* on 18 October 1016. The only other evidence for the foundation of the abbey is an entry in *Monasticon Anglicanum* the original of which has not been traced. Under the heading *In Evidences de Chateriz per Johannem Stivecle*, and with the source described as *Ex Munimentis Abbatie de Chateriz*, the entry begins:

> Item Alwen, le mere Aylwyn founda l'abbey de nonnes de Chatteriz per assent de luy, come en sa toumbe mencion est fait; et l'abbesse tenoit de roy en chefe auxi come fait l'abbe tanqe le roy H. le primier dona la patronage des ditz noneins a Henrie[3] euesqe de Ely.[4]

In contrast to the narrative in the cartulary, this extract ascribes the foundation to Ælfwen rather than to her brother Eadnoth. Camden and Tanner, too, state

---

1 *Liber Eliensis* ed. Blake, pp. 140–2. The narrative appears in Book II of the *Liber Eliensis* which was completed after 1154 (Ibid. p. xlviii).
2 No. 2, fo. 73r.
3 Recte *Hervie*.
4 *Mon. Ang.* ii, p. 616.

that Ælfwen was the foundress.[1] It is impossible to know which version is more true though Ælfwen may, perhaps, have been the instigator of the foundation and Eadnoth the actual founder.

Sally Thompson's work on post-Conquest nunneries may be equally applicable to Chatteris abbey. She emphasizes the obscurity of the early years of many nunneries and argues that this obscurity does not necessarily derive solely from the scarcity of relevant sources, but may sometimes result from houses having evolved slowly around an anchoress or in association with hospitals or monasteries.[2] In many cases, the very concept of foundation at a particular time and place and by a particular person may be misleading since it suggests that the creation of a religious house was a single event rather than a gradual process.

A late twelfth-century kalendar for Ely provides a tantalizing suggestion of a link between the abbey and at least one religious woman. An entry in the kalendar reads, *xi kal. Mar. Ob. Ægelmer' comes et soror nostra Herewen anachorita*.[3] It is tempting to speculate that this may be evidence that Ely abbey was associated with one or more local religious women in the pre-Conquest period, perhaps before the foundation of Chatteris abbey. More speculatively still, other such women could perhaps have been the nucleus around which Eadnoth, bishop of Dorchester and former abbot of Ramsey, formally established a nunnery at Chatteris. In the absence of other evidence, there can be no proof. It is not possible even to assess how genuine the link between Eadnoth and Chatteris abbey was and whether he did indeed, if not necessarily found the abbey, at least formalize the establishment of a community of religious women there. However, the inclusion in the cartulary of the narrative about Eadnoth, which refers briefly to his foundation of the abbey, shows at least that the compiler of the cartulary thought it important to define the origin of the abbey. The cartulary not only records the acquisition by the abbey of property and privileges, it also seeks to assign the foundation of the abbey to a particular, noteworthy person. The reality of the creation of the nunnery may have been more complicated, but the details of this early history had probably been lost by the time of the compilation of the cartulary.

In the early twelfth century, Chatteris abbey became associated with the bishop of the newly created diocese of Ely. Having established the diocese in 1109 from part of the enormous diocese of Lincoln, Henry I gave rights over

---

[1] W. Camden *Britannia* 2nd edn, ii (London, 1806) p. 235; T. Tanner *Notitia Monastica* (London, 1744) p. 40.

[2] Thompson *Women Religious*, part 1.

[3] Cambridge, Trinity College MS O. 2. 1, fo. k2v.

Chatteris abbey to Ely cathedral and Hervey, the first bishop, in 1127 × 1129 (no. 5). The motivation behind this gift is obscure but, by the time of the creation of the diocese of Ely, the king no longer had the extensive lands at his disposal which had been available for royal patronage immediately after the Conquest. By giving rights over Chatteris abbey to the bishop, the king could appear munificent without giving away any more land.

The wording of Henry I's charter suggests that the rights granted over the abbey were very extensive, amounting to the subordination of the abbey to the bishop:

> Sciatis me dedisse et concessisse Deo et Elyensi ecclesie et Herveo episcopo in elimosinam abbatiam de Chateriz cum terris et possessionibus et omnibus rebus eidem abbatie pertinentibus. Et volo et precipio firmiter ut bene et in pace et quiete et honorifice teneat cum saca et socha et toll et theam et infanganetheof et omnibus consuetudinibus et libertatibus sicut melius et quietius et honorificentius tenet alias terras suas de episcopatu de Ely.

The impression created by this charter is reinforced by two papal privileges issued by popes Innocent II and Lucius II, in 1138 and 1144 respectively (nos. 270 and 269). These privileges, which were copied into the *Liber Eliensis* as well as into the cartulary, include the confirmation to bishop Nigel and Ely cathedral of their possession of Chatteris abbey. The privilege of Lucius II also confirms to Nigel and Ely cathedral the remission of the ward-penny owed by Chatteris abbey. When Henry I granted the remission of the ward-penny to the abbey, he stated that he did so at the petition of bishop Hervey (no. 6). An entry on the pipe roll for Michaelmas 1130 shows that the bishop became responsible for its payment: *Et idem episcopus [Heveius episcopus de Ely] debet CC et xl li. ut rex clamet eum quietum de superplus militum episcopatus et ut abbatia de Cateriz sit quieta de warpenna.*[1] These documents show that, in some respects, the ties between Chatteris abbey and the bishop and cathedral of Ely were close, but they do not mention patronage explicitly. Henry I's charter to bishop Hervey is very different from the charter in which king John granted the patronage of Thorney abbey to the bishop of Ely in 1215. Unlike Henry I, John spelt out all the rights of the bishop as patron.[2] Nevertheless it seems that the effect of Henry's charter was to confer the patronage of Chatteris abbey on the bishop.

---

1 *The Pipe Roll of 31 Henry I* ed. J. Hunter (Record Commission, 1833; reprinted 1929 from 1833 edn) p. 44.
2 *Mon. Ang.* ii, pp. 605–6.

John Stukeley's *Evidences de Chateriz* state that *le roy H. le primier dona la patronage des ditz noneins a Hervie.*[1] Also, an inventory of the charters of Ely cathedral – compiled in the late thirteenth century or soon afterwards – uses the phrase 'concerning the patronage of the abbey' to describe the king's charter: *Carta eiusdem [Henrici primi regis Anglorum] eidem [Herveo episcopo] facta de patronatu abbatie de Chateryce.*[2] The compiler of the inventory thought that Henry I had made the bishop the patron of the abbey and his assumption is supported by the language of another extract from the *Liber Eliensis* in the cartulary (no. 4). This extract is a narrative which attributes the acquisition of the patronage of the nunnery to the efforts of bishop Hervey. It claims that the nunnery was suffering by remaining in the king's hand, *quamdiu sub manu regia versabatur, gravissimis angariis premebatur,* and that the nuns would not be able to continue living there without better patronage, *sine meliore patrocinio.* This shows that the compiler of the *Liber Eliensis* believed that the king had become the patron of the abbey between the death of Eadnoth and the reign of Henry I. The narrative describes how Hervey persuaded Henry I to give this patronage to him and the rights he acquired: *ut locum illum Eliensi ecclesie jure perpetue possessionis ascriberet et deinceps matres ibi statuendi et monachas imponendi principalem potestatem haberet.* It goes on to emphasize the importance to a nunnery of an effective male patron, claiming that Hervey did not have ulterior motives in seeking the patronage and that he merely wanted the nuns not to have to think of the morrow: *non, ut terreno commodo consuleret, sed, ut ancille Dei de crastino non cogitarent, allaboravit.* Despite such assurances, a patron could expect to benefit from his position, though what exactly the bishop of Ely gained is unclear: he may have been owed rent, renders or services by the nunnery, evidence for which is now lost, or else may have received only the prayers to which all patrons were entitled.

Although the compiler of the *Liber Eliensis* thought that the patronage of the abbey had passed into royal hands by the time of Henry I, Henry's charter may, in fact, have confirmed rather than given the patronage to bishop Hervey: the bishop of Ely may have inherited the patronage from the bishops of Dorchester and Lincoln. Since Eadnoth was bishop of Dorchester when the abbey was founded, and remained bishop until his death, it is likely that his successors in the see would indeed have inherited the patronage of Chatteris abbey. When the see was transferred from Dorchester to Lincoln *c.* 1067, the patronage of the abbey would presumably have passed to the bishop of Lincoln. In 1109 Henry I

---

[1] Ibid. p. 616.
[2] BL Cotton MS Nero C. iii, fo. 202r.

created the diocese of Ely from part of the diocese of Lincoln. Since Chatteris abbey lay within the new diocese of Ely, the acquisition of the patronage of the nunnery by the bishop of Ely may have been a transfer of patronage, confirmed by the king, from the bishop of Lincoln to the bishop of Ely, rather than a gift from the king.

The establishment of the bishop of Ely as the patron of Chatteris abbey in the late 1120s coincided with a period in which Norman bishops were the principal founders of nunneries in England. Between 1090 and 1130 bishops and archbishops founded six houses for women whilst archbishop William de Corbeil seems to have been instrumental in the refoundation of the ruined house at Minster in Sheppey (Kent).[1] This number of episcopal foundations is remarkable because lay people probably founded only two nunneries between the Conquest and 1130. Judith, niece of the Conqueror, founded Elstow abbey (Beds.) and Emma, daughter of the lord of Redlingfield, founded Redlingfield priory (Suff.); in addition, Roger de Montgomery may have played a part in the foundation of the priory at Lyminster (Sussex).[2] Therefore bishop Hervey of Ely became patron of Chatteris at a time when the bishops rather than the laity were most active in extending provision for, and authority over, religious women.

Despite the extent of the rights over Chatteris abbey which Henry I granted or confirmed to the bishop of Ely, few episcopal documents occur in the cartulary. Under the patronage of the bishop, the abbey continued to function as an independent house without interference from the bishop in the administration of its estates. There is no evidence that the bishop ever appointed a male *custos* to oversee or regulate the nunnery. Nevertheless, the patronage of the bishop did have wide-ranging effects on the abbey, one of which was tenurial. Henry I's charter to bishop Hervey seems to have changed the tenurial status of the abbess of Chatteris and, in particular, to have created a tenurial relationship between the abbess and the bishop of Ely. In 1086, the abbess was a tenant-in-chief of the king in Foxton, Burwell, Barrington, Shepreth, Orwell and Over (Cambs.), in Barley (Herts.) and in Kersey (Suff.).[3] The evidence which survives for some of these estates in the hundred rolls of 1279 shows that other tenants-

---

1 The six houses founded by bishops were: Malling abbey (Kent); the priory of St Sepulchre, Canterbury (Kent); Stratford-at-Bow priory (Middx); St Margaret's priory, Ivinghoe (Bucks.); Brewood Black Ladies priory (Staffs.) and Clementhorpe priory, York (Elkins *Holy Women*, pp. 14–18).

2 Ibid. pp. 13–14.

3 *Domesday Book* i, fos. 193a, 136b; ii, p. 389a.

in-chief, most notably the bishop of Ely, had been interposed between the king and the abbess after 1086.[1] In 1279, the lands of the nunnery's largest manor at Foxton were held in alms of the bishop:

> Dicunt quod abbatissa de Chateriz tenet in Foxton CCC acras terre arabilis, xxxij acras prati, xv acras pasture in puram et perpetuam elemosinam episcopi Elyensis, de quo episcopo non exstat memoria, et tenet visum franci plegii, assisam panis et cervisie per libertatem Elyensis, nescimus quo warranto.[2]

The hundred rolls also state that the abbess held her four virgates of land in Over of the bishop of Ely. The tenurial position of the abbess in Barrington and Shepreth was less straightforward. In 1279, the abbess of Chatteris was said to hold a fourth part of the vill of Barrington of the barony of Mountfitchet, but the nunnery's connection with the bishop meant that she was able to avoid most services *per libertatem Eliensem*. Similarly, the hundred rolls state that her hide and a half in Shepreth had been held of the fee of Boulogne but that it had been drawn into the liberty of Ely.[3]

The bishop of Ely was overlord of the nunnery's estate in Suffolk too: a presentment by the half-hundred of Cosford shows that, in the first half of the thirteenth century, Nesta de Cockfield held Kersey of the nuns of Chatteris and the bishop of Ely (no. 189). Although, in general, the cartulary shows that the abbey managed its lands independently, another document relating to Kersey suggests that in the mid-twelfth century the bishop may have exerted more influence. At the end of the century, the abbey confirmed the manor of Kersey to Adam son of Robert de Cockfield (no. 186). The confirmation states that previously Nigel, bishop of Ely, and Hadewisa, prioress of Chatteris, had granted and confirmed the manor to Adam de Cockfield, grandfather of Adam:

> Et volumus et concedimus ut manerium illud bene et honorifice teneat, in hominibus et bosco et plano et pratis et pasturis et omnibus aliis consuetudinibus eidem manerio juste pertinentibus, sicut episcopus Nigellus Eliensis ecclesie et Hadewisa quondam priorissa ecclesie nostre et conventus concesserunt Ade de Cokefeld' avo predicti Ade et heredibus suis et cartis suis confimaverunt.

---

[1] The imposition of a tenant-in-chief on a religious house founded before the Conquest is not unparalleled. For example, the minster of secular clerks at Wenlock (Shrops.), which was refounded by earl Roger de Montgomery as a Cluniac priory c. 1079 × 1082, appears in Domesday Book as one of his under-tenants (*VCH Shrops.* i, p. 291; ii, pp. 38–40). This is not directly comparable to the case of Chatteris abbey, though, since the nunnery was clearly still a tenant-in-chief in 1086 and refoundation was not involved in the alteration of its status.

[2] *Rot. Hund.* ii, p. 548.

[3] Ibid. ii, pp. 478, 560, 562.

It is possible that Hadewisa made the grant and that Nigel confirmed it, but the wording seems to imply that Nigel and Hadewisa together granted and confirmed the manor to Adam. If the latter is correct, the bishop's patronage of the abbey may have restricted the abbey's administrative autonomy in the mid-twelfth century. However, it seems that the abbey had asserted its independence by the later twelfth century since none of the other documents in the cartulary shows the bishop intervening in the administration of the abbey's estates.

In Chatteris itself, the tenurial relationship between the nunnery and the bishop was simpler because the nunnery acquired its manor there from the church of Ely. In 1086 there were two manors in Chatteris, one held by the abbot of Ely and the other by the abbot of Ramsey.[1] The gift of Ely's manor to the nunnery was probably made by one of the twelfth-century bishops of Ely, possibly as a demonstration of his newly acquired patronage of the nunnery. The cartulary contains two copies of the charter of bishop Nigel which gave the lordship (*dominium*) and advowson of the church of St Peter in Chatteris to the nuns (nos. 10 and 76). This charter may be the record of the gift of the bishop's manor in Chatteris to Chatteris abbey. It is possible, though, that the links between the church of Ely and Chatteris abbey predated the creation of the diocese of Ely in 1109 and that either Simeon or Richard, the last two abbots of Ely, gave the manor to the nunnery. Whichever was the case, the nuns' manor in Chatteris was never held in chief of the king by the abbess. A copy of an inquisition *ad quod damnum* held in 1387, which was copied into the cartulary (no. 257), makes the tenurial relationship explicit. The jurors said that John Dreng held of the abbess of Chatteris three messuages, two acres and three roods of land and 22d. of rent in Chatteris, *Et dicunt quod dicta abbatissa ea ultra tenet de episcopo Eliensi et episcopus ea ultra tenet de domino rege in capite*. The history of the tenure of the nuns' manor in Chatteris is clearly distinct from that of many of its other estates because the abbess had never been tenant-in-chief there. It is probable that the nunnery's loss of tenant-in-chief status after 1086 in Foxton, Over, Barrington and Shepreth – which may well have been paralleled in some of its other property – derived from Henry I's charter giving rights over Chatteris abbey to the bishop of Ely.

Royal patronage which gave the beneficiary the overlordship of an existing tenant-in-chief was efficient for the king and was bestowed on secular as well as ecclesiastical landholders. For example, Henry I made Nigel d'Aubigny over-

---

lord of Gilbert Tison and William de Arches, both previously tenants-in-chief.[1] Whereas secular lords could claim feudal incidents from their tenants, these profits could not be exacted by the bishop of Ely from Chatteris abbey. However, the bishop could claim jurisdictional rights in the same way as secular lords and the holding of courts generated income.

The bishop was lord of the hundred of Witchford in which Chatteris lay and so had the right to hold a court there: the inquisition *ad quod damnum* (no. 257) includes a reference to suits owed for property in Chatteris, Doddington and Wimblington at the Witchford hundred court and at the court of the palace of Ely.[2] In Wisbech hundred, where the bishop was the predominant manorial lord as well as lord of the hundred, the hundred court dealt with some domanial business.[3] In contrast, since the bishop was not lord of the majority of the manors in Witchford hundred, its hundred court did not deal with tenurial matters. A charter in the cartulary (no. 15) provides evidence for rent owed to the bishop of Ely being paid to the hundred, but the surviving medieval court rolls for the hundred, which date only from the later fourteenth century, are dominated by pleas of debt.[4]

In addition to the hundred court, the bishop had the view of frankpledge in Witchford hundred. A few late fourteenth and fifteenth-century records survive from the biannual sheriff's tourn held by the bishop's steward.[5] An entry in 1429 shows that the abbess of Chatteris owed suit at the tourn: *Preceptum quod abbatissa de Chateriz debet sectam et predicta abbatissa venit per eius ballivum*

---

[1] *Charters of the Honour of Mowbray 1107–1191* ed. D. E. Greenway (British Academy, 1972) p. xxv.

[2] The two hundreds of Ely and Witchford were not clearly distinguished from one another before the thirteenth century and may have had only one court. The court of the palace of Ely, which had jurisdiction over both hundreds, seems to have been an anachronistic survival from this time. From the thirteenth century, each hundred in the Isle of Ely had its own distinct hundred court: the court of the palace of Ely was held in addition, but it exercised only a trace of the jurisdiction formerly belonging to the single court of the two hundreds (*VCH Cambs.* iv, p. 11, and E. Miller *The Abbey and Bishopric of Ely. The Social History of an Ecclesiastical Estate from the Tenth Century to the Early Fourteenth Century* (Cambridge, 1951) pp. 221–5.)

[3] Cambridge UL, EDR C 13/1–5.

[4] No. 15: *reddendo inde nobis annuatim et successoribus nostris et hundredo nostro de Ely decem denarios ubi prius reddi solebant quinque denarii ad quatuor terminos censuales pro sectis curie consuetudinibus et demandis*; *VCH Cambs.* iv, p. 12; Cambridge UL, EDR C 7/28, 30–1 (1366–7, 1373–4, 1389–90).

[5] Cambridge UL, EDR C 7/29, 34.

gracia domini.[1] The bishop also held courts leet in his four demesne manors in Witchford hundred and in Coveney, Little Thetford and Chatteris.[2] The surviving medieval court rolls for the bishop's leets in Chatteris date from the late fourteenth and early fifteenth centuries.[3] The abbess of Chatteris appears several times: for example, in 1385 she was presented for not having maintained her channel (*guttera*) at 'Modirston' and for having blocked a right of way at 'Mille Cote', and in 1400 she was presented for having enclosed a croft called 'Wodecroft' as her own severalty.[4] No pre-Dissolution rolls survive for the manorial courts held by the abbess herself in Chatteris, but records do exist for courts held in the manor, by then known as Chatteris Regis, in 1539–43.[5] These courts were courts baron, concerned solely with tenurial business, so it is likely that before the Dissolution the abbess held a court dealing with seignorial matters whilst the bishop exercised the leet jurisdiction. The origin of this divided jurisdiction probably lies in the gift to the nunnery by the bishop of Ely – or by one of the last two abbots – of the manor in Chatteris which the abbot of Ely held in Domesday Book. It seems that the bishop may have retained his view of frankpledge in the manor and transferred only the right to deal with tenurial matters to the abbess.

The abbess of Chatteris did, though, deal with both leet and baronial matters in her manorial courts at Foxton – to which her tenants from Foxton, Shepreth, Barrington, Madingley and Over owed suit – and at Barley.[6] The hundred rolls for 1279 state that the abbess of Chatteris held the view of frankpledge and the assize of bread and ale in Foxton under the liberty of the bishop of Ely, and that she also held the view of frankpledge in Shepreth, presumably also under the bishop's liberty, although the jurors were not certain: *nesciunt quo waranto nisi per Elyensem.*[7] The pattern of manorial jurisdiction in Over was less straightforward than in the abbey's lands in Foxton, Shepreth, Barrington and Madingley which, together with Over, made up the manor later known as Foxton with members. Two fifteenth-century sources contain a memo-

---

1 Cambridge UL, EDR C 7/29, rot. 2d.
2 *VCH Cambs.* iv, p. 11. The bishop's leet jurisdiction in Chatteris applied only to the manor of the nunnery and not to the manor of the abbot of Ramsey who held his own courts leet in his manor there (Ault ed. *Ramsey Court Rolls*, pp. 260–80).
3 Cambridge UL, EDR C 12/4/1–7 (1385, 1388–9, 1391–2, 1394–1400, 1403, 1406).
4 Cambridge UL, EDR C 12/4/1, 5.
5 Cambridge, Trinity College Archives, Foxton 6, rott. 3d, 5, 6, 7; CCRO L 63/18, rot. 26.
6 Cambridge, Trinity College Archives, Foxton 1–5; PRO SC 2/177/1.
7 *Rot. Hund.* ii, pp. 548, 562.

randum stating that the tenants of the abbess in Over were subject to the leet jurisdiction of the bishop, who was the overlord, at Willingham:

> Memorandum quod abbatissa de Chateriz tenet iiij^{or} virgatas terre cum tenentibus in Overe de domino episcopo Eliensi in capite qui quidem tenentes faciunt sectam ad letam dicti domini episcopi apud Wyvelyngham.[1]

Manorial court rolls relating to the nunnery's estate in Over survive from 1293–1324 and 1523–43.[2] Most of these courts were courts baron, but in 1294 and 1301 the abbess held a view of frankpledge there.[3] It seems, therefore, that the abbess's leet jurisdiction in Over was probably transferred to the bishop during the fourteenth or fifteenth-centuries.

All bishops had quite extensive spiritual jurisdiction over the nunneries in their diocese: they heard the profession of nuns, appointed confessors for them, visited them and confirmed the election of new heads of houses. The Ely episcopal registers contain examples of the exercise of all these functions in relation to Chatteris abbey. For instance, in 1398 bishop Fordham appointed Thomas Dounham, a monk of Ely, to hear confessions at the nunnery, whilst in 1388 the same bishop had granted the abbess and nuns a licence to elect for themselves a suitable chaplain to be their confessor.[4] Bishop Grey received the profession of four nuns of Chatteris in 1467, whilst bishop Fordham licenced his suffragan, Thomas Barrett, bishop of Killala (*Aladensis*), to receive the profession of three nuns in 1401 and of three more in 1406.[5] That these nuns made their profession in small groups suggests that women did not feel an urgent need to be professed and so did not seek profession as soon as possible after entering the nunnery.

Few visitation records for Chatteris abbey contain substantial detail. The injunctions in bishop de Lisle's register, dating from 1347, are an exception.[6] They include orders to the abbess not to begin new work costing more than 10 marks and not to spend the convent's money without the consent of the nuns;

---

[1] Cambridge UL, EDR G 3/27 'The Old Coucher Book', fo. 240v; BL Cotton MS Claudius C. xi, fo. 358v.

[2] Cambridge, Trinity College Archives, Foxton 1, rott. 1, 3, 4d; Foxton 2, m. 1; Foxton 3, rot. 3d; Foxton 4, rot. 1d; Foxton 5, rot. 1; Foxton 6, rott. 4d–6, 7d. CCRO L 63/18, rott. 16d, 17d, 26d.

[3] Cambridge, Trinity College Archives, Foxton 1, rot. 1; Foxton 3, rot. 3d.

[4] Cambridge UL, EDR G/1/3, Fordham register, fos. 189v, 4v.

[5] Cambridge UL, EDR G/1/5, Grey register, fo. 69r; EDR G/1/3, Fordham register fos. 193r, 203r.

[6] Cambridge UL, EDR G/1/1, de Lisle register, fo. 47v.

the abbess and prioress are both ordered to be modest, sincere and charitable in correcting the nuns who, in turn, are to accept correction; old and infirm nuns are to be treated with compassion; the doors of the choir are to be closed during services except at the elevation of the host; the abbess is to look after the nunnery's income fittingly; she may deal with the convent's possessions only if she has the convent's consent and she must not unduly enrich her relatives or anyone else; the nuns are not to keep birds or dogs and no servant removed from the nunnery for immorality is to be readmitted. The other significant visitation material relating to the abbey is archiepiscopal: the register of archbishop Whittlesey records the *comperta* from the visitation of the nunnery in 1373 during a vacancy in the see of Ely.[1] It was presented that certain nuns were disobedient including, in particular, Cecilia Aubyn; that the abbess did much important business concerning the convent without seeking its advice, following instead the wishes of Edward Dreng; that she had withdrawn an annual sum of 10s. intended for the nuns' clothing; and that there was insufficient bread and ale. The abbess, Margaret Hotot, replied to the charges made against her. She said that in convent business, she did nothing without the advice of the nuns, but that she consulted Dreng about other business in which he was an expert. She also explained that she had been forced to use the 10s. to help to pay tithes and subsidies which the resources of the abbey could not otherwise have met.

The bishop's patronage of the nunnery does not seem to have affected his role as diocesan in visitations. Comparison with visitation material for nunneries in the diocese of Lincoln in the fifteenth century shows that the bishop of Ely and the archbishop of Canterbury were exercising standard supervisory and corrective authority at Chatteris abbey. For example, the heads of nunneries in the diocese of Lincoln were often enjoined to render annual accounts of their administration and the abbess of Elstow was ordered not to transact any business concerning the abbey's property without the express consent of the majority of the convent.[2] The prioress of Ankerwyke (Bucks.) admitted that she had never rendered an account and had administered everything without informing the convent.[3] The prioress of Legbourne (Lincs.) was similarly charged with not accounting for her administration and also with putting the common property of the priory to her own use. She was enjoined to 'do no grete nedes of your house ne lete no ferme ne susteyn none of your kynne or

---

1 Lambeth Palace Library, Whittlesey register, fos. 152v–153r.
2 *Visitations of Religious Houses* ed. Thompson, i, p. 50.
3 Ibid. ii, p. 3.

allyaunce wythe the commune godes of the house, wythe owten the hole assent of the more hole parte of the covent'.[1] The same prioress was accused of lacking impartiality when correcting nuns and was ordered to be 'indifferent, not cruelle to some and to some favoryng agayn your rule'. She was also ordered to ensure that sick and aged nuns were cared for in the infirmary.[2] The keeping of both dogs, at Langley priory (Leics.), and birds, at Legbourne priory, arises in the Lincoln visitation material, although in both cases the animals belonged to secular boarders rather than nuns.[3] There are also instances of insufficient provision for nuns' clothing: at Langley priory the nuns allegedly received nothing from the house for their clothing; at Ankerwyke priory the nuns had patched clothes because the prioress had not provided new habits for three years; and at Stixwould priory (Lincs.) the nuns, who had formerly received half a mark annually for clothing, had had nothing for several years.[4] The Lincoln records contain several reports of insufficient food together with injunctions regulating the amount of food nuns were to have. For example, at Elstow abbey (Beds.), every nun was to have a meat or fish dish three times a week, together with five measures of better beer weekly, and the bread of the abbess and of the convent was to be of equal quality.[5]

Despite such parallels, there is nothing in the visitation material which survives from Chatteris to compare with the reported 'acts of adultery, incest, sacrilege and fornication' at Sewardsley priory (Northants.), nor with Mary Browne, a pregnant nun from Godstow abbey (Oxon.).[6] In her history of medieval nunneries, Eileen Power draws many of her examples from visitation records which inevitably dwell on the shortcomings of religious houses. She argues that the significant number of nuns who broke their vows and disobeyed the rule of their order shows that moral laxity was widespread.[7] John Tillotson, whilst not denying the validity of Power's examples, thinks that her catalogue of the defects found in medieval nunneries is misleading. He believes that Power's analysis gives too much weight to the relatively small number of nuns who were guilty of serious maladministration or immorality. He argues instead that, although some individual nuns behaved badly, the late medieval visitation

[1] Ibid. ii, pp. 185, 187.
[2] Ibid. ii, pp. 185–6.
[3] Ibid. ii, pp. 175, 185.
[4] Ibid. ii, pp. 175, 4; iii, p. 357.
[5] Ibid. ii, p. 49.
[6] Ibid. ii, pp. 112, 65.
[7] Power *Medieval English Nunneries*, chs. 7–11.

evidence shows that all the Yorkshire nunneries managed to remain fairly respectable most of the time.[1] Although the visitation evidence for Chatteris is scanty – and it is impossible to know how observant and disciplined the nuns were – Chatteris did not produce a single recorded example of immorality or apostasy.

As well as visiting Chatteris abbey, the bishop of Ely can be seen exercising his spiritual jurisdiction over the nunnery by confirming the election of abbesses but, as patron, he had additional rights: he granted the licence to elect and he had oversight of the election process. The nuns of Ickleton priory similarly had to seek their licence to elect from the bishop of Ely, their patron, whereas the nuns of Swaffham Bulbeck priory sought theirs from their patron, the earl of Oxford.[2] In the case of nunneries such as the abbeys at Barking (Essex), Shaftesbury (Dorset), Wherwell (Hants.) and Wilton (Wilts.) which, like Chatteris, were pre-Conquest Benedictine foundations, the king was patron and issued licences to elect abbesses and writs *de intendendo* for the restitution of their temporalities.

The episcopal registers record the election of only two abbesses of Chatteris: Matilda Bernard in 1347 and Anne Basset in 1488.[3] In both accounts the bishop is referred to as the patron of the abbey and bishop Alcock calls the abbey *domus sive monasterium vestrum predictum nostre fundationis*, which shows how far the concept of the bishop's claims over the abbey extended.[4] These elections were organised and confirmed by the bishop's commissary, but in neither does the bishop seem to have interfered unduly in the election process: the nuns were apparently free to choose their own abbess. On the retirement of abbess Alice de Shropham in 1347, the nuns received a licence from the bishop's commissary to elect her successor. Seven of the nuns were delegated to vote *per viam com-*

1 J. H. Tillotson 'Visitation and Reform of the Yorkshire Nunneries in the Fourteenth Century' *Northern History* xxx (1994) p. 19.
2 Cambridge UL, EDR G/1/4, Bourgchier register, fo. 61r; EDR G/1/1 Montacute register, fo. 22v.
3 Cambridge UL, EDR G/1/1 de Lisle register, fos. 51r–52r; EDR G/1/6 Alcock register, pp. 147–53.
4 Cambridge UL, EDR G/1/6, Alcock register, p. 147. The register of bishop Bourgchier records a similar extension of rights claimed in respect of Ickleton priory. Although a member of the Valoignes family founded this nunnery in the twelfth century, the bishop of Ely was its patron by the later Middle Ages. In the account of the election of a prioress in 1444 the bishop is called the patron and the priory is said to be of the foundation of the bishops of Ely (*VCH Cambs.* ii, p. 223–4; Cambridge UL, EDR G/1/4, Bourgchier register, fo. 61r).

promissi. Five of the seven voted for Matilda Bernard who was thereby elected. The two electors who voted for other nuns were Matilda Bernard, who did not vote for herself, and, more significantly, the retiring abbess Alice de Shropham, who was still alive in 1355 when she was granted a papal indult to choose her confessor at her death.[1] In 1488, following the death of Margery Ramsey, the bishop himself granted to the nuns a licence to elect a new abbess. They unanimously and *per inspirationem spiritus sancti* chose the prioress, Anne Basset. The bishop's commissary, James Hutton, confirmed the election and installed the new abbess who swore an oath of obedience to the bishop and his ministers.[2]

The register of archbishop Winchelsey sheds further light on the rights of the bishop of Ely as patron during an election. In 1298, during a vacancy in the diocese of Ely, Winchelsey issued a mandate to his official to inquire into the election of the new abbess and to confirm or invalidate it.[3] The following year, on 18 March 1299, the archbishop notified the abbey that, although he had nominated Idonea de Chilham, an illiterate, for admission as a lay-sister, this was not a precedent for bishops of Ely to nominate lay-sisters instead of nuns in the future.[4] This shows, again, that the bishop normally had the right to oversee the election of the abbess of Chatteris, but it is also evidence of his right to nominate a nun when he confirmed the election.

The patron of a religious house had the potentially valuable right to the custody of its temporalities when the position of head of the house fell vacant. This right encouraged some houses to separate the properties of the head from those of the convent so that the patron could claim only the head's temporalities during vacancies. By the second half of the twelfth century, all the large Benedictine houses for men had divided their lands and revenues between the abbot and convent, but it is not clear how far this arrangement was adopted by smaller monasteries.[5]

In the case of nunneries it seems that even the largest houses did not divide their revenues in this way, but some nunneries made other arrangements to protect their interests during vacancies. In 1382 the abbess and convent of the

---

[1] Cambridge UL, EDR G/1/1, de Lisle register, fos. 51r–52r; *Calendar of Entries in the Papal Registers Relating to Great Britain and Ireland* iii *Papal Letters 1342–62* eds W. H. Bliss and C. Johnson (PRO Texts and Calendars, 1897) p. 553.

[2] Cambridge UL, EDR G/1/6, Alcock register, pp. 147–53.

[3] *Registrum Roberti Winchelsey Cantuariensis Archiepiscopi 1294–1313* ed. R. Graham (Canterbury and York Society li, 1952) pp. 262–3.

[4] Ibid. pp. 324–5.

[5] D. Knowles *The Monastic Order in England. A History of its Development from the Times of St Dunstan to the Fourth Lateran Council 940–1216* 2nd edn (Cambridge, 1963) pp. 434–7.

wealthy abbey at Shaftesbury (Dorset) petitioned Richard II to grant to the prioress and convent the right to retain the temporalities of the abbey on the occasion of all future vacancies.[1] In 1307, after the death of Philippa, abbess of Romsey (Hants.), Edward II upheld the grant previously made to Philippa by Edward I that the prioress and nuns of Romsey should have custody of the abbey's temporalities in the next vacancy.[2] Similarly, in 1331 Edward III granted to prioress Isabella de Wytereshulle and the convent of Wherwell abbey (Hants.) the right to the custody of the abbey and its possessions during vacancies.[3] In all these cases the income of the abbess and convent must have been undivided since the king – who was their patron – clearly had the right to claim it all in a vacancy. At Barking abbey (Essex), too, the nuns' income was not separated from that of the abbess. During a vacancy of six months in 1199–1200, the royal keeper of the abbey's estates collected a total of £219 8s. 5d. from which he paid £70 to the prioress and nuns for their maintenance.[4] Had the convent had its own income such a payment would not have been necessary. The abbess of Barking managed all the resources of the abbey, although she did also have some limited resources assigned specifically to her office.[5]

The evidence relating to Chatteris, where the bishop of Ely rather than the king was patron, is less conclusive. It suggests, though, that the abbey's financial arrangements were similar to those in the nunneries discussed above. The visitation injunctions issued by bishop de Lisle in 1347 forbade the abbess of Chatteris from spending the convent's money and from dealing with its possessions without the consent of the nuns.[6] This order does not state explicitly whether or not the abbess's funds were separated from those of the convent, but it seems most likely that the resources of the abbess and convent were pooled and that the abbess was not supposed to exercise independent authority over their expenditure. The evidence from the cartulary supports this interpretation: none of the benefactors in the cartulary made donations specifically to the abbess or to the convent, rather than to the abbess and convent together. Whichever was the case, the vacancies which preceded the two recorded elec-

---

1 *Rotuli Parliamentorum; ut et Petitiones, et Placita in Parliamento* iii (Record Commission, [1783]) p. 129.
2 *CCR 1307–13*, p. 1.
3 *CPR 1330–34*, p. 72.
4 *Pipe R.* 2 John, p. 266; W. M. Sturman 'Barking Abbey. A Study in its Internal and External Administration from the Conquest to the Dissolution', Ph.D. thesis (University of London, 1961) pp. 262–3, 378.
5 Sturman 'Barking Abbey', p. 264.
6 Cambridge UL, EDR G/1/1, de Lisle register, fo. 47v.

tions at Chatteris would have allowed the bishop of Ely little or no scope to profit from the custody of the temporalities. In 1347, Matilda Bernard was elected on the same day that Alice de Shropham retired while, in the election of 1488, Margery Ramsey died on 27 January and her successor, Anne Basset, was elected on 4 February and had her temporalities restored on 13 February.[1]

The extent to which the bishop of Ely represented the interests of Chatteris abbey as its patron is unclear. The register of archbishop Kempe contains the record of the convocation of 1453. This is the only convocation of the province of Canterbury before 1529 which preserves a list of those who were to appear.[2] 140 abbots and 139 priors are listed altogether: the abbot of Thorney and the priors of Ely, Barnwell and Anglesey attended from the diocese of Ely, but the abbess of Chatteris did not send a proctor.[3] Unfortunately, the absence of a proctor for the abbess does not prove that the bishop of Ely, as patron, was representing the nunnery. Although the numbers attending the convocation were substantial, many religious houses were not represented. None of the other nunneries in the diocese of Ely – St Radegund's priory in Cambridge, Ickleton priory, Swaffham Bulbeck priory and Denny abbey – sent a proctor and several heads of the male houses in the diocese were absent. More significantly, all the nunneries in the whole province were unrepresented at the convocation.

One of the functions of the patron of a religious house was to uphold its claims in land disputes. Although there is no record of the bishop of Ely having intervened in a law-suit on behalf of Chatteris abbey, bishop Orford did support the abbey following a devastating fire at the nunnery in 1306 × 1310. He wrote to ask Ralph Baldock, bishop of London, to remit the tithes which the nuns owed to him because the fire had destroyed buildings at the abbey together with all the produce of its manors stored there.[4] However, Robert Orford did not state that he was acting as patron of the nunnery. He referred to the nunnery as being of his diocese rather than of his patronage, which may mean that he would have acted similarly on behalf of the abbey in this case even if he had not been its patron.

---

[1] Cambridge UL, EDR G/1/1 de Lisle register, fo. 51v; EDR G/1/6 Alcock register, p. 152.
[2] E. W. Kemp 'The Archbishop in Convocation' in *Medieval Records of the Archbishops of Canterbury*, usually catalogued under I. J. Churchill, author of the first lecture (London, 1962) pp. 24–5.
[3] Lambeth Palace Library, Stafford and Kempe register, fo. 230v.
[4] *Mon. Ang.* ii, pp. 618–19, no. 10 (BL Cotton Ch. xxi. 12).

The appropriation to Chatteris abbey of the churches of Chatteris and Shepreth also blurred the bishop's role as diocesan and patron (nos. 10/76 and 160). It is probable that bishops Nigel and Eustace were motivated by their patronage of the nunnery when they granted the appropriations, but it is again difficult to disentangle the dual roles of bishop and patron in relation to the nunnery. In many respects, the two roles were complementary: they tended to strengthen the bishop's influence over the nunnery and to enhance the benefits which the nunnery could expect from its patron.

III

The Endowment

Temporalities

In 986 Æthelstan Mannessune, a powerful thegn of the eastern Danelaw, left land in Chatteris to Ramsey abbey in his will.[1] According to the *Liber Eliensis*, Eadnoth, who was the son of Æthelstan and the second abbot of Ramsey, founded Chatteris abbey between 1007 × 1009 – when he became bishop of Dorchester – and 1016 when he was killed at the battle of *Assandun*.[2] Eadnoth seems to have used the estate which his father had given to Ramsey abbey to provide a site for Chatteris abbey, but Ramsey abbey retained its manor in Chatteris and the nunnery did not have its own estate there when Domesday Book was compiled. Only in the twelfth century did Chatteris abbey acquire a manor in Chatteris itself. It was probably bishop Hervey or bishop Nigel of Ely who gave to the nunnery the manor which the abbot of Ely had held in Chatteris in 1086.[3]

Although Chatteris abbey did not acquire its property in Chatteris from Ramsey abbey, Cyril Hart argued that Chatteris abbey's Domesday estates in Over and Barley (Herts.) were derived from gifts made by members of Eadnoth's family to Ramsey abbey. Æthelstan Mannessune left land in Over to his wife in his will.[4] Ælfwaru, Æthelstan's eldest daughter, died in 1007 and, like her father, she left property to Ramsey abbey in her will. This property included 'Chinnora' and her share of the land in Barley (Herts.) which she held

---

[1] *Chronicon Abbatiæ Rameseiensis* ed. W. D. Macray (Rolls Series lxxxiii, 1886) p. 59.
[2] No. 2; *Liber Eliensis* ed. Blake, pp. 140–2.
[3] *Domesday Book* i, fos. 192d, 193a, 191d.
[4] *Chronicon Abbatiæ Rameseiensis*, p. 59.

jointly with another Eadnoth, a monk of Ramsey.[1] Hart argued that 'Chinnora' should be identified with Over, and that Ælfwaru had inherited part of her mother's estate in Over, but according to the *Victoria County History* 'the etymological grounds for linking 'Chinnora' with Over are slight'.[2] In any case, Over seems to have been given to Ramsey abbey by Eadnoth, the former monk of Ramsey who was bishop of Dorchester from 1034 to 1049; this Eadnoth may also have given part of Over to Chatteris abbey.[3] However, Ælfwaru's bequest to Ramsey of her share of the land she held in Barley may have been the origin of Chatteris abbey's estate there. In 1086, Chatteris abbey held three and a half hides in Barley whereas Ramsey abbey held none, which suggests that Ælfwaru's bequest may have been transferred to Chatteris.[4] Part of Ramsey's holding in Burwell may also have been given to Chatteris abbey: king Edgar gave five hides in Burwell to Ramsey in 969 and St Oswald bought another five hides there for his abbey in the late tenth century, but Chatteris abbey acquired half a hide in Burwell before 1086.[5] The source of most of Chatteris abbey's Domesday holdings remains unclear, but it is possible that members of Eadnoth's family provided lands other than those in Barley. This is perhaps particularly plausible given that Eadnoth's sister, Ælfwen, became the first abbess. The core of the nunnery's Domesday estates, which lay in the adjacent south Cambridgeshire parishes of Foxton, Shepreth and Barrington, may have been Ælfwen's dowry, but it is impossible to be sure.

The narrative about Eadnoth in the *Liber Eliensis* states that he founded Chatteris abbey after he had become bishop of Dorchester in 1007 × 1009, but the evidence for the early endowment of the nunnery suggests that he may, in fact, have founded it whilst he was still abbot of Ramsey. If the nunnery's lands in Barley were those which Ælfwaru had bequeathed to Ramsey abbey in 1007, it seems unlikely that they would have been transferred to the nunnery if Eadnoth were no longer abbot, even though he subsequently became bishop of the diocese in which Ramsey lay. If Eadnoth did found Chatteris abbey after

---

1 Ibid. p. 84; *Cartularium Monasterii de Rameseia* ed. W. H. Hart and Rev. P. A. Lyons, iii (Rolls Series lxxix, 1893) p. 167.

2 C. Hart 'Eadnoth, First Abbot of Ramsey, and the Foundation of Chatteris and St Ives' *Proceedings of the Cambridge Antiquarian Society* lvi–lvii (1964) p. 63; *VCH Cambs.* ix, p. 344.

3 *Chronicon Abbatiæ Rameseiensis*, p. 159.

4 *Domesday Book* i, fo. 136b.

5 *Chronicon Abbatiæ Rameseiensis*, pp. 47–9; *Domesday Book* i, fo. 193a.

the death of Ælfwaru in 1007, but before he became bishop of Dorchester, the date of the abbey's foundation must be 1007 × 1009.

Domesday Book contains the earliest detailed information about the endowments of Chatteris abbey. In 1086, the abbess was a tenant-in-chief of the crown and the abbey's lands lay mainly in Cambridgeshire (see figure 1). Within Cambridgeshire, most of the abbey's lands were clustered in a small area in the south of the county. The abbess held five hides and 40 acres of land and half a mill in Foxton; she held two hides and a mill in Barrington; in Shepreth she held one hide and one and a half virgates of land and a mill; and in Orwell she held a quarter of a virgate. The abbey's other lands in Cambridgeshire lay in Burwell, in the east of the county, and in Over, in the west. The abbess held half a hide in Burwell and one hide in Over.[1] The abbey also had lands in Hertfordshire and Suffolk in 1086. The abbey's land in Hertfordshire was a manor in Barley consisting of three and a half hides of land.[2] Since Barley lies just inside Hertfordshire's boundary with Cambridgeshire, the abbey's manor in Barley lay only a few miles from the abbey's property in south Cambridgeshire. In south Suffolk, far removed from its other properties, the abbey held Kersey with three and a half carucates of land, a mill and the church.[3] The abbey had yet to acquire its manor in Chatteris in 1086 when the two landholders were the abbots of Ramsey and Ely. The abbot of Ramsey held three hides less half a virgate in Chatteris, whilst the abbot of Ely held two hides and half a virgate.[4] The manor of the abbot of Ely was later transferred to Chatteris abbey, probably not long after Henry I granted the patronage of the nunnery to the bishop of Ely.

The privilege *Religiosam vitam eligentibus* of pope Innocent IV (1243–54), which confirmed the possessions of Chatteris abbey, provides a mid-thirteenth-century list of the properties of the abbey (no. 3). Although Innocent's privilege does not specify the extent of the properties which it lists, it does show that the abbey had acquired more property than it had in Domesday Book. In addition to its lands in Foxton, Barrington, Shepreth, Orwell, Burwell, Over, Barley (Herts.) and Kersey (Suff.), by the mid-thirteenth century, the abbey had gained land and rents in Chatteris itself, land in Lincoln and Huntingdon, land with a mill in Thriplow and land with a harbour (*portus*) in Cambridge (see figure 1). The privilege also lists the spiritualities acquired by the abbey: the churches of

[1] *Domesday Book* i, fo. 193a.
[2] Ibid. i, fo. 136b.
[3] Ibid. ii, p. 389a.
[4] Ibid. i, fos. 192d, 191d.

Figure 1: Map showing the location of the estates of Chatteris abbey

Chatteris and Shepreth and the chapel of Honey Hill in the parish of Chatteris, together with its tithes.

It is possible to link the acquisition of some of these properties with documents in the cartulary. In 1220 × 1225 John of Fountains, bishop of Ely, confirmed to the abbey both the possessions which it held of his fee and all the gifts made from his fee in Chatteris (no. 13). A significant number of donations of property in Chatteris by other benefactors seems to have been made before Innocent IV issued his confirmation. The donations recorded in nos. 19, 23–5, 55, 68 and 88 were probably all made before the mid-thirteenth century; several other grants which cannot be dated very precisely were probably made before then too. No. 227 records the grant made in the second half of the twelfth century by Hugh de Cranwell to the abbey of a rent of 10s. from houses in Lincoln; nos. 229 and 230 are early fourteenth-century documents dealing with property which the abbey had previously acquired in Huntingdon; and no. 166 is the gift made by bishop Nigel *c.* 1150 × *c.* 1158 of land with a mill in Thriplow.

The rubric above the privilege of Innocent IV in the cartulary claims that the document is a renovation of a bull of Alexander III, who was pope from 20 September 1159 to 30 August 1181, but no trace of an earlier bull remains nor is it mentioned in Innocent IV's privilege. The list of properties in Innocent IV's document cannot merely be a repetition of a later twelfth-century list from a bull, now lost, of Alexander III because Innocent IV confirmed the abbey's possession of Shepreth church. The church was not appropriated to the abbey until 8 March 1198 × 3 Feb. 1215, well after Alexander's death (no. 160). However, Innocent's privilege does not list all the parishes in which the abbey acquired property before the mid-thirteenth century. It omits, for example, the tenement in Bircham (Norf.) which was given with Richard de Bircham by William of Ely in 1201 × 1222 (nos. 91/223). Also missing is the abbey's property in Madingley (Cambs.). Richard FitzNeal confirmed *c.* 1159 × 30 May 1169 one hide of land in Madingley given by Robert his brother and, in 1196 × Aug. 1215, 'R.' gave five acres of land and half an acre of meadow in Madingley to the abbey (nos. 109 and 239). In addition, Aubrey son of Eustace de Madingley twice sold land in Madingley to the abbey and both these sales may have been made before Innocent IV's privilege (nos. 110 and 238). The exclusion from the privilege of the abbey's property in Bircham and Madingley may be significant. It suggests that the list of properties in the mid-thirteenth-century privilege may indeed be a copy of a list contained in a privilege, now lost, issued by pope Alexander III in 1159 × 1181, to which list was added only the recently appropriated church of Shepreth.

Unlike Innocent's privilege, the taxation of pope Nicholas IV in 1291 records the abbey's temporal property in both Bircham and Madingley, but neither the 1291 taxation nor the privilege refers to the land in Lynn given to the abbey by William son of Wluric de Wootton in the first half of the thirteenth century which the abbey held until its dissolution.[1] Other properties and rents – none of them very sizeable – seem to have been given to the abbey before the mid-thirteenth century in Bilney (Norf.) (no. 82); in Stuntney, Little Thetford and in Upwell and Outwell (Cambs. and Norf.) (no. 91); in Fen Ditton (no. 94); and in Ely (nos. 92 and 99). None of these lands or rents was listed in Innocent IV's privilege, in the hundred rolls of 1279, in the taxation of 1291 or in the minister's accounts of 1539, which suggests that the abbey may not have retained them for long.

The hundred rolls specify the extent of some of the abbey's holdings in 1279. In Foxton the abbey held 300 acres of arable land, 32 acres of meadow and 15 acres of pasture in demesne; its freeholders held 77¼ acres; its villeins and other customary tenants held 351 acres and its cottars held nine acres.[2] In Shepreth the abbey held 160 acres of land and meadow in demesne; its freeholders held 28¼ acres; its villeins held 135 acres and its crofters held six and a half acres.[3] The abbey held a quarter of the vill of Barrington, its freeholders held 118¼ acres and its villeins 165½ acres.[4] All four virgates of the abbey's land in Over were held by tenants.[5] In Thriplow the heir of William Stonhard held of the abbess 30 acres, a messuage and a croft of two acres, whilst in Orwell Roger de Thorinton held 20 acres of the abbess.[6] Since the 1279 hundred rolls survive only patchily, they do not reveal the extent of the abbey's other lands. However, the existing rolls underline the importance of the abbey's holdings in Foxton, Shepreth and Barrington.

Although the cartulary is the richest source of information about the endowment of the abbey, it is not comprehensive. The absence of some of the abbey's properties is especially striking given that the extant cartulary was not

---

1 *Taxatio Ecclesiastica Angliae et Walliae Auctoritate Nicholai IV circa A.D. 1291* [ed. T. Astle et al.] (Record Commission, 1802) pp. 105, 268; no. 217; PRO SC 6/HenVIII/267, rot. 8d.

2 *Rot. Hund.* ii, p. 548.

3 Ibid. p. 562.

4 Ibid. p. 560.

5 Ibid. p. 478.

6 Ibid. pp. 543, 559.

compiled until the fifteenth century. Domesday Book shows that the abbey held a quarter of a virgate in Orwell in 1086 and the hundred rolls record that in 1279 Roger de Thorinton held of the abbess half a virgate of land containing 20 acres in Orwell for an annual rent of five shillings.[1] Orwell does not occur in the cartulary even though the hundred rolls state that Roger de Thorinton held the half virgate of the abbess *per cartam*. However the lands in Orwell are also absent from the 1291 taxation of pope Nicholas IV and from the post-Dissolution minister's accounts.[2] This may be because the abbey had leased the lands but was unable to enforce the payment of the rent which it was owed. Alternatively, the abbey may have alienated the lands and handed over the deeds at the same time, which would account for their absence from the cartulary.

The hundred rolls show that in 1279 the abbey also held land in Impington, though this land is not recorded in any other sources relating to the abbey. According to the hundred rolls, the abbey had nine tenants there in 1279, two of whom held a messuage and half a virgate of land, whilst the remaining seven had smaller holdings ranging in size from a messuage and six acres down to one rood of land.[3] Again it seems likely that the abbey may have alienated these lands before the compilation of the cartulary.

The abbey's income from property in Colne (Hunts.) and Benwick is recorded only in the minister's accounts after the dissolution of the nunnery. In 1539 the minister received 1s. in rent from one acre in Colne and one mark from the farm of a fishery in Benwick.[4] The records of the acquisition of these properties may simply have been omitted from the cartulary, or the abbey may have acquired them after the compilation of the cartulary. The sole reference to property owned by the abbey in Wilburton occurs in the 1291 taxation of pope Nicholas IV which values the unspecified property at only 6d.[5] The abbey may have acquired a little land or rent in Wilburton shortly before 1291 which it sold soon afterwards. Alternatively, the occurrence of Wilburton in the taxation of Nicholas IV may be a mistake: it is possible that Wimblington, also in Cambridgeshire, was meant. In 1539, the minister's accounts record that two shillings of rent were received for two acres of arable land in Wimblington.[6]

---

1 *Domesday Book* i, fo. 193a; *Rot. Hund.* ii, p. 559.
2 *Taxatio Nicholai IV*, p. 268; PRO SC 6/HenVIII/267, rott. 5–9.
3 *Rot. Hund.* ii, pp. 465–6.
4 PRO SC 6/HenVIII/267, rot. 8–8d.
5 *Taxatio Nicholai IV*, p. 268.
6 PRO SC 6/HenVIII/267, rot. 8.

Since Chatteris abbey was worth less than £200, it ought to have been dissolved in 1536, following the act for the suppression of the lesser monasteries.[1] However, it was one of 44 nunneries which gained exemption from the statute.[2] In August 1536 the abbey received a licence to continue unsuppressed, probably on payment of a substantial sum, but this is not recorded.[3] The nunnery survived for another two years, until it was dissolved on 3 September 1538.[4]

After the dissolution of the nunnery, the former abbey's properties were split up before being granted to new tenants. In 1551 the nuns' manor in Chatteris itself was granted to Edward lord Clinton and Saye for an annual rent of 29s. The crown also granted the rectory of Chatteris to lord Clinton for 14s. 5d. annually in 1551, but within a fortnight lord Clinton had regranted both the manor and rectory to Thomas Rowe, a merchant tailor of London. In 1554 Rowe granted the manor and rectory to William Bettys whose family held it into the seventeenth century.[5] The crown sold the abbey's manor in Foxton in 1544 to a group of London aldermen including Sir Ralph Warren who was the sole owner from 1545. When his son died childless in 1597, the heir was Sir Oliver Cromwell who gave the manor *c.* 1609 to his ward Henry Palavicino of Babraham, the husband of his daughter Catherine.[6] The abbey's manor in Shepreth and the advowson of the church were granted by the crown to Edward Elrington in 1543; in 1556 they were held by Sir William Laxton, an alderman of London. They descended through his family until the nineteenth century: one of the seventeenth-century holders of the manor was the antiquarian John Layer who died in 1641.[7] The crown sold the abbey's manor in Barrington in 1543 to the Cambridge college of Michaelhouse, which was already lord of the other lands in the parish. In 1546, when Michaelhouse was incorporated into Trinity College, the manor passed to the new college.[8] In 1540 Ralph Rowlatt the elder bought the nuns' manor of Mincingbury in

1   *Valor Ecclesiasticus* iii, p. 499.
2   K. Cooke 'The English Nuns and the Dissolution' in *The Cloister and the World: Essays in Medieval History in Honour of Barbara Harvey* eds J. Blair and B. Golding (Oxford, 1996) p. 295.
3   *Letters and Papers, Foreign and Domestic, of the Reign of Henry VIII* ed. J. Gairdner, xi (PRO Texts and Calendars, 1888) p. 156, no. 385. 22.
4   Ibid. xiii, part ii (1893) p. 109, no. 272.
5   *VCH Cambs.* iv, p. 105.
6   Ibid. ix, p. 166.
7   Ibid. v, p. 253.
8   Ibid. v, p. 148.

Barley (Herts.) from the crown. He had already bought the Barley manor of Hoares in 1539. His son Ralph inherited both and bought Abbotsbury, another manor in Barley, in 1544. The whole estate descended together after Rowlatt's death in 1571.[1]

Spiritualities

In common with many religious houses, Chatteris abbey derived a significant proportion of its income from churches and tithes. The abbey became the appropriator of the parish churches of Chatteris and Shepreth, it acquired the advowson of Barley (Herts.) and had the right to tithes in Barley, Barrington and Honey Hill in the parish of Chatteris. In addition, the church of Kersey (Suff.) originally belonged to the abbey as, probably, did the church of Foxton.

The only church which Domesday Book lists amongst the possessions of Chatteris abbey is the church of Kersey (Suff.). The abbey did not retain this church for long. A late twelfth-century confirmation shows that the abbey granted their manor of Kersey in fee-farm to Adam de Cockfield in the mid-twelfth century (no. 186). The abbey probably granted Kersey church along with the manor since the church was in the possession of Nesta de Cockfield, great-granddaughter of Adam, in the early thirteenth century. Before her second marriage in 1240, Nesta de Cockfield, widow of Thomas de Burgo, granted the church to Kersey priory.[2]

The church of Foxton may once have belonged to Chatteris abbey too. Foxton was important to the nuns: the abbey held more land there than in any other parish and it held the manorial court for its extensive lands in Foxton, Shepreth and Barrington at Foxton. It would not be surprising if the abbey had originally been the patron of the church and three late twelfth or early thirteenth-century documents in the cartulary suggest that this may have been the case. There was a quarrel between the abbey and Richard son of Ilbert, rector of Foxton, concerning the tenure of one hide and nine acres of land in Foxton. In the ensuing agreement, the rector acknowledged that he did not hold the land in the right of his church, but that he held it of the abbey for his life, for one talent of gold annually (no. 131). In another agreement rector Peter de Shelford similarly admitted that two virgates and nine acres of land, three messuages and a meadow which he held in Foxton belonged to the abbey's demesne. He admitted that he held them for his life only, for a payment of one

---

1 *VCH Herts.* iv, pp. 38, 40–1.
2 *Mon. Ang.* vi, p. 592.

gold coin annually to the abbey (no. 130). Despite these two agreements the
dispute between the abbey and the rectors of Foxton continued. The next
rector, Simon, claimed that the same properties described in no. 130 belonged
to Foxton church. The matter seems finally to have been settled when bishop
Geoffrey – probably de Burgo (1225–8) – confirmed these properties to the
abbey (no. 129). The land in Foxton which the rectors held of the nuns was
probably the glebe. This suggests that Chatteris abbey had once been the
church's patron, but by the second half of the thirteenth century the bishop of
Ely was patron of Foxton church.[1] In addition to his spiritual jurisdiction over
the parishes in his diocese, the bishop of Ely also had a spiritual jurisdiction
over Chatteris abbey. He may have taken this spiritual authority over the
nunnery as the basis for taking over the patronage of Foxton church. Alternatively, since the bishop was the overlord of the abbey, it may have been in this
capacity that he took possession of the advowson at Foxton. In 1269 bishop
Hugh de Balsham undertook to appropriate Foxton church to the almonry of
Ely priory.[2] The rector at that time was the Italian, Manuel de Bagnaria, but
the church was held at farm by the prior and convent of Ely (no. 147). In 1275
Hugh de Balsham carried out the appropriation and ordained a vicarage whose
collation he reserved to himself and his successors.[3]

Chatteris abbey gained the income from two churches when the parish
churches of Chatteris and Shepreth were appropriated to the abbey. Nigel,
bishop of Ely, gave the lordship (*dominium*) and the advowson of the church of
St Peter in Chatteris to the abbey between *c.* 1158 and 30 May 1169 (nos.
10/76). In his charter Nigel ordered that, after the death of the two current
parsons, the profits of Chatteris church should be used to support the nunnery,
but he did not use the terminology of appropriation nor deal with the establishment of a vicarage. The issue of the vicar's income was addressed when
bishop William Longchamp confirmed the settlement reached between Chatteris abbey and Alan, vicar of Chatteris, between 5 June 1190 and 17 March
1195 (no. 79). Under this settlement Alan received the altar-dues and a third of
the tithes, whilst the abbey received all the other tithes and all the land pertaining to the church. However, the settlement also stated that the next vicar would
receive only the altar-dues and that, after Alan's death, the abbey would have all
the other revenues from the church. The vicar's income was fixed more precisely between 8 March 1220 and 6 May 1225 when bishop John of Fountains

1 *Rot. Hund.* ii, p. 548.
2 Cambridge UL, EDR G/3/28 'Liber M', pp. 195–6.
3 Ibid. pp. 197–8.

confirmed the appropriation of the church to the abbey (no. 11). The confirmation specified that the nuns should present a chaplain to the vicarage and that
he should have four marks annually from alter-dues, together with the house
which had formerly belonged to Matilda de Barley.

Chatteris abbey seems to have held the advowson of Shepreth church in the
twelfth century since Robert Martin tried, unsuccessfully, to claim the advowson from the abbey in 1214, following the death of the incumbent.[1] Eustace,
bishop of Ely, appropriated Shepreth church to the nunnery between 8 March
1198 and 3 February 1215 (no. 160), although it is unlikely that he would have
appropriated it during the papal Interdict of 23 March 1208–2 July 1214.
Neither Eustace's charter nor the entries on the Curia Regis rolls reveal
whether Robert Martin tried to claim the advowson before or after the
appropriation.

The charter of appropriation does not mention a vicarage but on 14 August
1269 bishop Hugh de Balsham settled a dispute between the vicar of Shepreth
and Chatteris abbey about the augmentation of the vicarage (no. 161). The
settlement awarded five acres of arable land previously held by the abbey to the
vicar, together with all the lesser tithes and 20s. annually from the abbey; the
abbey was awarded the tithe of corn and retained a villein and croft from the
five acres of land. In addition, the settlement safeguarded the right of the vicar
and his successors to live in the house then inhabited by the vicar. The abbey
took care to protect its income from Shepreth church. When the abbey confirmed to William de la Haye the chantry in his chapel in Shepreth, c. 1265 ×
1297, it stipulated that the parish church should lose nothing because of the
chapel, that all the obventions from the chapel should be paid to Shepreth
church and that William should give one pound of wax annually to the church
(no. 162). In 1533 the abbey granted the next right of presentation to Shepreth
vicarage to Robert Cooper, John Pory and Robert Davy who presented Richard
Rayment in 1536.[2]

As well as holding the rectories of the parish churches of Chatteris and
Shepreth, the abbey also received the tithes of the chapel of Honey Hill in the
parish of Chatteris. It is not clear when the abbey began to receive the tithes but
they may have been included in bishop Nigel's grant of the parish church in
c. 1158 × 1169 (nos. 10 and 76). In 1216 the prior and convent of Ramsey issued
a remission to the abbess of Chatteris of all disputes between them – including
that concerning the chapel of Honey Hill – until the election of an abbot (no.

---

1 *Cur. Reg. R.* vii, pp. 246, 248, 303.
2 Cambridge UL, EDR G/1/7, Goodrich register, fos. 104v–105r.

164). The remission contained an assurance that the abbess should meanwhile have all oblations and tithes pertaining to the chapel. The privilege of pope Innocent IV confirmed the abbey's right to these tithes in the mid-thirteenth century (no. 3). The tithes are not mentioned separately in the post-Dissolution minister's accounts, but they may have been included in the sum given for the issues of the rectory of Chatteris.[1]

Chatteris abbey held one of the manors in Barley (Herts.) and had the right to some of the tithes there. This right was confirmed during the reign of Henry II when a tithe dispute between Osbert, the rector, and the abbey was settled. The settlement allowed the nuns to retain the tithes from the lands which they had held in the time of Henry I, but it awarded to the rector all the other tithes, including those accumulated by the nuns since the reign of Henry I (no. 180). This settlement did not resolve the matter permanently though. In 1238, the dean and chapter of St Paul's confirmed a settlement agreed before papal judges delegate between Herbert, rector of Barley, and Chatteris abbey which concerned the ownership of greater and lesser tithes in Barley (no. 182). Only eight years later, in 1246, papal judges delegate dealt with another suit relating to the tithes in Barley (no. 181). In this case Richard, rector of Barley, charged the abbey with the loss which he claimed his church had suffered owing to the previous settlement between Herbert and the abbey. However, the judges confirmed the earlier settlement and Richard swore that he would observe it. There is no evidence that any subsequent rector of Barley challenged the abbey over tithes in the parish.

The abbey's tithes in Barley were not the only spiritual property which it acquired there. In 1268 Ralph son of Ralph son of Fulk de Broadfield granted the advowson of the church, together with three acres and three roods of arable land, to Chatteris abbey (nos. 177–8). In 1281, when the church was vacant, the abbess paid 40s. to Ralph for the release of his claim in the advowson (no. 179). Thereafter, the abbey retained the advowson until the early sixteenth century but, in 1506 × 1515, it granted its tithes in Barley and the right of presenting the next rector of Barley to James Stanley, bishop of Ely, and Walter Berkoke (no. 277).

The abbey also had rights over some tithes in the parish of Barrington. In a tithe-suit heard by papal judges delegate in 1249, Robert Passelewe, archdeacon of Lewes and rector of Barrington, accused the abbey of withholding from him the tithes from one carucate of land in Barrington (no. 112). The judgement in

---

[1] PRO SC 6/HenVIII/267, rot. 9.

the case was made by Hugh de Northwold, bishop of Ely, who ordained that Robert Passelewe should have the greater tithes from the nuns' lands in Barrington but that the nuns should have the tithes from their mill together with the lesser tithes.

THE VALUE OF THE ABBEY'S TEMPORALITIES AND SPIRITUALITIES

Domesday Book provides the earliest indication of the value of the endowment of Chatteris abbey. More than half of the nunnery's income came from its cluster of properties in the south Cambridgeshire parishes of Foxton, Barrington, Shepreth and Orwell. The value of the abbey's lands and half-mill in Foxton was £6 in 1086 and £7 before 1066; the value of its lands and mill in Barrington was £3 in 1086 and £4 before 1066; in Shepreth its lands and mill were worth £1 10s. in 1086 and £2 before 1066; and in Orwell its land was worth 1s. The abbey's other Cambridgeshire lands lay in Burwell and Over. The former were worth 10s. and the latter 16s. in 1086.[1] Although the abbey derived well over half its revenue from its Cambridgeshire properties, its two manors in Hertfordshire and Suffolk also generated a significant proportion of its income. The abbey's manor in Barley (Herts.) was valued at £3 10s. in 1086 and at £4 before 1066.[2] In south Suffolk, the abbey's lands, mill and church at Kersey, which had been worth £4 in 1066, were worth £5 by 1086; there was also one free man at Kersey worth 3s. 8d.[3] Kersey was the second most valuable of the abbey's possessions whose total value was £20 10s. 8d. in 1086 and had been £22 10s. 8d. before 1066.

Domesday Book records the gross income of eight nunneries which, in descending order of wealth, were Wilton (Wilts.), Shaftesbury (Dorset), Barking (Essex), Romsey (Hants.), Winchester (Hants.), Amesbury (Wilts.), Wherwell (Hants.) and Chatteris. Wilton and Shaftesbury were the only nunneries to owe knight-service: Wilton had a quota of five knights and Shaftesbury of ten, subsequently seven. Wilton had a gross income of £246 15s. and Shaftesbury of £234 5s. In 1086, Chatteris was much the poorest of the pre-Conquest houses with an income of only £20 10s. 8d.: the income of the second poorest house, Wherwell abbey, was £52 4s. Although Wilton abbey, the richest nunnery in 1086, had an income 12 times greater than that of Chatteris abbey, the range in the income of religious houses for men was much greater. The wealthiest

---

[1] *Domesday Book* i, fo. 193a.
[2] Ibid. i, fo. 136b.
[3] Ibid. ii, p. 389a.

monasteries were Glastonbury, with an income of £827 18s. 8d., and Ely, with
an income of £768 17s. 3d., both of which were much richer than Shaftesbury.
In contrast, the poorest monasteries were even poorer than Chatteris: Horton
had only £12 5s. 5d. whilst Swavesey had a mere £2.[1]

The two manors in Chatteris itself in 1086 were held by the abbots of Ramsey and Ely. They were valued at £3 and £2 respectively in 1086 but had been
worth £4 and £2 10s. before 1066.[2] The nunnery subsequently acquired the
manor in Chatteris which had belonged to the abbot of Ely; this acquisition
probably occurred quite soon after Henry I had granted the patronage of
Chatteris abbey to bishop Hervey of Ely. However, even after the addition of a
manor in Chatteris to their endowments, the nuns still received the core of
their revenues from the abbey's lands in south Cambridgeshire.

From the thirteenth century onwards, taxation records provide valuations
of the abbey's income, both temporal and spiritual. The first surviving valuation of the abbey's spiritual income was probably made in 1217. It valued the
church of Chatteris at £4 and that of Shepreth at £11.[3] In 1254 the valuation of
Norwich valued Chatteris church at £13 6s. 8d. and the church of Shepreth at
£10.[4] The next extant valuations, made in 1276, were much greater: Chatteris
church was valued at £20 10s. and Shepreth at £23 6s. 8d.[5] However, in the
taxation of pope Nicholas IV in 1291 the valuation of Chatteris church was
reduced to £16 13s. 4d. and that of Shepreth to £13 6s. 8d. In 1291 the abbess
also received a share, valued at £4, of the revenues of Barley church (Herts.).[6] In
the case of Chatteris abbey, the *Valor Ecclesiasticus* of 1535 does not differentiate
between the abbey's spiritual and temporal revenues but gives only the total net
income of the nunnery, which was £97 3s. 4d.[7] The minister's accounts produced after the dissolution of the abbey show that in 1539 the revenue from
Chatteris church was £7 4s. and that in addition the minister received a pension
of 6s. 8d. from the vicarage of Chatteris. In the same year Richard Ingreth' paid

---

[1]   D. Knowles *The Monastic Order in England. A History of its Development from the Times of St
      Dunstan to the Fourth Lateran Council 940–1216* 2nd edn (Cambridge, 1963) pp. 702–3; *VCH
      Wilts.* iii, p. 233.
[2]   *Domesday Book* i, fos. 192d, 191d.
[3]   BL Cotton MS Tib. B. ii, fo. 235r–v, printed in W. E. Lunt *The Valuation of Norwich*
      (Oxford, 1926) appendix i, pp. 536, 539.
[4]   Lunt *Valuation of Norwich*, pp. 210, 217.
[5]   BL Cotton MS Claud. C. xi, fo. 22r, printed in Lunt *Valuation of Norwich*, appendix ii, pp.
      554–5.
[6]   *Taxatio Nicholai IV*, pp. 18, 265, 267.
[7]   *Valor Ecclesiasticus* iii, p. 499.

£10 for the farm of the more distant rectory of Shepreth which, unlike the rectory of Chatteris, seems to have been leased by the abbey before its suppression.[1]

As well as valuing the spiritualities of the abbey, the taxation of pope Nicholas IV also gives detailed valuations of its temporalities. The valuations show that in 1291 the abbey had temporalities worth £79 5s. 8d and that the abbey derived £73 2s. 6d. of this income from five parishes: in Foxton its temporalities were valued at £25 12s. 2d.; in Chatteris they were valued at £16 4s. 5d.; in Barrington at £11 3s. 1d.; in Barley (Herts.) at £10 2s. 10d. and in Kersey (Suff.) at £10.[2] However Shepreth appears to have been omitted from the valuations. It must have been another important source of temporal income because in 1279 the abbey held 160 acres of land there in demesne, whilst its free tenants held 28¼ acres and its villeins another 135 acres.[3] The other parishes which were listed in the taxation of Nicholas IV, and which together provided £6 3s. 2d. of temporal income for the abbey, were Huntingdon, Bircham (Norf.), Burwell, Kingston, Over, Madingley and Wilburton.[4]

The minister's accounts for Michaelmas 1539 list the revenues from the former nunnery's properties in the first full year after the dissolution of the abbey. They show that the gross income was £122 7s. 11¾d. Spiritualities accounted for £17 10s. 8d. of this amount and perquisities of the courts for another £4 15s. 6d. The gross income from temporalities was therefore £104 17s. 3¾d. As in the thirteenth century, it was property in the parishes of Foxton, Chatteris, Barley (Herts.), Shepreth, Barrington and Kersey (Suff.) which produced the greater part of the revenue. Property in Foxton alone generated a total of £28 11s. 4½d., more than any other parish, whilst property in the three south Cambridgeshire parishes of Foxton, Shepreth and Barrington together produced a sum of £53 8s. 2¾d., over half of the total temporal income from the former abbey's property. This shows that the abbey's estate in south Cambridgeshire remained its core source of income throughout its history. In contrast, in 1539, the former abbey's temporal property in Chatteris itself and in the nearby villages of Benwick, Doddington and Wimblington was worth only £15 1s. 9d.[5]

---

1 PRO SC 6/HenVIII/267, rot. 9.
2 *Taxatio Nicholai IV*, pp. 15, 133, 268.
3 *Rot. Hund.* ii, p. 562.
4 *Taxatio Nicholai IV*, pp. 51, 105, 130, 268.
5 PRO SC 6/HenVIII/267, rott. 5–9.

Despite the additions to its endowment after the Conquest, Chatteris abbey remained the poorest of the nunneries founded before 1066. The net income of Chatteris abbey in the *Valor Ecclesiasticus* of 1535 was over £97, that of Wherwell – the second poorest nunnery in 1086 – was over £339, that of Wilton over £601 and that of Shaftesbury over £1166. In 1535 the richest nunnery, with a net income of over £1731, was Syon abbey (Middx), founded in 1415.[1] However, the foundation of many, very poorly-endowed nunneries after the Conquest made the endowment of Chatteris abbey seem less meagre by comparison. By the fourteenth and fifteenth centuries there were over 140 houses of nuns and canonesses in England and Wales.[2] Chatteris was the second wealthiest of the five Cambridgeshire nunneries in existence at the end of the Middle Ages. Denny abbey, a Franciscan house, was the wealthiest nunnery in the county and had a net income of over £172 in 1535, but Chatteris abbey, with its income of over £97, was richer than Ickleton priory whose income was over £71 and Swaffham Bulbeck priory whose income was over £40. Chatteris had also been wealthier than the Cambridge priory of St Radegund, dissolved in 1496, which had an income of *c.* £75 in 1450. There were some nunneries which were even poorer than the those in Cambridgeshire: for example, the nearby Benedictine nunnery at Hinchingbrooke (Hunts.) had an income of less than £18 in 1535.[3] Chatteris abbey's endowment was always modest, but from the twelfth century onwards there were many other nunneries with similar or lesser incomes. The gross income of Chatteris in 1535 – like that of the other houses in Cambridgeshire – was not recorded in the *Valor*, but the post-Dissolution minister's accounts show that it was £122 7s. 11¾d. in 1539.[4] In 1535, two-thirds of nunneries had a gross income of less than £100 a year and over a third had less than £50 a year.[5] Therefore at the end of its life, Chatteris abbey was wealthier than two-thirds of the nunneries in the country, but was still far less well-endowed than the richest nunneries.

---

1   Knowles and Hadcock *Medieval Religious Houses* 2nd edn, pp. 202, 253, 255.
2   Ibid. p. 494.
3   Ibid. pp. 253–4, 257, 286.
4   PRO SC 6/HenVIII/267, rot. 9.
5   J. H. Tillotson *Marrick Priory: a Nunnery in Late Medieval Yorkshire* (Borthwick Paper no. 75; York, 1989) p. 2.

THE CHRONOLOGY, TYPE AND SIZE OF DONATIONS MADE TO THE ABBEY

The cartulary shows that many benefactors made additions to the estates of Chatteris abbey in the centuries after the Conquest, but it is difficult to date the majority of their donations exactly. This is partly because most of the witness-lists from the charters have been lost: none of the original charters survives and the scribe who copied the charters into the cartulary omitted almost all the witness-lists. In addition, many donors came from obscure local families rather than from noble or knightly families whose members are usually easier to date. The imprecision in the dating of so many charters means that it is impossible to analyse in detail the chronology of donations to the abbey. Nevertheless, general patterns do emerge. It is clear that there were no significant geographical variations in the chronology of donations and that most donations were made between the last quarter of the twelfth century and the third quarter of the thirteenth century. Several donations date from the mid to late twelfth century and from the late thirteenth century, whilst a few date from the fourteenth century. Although the abbey probably received other gifts in the twelfth century for which no documentary evidence survives, most of the post-Conquest donations still seem to have been made between the late twelfth century and the statute of mortmain in 1279. The fourteenth century charters show that the statute of mortmain did not halt donations to the abbey but, in common with most religious houses, the main phase of territorial expansion at Chatteris abbey had ended by the later thirteenth century.[1]

Despite the many donations which the cartulary records, the abbey attracted few substantial endowments after Domesday Book. One of the twelfth-century bishops of Ely – probably Hervey (1109–31) or Nigel (1133–69) – seems to have given his manor in Chatteris to the abbey, but most benefactors gave only small parcels of land. Of the 13 gifts of land in Chatteris which specify the extent of the land given, six were gifts of only a quarter of an acre (one rood) and five were of half an acre; the other two gifts were of five and a quarter acres and eight acres.[2] The cartulary shows that the abbey also received four gifts of one selion in Chatteris and one each of two, three and four selions, together with one gift of one *cultura* and one of one *cultura* with half an acre.[3] In addition,

---

1   S. Raban *Mortmain Legislation and the English Church 1279–1500* (Cambridge, 1982) pp. 166–9.
2   Gifts of ¼ acre: nos. 31, 48–9, 54, 57 and 65; gifts of ½ acre: nos. 24/45, 38–9, 46 and 62; gift of 5¼ acres: no. 34; gift of 8 acres: no. 68.
3   Gifts of 1 selion: nos. 33, 53, 58 and 67; gift of 2 selions: no. 25/41; gift of 3 selions: no. 66; gift of 4 selions: no. 63; gift of 1 *cultura*: nos. 27/40; gift of 1 *cultura* and ½ acre: no. 28.

two gifts of one messuage in Chatteris, two of two messuages and one of three were made.[1] The abbey received very small parcels of land elsewhere in the Isle of Ely: it acquired one and a half acres each of land and meadow in Stuntney and a messuage in Ely (nos. 91–2). The nunnery's most local benefactors tended to make very small donations but there were exceptions to this pattern: in 1387 John Dreng gave 15 messuages, one toft, almost 21½ acres of land and nine and a quarter acres of meadow in Chatteris, Doddington and Wimblington to the abbey (nos. 256–8).

Most gifts to the nunnery of land outside the Isle of Ely were small, but few benefactors outside the Isle made gifts of tiny parcels of land containing an acre or less. For example, none of the gifts of land in Foxton was large but none was a mere fraction of an acre: the abbey received one gift of three acres, two of five and one of 10 acres with five roods of meadow, a messuage and a croft.[2] In Madingley, the abbey bought one acre of land and another eight selions of land with one rood of meadow; it was also given five acres of land with half an acre of meadow (nos. 110 and 238–9). As well as these smaller acquisitions, the abbey received two substantial endowments in Madingley. Robert brother of Richard FitzNeal gave one hide of land to the abbey in the mid-twelfth century and Ernald Picot pledged another hide when he died on pilgrimage to Jerusalem *c.* 1180: this hide was divided between the abbey and Ernald's son Ranulph in 1205.[3] The cartulary shows that the abbey received several smaller donations in Shepreth of 11¾ acres, five and three-quarter acres and half an acre of land together with one larger gift of 40 acres made by Simon son of Walter Martin *c.* 1250 (nos. 150, 152, 158, 149). In Barley (Herts.) the abbey was given four acres and three and three-quarter acres of land (nos. 175, 177); in Elm it was given five acres (no. 235); and in Hemingford[4] (Hunts.) it received with Peter Bonem 16 acres of arable land, two acres of meadow and a messuage (no. 272).

Given that most of the abbey's lands always lay in Cambridgeshire, it is not surprising that the overwhelming majority of gifts of land in the cartulary were in Cambridgeshire too. The endowments which the abbey received after the Conquest created a significant estate in Chatteris itself but otherwise reinforced

---

[1] Gifts of 1 messuage: nos. 23 and 68; gifts of 2 messuages: nos. 17/59 and 18; gift of 3 messuages: no. 55.
[2] Gift of 3 acres: no. 127; gifts of 5 acres: nos. 143 and 152; gift of 10 acres and 5 roods of meadow: no. 140.
[3] No. 109; *VCH Cambs.* ix, p. 168; *Cur. Reg. R.* iii, p. 189.
[4] The charter does not make clear whether this land lay in Hemingford Abbots or Hemingford Grey.

the pre-Conquest pattern of endowment. The core of the abbey's estates remained the lands in the south of the county, despite the numerous twelfth and
thirteenth century gifts of property in Chatteris and the scattered gifts of
property elsewhere.

Most benefactors gave land to the abbey but some provided fixed sources of
income by granting rents which ranged in value from ½d. to 40s. annually. The
abbey was granted rents of: ½d. and 4d. in Chatteris (*s.* xiii[1-2]); 3d. each in
Stuntney and Little Thetford (1201 × 1222); a prebend of 20s. in Fen Ditton
(1174 × 1189); 2s. and four capons annually in Ely (*s.* xii[4] × *s.* xiii[2]); half a mark
of quitrent from a messuage and 5s. from a tenement in Cambridge (*s.* xiii[1-2]; *s.*
xiii[2-4]); 9s. 4d. in Pinchbeck (Lincs.) together with rents of 6d. and 2d., probably
also in Pinchbeck (*s.* xiii[2] × 1265); 10s. in Lincoln (*s.* xii[4] × 1188); 5s. in Hemingford[1] (Hunts.) (*s.* xiii[2] × 1265); 4s. in Kingston (1239 × *s.* xiii[3]); and 2s. 2d.
of rent in Chatteris, Doddington and Wimblington (1387).[2] The abbey also
received, in the last decade of the twelfth century, 4s. annually from Ralph son
of William of Ely, whilst Adam son of Robert de Cockfield granted a rent of
40s. from his first church to fall vacant, excepting Kersey and the chapel of
Lindsey (Suff.), but meanwhile giving one mark annually to the abbey (nos. 72
and 73/188).

Turfs were valuable because of the dearth of alternative sources of fuel in the
fenland but the cartulary records no grants of turbaries to the abbey. The abbey
did, though, receive several fisheries, most of which were granted during the
thirteenth century. All bar one of the grants of fisheries are grouped together in
the cartulary between fos. 99v and 103r (nos. 83–9 and 91). The other grant is
one of the charters which were added in another hand after the completion of
the main part of the cartulary (no. 211). Most of the grants are of fisheries in
Chatteris, but at least one, and possibly two, are in Upwell and Outwell
(Cambs. and Norf.) (nos. 87 and 91). These grants meant that by the later
thirteenth century the abbey had acquired a significant number of local fishing
rights, the catch from which doubtless provided an important element in the
nuns' diet, particularly given the abbey's isolated location.

The cartulary contains nine charters in favour of the abbey in which the
donor reserved a rent.[3] These rents ranged from ½d. annually for one rood of
land in Chatteris (no. 57) to 6s. annually for land with a mill in Thriplow (no.
166). Although the cartulary does not provide a complete record of all do-

---

1 Again, this charter could refer to Hemingford Abbots or Hemingford Grey.
2 Nos. 20, 21/70, 91, 94, 99, 104, 108, 226–7, 232, 240 and 256–8.
3 Nos. 54, 57, 62, 91/223, 105, 125, 166, 175 and 217.

nations made to the abbey, it is unlikely that reserved rents were a significant financial burden since most of those recorded in the cartulary were only fractions of a shilling. Even the 6s. owed to the bishop of Ely from the mid-twelfth century for land with a mill in Thriplow was far from onerous because the ownership of a mill was likely to generate considerable profit. At some point between 1243 and 1286, the abbey gave this mill back to the bishop of Ely, reserving a rent of 16s. (no. 95).

Several charters in the cartulary released the abbey from other rents which it owed. For example, in 1298 × 1306 John Fithien surrendered the annual rent of 2½d. which the abbey used to pay to him for the houses and two roods of land given to it by Geoffrey le Spenser (no. 38). In a document which probably dates from the late fourteenth or early fifteenth century, John Winwick, John Cokerell and Nicholas Tyd released the abbey from payment of a rent of 2s. 2d. annually for lands in Chatteris, formerly paid to Richard Radewyn' of Swaffham Prior and his ancestors (no. 80). Sometimes, a payment was made in return for a release from a rent. In the late thirteenth century Amicia de Cambridge, who was then sacrist of the abbey, paid 6d. to Ralph son of Katherine Coveney when he released her from the payment of ½d. annually for one rood of arable land in Chatteris (no. 47). The cartulary also includes a document in which the abbey paid for the quittance of a widow's dower rights in 1235 × *s*. xiii[4]: Aveline, the former wife of Henry Briston of Chatteris, quitclaimed to the abbey her dower rights relating to the abbey, within or without Chatteris, for 12d. (no. 44). However, the abbey did not always pay for such a reinforcement of its rights. Juliana the widow of Henry Fithien quitclaimed to the abbey a *cultura* of land called Stocking in Chatteris, which had belonged to her husband, without taking any payment from the abbey (no. 29; *s*. xiii[3] × 1290).

Many charters in the cartulary are background deeds showing the history of the ownership of properties which were given to the nunnery. It is sometimes possible to trace in the cartulary several previous owners of a piece of land through the background deeds which benefactors passed on with the property. For example, nos. 81, 52 and 54 record the passage in the thirteenth century of one rood of land in Chatteris through the hands of Thomas Alberd', Thomas, dispenser of Chatteris, and Isabel daughter of Hervy de Foxton who gave the rood to Chatteris abbey. These three charters also show that the scribe who compiled the cartulary did not always group together charters relating to the same property.

A few charters in the cartulary do not seem to relate to lands given to the nunnery. These charters are gifts from one individual to another of: a messuage in Chatteris; a messuage and nine acres of land in Barrington; a messuage with a croft and land with a meadow in Barrington; and four selions of land with headlands of meadow and an acre of meadow in Chatteris (nos. 56, 116/122, 121, 234). These documents may be background deeds for gifts to the nunnery which are now unrecorded.

THE ABBEY'S BENEFACTORS

Henry I granted to Chatteris abbey the remission of the half-mark of ward-penny which it owed to the crown, but the abbey received no additions to its endowment from royalty. Nor did the abbey attract noble benefactors. The only tenants-in-chief of the crown who made recorded donations to the abbey were three of the early bishops of Ely: Nigel (1133–69), Geoffrey Ridel (1174–89) and Eustace (1198–1215).[1] It was probably Nigel or his predecessor, Hervey (1109–31), who also gave Ely's manor in Chatteris to the abbey, but this gift does not occur in the cartulary. As well as these bishops, a significant number of other clerical benefactors occurs in the cartulary. William of Ely, archdeacon of Cleveland (1201–1222); Simon, parson of Cranfield (Beds.) (s. xii^4 × s. xiii^2) and Ralph de Cardington, parson of Barley (1329–1359), all made donations as did the chaplains Ebrard, son of Robert Briston (s. xiii$^{1-3}$); John son of Absolon de Cambridge (s. xiii$^{1-2}$); John Percy (s. xiii$^{2-4}$) and Roger le Fraunceys of Foxton (s. xiii^2 × 1290).[2]

The majority of the abbey's benefactors came from local families. Some were of knightly status, but others seem to have come from lower orders of society. Knightly donations included those made by Adam son of Robert de Cockfield (c. 1190 × c. 1198), Roger Gaugi, Simon de Insula and Richard Muschet (s. xiii$^{1-2}$), Thomas de Bancis (s. xiii$^{2-3}$), Simon son of Walter Martin of Shepreth (c. 1250) and Ralph son of Ralph son of Fulk de Broadfield (1268).[3] It is difficult to be sure of the status of many of the abbey's donors, but most of the numerous tiny parcels of land which the abbey acquired were probably given by modest, local land-holders. Some of these donors were of lesser gentry status but others seem to have been drawn from the ranks of the more substantial free peasantry.

---

[1] Donations by Nigel: nos. 10/76, 89, 166; donations by Geoffrey Ridel: no. 94; appropriation to Chatteris abbey by Eustace: no. 160.

[2] Nos. 91, 236, 254, 88, 104, 108 and 140.

[3] Nos. 73/188, 55, 68, 92, 115, 125, 149 and 177.

Brian Golding found that free peasants made many of the surviving donations to the Gilbertine priory of Alvingham (Lincs.) and some of those to the
Gilbertine priory of Bullingham (Lincs.). In the case of both priories, almost all
the peasant donors came from the upper ranks of the local peasantry and most
made very small donations.[1] Golding used seals and witness-lists as two of his
criteria for establishing whether obscure donors were likely to be peasants.
Peasants tended to have much simpler devices on their seals – often a fleur-de-lis
– whilst both peasants and gentry usually drew witnesses to their charters from
their own ranks. In the case of Chatteris abbey, the lack of original charters and
the omission of most witness-lists prevents the use of these indicators in the
detection of peasant donors. However Golding also used the size of donations
to help determine the rank of donors.[2] It would be dangerous to assume that all
donations of small parcels of land were made by peasants, since higher ranking
individuals might also make such gifts, but the size of donations may be taken
as a very general guide to the rank of obscure donors. The majority of gifts to
Chatteris abbey of very small plots of land were made by donors from Chatteris
itself. As described above, 13 gifts of land in Chatteris specify precisely the
extent of the land given, of which six were gifts of only a quarter of an acre (one
rood) and five were of half an acre.[3] The abbey also received four gifts of one
selion in Chatteris.[4] Most if not all of these gifts were probably made by
peasants. Whilst many other gifts to the nunnery of land in Chatteris and
elsewhere were far from extensive, few benefactors outside the Isle of Ely gave
tiny parcels of land containing an acre or less. Some of the slightly larger gifts to
the abbey of a few acres or a *cultura* of land may also have been made by
wealthier peasants, but the large number of very small gifts of land in Chatteris
itself suggests that the abbey was able to attract most peasant donors from its
immediate vicinity.

Despite the number of gifts of land which seem to have been made by
peasants, the cumulative impact of peasant donations on the size of the abbey's
estate cannot have been great. However, small donations could be more valuable than their size would suggest if they consolidated separate plots of land
already held by the abbey. In addition, these donations are important because
they show the significance of the abbey to lower-ranking local people. The

---

[1] B. Golding 'The Gilbertine Priories of Alvingham and Bullington: their Endowments and
Benefactors', D.Phil. thesis (University of Oxford, 1979) pp. 291–329.

[2] Ibid. pp. 275–8.

[3] Gifts of ¼ acre: nos. 31, 48–9, 54, 57 and 65; gifts of ½ acre: nos. 24/45, 38–9, 46 and 62.

[4] Gifts of 1 selion: nos. 33, 53, 58 and 67.

abbey was essentially a local institution which was able to attract support from the richer members of the local peasantry as well as from local knightly families.

Since most of the abbey's donors were local people of limited means, whether or not they were peasants, the abbey's estates remained concentrated in Cambridgeshire. Moreover, given that the majority of the abbey's benefactors lived nearby, the absence of other nunneries in the vicinity may have worked to the abbey's advantage as it built up its endowment. There were no other nunneries within a 12 mile radius of Chatteris. The nearest were the tiny Benedictine priory at Hinchingbrooke (Hunts.) and the Franciscan abbey which was founded at Waterbeach in 1294 but abandoned in favour of Denny in the mid-fourteenth century.[1] The other nunneries in Cambridgeshire were the priories of St Radegund in Cambridge, Swaffham Bulbeck to the east of Cambridge and Ickleton near the border with Essex. There was also a cluster of four nunneries in west Norfolk at Blackborough, Crabhouse, Marham and Shouldham, and in north-east Northamptonshire was the Benedictine priory of Stamford.[2]

The great majority of the donors to Chatteris abbey who appear in the cartulary made only one gift each; a few made two and Nigel, bishop of Ely (1133–69), made three. However Ismaena, daughter of Ralph Briston (s. xiii$^{1-2}$), and John Vivien (s. xiii$^{2-4}$) each made four separate donations, all of property in Chatteris.[3] They made grants of small rents and fisheries and gifts of land ranging in extent from one rood to five and a quarter acres. Although both these local benefactors made four recorded donations to the nunnery, the small scale of their gifts meant that some other donors made more substantial gifts in a single charter.

The Briston family, who made several donations of property in Chatteris to the abbey, is particularly interesting because some of the many variants of their name – Brickeston', Bricston', Brixston' and Brixton' – suggest that the family may have been descended from Bricstan. Bricstan lived in Chatteris in the early twelfth century and, when he was imprisoned in London, was reputedly freed from his shackles by a miracle of St Etheldreda.[4]

---

[1] Knowles and Hadcock *Medieval Religious Houses* 2nd edn, p. 286.
[2] Ibid.: map of 'The Nuns in England and Wales', following p. 565.
[3] Donations by Ismaena daughter of Ralph Briston: nos. 20, 21/70, 24/45 and 84; donations by John Vivien: nos. 31, 33, 34 and 83.
[4] *Liber Eliensis* ed. Blake, pp. 266–9.

Thomas de Bancis, another of the abbey's benefactors from Cambridgeshire, is notable because his family also endowed a convent in London. The Chatteris cartulary records two gifts by Thomas de Bancis to the abbey in the mid-thirteenth century (nos. 115 and 125). Previously, in the second half of the twelfth century, Eustace, Roger and William de Bancis had made several donations of property in Wimpole and Kingston to the London priory of St Mary, Clerkenwell, which seems to have been a house for Augustinian canonesses.[1] These gifts show that, although one member of this Cambridgeshire knightly family supported Chatteris abbey, some of his ancestors had chosen to make donations to another distant, though admittedly wealthier, house for women. It seems that the de Bancis family may also have preferred to send its daughters to the priory of St Mary, Clerkenwell. Although one of the thirteenth-century abbesses of Chatteris was called Mabel de Bancis, three women from the family were canonesses at Clerkenwell in the second half of the twelfth century: Margaret and Hawisa, daughters of William de Bancis, and Avice, daughter of Eustace de Bancis, all entered the priory.[2]

A significant proportion of the abbey's benefactors were women. Given the preponderance in the cartulary of gifts to the abbey of property in Chatteris, it is not surprising that most of the female benefactors who appear in the cartulary gave property in Chatteris too. The cartulary contains evidence of 40 donations of land, rents, fisheries and other rights in Chatteris, of which 11 were made by women.[3] These 11 donations were all made in the thirteenth century apart from one which seems to have been made in the early fourteenth century (no. 66). The abbey had eight female benefactors: seven women each made one gift of land and one woman, Ismaena daughter of Ralph Briston, made four donations of land, fisheries, rents and homage in the first half of the thirteenth century (nos. 20, 21/70, 24/45, and 84). All the gifts of land in Chatteris made by women were small. Four women gave only one rood of land each, three gave half an acre and one gave three selions.[4] In another thirteenth-century charter, Andrew son of Henry, priest, and Alice his wife, the daughter of Ralph Briston, jointly granted four fisheries in Chatteris to the abbey (no. 86). As well as the women who gave property in Chatteris to the abbey, the

1 *Cartulary of St Mary Clerkenwell* ed. W. O. Hassall (Camden 3rd ser. lxxi, 1949) p. viii and nos. 120–25, 130–33.
2 Ibid. nos. 125, 130 and 133.
3 Nos. 20, 21/70, 24/45, 39, 46, 48–9, 54, 57, 66 and 84 record donations by women.
4 Gifts in Chatteris by women of 1 rood: nos. 48–9, 54 and 57; gifts of ½ acre (2 roods): nos. 24/45, 39, 46; gift of 3 selions: no. 66.

cartulary records several other donations by women. Cecilia Godsho and her sister Amicia gave land in the Cambridge parish of St John Zachary to the abbey (s. xiii[1-2]); Isabel de Indyngword' granted 5s. rent in Hemingford (Hunts.) (s. xiii[2] × 1265); Beatrice the former wife of Jolanus de Bradehous granted 4s. rent in Kingston (1239 × s. xiii[3]); and Isabel de Hemingford gave Peter Bonem with the lands and messuage which he held of her in Hemingford (1242 × s. xiii[3]).[1] It is striking, though, that none of the benefactors in the cartulary who gave property in Foxton, Shepreth and Barrington were women.

Two gifts to the abbey in the cartulary were made by men with the explicit consent of their wives. In the first half of the thirteenth century, Robert le Noreis gave two selions of land, probably in Chatteris, to the abbey, with the assent of his wife, Margaret, and heir, Azo (nos. 25/41). In the same period, Richard Muschet gave a messuage in Potter's Lane, Ely to the abbey's infirmary, with the assent of his wife (no. 92). The inclusion of the wives' consent may indicate that Robert le Noreis and Richard Muschet made these gifts from their wives' marriage-portions. The cartulary also has an example of a gift of land by an unmarried woman together with a later surrender of the land by her husband after their marriage. In the early thirteenth century, Ismaena daughter of Ralph Briston made a gift in free alms of two roods of land in Chatteris to the nunnery in a charter which included a warranty clause (nos. 24/45). Henry de Merchyt, her husband, subsequently surrendered the two roods given by Ismaena and swore that he would warrant the land to the abbey (nos. 22/64).

DONATIONS TO THE ABBEY FOR PURPOSES SPECIFIED BY THE BENEFACTORS

Most benefactors did not require the income from their donations to Chatteris abbey to be used in a particular way. However, the cartulary contains 15 charters which specify how the revenue derived from them was to be spent. Three charters state that the donations were to be used to support the convent's infirmary; five were assigned to the conventual church; six were to be used to support the almonry or its activities; and, in a gift of two roods of land, one rood was allocated to the almonry and the other to the church.[2] Of the donations to the conventual church, one was made to maintain the light of the high altar, another for the light of St Katherine and four for the lights of St Mary.

---

[1] Nos. 105, 232, 240 and 272.

[2] Donations to the infirmary, nos. 72, 91/223 and 92; donations to the conventual church, nos. 54, 57, 65, 115 and 240; donations to the almonry, nos. 21/70, 33, 49, 53, 58 and 67; donation of 2 roods to the almonry and the church, no. 62.

One of the latter donations towards a light for the mass of St Mary was also to be used to pay a chaplain to celebrate the mass of St Mary there perpetually (no. 115).

Nine of the 15 charters described above are donations of land or rent in Chatteris and another is a grant of rent probably also in Chatteris (nos. 21/70). Since the overwhelming majority of donations to the abbey in the cartulary relate to property in Chatteris itself, it is not surprising that most of the donations allocated to specific uses relate to Chatteris too. It is significant, though, that all seven donations in favour of the almonry concern property in Chatteris. Although the core of the abbey's estate lay in Foxton, Shepreth and Barrington in south Cambridgeshire, no recorded donations of property in these parishes are directed to the almonry. It seems that benefactors from Chatteris itself may have viewed their donations differently because of the proximity of the abbey. The abbey's local importance as a social and economic, as well as religious, institution seems to be reflected in the specific requirements of local benefactors. One of the donations assigned to the almonry was made principally for the support of poor women under the authority of the abbey (no. 49). This suggests that the nunnery had a system for administering alms to local poor women which required the women to submit to the jurisdiction of the nuns. Whilst local and more distant patrons alike doubtless sought to support the nuns and to ensure the salvation of themselves and their families through their endowments, some local patrons seem to have used the abbey as an institutional means of providing for the local poor. The nunnery not only provided spiritual services, it was also a medium for local charity. The cartulary reveals another function which Chatteris abbey fulfilled for its benefactors. In common with many other religious houses, the nunnery allowed benefactors to be buried in the conventual church. In the later thirteenth or early fourteenth centuries, Geoffrey de Barnwell made a gift of two roods of land in Chatteris, one for the almonry and one for the light of St Mary, *cum corpore meo* (no. 62). In addition Robert Bollonde stated in his will, which was proved in 1533, that he wished to be buried in the abbey, before the blessed rood.[1]

As well as the seven donations in favour of the almonry, the cartulary also contains a confirmation by abbess M. and the convent of Chatteris of 5s. annually in Hemingford (Hunts.) which Agnes, a former abbess, had assigned to the alms-house (no. 232). This annual sum of 5s. was half that given to the abbey by Isabel de Indyngword'. The confirmation was made on the inter-

---

1 CCRO Ely consistory court probate register, vol. 7, fo. 94r.

cession of Ralph de Barley who gave and quitclaimed to the abbey 10 acres of land which he held of them in Foxton and Barrington. It shows that even donations which were not initially allocated to specific uses might subsequently be diverted to them.

DOWRY-GRANTS

In common with the benefactors of other religious houses, donors who gave property in free alms to Chatteris abbey hoped to receive in return the spiritual reward of a share in the prayers of the community. Gifts in free alms often included formulaic phrases in which benefactors sought prayers for the salvation of themselves and their relatives. However some benefactors made donations to Chatteris abbey specifically to accompany the reception of a female relative by the convent, rather than for general spiritual benefits. The rule of St Benedict did not require entrants to the religious life to make a donation to their house, but neither did the rule preclude such gifts. Postulants could either offer their property to the poor or make a formal donation to the house they were to enter, keeping nothing for themselves.[1] In the eleventh and early twelfth centuries, both male and female entrants to religious houses commonly brought with them gifts of property from their relatives. For example, the cartulary of Shaftesbury abbey shows that the nunnery received 18 dowry-grants from the relatives of women who entered the convent in *c.* 1086– *c.* 1121.[2] Similarly, the register of Godstow abbey records 19 dowry-grants dating from the twelfth and thirteenth centuries.[3] From the second quarter of the twelfth century onwards, such gifts increasingly came to be categorized as simoniacal by canon lawyers. This trend culminated in the sixty-fourth canon of the fourth Lateran council which forbade dowry-grants to nunneries in 1215. Before 1215, both nunneries and monasteries had been criticized for accepting gifts on the reception of new members, but following the ruling of 1215 the accusations of simony were directed primarily at nunneries.

Despite the canon and the subsequent action to enforce it, there is considerable evidence that benefactors continued to make dowry-grants, particularly to poorer houses, well into the thirteenth century. The practice continued partly

---

[1] *The Rule of St Benedict* ed. D. O. H. Blair, 2nd edn (Fort-Augustus, 1906) pp. 156–7.
[2] K. Cooke 'Donors and Daughters: Shaftesbury Abbey's Benefactors, Endowments and Nuns *c.* 1086–1130' in *Anglo-Norman Studies* xii *Proceedings of the Battle Conference 1989* (Woodbridge, 1990) pp. 29–30.
[3] Power *Medieval English Nunneries*, p. 17.

because the canon was directed at those dowry-grants which were mandatory or were the product of negotiated agreements: grants which were made freely, without a pact between the benefactor and nunnery, were likely to be tolerated. However, dowry-grants also persisted for the practical reason that many nunneries were very poorly endowed and the number of places in them limited. Small, poor convents which grew through the admission of new members needed additional revenue to prevent them from becoming poorer still.[1] This need accounts for the substantial number of dowry-grants which survive from the many small nunneries in Yorkshire.[2] Visitation evidence from the diocese of Lincoln suggests that some nunneries were still requiring dowry-grants in the early fifteenth century despite the efforts to eradicate them. Bishop Fleming issued an injunction to Elstow abbey (Beds.) *c.* 1421–2 ordering that only suitable women were to be admitted as nuns and that no money or anything else was to be demanded on their entry. In addition, in 1440, the visitation of Nun Cotham priory (Lincs.) revealed that the house used to require about £20 from novices on admission. As a result, the prioress was enjoined not to receive more nuns than could be supported by the income of the house and not to exact payment. The bishop did, though, allow the prioress to accept offerings made to the house by new members or their friends if they were made charitably and no pre-arranged pact or promise existed.[3]

The Chatteris cartulary provides several examples of gifts made by benefactors to the abbey when female relatives entered the convent. Michael Peregrinus confirmed a tenement, probably in Chatteris, which his father, Henry, had given to the nunnery with Tecla, Michael's sister (no. 26). Robert de Insula gave two fisheries and a fee in Upwell and Outwell (Cambs. and Norf.) with Alice daughter of Richard Moler, his kinswoman (*consanguinea*) who became a nun at his request: *que habitum religionis ad petitionem meam in eadem ecclesia suscepit* (no. 87). Alan son of Robert de Shepreth gave 15 roods and two acres of land in Shepreth, five acres in Foxton, a croft in 'Hulmo', one acre of meadow, and a messuage in Cambridge, when he gave his daughter Agatha to the convent (no. 152). Richard de Columbers granted a weight of cheese annually to the abbey in which his daughters, Rose and Margaret, were received as nuns (no. 170).

---

1 J. H. Lynch *Simoniacal Entry into Religious Life from 1000–1260: a Social, Economic and Legal Study* (Columbus, Ohio, 1976), especially chapters 6–8.

2 J. Burton *The Yorkshire Nunneries in the Twelfth and Thirteenth Centuries* (Borthwick Paper no. 56; York, 1979) pp. 19–23.

3 *Visitations of Religious Houses* ed. Thompson, i, p. 49; iii, pp. 249, 252.

It is not possible to know whether these gifts were made before or after 1215, nor is it clear whether the abbey required them as a condition of entry. Although Chatteris abbey was far from being one of the poorest nunneries, a significant increase in the number of nuns would inevitably have caused extra expenditure and may have led the abbey to seek new sources of income. The wording of the documents suggests that the donations in nos. 87 and 152 and the gift confirmed in no. 26 were made when women entered the convent, but that the grants of cheese in no. 170 and rent in no. 227 may have been made after the daughters of the donors had become nuns. However, given the potentially simoniacal implications of dowry-grants, the lack of precision in the wording may be deliberate. Benefactors' wariness of accusations of simony may also mean that other gifts in the cartulary were in fact linked to the reception of women by the abbey even though they make no mention of nuns who were related to the donor. The grant by Thomas de Bancis to the abbey of the homage and service of John Glenman, Henry son of Aveline and Elloria de la Lawe (no. 115) or his gift of land in Foxton (no. 125) may perhaps have been connected to the entry to the nunnery of Mabel de Bancis who later became abbess, although there is no evidence to show how Thomas and Mabel were related. However, given that the earliest list of the members of the convent dates from the mid-fourteenth century and that most gifts to the abbey were made in the twelfth and thirteenth centuries, it is not possible to speculate about how many nuns may have been related to benefactors. Even if it were possible to link the names of nuns and benefactors, this would not necessarily mean that the donations made had been dowry-grants since the entry of a female relative to the convent may merely have strengthened an existing relationship between a benefactor and the abbey.[1]

The only other example of a donation to Chatteris abbey by a relative of a nun is the grant by Hugh de Cranwell of a rent of 10s. in Lincoln (no. 227). This charter differs significantly from the other dowry-grants. It states that Hugh made the grant on condition that Adelicia his daughter, a nun of Chatteris, should have the rent for her life *ut inde faciat quod voluerit* and that her prebend should not be reduced on account of it; after her death the rent was to remain to the abbey. It is not clear whether Adelicia had entered the convent shortly before this grant was made, and that the grant was related to her entry, or whether she had been a member for some time. Whichever was the case, this grant shows both a benefactor providing for an individual nun, rather than

---

[1] Thompson *Women Religious*, pp. 187–9.

adding to the resources of the convent as a whole, and a nun holding private property in contravention of her vow of poverty. The grant is particularly significant because it dates from the second half of the twelfth century and is therefore a very early example of a nun in receipt of a private income. Eileen Power collected many later instances of gifts and legacies in favour of individual nuns and showed that 'there was a considerable approximation to private life and to private property' in nunneries in the fourteenth and fifteenth centuries.[1] Similarly, Catherine Paxton found 24 examples of relatives providing pensions for individual nuns at six nunneries in or near London in 1370–1540.[2] In 1456 Henry Buckworth, vicar of Chatteris, bequeathed 40d. each to the abbess and prioress of Chatteris and 12d. to each professed nun, whilst in 1519 Richard Boneyerd left 12d. to the abbess, 8d. to the prioress and 4d. to each nun in his will.[3] These bequests show the continuing existence of private property at Chatteris abbey in the fifteenth and early sixteenth centuries.

BEQUESTS TO CHATTERIS ABBEY

Probate records show that Chatteris abbey continued to receive several small additions to its income from bequests made in the late fifteenth and early sixteenth centuries. The wills of two testators from Chatteris were proved in the prerogative court of Canterbury before the dissolution of the abbey. One of these wills contains a bequest in favour of the nuns: John Mathewe left 10s. to the abbess and nuns, to be divided equally between them, in his will proved in 1525.[4] The audience court of the bishop of Ely proved a small number of wills made by clerics and wealthy inhabitants of the diocese. Of the 26 wills proved in this court in 1382–1527, three contain bequests to the abbey. William Bray, vicar of Chatteris, left 10 marks for the repair of the chapel of St Mary at the abbey in 1490; Richard Bradwey of Ely left 13s. 4d. to the abbey, also in 1490; and William Thornbrowgh left 10s. to Chatteris for a mass and 'Dirige' in 1525.[5] The court of the archdeacon of Ely dealt with wills from the deaneries of

1	Power *Medieval English Nunneries*, pp. 14–15, 322–340; quotation p. 331.
2	C. Paxton 'The Nunneries of London and its Environs in the Later Middle Ages', D.Phil. thesis (University of Oxford, 1992) p. 40.
3	CCRO Ely consistory court probate registers, vol. 1, fo. 14v; vol. 6, fo. 49r.
4	PRO PROB 11/21/36.
5	Cambridge UL, EDR G/1/6 Alcock register, pp. 56–7; G/1/7 West and Goodrich register, fo. 78r; printed in A. Gibbons *Ely Episcopal Records. A Calendar and Concise View of the Episcopal Records Preserved in the Muniment Room of the Palace at Ely* (Lincoln, 1891) pp. 205–6, 219.

Bourne, Shingay and Cambridge and the parishes of Haddenham and Wilburton. The probate records from this court begin only in 1513 and contain no wills made by testators from Chatteris.

The overwhelming majority of Cambridgeshire wills were proved in the consistory court of the bishop of Ely whose probate registers begin in 1449.[1] Because they are so numerous, these wills have not been searched exhaustively for legacies to Chatteris abbey, but probate evidence from the adjoining diocese of Norwich shows that testators who made bequests to religious houses for women usually came from the same parish or town as the houses concerned.[2] The Ely probate registers have been searched for all the pre-1538 testators from Chatteris itself and for the vicars of Chatteris and Shepreth churches. The wills of 18 testators from Chatteris occur in the probate registers before 1538, five of which contain legacies to the abbey. Four of these testators were lay people and one was a vicar of Chatteris.

Some testators left money to the nuns themselves whilst others directed their legacies to the conventual church or to the fabric of the abbey. In his will, proved in March 1519, Richard Boneyerd left 12d. to the abbess, 8d. to the prioress and 4d. to each nun.[3] Only two years before the dissolution of the abbey, Margaret Measse left 3s. 4d. towards the repair of the abbey's clock in her will which was proved in April 1536.[4] The inventory of the abbey compiled in September 1538 states that this clock was located in the north aisle of the conventual church.[5] Both Richard Boneyerd and Margaret Measse asked to be buried at the parish church in their wills. However the two other lay testators, Robert Bollonde and his wife Olliff, asked to be buried at Chatteris abbey. Robert Bollonde asked specifically, in 1533, for his body to be buried in the monastery, before the blessed rood, and he gave 6d. to the high altar 'for tythes forgotten.'[6] He went on to make several bequests to the parish church, but he made detailed arrangements for his commemoration in the nuns' church. He appointed Thomas and Margaret Brye and their heirs to ensure that a standing 'Dirige' was sung annually in the abbey church in perpetuity. Thomas and Margaret were to pay 20d. annually to the priest and clerks for singing, 4d. for bell-ringing, 3d. in bread and ale to the ringers and 2d. to the bellman for

---

1 J. S. W. Gibson *Wills and Where to Find Them* (Chichester, 1974) pp. 18–19.

2 Oliva *Convent and Community*, p. 177.

3 CCRO Ely consistory court probate register, vol. 6, fo. 49r.

4 Ibid. vol. 10, fo. 49v.

5 PRO E 117/11/13, fo. 4r.

6 CCRO Ely consistory court probate register, vol. 7, fo. 94r.

organising the ringers. In addition, four dozen farthing-loaves, worth 12d., were to be made annually and given to the poor at the church door, and a wax taper weighing three pounds was to be set yearly before the sepulchre in the abbey for all the Easter holidays, after which the remainder was to be set on Bollonde's hearse on his anniversary every year.[1] However, Bollonde's instructions could not be carried out in perpetuity since the abbey was dissolved only five years after his death. Olliff Bollonde died shortly after her husband, in February 1534, and her will was proved the following June. She asked for her body to be buried in the churchyard of the abbey and she gave 4d. each to the high altar of the abbey, to the altar of St John and to the altar of St Andrew.[2] This will and the one which precedes it in the register were copied again in a later probate register. The second copy states that, in addition to her gifts to the high altar and to the altar of St Andrew, Olliff left 4d. to the altar of St Thomas rather than to that of St John.[3] The error in one copy may have arisen because of confusion between the abbreviations *Ioh'* and *Tho'* in the original. Whether St Thomas or St John is correct, it seems that the abbey had two altars dedicated to male saints which are not recorded in other sources.

The vicar of Chatteris whose will was proved in the consistory court and who made bequests to the abbey was Henry Buckworth. He was the vicar who, together with abbess Agnes Ashfield, was behind the production of the abbey's cartulary (no. 1). He died in 1456 and asked to be buried at the parish church to which he left a new antiphonary, legendary and processional. He left 6s. 8d. to the high altar of the conventual church and, like Richard Boneyerd, made bequests to the members of the convent, leaving 40d. each to the abbess and prioress and 12d. to each professed nun.[4] Wills for vicars of Chatteris, proved before the Dissolution, survive only for Henry Buckworth and William Bray, whilst none survive for pre-Dissolution vicars of Shepreth.

Catherine Paxton's survey of 562 wills proved in the court of Husting in 1370–1420 revealed that 50 (8.9%) of the testators left bequests to nunneries in or near London. Most of these testators – who were primarily wealthier freemen and their widows – left cash to the nunnery as a whole, but some left specific amounts to each nun and 12 made bequests to individual, named nuns.[5]

1 Ibid. vol. 7, fo. 94v.
2 Ibid. vol. 8, fo. 183v.
3 Ibid. vol. 10, fo. 16r.
4 Ibid. vol. 1, fo. 14v.
5 C. Paxton 'The Nunneries of London and its Environs in the Later Middle Ages', D.Phil. thesis (University of Oxford, 1992) pp. 97–103.

Paxton also surveyed the wills from the prerogative court of Canterbury and the commissary court of London. She examined the wills made by testators who seem to have lived in the parishes of the three London nunneries – St Helen's, Clerkenwell and Stratford – which shared their conventual church with their parish. An average of 51% of these wills proved in the prerogative court of Canterbury included bequests to the nunneries, as did an average of 27% of those proved in the commissary court of London, showing the local importance of these nunneries.[1]

The Norwich probate registers show that testators from Norfolk and Suffolk made significantly more bequests to nunneries than to monasteries, even though there were 63 monasteries and only 11 nunneries in the diocese.[2] These bequests, which were made mainly by local people and which continued until the Dissolution, show the continuing significance of these nunneries in their own localities.[3] Clementhorpe priory, which lay just outside York, also benefited from a stream of late medieval bequests from local testators.[4]

The bequests in favour of Chatteris abbey made by testators from Chatteris itself show that it too attracted small local donations even in the early sixteenth century. The wills of Robert Bollonde, Olliff Bollonde and Margaret Measse are particularly significant since they were all proved between 1533 and 1536, in the last five years of the life of the abbey. It is clear that the nunnery remained an important economic institution in Chatteris in the late fifteenth and early sixteenth centuries, and that it still fulfilled a spiritual function for at least some local testators.

---

[1] Ibid. pp. 148–53.
[2] Oliva *Convent and Community*, pp. 175–7.
[3] Ibid. p. 183.
[4] R. B. Dobson and S. Donaghey *The History of Clementhorpe Nunnery* (The Archaeology of York ii, fasc. i, 1984) pp. 22–5.

IV

The Management of the Estate

PURCHASES, SALES AND EXCHANGES MADE BY THE ABBEY

The documents in the cartulary record not only benefactors' gifts to the abbey but also the abbey's own activity in the land-market in which it bought, sold and exchanged land. Five purchases of property by the abbey are recorded in the cartulary. The abbey bought an acre of land in Madingley for 7s. and eight selions of land and one rood of meadow in Madingley for 40s. in the thirteenth century (nos. 110 and 238). Probably in the second half of the century, the abbey paid 40s. for the surrender and quitclaim by William son of Robert de Shepreth of a tenement in Shepreth which he had previously bought from the abbey (no. 154). In Barley (Herts.), the abbey paid 10 marks c. 1280 to Richard son of Richard de Myldeborn' for lands, tenements, meadows and pastures formerly belonging to John de Beauchaump and, also in the thirteenth century, it paid one mark in advance and 2d. annually to John son of John Pompun for another four acres of land there (nos. 172 and 175).

In the case of the thirteenth-century purchase by the abbey of one acre of land in Madingley from Aubrey son of Eustace de Madingley for 7s., the charter states that the payment was to be put towards the vendor's pilgrimage to Jerusalem (no. 110). This charter seems therefore to be an example of the abbey acting as a provider of liquidity. In the charters relating to the abbey's other purchases, no reason is given for the sales. The hospital of St John the Evangelist in Cambridge seems regularly to have supplied liquid funds to benefactors in return for donations of property to the hospital.[1] However, in the case of Chatteris abbey there are too few documented purchases to determine whether it often provided cash for local landlords who were willing to sell property.

It is unclear what other factors motivated the abbey to buy land, but Sandra Raban has argued that thirteenth-century records of activity in the land-market

---

[1] M. Rubin *Charity and Community in Medieval Cambridge* (Cambridge, 1987) pp. 217–26.

do not indicate that land was seen as an investment.[1] The evidence in the Chatteris cartulary, if accurate, certainly suggests that the abbey bought little land. The cartulary may be somewhat misleading, though, because it contains relatively few documents dating from the twelfth century when the abbey may have bought more land. In the second half of the twelfth century, Gilbertine priories made large numbers of purchases of land, particularly in order to consolidate their granges.[2] However, the Gilbertine priories were recent foundations in the later twelfth century and were still in the process of establishing their estates. Chatteris abbey, in contrast, had existed since the early eleventh century and did not practise the grange system of farming. It did not face the same pressure as most Gilbertine houses to expand its holdings into viable estates. It may, nevertheless, have made additional, unrecorded purchases in order to consolidate its lands.

Few sales or grants in fee-farm by Chatteris abbey occur in the cartulary. In the first half of the thirteenth century, the abbey sold a messuage in Potter's Lane, Ely for 5s. and an annual rent of 2s. 6d. (no. 93). In the thirteenth century, the abbey gave its water-mill in Thriplow to the bishop of Ely for 16s. annually (no. 95). In the mid-thirteenth century, abbess Mary de Sancto Claro and the convent sold a messuage and 10 acres of land in Foxton for an annual rent of 4s. 6d. and six hens (no. 141). The same abbess and the convent also sold all their land in Hemingford Grey[3] (Hunts.) for one mark annually and scutage of 40s. (no. 231). Between 1275 and 1290 the abbey sold a croft with a messuage and meadow in Barrington for two marks in advance and 16d. annually (no. 120). The abbey also made a grant in fee-farm, probably in 1268 × 1280, of their half of a water-mill in Barrington and Foxton, together with two pieces of meadow in Foxton towards the repair of the mill, for 2s. annually (no. 119). It is difficult to know how many of these sales were prompted by immediate financial necessity. However, most of the sales were made in return for an annual rent or for a relatively modest initial payment together with an annual rent. Only the sale of the croft, messuage and meadow in Barrington was made

---

[1] S. Raban 'The Land Market and the Aristocracy in the Thirteenth Century' in *Tradition and Change. Essays in Honour of Marjorie Chibnall Presented by her Friends on the Occasion of her Seventieth Birthday* eds D. E. Greenway, C. Holdsworth and J. Sayers (Cambridge, 1985) p. 260.

[2] B. Golding *Gilbert of Sempringham and the Gilbertine Order* c. 1130–c. 1300 (Oxford, 1995) pp. 288–92.

[3] The two other charters relating to Hemingford (nos. 232 and 272) do not make clear whether the endowments lay in Hemingford Grey (East Hemingford) or Hemingford Abbots (West Hemingford).

for a substantial initial payment and a relatively low annual rent, which may imply that the abbey was in financial difficulties and needed cash at that time.

The scarcity of alienations by the abbey in the cartulary does not necessarily show that the abbey rarely sold property, since it was much more important for the abbey to keep a careful record of its acquisitions than of its alienations. It is possible to prove that the cartulary is not a comprehensive collection of every land-transaction in which the nunnery was involved. For example, the archive of St John's College, Cambridge contains an original charter issued by the nunnery which does not occur in the cartulary. It is a sale by the abbey before 1233 of half an acre of land in Madingley for half a pound of pepper annually at Easter (no. 281).[1] This land was later given to the hospital of St John, Cambridge and at the beginning of the sixteenth century the hospital was refounded as St John's College which explains why the nunnery's charter survives in the college's archive. Another transaction not recorded in the cartulary is the probable alienation by the abbey of its lands in Orwell. The abbey held a quarter of a virgate in Orwell in 1086 and the hundred rolls record that by 1279 the abbey had let half a virgate of land there for an annual rent of 5s.[2] Since no income from property in Orwell occurs in the 1291 taxation of pope Nicholas IV nor in the post-Dissolution minister's accounts, it seems likely that the abbey either sold its lands in Orwell or leased them but could not exact its rent. However, neither a sale nor a lease is recorded in the cartulary.[3] These examples suggest, therefore, that the abbey may have been more active in the land-market than the cartulary reveals.

The cartulary does show, though, that in one case the abbey alienated property which it had probably been given only shortly before. Richard Muschet gave a messuage in Potter's Lane in Ely to the infirmary of the abbey in the early thirteenth century (no. 92). Although this gift was made in pure and perpetual alms, the abbey seems to have sold the messuage soon afterwards to Alan de Ely and Alice his wife for a cash payment of 5s. and an annual rent of 2s. 6d. (no. 93). The occurrence of Richard Muschet's charter in the cartulary suggests that it was not passed on with the messuage when it was sold, but was retained with the abbey's muniments instead. In the case of the other property sold by the abbey, it is not possible to tell how long the abbey had held the

---

1 Cambridge, St John's College Archives D 25. 22. For a discussion of the seal attached to this charter, see p. 93.
2 *Domesday Book* i, fo. 193a; *Rot. Hund.* ii, p. 559.
3 *Taxatio Nicholai IV*, p. 268; PRO SC 6/HenVIII/267, rott. 5–9.

lands. Nor is there enough evidence about sales by the abbey to be able to detect any pattern in the alienation of its property.

The cartulary does not contain a grant in fee-farm of the manor of Kersey (Suff.), but the documents relating to Kersey show that the manor had been granted in fee-farm by the mid-twelfth century at the latest. In the last decade of the twelfth century, Chatteris abbey confirmed the manor of Kersey – which was to be held in fee-farm for £10 annually – to Adam son of Robert de Cockfield (no. 186). The confirmation states that Nigel, bishop of Ely, and Hadewisa, prioress of Chatteris, had granted and confirmed the manor to Adam de Cockfield, grandfather of Adam son of Robert, who probably died in the mid-1150s. This manor lay in south Suffolk and was doubtless granted in fee-farm because of its remoteness both from Chatteris itself and from all the other properties of the abbey. It is not clear whether the manor was at farm before Adam de Cockfield held it, but the cartulary shows that the manor remained at farm from the second half of the twelfth century through to the mid-fifteenth century.[1] The minister's accounts after the Dissolution confirm that the manor was still at farm in 1539.[2] Additional information about the tenure of the manor in the 1320s comes from two documents in the series of ancient deeds in the Public Record Office. In 1322 Hugh le Despenser senior exchanged the manor of Barnwell (Northants.) and his rent of £10 in Kersey for two manors and other lands belonging to Sir Giles de Wattisham in Oxfordshire, for their lives.[3] An inquisition in the cartulary of 1327 × 1328 shows that Hugh le Despenser subsequently gave the manor of Kersey to Hugh le Despenser junior (no. 191). Although the abbey had solved the problem of managing a distant, isolated manor by granting the fee-farm of Kersey to Adam de Cockfield in the twelfth century, the grant fixed the heritable farm of the manor at £10. Price-rises from the late twelfth century onwards must have meant that the abbey suffered considerable losses of income from the manor. However there is no evidence that the abbey ever tried to redeem this fee-farm, unlike the monks of Westminster who pursued a policy of attempting to recover their numerous fee-farmed estates in the thirteenth and fourteenth centuries.[4]

The cartulary contains six exchanges made by Chatteris abbey, most of which involved small parcels of land. In Chatteris itself the abbey exchanged a croft for half an acre of land belonging to Ralph de Barley in the thirteenth

[1] Nos. 187, 189–203, 205, 208 and 212.
[2] PRO SC 6/HenVIII/267, rot. 8d.
[3] PRO E 40/10769; E 40/10907.
[4] B. Harvey *Westminster Abbey and its Estates in the Middle Ages* (Oxford, 1977) pp. 166–7.

century; in Over it exchanged one toft for another belonging to the rector, Roger de Seaton, between 1268 and 1280; and in Barrington it exchanged a messuage and croft for three selions belonging to John Waryn between 1275 and 1290 (nos. 30, 101 and 113). In Foxton, the abbey exchanged one *cultura* for five and three-quarter acres of land belonging to Reginald Binel in the mid-thirteenth century and another *cultura* for two belonging to Alan son of Alan de Shepreth in the late twelfth or early thirteenth centuries (nos. 145–6). The abbey probably made these exchanges in order to consolidate small and previously scattered holdings which it had been given into more easily manageable blocks of land. Exchanges were therefore likely to be particularly effective transactions for the nunnery. The other exchange in the cartulary is of fishing rights: Nigel, bishop of Ely (1133–1169), exchanged 20 sticks of eels in the fishery of Polwere for 20 sticks belonging to the abbey in three other fisheries in Chatteris (no. 89). In the same charter, Nigel granted another 10 sticks of eels yielded by the fishery of Polwere to the abbey, which meant that he had both consolidated and extended the abbey's fishing rights in a single charter.

THE ABBEY'S METHODS OF EXPLOITING ITS ESTATES

The abbey needed a supply of food for the nuns as well as an income in cash with which to pay wages and to buy goods and services. In common with other landlords, it could choose whether to exploit its demesne lands directly, whether to commute labour services to cash payments, and whether to lease its demesne lands and lands formerly held by villeins. When the abbey exploited its demesnes directly, using a combination of villein and hired labour, it produced a supply of food for the convent and a surplus which could be sold to generate a cash income. Conversely, when the abbey leased its demesnes, it had to spend a proportion of its income from rents to buy food for the nuns. In practice, the situation was less clear-cut since the abbey leased some land even when it was farming much directly, whilst in its final years it still retained a little demesne land when almost all the rest had been leased. The lack of surviving rentals and account rolls from the abbey precludes a systematic analysis of the nunnery's economy. It is difficult, moreover, to draw parallels from the financial records of other nunneries since Jackie Mountain has demonstrated that there was wide diversity in the late medieval economic circumstances of three nunneries – Romsey abbey (Hants.), Catesby priory (Northants.) and Marrick priory

(Yorks. N.) – whose early fifteenth-century account rolls survive.[1] Despite these problems, it is possible to investigate the way in which Chatteris abbey exploited its lands by using the cartulary together with the hundred rolls, manorial court rolls and the post-Dissolution minister's accounts.

Evidence of the leasing of land by Chatteris abbey occurs in the cartulary in several forms. As well as leases of both demesne land and tenements formerly in villeinage, there are recognitions by tenants of their tenancies, a charter worded as a grant in fee-farm but which created only a life tenancy, letters of attorney appointing a rent-collector and acquittances of rents paid. Given that the core of the abbey's estates lay in a few adjacent south Cambridgeshire parishes, it is not surprising that a substantial proportion of the leases came from these parishes. Whereas there are four leases by the abbey of land in Chatteris in the cartulary, there is evidence of six in Foxton and one each in Barrington and Shepreth.[2] One lease is of property and rights in both Foxton and Shepreth (no. 163). The cartulary also contains evidence of one lease each in Barley (Herts.), Lincoln, Bircham (Norf.) and Huntingdon, and of three in Lynn (Norf.).[3] The abbey may once have had a separate book in which more leases were recorded but, if so, it has not survived.

The relatively small number of leases in Chatteris itself, compared with the larger number in south Cambridgeshire, may mean that the abbey was more likely to lease its more distant lands and to keep a greater proportion of land nearby in demesne. Unfortunately, the total number of leases in the cartulary is far too small for secure conclusions to be drawn about geographical variations in the abbey's leasing policy within Cambridgeshire. The cartulary does show, though, that the abbey consistently leased some of its most distant properties. In the early thirteenth century, William son of Wluric de Wootton gave a messuage in Lynn (Norf.) to Chatteris abbey and reserved a rent of 6d. annually. The cartulary shows that the abbey was letting this messuage for one mark in the first half of the thirteenth century, in 1300 and in 1425. The messuage was still yielding one mark of rent annually in 1539 after the dissolution of the abbey.[4] The documents do not make clear whether the messuage had been

---

[1] J. Mountain 'Nunnery Finances in the Early Fifteenth Century' in *Monastic Studies* ii *The Continuity of Tradition* ed. J. Loades (Bangor, 1991) pp. 263–72.

[2] In Chatteris: nos. 51, 60, 69 and 71; in Foxton: nos. 128, 130–2 and 138–9; in Barrington: no. 118; in Shepreth: no. 151.

[3] In Barley: no. 176; in Lincoln: no. 228; in Bircham: no. 225; in Huntingdon: no. 230; in Lynn: nos. 218–20.

[4] Nos. 218–20; PRO SC 6/HenVIII/267, rot. 8d.

granted in fee-farm or whether the abbey had granted a succession of leases. It seems likely though that, as with the manor of Kersey (Suff.), the abbey was content to receive a regular, fixed income from a distant, isolated property.

Few of the leases for which evidence survives can be dated precisely. The majority of them date from the thirteenth century and about one third of the total date from the middle of that century. Of the four leases in Chatteris itself, two date from the mid-thirteenth century, one is dateable only to the thirteenth century and the fourth dates from the first half of the fourteenth century.[1] Of the six leases in Foxton, one dates from the late twelfth or early thirteenth century, one from 1225 × 1228 and three date from the mid and one from the late thirteenth century.[2] The lack of a significant number of accurately dateable leases in the cartulary means that it is no easier to detect chronological than geographical patterns in the abbey's leasing policy.

Although the timing of alterations in the management of the nunnery's estates is obscure, two disputes recorded in the cartulary provide evidence that Chatteris abbey was farming its own demesnes in the thirteenth century. In 1238 dean Geoffrey de Lucy and the chapter of St Paul's, London confirmed a settlement agreed between Herbert, rector of Barley (Herts.), and Chatteris abbey before judges delegate concerning the ownership of lesser and greater tithes in Barley. The confirmation states that the settlement had been made:

> super decimis minutis de dominico earundem et omnibus majoribus de terris earum quas [sanctimoniales] excolunt propriis sumptibus in villa de Berle provenientibus, et de intentione decimarum majorum provenientium ex viginti septem acris terre in eadem villa, quas homines predictarum monialium excolunt et tenent de dominico predicto.[3]

This shows that the abbey directly exploited lands in Barley in the 1230s. Another tithe-suit heard by papal judges delegate also suggests that the abbey was farming some of its lands in Barrington directly in 1249. Hugh de Northwold, bishop of Ely, who gave the judgement in the case, ordered that Robert Passelewe, archdeacon of Lewes and rector of Barrington, should receive all the tithes of corn and hay from the nuns' lands in Barrington *sive excolantur propriis manibus sive per manus aliorum* (no. 112).

A mid-thirteenth-century agreement relating to two semi-free men who held land of the abbey in Foxton (no. 144) sheds light on the flexible methods by

---

1 Nos. 51 and 69; 60; and 71 respectively.
2 Nos. 131; 130; 132, 138 and 139; and 128 respectively.
3 No. 182, fo. 143v.

which the nunnery could exploit its estates.[1] In the agreement, the abbey leased to Roger, smith, and Roger his son half a virgate of land in Foxton. The abbey received a payment of 40s., an annual rent of 4s., a small number of seasonal labour services and the servile dues of tallage and merchet. Despite these dues, which suggest that Roger and his son were villeins, the agreement does not contain substantial labour services. Moreover, Roger and his son held the land in perpetuity and by charter, in the manner of free tenants. It seems therefore that Roger and his son must have been semi-free men. Although they did not have to perform onerous labour services, the inclusion of some plough-services and boon-works shows that the abbey was farming land in Foxton directly in the mid-thirteenth century.

Another document in the cartulary shows that the abbey was still exploiting lands directly later in the thirteenth century. In an agreement made between November 1287 and November 1288, Roger de Foxton, chaplain, gave all his land – presumably in Foxton – to the abbey on condition that the abbey sowed half of it and manured three acres of fallow land annually during Roger's life (no. 136). Roger, for his part, was to reap and collect the corn from all the land and was to receive half of the cost from the abbess, together with half of the corn from the land. This agreement reveals the detailed arrangements for cultivating land which the abbey made with an individual, as well as showing that the abbey must still have been farming land directly in the 1280s.

The hundred rolls shed light on the abbey's lands in south and west Cambridgeshire in 1279. In Shepreth the abbess held 160 acres in demesne. She had three free tenants who held 28¼ acres between them, though 27½ of these acres were in the hands of one man, Osbert Goudleg. She also had 16 villeins who held a total of 135 acres: 13 of the villeins held nine acres of land each, one held eight acres of meadow and two held five acres of land each. The rolls do not specify the works and customs owed but they do list their value, which for 10 of the 13 holders of nine acres was 6s. 6d. As well as the villeins, the abbess had seven crofters who held only six and a half acres between them.[2] In Barrington, the abbess held a quarter of the vill, her eight free tenants held a total of 118¼ acres and her 12 villeins held 165½ acres. Two of the free tenants each owed two autumn boon-works but, as in the case of Shepreth, the rolls do not list the services owed by villeins. The rolls do list the values of the services though: the works and customs of the five villein holders of 20 acres of land were worth

1 E. Miller and J. Hatcher *Medieval England – Rural Society and Economic Change 1086–1348* (London, 1978) p. 118.
2 *Rot. Hund.* ii, p. 562.

10s. each annually, those of the six holders of 10 acres of land were worth 8s. each, and those of the single holder of five and a half acres were worth 4s.[1]

Whereas the hundred rolls for Shepreth and Barrington list only the value of the services owed to landlords, for Foxton the rolls describe the services in detail. In Foxton the abbess held 300 acres of arable land, 32 acres of meadow and 15 acres of pasture in demesne. The abbess's nine free tenants held a total of 77¼ acres, though five held only an acre or less. John Frances, who held 10 acres, owed six capons annually in addition to his rent of 4s. 2d. whilst William Luton, who held one acre, owed two boon-works annually in addition to his rent of 1s. The hundred rolls name 13 villeins of the abbess in Foxton who held 18 acres of land and a messuage. All these villeins owed the same works and customs: they had to do 52 works annually; they had to plough the abbess's land for two days and perform two boon-works in autumn; they had to mow her meadow for two days, do carriage-service, roof her court and harrow the land sown with oats; they owed one hen and 16 eggs annually and were henceforth to pay a rent of 2s. 6d. These customs, excluding the rent, were valued at 9s. 8d. As well as her 13 villeins who each held 18 acres and a messuage, the abbess had another 13 customary tenants who each held nine acres and a messuage. These tenants had to do 100 works annually, plough one acre of land, perform carrying-service on foot, give one hen, and perform mowing and stacking services. In addition to the works, which were worth 10s., these tenants had to pay 3d. in rent.[2] Furthermore, the abbey's manorial court rolls show that the abbess was able to exact large entry-fines from her villeins in Foxton. For example, in 1316 Agnes daughter of Robert le Ro paid an entry-fine of 60s. when she received a messuage and 18 acres of land, whilst in 1300 William Overhawe and Basilia his wife paid 26s. 8d. when they were admitted to a messuage and nine acres of land.[3] As well as the free and villein tenants on the abbey's manor in Foxton in 1279 there were also six cottars, five of whom held one acre and another who held four acres. One of the holders of a single acre paid a rent of 12d. and a hen, but the other cottars all owed services. Three of the holders of one acre performed 48 works and other customary services as well as giving a hen and four eggs, whilst the other holder of one acre owed half as much. The cottar who held four acres, Henry Dalibon, owed 96 works and a hen, together worth 3s. 9d.[4]

---

[1] Ibid. ii, p. 560.
[2] Ibid. ii, p. 548.
[3] Cambridge, Trinity College Archives, Foxton 5, rot. 4d; Foxton 4, rot. 5.
[4] *Rot. Hund.* ii, p. 548.

Although the works, services and payments owed by the abbess's villeins are described in detail for Foxton, whereas their value only is given for Shepreth and Barrington, this does not mean that villein services had been commuted to money payments in Shepreth and Barrington. The value of the services in Foxton is always noted in addition to a description of the services themselves. Moreover the details of services owed are included for the tenants of all lords in Foxton but for the tenants of none in Shepreth. Sandra Raban has emphasized the inconsistency in the amount and type of information preserved in the returns of the 1279 hundred rolls.[1] Shepreth and Barrington both lay in the hundred of Wetherley, whilst Foxton lay in the hundred of Thriplow. It is striking that all the returns for Thriplow hundred describe the services owed in great detail, but those for Wetherley hundred either record them briefly or else note only their valuation.[2] It seems, therefore, that the differences between the description of services in Foxton, on the one hand, and in Shepreth and Barrington, on the other, were ones of scribal idiosyncrasy in the compilation of the rolls, rather than the result of the commutation to money payments of services in Shepreth and Barrington.

Entries on the manorial court rolls for the abbey's lands in Foxton, Shepreth and Barrington make clear that in the late thirteenth and early fourteenth centuries holders of villein tenements did indeed owe works, rather than money payments, in Shepreth and Barrington as well as in Foxton. For example in 1313 John son of William le Parmenter' of Shepreth received at the abbess's court the messuage with croft and two selions of land which his father had held. The court roll states that John was to hold the messuage and lands in villeinage, by doing works and customs. He paid an entry-fine of five shillings, but owed no cash rent.[3]

The description in the hundred rolls of the abbey's four virgates of land in Over shows that the land was divided between 11 tenants who held between one acre and half a virgate each and who all owed cash rents. For three tenants the rolls state simply the rent for which their lands were held, whilst for the remaining eight tenants the rolls note the rent and also that the tenants owed carrying-service.[4] It is unclear whether the abbey had leased these lands or whether it was farming them directly with hired labour, but it is possible that

---

1   S. Raban 'The Church in the 1279 Hundred Rolls' in *Medieval Ecclesiastical Studies in Honour of Dorothy M. Owen* eds M. J. Franklin and C. Harper-Bill (Woodbridge, 1995) pp. 192–3.
2   *Rot. Hund.* ii, pp. 542–69.
3   Cambridge, Trinity College Archives, Foxton 4, rot. 2d.
4   *Rot. Hund.* ii, p. 478.

the abbey had never practised demesne farming on relatively isolated lands such as those in Over, in west Cambridgeshire.

The abbey's earliest manorial court rolls, which date from 1276 to 1325, deal with its lands in Foxton, Barrington, Shepreth, Madingley and Over. The rolls contain many entries relating to the enforcement of the labour services which were needed to cultivate the abbey's demesne lands.[1] For example, Ace the reap-reeve (*messor*) occurs in the court roll for 5 August 1294 because he had not come to weed the abbess's corn. The same court dealt with William de Barley, Beatrix Goffe, Alan Asselote and Henry Werry because they had failed to come with their cart to carry the abbess's hay.[2] On 7 October 1319 Walter the miller occurs in the court roll for having gleaned badly and on 2 November 1325 Robert Obsty, Nicholas Gerold and Alan Man, all of Shepreth, were presented for having reaped her corn badly that autumn.[3] The plentiful evidence in the court rolls for the persistence of labour services shows that the abbey still practised demesne farming in Foxton, Barrington and Shepreth at least until the end of the first quarter of the fourteenth century. The same court rolls also include numerous instances of the imposition of merchet, leyrwite and other servile dues which were indicative of personal unfreedom on the abbey's villeins. For example, on 5 May 1297 William le Man paid 4s. for the marriage of his daughter and for leyrwite; on 3 June 1308 Alice Reynold of Madingley paid 12d. for permission to marry her daughter Isabel to Robert de Foxton of Chesterton; and on 4 December 1307 Henry Swan was presented at the court because his son Henry had been ordained without the permission of the court.[4]

The decline in demesne farming began on many estates in the late thirteenth century, but between 1380 and 1420 it was abandoned altogether in most places.[5] In the case of Chatteris abbey, it is impossible to know precisely when the transition occurred, owing to the complete absence of surviving account rolls, together with the lack of manorial court rolls for the period 1325–1463. Towards the end of the cartulary there are two manumissions of villeins. The first, dated 1436, released from serfdom John Hulot, a villein of the nuns' manor in Barley (Herts.), whilst the second, dated between September 1435 and August 1436, released John Whiteheed', a villein of their manor in Chatteris

---

1 Cambridge, Trinity College Archives, Foxton 1–5.
2 Ibid. Foxton 1, rot. 1d.
3 Ibid. rott. 4–5.
4 Ibid. rott. 3, 7–7d.
5 *The Agrarian History of England and Wales* iii *1348–1500* ed. E. Miller (Cambridge, 1991) pp. 573–6.

(nos. 271 and 274). These documents show that in the 1430s at least two of the abbey's villeins were prepared to bear the expense of acquiring a charter from the abbey to formalize their release from servile status.

The minister's accounts compiled in 1539 confirm that, as would be expected, the abbey had leased almost all of its demesne land before its dissolution. They show that the minister received £8 in Foxton, £5 6s. 8d. in Barrington and £13 6s. 8d. in Barley for the farm of the demesne lands.[1] The minister also collected fixed rents from the former abbey's customary tenants. In 1539 these fixed rents amounted to £7 15s. 4d. in Chatteris, £20 11s. 4½d. in Foxton, £6 4s. 6d. in Barrington, £10 15s. 8¼d. in Shepreth, £2 4¼d. in Madingley and £2 7s. 1¾d. in Over.[2] However, even in the 1530s, the abbey was still farming a little land directly. In 1539, the minister's accounts record the receipt of the sum of £5 3s. 11d. for the farm of the site of the former abbey and all the buildings within its precinct, together with all the demesne lands adjacent to the site formerly cultivated by the abbess and convent *ad usum hospitii sui*.[3] The inventory taken at the dissolution of the abbey shows that this land was cultivated with hired labour. It records that a total of £1 14s. 9d. was paid to 10 harvest labourers in 1538; five of the labourers were men and five were women, and the sums paid to them ranged from 10s. to 3d.[4]

Documents in the cartulary suggest that links between abbesses and local families may sometimes have influenced the management of the abbey's estates. In particular, Mabel de Bancis, who was abbess in the mid-thirteenth century, granted two leases to Thomas de Bancis: she leased to him a messuage and 12 acres of land in Foxton for 4s. annually and a messuage, five acres of land and five acres of meadow, also in Foxton, for 3s. 6d. annually (nos. 132 and 139). Since many abbesses seem to have been drawn from local families, it is not surprising to find members of these families as tenants of the abbey. It is tempting to think, though, that abbesses may have been particularly willing to lease land to people whom they knew well or to whom they were related. Although the leases made to Thomas de Bancis do not seem to have been made on especially beneficial terms, such leases must nevertheless have strengthened the links between local families and the abbey.

As well as being a lessor, Chatteris abbey also rented property, latterly at least. The minister's accounts show that at the end of its life the abbey was

1 PRO SC 6/HenVIII/267, rott. 6d-7, 8d-9.
2 Ibid. rott. 5d, 6d, 7-8.
3 Ibid. rot. 5d.
4 PRO E 117/11/13, fo. 7r.

renting lands in Chatteris from five lords, including the bishop and the prior of Ely and the abbot of Ramsey. The abbey owed a total of £1 17s. 1d. for these lands, £1 8s. 4d. of which was owed to the abbot of Ramsey who was the lord of the other manor in Chatteris.[1] It is not clear whether Chatteris abbey rented much property earlier in its history, but the abbess does not occur as a tenant in 1472 in a rental for Ramsey abbey's possessions in Chatteris.[2] Chatteris abbey may, therefore, have rented land from Ramsey abbey only later in the fifteenth or in the early sixteenth century.

THE SALE AND CONSUMPTION OF AGRICULTURAL PRODUCE

It is difficult to judge the extent to which produce from the nunnery's estates was sold or consumed by the abbey. A charter in the archives of St John's College Cambridge contains an enigmatic reference which suggests that the abbey may have transported the grain harvested from its south Cambridgeshire demesnes to Chatteris via Cambridge. The charter, which seems to date from the early or mid-thirteenth century, is a gift in free alms by Geoffrey son of Walter son of Scolicia to the hospital of St John, Cambridge of a messuage with buildings in the parish of St Michael, Cambridge.[3] Geoffrey reserved an annual rent of 12d. and four capons which the hospital was to pay to the nuns of Chatteris; he also reserved the nuns' right of free entry into the courtyard of the messuage and he excepted from his gift the building (*domus*) in the courtyard in which the nuns stored their corn and other goods when their boat was away. Since the nuns needed somewhere to store their corn before rather than after the arrival of their boat, this charter suggests that the nuns may not have been using Cambridge markets at this date to sell their agricultural produce. Instead it seems that grain from their south Cambridgeshire manors was transported to Cambridge for storage until their boat came to take it by water to Chatteris. It is possible, though, that the abbey needed to use the markets of Cambridge to buy corn which was then stored in the town until it could be shipped to Chatteris. Brian Golding has shown that the urban property of Gilbertine houses not only provided income from rents and accommodation for travelling canons and lay brothers, but that it was also used as a base for the houses' commercial activities and for storing agricultural produce.[4]

---

1 PRO SC 6/HenVIII/267, rot. 9.
2 PRO SC 11/91.
3 Cambridge, St John's College Archives, D 20. 130.
4 Golding *Gilbert of Sempringham and the Gilbertine Order*, pp. 432–43.

In the case of Chatteris, an early fourteenth-century letter from the bishop of Ely to the bishop of London suggests that the abbey transported the produce of its demesnes to Chatteris for consumption there. In 1306 × 1310 Robert Orford, bishop of Ely, wrote to ask Ralph Baldock, bishop of London, to remit the tithes owed to him by the nuns following a fire at the abbey. Orford's letter describes the damage caused by the fire and states that it completely devastated the abbey's church, its buildings and *omnia bona maneriorum suorum pro earum sustentatione ibidem collocata.*[1] This description shows that, at the beginning of the fourteenth century, the abbey still consumed directly at least part of the produce from its own demesnes.

MILLS

The possession of mills was important partly because the abbey could use them to grind its own corn, but also because they could generate significant additional revenue for the abbey. This revenue came either from multure payments, if the abbey retained its mills in its demesne, or from substantial rents if it decided to lease them. In Domesday Book the abbess held half a mill in Foxton as well as one mill in Barrington, one in Shepreth and another in Kersey (Suff.).[2] Although the abbey later acquired a number of other mills, there are relatively few charters relating to mills in the cartulary.

Between 1268 and 1306, the abbey granted in fee-farm to Warin de Barrington their half of a water-mill called 'le Estmelne' in Barrington and Foxton, together with two pieces of meadow in Foxton towards the repair of the mill, for 2s. annually (no. 119). This mill, which seems to be the half-mill in Foxton which occurs in Domesday Book, appears only once in the cartulary. The abbey's mill in Barrington occurs twice. It is mentioned first in a tithe-suit between Robert Passelewe, archdeacon of Lewes, and Chatteris abbey which was heard before papal judges delegate in 1249. The dispute was resolved by a settlement which divided the tithes in the parish and which allocated to Chatteris abbey the lesser tithes and the tithes from its mill in Barrington (no. 112). The mill occurs again in the cartulary when the abbey leased it and a messuage in Barrington to Warin de Barrington c. 1253 × c. 1307 for a payment of half a mark and an annual rent of 44s. (no. 118).

---

[1] *Mon. Ang.* ii, pp. 618–19, no. 10 (BL Cotton Ch. xxi. 12).
[2] *Domesday Book* i, fo. 193a; ii, p. 389a.

The cartulary also contains an agreement made in 1265 in which the abbey leased its mill called 'Mepus' in Shepreth for 10 years to William de Fowlmere, carpenter, for 40s. annually (no. 163). Along with the mill, the abbey leased a rood of land, all the multure of the abbey's court in Foxton and the suit of all their tenantry in Foxton and Shepreth to William. The lease makes clear that the mill in Shepreth was a water-mill because it includes references to the mill-pond and the source of its water. In 1539, the minister's accounts show that the former abbey's water-mill in Shepreth was let for a farm of 50s. annually.[1]

The abbey's mill in Kersey was probably at farm together with the rest of the manor from at least the twelfth century. It occurs only once in the cartulary in an inquisition which states that Hugh le Despenser held the manor, including the mill, in fee-farm of Chatteris abbey in the early fourteenth century (no. 191). The privilege *Religiosam vitam eligentibus* of pope Innocent IV (1243–54), which confirmed the possessions of Chatteris abbey, refers to the vill of Kersey with its appurtenances but does not mention the mill specifically (no. 3).

Innocent IV's privilege does, though, include the nunnery's mills in Barrington and Shepreth and its half-mill in Foxton, as well as the land with a mill which the abbey held in Thriplow (no. 3). Nigel, bishop of Ely, gave land and a mill in Thriplow to Chatteris abbey *c.* 1150 × *c.* 1158 (no. 166). He made this gift at the request of Richard de Stuntney, a clerk of archdeacon William de Lavington, who held the land and mill of the bishop. Richard de Stuntney had owed Nigel an annual rent of 6s. for the land and mill (no. 165). Nigel reserved this rent again when he gave the land and mill to Chatteris abbey. At some time after Innocent's privilege of 1243 × 1254, the abbey gave their mill in Thriplow back to the bishop of Ely during the episcopate of Hugh, reserving a rent of 16s. annually (no. 95). The bishop who received the mill was either Hugh de Northwold or Hugh de Balsham, so the abbey must have alienated it in either 1243 × 1254 or 1257 × 1286.[2]

Two mills not included in the privilege of Innocent IV are those in Chatteris and Bilney (Norf.). Evidence that the abbey had a windmill in Chatteris is provided by a gift which John Fithien made to the abbey in the late thirteenth century (no. 28). Fithien gave half an acre of land called 'le Wellestolt' which lay in the field of the abbess's windmill in Chatteris. This windmill also occurs in 1539 in the post-Dissolution minister's accounts which state that the mill of

---

[1] PRO SC 6/HenVIII/267, rot. 7d.

[2] Innocent IV was pope 1243–54, Hugh de Northwold was bishop of Ely 1229–54 and Hugh de Balsham was bishop of Ely 1257–86.

the former abbey in Chatteris was at farm for 20s. annually.[1] The cartulary shows that the abbey was given part of a mill in Bilney (Norf.) by William de Bek in the late twelfth or early thirteenth century (no. 82). The abbey may initially have leased their share in this mill which was not close to any of the abbey's lands. However, the mill does not occur in any other sources relating to the abbey, so it seems likely that the abbey alienated it during the thirteenth century, probably before Innocent IV issued his privilege in 1243 × 1254.

Documents in the cartulary show that the abbey granted in fee-farm or leased its mills in Barrington, Foxton and Shepreth at least once each in the later thirteenth or very early fourteenth centuries.[2] These documents cannot, though, be taken to indicate that the abbey was also leasing its demesnes in these places then, since the abbey seems sometimes to have used its windmill in Chatteris to grind corn from its other estates. The charter at St John's College Cambridge, which refers to the building (*domus*) in Cambridge where the nuns stored their corn when their boat was away, suggests that the abbey transported demesne grain from south Cambridgeshire to Chatteris via Cambridge.[3] It also implies that the grain was ground in Chatteris. If the abbey used its mill in Chatteris to grind corn from other lands, it would have been able simultaneously to maintain demesne production in south Cambridgeshire and to lease its mills there.

Too few relevant documents survive to show how regularly the abbey leased its mills, but a court roll dating from 1294 sheds light on how the abbey might decide whether to manage a mill directly or to lease it. In February 1294, the abbey's court at Foxton noted that it had been found by inquiry that the multure and meadow pertaining to the mill of Barrington was worth 24s. annually. The following month, the court held another inquiry to determine whether it would be to the advantage of the abbess to hold the mill in her demesne or to lease it as before. The court decided that it was in the abbess's interests to continue to lease the mill for 20s. annually, even though this rent was 4s. less than the value of the mill's multure and meadow.[4] It is possible that the court may also have held similar inquiries when the abbey was deciding whether or not to retain land in demesne.

---

[1] PRO SC 6/HenVIII/267, rot. 5d.
[2] Nos. 118–19 and 163.
[3] Cambridge, St John's College Archives, D 20. 130.
[4] Cambridge, Trinity College Archives, Foxton 2, m. 2d.

MANORIAL COURTS

Chatteris abbey seems to have had three main manorial courts: one in Chatteris itself, one in Foxton and another in Barley (Herts.). The rolls of these courts survive only patchily, but there are more records from the court held at Foxton than from those held at Chatteris or Barley. There are Foxton court rolls for many, but not all, years between 1276 and 1325 and between 1492 and 1533, as well as for 1537 and 1538.[1] Evidence for the court in Chatteris comes only from the records of the court of Chatteris Regis, which replaced the nuns' court after the suppression of the abbey. These rolls survive for the years 1539–43.[2] For the nuns' manor in Barley, there are pre-Dissolution rolls for the years 1463, 1469, 1505–8 and 1520.[3] The abbey held courts leet and baron at Foxton and Barley, but at Chatteris the bishop exercised the leet jurisdiction whilst the abbey's court dealt only with tenurial matters.

The court in Foxton always dealt with the abbey's lands and tenants in Foxton, Shepreth and Barrington, but the court rolls show that it sometimes dealt with the abbey's lands in Madingley and occasionally with those in Over too. In all the existing court rolls Madingley occurs only as a member of the manor of Foxton. Over is also always a member of the nuns' manor in Foxton in the late thirteenth and early fourteenth-century rolls, but there are two pre-Dissolution examples of separate courts held by the abbey at Over in 1523 and 1524.[4]

The court rolls for 1539 show that, in the year after the dissolution of the abbey, a steward held courts on successive days in the manors formerly belonging to the abbey. On 6 May, the first court was held at Chatteris, followed by a court at Over on 7 May, a court at Foxton on 8 May for the former abbey's lands in Foxton, Shepreth and Barrington, and on 9 May the last court in the series was held at Barley.[5] Although the majority of the surviving pre-Dissolution court rolls relate to the manor of Foxton with members and none survives from the abbey's manor in Chatteris, there are signs that before the Dissolution the abbey's steward made court-holding circuits similar to that undertaken by the steward in 1539. For example, in April 1507, June 1508 and

1 Cambridge, Trinity College Archives, Foxton 1–5, 6 rott. 1–2; CCRO L 63/17 and L 63/18, rott. 1–25d.
2 Cambridge, Trinity College Archives, Foxton 6, rott. 3d, 5–7; CCRO L 63/18, rot. 26.
3 PRO SC 2/177/1; CCRO L 63/18, rot. 12d.
4 Cambridge, Trinity College Archives, Foxton 1–5; CCRO L 63/18, rott. 16d, 17d.
5 Cambridge, Trinity College Archives, Foxton 6, rott. 3–4d.

June 1520, the abbey's steward held manorial courts on successive days at Foxton and Barley.[1]

The abbey administered its estates and enforced its leet jurisdiction through its manorial courts. As a result of the fines and other payments made, the courts were a source of revenue for the abbey. The minister's accounts rendered in Michaelmas 1539 state that the profits from the two courts held during the preceding year were £4 15s. 6d.[2] The surviving court rolls for that year show that the profits of the court of Foxton Regis, which dealt with the former abbey's lands in Foxton, Shepreth and Barrington, were £3 2s. 6d., before the deduction of the steward's expenses. The profits of the court of Chatteris Regis were 3s. 4d., those of Barley Regis were 9s. 4d. and those of Over Regis were 13s. 4d., again before the deduction of expenses in each case.[3] The sum of these profits according to the court rolls was £4 8s. 6d. Other rolls from the late fifteenth and early sixteenth centuries show that there were considerable inter-annual variations in the revenue which the abbey derived from its courts. For example, in contrast to the 9s. 4d. which the manor of Barley Regis yielded in 1539, the abbey's courts leet and baron held at Barley on 29 October 1505 produced profits of £2 3s. 10d.[4] There were variations also in the receipts from the nuns' manor of Foxton with members. In the year to Michaelmas 1496, the courts leet and baron held at Foxton on 13 October 1495 and 9 June 1496 produced a total of £6 14s. 4d.[5] In the year to Michaelmas 1528, the same courts held on 8 October 1527 and 26 May 1528 produced only £3 15s.[6] Similar variations existed in the earlier surviving court rolls for the same manor. For example, in the year to Michaelmas 1304, the courts leet and baron held at Foxton on 13 April and 17 September 1304 raised a total of £6 1s., but the courts for the year to Michaelmas 1320 held at Foxton on 7 October 1319 and 14 May 1320 raised a total of only £3 9s.[7]

A notebook of John Layer, who was rector of Shepreth in the early seventeenth century, contains abstracts of medieval charters which he had inherited. One of these abstracts relates to a thirteenth-century gift of nine acres of arable land and a messuage in Foxton lying *juxta curiam monialium de Chateris*.[8] This

1 CCRO L 63/17, rott. 12, 14; CCRO L 63/18, rot. 12–12d, 14; PRO SC 2/177/1, rott. 5–6.
2 PRO SC 6/HenVIII/267, rot. 9.
3 Cambridge, Trinity College Archives, Foxton 6, rott. 3–4d.
4 PRO SC 2/177/1, rot. 3.
5 CCRO L 63/17, rott. 4–5.
6 CCRO L 63/18, rott. 20–20d, 22–22d.
7 Cambridge, Trinity College Archives, Foxton 4, rot. 4; Foxton 1 rot. 4–4d.
8 Oxford, Bodl. MS Rawl. B 278, fo. 132r.

building probably had several functions: the steward would have held the abbey's manorial courts in it and he may have stayed there whilst in Foxton on the abbey's business; the bailiff may have collected the abbey's rents in the building; and it could also have been used as a temporary store for agricultural produce.

THE ABBEY'S OFFICIALS

In common with other substantial landlords, the abbey employed a hierarchy of officials to run its estates. At the top of this hierarchy was the steward who had a dual responsibility for the administration of the abbey's demesne and the supervision of its household. The names of four of the abbey's stewards survive, one in the cartulary, two in court rolls and a fourth in the post-Dissolution minister's accounts. In the cartulary, Hugh de Impington occurs as a witness in two mid-thirteenth-century charters: the sale by the abbey of their land in Hemingford Grey (Hunts.) and the grant to the abbey of a rent of 4s. in Kingston (nos. 231 and 240). The court rolls of the abbey's manor of Foxton show that John de Cambridge and Walter Bercok were also stewards. John de Cambridge occurs from 1305 to 1320, presiding over the abbey's court in Foxton, and Walter Bercok occurs in the same role from 1510 to 1518.[1] The steward called John de Cambridge is probably the same as the John de Cambridge to whom Mary de Shouldham leased a messuage and close in Chatteris in the first half of the fourteenth century (no. 71). The lease, which did not require the payment of rent, may have been made to provide the steward with somewhere to stay whilst attending to the abbey's business in Chatteris. This steward may possibly also have been the John de Cambridge who in 1311 bought a piece of land with a stone house in Cambridge which subsequently became part of the site of Gonville and Caius college, but the commonness of his name makes this identification far from certain.[2] In contrast it seems very likely that Walter Bercok, the other steward who occurs in the abbey's manorial court rolls, should be identified with the Walter Berkoke who occurs in the cartulary: in 1506 × 1515 Chatteris abbey granted to James Stanley, bishop of Ely, and Walter Berkoke, gentleman, the tithe of the church of Barley (Herts.) and the next presentation to it (no. 277). The fourth known steward is John Goodryke who in 1539 occurs in the minister's accounts as the chief steward of the pos-

---

[1] Cambridge, Trinity College Archives, Foxton 4, rot. 3; Foxton 1, rot. 4d; CCRO L 63/18, rott. 2, 11d.

[2] C. N. L. Brooke *A History of Gonville and Caius College* (Woodbridge, 1985) p. 14.

sessions of the suppressed abbey. The abbey had appointed Goodryke to the office of steward for life and paid him 40s. annually. The minister's accounts also show that Thomas Donolt was the under-steward of the nuns' court and that he was paid 26s. 8d. annually.[1]

Below the steward in the hierarchy of estate administration was the bailiff. The bailiff and rent-collector who occurs in 1539 in the post-Dissolution minister's accounts is Ralph Jhoneson.[2] He was paid 53s. 4d. annually and, like the chief steward, had been appointed for life by the abbey. He seems to have dealt with almost all the abbey's lands but a second bailiff also occurs in the 1539 accounts: Robert Wingefeld was bailiff of the distant manor of Kersey (Suff.). He was paid 20s. annually, which was a tenth of the £10 received for the farm of the manor.[3] In 1539, a total of £7 was paid to officials of the former abbey from an income which amounted to £122 7s. 11¾d.[4]

In addition to its stewards and bailiffs, the abbey would have had a reeve on each of its manors. The reeve was usually a villein and was the chief unfree officer. Reeves were normally appointed, or elected, to serve for a year, although from the later thirteenth century they sometimes served for longer periods.[5] A few reeves occur in the cartulary but none can be proved to have been reeves for the abbey's manors.

As well as the officials who administered the abbey's estates, the nuns also had household officials, though these figures are poorly documented. There are no known chamberlains from Chatteris but there is evidence of one dispenser (*dispensarius*). He was probably responsible for organising the abbey's provisions, perhaps under the authority of the steward. The only known holder of the office is Thomas, dispenser of Chatteris, who received one rood of land in Chatteris from Thomas Alberd' between the mid and the late thirteenth century (no. 81). Subsequently Thomas – who was by then the former dispenser of Chatteris – gave the same rood of land to Isabel daughter of Hervy de Foxton (no. 52).

Another household official of the abbey who occurs in the cartulary is the *serviens*. Jocelin, who occurs as a witness in a mid-thirteenth-century charter, is described as *tunc serviente domus de Chatriz* (no. 240). He occurs again in a mid-thirteenth-century power of attorney where Mabel de Bancis refers to him as

---

1 PRO SC 6/HenVIII/267, rot. 9d.
2 Ibid. rot. 5.
3 Ibid. rot. 9d.
4 Ibid. rot. 9–9d.
5 Miller and Hatcher *Rural Society and Economic Change*, p. 193.

dilectum et fidelem servientem nostrum, procuratorem et attornatum nostrum (no. 228). The letters of attorney appointed Jocelin to be the manager and collector the abbey's rent in Lincoln. Thomas de Bancis, too, was called the *serviens* of the abbey when abbess Mabel de Bancis and the convent leased to him a messuage and five acres of arable land with five acres of meadow in Foxton before October 1247 (no. 139). These men seem to have been more the abbey's serjeant than its servant. Their role may have been executive, though the precise scope of their duties is elusive. Jocelin occurs only in this capacity in the cartulary, but Thomas de Bancis also occurs twice as a benefactor of the abbey (nos. 115 and 125). Unfortunately it is not clear whether he made his donations before, whilst or after he served the abbey.

V

The Abbey

Chatteris lies about 12 miles north-west of Ely, on raised ground which was formerly an island until the draining of the fens. The abbey was sited near the centre of the village, to the south-west of the parish church. The settlement at Chatteris already existed when the abbey was founded. Although the foundation narrative copied into the cartulary from the *Liber Eliensis* does not make clear which came first, the nunnery or the village, there is other evidence to prove that the settlement pre-dated the abbey. Æthelstan Mannessune gave part of Chatteris to Ramsey abbey (Hunts.) between 969, when the monastery was founded, and 974, when king Edgar confirmed the gift together with all the other privileges of Ramsey abbey.[1] The chronicle of Ramsey abbey makes clear that this was not merely a gift of unsettled pasture but that there was an established settlement at Chatteris:

> Imprimis Æthelstan Mannessone concessit Sancto Benedicto Ramesiæ terram de Chateriz, pro animæ suæ salute, cum dominio et hominibus, cum gurgitibus et piscariis, sicut ipse et pater suus eam unquam melius et plenius habuerunt.[2]

Domesday Book shows that there were two manors in Chatteris, one of which belonged to the abbot of Ramsey and the other to the abbot of Ely.[3] In 1086, the abbess of Chatteris had yet to acquire her manor there from the church of Ely. If the nunnery had been founded in isolation, there would almost certainly have been only one manor in Chatteris and the abbess, rather than the abbots of Ramsey and Ely, would have held it in 1086. The existence of the two manors

---

[1] *Chronicon Abbatiæ Rameseiensis* ed. W. D. Macray (Rolls Series lxxxiii, 1886) p. 59; *Cartularium Monasterii de Rameseia* eds W. H. Hart and P. A. Lyons, ii (Rolls Series lxxix, 1886) p. 56.

[2] *Chronicon Abbatiæ Rameseiensis*, p. 59.

[3] *Domesday Book* i, fos. 192d, 191d.

reinforces the argument that Chatteris had a considerable pre-Conquest history and that its origins long pre-dated the foundation of the nunnery in the early eleventh century. In addition, although some medieval settlements were established very rapidly, the extent of the settlement at Chatteris revealed by Domesday Book suggests that it had existed for more than the three generations since the arrival of the nuns. In 1086 the abbot of Ramsey held in Chatteris three hides less half a virgate, with land and meadow for four ploughs, woodland for 100 pigs, and 3000 eels; there were 10 villeins, five bordars and two serfs. The abbot of Ely held two hides and half a virgate, with land and meadow for three ploughs, woodland for 20 pigs and 1500 eels; there were six villeins, two bordars and two cottars.[1] All the evidence shows that Roberta Gilchrist is mistaken in her belief that the abbey was founded in isolation and that its existence alone produced the surrounding settlement.[2] However, whilst Chatteris abbey was not responsible for creating a village on the island, its agricultural and economic activity must have promoted the development of the village. The topographical evidence of the street-pattern in Chatteris suggests that the settlement was originally linear, with the main road running approximately north-south (see figure 2).[3] It is likely that the foundation of the abbey led to the development of other streets in its vicinity.

None of the abbey's medieval structures now survives but the abbey was not wholly demolished at its dissolution. Some of the buildings were left standing and were converted into a house which the Gascoyne family acquired and extended in the seventeenth century. In 1657, William Dugdale visited Chatteris on a journey around the fens. He wrote, 'From Dudington we went to Charteriz where there is no vestigia of the monasterie now left; one Mr Gascoyne who dwelleth there having transformed it into a new house.'[4] In the mid-eighteenth century, Cole noted that the fish-house in which the nuns dried their fish and the granary of the abbey were both still intact.[5] The second volume of the revised edition of *Monasticon Anglicanum* published in 1819 states that, 'The present vestiges of Chaateriz nunnery consist of little more than a few walls.'[6] Even the house built by the Gascoynes, which was known as

---

[1] Ibid.
[2] R. Gilchrist *Gender and Material Culture: the Archaeology of Religious Women* (London, 1994) p. 69.
[3] Ordnance Surveyors' Drawings, 2 inch, Cambs., Hunts. and Norf.: sheet 250 (1810).
[4] BL Lansdowne MS 722, fo. 34r.
[5] BL Add. MS 5809, fo. 112r.
[6] *Mon. Ang.* ii, p. 616. This information is not included in the first edition.

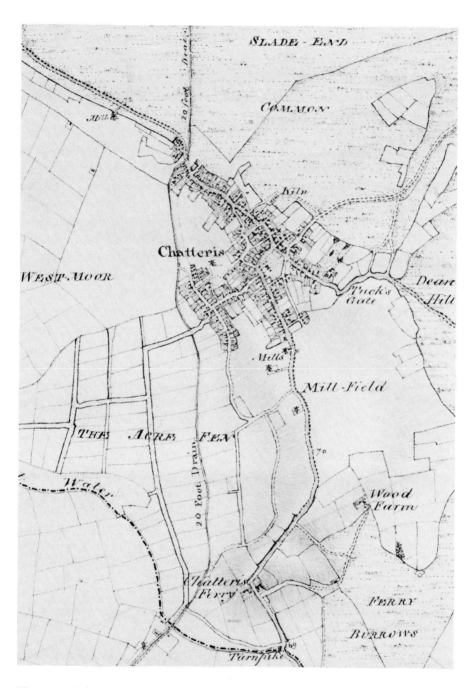

Figure 2:   Ordnance Surveyors' Drawings, 2 inch, Cambs., Hunts. and Norf.: sheet 250 (1810)

Park House, was derelict by the early nineteenth century; in 1847 it was pulled down.

An ordnance surveyor's drawing made in 1810, on a scale of two inches to the mile, shows the enclosure of the nunnery very clearly: it stands out as a large open space containing few buildings in the centre of the town.[1] The large building visible in the western half of the enclosure is Park House (see figure 2). The 25 inch Ordnance Survey map of 1888 shows the location of the abbey more precisely (see figure 3).[2] It lay south of Park Street and just north of a new road, later called Victoria Street, which divided the enclosure in two. Park Street and West, South and East Park Streets mark the boundary of the nunnery's enclosure. The Ordnance Survey maps of both 1888 and 1972 show the existence of an 'ancient wall' along part of the perimeter of the site of the abbey near the junction of East and South Park Streets.[3] These stretches of wall are not the abbey's original enclosing wall but were built from a combination of ragstone and stone quoins at some time after the demolition of much of the abbey at the Dissolution.[4]

By 1888, the north and west sides of the enclosure had already been built upon and during the twentieth century the whole site was built over. Despite the evidence of the Ordnance Survey maps, some confusion has arisen concerning the exact location of the nunnery. The *Victoria County History* for Cambridgeshire states that some of the last remains of the nunnery were removed when the Empress cinema was built in 1935.[5] But the site of the Empress cinema, now occupied by the Empress swimming pool, lay to the north of Park Street, on the site of a house called 'The Priory' which appears on the 25 inch Ordnance Survey map of 1888 (see figure 3).[6] The name of this house may have caused the confusion about the location of the abbey, but it is certain that the abbey lay to the south of Park Street.

Although none of the original buildings from the abbey survives, the inventory compiled when it was suppressed in 1538 contains much information about its layout and contents (see appendix 2).[7] The first room listed is the great guest chamber, which had beds for two guests, followed by an inward chamber

---

1 Ordnance Surveyors' Drawings, 2 inch, Cambs., Hunts. and Norf.: sheet 250 (1810).
2 Ordnance Survey, 25 inch, 1st edn, Cambs.: sheet 20. 16 (1888).
3 Ibid. and Ordnance Survey, 1: 2500: national grid plan TL 3885–3985 (1972).
4 I am grateful to A. P. Baggs for his advice on architectural matters in this chapter.
5 *VCH Cambs.* iv, p. 104.
6 *Kelly's Directory of Cambridgeshire 1937* (London, 1937) p. 144.
7 PRO E 117/11/13.

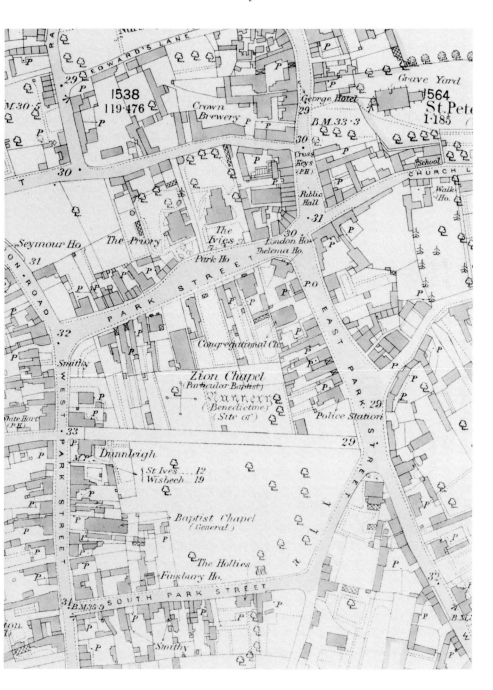

Figure 3: Ordnance Survey, 25 inch, 1st edn, Cambs.: sheet 20. 16 (1888)

with one further bed, and the maidens' chamber with four mattresses and 'certain old mattres for servauntes'. In 1343, bishop Montacute granted a licence to Elizabeth Peverel to hear mass in her chamber at Chatteris abbey or wherever else she should happen to stay in the diocese of Ely.[1] The bishop's register gives her the title *domina*, which could have been applied to a religious or a secular woman. The latter seems almost certain since the wording of the licence in the bishop's register suggests that she was a visitor at the abbey who travelled much locally. Moreover, there is no record of an abbess bearing her name and Alice de Shropham retired as abbess in 1347.[2] Elizabeth Peverel's room at the abbey seems, therefore, to have been the guest chamber rather than the abbess's lodging. The licence to hear mass there suggests that she may have been a regular boarder at the abbey. Boarders figure prominently in the Lincoln visitation material. Whilst their presence could cause disruption, they also produced revenue for the nunnery. The prioress of Langley (Leics.) stated during a visitation in 1440 that lady Audeley, a boarder, had dogs whose barking disturbed and frightened the nuns, but the sub-prioress reported that lady Audeley paid 40s. annually for her house within the priory and that she kept it in repair.[3] There is no evidence for Chatteris that the bishop of Ely sought to control the admission of boarders but regulation by licence was quite common elsewhere. For example, in the diocese of Lincoln bishop Flemyng enjoined the abbess of Elstow (Beds.) not to receive males or females over 12 years of age, particularly if married, without licence from him.[4] Such requirements for a licence seem to have been motivated by the dual concerns that boarders should not bring worldly influences into the convent and that they should be a source of financial support rather than strain to poorer houses.[5] It is not clear whether Chatteris abbey profited from the visits of Elizabeth Peverel and, since she is the only known guest of Chatteris abbey, it is impossible to tell how frequently the abbey's guest chamber was used and whether regular boarders or more transient visitors were the norm. Many religious houses had corrodians who paid a lump sum in return for the right to board there for the rest of their lives, but no evidence survives to show whether there were any at Chatteris.

1   Cambridge UL, EDR G/1/1 Montacute register, fo. 16v.
2   Cambridge UL, EDR G/1/1 de Lisle register, fo. 51r.
3   *Visitations of Religious Houses* ed. Thompson, ii, p. 175.
4   Ibid. i, p. 49.
5   J. H. Tillotson 'Visitation and Reform of the Yorkshire Nunneries in the Fourteenth Century' *Northern History* xxx (1994) pp. 15–19.

Archaeological remains at monastic sites show that heads of houses often had their own accommodation.[1] In nunneries, such lodgings were commonly located within the western range together with the accommodation for guests. The 1538 inventory of Chatteris abbey does not mention an abbess's lodging, but the detailed account of the election of Anne Basset as abbess in 1488 shows that there was an abbess's chamber in the late fifteenth century. After the publication of the election of Anne Basset, the new abbess was led *ad bassam cameram vulgariter nuncupatam* 'Thabbas Chamber'.[2] This suggests that the room was on the ground floor rather than the first floor where the guest-rooms were usually found. The existence of private accommodation for the abbess, although contrary to the rule of St Benedict, was far from unusual. Visitation material from the diocese of Lincoln reinforces the considerable archaeological evidence that many heads of houses slept separately. For example, in 1440 the prioress of Langley (Leics.) was accused of spending the night in her own private room rather than the dormitory. The bishop's injunction which followed, though corrective, also shows the degree to which separate quarters for heads of houses were accepted in the fifteenth century: 'Also we enjoyne yow, prioresse, ... that ye somtyme in the monethe or fourte nyght lyg by nyght in the dormytory, to se ther howe relygyone is keppede.'[3]

The inventory shows that the dormitory at Chatteris had been divided into cells.[4] Such divisions were common in later medieval Benedictine houses. In 1441, the prioress of Ankerwyke (Bucks.) was told to take down the parclose made in the dormitory and to see that every nun's cell was open towards the dormitory.[5] The east range at Littlemore priory (Oxon.) is a surviving example of a partitioned dorter with two rows of cells.[6] The sub-division of dorters was part of a move away from the common life, as was the introduction of separate lodgings for heads of houses and the development of informal households or *familiae* within later medieval nunneries. Bishop Gray's injunction to Godstow abbey (Oxon.) in 1432, which ordered that the abbey was to have only three households of nuns beside that of the abbess, was one of many injunctions

1 D. Knowles and J. K. S. St Joseph *Monastic Sites from the Air* (Cambridge, 1952) pp. xiv–xxvi.
2 Cambridge UL, EDR G/1/6 Alcock register, p. 149.
3 *Visitations of Religious Houses* ed. Thompson, ii, pp. 175, 177.
4 PRO E 117/11/13, fo. 3r.
5 *Visitations of Religious Houses* ed. Thompson, ii, p. 9.
6 R. Gilchrist 'The Archaeology of Medieval Nunneries: a Research Design' in *The Archaeology of Rural Monasteries in England and Wales* eds R. Gilchrist and H. Mytum (BAR British series 203; Oxford, 1989) p. 256.

dealing with households in nunneries in the diocese of Lincoln.[1] The abbeys at
Godstow and Chatteris were comparable in size: in 1445 Godstow had 17 nuns
including the abbess whereas Chatteris had 15 in 1379 and 13 in 1488.[2] Chatteris abbey may have had households similar to those at Godstow, even though
it was not a large house, but the only possible indications of their existence are
the abbess's chamber and the divided dorter.

Several rooms were used for the storage, production, preparation and consumption of food. The abbey had a cellarer's room, three butteries, a bake-
house and a brew-house, a kitchen, a hall and a frater. Barns are recorded and
the list of livestock and farm-implements implies that there were also buildings
for the animals and a cart-shed.

Despite appearing to be a thorough survey of the abbey, the inventory does
not list every room. There is no mention of the chapter house, possibly because
it did not contain significant movable furnishings. Proof of its existence seems
to be provided by documents dated there and by accounts of the election of two
abbesses which took place in it.[3] It is possible, though, that part of the north
aisle of the nuns' church acted as the chapter house: heads of religious houses
were commonly buried in their chapter houses and the Chatteris inventory
states that the north aisle contained gravestones.[4] As well as not naming a
chapter house, the inventory does not refer to the infirmary, although the
cartulary shows that William of Ely gave several properties to Chatteris abbey
for the support of sick nuns in the infirmary and Ralph, his son, gave a rent of
four shillings annually to it.[5]

The dedication of the church is usually given as St Mary in the cartulary
although several charters have St Mary and All Saints.[6] The cartulary records
one gift to the abbey for the maintenance of the light of St Katherine and four
for the light of St Mary.[7] One of the latter includes payment for a chaplain to
celebrate the mass of St Mary at the abbey.[8] The gifts for the maintenance of

1 *Visitations of Religious Houses* ed. Thompson, i, p. 68.
2 Knowles and Hadcock *Medieval Religious Houses* 2nd edn, p. 259; Palmer 'The Clerical Poll
   Tax of 1379 in Cambridgeshire', pp. 121–2; Cambridge UL, EDR G/1/6 Alcock register, p.
   148.
3 Nos. 266, 271, 274, 276; Cambridge UL, EDR G/1/1 de Lisle register, fo. 51r; G/1/6 Alcock
   register, p. 148.
4 PRO E 117/11/13, fo. 4r.
5 Nos. 91, 72.
6 Eg. nos. 54, 235.
7 For the light of St Katherine: no. 54; for the light of St Mary: nos. 57, 62, 115, 240.
8 No. 115.

lights suggest that, in addition to the high altar dedicated to St Mary, the nuns' church had another altar dedicated to St Katherine. Bequests made in the will of Olliff Bollonde in 1534 show that by the early sixteenth century the abbey also had two altars dedicated to male saints. The will was copied into two probate registers. According to the first copy, Olliff left 4d. each to the abbey's high altar, the altar of St John and the altar of St Andrew. In the second copy, gifts to three altars were recorded again, but one of these was to the altar of St Thomas rather than to that of St John.[1]

The inventory describes the abbey church in considerable detail.[2] The lead from the roof of the church and from its steeple was valued at £80 which suggests that it must have been quite a large building. The church consisted of a choir, two aisles and a vestry, together with the steeple. It is not clear from the inventory whether the north and south aisles lay on either side of the choir – in which case it is hard to understand why the inventory does not mention a nave – or whether the aisles lay alongside each other to the west of the choir. The south aisle seems to have been the part of the church which some townspeople used as their parish church: the inventory lists the contents of the choir, north aisle and vestry, as well as the plate, lead and bells, but for the south aisle it states merely, 'The sowth ile gyven'. The visitation injunctions issued by bishop de Lisle in 1347 include an instruction to keep the doors of the choir closed during services, except at the elevation of the host, which shows that people other than the nuns were attending services there.[3] The admission of parishioners to a conventual church would usually be financially advantageous to a religious house but, in the case of Chatteris, the abbey was already rector of the parish church and so would not have made money from attracting parishioners to its own church. Nevertheless, it is clear that some families in the town did attend the conventual rather than the parish church. On 3 September 1538 Dr Thomas Leigh, who had taken the surrender of the abbey, wrote to Thomas Cromwell and confirmed that 14 households from the town 'kept their parish church in the abbey'. Leigh suggested to Cromwell that these 14 households should go to the parish church instead.[4] Cromwell presumably agreed since the abbey church did not survive.

1 CCRO Ely consistory court probate registers, vol. 8, fo. 183v; vol. 10, fo. 16r.
2 PRO E 117/11/13, fos. 4r–5r.
3 Cambridge UL, EDR G/1/1, de Lisle register, fo. 47v.
4 *Letters and Papers, Foreign and Domestic, of the Reign of Henry VIII* ed. J. Gairdner, xiii, part ii (PRO Texts and Calendars, 1893) p. 110.

The question of whether the north and south aisles were choir aisles or whether they were parallel aisles to the west of the choir is problematic. Where nunneries shared their conventual churches with the laity, the convent commonly used the choir and the laity the nave as, for example, at Polesworth abbey (Warwicks.), where a crossing tower formed the division, and at Nun Monkton priory (Yorks. E.), where the nuns' choir and the aisleless parochial nave were divided by a screen. In some cases the division was reversed so that the nuns had the nave and the laity the choir, as at Marrick priory (Yorks. N.), Davington priory (Kent) and Nunkeeling priory (Yorks. E.). In contrast to such lateral divisions, the churches of the double houses of the Gilbertine order were parallelograms divided by a longitudinal wall into two wide aisles, one of which was used by the nuns and the other by the canons. Several nunneries which admitted parishioners to their services also had churches with two parallel aisles in which a screened arcade separated the nuns from the laity. Houses with such parallel-aisle churches were found mostly in the south and east of England and included the Benedictine priories of St Helen's, Bishopsgate (London); Minster-in-Sheppey and Higham (Kent); Wroxall (Warwicks.) and Ickleton (Cambs.). Chatteris abbey may have been similarly constructed. At St Helen's and Ickleton, as at Chatteris, the parishioners had the south aisle.[1] It is not possible to say whether the steeple of the conventual church at Chatteris was part of a western tower or whether the church had a crossing tower. Whichever was the case, it seems plausible that the church originally had a choir and an aisleless nave and that a screened aisle was added later alongside the nave. If this hypothesis is correct, the church would then have had a choir together with, in effect, a northern conventual aisle and a parallel southern parochial aisle. Such an arrangement would be consistent with bishop de Lisle's injunction to keep the doors of the choir closed during services except at the elevation of the host.[2] This injunction also suggests that the southern parochial 'aisle' may in fact have been the original aisleless nave and that it was the parallel northern conventual aisle which had been added later.

The use of the south aisle of the abbey church by parishioners suggests that the abbey's cloister must have lain to the north of the church. A north cloister was a departure from the standard monastic plan which positioned the cloister to the south of the church so that it received as much warmth and sunlight as possible. However, nunneries seem to have had a north cloister far more frequently than monasteries which usually had one only if the restrictions of

---

1 Gilchrist *Gender and Material Culture*, pp. 99–105.
2 Cambridge UL, EDR G/1/1 de Lisle register, fo. 47v.

the site made it unavoidable. Of all the nunneries with a north cloister, only Barking abbey can be shown to have required one because of the limitations of its site. Gilchrist has analysed the orientation of the cloisters in 61 nunneries and double house in which their position can be determined. She found that 21 of these 61 nunneries had their cloister to the liturgical north of the church. Her map of the distribution of north and south cloister nunneries shows that Chatteris lay within a discrete regional cluster of north cloister nunneries. The other members of the group were Crabhouse priory and Shouldham priory (Norf.), Hinchingbrooke priory (Hunts.) and Denny abbey, St Radegund's priory and Ickleton priory (Cambs.). There were two other regional groups of north cloister nunneries, one centred on London and one in the East and West Ridings of Yorkshire.[1] Gilchrist suggests that the choice of a north cloister may have been related to early traditions which linked women and female saints with the northern side of churches. She also argues that since there is no correlation between north cloisters and foundation-dates or particular orders, the regional groupings of north cloisters suggest that patrons or planners may deliberately have chosen them.[2] Given that Chatteris was the oldest member of its regional group, it may have acted as a model for other local nunneries. However there is insufficient evidence about the site of Chatteris abbey to know whether the position of the cloister was determined by the nature of the site itself or whether it was linked to the gender of the nuns.

The house later known as Park House, which was built in the sixteenth century and extended in the seventeenth century, incorporated some of the abbey's buildings within its fabric. In his history of the abbey, Philip Dickinson reproduced three water-colours of Park House which were painted just before its demolition in 1847.[3] One of the paintings shows two adjacent, blocked Norman arches, one of which is much larger than the other (see figure 4). It seems likely that these arches were part of the church and that they marked the division of the nave from the chancel. Another painting of Park House includes the parish church in the background (figure 5). This proves that the painting showing the Norman arches (figure 4) is a view from the east. If the rest of the

1 Gilchrist *Gender and Material Culture*, pp. 128–33.
2 Ibid. pp. 133–43.
3 P. G. M. Dickinson *A Little History of the Abbey of St Mary and the Parish Church of S. Peter and S. Paul, Chatteris, Cambridgeshire* (Chatteris, 1954) pp. 17–18. The paintings, which were formerly kept in the urban district council's chamber and elsewhere in Chatteris, are now in private hands. I am very grateful to Helen Pope for allowing me to see and photograph these watercolours which are the only known representations of Park House.

Figure 4: Watercolour of Park House from the east (privately owned)

Figure 5: Watercolour of Park House from the south-west (privately owned)

structure in figure 4 is part of the original abbey building, the painting suggests
– in contrast to the evidence from the inventory – that the abbey had a south
cloister. Moreover the two low arches in the south wall in figure 5 suggest a
vaulted undercroft beneath a southern frater. It is difficult to reconcile the
evidence relating to the location of the cloister in the sixteenth-century inventory with that in the nineteenth-century paintings. There is insufficient detail in
the paintings to prove whether the part of Park House lying to the south (i.e.
left) of the large arches in figure 4 was a section of the conventual complex, or
whether it was built on later with stone from other demolished parts of the
abbey, perhaps when the Gascoynes extended the sixteenth-century house in the
seventeenth century. It is also impossible to know whether the low arches
visible in figure 5 were, in fact, medieval structures. However the evidence from
the inventory, although not conclusive, does strongly suggest that the parishioners used the south aisle, which makes a north cloister at Chatteris more
likely.

The same painting which shows the blocked Norman archways (figure 4)
also shows clearly a large window, which may date from the late fifteenth or
early sixteenth centuries. Since this window cuts into the line of one of the
arches, it seems likely that the window was moved to the position shown in the
painting after the suppression of the abbey. It was probably saved from another
range of the conventual buildings which was pulled down at the Dissolution.
The window suggests that the claustral buildings were substantial stone structures. This is significant because poorer nunneries quite commonly had ranges
built of timber, half-timber or cob. For example, timber was used at Wilberfoss
priory (Yorks. E.) and cob at Crabhouse priory (Norf.).[1]

Most of the stone from the nunnery has disappeared and much of it may
have been used to maintain causeways in the fen near Chatteris.[2] After the
demolition of Park House, some of the stone was reused for other buildings in
Chatteris and in Doddington, a village four miles to the north. In Chatteris two
octagonal houses were built of stone at 46–8 London Road. Nearby, 14–19
Southampton Place – a row of houses built in 1857 – contained stones with
chevron carving which may have been taken from the blocked Norman archways in Park House.[3] These houses in Southampton Place and London Road

[1] Gilchrist *Gender and Material Culture*, p. 95.

[2] In 1490 William Bray, vicar of Chatteris, left 40s. in his will for the maintenance of the
parish's causeways (Cambridge UL, EDR G/1/6 Alcock register, p. 56).

[3] Dickinson *A Little History of the Abbey of St Mary, Chatteris*, pp. 14–15; D. Haigh *The Religious Houses of Cambridgeshire* (Cambridge, 1988) p. 18.

have now been demolished, but an old stone carved with two twelfth-century chevrons has been built into a modern gatepost in South Park Street.

Although most of the stone houses in Chatteris have now been demolished, a few are still standing. The five terraced houses at 34–42 London Road, which are known as Seymour Place, were built of rag-stone with free-stone quoins in 1847. Since 1847 was the year of the demolition of Park House, it seems almost certain that the stone in Seymour Place came from the abbey. Two late nineteenth-century, semi-detached houses at 24–6 Victoria Street are also built of stone, again probably from Park House. The side wall of no. 24 is particularly interesting. Whereas the front of the houses and the side of no. 26 are built with rectangular blocks of stone, the side wall of no. 24 contains many small triangular pieces. It is not clear what the original use of these stones could have been. There are similar triangular pieces of stone in the front wall of the house at 44 Benwick Street in Doddington. Three other houses in Newgate Street in Doddington have stone front walls and the front garden of 23 Station Road in Chatteris is bounded by a short stretch of stone wall with a stone gateway. Above the gateway is mounted a fragment of tracery which may have come originally from a window at the abbey.

Another stretch of stone wall in Chatteris, towards the west end of the south side of Victoria Street, was probably built with stone from the abbey following the demolition of Park House. It contains a scratch-sundial mounted upside-down which may have come from the nunnery. Some of the stones near the sundial have pink patches which suggest that they have been burnt in the past, possibly in the fire which occurred at the abbey in the early fourteenth century. The Norman arches from the abbey's church, which were preserved in Park House, must have survived the early fourteenth-century fire. The damage caused by the fire prompted Robert Orford, bishop of Ely, to ask Ralph Baldock, bishop of London, to remit the tithe owed to him by the nuns. Orford's request, which he made in 1306 × 1310, describes how the fire had devastated the nunnery's church, buildings and all the goods from its manors stored there. It also states that their dorter had been destroyed and that the nuns had only just enough food.[1] The abbey church was rebuilt and in 1352 bishop de Lisle consecrated both it and the parish church.[2] That the parish church was consecrated too suggests that the fire in Chatteris had not been confined to the nunnery but had spread through the town. Although much of the parish church was rebuilt in 1910, the remaining medieval work all dates from the mid-

---

[1] *Mon. Ang.* ii, pp. 618–19, no. 10 (BL Cotton Ch. xxi. 12).
[2] Cambridge UL, EDR G/1/1 de Lisle register, fo. 65v.

fourteenth century and later which is consistent with a rebuilding after the early fourteenth-century fire.[1] In 1490 the vicar of Chatteris, William Bray, left six marks towards the fabric of the parish church in his will, but he also left 10 marks for the repair of the chapel of St Mary at the abbey, showing the need for ongoing maintenance of the nunnery's church.[2]

Two impressions of the abbey's seal survive. The earlier impression is attached to an early thirteenth-century gift of land in Madingley made by abbess Agnes to Geoffrey son of Eustace (see figure 6).[3] The same twelfth-century matrix was used to make the seal for the surrender of the abbey in 1538.[4] The seal is a pointed oval and the device shows the Virgin crowned, holding a book in her left hand and a flowering staff topped with a cross in her right, seated on a throne whose sides terminate in animals' heads and feet; the legend is *SIGIL-LUM SANCTE MARIE*. The seal is part of a small group of nunnery seals which show the Virgin on her own with a book and a sceptre or cross. This iconography suggests that the seal dates from the last quarter of the twelfth century, whilst the style of the Virgin's long, trailing sleeves, which was popular from the mid-eleventh century until *c*. 1180–90, indicates that the matrix dates from before *c*. 1190.[5]

Gilchrist lists 136 nunnery seals classified according to their iconography and the Virgin appears on over half of these. 48 of the seals show the 'Throne of Wisdom' which depicts a crowned and enthroned Virgin with the child on her knee. Only five of the total 136 seals depict a seated Virgin without a child. These are the seals from the priories at Baysdale (Yorks. N.), Markyate (Beds.), Studley (Oxon.) and Swine (Yorks. E.) and the seal from Chatteris abbey.[6] Devices showing the Virgin with a book are unusual but there are three twelfth-century examples from nunneries in Yorkshire. The pointed oval seal of Nun Appleton, a Cistercian priory, has a standing, crowned Virgin holding a long cross in her right hand and a book in her left; the round seal of the Benedictine priory at Yedingham shows the Virgin standing, holding a fleur-de-lis in her right hand and an open book in her left; and the round seal of the Cistercian priory at Swine shows the Virgin sitting on a throne, with a lily in her right

1 *VCH Cambs.* iv, p. 107.
2 Cambridge UL, EDR G/1/6 Alcock register, p. 56.
3 No. 281: Cambridge, St John's College Archives D 25. 22. For a discussion of this charter, see p. 60.
4 PRO E 322/53.
5 T. A. Heslop 'Seals' in *English Romanesque Art 1066–1200* eds G. Zarnecki, J. Holt and T. Holland (London, 1984) p. 306.
6 Gilchrist *Gender and Material Culture*, pp. 143–6.

Figure 6: The seal attached to no. 281, the early thirteenth-century gift by abbess Agnes and the convent of Chatteris to Geoffrey son of Eustace of half an acre of land in Madingley (Cambridge, St John's College Archive, D 25. 22)

hand and an open book in her left.[1] The iconography of the seal of Swine priory – which was founded before 1153 – most closely resembles that of the Chatteris seal. Books are not uncommon on nunnery seals, but they occur with patron saints and heads of houses more frequently than with the Virgin. For example, the seal of Nunkeeling priory (Yorks. E.) shows St Helen holding a book and the seal of Aconbury priory (Herefords.) shows a prioress with a book, whilst the abbesses of Barking (Essex), Denny (Cambs.) and Nunminster in Winchester (Hants.) and the prioress of Nuneaton (Warwicks.) had personal seals with the head of the house holding a book.[2]

There are striking similarities between the seals of empress Matilda (1141–3) and Chatteris abbey which suggest that the former may have been a visual source for the latter.[3] Like the Chatteris Virgin, the empress is seated and is wearing an imperial crown of three points. The empress's dress is also similar to that of the Virgin, but the empress's sleeves, although long and trailing, are plainer and less exaggerated than those of the Chatteris Virgin. Matilda's left hand is empty and in her right hand she holds a sceptre at the top of which is a fleur-de-lis. Whilst the Chatteris Virgin holds a book in her left hand, in her right hand she holds a staff which parallels the sceptre in the empress's right hand. However the Virgin's staff has two sprays of flowers or leaves with a cross at its tip. The design of this staff has an affinity with Richard I's first seal, which dates from 1189. Richard's seal includes a stem with four sprays and with a cross at its tip; the stem rises from the orb which the king holds in his left hand.[4] This great seal is the first to include a flowering stem with a cross and it is possible that it influenced the design of the Chatteris seal but, in the context of the Virgin, the flowering staff may be read as a *virga* (*virgo*) giving forth a cross.[5]

---

1 C. Clay 'The Seals of the Religious Houses of Yorkshire' *Archaeologia* lxxviii (1928) pp. 28, 33–4; R. H. Ellis *Catalogue of Seals in the Public Record Office. Monastic Seals* i (London, 1986) pp. 86, 103.
2 Ellis *Monastic Seals* i, pp. 69, 2, 5, 30, 99, 68.
3 A. B. and A. Wyon *The Great Seals of England from the Earliest Period to the Present Time* (London, 1887) p. 14; pl. iv, no. 29.
4 Ibid. pp. 18–19; pl. v, no. 35.
5 I am grateful to Sandy Heslop for his comments on the abbey's seal.

THE NUNS

Chatteris abbey was not a large nunnery. The abbey had 15 nuns in 1347, when Matilda Bernard was elected abbess following the retirement of Alice de Shropham, and it still had 15 in 1379.[1] By 1488, there were only 13 nuns and the death of abbess Margery Ramsey on 27 January of that year reduced the number to 12.[2] When dissolved in 1538, the abbey had 11 nuns, including the abbess.[3] The number of nuns at the abbey declined gradually in the later Middle Ages, but the reduction was not so great as to suggest that the abbey found it difficult to recruit novices in the early sixteenth century. There is no evidence for the number of nuns before 1347 but the relatively slender endowment of the nunnery suggests that its population could never have been large. Some of the other Benedictine nunneries founded before the Conquest had far more nuns: Shaftesbury (Dorset), the largest nunnery in the country, had over 100 in the thirteenth and early fourteenth centuries when Nunminster in Winchester (Hants.) probably had between 70 and 80; Wilton (Wilts.) may have had over 80 nuns in the twelfth and thirteenth centuries and Romsey (Hants.) had 90 in 1333. The numbers at Chatteris seem small by comparison with those at these great abbeys, but many post-Conquest foundations had similar numbers of nuns to those found at Chatteris, and some had even fewer. For example, Ickleton priory, another Cambridgeshire Benedictine nunnery, had nine nuns in 1379, 12 in 1444 and nine in 1490; St Sepulchre's, Canterbury had six in 1379 and 1511 and eight in 1535; and Hinchingbrooke priory (Hunts.), always a small house, had only four nuns in 1536.[4]

Appendix 1 is a list of all the known abbesses and nuns from Chatteris. The list has been compiled from the cartulary itself, the registers of the bishops of Ely and the archbishops of Canterbury, court rolls from the abbey's manors and central government records relating to taxation and the dissolution of the abbey. The names of a substantial number of later medieval abbesses are known, often from several references, but the only known abbess who definitely occurred before the thirteenth century is Ælfwen, the first head of the house. Unlike the abbesses, most known nuns appear only in one source, and the identity of the majority of the nuns ever to have lived at the abbey is not

---

1 Cambridge UL, EDR G/1/1 de Lisle register, fo. 51r; Palmer 'The Clerical Poll Tax of 1379 in Cambridgeshire', pp. 121–2.
2 Cambridge UL, EDR G/1/6 Alcock register, p. 148.
3 All 11 nuns signed the surrender of the abbey (PRO E 322/53).
4 Knowles and Hadcock *Medieval Religious Houses* 2nd edn, pp. 257–9.

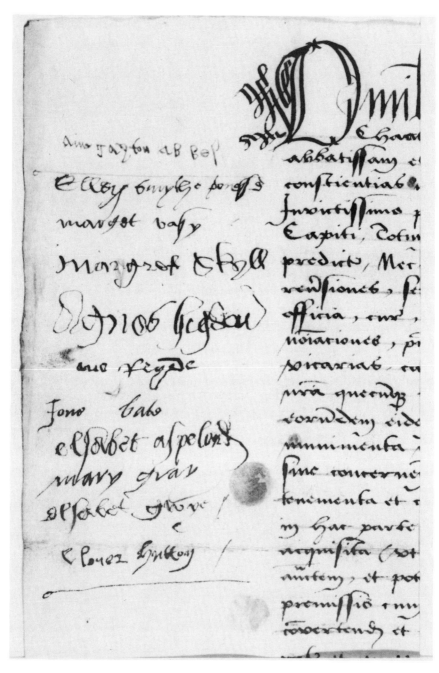

Figure 7: The signatures of the abbess, prioress and nuns of Chatteris abbey in the margin of the surrender of the abbey, 3 September 1538 (PRO E 322/53)

recorded. In a few cases, it is possible to trace individual nuns over time. For example, Margaret Hotot (Houtoft), Agnes Richard, Margaret Poleyn and Agnes de Offton were four of the 15 nuns of Chatteris in 1347, when Matilda Bernard was elected abbess, although Agnes de Offton did not attend the election through ill-health.[1] The record of the clerical poll-tax of 1379 shows that all four women were still at the abbey 32 years later and that Margaret Hotot had become abbess.[2] Agnes Ashfield, one of the other nuns at the time of the 1379 poll-tax, was abbess by the early fifteenth century: the latest source for her as abbess is dated 20 July 1437 by which time she must have been very elderly.[3] Another long-lived nun was Elizabeth Asplond for whom two pieces of evidence exist: she was a nun when Anne Basset was elected abbess in 1488 and also at the surrender of the abbey in 1538.[4]

The longevity of Elizabeth Asplond is interesting because of the light it casts on the literacy of the nuns. She, together with all her fellow nuns, signed the margin of the surrender of the abbey in 1538 (see figure 7). Her signature is large and uneven but, given her age and that all the nuns were able to sign, the style of her signature is more probably the product of an elderly woman struggling with poor eye-sight than that of a woman who could barely write. The same may be true of the wobbly signature of Agnes Higdon, although there is no evidence for her age. The italic hands of Mary Gray and Joan Bate suggest that they were the most recently educated members of the convent.

During a visitation in 1440, the sacrist of St Michael's priory in Stamford stated that the prioress had seven or eight boys and girls under the age of 12 boarding with her and being taught by her.[5] There is no evidence to show whether the nuns of Chatteris taught children. Indeed there is little evidence relating to the level of education attained by the nuns themselves. The literacy of the nuns in Latin may be implied by the Latin visitation injunctions issued to the abbess in 1347.[6] Bishops Fleming and Gray of Lincoln also issued injunctions to nunneries in their diocese in Latin in the early fifteenth century. In contrast, the injunctions of Gray's successor, Alnwick, were in Latin for

---

[1] Cambridge UL, EDR G/1/1 de Lisle register, fo. 51r.
[2] Palmer 'The Clerical Poll Tax of 1379 in Cambridgeshire', pp. 121–2.
[3] No. 276.
[4] Cambridge UL, EDR G/1/6 Alcock register, p. 148; PRO E 322/53.
[5] *Visitations of Religious Houses* ed. Thompson, iii, p. 349.
[6] Cambridge UL, EDR G/1/1 de Lisle register, fo. 47v.

monasteries and in English for nunneries which may have been a response to falling standards of Latin literacy in late medieval nunneries.[1]

There is scant evidence of a library at Chatteris abbey. The inventory produced at the dissolution of the abbey refers only to 'seytes in the quere wyth certen old bookes' which were presumably liturgical books.[2] However the cartulary contains a short paraphrase of a passage from St Augustine's *Enarratio in Psalmum XCI* and a stanza from an English translation of 'The Mirror of Simple Souls', a French, mystical tract by Margaret Porete (nos. 206–7). These entries in the cartulary suggest that the abbey may have had copies of these works in its library, though it is possible that they belonged to chaplains of the abbey.

Whilst there is little to suggest that Chatteris was a significant centre of learning, it is possible that an Anglo-Norman life of St Etheldreda, written in verse, was produced at Chatteris by a nun called Mary.[3] The author of 'La Vie Seinte Audrée' gives her name at the end of her work,

> Ici escris mon nom Marie
> Pur ce ke sois remembree.[4]

Although there is no proof that the author was a religious, M. D. Legge argues that she probably was a nun. If so, she may have come from Chatteris since the nunnery's patron was the bishop of Ely and his church was founded by St Etheldreda.[5] Moreover 'La Vie Seinte Audrée', which is a reworking of sections of the Latin *Liber Eliensis*, includes a reference to Chatteris which is absent from the Latin source,[6]

> En cest mareis est Rameseie
> Et l'abbeie de Thorneie,
> Plusurs autres ke jeo ne puis
> Nomer, si cume escrit le truis.
> Chateriz est en ydle de Ely,
> Ceste matere lais issi.[7]

---

1 *Visitations of Religious Houses* ed. Thompson, i–iii.
2 PRO E 117/11/13, fo. 4r: see appendix 2.
3 Ö. Södergård ed. *La Vie Seinte Audrée, Poème Anglo-Normand du XIIIe Siècle* (Uppsala, 1955).
4 Ibid. p. 181, ll. 4619–20.
5 M. D. Legge *Anglo-Norman Literature and its Background* (Oxford, 1963) p. 264.
6 J. Wogan-Browne '"Clerc u Lai, Muïne u Dame": Women and Anglo-Norman Hagiography in the Twelfth and Thirteenth Centuries' in *Women and Literature in Britain, 1150–1500* ed. C. M. Meale (Cambridge, 1993) p. 82, n. 35.
7 Södergård ed. *La Vie Seinte Audrée*, p. 64, ll. 313–18.

Legge shows that the life must have been written after 1189 because it includes a miracle which took place in the time of bishop Geoffrey Ridel who died in that year. According to Legge, the life probably dates from the first half of the thirteenth century and may possibly have been the work of Mary de Sancto Claro who was abbess in the middle of the century.[1] Only two other hagiographies written by women survive from twelfth or thirteenth-century England. The authors of these Anglo-Norman lives were both nuns at Barking abbey (Essex) and both lived in the late twelfth century. One wrote a life of Edward the Confessor anonymously and the other, Clemence, wrote a life of St Catherine. Although the life of St Etheldreda may have been produced by a nun at Chatteris, there is nothing else to indicate that the abbey sustained the same level of learning as the much larger and more aristocratic abbey at Barking.[2]

The list of all the nuns (appendix 1) reveals family links between some of them. The sisters Margaret and Rose de Columbers were nuns of Chatteris at the same time and it is probable that other nuns who shared the same surname were also related, such as Juliana, Margaret and Rose Hotot and Agnes and Isabel Norton. However, evidence from the diocese of Norwich suggests that kinship ties were not very influential in the choice of a nunnery: of the 22 identifiable nuns from the diocese who had relatives who were also nuns, only seven entered the same house as their relatives.[3]

Nuns' names provide interesting evidence about the geographical origins of the abbey's population. It is not surprising, given the local origins and relatively moderate means of most of the abbey's benefactors, that many of the women who entered the convent seem to have been local too. The toponyms of several abbesses – Emma de Somersham, Agnes de Ely, Amicia de Cambridge, Agnes de Burwell and Margery Ramsey – suggest Cambridgeshire and Huntingdonshire origins, whilst abbesses Alice de Shropham and Mary de Shouldham seem to have come from Norfolk. Apart from the first abbess, Ælfwen, who was the daughter of the thegn Æthelstan Mannessune, none of the known abbesses had noble, still less royal, connections. In contrast, other much richer Anglo-Saxon foundations for women sometimes had royal abbesses. For example, Mary of Blois, daughter of king Stephen, was abbess of Romsey in the mid-twelfth century; Mary, the half-sister of Henry II, was abbess of Shaftesbury in the late

---

[1] Legge *Anglo-Norman Literature*, p. 264.
[2] Wogan-Browne 'Women and Anglo-Norman Hagiography', pp. 61, 67 and 75, n. 2.
[3] Oliva *Convent and Community*, p. 61.

twelfth and early thirteenth centuries; and Maud, sister of Henry III, was elected abbess of Barking in 1247.[1]

The names of Chatteris nuns are recorded in significant numbers only from the fourteenth century onwards. Many of these nuns, like the abbesses, had surnames which suggest that, at least in the later Middle Ages, the abbey's recruits were predominantly local women. Agnes Caldecote, Katherine de Cambridge, Elizabeth Chesterton, Margaret de Conington, Margaret Fordham, Lucy Over and Agatha de Shepreth and the prioress, Joan de Drayton, all seem to have come from Cambridgeshire. Almost all the nuns with toponyms, who were not from Cambridgeshire, were from Huntingdonshire, Norfolk or Suffolk. Other nuns, such as Mabel de Bancis and Etheldreda de Sancto Georgio, were connected to prominent local families. Elizabeth Asplond, a nun in 1538, was presumably a relation of John Aspelond, who appears as a creditor of the abbess in 1538 and a tenant in Chatteris in 1539, and Joan Bate, another nun in 1538, was probably related to John Bate who was an executor of the will of William Bray, late vicar of Chatteris, in 1490.[2] The evidence from Chatteris is consistent with that from the 11 nunneries in the diocese of Norwich. Marilyn Oliva found that the majority of nuns in that diocese had entered the house which lay nearest to their previous home, showing that geographical proximity could have a considerable influence on the selection of a nunnery by recruits.[3]

The cartulary provides evidence of the family connections of some nuns in copies of gifts made by benefactors to the abbey on the entry of a female relative into the nunnery. Tecla Peregrinus became a nun when her father, Henry, gave a tenement, probably in Chatteris, to the abbey; Robert de Insula gave two fisheries in Upwell and Outwell (Cambs. and Norf.) to the nunnery on the entry of Alice daughter of Richard Moler, his kinswoman; Alan son of Robert de Shepreth gave property in Shepreth, Foxton and Cambridge with his daughter Agatha; Richard de Columbers, father of Margaret and Rose, granted to the abbey a weight of cheese annually at Dunstable (Beds.), following the reception of his daughters as nuns; and Hugh de Cranwell gave a rent of 10s. in

1 D. Knowles, C. N. L. Brooke and V. C. M. London eds *The Heads of Religious Houses England and Wales 940–1216* (Cambridge, 1972) p. 219; *CPR 1232–47*, p. 506.
2 PRO E 117/11/13, fo. 8v; PRO SC 6/HenVIII/267, rot. 5; Cambridge UL, EDR G/1/6 Alcock register, p. 56.
3 M. Oliva 'Counting Nuns: a Prosopography of Late Medieval English Nuns in the Diocese of Norwich' *Medieval Prosopography* xvi, no. 1 (1995) pp. 49–51.

Lincoln to the abbey on condition that his daughter, Adelicia, a Chatteris nun, should have the rent for her life.[1]

Whilst relatives sometimes made a gift to the abbey to accompany the reception of a woman by the nunnery, relatives may also have derived some benefit from their links with a nun, particularly if she became abbess. Several members of the de Bancis family appear in the cartulary, most notably Mabel and Thomas. Thomas gave land in Foxton to the abbey and he granted the homage and service of three people for a light and a chaplain to celebrate the mass of St Mary.[2] Mabel, when abbess, was responsible for two leases of property in Foxton to Thomas.[3] It is impossible to show that any abbess of Chatteris actively favoured her own family in the management of the abbey's lands, but it is plausible that an abbess would have acted in the interests of her family.

It is not clear whether the payment of dowry-grants was always required on the reception of women by the nunnery, but entry may have been restricted to women whose families could afford to make a contribution towards the revenues of the house. This would have excluded the lower ranks of society but it did not mean that relatively small nunneries such as Chatteris were the preserve of the élite. Whilst wealthy nunneries such as Barking (Essex) did attract women from the nobility and upper gentry, most of Chatteris abbey's recruits probably came from the ranks of the lesser, local landowners, as was the case at the Benedictine priory of Marrick (Yorks. N.).[4] Noreen Vickers, who studied the social origins of the members of all 24 nunneries in Yorkshire, also concluded that their entrants did not come from poor or from very wealthy backgrounds but from local gentry families.[5] Similar findings emerged in a study of White Ladies priory, Worcester.[6] However, Marilyn Oliva's prosopography of late medieval nuns in the diocese of Norwich emphasizes the diversity in their social status. Oliva found that Bruisyard abbey (Suff.) was distinctive because it attracted far more upper gentry nuns than any other convent, despite being one of the poorer nunneries in the diocese. In contrast,

---

[1] Nos. 26, 87, 152, 170, 227.

[2] Nos. 125, 115.

[3] Nos. 132, 139.

[4] Oliva *Convent and Community*, pp. 54–5; J. H. Tillotson *Marrick Priory: a Nunnery in Late Medieval Yorkshire* (Borthwick Paper no. 75; York, 1989) pp. 6–7.

[5] N. Vickers 'The Social Class of Yorkshire Medieval Nuns' *Yorkshire Archaeological Journal* lxvii (1995) pp. 127–32.

[6] M. Goodrich 'The White Ladies of Worcester: their Place in Contemporary Medieval Life' *Transactions of the Worcestershire Archaeological Society* 3rd ser. xiv (1994) pp. 134–5.

the other nunneries in Norfolk and Suffolk housed a few upper gentry nuns but the vast majority of their entrants were women from local, lower gentry families.[1] Oliva has shown that, in keeping with the general social profile of nuns, the overwhelming majority of identifiable abbesses, prioresses and obedientiaries also came from the middling rather than the upper levels of society in the diocese of Norwich.[2]

No obedientary rolls survive from Chatteris, but evidence from nunneries in the diocese of Norwich suggests that even the smaller houses had well-developed administrative structures. These structures were based on the division of financial responsibilities between office-holders who were assigned their own sources of income.[3] Apart from the abbess and prioress, the only other offices at Chatteris for which direct evidence exists are those of the sacrist and cellarer. Amicia de Cambridge was described as the sacrist of the abbey in the last quarter of the thirteenth century when Ralph son of Katherine Coveney released her from ½d. of annual rent which she owed to him for one rood of arable land (no. 47). Evidence for the office of cellarer comes from the inventory produced when the abbey was dissolved. The inventory notes the cellarer's chamber and its contents, but no names of cellarers are known.[4] The cartulary contains no explicit references to an infirmarian or an almoner, but these offices seem to have existed since the cartulary records three donations in favour of the infirmary and seven in favour of the almonry or its activities.[5] The abbey would also have had a precentor, in charge of the choir. It may have had a treasuress and a chambress as well, though other office-holders may have been responsible for their functions since Chatteris was not a large house.

Each nun who was still living at Chatteris abbey when it was suppressed received a payment followed by an annual pension. The abbess, Anne Gayton, was paid £3 6s. 8d. in 1538 whilst the prioress and all the other nuns were paid £2. The abbess received a pension of £15 and both the prioress, Ellen Smyth, and Elizabeth Asplond, who had been a nun for at least 50 years, received £4. Six nuns received pensions of four marks each and two, Elizabeth Gye and Joan Bate, were given 40s.[6] Most of the Chatteris nuns received more than the sum

---

[1] Oliva *Convent and Community*, pp. 52–60.
[2] Ibid. pp. 105–7.
[3] Ibid. pp. 83–90.
[4] PRO E 117/11/13, fo. 2v.
[5] Donations to the infirmary, nos. 72, 91/223 and 92; donations to the almonry or its activities, nos. 21/70, 33, 49, 53, 58, 62 and 67.
[6] PRO E 117/11/13, fos. 5v, 8r; PRO E 315/233.

of 47s. which Marilyn Oliva calculated to be the average pension received by nuns, excluding heads of houses, in the diocese of Norwich. In the same diocese, the pensions received by heads of houses ranged from £23 6s. 8d. paid to the prioress of Campsey Ash, whose house was worth £182 in 1535, to £4 paid to the prioress of Crabhouse, whose house was worth only £24.[1] Whereas many former monks were able to move on to other positions within the church, this option was not open to former nuns. Some women may have returned to their families, whilst others may have sought employment, perhaps in towns. It is not clear what happened to the nuns of Chatteris after the dissolution of their abbey, but the abbess, the prioress and four nuns – Mary Gray, Elizabeth Gye, Elinor Hutton and Anne Rede – were still receiving their pensions in 1556 when cardinal Pole's certificate of pensions payable to the former religious was compiled.[2]

CHAPLAINS, SERVANTS AND LAY-SISTERS

Unlike monks, nuns could not be ordained. Nuns therefore relied on men to celebrate mass for them and to hear their confessions. Sally Thompson and Sharon Elkins have explored in detail the relationship between nunneries and the men upon whom they depended for priestly help. Both Thompson and Elkins concluded that the inherent dependence of nuns on men was problematic, but that nuns adapted to a variety of arrangements to secure the priestly support they required.[3] During the twelfth century some Benedictine and Augustinian nunneries seem to have had links with independent foundations for men whose monks and canons provided the nuns with sacramental services. Although these partnerships between male and female religious houses seem to have been quite common, growing unease about them in the later twelfth century made them less acceptable.[4] Around this time, the emergence of double houses of the new orders meant that religious women in such communities had canons on hand to say mass for them. However, Chatteris abbey, like the majority of independent houses for women depended on outside chaplains.

Nothing is known about most of the chaplains who must have served Chatteris abbey over the centuries. In the mid-thirteenth century, Thomas de Bancis made a grant to the abbey for a light at the mass of St Mary and for the

---

1 Oliva *Convent and Community*, pp. 195–201.
2 PRO E 164/31, fo. 12v.
3 Thompson *Women Religious*, pp. 211–16; Elkins *Holy Women*, pp. 161–4.
4 Thompson *Women Religious*, pp. 54–73.

payment of a chaplain to celebrate the mass of St Mary there perpetually (no. 115). Several named chaplains occur in the cartulary but it is not clear how many of these were the abbey's chaplains. The cartulary contains two sales by Aubrey son of Eustace de Madingley to the abbey of land in Madingley: in no. 110 the witnesses include the chaplains Ebrard, Alan and Roger whilst in no. 238 they include Ebrard, Roger and Ralph who are described as chaplains of Chatteris. Ebrard, chaplain of Chatteris, occurs again in no. 88, in which he granted four fisheries in Chatteris to the abbey. Thomas, another chaplain of Chatteris, occurs in the cartulary in a charter in which he gave one rood of land to his niece, Alice, whilst Alexander de Childerley, chaplain, represented the abbess in a final concord in 1268 (nos. 50 and 178). Although these chaplains may have been attached to the parish church rather than to the abbey, it seems likely that some at least may have been chaplains at the abbey. The vicars of Chatteris, who were all presented by the abbess and convent, may also have acted as chaplains to the nuns. In 1406, the bishop of Ely's official was commissioned to ascertain the names of all the chaplains and chantry priests in the city of Ely and the deaneries of Ely and Wisbech. The priests listed for Chatteris were the vicar, Warin West, and also Richard Hoor, John Taillour and Henry Neve, one or more of whom may have been a chaplain at the abbey.[1]

The cartulary contains a single reference to a female servant at the abbey. In the thirteenth century the abbey leased to Matilda de Elsworth, who was a maid of the abbess, a messuage with a yard and croft in Chatteris, for her life. Elsworth paid 20s. in advance and 2s. annually for the lease (no. 60). Despite this lone reference to a servant in the cartulary, the abbey would clearly have needed a significant number of people to maintain it and to supply it with goods and services. The inventory compiled after the dissolution of the abbey in 1538 lists 16 male and eight female servants of the abbey together with an unnamed cooper and 10 harvest labourers. The 'servants' ranged from Sir Barnard Hartely, who was paid 16s. 4d. for a quarter of a year, to Thomas Skoyte who received 3s. 4d. for half a year.[2] The existence of 25 servants in 1538 – when there were only 11 nuns at Chatteris – underlines the importance of the abbey to the local economy as a source of employment.

The only known lay-sister from Chatteris abbey is Idonea de Chilham, who was a nominee of the archbishop of Canterbury.[3] Whereas the majority of known nuns at Chatteris came from local families, Idonea seems to have come

---

[1] Cambridge UL, EDR G/1/3 Fordham register, fo. 160r.

[2] PRO E 117/11/13, fos. 6r–7r.

[3] For details of her nomination, see p. 21.

from Kent: Chilham lies six miles south-west of Canterbury, but it was not an archbishop's manor. The bishop of Ely was entitled, as patron of Chatteris abbey, to nominate a new nun when he confirmed the election of an abbess. During a vacancy in the see of Ely, archbishop Winchelsey nominated Idonea for admission to the convent between July 1298 and March 1299, following his confirmation of an election at the nunnery. Because she was illiterate Idonea was admitted as a lay-sister, rather than a nun, but it seems that she protested to the archbishop. On 16 June 1300, Winchelsey issued a mandate to the bishop of Ely requiring him to ensure that the abbess fed and clothed Idonea as though she were a professed nun. However, Winchelsey had already notified the abbey in March 1299 that his nomination of an illiterate did not set a precedent for future bishops of Ely to nominate lay-sisters rather than choir nuns on the confirmation of subsequent elections.[1]

[1] *Registrum Roberti Winchelsey Cantuariensis Archiepiscopi 1294–1313* ed. R. Graham, 2 vols (Canterbury and York Society li, 1952; lii, 1956) i, pp. 324–5; ii, pp. 711–12.

VI

The Production and Arrangement of the Cartulary

The cartulary of Chatteris abbey is now bound as fos. 72–188 of BL Cotton Julius A. i, fo. 188 being the last in the volume. The heading *Registrum Monasterii de Chateris* has been added in a seventeenth-century hand at the top of fo. 71r above a genealogical tree showing the descent of Henry II and his issue from Charlemagne, Rollo first duke of Normandy and king Alfred. However this folio has been wrongly bound: the genealogical tree is in the same hand as the Bury chronicle which begins on fo. 3 and should precede it.[1] The former owners of the cartulary and the exact date of its acquisition by Sir Robert Cotton are unknown, but it appears in the 1621 catalogue of Cotton's manuscript books, where it is listed together with the other manuscripts with which it is still bound, but without the press-mark Julius A. i.[2] There is no reason to suppose that the Chatteris cartulary had any connection with the other items in the volume before it was acquired by Cotton.

The other items in the volume are: a drawing – representing the origin of the Stywarde family arms – of an armed knight, standing on a broken sword, about to strike a lion rampant with a ragged staff, whilst a shield showing the knight's arms is held by a hand descending from the top left corner (fo. 2v);[3] the chronicle of Bury St Edmunds from the Creation to 1265,[4] written by John de Taxster who had become a monk of Bury in 1244[5] (fos. 3r–43v); a short chronicle from the Creation to 1317 (fos. 44r–50v); a fourteenth-century chronicle in Anglo-Norman French of the reign of Edward II and the beginning

---

[1] *The Chronicle of Bury St Edmunds 1212–1301* ed. A. Gransden (London, 1964) p. xxxvi.

[2] BL Harl. MS 6018.

[3] F. Martin 'Origin of the Tressure of Scotland' *Archaeologia* xxiii (1831) pp. 387–92; J. H. Round *Studies in Peerage and Family History* (Westminster, 1901) pp. 133–44; *British Heraldry, from its Origins to c. 1800* comp. and ed. R. Marks and A. Payne (London, 1978) p. 91, no. 143. I am grateful to Dr Nigel Ramsay for pointing out his identification of this drawing to me.

[4] *Chronicle of Bury St Edmunds 1212–1301* ed. Gransden, pp. xxxv–xxxvii, 1–33.

[5] Ibid. p. 13n; Taxster mentions this on fo. 38v of the manuscript.

of the reign of Edward III (fos. 51r–63v); and a register of charters and memoranda from Pipewell abbey in Northamptonshire, written in fourteenth- and
fifteenth-century hands (fos. 65r–70v).[1] The manuscripts included in the
volume are listed in a seventeenth-century hand on fo. 1r. This is not, though,
the hand of Richard James, Cotton's librarian from 1624, who compiled many
of the lists of contents found in the Cotton manuscripts.[2]

The binding of Julius A. i did not survive the fire which broke out in the
Cotton library in 1731. When the volume was repaired in March 1847, each
folio was inlaid into a paper frame and the frames rebound.[3]

The cartulary is the work of one principal scribe (see figure 8), to whose
manuscript other scribes subsequently added 21 more entries. The latest dated
document in the hand of the main scribe (no. 203) was issued 1428, whilst the
opening inscription, which is in another hand, provides a *terminus post quem
non* for the production of the greater part of the manuscript:

> Orate pro animabus venerabilis domine domine Agnetis Aschefeld quondam
> abbatisse monasterii de Chatriz et Henrici Bukworth decretorum bacularii,
> quorum sumptibus et industria est liber pre manibus in hanc formam redactus.

Henry Buckworth, who had become vicar of Chatteris in 1429, died in 1456.[4]
The main scribe must, therefore, have produced his part of the cartulary between 1428 and 1456. Agnes Ashfield first occurs, as a nun of Chatteris, in the
records of the clerical poll-tax of 1379.[5] In the cartulary, the latest document in
the main hand which refers to her as abbess dates from 1428 (no. 203), but a
document added afterwards by another scribe shows that she was still abbess in
1437 (no. 276). Although the date of her death is not known, she may not have
lived long after 1437, given that she had been a nun at least since 1379. Therefore it seems likely that the main part of the cartulary was copied between 1428
and the 1440s. The 21 documents added to the cartulary by later scribes were
copied throughout the later fifteenth century and into the early sixteenth
century. The latest datable document is no. 277, a grant made between 1506 and
1515.

1 *A Catalogue of the Manuscripts in the Cottonian Library Deposited in the British Museum*
   (London, 1802) p. 1.
2 I am grateful to Dr Nigel Ramsay for this information.
3 BL Add. MS 62577 (Cottonian MSS Repairing and Binding Account, from 1839) fos. 3v–4r.
4 A. B. Emden *A Biographical Register of the University of Cambridge to 1500* (Cambridge, 1963)
   p. 104.
5 Palmer 'The Clerical Poll Tax of 1379 in Cambridgeshire', p. 122.

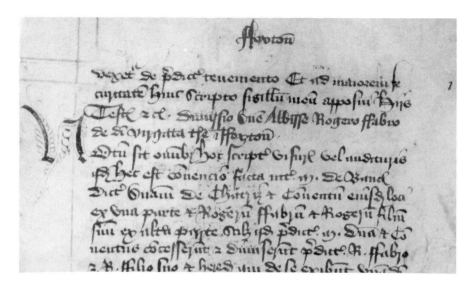

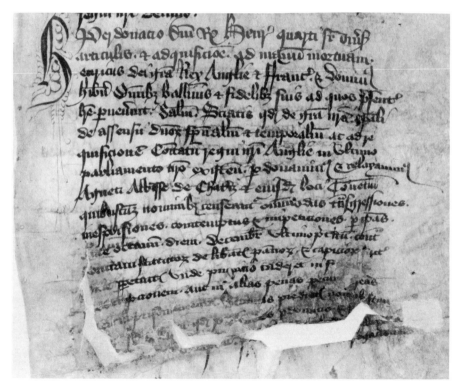

Figure 8: Examples of the main hand of the cartulary (details of fos. 126r and 175r)

The style of the hand which wrote most of the text changes gradually through the manuscript. At the beginning of the cartulary, 'a' and 'g' are double compartment letters and 'r' is short; in the central part of manuscript, 'a' takes both single and double compartment forms and long 'r' is introduced; towards the end of the cartulary, 'a' is more commonly in the single compartment form, 'r' can be short or long and secretary 'g' is used. In the first part of the manuscript the hand is quite upright, but towards the end the ascenders and descenders slant much more to the right. These changes are so gradual that the main hand shifts seamlessly between different styles of writing: there is no detectable break indicating a change of scribe. Nos. 2–204 and nos. 213–68 are all in the main hand, as are the majority of the rubricated headings, although these headings are in the form of the main hand which is found in the latter part of the manuscript.

The main scribe and rubricator does not identify himself explicitly but there are two clues in the manuscript which suggest that he could have been Henry Buckworth, vicar of Chatteris from 1429 to 1456. The rubricated heading for no. 200 reads, *Supplicatio domine abbatisse per Henricum Bucworth domino Johanni Holond comiti Huntidonie*. Although Buckworth's name occurs in this rubric, the petition itself, which is dated 1429 × 1447, does not mention him. It seems likely, therefore, that Buckworth was the scribe and that he included a reference to his own role in the matter when he added the rubric. It is possible, though, that the scribe and rubricator was someone else entirely who merely happened to know that Buckworth had been involved and so included him in the rubric, or else that an endorsement on the original charter noted that Buckworth had been the abbess's proctor.

However, the wording of the cartulary's opening inscription seems to reinforce the theory that Buckworth was the main scribe and rubricator. The request for prayers for the souls of Agnes Ashfield, formerly abbess of Chatteris, and Henry Buckworth, *quorum sumptibus et industria est liber pre manibus in hanc formam redactus*, probably means that Agnes Ashfield provided the money to cover the expenses of producing the cartulary, whilst the vicar, Henry Buckworth, undertook the work of copying the abbey's muniments himself. The considerable variation in the hand of the main scribe would be plausible if Buckworth were the main scribe since he was a secular clerk who would not have been working under supervision. Moreover, he must have been familiar with a wide variety of university hands since the inscription at the beginning of the cartulary states that he was a bachelor of canon law.

The other hands in the manuscript are found in marginal notes, in the opening request for prayers (no. 1), in the latter part of the gathering which seems to have ended at fo. 154 (nos. 205–12) and in the documents transcribed at the end of the cartulary on fos. 180r–188r (nos. 269–80). That is, they occur in those parts of the manuscript which were written some time after the main body of the text. Therefore these late medieval hands must date from the mid-fifteenth and early sixteenth centuries. The only exception is the seventeenth-century hand of the index on fo. 186r (no. 278). Most scribes who made additions to the cartulary seem to have copied only one document each, although one scribe copied nos. 206–10 and another copied nos. 269–71 and 274. It is tempting to think that a few of the documents at the end of the cartulary may have been added by nuns. The unpolished hand and examples of unconventional spelling in no. 277 on fo. 185v, which dates from 1506 × 1515, certainly suggest that this scribe was much less accomplished than the one who copied the main part of the cartulary.

The cartulary has a running heading in red ink at the top of each page throughout the part of the manuscript written in the main hand. Some of the headings, such as *Bulla papalis*, *Carta regis*, *Placita in scaccario* and *Presentatio*, describe the type of document copied below, but by far the majority of the headings are topographical, stating the parish to which the charters on that page relate. Two topographical headings may be given on a page where one charter relates to two places, for example fo. 102v. Also, where a charter beginning in the middle of a page concerns a different parish from the one preceding it, the heading at the top of the page generally gives the name of the parish in the new charter, but if a page has two charters beginning on it which relate to different parishes the heading may give both, as for example on fos. 99v, 106r, 161r and 164v. However, one of the headings on fo. 164v has been added after the other. The first charter beginning on the page relates to Elm and this heading is given at the top of the page. The second charter, beginning near the foot of the page and concerning the parish of Burwell, does not have a rubricated heading immediately above it. Instead, 'Burewelle' has been written in red in the margin and at the top of the page but apparently at a later date: the red ink is a different shade from that used elsewhere and the hand is different from that of the other rubrics. This different ink and hand also appear in other rubrics. They are used for quite a number of the headings at the top of pages, on fos. 73r–80v, fo. 95r, fo. 104r, fo. 105v, fo. 109r, fo. 111v, fo. 115v, fo. 116v, fos. 117v–118r, fo. 120r, fos. 128v–129r, fo. 132r, fo. 133v, fo. 135r, fo. 137v, fo. 139r, fo. 140v, fos. 142v–143r, fo. 144r, fo. 145r, fo. 146v, fo. 162v, fo. 164r–v, fo. 168r, fo. 172r, fo.

173r–178v, fo. 180r and perhaps fo. 184r. A few of the rubricated headings before charters also appear to have been added afterwards, including those for nos. 61, 123-5, 129, 137 and 261-3. In the case of fos. 117v–118r, which contain nos. 123-4 and the heading for no. 125, it seems likely that the scribe accidentally turned over two pages at once when he was adding the rubrics. Many of the folios not written in the main hand of the manuscript do not have a running heading, but there are headings in black ink on fos. 151v–153r and fos. 187v–188r, as well as one in red on fo. 184r.

Some of the headings have been corrected. On fo. 105v, 'Chatriz' was written first, but it was expunged in red and 'Ely' added after it. This correction is in the hand and ink of the second rubricator, but not all errors in rubrics are corrected in red: on fo. 106v the incorrect heading *Terre Chatriz et tenementa* has been expunged later in black. Proof that the headings were added after the text had been copied is provided by the correction to the heading on fo. 126v. The incorrect heading 'Sepereye' has been expunged in black, as has 'Scheperede' in the rubric above the copy of the charter. The field names show that the charter is in fact an exchange of lands in Foxton which was made between the abbess and convent of Chatteris and Reginald Bynel of Shepreth (no. 145). It seems that the scribe picked out the name Shepreth from the document when he came to add the rubric and wrongly assumed that the lands concerned lay in this parish. The headings have been included in the footnotes to the transcription but they are also listed below:

fo. 73r	Chateriz
fo. 73v	Bulla
fo. 74r	Papalis
fo. 74v	Bulla
fo. 75r	Papalis
fo. 75v	Cronica de Herveo episcopo
fo. 76r–v	Carta regis
fo. 77r	Carta regis ad manum mortuam
fos. 77v–80v	Chateriz
fos. 81r–91v	Chatriz
fo. 92r	Terre Chatriz et tenementa
fos. 92v–94v	Chatriz
fo. 95r	Chateriz
fo. 95v	Terre Chatriz et tenementa
fos. 96r–98v	Chatriz
fo. 99r	Terre Chatriz et tenementa

fo. 99v	Chatriz Bylneye
fos. 100r–101r	Chatriz piscarie
fo. 101v	iij denarii in Heverhille
fo. 102r	Thetforth' Parva infra Insulam
fo. 102v	Briccham Stunteneye
fo. 103r	Ely
fos. 103v–104r	Ditton'
fo. 104v	Chatriz Ditton'
fo. 105r	Elm
fo. 105v	Ely[1]
fo. 106r	Barenton'[2] Over'
fo. 106v	Terre Chatriz et tenementa[3]
fo. 107r	Over'
fos. 107v–108v	Cantabrig'
fo. 109r	Cantabr'
fo. 109v	Cantabrig'
fo. 110r	Maddynglee
fo. 110v	Kyngston'
fo. 111r	Barenton'
fo. 111v	Barengton'
fos. 112r–115r	Barenton'
fo. 115v	Baryngton'
fo. 116r	Barenton'
fo. 116v	Baryngton'
fo. 117r	Barenton'
fo. 117v	Baryngton'
fo. 118r	Barynton'
fos. 118v–126r	Foxton'
fo. 126v	Sepereye[4]
fos. 127r–128r	Foxton'
fos. 128v–129r	Scheperey
fos. 129v–130v	Sepereye
fo. 131r	Scheper'
fo. 131v	Sepereye

[1] Preceded by *Chatriz*, expunged.

[2] Preceded by *O*, expunged in black.

[3] *Terre ... tenementa*, expunged in black.

[4] Expunged in black, as is *Scheperede* in the rubric above the charter beginning on this folio.

fo. 132r	Scheperey
fos. 132v–133r	Sepereye
fo. 133v	Scheperede
fo. 134r–v	Sepereye
fo. 135r	Scheperey
fo. 135v	Pro capella de Honneye
fo. 136r–v	Trippelowe
fo. 137r	Dodyngton'
fo. 137v	Dunstapyl
fo. 138r	Berle
fos. 138v–143v	Berlee
fo. 144r	Keresey
fo. 144v	Kerseye
fo. 145r	Keresey
fo. 145v	Kerseye
fo. 146r	Kereseye
fo. 146v	Kerisey
fo. 147r	Kerseye
fos. 147v–151r	Kereseye
fos. 151v–153r	Kersey[5]
fo. 155r[6]	Leen
fos. 155v–157r	Lenna
fo. 157v	Leen
fos. 158r–159v	Brecham
fo. 160r	Pynchebec
fo. 160v	Lincolnie
fo. 161r	Lincoln' Huntyngdon'
fo. 161v	Huntyndon'
fo. 162r–v	Hemyngford'
fo. 163r–v	Chatriz
fo. 164r	Chateriz
fo. 164v	Elm Burewelle
fo. 165r	Barenton'
fo. 165v	Maddynglee
fo. 166r	Kyngeston
fo. 166v	Foxton'

5 In black.
6 Fos. 153v–154v have no headings.

fo. 167r	Berlee
fo. 167v	Dodyngton'
fo. 168r	Wymlygton'
fo. 168v	Dodynton'
fo. 169r	Dudyngton
fos. 169v–171r	Dodyngton'
fo. 171v	Chatriz Dodyngton'
fo. 172r	Carte Edwardi et Ricardi regum
fo. 173r[7]	Certificatio inquisitionis[8]
fo. 173v	Certificatio
fo. 174r–v	Carta confirmationis
fos. 175r–176r	Perdonatio regis Henrici iiij[ti]
fos. 176v–177r	Placita in scaccario
fo. 177v	Placita
fo. 178r	In scaccario
fo. 178v	Placita in scaccario
fo. 179v[9]	Berle
fo. 180r	Presentatio
fo. 184r[10]	Hemyngford'
fo. 187v	Chateriz[11]
fo. 188r	Chateriz[12]

The majority of the rubrics which appear before each charter are in the same hand as most of the running headings and most of the text. As with the running headings, they were added after the charters and other documents had been copied. There are many examples of the red ink overlapping the black. Moreover some rubrics are abbreviated by a phrase such as *ut infra in nigro* found on fo. 148v (no. 196) and many do not start at the left-hand margin but begin instead immediately after the last word of the previous charter, in the middle of the line. The scribe did not always leave enough space between charters so some rubrics run over into the right-hand margin. However, it appears that the scribe did deliberately leave some space for rubrics, rather than simply leaving a gap between charters into which rubrics were inserted. Where a charter finished

7 Fo. 172v has no heading.
8 MS *inquisionis*.
9 Fo. 179r has no heading.
10 Fos. 180v–183v and fos. 184v–188v have no headings.
11 In black.
12 In black.

near the foot of a page, the scribe left the last line or lines blank for the rubric and began the next charter on the second ruled line of the following page, as on fo. 88r–v; but where a charter finished on the very last line of a page, the scribe left the second ruled line the following page blank for the rubric, as on fos. 130v–131r.

There are often differences between the information in the rubrics and that in the charters which they precede. Some differences are minor scribal variations. Whereas the rubrics often use Arabic and Roman numerals in their descriptions of property, the charters use words rather than figures. Also, whereas both *Eliensis* and *Elyensis* occur in the text, the rubrics always have *Eliensis*. This suggests that the scribe copied the spelling from the originals in the text, but standardized the spelling when he added the rubrics. There are rubrics, though, which are inaccurate. The inaccuracies are sometimes simple cases of omission. For example, the rubric for no. 55 is *Donatio Rogeri Gaugi de duobus mesuagiis,* but the text shows that Roger gave to the abbey two messuages of Stephen de Chettisham and one of William son of Agnes. Similarly, no. 140 has the rubric, *Carta Rogeri le Fraunceys de uno mesuagio et 5 rodis prati,* but the charter itself lists a messuage, 10 acres and five roods of meadow. However, some rubrics are very misleading. The rubric for no. 72 begins, *Concessio Ricardi de Ely...,* whilst in the text the grantor is called *Radulphus de Hely filius Willelmi de Ely*; the rubric for no. 73, which begins *Donatio Roberti de Cokefeld'...,* is followed by a text reading *Adam filius Roberti de Cokefeld'*; the rubric for no. 90 claims that what follows is *Quieta clamantia Alexandri episcopi Eliensis...,* but the address begins, *Alexander filius Ingelrammi sturesmanni episcopi Elyensis*; and the rubric for no. 259 reads *Perdonatio domini regis Henrici quarti...,* but the document must date from the reign of Henry V, when John, duke of Bedford, was keeper of England. In some cases, the errors made by the scribe when he came to add the rubrics mean that the rubrics do not make sense at all. The scribe extracted the wrong piece of information from the description of the property in no. 213 and wrote in the rubric, *Carta Willelmi cordewanerii Willelmo filio Wlurici versus cimiterium ecclesie Sancte Margarete in Lenna.*

Occasionally, though, the rubrics correct the text, both directly and indirectly. In no. 45 a red 'i' has been added in the text above the 'o' of *in campos* in the text. In contrast, the rubric for no. 235 makes an indirect correction. The rubric begins with the words *Carta Roberti de Rosebi,* correcting the text in which the donor's name was miscopied as Robert de Boseby. The confirmation of this gift (no. 98) by Robert's daughter, Agnes de Roseby, shows that Roseby is correct.

All the original documents reproduced in the Chatteris abbey cartulary seem to have been lost: despite extensive searches none has come to light.[1] However, in the case of cartularies with surviving originals, the rubrics can be compared with the endorsements on the originals. Such comparisons demonstrate that rubrics were sometimes copied directly from endorsements. For example, Alexander Rumble has shown that in the earliest section of the cartulary of Winchester cathedral priory, which was copied in the second quarter of the twelfth century, it is likely that most of the rubrics, which are in Old English, Latin and a combination of the two, were taken from endorsements. Rumble goes on to suggest that endorsements were the source of Old English rubrics in the fourteenth-century cartulary of Wilton abbey and the twelfth-century cartulary of Sherborne abbey, although the loss of the relevant originals prevents proof.[2] Since the purpose of endorsements is to make it easier to refer to a collection of charters, they need to be accurate. The very considerable inaccuracy in some of the rubrics in the Chatteris cartulary not only undermines their own usefulness as a reference device, but also suggests that they were not copied from endorsements. Occasionally, though, the heading above a charter is written in black and underlined in red, as in no. 26. It is possible that such a heading was taken from an endorsement and copied by the scribe before he copied the text of the charter. When he came to add his rubrics, the scribe then had only to underline in red the heading he had already provided when he copied the text.

There are three series of foliation, all of which use Arabic numerals. The most modern foliation is in pencil on the paper frames around the folios and, in the Chatteris cartulary section of the volume, it runs from 72–188. There is an earlier foliation in ink on the top right hand corner of the parchment folios which also post-dates the binding together of the manuscripts found in Julius A. i. In this series, the Chatteris cartulary folios are numbered 70–186. The earliest foliation, in ink, is not visible throughout the manuscript and many of

---

[1] Searches in the Bodleian Library, the British Library, the Public Record Office and in Cambridge – in the college archives, the County Record Office and the University Library – revealed no originals from the Chatteris abbey muniments. However, a single original charter issued by the abbess, but not copied into the cartulary, is preserved in the archives of St John's College Cambridge and transcribed here as no. 281 (Cambridge, St John's College Archives D 25. 22). In addition, an original of no. 6 survives in the archives of the dean and chapter of Ely (Cambridge UL, EDC 1/B/5).

[2] A. Rumble 'The Structure and Reliability of the Codex Wintoniensis (BM Add. MS 15350; the Cartulary of Winchester Cathedral Priory)', Ph.D. thesis, 2 vols (University of London, 1979) i, pp. 132, 215–22.

the numerals are very faint. The first numeral visible is 12 which appears on modern fo. 84. Therefore, 1 in this series would have appeared on modern fo. 73 which is the first page of full text and that on which the foundation chronicle begins; fo. 72 is blank on the recto and on the verso has only the request for prayers of intercession. After 12, the majority of the numerals are visible and 112 is the last which can still be seen. Originally, the series ran from 1–115, with 61 being used twice. This foliation, pre-dating the binding together of the Julius A. i manuscripts, probably dates from the seventeenth century since it is used in the index on fo. 186r which is written in a seventeenth-century hand.

All the folios have suffered at least some fire-damage to their margins, the effects generally being worse at the outer margins. Because some folios are badly distorted and many are irregularly shaped, it is not possible to give simple measurements for the size of the manuscript. In addition, the mounting of the folios into their paper frames means that many folios do not have identical measurements on the recto and verso. Therefore, the maximum height and width measurements are given below for the recto of the first folio, every tenth folio thereafter and the last folio.

fo. 72r	c. 199 × 133 mm
fo. 82r	c. 196 × 137 mm
fo. 92r	c. 207 × 139 mm
fo. 102r	c. 205 × 142 mm
fo. 112r	c. 203 × 140 mm
fo. 122r	c. 195 × 136 mm
fo. 132r	c. 197 × 136 mm
fo. 142r	c. 196 × 136 mm
fo. 152r	c. 208 × 137 mm
fo. 162r	c. 204 × 140 mm
fo. 172r	c. 197 × 132 mm
fo. 182r	c. 204 × 136 mm
fo. 188r	c. 204 × 129 mm

The ruling is in ink and on both sides of the folios but it is not clearly visible on every folio. The measurements of the ruled space are taken from fo. 100r because the ruling is relatively clear there and the folio is little damaged. There are vertical and horizontal double bounding-lines extending to the edges of the folio. These bounding lines are 5.5 mm apart on the left and 5 mm apart on the right, at the top and at the foot of the folio. The dimensions of the ruled space are *c.* 153–163 × 87.5–98 mm, with 31 horizontal lines which are 5–6 mm apart.

The text is written in a single column of, usually, 30 lines, although a few pages have 29 or 31 lines of text. They begin on the second ruled line, to the right of the second bounding line on the left, but there is no clear margin on the right-hand side where the text often crosses the first and second bounding lines. No pricking is visible but there are some small holes, not coinciding with the ruling, in the upper, lower and outer margins which may possibly be fixing points for a ruling device. Alternatively, these holes may have been made when the manuscript was repaired in the nineteenth century.

The sheets are arranged so that the flesh-side faces flesh and the hair-side faces hair. Despite the loss of the earlier binding, the presence of catchwords allows most of the manuscript to be collated. There are catchwords on folios 80v, 88v, 98v, 106v, 114v, 122v, 130v, 138v, 146v, 162v and 170v. Although there are no catchwords on fo. 154v, where they would have been expected, this folio seems likely to mark the end of a gathering: fos. 151v–154v are written in different hands from the main hand of the manuscript which resumes on fo. 155r. Presumably the last folios of this gathering had been left blank when the cartulary was compiled and other documents were copied on to them later. Therefore, the collation up to fo. 170 seems to be: $1-2^8$, 3^{10}, $4-12^8$. There may have been another gathering of eight or ten leaves which began with fo. 171, but there are no catchwords after those on fo. 170v and there is no change in the hand between fo. 178v and fo. 179r nor between fo. 180v and fo. 181r which might indicate the end of a gathering after eight or ten leaves. The structure of the very last part of the manuscript, up to fo. 188, is also obscure, but there is evidence that at least one folio has been lost. The grant by abbess Margaret Develyn to James Stanley, bishop of Ely, and Walter Berkoke of the tithe of the church of Barley (Herts.) and the next presentation to it begins on fo. 185v (no. 277). Since the text of this grant breaks off at the foot of the page, it seems very likely that one or more folios which no longer survive once lay between the extant fos. 185 and 186.

The manuscript is not highly decorated. Red ink is used to highlight upper and some lower case letters on fo. 72v and capital letters only on fos. 73r–76r. In addition, the initial letter of each document copied on fos. 72v–178r and on fo. 179v is enlarged, set into the left margin and decorated in black ink. Similar decoration in black ink is applied to a 'b' and an 'A' in the first line of the opening passage of the cartulary on fo. 72v. Guide-letters for the decorated initials are sometimes visible in the left margin: the initials were drawn on top of the guide-letters after the text had been copied. Document no. 15 begins with the word *Omnibus* but it has a decorated initial 'U', following the incorrect guide-letter provided by the scribe. The initials with significant decoration are found only in the part of the manuscript written in the main hand. Of the documents written in other hands, only nos. 270 and 277 have decorated initial letters and these are smaller and much less ornate than those earlier in the cartulary.

The manuscript contains many scribal corrections. Expunctions, insertions in the margin and interlineations occur frequently; there is some cancellation and *vacat* is used twice on fo. 79r. Often, scribal emendations seem to be simple corrections of misreadings of the original document but, in some cases, it appears that the errors resulted from the monotony of copying many similar documents whose formulae, though often standardized, were not always identical. For example, in no. 74 the scribe at first wrote, *Et ut hec mea concessio...*, but had to expunge *mea* and, in no. 233, in the sentence, *In cuius rei testimonium presens scriptum quiete clamationis sigilli mei munimine roboravi,* the scribe originally wrote the more commonly occurring *impressione* after *mei,* then expunged it and wrote *munimine*. Another problem for the scribe is indicated by occasional spaces in the text, as in no. 231 on fo. 162v where two spaces of 43 and 17 mm have been left. It may be that the original document he was copying was damaged here.

The arrangement of the documents in the cartulary is primarily topographical, with charters grouped by parish, but this scheme does not obtain throughout. The manuscript opens with the passage asking for prayers for the souls of Agnes Ashfield, abbess of Chatteris, and Henry Buckworth, vicar of Chatteris. After this comes a short narrative taken from the *Liber Eliensis* about Eadnoth, abbot of Ramsey.[1] It describes the discovery of the body of St Ivo at St Ives (Hunts.) and contains a reference to the foundation of Chatteris abbey. This narrative is followed by: a copy of a bull of Innocent IV; an account from the *Liber Eliensis* of how bishop Hervey secured the patronage of the abbey for the bishops of Ely;[2] a group of royal charters (nos. 5–9) and a group of episcopal charters (nos. 10–16).

The main topographically arranged section of the cartulary (nos. 17–258) follows the episcopal charters. This section is arranged by county and by parish within each county. The counties occur in the following order: Cambridgeshire, Bedfordshire, Hertfordshire, Suffolk, Norfolk, Lincolnshire, Huntingdonshire and finally a second Cambridgeshire section. This order may have been administratively significant since it represents a circular tour. The first,

---

[1] *Liber Eliensis* ed. Blake, pp. 140–2.
[2] Ibid. p. 257.

and main, series of Cambridgeshire documents begins with the lay charters for the parish of Chatteris which, not surprisingly, form the largest part of the topographical section. Charters relating to other parishes follow, with the topographical groupings being observed reasonably consistently up to the latter part of the cartulary. However nos. 233–42 are charters relating to parishes in Cambridgeshire, all of which – apart from no. 236 relating to Burwell – have sections allotted to them earlier in the topographical arrangement. In addition, nos. 243–54 and 256–8 are a group of charters relating to the Cambridgeshire parishes of Doddington, Wimblington and Chatteris which date from the late thirteenth to the mid-fourteenth centuries. The final folios contain a variety of types of document, the majority of which date from the fourteenth and fifteenth centuries (nos. 259–80).

The first part of the cartulary, up to the last document relating to Barley (Herts.) (no. 182), may represent a fifteenth-century copy of an earlier cartulary which no longer survives. The cartulary's opening passage may be significant. It requests prayers for the former abbess and the vicar of Chatteris *quorum sumptibus et industria est liber pre manibus in hanc formam redactus.* The words *in hanc formam redactus* could imply that this cartulary was, in part, a copy of an earlier cartulary. It is even possible that there was no alternative but to use the earlier cartulary as the abbey may have lost many of its original documents in the fire at the nunnery in 1306 × 1310.[1]

There may indeed have been two earlier cartularies which were recopied in the fifteenth century, with more charters and other documents added at the end (nos. 213–80). If there were two such earlier cartularies, the first seems to have contained the charters up to the end of the section for Barley (nos. 2–182) and the second, much shorter manuscript seems to have contained most of the Kersey charters (nos. 183–204). The opening of the Kersey section certainly suggests that it may originally have marked the beginning of an earlier manuscript. The section begins, after a blank space of six lines, with the first few words of the foundation chronicle and the bull of Innocent IV which are copied in full at the beginning of the cartulary (nos. 2–3). At the beginning of the Kersey section, the opening words of these documents are followed in each case by *vide hanc cronicam [bullam] in principio libri* (nos. 183–4). This strongly suggests that there was an earlier manuscript containing the Kersey charters which began with copies of the chronicle and papal privilege and which was recopied by the scribe of the fifteenth-century manuscript. In addition, the hand

---

[1] *Mon. Ang.* ii, pp. 618–19, no. 10 (BL Cotton Ch. xxi. 12).

of the main scribe breaks off on fo. 151v, after no. 204, and the rest of the gathering is filled with documents in other hands, most of which relate to Kersey. This suggests that the last charter in the supposed earlier collection was no. 204 in the extant cartulary. The abbey's manor at Kersey was so far removed geographically from its other properties that it was probably administered separately: the existence of an earlier cartulary for Kersey would have enabled the abbey's steward to have a copy of the Kersey charters with him in Suffolk. The copy of the chronicle and privilege at the beginning of both of the supposed earlier cartularies suggests that there must have been a conscious decision to set these manuscripts out in a similar way and that their layout was important to their compilers.

Despite the apparently common form of these two supposed earlier cartularies, the structure of the extant manuscript seems to reflect a degree of disorganisation in the archives of the abbey. The position in the manuscript of nos. 233–5 and 237–42 – the charters relating to parishes in Cambridgeshire and Hertfordshire which have sections allotted to them earlier in the topographical arrangement – may be significant. The scribe of the extant manuscript, having realised perhaps that the first supposed earlier cartulary omitted these charters, may have decided to include them after copying the earlier cartularies and after adding his topographical sections relating to Lynn and Bircham (Norf.), Pinchbeck and Lincoln (Lincs.), and Huntingdon and Hemingford (Hunts.). One of these charters dates from the mid-fourteenth century and another may date from the early fourteenth century, but all the rest date from the twelfth and thirteenth centuries. They were not, therefore, omitted from the supposed earlier cartulary because they were written too late. The confusion in the topographical arrangement could have arisen if the earlier cartulary had not been bound and subsequently fell apart. Alternatively, some of the original charters may once have been arranged into topographical bundles, whilst others had not, which could have caused omissions from the earlier cartulary.

Disorganisation in the archives could explain, for example, why the gift of five acres of land in Elm by Robert de Roseby was copied towards the end of the manuscript on fo. 164v (no. 235), whereas the confirmation of this gift by his daughter, Agnes, appears on fo. 105r–v (no. 98). Within the main, topographically arranged section of the cartulary, charters relating to the same property are sometimes grouped together – for example nos. 213–17 which concern a piece of land in Lynn (Norf.) – but such linking of related documents is not always observed. For example, the gifts to the abbey by John de Cambridge of land in Chatteris on fo. 90r–v (no. 53) and on fo. 95r (no. 67) are confirmed by John Vivien in a document copied both on fo. 83r–v (no. 32) and on fos. 85v–86r (no. 37). This scattering of connected documents reinforces the impression of a lack of care in the arrangement of the archives.

Although it is quite common for cartularies to contain a section devoted to final concords, they are not treated separately in the Chatteris cartulary, perhaps because the small number of original final concords at Chatteris was not kept separately in the archives of the abbey. Had any of the original documents kept at the abbey survived, their endorsements might have provided more clues about the arrangement of the nunnery's archive. The Chatteris cartulary, in contrast to some, seems not to have served as a finding-aid for the originals because it does not have reference numbers alongside each of its copies.[1] It was probably used as a reference book itself rather than as a means of referring to the originals.

The final folios of the cartulary contain copies of a variety of types of document including: a general royal pardon; exchequer pleas; extracts from the *Taxatio* of pope Nicholas IV; presentations and an exchange of benefices; two papal privileges addressed to bishop Nigel of Ely which mention Chatteris abbey; manumissions and more lay charters. From no. 269 on fo. 180r up to the end of the manuscript, a variety of hands occurs, there is only one more rubricated heading and there are no more examples of the decorated type of initial which appears up to this point. It is clear, therefore, that these final documents were copied after the rest of the manuscript. Although some date from after the compilation of the main part of the cartulary – for example no. 277 dates from 1506 × 1516 and no. 280 dates from 1473 – others pre-date the compilation of the cartulary – for example nos. 272 and 275 both date from the thirteenth century. This shows that the last folios were not only used for copies of documents produced after the creation of the cartulary; they also contain earlier documents which had previously been omitted and which must have survived the fire of 1306 × 1310.

A striking feature of the arrangement of the cartulary is that 17 charters were copied twice.[2] It is difficult to be sure exactly why these duplicate copies were made. Their occurrence suggests that the production of the cartulary was not undertaken with very great care. However, the scribe may have been

---

[1] D. Walker 'The Organization of Material in Medieval Cartularies' in *The Study of Medieval Records: Essays in Honour of Kathleen Major* eds D. A. Bullough and R. L. Storey (Oxford, 1971) pp. 139–44, 149.

[2] Nos. 8/255; 10/76; 12/78; 13/14; 16/77; 17/59; 21/70; 22/64; 24/45; 25/41; 27/40; 32/37; 73/188; 75/137; 91/223; 100/123; 116/122.

working from a very disorganised collection of charters and may mistakenly have copied some charters twice. Equally, it is possible that the abbey possessed two copies of some charters and that both were copied into the cartulary. Even if this were the case, it still seems likely that the abbey's muniments were not well organised since in all cases bar one the duplicate copies found in the cartulary were not copied consecutively.

Most of the charters which have been copied twice relate to properties in the parish of Chatteris and, usually, both copies are to be found within the main topographical section devoted to it. There is one case in which it seems very likely that the scribe erroneously copied a single charter twice: no. 13, the confirmation charter of John, bishop of Ely, is followed immediately by another copy which the scribe has corrected by writing *va...cat* in the margins. However, the abbey may have had two copies of some original documents, which could account for duplicate copies in the cartulary. This could well be the case with important charters such as the grant by bishop Nigel of the lordship and advowson of the church of St Peter in Chatteris which appears as no. 10 on fos. 77v–78r, with the other episcopal charters, and again as no. 76 on fos. 97v–98r amongst the lay charters. It is, though, impossible to tell whether the abbey had two copies of most of the duplicated charters or not.

There are nine other charters which appear twice within the group of episcopal charters and the main Chatteris section which follows it.[1] Another charter is duplicated within the Barrington section (nos. 116/122), but some charters have two copies in completely different parts of the manuscript. For example, no. 91 is a long charter of William of Ely in which he made four gifts to the abbey. The beginning of this charter, recording the gift of Richard de Bircham and his tenement to Chatteris abbey, reappears as no. 223, between two other charters which show how William of Ely had acquired Richard and his tenement. This recopied section is followed by the words '*etc. ut supra in carta domini Willelmi de Ely*' and was evidently added here to aid readers by grouping together related documents. Similarly, letters patent of Edward III allowing the abbey to acquire lands in mortmain are copied both with the other royal charters (no. 8) and again near the end of the manuscript with documents relating to inquisitions into the abbey's acquisitions (no. 255). However, the reasons for other duplications are not always so clear. For example, no. 75, an agreement in the Chatteris section, reappears as no. 137 amongst the Foxton

---

[1] Nos. 12/78; 16/77; 17/59; 21/70; 22/64; 24/45; 25/41; 27/40; 32/37.

documents, but in both cases without indicating the location of the land concerned.

Where two copies of the same document exist, they are not always identical. Although some discrepancies between double copies must have arisen from differences between two separate exemplars, others were clearly the result of scribal inconsistency when copying one original twice. For example, the verb *persolvit* and the phrase *ab eodem Radulfo* are included in no. 70 but omitted from the first copy of the charter (no. 21); in addition Ralph is spelt *Radulfus* in no. 21 but *Radulphus* in no. 70. The charter copied first as no. 17 refers to the messuage of Robert le Vite, but in the second copy (no. 59) the messuage belongs to Robert Hotte, which is a plausible misreading of le Vite. The words *cum tota sequela et catallis ipsius. Et ipsa domina et conventus* occur in no. 75 but not in the second copy of the agreement (no. 137). Similarly, there are significant discrepancies between nos. 32 and 37, a duplicated confirmation. No. 32 includes the phrase *sine omni retinemento vel conditione mei vel heredum meorum* which is omitted from no. 37 and, whereas no. 37 reads *Huic scripto sigillum meum apposui*, no. 32 reads *Huic scripto in modum carte confirmationis confecto sigillum meum duxi apponendum*. The validation clauses are very different too: no. 32 has *Huic scripto in modum carte confirmationis confecto sigillum meum duxi apponendum*, whereas no. 37 has *Huic scripto sigillum meum apposui*. In the second copy of letters patent of Edward III (no. 255), the name of the scribe, 'Rasen', and the phrase *Per breve de privato sigillo* occur after the date, but this information is not provided in the first copy (no. 8). In the absence of originals, documents which were copied twice give an indication of how precisely the scribes copied their texts. The striking differences between some double copies show that it would be dangerous to assume that charters which occur only once in the cartulary are exact copies of the originals.

Despite the lack of surviving original documents, there are other copies of some cartulary texts in the records of central government and the records of the bishop and the dean and chapter of Ely. These copies allow collations to be made which shed light on the source of some of the texts found in the cartulary and, sometimes, on the accuracy of the cartulary scribe. Where two copies are being compared, the scope for assessing the accuracy of the scribe is limited. Even so, cases of errors in the cartulary can be seen. For example, a comparison of nos. 256-8 with the copy of the inquisition and related documents preserved in the Public Record Office shows that the surname Drenge was miscopied as Brenge in nos. 256 and 257, perhaps because of confusion over the form of the capital letter, although the scribe did write Dreng in no. 258.[1] Confusion also arose in no. 269, where the scribe twice miscopied an ampersand from the *Liber Eliensis* as *in*, presumably because the ligature was unfamiliar to him.[2]

Nos. 2, 4, 5, 6, 269 and 270 in the cartulary have been collated with all of the copies of these documents which exist in the various manuscripts of the *Liber Eliensis* and no. 6 has also been collated with an original charter preserved in the archives of the dean and chapter of Ely. The references for these copies in the Ely manuscripts are given above the transcription of each charter. As with the collations made for other documents in the cartulary, these collations can be used to examine the accuracy of the cartulary scribe. However, in the case of the documents in the cartulary which appear in the *Liber Eliensis*, the collations are more significant since it is likely that the Ely manuscripts were the source from which the Chatteris copies were taken. The Chatteris copies may not, though, have been made directly from the manuscripts at Ely: it would be interesting to know whether a scribe could go to Ely, consult the manuscripts and make copies there, or whether copies of parts of the *Liber Eliensis* were in circulation locally and available for recopying. Even though the copies in the Chatteris cartulary may well not have been taken directly from the manuscripts at Ely, the collations still sometimes seem to show which manuscripts were the original source.

In the case of no. 6, Henry I's remission of the ward-penny owed by the nunnery, the cartulary scribe should have had no need to rely on an Ely manuscript provided that no harm had befallen the original issued to the abbey. The collations suggest, though, that the cartulary scribe did use one of the copies made at Ely as his source. He does not seem to have used the surviving original of the charter at Ely because it is significantly different from the copy in the Chatteris cartulary. Since all the originals issued by Henry I ought to have been at least very similar, if not identical, the differences between the Ely original and the Chatteris copy also suggest that the scribe was not copying a Chatteris original. The Chatteris copy is much more similar to the Ely copies than to the Ely original: for example, only the original omits *mei*, has *quoque* instead of *unoquoque*, and has *episcopi* in a different position in its sentence. Also, the Ely original and 'Liber M' (Cambridge UL, EDR G/3/28) alone give the ward-penny as 6s. 8d. (half a mark), whereas all the other copies have the less plausible sum of 6s. 7d. Close examination of the collations shows that manuscripts E, F and G (Cambridge, Trinity College MS O. 2. 1; Cambridge UL, EDC 1

---

[1] PRO C 143/405/10; C 66/323 m. 11.
[2] *Liber Eliensis* ed. Blake, p. 330.

and BL Cotton MS Titus A. i) are most similar to the copy in the Chatteris cartulary. Therefore the source of the Chatteris copy is likely to be E, F or G, or a related manuscript which has not survived.[1]

There is no extant original from Ely or Chatteris of the gift by Henry I to bishop Hervey of rights over Chatteris abbey, but it is probable that the nunnery would have had its own original of such an important document (no. 5). However, since the remission of ward-penny (no. 6) was issued to the abbey itself and yet seems to have been copied from a *Liber Eliensis* manuscript, it is likely that the Chatteris copy of Henry I's charter to Hervey would have been taken from a copy at Ely too. Moreover, nos. 4–6 in the cartulary also occur sequentially in the Ely manuscripts E, F and O (Cambridge, Trinity College MS O. 2. 1; Cambridge UL, EDC 1 and Oxford, Bodl. Laud. Misc. 647) which may be a sign that all three documents were copied together. The collations show that the copies of no. 5 in E and F are most similar to the Chatteris copy.

It seems certain that nos. 2 and 4, both narrative extracts, would have been copied, directly or not, from the *Liber Eliensis*. There are three copies of no. 2 and four of no. 4 in the *Liber Eliensis* manuscripts. The collations show that no. 2 in the Chatteris cartulary is most closely related to manuscript E (Cambridge, Trinity College MS O. 2. 1). The wording of the dating clause in the cartulary is identical to that in E and, whereas manuscripts F and O have *assumpus est* near the beginning of the document, E and the cartulary have *est assumptus*. However E cannot have been the direct source for no. 2 since it uses *credendas* where all the other copies and the cartulary have *condendas*. Therefore the source for no. 2 seems to have been a lost manuscript which was more closely related to E than to F or O.

The collations of document no. 4, which appears in manuscripts A, E, F and O, are less revealing. Whilst the variants in the penultimate sentence beginning *Nemo igitur* show that the source definitely was not A (BL Cotton MS Vesp. A. xix), the collations do not point strongly towards E, F or O as the particular source. If nos. 4, 5 and 6 were copied together from one Ely manuscript, then O can be eliminated since the copies of nos. 5 and 6 were definitely not taken from it. The use of *concessisse* in no. 6 in both E and the Chatteris cartulary suggests a link with E, but the evidence is not conclusive.

The collations for nos. 269 and 270 are more successful in isolating the source of the documents. Seven of the *Liber Eliensis* manuscripts have a copy of no. 269 and eight have a copy of no. 270. They show that manuscripts C, D and

---

[1] The sigla are those used in *Liber Eliensis* ed. Blake and *Papsturkunden in England* ii.

M (Cambridge, Trinity College MS O. 2. 41; BL Cotton MS Tib. A. vi and Cambridge UL, EDR G/3/28 'Liber M') are most similar to the copies in the cartulary. It is possible that, as with the charter of Henry I to bishop Hervey, Chatteris abbey may always have had its own copies of the originals of these papal privileges which confirmed to bishop Nigel the possessions of the church of Ely, including Chatteris abbey. The bishop of Ely himself may have had more than one copy of the original, but it is very unlikely that discrepancies between different copies of the original could have been behind the variants in the numerous *Liber Eliensis* and the Chatteris abbey cartulary copies. The papal chancery took great care to ensure that if several copies of an original document were issued they were all identical. The variants must therefore have been introduced at the recopying stage. The similarities between the Chatteris versions of nos. 269 and 270 and the copies in C, D and M seem too great to be coincidental and so suggest that either C, D or M, or a related manuscript, was indeed the source.

Whilst the collations show that neither no. 269 nor no. 270 could have been copied from the other Ely manuscripts (A, E, F, G and O), the variants do not isolate C, D or M specifically as the source of no. 270. In the case of no. 269, though, the collations suggest that C was the source: there are strong similarities between C, D and M and the cartulary – they all have *legitime* and *atque* where E, F, G and O have *religiose* and *ac* – but the cartulary copy is closest to C. Whereas the cartulary and C have *servicium*, D and M have *servicii*. D and M also add *rege* which both the cartulary and C omit, and it is only C which shares the cartulary spelling of *sacca et socca*. Furthermore, no. 269 contains several lists of place-names for which the collations produced many variants: more of these names in C than in the other manuscripts are spelt in a similar way to that found in the cartulary. Since the scribe of the cartulary apparently copied no. 269 from C, or from another closely related manuscript, it is probable that C was also the source of no. 270, although the lack of significant differences between the versions of this document in C, D and M preclude certainty. It is not very surprising that the copies of the narratives, nos. 2 and 4, are related to a different version of the *Liber Eliensis* from the copies of the papal privileges, nos. 269 and 270. The two privileges, like the other documents in the last part of the cartulary, were added in a different hand after the main part of the manuscript had been written.

Collations for the three other cartulary copies of no. 147, an agreement between the prior and convent of Ely and Chatteris abbey concerning the pasturing of their cattle in Foxton, suggest that the source for the copy in the

Chatteris cartulary was M (Cambridge UL, EDR G/3/28 'Liber M'), rather than either of the copies of the cartulary of the almoner of Ely (BL Cotton MS Vesp. A. vi and Cambridge UL, EDC 1/A/2).

It seems likely that the scribe often standardized the spelling of Chatteris to 'Chatriz' or 'Chateriz' in the cartulary. Although other spellings sometimes occur in the manuscript, such as 'Catricia' in no. 129 and 'Chatrich' in no. 152, there is evidence that standardization occurred elsewhere. For example, whereas no. 4 has 'Chateriz', the manuscript from which it was copied has 'Chateriht'.[1] The copies of nos. 8 and 258 on the patent rolls have 'Chaterice' whereas the scribe of the cartulary wrote 'Chateriz' and 'Chatriz' respectively, and the copy on the close roll of no. 7 has 'Chateric'' but the scribe again wrote 'Chateriz'. It is possible that the letters sent to Chatteris contained different spellings from those which occur on the enrolments but the overwhelming prevalence of 'Chatriz' and 'Chateriz' in the cartulary, despite the considerable number of variants in existence, adds weight to the case for standardization having been imposed.

The manuscript contains many marginal notes, not written by the main scribe, which suggest that the cartulary was not merely compiled for its own sake, but was also used as a work of reference. These notes occur most often alongside the Chatteris parish charters – which may be because the local charters were consulted most frequently – and they take several forms. Sometimes a note is a place-name where a charter refers to property in more than one parish. For example, in no. 91, the place-names 'Briccham', 'Stunteneye', 'Welle' and 'Parva Thetford' occur in the margin alongside the appropriate parts of the charter, presumably to guide the reader since the rubric above this charter reads only, *Carta Willelmi de Ely de Ricardo de Brecham cum tenemento suo in Brecham*. Many other marginal notes act as reference aids by picking out information about the subject of a charter which is not contained in the rubric above it, such as *Carta rode ad lumen Sancte Katerine* in the case of no. 54 and *Redditus vj altilium ad Natale Domini* for no. 141.

Marginal notes are also used to supply cross-references. No. 81 on fo. 99v, a charter relating to Chatteris, is followed by the note, *Vide literam pro capella de Hunney infra folio xxxvij°*, written in a different hand from that of the main scribe. This is a reference to no. 164 on fo. 135v which is 37 folios below, counting inclusively. The reference seems to have been added on fo. 99v to link the main group of Chatteris charters to the later document concerning the

---

[1] The source may have been Cambridge UL, EDC 1, or Cambridge, Trinity College MS O. 2. 1, both of which have *Chateriht* in this document.

chapel of Honey Hill, which lay in the parish of Chatteris. The use of this system of cross-referencing shows that the manuscript had not been foliated when the note was written. However, after the manuscript had been foliated in the seventeenth century, '62' – which corresponds to modern folio 135 – was added to the end of the reference. There are several cross-references which follow the *vide infra* or *supra* pattern. Sometimes they draw together documents relating to the same place, as in the case above. Similarly, the note alongside no. 99 on fo. 105v states: *vide aliam cartam de Ely supra folio iij°*. In addition, cross-references are used to connect different transactions relating to the same property. For example, on fo. 101r there is a note beside no. 89 which reads, *Et dimissionem ad firmam eiusdem piscarie vide infra folio xxxvij°*, whilst on fo. 137r, beside no. 169, is the note, *Donationem istius piscarie vide supra folio xxxvij°*.

Rather more oblique evidence of the self-referential aspect of the cartulary is provided by two documents towards the end of the manuscript. The clause, *unde scrutatis evidenciis et munimentis et nostris examinatis*, is used in no. 276, a document issued by the abbess to counter the allegation that John Reynold was a villein of the abbey. Also, no. 279 begins, *Mete de communia de Chateriz ut per libros et evidencias de Chateriz et de Rameseya*. These examples show that sometimes the archives of the abbey were indeed consulted. It is even possible that reference may have been made to the cartulary itself before the composition of these documents because they were added to the last folios of the manuscript after the main part of the text had been completed.

Some religious houses, when given property, produced charters to record these gifts which the benefactors merely authenticated.[1] This practice, which tended to lead to standardization in phrasing or style, does not seem to have been employed at Chatteris. The variety, in particular, in the address clauses in the cartulary suggests that the charters had been composed by the benefactors' scribes, rather than by the abbey's scribes. If a collection of the original charters granted to the abbey survived, it would be possible to determine with more certainty, on palaeographical grounds, whether the abbey had its own scribes producing charters for its benefactors. It is usually impossible to say who wrote the original documents but one of the witnesses in no. 227, a charter of Hugh de Cranwell, is *Turstanus clericus de Templo qui hanc cartam scripsit*. However, some charters display local peculiarities which reinforce the impression that they had been written locally and that there were local formulae which gener-

---

[1] *Charters of the Honour of Mowbray 1107–1191* ed. D. E. Greenway (British Academy, 1972) pp. lxix–lxx.

ations of local scribes persisted in using. The clause *quantum pertinet ad tantam terram eiusdem feodi* appears in three different Barrington charters – one of which was recopied – but nowhere else. Local customs are reflected too: in many of the charters relating to Kersey, Palm Sunday appears as one of the four terms of the year on which rent was to be paid, but this term is not used elsewhere. Similarly, the feast of St Nicholas is often used in the Kersey charters but it is found in only two other charters in the rest of the manuscript.

It is unfortunate that none of the original documents copied into the cartulary survives since the scribe omitted most of the witness-lists, but there is a seventeenth-century copy of one original charter issued by the abbey. John Layer, lay rector of Shepreth, made a transcript, with witnesses included, of a confirmation by the abbey to William de la Haye of a chantry in his chapel in Shepreth (no. 162).[1]

Although the court of augmentations was entitled to receive the archives of all dissolved houses, most were probably never transferred to it. The apparent disappearance of all of the original documents in the cartulary suggests that those granted to the abbey may have been destroyed at or soon after its dissolution in 1538. This loss of the muniments is paralleled at other monasteries. For example, almost 1200 documents were copied into the cartulary of Thurgarton priory, but none of these originals survives.[2]

The motivation for the production of this cartulary is not explicitly stated but may well have been a combination of several factors. A cartulary could make documents more accessible. It could protect the abbey's lands and rights more effectively and show successors the history of those lands and rights. Additionally, a cartulary could be a safeguard against loss of or damage to the muniments. In the case of Chatteris abbey, and of other houses whose archives have disappeared, this last function has been particularly effective.

---

[1] Oxford, Bodl. MS Rawl. B. 278, fo. 132.
[2] T. Foulds 'Medieval Cartularies' *Archives* xviii, no. 77 (1987) p. 10.

VII

Editorial Method

The editor of a medieval manuscript has to extend abbreviations in the text, but the nature of a cartulary makes the extension of problematic abbreviated words particularly difficult. The standard practice of following the example of the scribe, and looking for instances where abbreviated words are spelt out in full elsewhere, falls down in the case of a cartulary, unless the scribe compiling it consistently imposed his own spelling and grammar on the documents he was copying. The original documents in a cartulary would have been written by many different scribes over several centuries. If the scribe who compiled the cartulary reproduced the spelling of these originals, a search for cases where a word is spelt out in full will not necessarily provide a good guide to how an abbreviated word would have been spelt in any other entry. Moreover, such a search may well produce a number of varying examples of how a word could be written.

However, it was not only the differences between the spelling and grammar of the original documents which led to the variations which are found in the manuscript since the main scribe was not always consistent with himself. As is mentioned above, Ralph is spelt *Radulfus* in no. 21 whereas in no. 70, another copy of the same charter, it is spelt *Radulphus*. Since *Radulphus* occurs more frequently than *Radulfus* in the manuscript as a whole, the former spelling has been used to extend abbreviations in charters where the name is not spelt out in full.

It is not only proper nouns which are spelt inconsistently in the cartulary. The spelling of many words is eccentric. Both *elemosina* and *elimosina* occur frequently, with an example of each in successive lines on fo. 84r (no. 33). Similarly, both *contraversia* and *controversia* are found on fo. 120v (nos. 130 and 131). Other non-standard spellings include *territario* in no. 35, *eidificiis* in no. 69, *avariis* in no. 147, *disparsis* in no. 180 and *fuudi* in no. 223. All such variant spellings have been retained in the transcription. In the case of minor scribal errors, as distinct from scribal peculiarities, the correct reading has been given in the text with the manuscript reading in the footnote. Footnotes have also been used to indicate where the scribe has corrected his own mistakes.

The editorial conventions used are, in general, those recommended by R. F. Hunnisett.[1] All place-names have been left unextended, except where they are used adjectivally. Personal names which have been abbreviated to an initial are expanded silently if they occur in full in the same document, but if the rest of the name has been supplied from elsewhere in the manuscript, or from another source entirely, the letters supplied are given within round brackets. Abbreviation marks after proper nouns have been retained. It is hard to judge how meaningful these marks were and it seems likely that many were no more than final flourishes. However Foxton, which is almost always written with a final abbreviation-mark, occurs once as *Foxtona* in no. 134, so at least some of the other abbreviation-marks may be meaningful. In addition, although the cartulary is a fifteenth-century manuscript, and it may often be safe to disregard such abbreviation marks in texts of this date, the scribes may have been reproducing them from the documents they were copying, many of which were composed in the twelfth or thirteenth centuries. For the sake of consistency, and because it is hard to date some charters accurately, such marks are preserved after proper nouns in all entries.

In the transcription of financial documents such as extents, exchequer pleas and returns for the *taxatio* of 1291, where sums of money occur frequently, the abbreviations *li. s. d. ob. qu.*, which were usually adopted by the scribe, have been used for sums of money. However, in those cases where the scribe spelt out the denominations in full or where the numbers were in words rather than figures, as at the foot of fo. 177v in no. 260, these extended forms have been retained. In all other documents, these words have always been fully extended.

The extension of abbreviated adjectives which precede more than one noun is problematic, again because of the inconsistency either of the scribes of the original documents or of the cartulary. Sometimes the scribes, when spelling such adjectives out in full, made them agree with all of the nouns but sometimes only with the first, with no regular pattern being observed even within single charters. Because of this variability, abbreviated adjectives have generally been extended in the transcription to agree with all of their the nouns, even if there is an example of agreement only with the first noun in a particular charter. An exception has been made, however, in the case of phrases such *quietum clamasse*

---

[1] R. F. Hunnisett *Editing Records for Publication* (British Records Association, Archives and the User series, iv; London, 1977).

totum jus et clamium where both of the nouns refer to a single concept and where the adjective, when spelt out, is never plural.

The extension of adjectives is particularly awkward in the case of *dictus*, its compounds and similar adjectives such as *prefatus* when they occur, as inevitably they do very frequently, before the phrase *abbatissa et conventus*. The common use of abbreviation marks at the end of adjectives not only saved space, it also saved the scribes from having to make a decision. When spelt out in full, the scribes sometimes made these adjectives singular, agreeing only with the first noun, and sometimes plural, agreeing with both: for example, the singular *dicta abbatissa et conventus* is found in no. 118, whereas the plural *predicte abbatissa et conventus* occurs in no. 218. The scribes also showed no consistency regarding the gender of *conventus*, which should strictly be a masculine noun. Indeed, there are several documents in which it occurs in masculine and feminine forms: for example, no. 124 contains both *dictorum abbatisse et conventus* and *dictarum abbatisse et conventus*. It seems that *conventus* could be regarded, logically enough in the case of a convent of nuns, as feminine. The variations within documents where endings are given make it impossible to conjecture what the scribe would have written when endings are lacking. Therefore, in the interests of consistency and logic, all such unextended adjectives have been made feminine plural in the transcription.

When *dictus*, its compounds and synonyms are found before two or more personal names they, again, sometimes agree only with the first and sometimes with all of the names. Endings have been supplied to such unextended adjectives so that they agree with all of the names. In the case of a male and female name, masculine plural adjectives are used, as in *sepedicti Alicia et Jacobus* in no. 120.

In the transcription, 'i' and 'u' are used for vowels and 'j' and 'v' for consonants. The transcription of the letters 'c' and 't', although usually written as distinct letters in the manuscript, is determined by the pronunciation of the Latin words or of the modern derivatives from them. This principle is also used for ambiguous cases of 'i' and 'j', giving *juxta*, *iam* and *eius*. However, in proper nouns, 'c' and 't' are transcribed as written, partly because the use of 'c' and 't' in the text and rubrics is not always consistent. Sometimes, the scribe appears to have been trying to reproduce the names he found in the documents very precisely: he often seems to have written 'c' whenever he read 'c' but, in the earlier hands used in the original documents, both 'c' and 't' would probably have been written as 'c'. Although the rubrics frequently follow the text, they sometimes seem to reflect the pronunciation of proper nouns. For example, the surname 'Fithien' occurs in the rubric above no. 38 whereas the text has 'Fichien'.

The use of capital letters has been regularized. The lower case has been used for *sanctus* and *beatus*. Otherwise, Hunnisett's advice on capitalization has been followed. The minimum amount of modern punctuation has been added to achieve clarity.

Some of the text in the cartulary has been lost because of the damage suffered by the manuscript in the Cotton library fire of 1731. Footnotes are used to indicate where the text is lacking or illegible. The length of each lacuna has been given in millimetres in the footnotes and the type of lacuna is indicated by 'hole', 'damaged' or 'unclear'. 'Hole' is used where there are distinct holes, 'damaged' where the parchment has been damaged but has not broken up completely, and 'unclear' where the manuscript is illegible because the ink has been lost from the surface of the parchment even though the parchment itself is intact.

Square brackets are used to enclose text which has been supplied because of any sort of damage to the manuscript. In the case of some damaged entries in the cartulary, it has been possible to supply text from other copies of the documents. For example, no. 260 is an exchequer plea from the reign of Edward III. The text in the cartulary is much abbreviated and in poor condition but a much fuller copy survives in good condition on the exchequer plea roll for 27 & 28 Edward III.[1] Where the manuscript is damaged, the words lacking have been supplied in square brackets and, where the text is abbreviated, the sections omitted have been included in the footnotes. The next document in the cartulary, no. 261, is another exchequer plea from the following year and it too has been badly damaged: unfortunately the exchequer plea roll for that year has been lost. This part of the cartulary is in a particularly bad state and a number of words in entry no. 259, a general pardon to Chatteris abbey by Henry IV, are also illegible. This pardon was issued as letters patent, but does not occur in the patent rolls. However, a very similar pardon issued in the following year was enrolled and has been used to supply the words lacking in the Chatteris abbey pardon.[2]

Alternative copies of damaged entries do not exist in all cases, but conjectural readings have been given, where possible, again enclosed in square brackets. In some cases, the words supplied may not be exactly those which the

---

1 PRO E 13/79, rot. 42.
2 PRO C 66/299, m. 39.

scribe wrote. For example, in no. 99 *et predictis* has been added even though the actual word lost may have been *dictis, memoratis, prefatis* or another similar word. Words have been supplied only when their meaning is beyond doubt and in order to make the text easier to read.

Where the scribe omitted parts of the text, and where it is possible to make conjectural readings, the missing words have been supplied within angled brackets, as in no. 180, where the sense dictates that *que* was omitted. In this case, the scribe left a short space after the preceding word suggesting, perhaps, that the original document he was copying was illegible at this point. There is also a space where an omission was made in no. 256, but *datis* has been supplied from a similar phrase in no. 257. In cases where missing words can be supplied, footnotes are given to indicate the source of the words. However, where the scribe omitted longer passages, which cannot be reconstructed with certainty, a footnote only has been added, as in no. 93 where the end of the *habendum* clause and the beginning of the *reddendo* clauses are lacking.

Some words in the cartulary can be read only with the aid of an ultra-violet light or an optical fibre light-cable. The former is useful where ink has flaked off the surface of the parchment, whereas the latter often increases the legibility of text obscured by repair-tissue applied in the nineteenth century. The use of these lights has not been signalled in the footnotes to the transcription, partly because it is impossible to draw a clear distinction between words which are and are not legible to the naked eye, and partly because the lights have to be used so extensively on some folios.

Marginal notes in the manuscript have been printed in the footnotes, with the footnote hanging from the word at the beginning or end of the line where the note occurs. The headings, usually rubricated, which are found at the top of each page have been printed in the footnotes and are also listed above in the description of the arrangement of the manuscript. The turns of the folios are indicated by the number of the new folio, enclosed within round brackets.

There is a general index for people, places and subjects. Individuals are indexed by surname, patronymic or toponym, with *de* being retained rather than translated as 'of' before toponyms. Peers and office holders are indexed under their family names, or their fore-names in the case of some countesses whose family name is unclear. Family relationships described in the text have been preserved in the index.

The indexing of occupational names is problematic, since it is often unclear which are merely descriptive and which are true surnames. Some, such as *clericus* and *capellanus* seem to be occupational descriptions, but others, such as *molendinarius* and *carectarius,* may not be. Since there is a wide chronological range of documents in the cartulary, and since many entries are impossible to date precisely, it is difficult to adopt a workable rule. For the sake of consistency, and at the risk of disguising some true surnames, all individuals with Latin occupational names have been indexed under their fore-name with a cross-reference under their occupation. An exception has been made in the case of fifteenth-century documents where it seems clear that occupational names are true surnames. English occupational names present more problems. Ralph 'le taillur" also appears as Ralph *cissor*: he, and others with plausible descriptive names, such as 'le smyth', 'le cobeler", 'le pottere' and 'le clerk', are indexed under their fore-names. However, other English names in the cartulary which were medieval family names, such as 'le Vavasour', have been treated as surnames in the index.

Place-names are indexed under their parish, where known, and all parishes are in Cambridgeshire, unless otherwise indicated. Places outside Cambridgeshire are identified according to their pre-1974 county. All variant spellings for personal and place-names have been given.

English summaries have been supplied above each document. In the summaries, as in the index, the county has been added only for places outside Cambridgeshire. The spelling of proper nouns in the summaries has been standardized to conform with the index. 'Chatteris abbey' has been used for abbess and convent, church and nuns, and nuns of Chatteris.

The undated documents in the cartulary have been dated as accurately as the evidence allows. However, reasonably precise dating is often impossible with this cartulary because many of the benefactors of the abbey were neither substantial land-owners nor office-holders, and the compiler of the cartulary omitted most of the witness-lists. Where exact dates cannot be found, documents are dated to the nearest quarter-century using the convention *s.* xii[4] to indicate 1175–1200 and *s.* xiii[2-3] for 1225–75. The *habendum et tenendum* clause may indicate whether a gift dates from before or after 1290: the wording *de me et heredibus meis* was used before the 1290 statute of *Quia Emptores* whereas *de capitalibus dominis feodi* was used afterwards. In addition, it was not possible to reserve a rent in a deed of gift after 1290. All sources used for dating are given in the note at the foot of each document, except for references to the *Handbook of British Chronology* for the dates of royal officials, bishops and peers, which have been omitted.[1]

[1] *Handbook of Bristish Chronology* eds E. B. Fryde, D. E. Greenway, S. Porter and I. Roy, 3rd edn (London, 1986).

VIII

The Cartulary of Chatteris Abbey

1 *Request for prayers of intercession for the souls of Agnes Ashfield, abbess of Chatteris, and Henry Buckworth, [vicar of Chatteris], at whose expense and by whose industry the book was formerly rendered into this form.*
fo. 72v [April 1456 × s. xv³]

Orate pro animabus venerabilis domine domine Agnetis Aschefeld quondam abbatisse monasterii de Chatriz et Henrici Bukworth decretorum bacularii, quorum sumptibus et industria est liber pre manibus in hanc formam redactus. (fo. 73r)[1]

> Note. Henry Buckworth died before 29 April 1456 when Thomas Holand became the next vicar of Chatteris (Cambridge UL, EDR G/1/5 Grey register, fo. 14r).

2 *Narrative concerning the life, death and burial of Eadnoth, abbot of Ramsey and bishop of Dorchester, the discovery of the body of St Ivo at St Ives, Hunts., and its translation to Ramsey, Hunts., the building of a church at St Ives, the foundation of Chatteris abbey [1007 × 1016] and the burial of St Ælfheah in London.*
fo. 73r–v [See note below for date]

> Cartulary copies: (E) Cambridge, Trinity College MS O. 2. 1, fo. 68r–v; (F) Cambridge UL, EDC 1, fo. 67r–v; (O) Oxford, Bodl. MS Laud. Misc. 647, fos. 42v–43r.
> Printed in *Mon. Ang.* ii, pp. 616–17, no. 3; *Liber Eliensis* ed. Blake, pp. 140–2.

Cronica fundationis monasterii seu abbathie de Chatriz.

Sequitur Ednodus, vir in Christo fa[mo]sus[2] et monasti[ce][3] religionis cultor egregius, qui a beato Oswaldo Eboracensi archiepiscopo et glorioso duce Egcl-wino in Ramisiensem[4] ecclesiam, quam ipsi construxerant,[5] de Wigorniensi[6]

---

[1] Heading *Chateriz.*
[2] Hole 5 mm.
[3] Hole 2 mm.
[4] EFO *Ramesiensem.*
[5] O *constituerant.*
[6] EFO *Wigornensi.*

monachatu ad officium abbatis est assumptus.[1] Ubi cum in omni honestate sub Christo floreret et gregem Domini fideli cura salubriter gubernaret, facta est cuidam fabro divina revelatio de corpore beati Ivonis[2] et sociis eius simul cum ipso apud villam de Slepa quiescentibus. Apparens enim fabro in episcopi specie, beatus Yvo et se et socios suos in eadem villa ab antiquissimo tempore jacuisse indicavit et, ut Ednodo id indicaret, imperavit. Ac ille statim evigilans, viro Dei visionem revelavit et de oblata su[o tempor]i[3] gracia nimis eum letificavit. Qui tantam sanctorum gloriam non passus est diutius in ceno latitare, sed, convocato clero et populo, ad effodiendum celestem thesaurum cum ecclesiasticis apparatibus properavit et beatum Yvonem propriis manibus, ceteris ceteros ferentibus, ipse usque in Rameseiam portavit et postea in ipsa Slepa[4] ecclesiam in nomine eiusdem sancti edificavit. Nec multum postea defuncto Lincolniensi antistite, in episcopum promovetur, pro qua potestate nichil minuit de antiqua religione, sed quanto altior, tanto melior effectus,[5] circa condendas[6] ecclesias et augendas congregationes assiduus insistebat, quarum unam apud Chatriz[7] ob amorem sancte Dei genetricis[8] Marie et Alfwenn[e],[9] sororis sue, cognomento domine, ad ponendas ibi cum ipsa sanctimoniales construxit et rebus necessariis ampli[avit].[10] Ipse quoque corpus beati Alphegi[11] martiris et archiepiscopi, [apud][12] Grenewicum a Dani[s][13] lapidatum, pietate [succ]ensus[14] (fo. 73v)[15] et fide armatus collegit atque Londoniis sepelivit. Tandem vero mar[tirii glori]a[16] pro gloriosa conversatione decorandus in bello, quod fuit inter Edmundum regem et Canutum apud Ass[a]ndun,[17] dum missam cantaret, a Danis Canuti

1 FO *assumptus est.*
2 EFO *Yvonis.*
3 Hole 15 mm; *lacunae* in chronicle supplied from transcript in Oxford, Bodl. MS Dodsworth 78, fo. 54r–v.
4 F *Flepa.*
5 O *affectus.*
6 E *credendas.*
7 EF *Chateriz.*
8 O *genitricis.*
9 Edge of folio lacking; F *Ælwene.*
10 Hole 7 mm.
11 EFO *Ælfegi.*
12 Hole 9 mm.
13 Hole 3 mm.
14 Hole 7 mm.
15 Heading *Bulla.*
16 Hole 12 mm.
17 Hole 2 mm.

sociis,[1] prius dextera manu[2] propter annulum amputata, deinde toto corpore
scisso interfectus est cum abbate Wlsio qui, secundum cronicam, ad ador-
andum[3] Deum pro milite bellum agente commemorant.[4] Huius corpus cum ad
hanc Elyensem ecclesiam a suis fuisset allatum, ut confestim hinc ad Ram-
eseyam,[5] ubi abbas fuerat, deferetur, Alfgarus vir sanctus, qui tunc temporis
relicto Helmanensi episcopatu hic ex toto se dederat, corpus illud ad augendam
loci huius dignitatem, inebriatis[6] custodibus, in secreto loco sepelivit, tum quia
illum s[anctas nostra]s[7] valde dilexisse cognoverat, tum quia martirem eum esse
credebat. Qui et ipse de veteri sepultura inter alios translatus magno nobis
honori habetur. Passus est[8] anno ab incarnatione Domini[9] millesimo xvj[mo], et
fuit in diebus Ethelredi et Edmundi regum temporibus.

Note. This account is taken from Book II of the *Liber Eliensis* which was compiled 1154 × s.
xii[3]. The earliest surviving *Liber Eliensis* manuscript (E) dates from the late twelfth century
(*Liber Eliensis* ed. Blake, pp. xxiii, xlviii).

3 *Privilege 'Religiosam vitam eligentibus' of pope Innocent IV confirming to
Chatteris abbey their possessions in Chatteris, Foxton, Barrington, Kersey (Suff.),
Shepreth, Barley (Herts.), Over, Lincoln, Huntingdon, Burwell, Thriplow, Cambridge and Honey Hill (par. Chatteris).*
fos. 73v–75v   [28 June 1243 × 7 Dec. 1254]

Printed in *Mon. Ang.* ii, p. 618, no. 8.

Bullam per subsequentem, videlicet Innocentii quarti qui tenuit pontificatum
anno Domini M° CC° quadragesimo secundo,[10] renovatur bulla Alexandri tertii
qui tenuit pontificatum anno Domini M° C° lxij°.[11]

Innocentius episcopus servus servorum Dei dilectis in Christo filiabus abbatisse
monasterii de Chateriz eiusque sororibus tam presentibus quam futuris regu-
larem vitam professis inperpetuum. Religiosam vitam eligentibus apostolicum

1 *-is* abbreviation unclear.
2 EFO omit.
3 E corrects from *ad orandum*.
4 EFO *convenerant*.
5 EO *Rameseiam*, F *Remeseiam*.
6 Followed by *con*, expunged.
7 Hole 14 mm.
8 O adds *autem*.
9 F omits *anno ... Domini*, adds *autem anno incarnationis*.
10 Recte *tertio*.
11 Recte *lxix°*.

convenit adesse presidium, ne forte cuiuslibet te[mer]itatis[1] incursus, aut [eos a][2] proposito revocet, [aut][3] robur, quod absit, (fo. 74r)[4] sacre religionis enervet. Eapropter dilecte in Domino filie, vestris justis postulationibus clementer annuimus et monasterium de Chateriz Elyensis diocesis, in quo divino estis obsequio mancipate, sub beati Petri et nostra protectione suscepimus, et presentis scripti privilegio communimus. In primis siquidem statuentes, ut ordo monasticus, qui secundum Deum [et][5] beati Benedicti regulam in eodem monasterio institutus esse dinoscitur, perpetuis ibidem temporibus inviolabiliter observetur. Preterea quascunque possessiones,[6] quecunque bona idem monasterium impresentiarum juste ac canonice possidet, aut in futurum concessione pontificum, largitione regum vel principum, oblatione fidelium seu aliis justis modis, prestante divino poterit adipisci, firma vobis et eis que vobis successerint et illibata permaneant. In quibus hec propriis duximus exprimenda vocabulis: locum ipsum in quo[7] prefatum monasterium situm [e]st[8] cum omnibus pertinenciis suis, ecclesiam quam habetis in villa de Chateriz cum omnibus pertinenciis suis, terram et redditus quos habetis in eadem villa de Chateriz, terram quam habetis in villa de Foxton' cum medietate unius molendini et pertinenciis suis, terram quam habetis in villa de Barantun' [cum uno][9] molendino et pertinenciis suis, villam de Kareseya cum pertinenciis suis, ecclesiam terram et[10] molendinum que habetis in villa de Scepereye cum omnibus pertinenciis eorumdem, terras quas habetis in Berele, Overe, Lincolnie, Huntedun' et Borewelle villis cum omnibus pertinenciis earumdem, terram cum molendino que habetis in villa de Trippelowe cum pertinenciis earumdem, terram cum portu quos habetis in burgo de Cantebrig' (fo. 74v)[11] cum omnibus suis pertinenciis, capellam de Honezeh' cum decimis et omnibus pertinenciis, cum pratis vineis terris nemoribus usuagiis et pascuis, in bosco et plano, in aquis et molendinis et viis et semitis et omnibus aliis libertatibus et immunitatibus suis.

---

1 Unclear 4 mm; *lacunae* in this charter supplied from transcript of this manuscript in *Mon. Ang.* ii, p. 618.
2 Damaged 11 mm.
3 Damaged 7 mm.
4 Heading *Papalis*.
5 Hole 3 mm.
6 Final *s*, interlined.
7 *in quo*, ins. marg.
8 Hole 2 mm.
9 Hole 13 mm.
10 Interlined.
11 Heading *Bulla*.

Sane novalium vestrorum que propriis sumptibus colitis, de quibus aliquis hactenus non[1] percepit, sive de vestrorum animalium nutrimentis nullus a vobis decimas exigere, sive extorquere presumat. Liceat quoque vobis personas liberas et absolutas e seculo fugientes ad conversionem recipere, et eas absque contradictione aliqua retinere. Prohibemus insuper, ut nulli sororum vestrarum post factam in monasterio vestro professionem fas sit sine abbatisse sue licencia de eodem loco, nisi artioris religionis obtentu discedere, discedentem vero absque communium litterarum vestrarum cautione nullus audeat retinere. Cum autem generale interdictum terre fu[erit],[2] liceat vobis clausis januis, exclusis excommunicatis et [interdicti]s,[3] non pulsatis campanis, suppressa voce, divina o[f]ficia[4] celebrare dummodo causam non dederitis interdicto. Crisma vero, oleum sanctum, consecrationes altarium seu basilicarum, benedictiones monialium a diocesano suscipietis e[piscopo],[5] siquidem catholicus f[uerit, et g]raciam[6] et communionem sacrosancte Romane sedis habuerit, et ea nobis voluerit sine pravitate aliqua exhibere. Prohibemus insuper ut infra fines [par]ochie[7] vestre nullus, sine asscensu diocesani episcopi et vestro, capellam seu oratorium de novo construere audeat, salvis privilegiis pontificum Romanorum. Ad hec novas et indebitas exactiones ab archiepiscopis episcopis archidiaconis seu decanis aliisque omnibus ecclesiasticis secularibusve personis a vobis omnino[8] fieri prohibemus. Sepulturam quoque ipsius loci liberam (fo. 75r)[9] esse decernimus, ut eorum devotioni et extreme voluntati qui se illic sepeliri deliberaverin[t, nisi][10] forte excommunicati vel interdicti sint, aut etiam publice usurarii, nullus obsi[st]at,[11] salva tamen justicia illarum ecclesiarum a quibus mo[r]tuorum[12] corpora assumuntur. Decimas preterea et possessiones ad jus ecclesiarum vestrarum spectantes, que a laicis detinentur[13] redimendi, et legitime deliberandi de manibus eorum, et ad ecclesias ad qu[a]s[14] pertinent revocandi, libera sit vobis

---

1　*decime* marginated before *non.*
2　Unclear 8 mm.
3　Damaged 11 mm.
4　Damaged 2 mm.
5　Unclear 4 mm.
6　Hole 14 mm.
7　Damaged 7 mm.
8　Ins. marg.
9　Heading *Papalis.*
10　Hole 9 mm.
11　Damaged 2 mm.
12　Damaged 1 mm.
13　*decime* marginated after *de-.*
14　Hole 1 mm.

de nostra auctoritate facultas. Obeunte vero te nunc eiusdem loci abbatissa, vel earum aliqua que tibi successerit, nulla ibi qualibet subreptionis astutia, seu violentia prepon[a]tur,[1] nisi quam sorores communi consensu, vel [earum][2] ma[jo]r[3] pars consilii sanioris, secundum Deum et beati Benedicti regulam, providerint eligendam. Paci quoque et tranquillitati vestre paterna in posterum sollicitudine providere volentes,[4] apostolica auctoritate prohibemus, ut infra clausuras locorum vestrorum nullus rapinam seu furtum facere, ignem apponere, sanguinem fundere, hominem temere capere vel interficere, seu violenciam audeat excercere. Preterea omnes libertates et immunitates a predecessoribus nostris Romanis ponti[ficibus][5] monasterio vestro concessas, necnon libertates [et][6] exemptiones secularium exactionum[7] a regibus et principibus vel aliis fidelibus rationabiliter vobis indultas, auctoritate apostolica confirmamus et presentis scripti privilegio communimus. Decernimus ergo ut nulli omnino hominum liceat prefatum monasterium temere perturbare, aut eius possessio[n]es[8] auferre, vel [ablatas r]etinere,[9] minuere seu quibuslibet vex[ati]onibus[10] fatigare,[11] s[ed][12] omnia integ[ra con]s[erv]entur,[13] (fo. 75v)[14] [earum][15] pro quarum gubernatione ac sustentatione concessa sunt usibus om[nimodis][16] profutura, salva sedis apostolice a[uctoritat]e,[17] et diocesani episcopi canonica justicia, et [i]n[18] predictis decimis moderatione consilii generalis. Si qua igitur in futurum ecclesiastica ⟨secularis⟩ve persona hanc nostre constitutionis paginam sciens contra eam temere venire temptaverit, secundo tertiove commonita, nisi reatum suum congrua satisfactione correxerit, potestatis honorisque sui careat

---

1 Hole 3 mm.
2 Hole 5 mm.
3 Hole 3 mm.
4 Followed by *auctoritate*, expunged.
5 Hole 3 mm.
6 Hole 3 mm.
7 MS *exactionem*.
8 Damaged 2 mm.
9 Damaged 16 mm.
10 Damaged 4 mm.
11 Ins. marg.
12 Damaged 4 mm.
13 Hole 16 mm.
14 Heading *Cronica de Herveo episcopo*.
15 Damaged 5 mm.
16 Hole 9 mm.
17 Damaged 13 mm.
18 Damaged 1 mm.

dignitate, reamque se divino judicio[1] existere de perpetrata iniquitate cognoscat, et a sacratissimo corpore ac sanguine Dei et Domini redemptoris nostri Jesu Christi alien[a fiat, atque i]n[2] extremo examine districte subjaceat ultioni. Cunctis autem eidem loco sua jura se[rvant]ibus, sit pax Domini nostri Jesu Christi, quatinus et hic [f]ruc[tum bone][3] actionis percipiant, et aput districtum judi[cem][4] premia eterne pacis inveniant. Amen.

> Note. The privilege was not registered. No trace remains of the earlier bull of Alexander III which is mentioned in the rubric but not in the text of the privilege of Innocent IV. Innocent IV was pope 28 June 1243–7 Dec. 1254.

4 *Narrative concerning the acquisition by Hervey, bishop of Ely, of rights for Ely cathedral over Chatteris abbey.*
fos. 75v–76r [See note below for date]

> Cartulary copies: (A) BL Cotton MS Vesp. A. xix, fos. 32v–34r; (E) Cambridge, Trinity College MS O. 2. 1, fo. 114r; (F) Cambridge UL, EDC 1, fo. 114r; (O) Oxford, Bodl. MS Laud. Misc. 647, fo. 77v.
>
> Transcript in Oxford, Bodl. MS Dodsworth 78, fos. 54v–55r.
>
> Printed in *Mon. Ang.* ii, p. 617, no. 5; *Liber Eliensis* ed. Blake, p. 257.

Quomodo Herveus primus episcopus Eliensis monasterium de Chatriz optinuit et Eliensi ecclesie jure perpetue possessionis de manu regia temporibus perpetuis attribuit.

Est autem Chateriz[5] circa insulam Elyensem[6] s[ancti]monialium[7] habitatio ubi monasterium sub nomine [abbathi]e[8] constitutum, quamdiu sub manu [regia][9] ve[rsaba]t[ur],[10] gravissimis angariis premebatur. Viden[s ita]que[11] vir discretissimus locum districtioni[12] proximum et [pauperes][13] Dei ancillas nimium inqui-

---

1 *reatum ... judicio,* ins. marg.
2 Damaged 19 mm.
3 Damaged 23 mm.
4 Unclear 4 mm
5 A *Chatericht,* EF *Chateriht.*
6 E *Eliensem,* F *Helyensem.*
7 Unclear 2 mm; *lacunae* in this charter supplied from transcript in Oxford, Bodl. MS Dodsworth 78, fos. 54v–55r.
8 Unclear 10 mm; Dodsworth *abbathie,* AEF *abbatie,* O *abbate.*
9 Hole 2 mm.
10 Unclear 14 mm.
11 Damaged 8 mm; Dodsworth *Vidensque utique,* but MS seems to read *Videns* and *Liber Eliensis* has *itaque,* which makes more sense.
12 A *discretioni,* EFO *destructioni.*

etari nec posse [ul]lo[1] modo sine meliore patrocinio locum incoler[e, pater]na[2] pietate ductus episcopalem solicitudinem ad liberandam Christi fa[mil]iam[3] [app]osuit[4] et mira efficacia regium favorem ad sui [de]siderii[5] modum aptavit. Tantoque pondere suscepto, ne[gotio in]stitit,[6] ut locum illum Eliensi[7] ecclesie jure[8] (fo. 76r)[9] perpetue possessionis ascriber[et et deincep]s[10] [matres ibi sta]t-uendi[11] et monachas imponendi principa[lem potesta]tem[12] haberet.[13] Egit hoc itaque[14] misericors manus Domini, ut pater animarum pater esset et rerum et in [omnibus][15] necessitatibus[16] suis, [quibus][17] manus feminea non sufficiebat, filie ad patrem recurrerent et congruum auxilium invenirent. Nemo igitur tantum episcopum putet[18] rebus quidem[19] terrenis multipliciter abundantem aliquam sinistram intentionem in hac causa fuisse sequutum,[20] qui non, ut terreno com-modo[21] consuleret, sed, ut ancille Dei de crastino non cogitarent, allaboravit. Quanto autem[22] robore locum illum sibi suisque successoribus vendicaverit,[23] quanta utilitate locus ille illi cesserit, due sequentes carte testantur, quas regia largitas Elyensi[24] dedit ecclesie.[25]

13 Damaged 12 mm.
1 Hole 4 mm.
2 Damaged 12 mm.
3 Unclear 3 mm.
4 Hole 4 mm.
5 Hole 3 mm.
6 Hole 14 mm.
7 AO *Elyensi*, F *Helyensi*.
8 MS and Dodsworth *vice*.
9 Heading *Carta regis*.
10 Hole 18 mm.
11 Hole 15 mm.
12 Hole 15 mm.
13 F *h'nt*, *haberet* ins. marg.
14 EFO *utique*.
15 *in* followed by caret, but *omnibus* lacking, probably because of damage to margin. Supplied from *Mon. Ang.* ii, p. 617b: omitted from Dodsworth's transcript.
16 E *necessitabus*.
17 Damaged 3 mm.
18 AEFO *putet tantum episcopum*.
19 A omits.
20 A *consecutum*, EFO *secutum*.
21 A *quomodo*.
22 A *etiam*.
23 A *vindicaverint*, EFO *vindicaverit*.
24 E *Eliensi*, F *Helyeni*.
25 A adds *Et de huius sunt*, EFO add *Et hec huius modi sunt*.

Note. This account is taken from Book III of the *Liber Eliensis* which was compiled after 1169 when bishop Nigel died and before 1174 when Geoffrey Ridel, who is not mentioned in the book, became bishop. The earliest surviving *Liber Eliensis* manuscript (E) dates from the late twelfth century (*Liber Eliensis* ed. Blake, pp. xxiii, xlviii).

5 *Gift in alms by Henry I to Ely cathedral and bishop Hervey of Chatteris abbey with its lands and possessions.*

fo. 76r   At St-Pierre-sur-Dives, France [Sept. 1127 × July 1129, perhaps Aug. × Sept. 1127]

> Cartulary copies: (C) Cambridge, Trinity College MS O. 2. 41, pp. 126–7; (D) BL Cotton MS Tib. A. vi, fo. 109r–v; (E) Cambridge, Trinity College MS O. 2. 1, fo. 114r–v; (F) Cambridge UL, EDC 1, fo. 114r; (G) BL Cotton MS Titus A. i, fo. 32r; (M) Cambridge UL, EDR G/3/28 'Liber M', p. 79; (O) Oxford, Bodl. MS Laud. Misc. 647, fo. 77v.
> Cartæ Antiquæ copy: (Y) PRO C 52/2, m. 3d, no. 32a.
> Printed in *Mon. Ang.* ii, p. 617, no. 6; *Liber Eliensis* ed. Blake, p. 258.

Carta regis Henrici de connectione ecclesie de Chatriz monasterio de Ely cum omnibus ad eam pertinentibus.

Henricus rex Anglorum archiepiscopis episcopis abbatibus comitibus vice-comitibus baronibus et omnibus fidelibus[1] totius Anglie[2] salutem.[3] Sciatis[4] me[5] dedisse et concessisse Deo et Elyensi ecclesie[6] et Herveo[7] episcopo in elimosinam abbatiam de Chateriz[8] cum terris et possessionibus et omnibus rebus eidem[9] abbatie[10] pertinentibus. Et volo et precipio firmiter ut bene et[11] in pace[12] et quiete et honorifice teneat[13] cum[14] saca[15] et socha[16] et toll et

---

1   CDM adds *suis.*
2   O omits *abbatibus ... Anglie,* adds *etc.*
3   Y omits *rex ... salutem,* adds *Dei gracia etc.*
4   Followed by *d*, expunged.
5   Y *nos.*
6   F *ecclesie Helyensi*, EG *ecclesie Eliensi*, CDMOY *ecclesie Elyensi.*
7   Y *Herveio.*
8   CD *Chatriz*, E *Chateriht*, F *Chaterhit*, G *Chateric.*
9   D *eiusdem.*
10 Y *ecclesie.*
11 G omits *bene et.*
12 M adds *teneat.*
13 M omits.
14 D omits.
15 CDFGO *sacha*, Y *saka.*
16 D *soccha*, M *soca*, O *soka*, Y *soka.*

theam[1] et infanganetheof[2] et omnibus consuetudinibus et libertatibus, sicut melius et quietius et honorificentius tenet alias terras suas de episcopatu de Ely.[3] Testibus[4] Gauferido[5] cancellario,[6] Willelmo de Alb[eneio][7] pincerna,[8] Gauferido[9] de Clint[une], Pagano filio Johannis.[10] Apud Sanctum Petrum desuper Divam.[11]

Note. The dating is taken from *Liber Eliensis* ed. Blake, p. 258, n. 1.

6 *Grant by Henry I, at the petition of Hervey, bishop of Ely, to Chatteris abbey of the remission of its ward-penny of 6s. 7d. [recte 6s. 8d.].*
fo. 76r–v [At Eling (Hants.), *in transitu meo, c.* August 1127]

Original charter (Ely archive): (X) Cambridge UL, EDC 1/B/5.
Cartulary copies: (C) Cambridge, Trinity College MS O. 2. 41, pp. 127–8; (D) BL Cotton MS Tib. A. vi, fo. 109v; (E) Cambridge, Trinity College MS O. 2. 1, fo. 114v; (F) Cambridge UL, EDC 1, fo. 114r–v; (G) BL Cotton MS Titus A. i, fo. 32r–v; (M) Cambridge UL, EDR G/3/28 'Liber M', p. 79; (O) Oxford, Bodl. MS Laud. Misc. 647, fos. 77v–78r.
Printed in *Mon. Ang.* ii, p. 617, no. 7; *Liber Eliensis* ed. Blake, p. 258.

Carta regis Henrici de relaxatione[12] pecunie de ecclesia de Chatriz quam condonarat sancte Etheldrede. (fo. 76v)[13]

[Henricus re]x[14] Angl[orum ar]chiepiscopis[15] episcopis abbatibus comi[tibus vice]comitibus[16] baronibus[17] et omnibus fidelibus suis [Francis][18] et Anglis

---

1 M *team,* D omits *et toll et theam.*
2 CD *infangentheof,* G *infangathof,* MO *infangenetheof,* Y *infongenþef.*
3 CF *Hely,* Y omits *de Ely,* adds *Elyensi.*
4 CDM *Teste.*
5 CD *Gausfrido,* EF *Gauf',* G *Gaufr',* MO *Gaufrido,* Y *Galfrido.*
6 DM add *et.*
7 G *Aben'.*
8 DM add *et.*
9 CD *Gausfrido,* EF *Gauf',* G *Gaufr'.*
10 O omits *Willelmo ... Johannis,* adds *et aliis.*
11 Y omits *Willelmo ... Divam,* adds *et pluribus aliis.*
12 *Cartam Ricar[di] vide infra folio [ij°],* marginated after *relax-*; edge of folio lacking.
13 Heading *Carta regis.*
14 Hole 14 mm.
15 Hole 9 mm.
16 Hole 12 mm.
17 XCDEFGM *baronibus vicecomitibus.*
18 Damaged 10 mm.

totius Anglie[1] salutem. Sciatis me [con]cessisse[2] ecclesie sancte Marie de Chateriz,[3] quam concessi et dedi in elimosinam ⟨ecclesie⟩[4] de Ely,[5] pro Dei amore[6] et pro[7] anima patris mei[8] et matris mee et pro redemptione peccatorum meorum et petitione Hervei episcopi[9] eiusdem ecclesie primi sex solidos et vij[10] denarios de warpeni,[11] quos predicta ecclesia de Chateriz[12] unoquoque[13] anno dare solebat, ita quod amodo imperpetuum sit[14] inde in pace et quiete. A'.[15]

> Note. The dating is taken from *Liber Eliensis* ed. Blake, p. 258, n. 2. Although this copy and most of the Ely copies of the grant state that the ward-penny was 6s. 7d., the Ely original and the copy in 'Liber M' have 6s. 8d. The latter amount is not only more plausible, being half a mark, but is also the sum given in Richard I's confirmation of the remission of ward-penny (no. 9). The pipe roll for Michaelmas 1130, in an entry for a sum owed by the bishop of Ely, shows that the bishop had assumed responsibility for the abbey's ward-penny (*The Pipe Roll of 31 Henry I* ed. J. Hunter (Record Commission, 1833) p. 44).

7 *Order by Edward III to John de Weasenham, farmer of the temporalities during a vacancy in the see of Ely, to pay to Chatteris abbey the arrears of an annual rent of 20s. from Thriplow mill.*
fos. 76v–77r   At Westminster, 8 May 1358

Copy: (Q) PRO C 54/196, m. 22.

Carta Edwardi regis de allocatione xx[ti] solidorum apud scaccarium Eliensem vacante sede episcopali.

1   O omits *abbatibus ... Anglie*, adds *etc.*
2   XCDMO *condonasse*; F expunges *concedisse* and interlines *condonasse* in a different hand.
3   X *Catriz*, D *Chatriz*, EF *Chateriht*, GO *Chaterich*.
4   XCDEFGMO add *ecclesie*.
5   X *Eli*, F *Hely*.
6   D *amore Dei*.
7   XCDEFGMO omit.
8   X omits.
9   X omits *episcopi* and adds after *primi*.
10 X *viij*, M *octo*.
11 Followed by *ecclesia*, expunged; X *warpeini*, CDMO *wardpeni*.
12 XC *Catriz*, EF *Chateriht*, GO *Chaterich*.
13 X *quoque*.
14 O *sit imperpetuum*.
15 XCDEFGMO omit; XCDEFGM add *Teste Rogero episcopo Saresberiensi et Gaufrido cancellario et Roberto de Sigillo et Willelmo de Tancarvilla et Willelmo de Albeneio pincerna et Radulpho Basset et Gaufrido de Clintune et Willelmo de Ponte Largo. Apud Hellingas in transitu meo.* (For variants in witness-list and dating clause, see *Liber Eliensis* ed. Blake, pp. 258–9); O adds *Test' Rogero episcopo Sarebiriensi et aliis apud Hellingas in transitu meo.*

Edwardus Dei gracia rex Anglie et Francie dominus Ybernye dilecto[1] sibi Johanni de Wesenham firmario[2] temporalium episcopatus Elyensis[3] certis de causis in manu nostra existentium salutem. Quia, per certificationem thesaurarii et baronum de scaccario nostro nobis in cancellaria nostra de mandato nostro missam, est compertum quod tempore domini Henrici quondam regis Anglie proavi et domini Edwardi quondam regis Anglie avi et domini Edwardi nuper regis Anglie patris nostrorum, temporalibus episcopatus predicti tempore predicte vacationis[4] eiusdem in manibus ipsorum progenitorum nostrorum existentibus, allocati fuerunt custodibus temporalium eorundem viginti solidi per annum, soluti abbatisse et monialibus de Chateriz[5] de redditu eis debito de molendino de Trippelowe,[6] qui[7] de pertine[n]c[ii]s[8] temporalium predictorum existunt, et quem quidem redditum [ad][9] scaccarium Elyensem[10] percipere consueverunt ad terminos sancti Michaelis, sancti Andree, Annunciationis beate Marie et sancti Johannis Baptiste, vobis mandamus quod eisdem abbatisse et monialibus id quod eis a retro est de predictis viginti solidis annuis a tempore captionis tempo/ralium (fo. 77r)[11] predictorum in manum nostram de exitibus temporalium eorundem[12] solvi et habere faciatis, prout eis temporibus[13] d[ic-to]rum[14] progenitorum nostrorum solvi consueverunt, r[e]cipiens[15] ab eisdem abbatissa et monialibus litteras suas acqui[etan]cie[16] que sufficientes fuerint in hac parte. Et nos vo[bis][17] inde[18] ad scaccarium nostrum debitam allocationem habere faciemus. [Teste][19] meipso[20] apud Westm' viij die maii anno regni nostri

---

1 Q begins *Rex dilecto.*

2 Q *custodi.*

3 Q *Eliensis.*

4 Q *tempore vacationum*; since *predicte* does not occur in Q and the vacancy is not previously mentioned, the cartulary scribe probably added *predicte* in error here.

5 Q *Chateric'.*

6 Q *Trippelawe.*

7 MS *que.*

8 Holes 2 mm and 3 mm.

9 Unclear 5 mm.

10 Q *Eliensem.*

11 Heading *Carta regis ad manum mortuam.*

12 Q *predictorum.*

13 MS *temporalibus.*

14 Unclear 3 mm.

15 Hole 1 mm.

16 Damaged 5 mm.

17 Hole 4 mm.

18 Q adds *in compoto vestro.*

19 Damaged 5 mm.

Anglie tricesimo secundo, regni nostri Francie decimo nono. Consimile breve pro abbatissa perquisitum est[1] iiij[to] die februarii anno xxx[mo] iiij[to] et irrotulatur in cancellaria.[2]

8 *Grant by Edward III to Chatteris abbey of a licence to acquire property to the value of £10 annually, the statute of mortmain notwithstanding.*
fo. 77r At Westminster, 27 Jan. 1331/2

    Copy: (R) PRO C 66 178, m. 29.

Carta Edwardi regis de adquirendo ad manum mortuam statuto non obstante.

Edwardus Dei gracia rex Anglie dominus Hibernye et dux Aquietannie omnibus ad quos presentes littere pervenerint salutem.[3] Sciatis quod de gracia nostra speciali concessimus et licenciam dedimus pro nobis et heredibus nostris, quantum in nobis est, dilectis nobis in Christo abbatisse et conventui de Chateriz[4] quod ipsi terras tenementa et redditus cum pertinenciis ad valentiam decem librarum per annum juxta verum valorem eorumdem, tam de feodo suo proprio quam alieno, exceptis terris tenementis et redditibus que de nobis tenentur in capite, adquirere possint, habenda et tenenda sibi et successoribus suis imperpetuum, statuto de terris et tenementis ad manum mortuam non ponendis edito non obstante. Dum tamen per inquisitiones inde in forma[5] debita faciendas, et in cancellaria nostra vel heredum nostrorum rite retornandas, compertum sit quod id fieri poterit absque damno et prejudicio nostro et heredum nostrorum ac alterius cuiuscumque. In cuius rei testimonium has litteras nostras fieri fecimus patentes.[6] Teste [me]ipso[7] apud Westm' vicesimo septimo die jan[uarii ann]o[8] regni nostri sexto.[9]

    Note. Another copy of no. 255.

---

20 Q *rege.*
1 Interlined.
2 Q omits *anno regni ... cancellaria.*
3 R begins *Rex omnibus ad quos etc. salutem.*
4 R *Chaterice.*
5 Followed by *ta*, expunged.
6 Ins. marg.; R omits *rei ... patentes*, adds *etc.*
7 Unclear 4 mm; R *rege.*
8 Hole 15 mm.
9 R omits *anno ... sexto*, adds *per breve de privato sigillo.*

9 *Confirmation by Richard I to Ely cathedral and bishop elect William [Longchamp] of Chatteris abbey and of the remission of its ward-penny of 6s. 8d.*
fo. 77r–v   At Westminster, 10 Oct. 1189

Cartulary copy: a copy of the renovation of this charter, dated 2 July 1198, is in Cambridge UL, EDR G/3/28 'Liber M', p. 94.

Confirmatio regis Ricardi super (fo. 77v)[1] connectione ecclesie de Chatriz monasterio Eliensi.

Ricardus Dei gracia rex Anglie dux Normannie et Aquietannie comes Andegavie archiepiscopis episcopis abbatibus comitibus baronibus justiciariis vicecomitibus ministris et omnibus balivis et fidelibus salutem. Sciatis nos concessisse et presenti carta nostra confirmasse Elyensi ecclesie et Willelmo eiusdem ecclesie electo, pro salute anime nostre et Henrici regis patris nostri et a[ntec]essorum[2] nostrorum, donationem quam Henricus rex proavus noster dedit et concessit Herveo primo Elyensi episcopo in elimosinam, scilicet abbathiam de Chateriz cum terris et possessionibus et omnibus rebus eidem abbathie pertinentibus. Et volumus et firmiter precipimus quod iam dictus electus habeat et teneat bene et in pace libere et quiete integre plenarie et honorifice prenominatam abbathiam cum sok et sak et toll et them infongenethef et omnibus libertatibus et consuetudinibus quas habet in aliis terris suis de episcopatu Elyensi, et sit ipsa abbathia de Chateriz quieta de vj solidis viij denariis de warpeny quos ecclesia unoquoque anno dare solebat. Testibus H(ugone) Dunelmensi episcopo, Ricardo London' electo, Willelmo de Sancto Johanne, Hugone Bardolf, Gaufrido filio Petri, Roberto de Whitefeld'. Data per manus eiusdem Willelmi de Longo Campo cancellarii nostri[3] Elyensis electi, apud Westm' x° die octobris anno primo regni nostri.

Note. Hugh du Puiset was bishop of Durham in 1189. No. 5 is the gift by Henry I to bishop Hervey of Chatteris abbey; no. 6 is Henry I's grant of the remission of ward-penny to Chatteris abbey.

10 *Grant by Nigel, bishop of Ely, to Chatteris abbey of the lordship and advowson of the church of St Peter, Chatteris.*
fos. 77v–78r   [*c.* 1158 × 30 May 1169]

[1] Heading *Chateriz.*
[2] Hole 4 mm.
[3] MS *cancellarii r nostro.*

Donatio domini Nigelli episcopi Eliensis de dominio et advocatione ecclesie parochie beati Petri in Chatriz.

Nigellus Dei gratia etc. Sciatis nos dedisse et presenti carta confirmasse sanctimonialibus Deo et ecclesie sancte Marie in ecclesia de Chateriz servientibus dominium et advocationem ecclesie beati Petri in Chateriz. Quare volumus et firmiter precipimus ut beneficia prefate ecclesie, post decessum personarum eiusdem ecclesie Walteri Phil' et Rogeri Crochem, ad usum et ad (fo. 78r)[1] [nec]essit[ates ecclesie earum sustentandas cum omnibus][2] pertinenciis suis perveniant. Testibus etc.

Note. Another copy of no. 76. For dating and annotation see no. 76n.

11 *Confirmation by John [of Fountains], bishop of Ely, to Chatteris abbey of the appropriation of the church of St Peter, Chatteris, to the vicarage of which church the nuns will present a chaplain who will have 4 marks annually from altar-dues with the house formerly of Matilda de Barley.*
fo. 78r [8 March 1220 × 6 May 1225]

Carta collationis seu confirmationis eiusdem ecclesie beati Petri per episcopum Johannem.

Universis Christi fidelibus ad quos presens scriptum pervenerit Johannes Dei gracia Elyensis episcopus salutem in Domino. Quoniam ex cura nobis commissa inopie et egestati pauperum et maxime religiosorum paterna affectione providere tenemur, nos attendentes paupertatem et honestatem dilectarum in Christo filiarum monialium de Chateriz, ecclesiam [sancti][3] Petri eiusdem ville cum omnibus pertinenciis suis, domus pietatis intuitu et pro salute animarum virorum venerabilium episcoporum Elyensium predecessorum nostrorum et [nostr]a,[4] eisdem monialibus ad sustentationem domus sue, in proprios usus habendam, contulimus et presenti carta nostra confirmavimus, salva vicaria cuidam capellano quem ipse moniales ad dictam vicariam presentabunt, qui curam habebit animarum, videlicet quatuor marcis de altaragio ipsius ecclesie annuatim percipiendis cum mansione que fuit Matill' de Berlee, salvis etiam nobis et successoribus nostris jure pontificali et parochiali. Ut igitur hec nostra

---

1 Heading *Chateriz.*
2 Damaged 66 mm; supplied from no. 76, the other copy of this charter.
3 Damaged 4 mm.
4 Damaged 4 mm.

collatio et confirmatio perpetuum firmitatis robur optineant, eam presentis scripti munimine et sigilli nostri appositione communimus. Hiis testibus etc.

Note. John of Fountains was bishop of Ely 8 March 1220–6 May 1225.

12 *Confirmation by Roger [de Bergham], prior of Ely, to Chatteris abbey of no. 11.* fo. 78r–v [8 March 1220 × early 1229]

Confirmatio domini Rogeris prioris et totius conventus[1] Eliensis de eadem ecclesia.

Universis etc. Rogerus prior Eliensis ecclesie et totus conventus eiusdem loci salutem in Domino. Noverit universitas vestra nos, a solo Deo remunerationem expectantes et venerabilis patris nostri Johannis Elyensis episcopi dona/tionem (fo. 78v)[2] et con[firmationem ratam et gratam habentes],[3] monialibus de Chateriz hac presenti carta nostra confirmasse ecclesiam sancti Petri eiusdem ville, quam venerabilis pater noster Johannes episcopus Elyensis in proprios usus habendam cum omnibus pertinenciis suis eisdem monialibus contulit et confirmavit, sicut in eiusdem carta continetur, salvis vicarie quatuor marcis de altaragio, quas quidam capellanus, quem ipse moniales ad dictam vicariam presentabunt, cum mansione que fuit Matill' de Berlee annuatim percipiet, qui eidem ecclesie [de]ser[viet][4] et curam habebit animarum, salvo etiam venerabili pa[tre][5] nostro Elyensi episcopo et successoribus suis jure pontificali et parochiali. Ut igitur hec nostra confirmatio perpetuum robur optineat, presens scriptum sigillo capituli nostri roboravimus. Hiis testibus etc.

Note. Another copy of no. 78. Roger de Bergham was prior of Ely before Feb. 1215–early 1229 (*Fasti 1066–1300* ii, p. 49); John of Fountains was bishop of Ely 8 March 1220–6 May 1225.

13 *Confirmation by John [of Fountains], bishop of Ely, to Chatteris abbey of whatsoever the abbey possesses in Chatteris and of his fee, and of all gifts made from his fee.* fo. 78v [8 March 1220 × 6 May 1225]

Carta domini Johannis episcopi Eliensis de terris tenementis piscariis et aliis in Chatriz.

1 Followed by *et conve*, expunged.
2 Heading *Chateriz*.
3 Damaged 50 mm; *lacunae* in this charter supplied from no. 78, the other copy of the charter.
4 Holes 4 mm and 6 mm.
5 Hole 2 mm.

Universis etc. Johannes Dei gracia etc. Noverit universitas vestra nos intuitu caritatis concessisse et presenti carta nostra confirmasse Deo et ecclesie beati Marie de Chateriz et monialibus ibidem Deo servientibus quicquid habent et de jure possident in villa de Chateriz et de feodo nostro, necnon et omnes donationes in terris in redditibus in piscariis in pratis in pascuis et pasturis et omnibus aliis, que de feodo nostro sunt eisdem factas et concessas, sicut in cartis donatorum plenius testatis. Et ut hec nostra concessio et confirmatio futuris temporibus valitura permaneat, eam presentis[1] scripti munimine et sigilli nostri appositione roboravimus. Hiis testibus etc.

> Note. The relatively simple language of this charter suggests that it must have been issued by John of Fountains, bishop of Ely 8 March 1220–6 May 1225, rather than by one of the later Johns who were bishop of Ely.

14 *Cancelled duplicate of no. 13.*
fos. 78v–79r

Universis sancte matris ecclesie etc. Johannes Dei gracia Elyensis episcopus salutem in Domino. Noverit universitas vestra (fo. 79r)[2] nos intuitu caritatis concessisse et presenti carta nostra confirmasse[3] Deo et ecclesie sancte Marie de Chateriz et monialibus ibidem Deo servientibus quicquid habent et de jure possident in villa de Chateriz de feodo nostro, necnon et omnes donationes in terris et redditibus in piscariis in pratis in pascuis et pasturis[4] et in omnibus aliis, que de feodo sunt eisdem factas et concessas.

15 *Confirmation by Hugh [de Northwold], bishop of Ely, to Chatteris abbey of the land in Chatteris given to the abbey by William Owen; for 10d., formerly 5d., annually.*
fo. 79r [10 June 1229 × 6 Aug. 1254]

Confirmatio domini Hugonis episcopi Eliensis de terra Willelmi Owe'[5] in Chatriz.[6]

---

1 MS *presenti.*
2 Heading *Chateriz.*
3 Recopying of charter corrected by use of *vacat:* -*cat* marginated after *con*-; but *va*- lacking in damaged left margin.
4 *et pasturis*, ins. marg. after *pascuis.*
5 End of name lost at edge of folio.

Omnibus[1] Christi fidelibus etc. Hugo Dei gracia Elyensis episcopus salutem in Domino. Noveritis nos concessisse et hac presenti carta nostra confirmasse Deo et beate Marie et abbatisse et monialibus de Chateriz totam illam terram cum pertinenciis quam Willelmus Oeyn dedit eisdem, tenendam et habendam dictis abbatisse et monialibus de nobis et successoribus nostris libere quiete bene et[2] in pace, reddendo inde nobis annuatim et successoribus nostris et hundredo nostro de Ely decem denarios, ubi prius reddi solebant quinque denarii, ad quatuor terminos censuales pro sectis curie consuetudinibus et demandis. In cuius rei testimonium presenti scripto sigillum nostrum fecimus apponi. Hiis testibus etc.

> Note. Hugh de Northwold was bishop of Ely 10 June 1229–6 Aug. 1254. The bishop doubled the rent he received when he confirmed the gift by William Owen to the abbey (nos. 17/59). This rent was paid to the hundred (Miller *Abbey and Bishopric of Ely*, pp. 107n, 117n).

16 *Declaration by Hugh [de Balsham], bishop of Ely, that Chatteris abbey acquired the parish churches of Chatteris and Shepreth canonically and that it is sufficiently strengthened by papal quthority and by these letters to possess them.*
fo. 79r–v At Little Downham, 5 Aug. 1262

Dimissio domini Hugonis episcopi Eliensis de ecclesiis de Chateriz et Scheperede in sua visitatione.

Universis Christi fidelibus presentes litteras visuris vel audituris Hugo Dei gracia episcopus Elyensis salutem in Domino sempiternam. Noverit universitas vestra quod nos, inspectis et examinatis instrumentis et cartis predecessorum nostrorum et capituli nostri Elyensis, que seu quas dilecte in Christo filie sanctimoniales de Chateriz coram nobis auctoritate apostolica ad docendum de jure quod habent in ecclesiis parochialibus de Chateriz et de Seperheye nostre diocesis legitime vocate in presentia nostra exhibuerunt, quod eedam moniales dictas ecclesias canonice (fo. 79v)[3] sunt assecute et quod sufficienter ad dicta beneficia optinenda sunt munite tam apostolica auctoritate quam nostra tenore presentium pronunciamus, ad futuram rei memoriam presens scriptum sigilli nostri appositione signatum predictis monialibus concedentes in testimonium. Dat' apud Douunham nonas augusti anno Domini M° CC° sexagesimo secundo.

---

6   *Confirmatio ... Chatriz*, ins. marg.; rubric above charter, *Dimissio domini Hugonis episcopi Eliensis de ecclesiis de Chatriz et Scheperede in sua visitatione*, corrected by *vacat*, in red in margin.
1   MS *Umnibus* (guide-letter and decorated initial both incorrect).
2   *nota x denarii hundredo de Ely*, marginated after *et*.
3   Heading *Chateriz*.

Note. Another copy of no. 77.

17 *Gift in free alms by William Owen to Chatteris abbey of 2 messuages and all his land with meadows and liberties in Chatteris.*
fo. 79v [*s*. xiii[1] × 6 Aug. 1254]

Donum Willelmi Owyn' de duobus mesuagiis in Chatriz.

Sciant presentes etc. quod ego Willelmus filius Owini dedi etc. domui beate Marie de Chateriz et sanctimonialibus ibidem Deo servientibus pro salute anime mee et animabus antecessorum meorum duo mesuagia in villa de Chateriz, scilicet unum mesuagium quod jacet inter mesuagium Roberti filii Gilberti et mesuagium Johannis coci, et unum mesuagium quod jacet inter mesuagium Radulphi de Berlee et mesuagium Roberti le Vite,[1] et totam terram quam tenui in villa de Chateriz, et cum pratis et libertatibus et omnibus pertinenciis ad predictam terram pertinentibus, tenenda et habenda in puram elimosinam libere et quiete, salvo servicio domini feodi. Et ego Willelmus et heredes mei warantizabimus[2] predicta mesuagia cum nominata terra supradictis monialibus et predictum servicium imperpetuum contra omnes gentes. Et ut hec mea donatio etc.

Note. Another copy of no. 59. For confirmation and dating see no. 15n.

18 *Gift in free alms by Ralph de Barley to Chatteris abbey of 2 messuages in Chatteris and a parcel of land with a croft [in Chatteris].*
fos. 79v–80r [*s*. xiii[1-3]]

Donum Radulphi de Berlee de duobus mesuagiis et una particula terre in Chatriz.

Sciant etc. quod ego Radulphus de Berlee dedi etc. Deo et ecclesie beate Marie de Chateriz et monialibus ibidem Deo servientibus duo mesuagia cum pertinenciis in Chateriz, scilicet mesuagium illud quod Johannes cocus de me tenuit in eadem villa cum crofta jacente et mesuagium quod Alicia Mayseynt similiter de me (fo. 80r)[3] tenuit in eadem villa. Preterea reddidi dictis monialibus quandam particulam terre jacentem in campo de Horshee juxta terram predicti Radulphi de Berle, et abuttat super terram quondam Willelmi Oen et super

---

1 *Roberti Hotte* in no. 59, the other copy of the charter.
2 Followed by *pres*, expunged.
3 Heading *Chateriz*.

terram Jacobi filii Willelmi le Ladman, una cum crofta earum quam habui de predicta terra, habenda et tenenda predictis monialibus in liberam et puram et perpetuam elimosinam de me et heredibus imperpetuum. Et ego Radulphus et heredes mei warantizabimus acquietabimus et defendemus predicta mesuagia et predictam terram cum pertinenciis predictis monialibus contra omnes mortales imperpetuum. Et ut hec mea donatio etc.

> Note. Ralph de Barley is a witness in 1239 × *s.* xiii[3] (no. 240) and occurs *s.* xiii[1] × 6 Aug. 1254 (no. 17).

19 *Gift in free alms by Robert son of John, scribe, with the assent of his lord, Ralph Briston, to Chatteris abbey of a croft and all his land and adjacent meadow beyond his dike [in Chatteris].*
fo. 80r [s. xii[4] × 1235]

Carta Roberti filii Johannis scriptoris de quodam crofto et prato in Chatriz.

Sciant presentes etc. quod ego Robertus filius Johannis scriptoris consilio et assensu domini mei Radulphi Briston' dedi etc. Deo et ecclesie sancte Marie de Chateriz et sanctimonialibus ibidem Deo servientibus croftum unum in puram et perpetuam elimosinam, pro animabus patris mei et matris et pro anima mea et uxoris mee, quod croftum jacet inter me et Robertum le Nor[eis][1] et abuttat super stratam, habens in latitudine versus stratam quatuor perticas et quinque pedes, et in latitudine versus mariscum quatuor perticas, et in longitudine novem perticas, et totam terram meam et pratum adjacens extra fossatum meum, habenda et possidenda imperpetuum libere et quiete et honorifice, sine omni servicio consuetudine et demanda. Ego autem et heredes mei[2] warantizabimus predicte ecclesie predictum tenementum contra omnes gentes. Et ut hec donatio mea etc.

> Note. Ralph Briston, father of Ismaena, seems to have died before 1235 (no. 24). Robert le Noreises occur in Cambs. in *s.* xiii[1] × 1233, and in 1235–6 and 1242–3 (no. 281; *Book of Fees* i, p. 493; ii, p. 924).

20 *Grant by Ismaena daughter of Ralph Briston to Chatteris abbey of the homage of John Cade and the rent of ½d. [?in Chatteris] which he used to pay to her.*
fo. 80r–v [s. xiii[1–2]]

---

[1] Unclear 5 mm.
[2] MS *me*.

Donatio Ismaene filie[1] Radulphi Briston' de homagio Johannis Cade.

Sciant presentes etc. quod ego Ismaena filia Radulphi Bryston' dedi etc. Deo et domui de Chateriz et sanctimoni/[ali]bus[2] (fo. 80v)[3] ibidem Deo servientibus pro animabus omnium predecessorum [m]eorum[4] in puram et perpetuam elimosinam homagium Johannis Cade et redditum cuiusdam oboli quem idem Johannes michi reddere consuevit in die sancti Michaelis. Et ego Ismaena et heredes mei warantizabimus prefatum homagium cum predicto redditu contra omnes homines. In cuius rei testimonium.

Note. For dating of Ismaena see nos. 21n and 24n.

21 *Grant by Ismaena daughter of Ralph Briston, for the souls of her parents and of Adelicia wife of Ralph de Barley, to the almonry of Chatteris abbey of an annual rent of 4d. [?in Chatteris] which Ralph de Barley pays to her, for 2s. from Ralph de Barley.*
fo. 80v [*s.* xiii[1-2]]

Sciant presentes etc. quod ego Ismaena filia Radulfi Briston' dedi etc. in puram et perpetuam elimosinam,[5] et pro anima patris[6] mei et matris mee et etiam pro anima Adilicie uxoris Radulfi de Berlee, redditum iiij[or] denariorum ad elimosinam domus[7] sancte Marie de Chateriz, redditum scilicet illum quem dictus Radulfus ⟨persolvit⟩[8] michi per annum ad quatuor terminos, ut idem redditus ⟨ab eodem Radulfo⟩[9] et a suis assignatis predicte elimosine sancte Marie de Chateriz persolvatur ad unum terminum anni, videlicet in vigilia Natalis Domini. Et ego Ismaena et heredes mei warantizabimus hanc concessionem[10] et donationem nostram tanquam puram elimosinam contra omnes. Pro hac autem concessione donatione et warentizatione, dedit michi predictus Radulfus de Berle duos solidos. Ut vero hec carta firma sit et stabilis etc.

---

1 MS *filia.*
2 Damaged 3 mm.
3 Heading *Chateriz.*
4 Damaged 3 mm.
5 MS *elesimosinam.*
6 *De iiij[or] denariis ad elimosinariam,* marginated before *patris.*
7 Followed by *sue,* expunged.
8 cf. no. 70.
9 cf. no. 70.
10 Followed by *et donationem,* expunged.

Note. Another copy of no. 70. Ralph de Barley is a witness in 1239 × s. xiii³ (no. 240) and occurs *s*. xiii¹ × 6 Aug. 1254 (no. 17). Ralph Briston, father of Ismaena, seems to have died before 1235 (no. 24). The Ralph de Briston who held half a knight's fee in Briston (Norf.) in 1242–3 seems to have been another man (*Book of Fees* ii, p. 906).

22 *Surrender by Henry de Merchyt to Chatteris abbey of 2 roods of land [in Chatteris] given by Ismaena, his wife.*
fos. 80v–81r [s. xiii¹⁻²]

Donum Henricy de Merthyt de duabus rodis terre in Chatriz.

Sciant presentes etc. quod ego Henricus de Merchyt¹ reddidi et liberavi pro animabus antecessorum meorum, per petitionem Ismanie uxoris mee, ad ecclesiam sancte Marie de Chateriz et conventum eiusdem loci illas duas rodas terre cum pertinenciis que Ismaena uxor mea dedit ad ecclesiam sancte Marie de Chateriz et conventum² eiusdem loci. Et ego predictus Henricus affidavi quod warantizabo contra omnes homines tota vita Ismaene uxoris m[ee]³ illas predictas rodas terre cum pertinenciis⁴ (fo. 81r)⁵ quas Ismaena predicta uxor mea dedit per concessionem ⟨meam ad ecclesiam sancte Marie de Chatriz et conventui loci eiusdem. Et propter istam concessionem⟩⁶ et confirmationem ratum⁷ esse tenetur. Et ego Henricus confirmo sigillo meo. Hiis testibus etc.

Note. Another copy of no. 64. Ismaena's gift is no. 24. For dating, see no. 24n.

23 *Gift in free alms by Robert son of John, scribe, with the assent of his lord, Ralph Briston, to Chatteris abbey of his messuage in Chatteris.*
fo. 81r [s. xii⁴ × 1235]

Donum Roberti filii Johannis scriptoris de quodam mesuagio.

Sciant presentes etc. quod ego Robertus filius Johannis scriptoris, consilio et assensu domini mei Radulphi Briston', dedi etc. Deo et ecclesie sancte Marie de Chateriz et sancti[monialibus]⁸ ibidem Deo servientibus totum mesuagium

---

¹ Followed by *Ysmanie*, erroneously copied here.
² Corr. from *conventui*.
³ Unclear 4 mm.
⁴ Followed by catchwords, *quas predicta*.
⁵ Heading *Chatriz*.
⁶ Omitted words supplied from no. 64, the other copy of the charter.
⁷ MS *rat'*: cf. penultimate sentence of no. 24.
⁸ Hole 7 mm.

meum in Chateriz integre quod jacet juxta Herbertum filium Gilberti apud A...lonem,[1] scilicet quod Johannes pater meus tenuit [o]mnibus[2] diebus vite sue, libere in puram et perpetuam eli[mo]sin[am][3] pro animabus patris mei et matris mee et pro anima uxoris mee, habendum et tenendum et possidendum imperpetuum libere quiete et honorifice, sine omni servicio consuetudine et demanda. Ego autem et heredes mei warantizabimus predicte ecclesie pred[ictum mesuagium][4] contra omnes homines. Et ut hec donatio m[ea][5] etc.

Note. For dating of Ralph Briston see no. 21n.

24 *Gift in free alms by Ismaena daughter of Ralph Briston to Chatteris abbey of 2 roods of land in Chatteris.*
fo. 81r–v [*s.* xiii[1] × 1235]

Donum Ismaene Briston' de duabus rodis terre.

Sciant etc. quod ego Ismaena filia Radulphi Briston' dedi etc. ad ecclesiam sancte Marie de Chateriz et conventum[6] eiusdem loci in elimosinam perpetuam duas rodas terre mee cum pertinenciis in campis de Chatriz, et p[ro animabus pat]ris[7] et matris mee et pro animabus antecessorum meorum et pro animabus heredum meorum, et quod istam elimosinam et[8] predictam[9] terram warantizabunt, scilicet illam rodam terre cum pertinenciis que jacet in campo de Horshee, que abuttat super alteram viam inter terram domini Wari[ni][10] de Saham et terram Roberti ⟨filii⟩[11] Stephani, et illam rodam[12] terre [cum][13] pertinenciis que jacet in campo de Horingsla[de][14] in[t]er[15] terram Katerine de Cov[neya] ...,[16] sci-

---

1 Damaged 6 mm.
2 Hole 2 mm.
3 Damaged 12 mm.
4 Hole 13 mm.
5 Hole 4 mm.
6 Corr. from *conventui*.
7 Hole 19 mm.
8 Ins. marg.
9 Followed by *et*, expunged.
10 Hole 3 mm.
11 Supplied from no. 45, the other copy of this charter.
12 MS *illa roda*.
13 Hole 3 mm.
14 Hole 3 mm.
15 Damaged 2 mm.
16 Hole 32 mm; perhaps *et Markis* lacking, cf. no. 45.

licet e[go]¹ Isma[ena et]² heredes [mei warantizabimus predictam terram cum pertinenciis]³ (fo. 81v)⁴ contra omnes homines et elemosinam predicte ecclesie et conventui eiusdem loci, et propter istam donationem et elimosinam et confirmationem ratum esse tenetur. Ego Ismaena confirmavi sigillum meum etc.

Note. Another copy of no. 45. See also no. 22. Warin de Saham occurs *c.* 1210 and died in 1235 (*VCH Cambs.* viii, p. 145). For dating of Ismaena see no. 21n.

25 *Gift in free alms by Robert le Noreis, with the assent of his wife, Margaret, and heir, Azo, to Chatteris abbey of 2 selions of land [?in Chatteris], 1 of which he bought from Robert son of John.*
fo. 81v [*s.* xiii¹⁻²]

Donum Roberti le Noreis de uno sellione terre.

Sciant presentes etc. quod ego Robertus le Noreis, consilio et assensu uxoris mee Margarete et Azonis heredis mei, dedi etc. in puram et perpetuam elimosinam Deo et ecclesie sancte Marie de Chateriz et monialibus ibidem Deo servientibus unum sellionem terre mee in Fligellis, que abuttat super fossatam, et unum sellionem in Frangkwode juxta Galfridum de Coveneye, quem emi de Roberto filio Johannis, pro salute anime mee et uxoris mee et parentum meorum. Ego Robertus et heredes mei warantizabimus predictas partes terre pre[dicte]⁵ ecclesie etc.

Note. Another copy of no. 41. For dating of Robert le Noreis see no. 19n; Azo le Noreis was dead by 1235 × *s.* xiii³ (nos. 32 and 67).

26 *Confirmation by Michael Peregrinus to Chatteris abbey of the tenement [?in Chatteris] given by his father, Henry Peregrinus, with Tecla, daughter of Henry and sister of Michael.*
fos. 81v–82r [*s.* xii⁴ × *s.* xiii²]

Confirmatio Michaelis Pere[grini]⁶ quam fecit super cartam patris sui.⁷

---

¹ Hole 5 mm.
² Hole 10 mm.
³ Hole 75 mm: the words lacking have been supplied from no. 45.
⁴ Heading *Chatriz*.
⁵ Hole 6 mm.
⁶ Unclear 6 mm.
⁷ Heading written in black, underlined in red.

Omnibus sancte matris etc. Michael Peregrinus salutem in Domino. Sciatis me concessisse etc. in puram et perpetuam elimo[sin]am[1] Deo et ecclesie s[anct]e[2] Marie de Chateriz et c[onve]ntui[3] eiusdem loci donationem totius tenementi quod pater meus Henricus Peregrinus[4] eidem[5] ecclesie[6] contulit cum Tecla filia sua, sorore mea, in terra in bosco et aliis pertinenciis, preter piscationem quam eis non dedit. Hanc autem concessionem et carte mee confirmationem predicto domui feci sicut heres socagii predicti Henrici patris mei, pro salute anime m[ee][7] et predecessorum meorum et heredum meorum. Et preterea quia conventus predicte d[omu]s[8] de Chatriz suscepit in ...[9] Teclam sor[or]em[10] (fo. 82r)[11] meam ad preces meas quousque in tempora mea habitum sanctimonialis suscipere detulerat. Et ideo volo et firmiter concedo quod predicta domus de Chatriz predictum teneat tenementum bene et in pace, liberum et absolutum ab omni servicio seculari quod ad me et heredes meos pertinet. Hiis testibus etc.

Note. The dating is based solely on the language of the charter.

27 *Gift in free alms by Azo son of Robert le Noreis, with the consent of his heirs, to Chatteris abbey of his* cultura *called 'Wodecroft' with a close and dike [?in Chatteris].*
fo. 82r [*s.* xiii[1-3]]

Donatio Azonis le Nores de cultura de Wodecroft.

Sciant etc. quod ego Azo filius Roberti le Noreis, consensu et voluntate heredum meorum, dedi etc. Deo et ecclesie sancte Marie de Chateriz et monialibus ibidem Deo servientibus in puram et perpetuam elemosinam totam culturam meam que vocatur Wodecroft, cum claustura[12] et fossa et eius pertinenciis, que jacet inter nemus predictarum monialium ex parte una et mariscum ex altera parte, tenendam et habendam de me et heredibus meis sibi et

1	Hole 8 mm.
2	Hole 8 mm.
3	Hole 11 mm.
4	Followed by *eiusdem*, expunged.
5	Ins. marg.
6	Repeated and expunged.
7	Hole 3 mm.
8	Hole 9 mm.
9	Hole 53 mm.
10	Hole 3 mm.
11	Heading *Chatriz*.
12	*vide culturam de Wodecroft*, marginated after *clau-*.

successoribus suis imperpetuum libere quiete honorifice hereditarie ab omni consu[e]t[u]dine[1] seculari et exactione. Et ego Azoto et heredes mei defendemus et warantizabimus illam predictam culturam dictis m[on]ialibus[2] et successoribus suis contra omnes etc. E[t][3] ut hec etc.

Note. Another copy of no. 40. Azo le Noreis was dead by 1235 × *s*. xiii[3] (nos. 32 and 67).

28 *Gift in free alms by John Fithien of Chatteris to Chatteris abbey of a* cultura *called* Stocking *with a headland and ½ acre of land called 'le Wellestolt" in Chatteris.*
fo. 82r–v [*s*. xiii[3] × 1290]

Donatio Johannis Fichyen de cultura de Stokkyng'.

Sciant et presentes etc. quod [eg]o[4] Johannes Fichien de Chateriz dedi et concessi etc. abbatisse et conventui et beate genitrici eiusdem et omnibus [sanctis in][5] monasterio de Chatriz famulantibus totam illam [c]ulturam[6] terre mee[7] que vocatur le Stokkyng cum omnibus pertinenciis suis, et cum una capitera que jacet de longo in longum ad capu[t][8] boreale predicte culture in campo qui dicitur [E]llemannesfeld'[9] [in villa de][10] Chatriz, et abuttat ...[11] culture super terram et (fo. 82v)[12] pratum domine Basilie de Saham, et unam dimidiam acram terre mee que vocatur le Wellestolt' cum omnibus suis pertinenciis, que jacet in campo de molendino ad ventum dicte abbatisse versus Horshethe, habendam et tenendam de me et heredibus meis vel meis assignatis in puram et perpetuam elimosinam totam predictam terram cum omnibus pertinenciis suis predictis abbatisse et conventui et omnibus suis successoribus libere quiete integre bene et in pace. Et ego predictus Johannes et heredes mei vel mei assignati warantizabimus defendemus et acquietabimus totam predictam culturam terre cum predictis capitera et dimidia acra et cum omnibus pertinenciis suis predictis

1 Two holes, both 3 mm.
2 Hole 4 mm.
3 Unclear 3 mm.
4 Hole 6 mm.
5 Damaged 12 mm.
6 Hole 2 mm.
7 *vide culturam de Stokkyng'*, marginated after *mee*.
8 Hole 2 mm.
9 Hole 2 mm.
10 Unclear 17 mm.
11 Hole 48 mm.
12 Heading *Chatriz*.

abbatisse et conventui et earum successoribus contra omnes gentes imperpetuum. In cuius rei testimonium etc.

Note. John Fithien occurs in 1289 and shortly before 8 July 1298 × 27 March 1306 (Ault ed.
Ramsey Court Rolls, pp. 278–9; nos. 38 and 63). Basilia de Saham occurs in 1271 (*Cal. IPM* i,
p. 273, no. 807).

29 *Quitclaim by Juliana formerly wife of Henry Fithien of Chatteris to Chatteris*
abbey of a cultura *called Stocking [in Chatteris], formerly of Henry her husband.*
fo. 82v [*s.* xiii³ × 1290]

Quieta clamantia Juliane Fichien de cultura le Stokking'.

Notum etc. quod ego J[uliana]¹ quondam uxor Henrici Fichien de Chatriz, in
ligi[tima vidueta]te² mea, imperpetuum quietum clamavi a[bbatisse et]³ conventui de Chateriz et omnibus earum succes[soribus]⁴ totum jus et totum
clamium quod habui vel habere ...⁵ potero in futurum nomine dotis in cultura
que vo[catur le]⁶ Stokking' seu in aliqua sui parte, que jacet in campo qui
vocatur Elmenesfeld', que fuit quon[dam]⁷ predicti Henrici viri mei, ita quod
nec ego nec aliqui[s nomine]⁸ meo de cetero aliquod jus vel clamium in dicta
[cultura]⁹ seu in aliqua sui parte aliquo modo exig[ere] valeamus. In cuius rei
testimonium etc.

Note. For dating see no. 28, the gift which probably precedes this quitclaim.

30 *Exchange between Ralph de Barley and Chatteris abbey of ½ acre of land in*
Chatteris for a croft formerly of Richard Fader'.
fos. 82v–83r [*s.* xiii¹⁻³]

Donatio Radulphi de Berle de dimidia acra in Gravesten'.¹⁰

---

¹ Hole 13 mm.
² Hole 18 mm.
³ Hole 13 mm.
⁴ Hole 9 mm.
⁵ Hole 17 mm.
⁶ Hole 12 mm.
⁷ Unclear 6 mm.
⁸ Hole 11 mm.
⁹ Unclear 12 mm.
¹⁰ Or *Granesten'*?

Sciant presentes etc. quod ego Radulphus de Berle dedi etc. conventui de Chatriz un[a]m[1] dimidiam acram terre mee in campo de C[hatriz qui][2] vocatur G[ravesten'],[3] jacentem inter terram ... ...i [4] (fo. 83r)[5] filii Margarete, tenendam et habendam predicto conventui pro crofta illa que fuit Ricardi Fader', inter tuftas Ricardi le Ray et Matill' de Wroh, imperpetuum escambium, quam[6] croftam[7] predictus conventus dedit et concessit michi et heredibus meis vel meis assignatis per cartam suam. Et ego dictus Radulphus et heredes mei war-antizabimus predictam dimidiam acram predicto loco pro dictis escambiis imperpetuum contra omnes gentes. Et ut predicta[8] escambia rata permaneat, huic scripto sigillum meum apposui. Hiis testibus etc.

Note. Ralph de Barley is a witness in 1239 × *s.* xiii[3] (no. 240) and occurs *s.* xiii[1] × 6 Aug. 1254 (no. 17).

31 *Gift in free alms by John Vivien of Chatteris to Chatteris abbey of 1 rood of land in the field behind Chatteris parish church.*
fo. 83r [*s.* xiii[2-4]]

Donatio Johannis[9] Vevien de una roda terre.

Notum sit etc. quod ego Johannes Vivien de Chatriz[10] dedi etc. Deo et ecclesie beate Marie de[11] Chatriz et monialibus ibidem Deo servientibus, pro salute anime mee et patris mei et matris mee et antecessorum meorum, unam rodam terre cum pertinenciis que jacet in campo subtus ecclesiam parochialem de Chat-riz et [prope][12] Comesdich,[13] juxta terram dictarum dominarum[14] et earum successorum,[15] libere et quiete imperpetuum in puram et perpetuam elimo-

1 Hole 1 mm.
2 Damaged 20 mm.
3 Hole 14 mm.
4 Hole 48 mm.
5 Heading *Chatriz.*
6 Followed by *predictam*, expunged.
7 Followed by *ped*, expunged.
8 MS *predictus.*
9 Followed by *D*, expunged.
10 MS *Chatrii.*
11 Followed by *Chad*, expunged.
12 Unclear 4 mm, cf. no. 34.
13 Recte *Tomesdich*, cf. no. 34.
14 Followed by *suarum*, expunged.
15 MS *successoribus.*

sinam cum omnibus suis pertinenciis integre. Et ego Johannes et heredes mei warantizabimus acquietabimus et defendemus totam predictam terram cum pertinenciis predictis monialibus et eorum successoribus contra omnes mortales imperpetuum, sicut liberam et perpetuam elimosinam. Et ut hec mea donatio concessio presentis carte mee confirmatio firma sit et stabilis, presenti scripto sigillum meum apposui. Hiis testibus etc.

Note. John Vivien occurs in 1235 × *s.* xiii[3] (no. 32) and in *s.* xiii[2] × 1291 (no. 275).

32 *Confirmation by John Vivien of Chatteris to Chatteris abbey of 2 selions of land in Chatteris, given by John de Cambridge.*
fo. 83r–v [1235 × *s.* xiii[3]]

Confirmatio Johannis Vivien de duobus sellionibus ut scriptum est supra.

Sciant presentes etc. quod ego Johannes Vivien de Chatriz ratam et gratam habeo et hac presenti carta mea confirmo (fo. 83v)[1] Deo et ecclesie sancte Marie et omnium sanctorum de Chatriz et monialibus eiusdem loci donationem et concessionem quam Johannes de Cantebr' in Chatriz eis fecit de una sellione terre cum pertinenciis in campo de Horingslade de Chatriz, jacente inter terram Henrici Bruston' et terram que fuit quondam Warini de Saham, et abuttat super capiteram Guinore Cade, et de uno alio sellione terre cum pertinenciis, sicut jacet in longitudine et in latitudine in campo versus Elmethe, juxta terram que fuit quondam Azotis le Noreys et terram abbatis de Rameseye, et extendit se juxta[2] viam tendentem versus Elmenswrth'. Volo igitur et concedo pro me et heredibus meis quod predicta ecclesia de Chatriz et moniales memorate habeant et teneant pacifice imperpetuum et imperpetuum possideant predictos seliones cum pertinenciis in liberam puram et perpetuam elimosinam, sicut carte prefati Johannis de Cantebr' quas memorate moniales inde habent testantur, quiete et absolute de me et heredibus meis imperpetuum, sine omni retinemento vel conditione mei vel heredum meorum. Et ego et heredes mei totam predictam ⟨terram⟩ cum pertinenciis prefate ecclesie et monialibus memoratis warantizabimus acquietabimus et defendemus erga omnes gentes imperpetuum. Et nec ego nec heredes mei in predicta terra cum pertinenciis aliquod jus vel clamium nobis de cetero vendicari possimus. Huic scripto in modum carte confirmationis confecto sigillum meum duxi apponendum. Hiis testibus.

1 Heading *Chatriz.*
2 Followed by *se,* expunged.

Note. Another copy of no. 37. See also nos. 53 and 67, the gifts by John de Cambridge. For dating see no. 53n.

33 *Gift in free alms by John Vivien of Chatteris to Chatteris abbey, for the support of its alms, of 1 selion of land [in Chatteris].*
fos. 83v–84r [s. xiii$^{2-4}$]

Donatio Johannis Vivien de uno sellione apud Horinslade ad sustentationem pauperum.

Notum sit omnibus quod[1] ego Johannes Vivien de Chatriz concessi dedi etc., pro salute anime mee et antecessorum meorum, Deo et ecclesie beate Marie de Chatriz et monialibus (fo. 84r)[2] ibidem Deo servientibus unum selionem terre mee in campo de Horingslade, sicut jacet in longitudine et in latitudine cum pertinenciis suis inter terram que fuit quondam Azotis le Noreys et terram Rogeri Sarle, quam tenet de abbate de Rames' et abuttat super Erche, habendum et tenendum eisdem dominabus et earum successoribus libere quiete et ab omni seculari servicio et demanda imperpetuum in puram et perpetuam elimosinam,[3] videlicet ad sustentationem elemosinarum suarum. Et ego Johannes et heredes mei warantizabimus acquietabimus et defendemus contra gentes imperpetuum. Et ut hec mea concessio donatio et presentis carte confirmatio robur optineat imperpetuum, scripto sigillum meum apposui. Hiis testibus etc.

Note. For dating of John Vivien see no. 31n. Roger Sarle occurs in 1289 (Ault ed. *Ramsey Court Rolls*, p. 277).

34 *Gift in free alms by John Vivien of Chatteris to Chatteris abbey of 5 acres and 1 rood of arable land in Chatteris.*
fo. 84r–v [s. xiii^2 × 1290]

Donatio eiusdem Johannis Vivien de quinque acris et una roda.

Sciant etc. quod ego Johannes Vivien de Chatriz dedi etc. Deo et ecclesie beate Marie genitrici eiusdem ac abbatisse et conventui de Chatriz, et pro salute anime mee et antecessorum meorum, in puram et perpetuam elemosinam quinque acras terre arabilis et unam rodam, sicut jacet in[4] campis per particulas de eadem

[1] Repeated.
[2] Heading *Chatriz*.
[3] *nota selionem ad elimosinariam*, marginated after *eli-*.
[4] *vide culturam de Stokkyng'*, marginated after *in*.

villa cum omnibus suis pertinenciis, quarum quatuor acre et[1] dimidia jacent in una cultura in longitudine et in latitudine que vocatur le Stokkyng', cum capitera jacente in campo qui appellatur Elmenefeld', cum omnibus suis pertinenciis in predicta villa de Chatriz, et extendit se in longitudine ex parte orientali per terram domine de Mephale et ex parte occidentali extendit se per capites que dicuntur Commannelond',[2] unum caput abuttat se ex parte[3] meridionali super terram et pratum dicte domine de Mephale, et aliud caput ex parte aquilonis super predictam capiteram, que extendit se ex parte meridionali, superextendit se per capites terre abbatis (fo. 84v)[4] de Rameys', et una roda terre cum pertinenciis que jacet in campo subtus ecclesiam parochialem de Chatriz et prope Tomesdych', juxta terram dicte abbatisse et conventus et terram Johannis Gerard', quam tenet de abbate de Rames' et abuttat super Burtefen,[5] et una dimidia acra terre cum pertinenciis que vocatur le Welstecche in eadem villa, et jacet inter terram dicte abbatisse ex una parte et terram Stephani filii Hugonis Serle ex altera parte, cuius unum caput abuttat super foveam que ducit versus Southwode versus orientem et aliud caput super viam que ducit versus occidentem, habendam et tenendam totam predictam terram cum omnibus suis pertinenciis dictis abbatisse et conventui suo in puram et perpetuam elemosinam de me et heredibus meis vel assignatis, libere quiete integre hereditarie bene et in pace. Et ego predictus Johannes et heredes mei vel mei assignati warantizabimus et defendemus et acquietabimus totam prefatam terram prout jacet et cum omnibus suis pertinenciis predictis abbatisse et conventui contra omnes gentes imperpetuum. Et ut hec mea donatio concessio et presentis carte confirmatio firmum et perpetuum robur optineat, presenti carte sigillum meum apposui. Hiis testibus etc.

Note. For dating of John Vivien see no. 31n. Stephen son of Hugh Sarle occurs in 1272 (Ault ed. *Ramsey Court Rolls*, p. 264). The land is to be held *de me et heredibus meis* so the gift must pre-date 1290. The last ½ acre of land described in this gift is probably the same as the ½ acre given in no. 36: see no. 36n.

35 *Gift by John Fithien of Chatteris to Geoffrey de Barnwell, cook, of 2 roods of arable land in Chatteris, for 20s. and an annual rent of ½d.*
fos. 84v–85r [*s.* xiii[3] × 1290]

[1] Interlined.
[2] 7 minims for *mm*.
[3] Followed by *meriona*, expunged.
[4] Heading *Chatriz*.
[5] Followed by *Bourtefen*, marginated.

Donum Johannis Fithien de duabus rodis terre.

Sciant etc. quod ego Johannes Plichien[1] de Chatriz dedi etc. Galfrido de Berne-welle coco duas rodas terre arabilis in territario de Chatriz, quarum una roda jacet in campo qui vocatur Horingslade, inter terram abbatisse de Chatriz ex una parte et terram Boreston' ex altera, et abuttat super Herberd' Hoved' Lond', et altera roda terre jacet in campo qui vocatur Horsethefeld', inter ter-ram Galfridi de Litton' ex parte una et terram Jordani Peit ex altera, unde unum caput abuttat super Horsethewere versus orientem (fo. 85r)[2] et aliud caput abuttat super Schipchirnefen versus occidentem, habendas et tenendas predictas rodas terre cum pertinenciis suis de me et heredibus meis predicto Galfrido et heredibus suis, vel cuicumque eas dare vendere legare vel aliquo modo assignare voluerit et quando, libere et quiete bene et in pace et hereditarie imperpetuum, reddendo inde michi annuatim et heredibus meis ille et heredes sui vel sui assignati unum obolum ad Pascha pro omnibus serviciis sectis curie consue-tudinibus et secularibus demandis. Et ego predictus Johannes et heredes mei warantizabimus acquietabimus et defendemus predictas duas rodas terre cum pertinenciis suis predicto Galfrido et heredibus suis vel suis assignatis pro prenominato servicio, sicut predictum est, contra omnes gentes imperpetuum. Pro hac autem concessione donatione et presentis carte mee confirmatione, dedit michi predictus Galfridus xx solidos in guersummam. Et[3] ut hec mea donatio concessio et presentis carte confirmatio perpetuum robur optineant, hanc presentem cartam sigilli mei inpressione roboravi. Hiis testibus.

Note. This gift is followed by no. 62. It pre-dates 1290 since the land is to be held *de me et heredibus meis* and an annual rent is reserved. Geoffrey 'de Loyton'' occurs in 1272, Jordan Peit in 1287 and John Fithien in 1289 (Ault ed. *Ramsey Court Rolls*, pp. 268, 272, 278–9). John Fithien occurs shortly before 8 July 1298 × 27 March 1306 (nos. 38 and 63).

36 *Gift in free alms by John Vivien of Chatteris to Chatteris abbey of ½ acre of arable land called 'le Welsteche' in Chatteris.*
fo. 85r–v [*s.* xiii[2] × 1290]

Donatio Johannis Vivien de dimidia acra aput Wellesteche.

Sciant etc. quod ego Johannes Vivien de Chatriz dedi etc. Deo etc. beate Marie genitrici eiusdem ac abbatisse et conventui de Chatriz, pro salute anime et ante-

---

1 The scribe may have misread an initial *F* or have miscopied an initial *Ph*.
2 Heading *Chatriz*.
3 Followed by *h*, expunged.

cessorum meorum, in puram et perpetuam elemosinam unam dimidiam ⟨acram⟩ terre mee arabilis que vocatur le Welsteche in villa de Chatriz, et jacet inter terram dicte abbatisse ex una parte et terram Stephani filii Hugonis Serle ex altera, cuius unum caput abuttat super foveam que ducit versus Horsechewode versus orientem, et aliud caput super viam que ducit versus Horseche versus occidentem, habendam et tenendam dictam terram cum omnibus pertinenciis suis dicte abbatisse et conventui suo ac successoribus suis in puram et perpetuam elemosinam de me et heredibus meis (fo. 85v)[1] vel meis assignatis, libere quiete integre hereditarie bene et in pace. Et ego predictus Johannes et heredes mei vel mei assignati warantizabimus defendemus et acquietabimus prefatam terram cum omnibus suis pertinenciis predictis abbatisse et conventui contra omnes gentes imperpetuum. Et ut hec mea donatio concessio ac presentis carte mee confirmatio firmum et perpetuum robur optineat, presenti carte sigillum meum apposui. Hiis testibus etc.

> Note. For dating see no. 34n. The ½ acre of land in this gift is probably the same as the last ½ acre described in no. 34. One gift may, in effect, be a confirmation of the ½ acre, but it is possible that no. 36 was produced after no. 34 by the abbey to strengthen its claim in the land.

37 *Confirmation by John Vivien of Chatteris to Chatteris abbey of 2 selions of land in Chatteris, given by John de Cambridge.*
fos. 85v–86r [1235 × s. xiii[3]]

Confirmatio Johannis Vivien de duobus selionibus terre apud Horynsslade.

Sciant etc. quod ego Johannes Vivian[2] de Chatriz ratam et gratam habeo et hac presenti carta mea confirmo Deo et ecclesie sancte Marie et omnium sanctorum de Chatriz et monialibus eiusdem loci donationem et concessionem quam Johannes de Cantebr' in Chatriz eis fecit de uno sellione terre cum pertinenciis in campo de Horingslade de Chatriz, jacente inter terram Henrici Bruston' et terram que fuit quondam Warini de Saham, et abuttat super capiteram Guinore Cade, et de uno alio selione terre cum pertinenciis, sicut jacet in longitudine et latitudine in campo versus Elmene, juxta terram que fuit quondam Azotis et terram abbatis de Rames', et extendit se juxta viam tendentem versus Elmenestirch' de Chatriz. Volo igitur quod predicta ecclesia de Chatriz et moniales memorate habeant et teneant et pacifice imperpetuum possideant predictos seliones cum pertinenciis in liberam et perpetuam elimosinam, sicut carte

1 Heading *Chatriz.*
2 MS *Viviam*, final minim expunged.

prefati Johannis de Cantebr' in Chatriz quas memorate moniales inde habent testantur, quiete et absolute de me et heredibus meis imperpetuum. Et ego et heredes mei totam predictam terram cum pertinenciis prefate ecclesie de Chatriz et monialibus memoratis warantizabimus acquietabimus defendemus contra omnes homines imperpetuum. Et ne ego vel heredes mei vel aliquis (fo. 86r)[1] alius nomine meo in predicta terra cum pertinenciis aliquod jus vel clamium nobis de cetero vendicare possimus.[2] Huic scripto sigillum meum apposui. Hiis testibus etc.

Note. Another copy of no. 32. See also nos. 53 and 67, the gifts by John de Cambridge. For dating see no. 53n.

38 *Release and quitclaim by John Fithien of Chatteris to abbess Amicia de Cambridge and the nuns of Chatteris of 2½d. of annual rent [?in Chatteris] which they used to pay to him for the houses and 2 roods of land which Geoffrey le Spenser gave to the abbey.*
fo. 86r [Shortly before 8 July 1298 × 27 March 1306]

Quieta clamantia Johannis Fithien de ij denariis et obolo annui redditus.

Omnibus Christi etc. ad quos presens scriptum pervenerit Johannes Fichien de Chatriz salutem in Domino sempiternam. Noverit universitas vestra me remisisse et penitus quietos clamasse pro me et heredibus meis Amicie de Cantebrig' abbatisse de Chatriz et monialibus ibidem Deo servientibus in puram et perpetuam elemosinam illos duos denarios et obolum annui redditus quos michi reddere consueverunt, pro domibus Galfridi le Spenser et duabus rodis terre quas dictus Galfridus eidem abbatisse et conventui in vita sua dedit et per cartam suam concessit, ita quod nec ego dictus Johannes nec aliquis heredum meorum in predictos duos denarios et obolum[3] de cetero aliquid inde exigere poterimus. Et ut hec mea concessio et quieta clamatio robur habeat imperpetuum, presenti scripto sigillum meum apposui. Hiis testibus etc.

Note. Amicia de Cambridge was abbess by Michaelmas 1300 (no. 219), so she was very probably the prioress who was elected abbess shortly before 8 July 1298 (*Reg. Winchelsey* i, pp. 262–3). Mary de Shouldham was abbess by 28 March 1306 (no. 230).

---

[1] Heading *Chatriz.*
[2] MS *posseimus*, *e* expunged.
[3] MS *obolo.*

39 *Gift in free alms by Agnes formerly wife of Azo le Noreis of Chatteris to Chatteris abbey of ½ acre of arable land in Chatteris.*
fo. 86r [*s.* xiii$^{2-3}$]

Carta Agnetis le Nores de una dimidia acra terre.

Notum sit omnibus etc. quod ego Agnes quondam uxor Azonis le Noreys de Chatriz dedi etc. abbatisse de Chatriz et monialibus ibidem Deo servientibus in puram et perpetuam elemosinam unam dimidiam acram terre arabilis in campo de Chatriz, que jacet inter terram Johannis Wlfrith' et terram Edithe vidue ex altera parte, habendam et tenendam cum pertinenciis pro salute anime mee et filiarum mearum salvatione. Et ut hec mea donatio stabilis et firma permaneat, presenti scripto sigillum meum apposui. Hiis testibus etc.

> Note. See also no. 42, the earlier confirmation of this land by Hingenolf' and Alice to Robert son of Azo le Noreis, and no. 43, the quitclaim which follows this gift. Azo was dead by 1235 × *s.* xiii^3 (nos. 32 and 67).

40 *Gift in free alms by Azo son of Robert le Noreis, with the consent of his heirs, to Chatteris abbey of his* cultura *called 'Wodecroft' with close and dike [?in Chatteris].*
fo. 86r–v [*s.* xiii$^{1-3}$]

Carta Azonis le Noreis de cultura de Wodecroft'.

Sciant presentes etc. quod ego Azo filius Roberti le Noreys, de (fo. 86v)^1 consensu et voluntate heredum meorum, dedi etc. Deo et sancte^2 Marie de Chatriz et monialibus ibidem Deo servientibus in puram et perpetuam elemosinam totam culturam meam que vocatur Wodecroft, cum claustura et^3 fossa et eius pertinenciis, que jacet inter nemus predictarum monialium ex una parte et mariscum ex altera, tenendam et habendam de me et heredibus meis sibi et successoribus suis imperpetuum libere quiete et honorifice et hereditarie ab omni seculari consuetudine et exactione. Et ego Azoto et heredes mei defendemus warantizabimus illam dictam culturam dictis monialibus et successoribus suis contra omnes homines. Et ut hec donatio et concessio et carte mee confirmatio rata et indiscussa permaneat, presens scriptum sigilli mei munitione corroboravi. Hiis testibus.

> Note. Another copy of no. 27. For dating see no. 27n.

---

1   Heading *Chatriz*.
2   Followed by *ecclesie*, expunged.
3   *vide culturam de Wodecroft'*, marginated before *et*.

41 *Gift in free alms by Robert le Noreis, with the assent of his wife, Margaret, and heir, Azo, to Chatteris abbey of 2 selions of land [?in Chatteris], 1 of which he bought from Robert son of John.*
fo. 86v [*s.* xiii$^{1-2}$]

Donum Roberti le Noreis de uno sellione terre.

Sciant presentes etc. quod ego Robertus le Noreys, consilio et assensu uxoris mee Margarete et Azonis heredis mei, dedi etc. in puram et perpetuam elemosinam Deo et ecclesie sancte Marie de Chatriz et monialibus ibidem Deo servientibus unum selionem terre mee in Fliggele, qui abuttat super fossatum, et unum sellionem in Frankewode juxta Galfridum de Coveneye, quem emi de Roberto filio Johannis, pro salute anime mee et uxoris mee et parentum meorum. Et ego Robertus et heredes mei warantizabimus predictas partes terre predicte ecclesie contra omnes homines et feminas. Hiis testibus etc.

   Note. Another copy of no. 25. For dating see no. 25n.

42 *Confirmation by Hingenolf' and Alice, his wife, to Robert son of Azo le Noreis of ½ acre of land in Chatteris, given by them to Azo le Noreis; for 1d. annually.*
fos. 86v–87r [*s.* xii^4 × *s.* xiii^2]

Carta Hingenolf' facta Roberto filio Azonis de dimidia acra que vocatur Slade.

Sciant etc. quod ego Hingenolf' et Alicia uxor mea concessimus et confirmavimus Roberto filio Azonis le Noreis dimidiam acram terre nostre cum pertinenciis[1] in campo de Chatriz quod vocatur Slade, que jacet inter terram Johannis Wlfr[i]ch[2] (fo. 87r)[3] et Edithe vidue, tenendam et habendam de nobis et heredibus nostris sibi et heredibus suis, vel cuicumque illam dare vel assignare voluerit, sicut continetur in carta dicti Azonis patris predicti Roberti [cu]i[4] predictam dimidiam acram dedimus pro homagio et servicio suo, reddendo inde nobis annuatim unum denarium in festo sancti Michaelis pro ommi servicio seculari. Et ego predictus Hingenolf et Alicia uxor mea et heredes nostri warantizabimus predictam dimidiam acram cum pertinenciis dicto Roberto et heredibus suis contra omnes gentes. In cuius rei testimonium presenti scripto sigilla nostra apposuimus. Hiis testibus etc.

1 Followed by *d*, expunged.
2 Hole 1 mm.
3 Heading *Chatriz.*
4 Hole 3 mm.

Note. In no. 39, Agnes widow of Azo le Noreis – who seems to have been the grandson of the Azo in this document – gave this land to Chatteris abbey. For dating of Robert le Noreis see no. 19n.

43 *Quitclaim by William Baldewelle of Swaffham to Chatteris abbey of ½ acre of arable land in Chatteris.*

fo. 87r [s. xiii²⁻³]

Quieta clamantia de dimidia acra terre Willelmi Baldewyn'.

Universis etc. Willelmus Ba[l]d[e]welle[1] de Swafham salutem in Domino sempiternam. Noverit universitas vestra me dedisse concessisse ac omnino quietum clamasse totum jus et clamium quod habeo[2] vel habere potero de me et heredibus meis seu assignatis abbatie de Chatriz et monialibus ibidem Deo servientibus in una dimidia acra terre arabilis, que jacet inter terram Johannis quondam Wlfrich et terram E[dithe vidue][3] in campo de Chatriz, ita silicet quod nec [eg]o[4] nec [a]l[iqui]s[5] nomine meo seu nomine heredum meorum seu assignatorum meorum aliquam juris exigenciam in dicta dimidia acra [terr]e[6] exigere seu vendicare de cetero poterim[us],[7] salvo servicio domini regis forinceco, videlicet tunc quod pertinet ad [me]am[8] terram eiusdem[9] feodi in ea[dem],[10] scilicet in feodo Azonis Noreys. Ad hanc concessionem et q[uietam clama]tionem[11] ratam et stabilem confirmandam, hoc [pre]s[ens][12] scriptum sigilli mei impressione corrobor[avi].[13] Hiis testibus.

Note. No. 39 is the gift which precedes this quitclaim. For dating see no. 39n.

44 *Quitclaim by Aveline formerly wife of Henry Briston of Chatteris to Chatteris abbey of her dower rights relating to the abbey, within or without Chatteris, for 12d.*

1 Two holes 1 mm and 2 mm.
2 Ins. marg.; *vel* preceded by *ho'*, possibly expunged.
3 Hole 24 mm; supplied from no. 39.
4 Hole 4 mm.
5 Hole 11 mm.
6 Hole 5 mm.
7 Hole 4 mm.
8 Unclear 5 mm.
9 Followed by *loci*, expunged.
10 Hole 3 mm.
11 Damaged 20 mm.
12 Damaged 11 mm.
13 Hole 5 mm.

fo. 87r–v [1235 × s. xiii⁴]

Quieta clamantia Aveline Brixton' de dote sua.

Omnibus etc. Avelina quondam uxor Henrici Brixton' de Chatriz salutem. Noveritis me in libera viduitate mea (fo. 87v)[1] dimisse et quietum clamasse abbatie et conventui ecclesie beate Marie de Chatriz, pro xij denariis argenti, totum jus et clamium meum quod vendicare potero de predicta abbatissa et de conventu predicto nomine dotis infra villam de Chatriz vel extra, ita videlicet quod nec ego predicta Av[e]l[i]na[2] nec aliquis pro me seu nomine meo in dicta dote aliquid de cetero exigere vel vendicare poterimus nec debemus. In cuius rei testimonium huic presenti scripto mediante mea sigillum meum apposui. Hiis testibus etc.

Note. Henry Briston occurs in Chatteris in 1235 × s. xiii⁴ (no. 53).

45 *Gift in free alms by Ismaena daughter of Ralph Briston to Chatteris abbey of 2 roods of land in Chatteris.*
fo. 87v [s. xiii¹ × 1235]

Carta Ismaene Brixton' de duabus rodis terre in perpetuam elemosinam.

Sciant etc. quod ego Ismaena filia Radulphi Brixton' dedi etc. ad ecclesiam sancte Marie de Chatriz et conventui eiusdem loci in elimosinam perpetuam duas rodas terre mee cum pertinenciis in campis[3] de Chatriz, et pro animabus patris et matris mee et pro animabus antecessorum meorum et propter animam meam et pro animabus heredum meorum, quod istam[4] elimosin[am et pre-dictam terr]am[5] warantizabunt, scilicet illam rodam[6] ⟨terre⟩ cum per[tinenciis][7] que j[ace]t[8] in campis de Horse, que abuttat super alteram viam inter terram Warini de Saham et terram Roberti filii Stephani, et illam rodam terre cum pertinenciis in campo de Horyngslade inter terram Katerine de Covneya et Markissilio.[9] Et ego Ismaena et heredes mei warantizabimus predictam terram

1 Heading *Chatriz*.
2 Hole 4 mm.
3 MS *campos*, *o* expunged and superscript *i* added in red.
4 MS *ista*.
5 Hole 21 mm; lacunae in this charter supplied from no. 24, the other copy of the charter.
6 MS *illa roda*.
7 Hole 6 mm.
8 Hole 7 mm.
9 Recte *Markis scilicet*? cf. no. 24.

cum pertinenciis contra omnes homines et elemosinam predicte ⟨ecclesie⟩ et conventui eiusdem loci, [et propter ista]m[1] donationem elemosinam et confirmationem ra[tum] ...[2] esse tenetur. Ego Ismaina presentem cartam sigilli mei impressione roboravi. Hiis testibus etc.

Note. Another copy of no. 24. For dating see no. 24n. See also no. 22.

46 *Gift in free alms by Alice Briston of Chatteris to Chatteris abbey of ½ acre of land in Chatteris.*
fos. 87v–88r [s. xiii[1–3]]

Carta Alicie Bruston' de dimidia acra terre. (fo. 88r)[3]

Omnibus etc. Alicia Bruston' de Chateriz salutem in Domino. Noverit universitas vestra me concessisse dedisse et presenti carta mea confirmasse pro salute anime mee et antecessorum meorum unam dimidiam acram terre in campo de Chatriz qui vocatur Horinglade Feld', et jacet juxta terram abbatisse de Chateriz et conventus, Deo et ecclesie beate Marie de Chateriz et monialibus Deo[4] ibidem servientibus, tenendam et habendam dictis monialibus in puram et perpetuam elemosinam. Et ego Alicia et heredes mei warantizabimus acquietabimus et defendemus totam predictam terram cum pertinenciis predictis monialibus contra omnes mortales imperpetuum. Et ut hec mea donatio et concessio robur optineat imperpetuum, presenti scripto sigillum meum apposui. Hiis testibus etc.

Note. The dating is based solely on the language of the charter.

47 *Release by Ralph son of Katherine Coveney to Amicia de Cambridge, sacrist of Chatteris abbey, of ½d. of annual rent in which she was bound to him for 1 rood of arable land which she held of him [in Chatteris]; for 6d.*
fo. 88r [s. xiii[4], before 1298]

Carta Radulphi filii Katerine Coveneye de uno obolo redditus.

Sciant presentes etc. quod ego Radulphus filius Katerine Coveye[5] dedi etc.[6] Amicie[7] de Cantebr' sacriste[8] ecclesie[9] de Chateriz et successoribus suis unum

---

1 Hole, 13 mm.
2 Hole 15 mm, though nothing added here in no. 24.
3 Heading *Chatriz.*
4 Followed by abbreviated *ibidem*, unfinished and expunged.
5 Or *Coneye?*

obolum annui redditus in quo michi tenebatur pro una roda terre arabilis quam de me tenuit in campo de Sladefeld', habendum et tenendum sibi et successoribus suis libere quiete bene et in pace, sine aliquo clameo mei et alicuius heredum meorum. Et ego dictus Radulphus et heredes mei dictam rodam et dictum obolum predicte Amicie et eius successoribus warantizabimus acquietabimus et defendemus. Pro hac autem donatione et concessione et carte mee confirmatione, dedit michi prefata Amicia sex denarios in guersummam. Et ut hec omnia predicta robur optineant imperpetuum, presens scriptum sigilli mei impressione roboravi. Hiis testibus etc.

> Note. Amicia de Cambridge was abbess by Michaelmas 1300 (no. 219), therefore the prioress who was elected abbess shortly before 8 July 1298 was very probably Amicia (*Reg. Winchelsey* i, pp. 262–3). If so, Amicia must have been sacrist in the late thirteenth century before she became prioress.

48 *Gift in free alms by Margaret wife of Stephen le Bray to Chatteris abbey of 1 rood of land in Chatteris.*
fo. 88r–v [s. xiii$^{1-3}$]

Donum Margarete Bray de una roda terre ad Willystub. (fo. 88v)[1]

Sciant etc. quod ego Margareta uxor Stephani le Bray dedi etc. Deo et ecclesie beate Marie de Chatriz et monialibus ibidem Deo servientibus pro salute anime mee unam rodam terre in campis de Chatriz, illam scilicet ad Wylystub jacentem inter terram Andree Ide ex una parte et terram Walteri Godyng' ex altera, habendam et tenendam sibi et successoribus suis et suis assignatis de me et heredibus meis in puram et perpetuam elimosinam libere quiete pacifice et hereditarie. Et ego dicta Margareta et heredes mei warantizabimus acquietabimus et defendemus predictam terram cum suis pertinenciis[2] dictis monialibus et successoribus suis et suis assignatis contra omnes mortales. Hiis testibus etc.

> Note. The dating is based on the language of the charter. A Walter Godyng occurs in nos. 50 and 57.

---

6 Followed by *Tho*, expunged.
7 Corr. marg., MS *Amic'*.
8 MS *sacracriste*, *cra* expunged.
9 *nota redditum oboli sacreste*, marginated after *ecclesie*.
1 Heading *Chatriz*.
2 Followed by *et*, expunged.

49 *Gift in free alms by Margaret le Freman of Chatteris to Chatteris abbey, prin-*
cipally for the support of poor women under the authority of the abbey, of 1 rood of
land [in Chatteris].
fos. 88v–89r [s. xiii² × 1290]

Donum Margarete Freman de una roda terre.

Notum sit omnibus etc. quod ego Margareta le Freman de Chatriz in libera
viduitate mea dedi etc., pro salute anime mee et antecessorum meorum, in
puram et perpetuam elemosinam Deo et ecclesie beate Marie de Chatriz et
monialibus ibidem Deo servientibus, et precipue ad sustentationem pauperum
que pro quocumque tempore fuerint[1] in obedientia[2] vestra, unam rodam terre
cum pertinenciis jacentem in campo[3] de Horyngglade, inter terram domine
abbatisse ex parte australi et terram Agnetis quondam uxoris Willelmi le Rede
ex parte boriali, habendam et tenendam predictam terram, sicut jacet in
longitudine et in latitudine, pro me et heredibus meis et nostris assignatis
eisdem dominabus et earum sustentricibus libere quiete bene et in pace
imperpetuum. Et ego predicta Margareta et heredes mei et nostri assignati
warantizabimus defendemus et acquietabimus predictam terram dictis monialibus et earum successoribus predictis elemosinarum sustentationi[4] contra omnes
homines imperpetuum. Et ut hec mea donatio concessio et presentis carte confirmatio perpetuum r[o]b[u]r optin[eant],[5] huic (fo. 89r)[6] carte presenti sigillum
meum apposui. Hiis testibus etc.

Note. The dating is based solely on the language of the charter.

50 *Gift by Thomas, chaplain of Chatteris, to Alice his niece of 1 rood of land in*
Chatteris, for ½d. annually.
fo. 89r [s. xiii² × 1290]

Carta Thome capellani de Chatriz de una roda terre.

Sciant presentes quod ego Thomas capellanus de Chatriz dedi etc. Alicie nepti
mee unam rodam terre mee in villa de Chatriz jacentem in campo qui vocatur

1   MS *fuerit.*
2   MS *inobedientia.*
3   *nota pro elimosina,* marginated before *campo.*
4   MS *elems' sust';* cf. no. 33, *ad sustentationem elemosinarum.*
5   Unclear 23 mm.
6   Heading *Chatriz.*

Sladeford', inter terram Willelmi fabri[1] ex una parte et terram Walteri Godyng' ex[2] altera parte, tenendam et habendam dictam rodam terre cum pertinenciis suis de me et assignatis meis predicte Alicie et heredibus suis, vel cuicumque predictam rodam terre cum pertinenciis dare vendere vel aliquo modo assignare voluerit, bene et in pace honorifice et hereditarie imperpetuum, reddendo michi inde annuatim et assignatis meis ipsa[3] et heredes sui ad festum sancti Michaelis unum obolum pro omni servicio consuetudine exactione et demanda seculari. Et ego predictus Thomas capellanus et assignati mei warantizabimus acquiet-abimus et defendemus predictam rodam terre cum pertinenciis predicte Alicie et heredibus suis et suis assignatis, sicut predictum est, contra omnes gentes imper-petuum. Et ut hec mea donatio concessio et presentis carte mee confirmatio perpetue firmitatis robur optineant, hanc presentem cartam sigilli mei impres-sione roboravi. Hiis testibus etc.

Note. See also no. 57 in which Alice gave this rood of land to Chatteris abbey. For dating see no. 57.

51 *Agreement whereby abbess Mary de Sancto Claro and the convent of Chatteris lease to John de Fransham, for his life, a messuage with buildings in Chatteris which Alan de Bassingbourn held of them; for 2s. annually.*
fo. 89r–v [s. xiii[2] × 28 Sept. 1265]

Scriptum feodi firme de terra tradita magistro Johanni de Franesham.

Hec est conventio etc. inter Mariam de Sancto Claro abbatissam de Chatriz et conventum[4] eiusdem loci ex una parte et magistrum Johannem de Franesham ex altera, videlicet quod predicta Maria et conventus predictus unanimi assensu concesserunt et dimiserunt predicto Johanni mesuagium illud in Chatriz cum edificiis et pertinenciis in eodem sitis quod Alanus de Bassingbourne tenuit de predicto conventu in eadem villa, habendum et tenendum predicto Johanni tota vita sua cum omnibus pertinenciis secundum quod Alanus de Bassingbourne prenominatus illud tenuit de predicto (fo. 89v)[5] conventu, reddendo inde annuatim predicto conventui duos solidos ad duos anni terminos, scilicet ad festum sancti Michealis xij denarios et ad Pascha xij denarios, pro omnibus serviciis consuetudinibus et secularibus demandis, ita quod non liceat predicto

---

1 MS *frabri*.
2 Followed by *ui*, expunged.
3 *Resolutio oboli per annum*, marginated after *ipsa*.
4 MS *coventum*.
5 Heading *Chatriz*.

Johanni vastum vel venditionem facere in domibus vel arboribus mesuagii predicti, nec edificia que in eo invenit vel postea construxerit ammovere, nec falces prosternere nisi ad edificandum in eodem mesuagio vel ad sustentationem eorundem edificiorum, cum fuerit necesse, per visum balivorum predicte domine et conventus. Et si contingat quod absit domos vel edificia predicti mesuagii conbustione vel pro defectu custodie vel sustentationis deperisse, dictus Johannes damnum edificiorum pro defectu suo[1] conventui predicto illatum se soliciturum fide media obligavit per visum proborum hominum. Et post decessum dicti Johannis totum predictum mesuagium cum omnibus pertinenciis et omnibus edificiis in eodem sitis predicto conventui quiete et sine alicuius contradictione revertatur. Hec autem omnia supradicta firmiter et sine dolo tenenda dictus Johannes[2] tactis sacrosanctis juravit. Et ad maiorem securitatem in posterum, prenominatus conventus et predictus Johannes sigilla sua huic cirographo alternatim apposuerunt. Hiis testibus etc.

> Note. For dating of Mary de Sancto Claro see no. 100n. Alan de Bassingbourn held the
> manor of Bassingbourn in Wimpole before 1223 and still held it *c.* 1235 (*VCH Cambs.* v, p.
> 265; *Liber de Bernewelle*, p. 251); his son Baldwin inherited the manor before 1264 (*VCH
> Cambs.* v, p. 265).

52   *Gift by Thomas, formerly dispenser of Chatteris, to Isabel daughter of Hervy de Foxton of 1 rood of land in Chatteris, for 3d. annually.*
fos. 89v–90r   [*s.* xiii[2] × 1290]

Carta Thome dispensarii de una roda terre in Chatriz.

Sciant etc. quod ego Thomas dispensarius quondam de Chatriz dedi etc. Isabelle filie Hervy de Foxton' pro servicio suo unam rodam terre cum pertinenciis in campis de Chatriz que jacet in campo qui vocatur Horynngsladefeld', scilicet inter terram Emme filie Azonis Noreys et terram Stephani de Chedesham, et abuttat super foreram Ricardi filii Stephani, habendam et tenendam predictam rodam (fo. 90r)[3] terre cum pertinenciis de me et heredibus meis sibi et heredibus suis vel assignatis et eorum heredibus, vel cuicumque illam dare vendere legare vel assignare voluerit, libere quiete integre et hereditarie bene et in pace imperpetuum, reddendo inde annuatim michi et heredibus meis vel meis assignatis tres denarios,[4] scilicet ad festum sancte[5] Marie Assumptionis duos

---

1   Writtem *suorum*, *rum* expunged.
2   MS *Johannis*, perhaps corr. to *Johannes*.
3   Heading *Chatriz*.
4   Followed by *pro omnibus*, expunged.

denarios et ad festum sancti Michaelis unum denarium, pro omnibus serviciis consuetudinibus sectis curiarum et secularibus demandis. Et ego predictus Thomas dispensarius et heredes mei warantizabimus defendemus et acquietabimus predictam rodam terre cum pertinenciis predicte Isabelle filie Hervy de Foxton' et heredibus suis vel suis assignatis et eorum heredibus contra omnes gentes per predictum servicium imperpetuum. Et ut hoc firmum sit et stabile permaneat, huic scripto sigillum meum apposui. Hiis testibus etc.

Note. This gift follows no. 81 and precedes no. 54. For dating see no. 81n.

53 *Gift in free alms by John de Cambridge to Chatteris abbey, for the support of its alms and for feeding the poor and beggars, of 1 selion of land in Chatteris.*
fo. 90r–v [1235 × s. xiii³]

Donatio Johannis de Cantabr' de uno sellione terre.

Omnibus sancte matris ecclesie etc. Johannes de Cantebr' in Chatriz salutem in Domino sempiternam. Noverit universitas vestra me concessisse dedisse et presenti¹ carta mea² confirmasse Deo et ecclesie beate Marie de Chatriz et monialibus ibidem Deo servientibus, pro salute anime mee et antecessorum meorum, unum sellionem terre mee cum pertinenciis in campo de Horyngslade de Chatriz jacentem inter terram Henrici Bryghston' et terram que fuit quondam Warini de Saham, et abuttat super capiteram Gunnore³ Cade, habendum et tenendum eisdem dominabus et earum succestricibus imperpetuum libere quiete ab omni seculari servicio et demanda, in puram et perpetuam elimosinam, ad sustentationem elimosinarum suarum et ad refectionem pauperum et mendicantium. Et ego Johannes et heredes mei (fo. 90v)⁴ warantizabimus acquietabimus et defendemus totam predictam terram cum pertinenciis omnibus predictis dominabus et earum successtricibus contra omnes mortales imperpetuum. Et ut hec mea concessio donatio et presentis carte mee confirmatio firma [sit]⁵ et stabilis imperpetuum, presenti scripto sigillum meum⁶ apposui. Hiis testibus etc.

5 Followed by *Michaelis*, expunged.
1 MS *predcsenti, dc* expunged.
2 MS *carte mee*; *a* written over each final *e*.
3 *nota pro elimosina*, marginated after *Gunnore*.
4 Heading *Chatriz*.
5 Unclear 4 mm.
6 Ins. marg.

Note. See also the two copies of the confirmation of this gift, nos. 32 and 37. Warin de Saham died in 1235 (*VCH Cambs.* viii, p. 145).

54 *Gift by Isabel [daughter of] Hervy de Foxton to Chatteris abbey, for the light of St Katherine, of 1 rood of land in Chatteris, for 1d. annually.*
fo. 90v [*s.* xiii^2 × 1290]

Donatio Isabelle de Foxton de una roda terre.

Sciant presentes etc. quod ego Isa[b]ella^1 Hervy de Foxton' dedi etc. Deo et ecclesie beate Marie et omnium sanctorum de Chatriz et monialibus ibidem Deo servientibus, ad lumen sancte Katerine in dicta ecclesia, unam rodam terre cum pertinenciis in campis^2 de Chatriz que^3 jacet in campo qui vocatur Horyngsladefeld', scilicet inter terram que fuit Emme filie Azonis Noreis et terram Stephani de Chedesham, et abuttat super foreram Ricardi filii Stephani, habendam et tenendam predictam rodam terre cum pertinenciis de me et heredibus meis sibi et succestricibus libere quiete^4 integre hereditarie bene et in pace imperpetuum, reddendo inde annuatim michi et heredibus meis vel meis assignatis unum denarium, scilicet ad festum sancti Michaelis, pro omnibus serviciis consuetudinibus sectis curiarum et secularibus demandis. Et ego predicta Isabella et heredes mei warantizabimus acquitabimus et defendemus predictam rodam terre cum pertinenciis predictis monialibus et succestricibus contra omnes gentes imperpetuum per predictum servicium. Et ut hoc firmum sit et stabile permaneat, presenti scripto sigillum meum apposui. Hiis testibus etc.

Note. This gift follows nos. 81 and 52. For dating see no. 81n.

55 *Gift in free alms by Roger Gaugi of Chatteris to Chatteris abbey of 3 messuages, all his land with all its liberties, and all his rent and rights in Chatteris.*
fos. 90v–91r [*s.* xiii$^{1-2}$]

Donatio Rogeri Gaugi de duobus mesuagiis.

Sciant etc. quod ego Rogerus dictus Gaugi de Chatriz dedi etc. domui beate Marie de eadem et sanctimonialibus (fo. 91r)^5 Deo servientibus, pro salute anime mee et animabus antecessorum meorum, duo mesuagia Stephani de

---

1 Hole 2 mm.
2 MS *camp'*.
3 *Carta rode ad lumen sancte Katerine*, marginated before *que*.
4 MS *quete*.
5 Heading *Chatriz*.

Chedesham et mesuagium Willelmi filii Agnetis coci et totam terram cum omnibus libertatibus ad predictam terram pertinentibus, tam in pratis quam in pasturis et piscariis, et totum redditum et totum jus meum quod habui vel habere potui in villa de Chatriz, tenenda et habenda in puram et perpetuam elimosinam libere honorifice hereditarie et in pace, salvo servicio domini feodi. Et ego predictus Rogerus et heredes mei duo predicta mesuagia cum tota predicta terra et pertinenciis predictis dictis monialibus per predictum servicium contra omnes mortales warantizabimus defendemus acquietabimus imperpetuum. Et ut ista concessio et carte mee confirmatio rata sit et stabilis, presens scriptum sigilli mei impressione roboravi. Hiis testibus etc.

Note. See also no. 60, the lease to Matilda de Elsworth of a messuage which Roger Gaugi had given to the abbey. In 1216 the land of Richard Gubion in Northants. and Leics. was committed to Roger Gaugi (Farrer *Honors* i, p. 85). Roger Gaugi died *c.* 1250 (*CCR 1247-51*, p. 394). Stephen de Chettisham occurs in 1270 (Ault ed. *Ramsey Court Rolls*, p. 262).

56 *Gift by Berenger le Moyngne to Geoffrey de Barnwell, cook, of a messuage in 'Northstrete', Chatteris, for 3d. annually.*
fo. 91r–v [s. xiii[3] × 1290]

Donatio Berengeri le Moyngne de quodam mesuagio in Northstrete.

Sciant presentes etc. quod ego Berengerus le Moyngne dedi concessi et hac presenti carta mea confirmavi Galfrido de Bernewelle coco pro homagio et servicio suo unum mesuagium in villa de Chatriz cum pertinenciis in vico qui vocatur Northstrete, jacens inter mesuagium Roginaldi le Blower' ex una parte et mesuagium Hugonis Bene ex altera parte, habendum et tenendum totum predictum mesuagium cum pertinenciis suis de me et heredibus meis predicto Galfrido et heredibus suis, vel cuicumque illud mesuagium cum pertinenciis suis dare vendere legare vel aliquo alio modo assignare voluerit et quando, libere quiete bene et in pace et hereditarie imperpetuum, reddendo inde annuatim michi et heredibus meis ille et heredes sui ⟨vel sui⟩ assignati tres denarios ad duos anni terminos, scilicet ad Pascha tres obolos et ad festum sancti Michaelis tres obolos, (fo. 91v)[1] pro omnibus serviciis sectis consuetudinibus et omnibus aliis secularibus demandis. Et ego predictus Berengerus et heredes mei warantizabimus acquietabimus et defendemus totum predictum mesuagium cum pertinenciis suis predicto Galfrido heredibus suis vel suis assignatis per prenominatum servicium, sicut predictum est, contra omnes gentes imperpetuum. Et ut hec

---

[1] Heading *Chatriz.*

mea donatio concessio et presentis carte mee confirmatio perpetuum robur
optineat, hanc presentem cartam sigilli mei impressione roboravi. Hiis testibus
etc.

> Note. Berenger le Moyne occurs in 1287 and 1289 (Ault ed. *Ramsey Court Rolls*, pp. 271,
> 277). Geoffrey de Barnwell occurs in *s.* xiii[3] × 1290 (no. 35). Hugh Bene occurs in 1270 and
> 1289 (Ault ed. *Ramsey Court Rolls*, pp. 260, 278).

57 *Gift by Alice formerly wife of Geoffrey le Moyngne to Chatteris abbey, for the
light of St Mary of Chatteris, of 1 rood of land in Chatteris, for ½d. annually.*
fo. 91v [*s.* xiii[2] × 1290]

Donatio Alicie le Moyngne de una roda terre ad lumen ecclesie beate Marie de
Chatriz.

Sciant presentes etc. quod ego Alicia quondam uxor Galfridi le Moyngne in
libera viduitate et legitima potestate mea dedi etc. ad lumen beate Marie de
Chatriz unam rodam terre mee cum pertinenciis in[1] villa de Chatriz, jacentem
in campo qui vocatur [Sladeford']² inter terram Willelmi fabri ex una parte et
terram Walteri Godyng' ex altera, habendam et tenendam de me et heredibus
meis libere quiete integre bene et in pace imperpetuum, reddendo inde annuatim michi et heredibus meis vel assignatis unum obolum,³ videlicet ad festum
sancti Michaelis, pro omnibus serviciis exactionibus et secularibus demandis. Et
ego predicta Alicia et heredes mei warantizabimus defendemus et acquietabimus
predictam rodam terre cum suis pertinenciis ad predictum lumen predicte
ecclesie de Chatriz contra omnes gentes per predictum servicium imperpetuum.
Et ut hec mea donatio concessio presentis carte mee confirmatio perpetue
firmitatis robur optineat, hanc presentem cartam meam sigilli mei impressione
roboro. Hiis testibus etc.

> Note. See also no. 50, the gift of this rood of land to Alice by Thomas, chaplain of Chatteris.
> A Geoffrey le Moyne, who held the manor of Little Paxton (Hunts.), occurs in 1279 and
> 1286 (*Rot. Hund.* ii, p. 672; *VCH Hunts.* ii, p. 333). If he and the Geoffrey in this charter are
> the same, this gift must date from 1286 × 1290.

58 *Gift in free alms by Alexander Briston to Chatteris abbey, for the support of the
almonry, of 1 selion of land [in Chatteris].*

---

1 *[n]o[ta] rodam ad lumen beate Marie*, marginated before *in.*
2 Space, 20 mm; supplied from no. 50.
3 Followed by *vil'*, expunged.

fos. 91v–92r ?[*s.* xiii$^{1-3}$]

Donatio Alexandri Brixston' de uno selione.

Notum sit omnibus Christi fidelibus quod ego Alexander Brickeston' in viduitate mea dedi etc. Deo et ecclesie beate Marie de Chatriz et monialibus ibidem Deo servientibus, pro salute anime mee (fo. 92r)[1] et antecessorum meorum, unum sellionem terre in campo de Slade que jacet inter terram abbatis de Ramesch' et terram domine Mabilie de Saham, tenendum et habendum dictis dominabus et succestricibus earum in puram et perpetuam elemosinam, scilicet[2] ad sustentationem elemosinarie sue imperpetuum. Et ego Alexander et heredes mei warantizabimus acquietabimus et defendemus totam predictam terram cum pertinenciis predictis dominabus et earum successtricibus imperpetuum contra omnes mortales. Et ut hec mea donatio et confirmatio robur optineat imperpetuum, presenti scripto sigillum meum apposui. Hiis testibus etc.

> Note. The scribe may have miscopied the forename of Alexander Briston, who made his gift *in viduitate mea,* but the suggested dating is based on no. 85, a grant by Alexander son of Ralph Briston.

59 *Gift in free alms by William son of Owen to Chatteris abbey of 2 messuages and all his land with meadows and liberties in Chatteris.*
fo. 92r [*s.* xiii^{1} × 6 Aug. 1254]

Carta Willelmi filii Oweini de duobus mesuagiis terris pratis libertatibus et omnibus pertinenciis.

Sciant presentes etc. quod ego Willelmus filius Owini dedi concessi et hac presenti carta mea confirmavi domui beate Marie de Chatriz et sanctimonialibus ibidem Deo servientibus, pro salute anime mee et pro animabus antecessorum meorum, duo mesuagia in villa de Chatriz, scilicet unum mesuagium quod jacet inter mesuagium Roberti filii Gilberti et mesuagium Johannis coci, et unum mesuagium jacet inter mesuagium Radulphi de Berle[3] et mesuagium Roberti Hotte,[4] et totam terram quam tenui in villa de Chatriz cum pratis et libertatibus et omnibus pertinenciis ad predictam terram pertinentibus, tenenda et habenda in puram et perpetuam elemosinam libere honorifice et quiete, salvo servicio domini feodi. Et ego Willelmus et heredes mei warantizabimus predicta

---

1 Heading *Terre Chatriz et tenementa.*
2 *vide selionem ad elemosinariam*, marginated after *scilicet.*
3 Corr. from *Serle.*
4 *Le Vite* in no. 17, the other copy of the charter.

mesuagia cum prenominata terra sepedictis monialibus per predictum servicium imperpetuum contra omnes homines et feminas. Et ut hec mea donatio et carte mee confirmatio rata sit et stabilis, presens scriptum sigilli mei impressione roboravi. Hiis testibus etc. (fo. 92v)[1]

Note. Another copy of no. 17. For confirmation and dating see no. 15n.

60 *Agreement whereby Chatteris abbey leases to Matilda de Elsworth, maid of the abbess, for her life, a messuage with a yard and croft [in Chatteris] which Roger Gaugi gave to the abbey; for 20s. in advance and 2s. annually.*
fo. 92v [s. xiii]

Littera conventionis inter dominam abbatissam et Matildam de Esewyth'.

Hec est conventio facta inter abbatissam et conventum de Chatriz ex una parte et Matill' de Eleswith' ancillam dicte abbatisse [tu]nc[2] temporis ex altera, videlicet quod predicte abbatissa et conventus [c]oncesserunt[3] et dimiserunt predicte Matill' illud mesuagium quod Rogerus Gaugi dedit in puram et perpet-uam elemosinam dictis abbatisse et conventui una cum curtillagiis et crofta pertinentibus ad illud mesuagium, prout jacet inter mesuagium Stephani de Thecesham ex una parte et mesuagium Willelmi Godyng' de feodo domine de Mephale ex altera, habendum et tenendum dictum mesuagium cum dictis curtil-lagiis et crofta abbatissa[4] et conventu predicte Matill' libere quiete et pacifice ad totam vitam suam, ita tamen quod post decessum eius prefatum mesuagium ad predictos abbatissam et conventum sine cuiuscumque contradictione integre revertatur, reddendo inde annuatim dictis abbatisse et conventui duos solidos ad quatuor terminos anni, videlicet ad festum sancti Michaelis sex denarios et sic ad alios terminos reddituales, pro omni servicio et exactione et demanda. Predicti autem abbatissa et conventus pro predicto servicio illud mesuagium cum predictis dicte Matill' usque ad decessum eius contra omnes homines waranti-zabunt acquietabunt et defendent. Pro hac autem concessione et dimissione et warantizatione dedit dicta Matill' prefatis abbatisse et conventui viginti solidos sterlingorum pre manibus. Et ut hec conventio sine dolo et fraude observetur, huic scripto ad modum cirographi confecto hincinde sigilla sua apposuerunt. Hiis testibus etc.

1 Heading *Chatriz.*
2 Hole 2 mm.
3 Hole 1 mm.
4 MS *abbia'.*

Note. See also no. 55 in which Roger Gaugi gave three messuages to Chatteris abbey. For dating see no. 55n.

61 *Gift by Queen daughter of Codewin de Horseheath to William Litelmold' of 1 rood of land in Chatteris, for 10s. in advance and 1d. annually.*
fos. 92v–93r [s. xiii^2 × 1290]

Carta Quene filie Codewyni de Horesethe de una roda terre Willelmo Lytel-mold'. (fo. 93r)[1]

Sciant presentes etc. quod ego Quena filia Codewyni de Horsethe concessi etc. et hac presenti carta mea c[on]firmavi[2] Willelmo Litelmold' et heredibus suis vel suis assignatis, pro servicio suo et pro decem solidis sterlingorum quos michi dedit pre manibus, unam rodam terre cum pertinenciis in campo de Chatriz que jacet in campo qui vocatur Hornyngsladefeld', scilicet inter terram[3] Emme filie Azonis ex parte una et terram Stephani, et abuttat versus occidentem super terram domine abbatisse de Chatriz, habendam et tenendam totam predictam terram cum pertinenciis de me et heredibus meis sibi et heredibus suis, vel assignatis vel cuicumque illam dare vendere legare vel assignare voluerit, libere integre quiete et hereditarie, reddendo michi inde annuatim et heredibus meis dictus Willelmus et heredes sui vel assignati sui unum denarium ad festum sancti Michaelis pro omnibus serviciis consuetudinibus sectis curialibus et secularibus demandis. Et ego et heredes mei predicto [Willelmo][4] et heredibus suis vel suis assignatis totam predictam rodam terre cum pertinenciis warantizabimus ac-quietabimus et defendemus per predictum servicium contra omnes gentes imperpetuum. Et ut hec mea concessio donatio warantizatio et presentis carte confirmatio perpetue firmitatis robur optineat, hanc presentem cartam meam in libera viduitate mea sibi feci eamque sigilli mei impressione corroboravi. Hiis testibus etc.

Note. William Litelmold' occurs in 1270 and 1272; Stephen de Chettisham occurs in 1270 (Ault ed. *Ramsey Court Rolls*, pp. 262, 266).

---

1 Heading *Chatriz*.
2 Hole 2 mm.
3 MS *interram* for *inter terram*.
4 Unclear 9 mm.

62 *Gift in free alms by Geoffrey de Barnwell, cook, to Chatteris abbey, with his body, of 2 arable roods in Chatteris, 1 for the almonry and 1 for the light of St Mary, for ½d. annually to the lord of the fee.*
fo. 93r–v [s. xiii³ × s. xiv¹]

Carta Galfridi de Bernewelle de duabus rodis.

Sciant presentes etc. quod ego Galfridus de Bernewelle cocus dedi concessi et hac presenti carta mea confirmavi domui sancte Marie de Chatriz duas rodas arabiles in campo de Chatriz cum corpore meo in libera elimosina et perpetua, quarum una jacet in campo qui vocatur Horyngslade inter terram abbatisse ex parte (fo. 93v)¹ una et terram Brixston² ex altera, et abuttat super Herber-hovedlond',³ et altera roda jacet in campo qui vocatur Horsedefeld' inter terram Galfridi de Luyton' ex una parte et terram Jordani Peyte ex altera, unde unum caput abuttat super Horsideweye versus orientem, videlicet⁴ unam rodam in Horsidefeld' ad almaneriam et [a]lteram⁵ in campo de Horyngslade ad luminare sancte Marie, habendas et tenendas predictas rodas terre cum pertinenciis, reddendo annuatim domino feodi unum obolum ad Pascha pro omnibus serviciis sectis consuetudinibus et secularibus demandis. Hiis testibus etc.

  Note. See no. 35n for dating of no. 35 which precedes this gift.

63 *Gift in free alms by John Fithien (Pichiun', Pychyun') of Chatteris to abbess Amicia de Cambridge and the nuns of Chatteris of 4 selions and 1 gore of arable land with meadow [in Chatteris].*
fos. 93v–94r [Shortly before 8 July 1298 × 27 March 1306]

Carta Johannis Pychyun' de quatuor selionibus et una gora.

Sciant presentes etc. quod ego Johannes Pichiun' de Chatriz dedi concessi et hac presenti carta mea confirmavi Amicie de Cantebr' abbatisse de Chatriz et monialibus ibidem Deo servientibus quatuor seliones et unam goram terre mee arabilis cum prato predicte terre pertingente in campo qui vocatur⁶ Horyng-slade, quorum duo seliones jacent inter terram dicte abbatisse ex una parte et terram abbatis de Rameseye ex altera, et duo selliones et gora inter terram dicte

---

1 Heading *Chatriz.*
2 Damaged, but *Brixston* appears correct.
3 MS *Herdeberhovedlond'*, *de* expunged; hole 1 mm between *ed*, but probably no letters lacking.
4 *vide ij rodas ad lumen sancte Marie*, marginated before *videlicet.*
5 Preceded by *ad*, possibly cancelled; unclear 2 mm; followed by *d* expunged.
6 MS has a *-ur* abbreviation after *o* and after *t.*

abbatisse[1] ex utraque parte, quorum unum caput abuttat super terram dicti abbatis et aliud caput cum prato super Horyngsladefen, tenendam et habendam dictam terram cum prato dicte abbatisse et conventui in puram et perpetuam elemosinam libere quiete bene et[2] pacifice imperpetuum. Et ego predictus Johannes et heredes mei predictam terram in predicto prato predicte abbatisse et conventui in puram et perpetuam elimosinam contra omnes mortales warantizabimus defendemus et acquietabimus imperpetuum. Et ut hec mea donatio (fo. 94r)[3] concessio et presentis carte mee confirmatio robur optineat imperpetuum, presens scriptum sigilli mei impressione roboravi. Hiis testibus etc.

Note. For dating see no. 38n.

64 *Surrender by Henry de Merchyt to Chatteris abbey of 2 roods of land [in Chatteris] given by Ismaena, his wife.*
fo. 94r [*s.* xiii[1-2]]

Carta Henrici de Meche de duabus rodis terre.

Sciant presentes et futuri quod ego Henricus de Mech baronus Ismayne reddidi et liberavi pro animabus antecessorum meorum, per petitionem Ismaene uxoris mee, ad ecclesiam sancte Marie de Chatriz et conventui eiusdem loci illas duas rodas terre cum pertinenciis quas Ismaena uxor mea dedit ad ecclesiam sancte Marie de Chatriz et conventui eiusdem loci. Et ego predictus Henricus affidavi quod warantizabo contra omnes gentes, post mortem et in tota vita Isamene uxoris mee, illas predictas rodas terre cum pertinenciis quas predicta Ismaena uxor mea dedit per concessionem meam ad ecclesiam sancte Marie de Chatriz et conventui loci eiusdem. Et propter istam concessionem et confirmationem ratificandam, ego Henricus confirmavi presentem cartam impressione sigilli mei. Hiis testibus etc.

Note. Another copy of no. 22. Ismaena's gift is no. 24. For dating see no. 24n.

65 *Gift in free alms by Pain de Wentworth to Chatteris abbey of 1 rood of land in Chatteris and grant of an annual rent of 2s., to maintain the light of the high altar.*
fo. 94r-v [*s.* xiii[2-4]]

Donatio Pagani de Wyntewrth' de una roda terre et duobus solidis.

---

1 *i* written over *e*.
2 Followed by *in pace*, expunged.
3 Heading *Chatriz*.

Notum sit omnibus sancte matris ecclesie filiis quod ego Paganus de Wyntewrth' concessi dedi et hac presenti carta mea confirmavi Deo et ecclesie beate
Marie de Chatriz et monialibus ibidem Deo servientibus pro salute anime mee
et antecessorum meorum unam rodam terre cum pertinenciis in Chatriz, que
jacet juxta terram Elicie Brygston' et croftam Willelmi de Hunneye, et annuum
redditum duorum solidorum percipiendum de Galfrido de[1] Lynton' (fo. 94v)[2]
et de suis heredibus,[3] duodecim denariorum ad quatuor terminos usuales,
scilicet ad festum sancti Andree tres denariorum, ad Pascha tres denariorum, ad
festum sancti Johannis Baptiste tres denariorum et ad festum sancti Michaelis
tres denariorum, pro terra quam tenet de feodo in eadem villa, tenenda et
habenda eisdem monialibus et earum succestricibus totam dictam terram et
redditum in puram et perpetuam elemosinam cum omnibus pertinenciis integre
ut homagiis wardis reveliis et escaetis et omnibus aliis, que michi vel heredibus
meis de dicto feodo de Maundevyle aliquo modo descendere debuissent aut
potuissent, bene et in pace imperpetuum, ad luminare sustinendum[4] magni
altaris predicte ecclesie. Et ego Paganus et heredes mei warantizabimus acquietabimus et defendemus totam predictam terram et redditum cum pertinenciis, ut
supradictum est, predictis monialibus et earum succestricibus contra omnes
gentes imperpetuum. Et ut hec mea concessio donatio et huius presentis carte
mee confirmatio robur optineat perpetuum, presenti scripto sigillum meum
apposui. Hiis testibus etc.

> Note. Pain de Wentworth occurs in *s.* xiii[2-4] (no. 275). The land and rent are to be held *de*
> *feodo Maundevyle*: since no forename is given for the holder of the fee, this charter may date
> from between 1275, when John I died, and 1281, when his son and heir, John II, came of age
> (I. J. Sanders *English Baronies. A Study of their Origin and Descent* (Oxford, 1960) p. 64).

66 *Quitclaim by Agnes widow of William son of Alexander de Horseheath to*
abbess Mary de Shouldham and the convent of Chatteris of 3 selions of land [?in
Chatteris] which the abbess acquired from Constance le Freman, but which Agnes
and her heirs will warrant to the abbess.
fos. 94v–95r [30 Sept. 1300 × 1347]

---

1 Followed by *Luyton'*, probably cancelled.
2 Heading *Chatriz.*
3 Part of the text seems to have omitted here, including the details of the payment of the other
  shilling of rent.
4 *Donatio ad luminare magni altaris*, marginated before *-nendum.*

Relaxatio Agnetis de Horsethe de tribus selionibus terre facta abbatisse et conventui.

Omnibus Christi fidelibus ad quos presens scriptum pervenerit Agnes relicta Willelmi filii Alexandri de Horsethe salutem in Domino sempiternam. Noveritis me in vera et legitima viduitate mea relaxasse et pro me et heredibus meis imperpetuum quietum clamasse Marie de Schuldham abbatisse de Chatriz et eiusdem loci conventui totum jus et clamium meum, quod umquam habui vel aliquo modo habere potui, in illis tribus selionibus terre quas predicta Maria abbatissa de Chatriz dudum perquisivit sibi et succestricibus suis de Constancia le Freman, ita quod nec ego dicta Agnes nec (fo. 95r)[1] aliquis heredum meorum de cetero aliquod jus seu clamium in predictis tribus selionibus terre vendicare poterimus nec debemus. Set ego predicta Agnes et heredes mei predictis Marie abbatisse et succestricibus suis predictas tres seliones terre cum omnibus pertinenciis suis contra omnes homines, ab omnibus secularibus demandis sectis curiarum et hundredorum imperpetuum warantizabimus et defendemus. In cuius rei testimonium huic quiete clamantie sigillum meum apposui. Hiis testibus etc.

Note. The last dated occurrence for Amicia de Cambridge, the abbess before Mary de Shouldham, is shortly after 29 Sept. 1300 (no. 219). The next dated abbess after Mary is Alice de Shropham who resigned as abbess on 13 Oct. 1347 (Cambridge UL, EDR G/1/1 de Lisle register, fo. 51r–v).

67 *Gift in free alms by John de Cambridge to Chatteris abbey, for the support of the almonry and for feeding the poor and beggars, of 1 selion of land [in Chatteris].* fo. 95r [s. xiii$^{2-3}$]

Carta Johannis de Cantabr' de uno selione terre ad sustentationem pauperum in elemosinaria.

Notum sit omnibus sancte matris ecclesie filiis[2] quod ego Johannes de Cantabr' in Chatriz concessi dedi et hac presenti ⟨carta⟩ mea confirmavi Deo et ecclesie beate Marie de Chatriz et monialibus ibidem Deo servientibus, pro salute anime mee et antecessorum meorum, unum selionem terre mee cum pertinenciis, sicut jacet in longitudine et latitudine in campo versus Elmene juxta terram que fuit quondam Azotis le Noreys et terram abbatis de Ramesh', que se extendit juxta viam tendentem versus Elmeneford', habendum et tenendum eisdem dominabus

1 Heading *Chateriz*.
2 MS *filius*.

et earum succestricibus imperpetuum libere quiete ab omni[1] seculari servicio et demanda in puram et perpetuam elemosinam, videlicet ad sustentationem ele- mosinarie sue[2] et ad refectionem pauperum et mendicantium. Et ego Johannes et heredes mei warantizabimus acquietabimus et defendemus totam predictam terram cum pertinenciis omnibus predictis dominabus et earum succestricibus contra omnes mortales imperpetuum. Et ut hec mea concessio donatio et pre- sentis carte mee confirmatio firma sit et stabilis imperpetuum, presenti scripto sigillum meum apposui. Hiis testibus etc. (fo. 95v)[3]

> Note. See also the two copies of the confirmation of this gift, nos. 32 and 37. For dating of John de Cambridge see no. 53n.

68 *Gift in free alms by Simon de Insula to Chatteris abbey of a messuage with 8 acres of land in Chatteris.*
fo. 95v [*s.* xiii[1-2]]

Carta Simonis de Insula de[4] uno mesuagio una cum octo acris terre in Chatriz.

Omnibus amicis et vicinis suis presens scriptum visuris vel audituris Simon de Insula salutem. Noverit universitas vestra me dedisse concessisse et presenti carta mea confirmasse, pro salute animarum patris mei et matris mee et pro salute anime mee et anime Amicie uxoris mee et pro animabus liberorum nostrorum et animarum omnium antecessorum et successorum nostrorum, Deo et ecclesie beate Marie de Chatriz et monialibus ibidem Deo servientibus in puram et perpetuam elemosinam mesuagium illud in villa de Chatriz cum octo acris terre et omnibus aliis pertinenciis quod Joecus cocus tenuit, habendum et tenendum imperpetuum libere quiete et pure, absque omni servicio et seculari exactione. Et in huius rei testimonium et securitatem hanc presentem cartam prefatis monialibus feci et impressione sigilli mei roboravi. Hiis testibus etc.

> Note. There were two men called Simon de Insula in the thirteenth century. The first occurs as a witness in *s.* xiii[1] × 1233 (no. 281) and occurs in 1206–1218 (*Rot. Litt. Pat.*, p. 63; *CPR 1216–25*, p. 208). The second occurs in 1253–86 (*CPR 1247–58*, p. 235; *CPR 1281–92*, p. 282). He also occurs in final concords in 53 Henry III (1268–9) and 1 Edward I (1272–3) with his wife Helen (*Elena*) (*Cambs. Fines*, pp. 42, 47). The later Simon may well have married more than once, but the language of the charter and the fact that the benefactor in this gift was married to Amicia both suggest that this is the earlier Simon.

1 Ins. marg.
2 *nota refectionem mendicantium*, marginated after *sue*.
3 Heading *Terre Chatriz et tenementa*.
4 Interlined.

69 *Notification and exemplification by Robert son of Robert de Lyndon' and Juliana his wife of a lease by abbess Mary de Sancto Claro and the convent of Chatteris to Robert and Juliana, for their lives, of 2 selions in Chatteris, for 20s. and an annual rent of 3s. and by providing annually 1 man for 1 day to mow their meadow and 1 man for 1 day to reap their corn.*
fos. 95v–96r [s. xiii² × 28 Sept. 1265]

Dimissio Marie de Sancto Clare abbatisse Roberto de Lyadon' de duobus selionibus juxta mesuagium Sichich'.

Omnibus hoc scriptum visuris vel audituris Robertus filius Roberti de Lyadon' et Juliana uxor eius salutem. Noveritis nos recepisse ex dimissione Marie de Sancto Claro abbatisse de Chatriz et eiusdem loci conventus duas selliones in villa de Chatriz juxta mesuagium Sichich' in hec verba: Omnibus hoc scriptum visuris vel audituris Maria de Sancta Clara abbatissa de Chatriz et eiusdem loci conventus salutem in Domino. Noverit universitas vestra nos unanimi assensu dimisisse concessisse et hac presenti carta mea confirmasse Roberto filio Roberti de Lyndon' et Juliane uxori sue, pro servicio suo et pro viginti solidis (fo. 96r)[1] quos nobis dedit, duas seliones cum pertinenciis in villa de Chatriz juxta mesuagium Sicheis, habendas et tenendas predicto Roberto et Juliane uxori sue ad totam vitam eorum libere quiete, reddendo inde nobis annuatim et successoribus nostris tres solidos ad quatuor anni terminos, scilicet ad festum sancti Andree novem denarios et ad Pascha novem denarios et ad festum sancti Johannis Baptiste novem denarios et ad festum sancti Michaelis novem denarios, et inveniendo nobis annuatim unum[2] hominem per unum diem integrum ad pratum nostrum falcandum ad cibum nostrum, et unum[3] hominem per unum diem integrum ad bladum nostrum metendum similiter ad cibum nostrum, pro omnibus serviciis consuetudinibus et secularibus demandis, salvo omni forinseco. Et post decessum predictorum Roberti et Juliane predicte seliones cum omnibus eidificiis in eisdem sitis nobis et succestricibus nostris quiete et sine alicuius contradictione revertentur. Et ego Maria et succestrices nostre warantizabimus predictam terram cum pertinenciis predicto Roberto et predicte Juliane tota vita sua per predictum servicium contra omnes gentes. Et ut hec dimissio et concessio rata sit et stabilis tota vita predictorum Roberti et Juliane, secundum quod predictum est, presens scriptum sigillo capituli nostri fecimus muniri. Hiis testibus etc.

---

[1] Heading *Chatriz.*
[2] Repeated.
[3] Followed by *d,* expunged.

Note. For dating of Mary de Sancto Claro see no. 100n.

70 *Grant by Ismaena daughter of Ralph Briston, for the souls of her parents and of Adelicia wife of Ralph de Barley, to the almonry of Chatteris abbey of an annual rent of 4d. [?in Chatteris] which Ralph de Barley pays to her, for 2s. from Ralph de Barley.*
fo. 96r–v [s. xiii$^{1-2}$]

Donatio Ismaene filia Raduphi Brixston' de iiij^{or} denariis annui redditus ad elimosinariam.

Sciant etc. quod ego Ismaena filia Radulphi Brigston' concessi dedi et hac pre-senti carta mea confirmavi in puram[1] et perpetuam elemosinam, pro anima patris et pro anima matris mee et etiam pro anima Adelicie uxoris Radulphi de Berl[e],[2] redditum quatuor denariorum ad elimosinariam domus sancte Marie de Chatriz, redditum scilicet illum quem dictus Radulphus (fo. 96v)[3] persolvit michi per annum ad quatuor terminos, ut idem redditus ab eodem Radulpho et a suis assignatis predicte elemosinarie sancte Marie de Chatriz persolvatur ad unum terminum anni, in vigilia videlicet Natalis Domini. Et ego Ismaena et heredes mei warantizabimus hanc concessionem et donationem nostram tan-quam puram elemosinam contra omnes homines. Pro hac autem concessione donatione et warantizatione, dedit michi predictus Radulphus de Berle duos solidos. Ut vero hec carta firma sit et stabilis imperpetuum remaneat, huic scripto sigillum meum apposui. Hiis testibus.

Note. Another copy of no. 21. For dating see no. 21n.

71 *Lease by abbess Mary de Shouldham and the convent of Chatteris to John de Cambridge, for his life, of a messuage with close [in Chatteris].*
fo. 96v [30 Sept. 1300 × 1347]

Donatio abbatisse et conventus Johanni de Cantabr' de uno mesuagio.

Sciant presentes et futuri quod nos Maria de Schuldham abbatissa de Chatriz et eiusdem loci conventus dedimus concessimus et hac presenti carta nostra confirmavimus Johanni de Cantebr' illud mesuagium nostrum quod jacet aput le Slade cum toto clauso et omnibus suis pertinenciis, scilicet illud mesuagium

---

[1] *Redditus iiij^{or} denariorum ad elimonariam*, marginated after *puram*.
[2] Hole in margin, 9 mm.
[3] Heading *Chatriz.*

quod Gilbertus Joce de nobis tenuit ad terminum vite sue, habendum et tenendum dicto Johanni ad[1] terminum vite sue de nobis et successoribus nostris, sine omni servicio seculari. Et nos dicta Maria et successores nostri dictum mesuagium cum omnibus suis pertinenciis dicto Johanni ad totam vitam suam ipsius Johannis contra omnes homines warantizabimus defendemus acquietabimus. In cuius rei testimonium huic presenti carte indentate sigillum nostrum commune apposuimus. Hiis testibus etc.

Note. This John de Cambridge is perhaps the steward recorded in the manorial court rolls of the abbey's manor of Foxton, 1305–20 (Cambridge, Trinity College Archives, Foxton 1 and 4–5). For dating of abbess Mary de Shouldham see no. 66n.

72 *Grant by Ralph son of William of Ely, treasurer, to the infirmary of Chatteris abbey of 4s. annually.*
fos. 96v–97r [1196 × Aug. 1215]

Concessio Ricardi[2] de Ely facta domui de Chatriz de quatuor solidis ad infirmarium.

Omnibus Christi fidelibus ad quos presens scriptum pervenerit. Notum [sit quod][3] ego Radulphus de Hely filius Willelmi de Ely thesaurarii domini regis, divine pietatis intuitu et pro salute (fo. 97r)[4] anime mee et patris mei et matris mee, dedi in puram et perpetuam elimosinam, et hoc presenti scripto confirmavi,[5] infirmatorio sanctimonialium de Chatriz quatuor[6] solidos argenti de camera mea annuatim ad festum sancti Nicholai donec in tanto vel uberiori beneficio eis providerunt[7] domui de Chatriz semper permansuro. Et ut hec mea donatio rata et inconcussa semper permaneat, presens scriptum sigilli mei appositione roboravi. Hiis testibus etc.

Note. See also nos. 90 and 91: Ralph is son of Alice, *alias* Edelyna, concubine of William. Ralph first occurs as archdeacon of Middlesex shortly after March 1198; his successor first occurs in 1217 × 1218 (*Fasti 1066–1300* i, p. 16). William was the royal treasurer 1196–Aug. 1215.

---

[1] Followed by *totam vitam ipsius Johannis*, expunged.
[2] Recte *Radulphi*.
[3] Unclear 8 mm.
[4] Heading *Chatriz*.
[5] Repeated.
[6] *de iiij^{or} solidis ad infirmatorium*, marginated after *quatuor*.
[7] *t* interlined.

73 *Grant by Adam son of Robert de Cockfield to Chatteris abbey of an annual rent of 40s. from the first church in his gift to fall vacant, excepting the church of Kersey and the chapel of Lindsey (Suff.), meanwhile giving to the abbey 1 mark annually.*
fo. 97r [c. 1190 × c. 1198]

Donatio Roberti de Cokefeld' de quadraginta solidis anui redditus quousque etc.

Universis sancte matris ecclesie filiis Adam filius Roberti de Cokefeld salutem. Noverit universitas vestra me dedisse et hac carta mea confirmasse in perpetuam elimosinam monialibus et sancte Marie in ecclesia de Chatriz servientibus, pro anima patris mei et predecessorum meorum et salute propria, redditum annuum quadraginta solidorum in prima ecclesia vacante que sit de donatione mea, excepta ecclesia de Kareseya et capella de Leleseya. Et interim dabo eis unam marcam argenti annuatim, videlicet quadraginta denarios in festo sancti Nicholai et quadraginta denarios in dominica Ramis Palmarum et octo diebus ante festum sancti Johannis Baptiste quadraginta denarios et ad festum sancti Michaelis xl denarios, quousque redditum predictorum xl solidorum annuatim in ecclesia que prima michi vacuerit cum exceptione premissa, illis determinate assignaverim in puram et perpetuam elimosinam et carta mea confirmaverim. Hanc autem donationem ego et heredes mei eis warantizabimus. Hiis testibus etc.

Note. Another copy of no. 188. See also no. 204, a confirmation of this grant. For dating see no. 186n.

74 *Gift in free alms by Ralph de Barley to abbess Mabel [de Bancis] and the convent of Chatteris of a parcel of land [?in Chatteris].*
fo. 97r–v [s. xiii² × 28 Sept. 1265]

Donatio Radulphi de Berlee de quadam particula terre quondam Stephani Alberd'.

Sciant presentes et futuri quod ego Radulphus de Berlee (fo. 97v)[1] concessi dedi et hac presenti carta mea confirmavi Mabilie dicte domine de Chatriz et conventui eiusdem loci quandam particulam terre mee, jacentem juxta terram quam tenuit quondam Stephanus Alberd' de dicta Mabilia dicta domina et conventu de Chatriz, habendam et tenendam de me et heredibus meis dicte Mabilie dicte domine et conventui in puram et perpetuam elemosinam. Et ego

1 Heading *Chatriz.*

dictus Radulphus et heredes mei warantizabimus dictam terram cum pertinenciis dictis Mabilie dicte domine et conventui de Chatriz contra omnes
homines et feminas imperpetuum. Et ut hec[1] concessio et donatio firma et
stabilis permaneat.

> Note. Ralph de Barley is a witness in 1239 × *s.* xiii[3] (no. 240) and occurs *s.* xiii[1] × 6 Aug.
> 1254 (no. 17). For dating of abbess Mabel de Bancis see no. 100n.

75 *Agreement between Chatteris abbey and John, carter, and Goditha his wife
whereby the abbey grants to them, for their lives, ½ virgate of land which William
son of Beatrice surrendered to the abbey, for the service performed by William and 1
mark; John becomes a villein of the abbey.*
fo. 97v   ?[*s.* xiii[1-3]]

Littera conventionis inter dominam abbatissam de Chatriz et Johannem carectarium.

Hec est conventio facta inter dominam de Chatriz et[2] conventum eiusdem loci
ex una parte et Johannem carectarium et Goditham uxorem eius ex altera parte,
videlicet quod predicta domina et conventus concesserunt Johanni et Godithe
uxori eius toto tempore vite eorum dimidiam virgatam terre quam Willelmus
filius Beatricis reddidit quietam in curia predicte domine et conventus, habendam et tenendam pro simili servicio quod idem Willelmus filius Beatricis
fecit. Et pro huius concessione sepedictus Johannes et Goditha dederunt unam
marcam argenti predicte domine et conventui et ille Johannes devenit[3] nativus
domine et conventus cum tota sequela et catallis ipsius. Et ipsa domina et
conventus warantizabunt predictam terram predicto Johanni et Godithe tota
vita eorum. Et post decessum eorum redeat predicta terra soluta et quieta ad
domum de Chatriz. In huius rei testimonium presenti scripto signa sua ambe
partes apposuerunt. Hiis testibus etc.

> Note. Another copy of no. 137. This agreement shows a free man becoming a villein which
> suggests that it probably dates from before the late thirteenth century.

76 *Grant by Nigel, bishop of Ely, to Chatteris abbey of the lordship and advowson
of the church of St Peter, Chatteris.*
fos. 97v–98r   [*c.* 1158 × 30 May 1169]

---

1 Followed by *mea*, expunged.
2 Interlined.
3 *vide nativum*, marginated before *devenit*.

Donatio dominii et advocationis ecclesie beati Petri de Chatriz per Nigellum episcopum Eliensem facta[1] Deo et monialibus.

Nigellus Dei gracia Eliensis episcopus Ricardo archidiacono Elyensi (fo. 98r)[2] totique clero episcopatus Eliensis salutem. Sciatis nos dedisse et presenti carta confirmasse sanctimonialibus Deo et sancte Marie in ecclesia de Chatriz servientibus dominium et advocationem[3] ecclesie beati Petri in Chatriz. Quare volumus et firmiter precipimus ut beneficia prefate ecclesie, post decessum personarum eiusdem ecclesie Walteri Pil' et Rogeri Crochem, ad usus et ad necessitates ecclesie earum sustentandas cum omnibus pertinenciis suis proveniant. Testibus etc.

> Note. Another copy of no. 10. Nigel was bishop of Ely 1 Oct. 1133–30 May 1169; Richard FitzNeal was archdeacon of Ely *c.* 1158–89 (*Fasti 1066–1300* ii, p. 50). The translation of *dominium* could be demesne or lordship, but the latter is probably correct. It is possible, though, that *dominium* may refer to the manor which the abbot of Ely held in Chatteris in 1086 and which later became the manor of Chatteris Nunns.

77 *Declaration by Hugh [de Balsham], bishop of Ely, that Chatteris abbey acquired the parish churches of Chatteris and Shepreth canonically and that it is sufficiently strengthened by papal authority and by these letters to possess them.*
fo. 98r   At Little Downham, 5 Aug. 1262

Dimissio domini Hugonis episcopi Eliensis de ecclesiis de Chatriz et Sepherede in visitatione sua.

Universis Christi fidelibus presentes litteras visuris vel audituris Hugo Dei gracia episcopus Elyensis salutem in Domino sempiternam. Noverit universitas vestra quod nos, inspectis et examinatis instrumentis et cartis predecessorum nostrorum et capituli nostri[4] Elyensis, que seu quas dilecte in Christo filie sanctimoniales de Chatriz coram nobis auctoritate apostolica ad docendum de jure quod habent in ecclesiis parochialibus de Chatriz et de Scheperheye nostre diocesis legitime vocate in presentia nostra exhibuerunt, quod eedem moniales dictas ecclesias canonice sunt assecute et quod sufficienter ad dicta beneficia optinenda sunt munite tam apostolica auctoritate quam nostra tenore presentium pronunciamus, ad futuram rei memoriam presens scriptum sigilli nostri

---

1 MS *factam*, *m* expunged.
2 Heading *Chatriz*.
3 *Advoca[t]io ecclesie sancti Petri de Chateriz*, marginated after *advo-*.
4 *Dimissio ecclesiarum de Chateriz et Scheperede*, marginated after *nostri*.

appositione signatum predictis monialibus concedentes in testimonium. Dat'
apud Dounham nonas augusti anno Domini M^{mo} CC^{mo} sexagesimo secundo.

Note. Another copy of no. 16.

78 *Confirmation by Roger [de Bergham], prior of Ely, to Chatteris abbey of no. 11.*
fo. 98r–v [8 March 1220 × early 1229]

Confirmatio prioris Eliensis et conventus super appropriatione ecclesie sancti
Petri de Chatriz.

Universis sancte matris ecclesie filiis presens scriptum visuris[1] Rogerus prior
ecclesie Eliensis et totus conventus eiusdem loci in Domino salutem. Noverit
universitas vestra nos,[2] (fo. 98v)[3] ⟨a solo Deo⟩[4] remunerationem exspectantes et
venerabilis patris nostri Johannis Eliensis episcopi donationem et confirmationem ratam et gratam habentes, monialibus de Chatriz hac presenti carta
nostra confirmasse ecclesiam sancti Petri eiusdem ville, quam venerabilis pater
noster Johannes episcopus Eliensis in proprios usus habendam cum omnibus
pertinenciis suis eisdem monialibus contulit et confirmavit, sicut in eiusdem
carta continetur, salva vicaria quatuor marcarum de alteragio, quas quidem
capellanus, quem ipse moniales ad dictam vicariam presentabunt, cum mansione
que fuit Matill' de Berlee annuatim percipiet, qui eidem ecclesie deserviet et
curam habebit animarum, salvo[5] etiam venerabili patre nostro Johanne Eliensi
episcopo et successoribus suis jure pontificali et parochiali. Ut igitur hec nostra
confirmatio perpetuum robur optineat, presens scriptum sigillo capituli nostri
fecimus corroborari. Hiis testibus etc.

Note. Another copy of no. 12. For dating see no. 12n.

79 *Confirmation by William [Longchamp], bishop of Ely and papal legate, of the
settlement of a dispute between Chatteris abbey and Alan, vicar of the church of St
Peter, Chatteris, by which settlement Alan is to have all the obventions of the altar
and a third of the tithes of the church of St Peter, and the abbey is to have all the
other tithes and all the land pertaining to the church; after the death of Alan, the
next vicar is to have only the obventions of the altar.*

---

1 Illegible marginal note, 21 mm, after *visuris*.
2 Followed by *venerabilis*, expunged.
3 Heading *Chatriz*.
4 Supplied from no. 12.
5 MS *salva*.

fos. 98v–99r [5 June 1190 × spring 1192]

Hec est concordia inter dominam abbatissam et Alanum quondam vicarium de Chatriz auctoritate legati sedis apostolice.

Omnibus sancte matris ecclesie filiis ad quos presens scriptum pervenerit Willelmus Dei gracia Eliensis episcopus, apostolice sedis legatus et domini regis cancellarius salutem. Ad universitatis vestre noticiam volumus pervenire controversiam, que in presentia nostra vertebatur, inter moniales de Chatriz et Alanum clericum super medietate ecclesie beati Petri de Chatriz, sub hac pacis forma sopitam fuisse, videlicet quod predictus Alanus omnes obventiones altaris eiusdem ecclesie et tertiam partem decimarum frugum ad ipsam pertinentium in perpetua vicaria tenebit, et prefate moniales omnes alias decimas et totam terram ad eandem ecclesiam pertinentem imperpetuum possidebunt. Post obitum vero predicti Alani ille, qui ad presentationem predictarum monialium predicte ecclesie perpetuam vicariam tenebit, non nisi tantum[1] (fo. 99r)[2] obventiones altaris habebit. Sed moniales ille [omni]a[3] alia ad eandem ecclesiam pertinentia tam in terra quam in aliis possidebunt. Ut igitur ista compositio rata in posterum habeatur, e[am][4] presentis scripti et sigilli nostri attestatione confirmamus. Hiis testibus etc.

> Note. William Longchamp was bishop of Ely 31 Dec. 1189–31 Jan. 1197 and chancellor Aug. 1189–31 Jan. 97. He was papal legate for England 5 June 1190–spring 1192 (L. Landon *The Itinerary of King Richard I* (Pipe Roll Society, new ser. xiii, 1935) pp. 215–18).

80 *Release and quitclaim by John Winwick, John Cokerell and Nicholas Tyd to abbess Agnes and the convent of Chatteris of 2s. 2d. of annual rent which Richard Radewyn' of Swaffham Prior and his ancestors used to receive for various parcels of land in Chatteris.*
fo. 99r–v ?[s. xiv[4] × s. xv[1]]

Relaxatio Johannis de Wynewyk, Johannis Cokerel et Nicholai Tyd de uno tenemento et duobus solidis et ij denariis.

Omnibus Christi fidelibus ad quos presens scriptum pervenerit[5] Johannes Wynewyk de Chatriz, Johannes Cokerell' et Nicholaus Tyd de eadem salutem

1 Followed by catchwords, *obventiones altaris*.
2 Heading *Terre Chatriz et tenementa*.
3 Damaged 5 mm.
4 Hole 4 mm.
5 *presentes littere pervenerint*, marginated after *pervenerit*.

in Domino. Noveritis nos remisisse relaxasse et omnino pro nobis et heredibus nostris imperpetuum quietum clamasse Agneti abbatisse de Chatriz et conventui eiusdem loci et eorum successoribus totum jus et clamium quod habuimus habemus seu quovismodo habere poterimus in duobus solidis et duobus denariis annualis redditus, quos Ricardus Radewyn' de Swafham Priour et antecessores sui pro diversis parcellis terre in campis de Chatriz de dicta abbatissa et conventu annuatim percipere solebant, quem quidem redditum duorum solid-orum et duorum denariorum, simul cum uno tenemento et diversis pratis et pasturis, nos Johannes, Johannes[1] et Nicholaus communitim habuimus in villis et campis de Chatriz, ex dono et feoffamento Willelmi Bokeland et Katerine uxoris sue de Swafham predicta, ita quod nec nos[2] Johannes, Johannes et Nicholaus nec heredes nostri nec aliquis per nos seu nomine nostro aliquod jus vel clamium in predicto annuali redditu duorum solidorum et duorum denariorum, vel in aliquo parcella eiusdem redditus, seu in aliquo alio servicio de dicta abbatissa et conventu vel earum successoribus de cetero exigere vel vendicare poterimus imperpetuum, sed ab omni actione juris et clamio sumus exclusi per presentem. In cuius rei testimonium presenti scripto nostro sigilla nostra apposuimus. Hiis testibus (fo. 99v)[3] Willelmo Hert de comitatu Norff', Ricardo Hyldresham de Hely etc.

Note. A John Cokerell occurs in a court leet in Chatteris in 1385 and a Nicholas Tyd occurs in a sheriff's tourn in Witchford hundred in 1395 (Cambridge UL, EDR C/12/4/1; EDR C/7/29, m. 7). If they are the same men who occur in this document, the abbess here could be Agnes Ashfield who occurs as abbess in 1415 and 1437 (nos. 259 and 276). However, the John Cokerell and Nicholas Tyd in this document could be ancestors of those who occur in the late fourteenth century.

81 *Gift by Thomas Alberd' of Chatteris to Thomas, dispenser of Chatteris, of 1 rood of land in Chatteris.*
fo. 99v [s. xiii² × 1290]

Carta Thome Alberd' de una roda terre cum pertinenciis.

Sciant presentes etc. quod ego Thomas Alberd' de Chatriz dedi concessi et hac presenti carta mea confirmavi Thome dispensar[io] de Chatriz pro servicio suo unam rodam terre cum pertinenciis in campo de Chatriz, que jacet in campo qui vocatur Horyngsladefeld inter terram Emme filie Azonis et terram Stephani de

---

1 Ins. marg.
2 MS *nobis, bi* expunged.
3 Heading *Chatriz Bylneye.*

Chedesham, et abuttat super foream Ricardi filii Stephani, habendam et tenendam predictam rodam terre cum pertinenciis de me et heredibus meis sibi et
heredibus suis vel assignatis et eorum heredibus.

Vide[1] literam pro capella de Hunney infra folio xxxvij°.[2]

> Note. Stephen de Chettisham occurs in 1270 (Ault ed. *Ramsey Court Rolls*, p. 262). This gift
> is followed by nos. 52 and 54. All three gifts must pre-date 1290 because the land is to be
> held *de me et heredibus meis*.

82 *Gift in free alms by William de Bek to Chatteris abbey of his part of the mill
which Richard son of Roland holds from him in Bilney (Norf.).*
fo. 99v [*s*. xii[4] × *s*. xiii[1]]

Carta Willelmi Bek de parte molendini quam habuit in Bylneye cum pertinenciis.

Sciant etc. quod ego[3] Willelmi de Bek concessi dedi et hac presenti carta mea
confirmavi totam partem meam molendini quam Ricardus filius Rodlandi tenet
de me in Bylneye in puram et perpetuam elemosinam, pro animabus[4] omnium
fidelium defunctorum monialibus de Chatriz. Et ut hec concessio rata et firma
permaneat, presentem cartam sigilli mei impressione roboravi. Hiis testibus etc.

> Note. William de Bek occurs in 28 Oct. 1198 (*Norf. Fines 1198–1202*, p. 86, no. 199) and 12
> Feb. 1209 (*Norf. and Suff. Fines*, p. 84, no. 174).

83 *Grant by John Vivien to Chatteris abbey of a fishery with meadow [in Chat-
teris], which was quit-claimed to him by Gonnora, his sister, to whom Henry, his
father, had given it as a marriage-portion.*
fos. 99v–100r [*s*. xiii[2–4]]

Carta Johannis Viven de piscaria inter Achenwere etc.

Sciant presentes etc. quod ego Johannes Vivien dedi concessi et hac presenti
carta mea confirmavi Deo et ecclesie beate Marie de Chatriz et monialibus
ibidem Deo servientibus, pro salute anime mee antecessorum et successorum

---

1 *Hunneye* marginated before *Vide*.
2 *62* marginated after *xxxvij°*: a reference to charter no. 164 on modern fo. 135v (fo. 62v according to earliest visible foliation).
3 Followed by *Johannes*, expunged.
4 Second *a* interlined.

meorum, in liberam puram et ⟨perpetuam⟩ elimosinam totam illam piscariam[1] quam Henricus Vivien pater meus aliquando dedit Gonnore sorori[2] mee in liberum maritagium [inter][3] Achenewere et Horse, cum toto prato ad pre-dictam (fo. 100r)[4] piscariam pertinente, et quam piscariam et quod pratum[5] predicta Gonnora michi per scriptum suum quieta clamavit cum omnibus pertinenciis suis, tenendam et habendam predictis monialibus et successtricibus suis libere quiete bene et in p[ace][6] et integre et hereditarie in liberam puram et perpetuam elemosinam, adeo liberius et quietius sicuti aliqua elimosina aliqui-bus viris religiosis dari potest vel conferri. Et ego predictus Johannes et heredes mei vel mei assignati warantizabimus acquietabimus et defendemus totam predictam piscariam, cum predicto prato ad predictam piscariam pertinente, predictis monialibus et successtricibus eius contra omnes gentes tam christianos quam judeos imperpetuum. Ut autem hec mea consessio et donatio robur optineat[7] imperpetuum, hanc cartam sig[illi] mei impression[e roboravi]. Hiis testibus.[8]

> Note. See also no. 275, the grant and quitclaim by Gonnora to John Vivien of the fishery and meadow. For dating see no. 275n.

84 *Grant by Ismaena daughter of Ralph Briston to Chatteris abbey of 2 fisheries [in Chatteris].*
fo. 100r [s. xiii[1-2]]

Carta Ismaene de piscariis in Horsewere et in gordo de Redesteche cum per-tinenciis.

Sciant etc. quod ego Ismaena filia Radulphi Bricston' dedi concessi et hac presenti carta mea confirmavi in puram et perpetuam elemosinam, pro me et animabus antecessorum meorum, Deo et domui de Chatriz totam piscariam quam habeo in Horsewere cum pertinenciis sine aliquo retenemento, et totam piscariam quam habeo in gordo de Rodesteche cum pertinenciis sine aliquo retenemento, tenendas et habendas libere et quiete imperpetuum. Et ego Is-

---

1 [vi]de aliam cartam [d]e eadem infra [fo]lio septuagesimo vijᵐᵒ, marginated before -riam.
2 MS sorore, e expunged, i interlined.
3 Hole 7 mm.
4 Heading Chatriz piscarie.
5 Interlined.
6 Hole 5 mm.
7 MS opertineat.
8 hanc ... testibus ins. marg.; right-hand egde of folio lacking.

maena et heredes mei warantizabimus predicte domui predictam piscariam cum pertinenciis contra omnes homines. Hiis testibus etc.

Note. For dating of Ismaena see nos. 21n and 24n.

85 *Grant by Alexander son of Ralph Briston to Chatteris abbey of 4 fisheries [in Chatteris].*
fo. 100r–v [*s.* xiii$^{1-3}$]

Carta Alaxandri de piscaria in Horswere cum aliis piscariis.

Sciant etc. quod ego Alexander filius Radulphi Brustin dedi etc. in puram et perpetuam elemosinam, pro me et animabus antecessorum meorum, Deo et sancte Marie et domui de Chateriz totam piscariam quam habeo in Horswere cum pertinenciis sine aliquo retenemento, et totam piscariam quam habeo in gordo de Redesteche cum pertinenciis sine aliquo retenemento, et totam pis-cariam (fo. 100v)^1 quam habeo in Ethenewere cum pertinenciis sine aliquo retenemento, et totam piscariam quam habeo in Newere sine aliquo reten-emento, tenendas et habendas libere et quiete imperpetuum. Et ego Alexander et heredes mei warantizabimus predicte domui predictam piscariam cum pertinenciis contra omnes homines. Hiis testibus etc.

Note. For dating of Ralph Briston see nos. 19n and 23n.

86 *Grant by Andrew son of Henry, priest, and Alice his wife, daughter of Ralph Briston, to Chatteris abbey of 4 fisheries [in Chatteris].*
fo. 100v [*s.* xiii$^{1-3}$]

Carta Andree de piscaria in Horsewere cum aliis.

Sciant presentes etc. quod ego Andreas filius Henrici sacerdotis et Alicia uxor mea filia Radulphi Bricston' dedi etc. in puram et perpetuam elimosinam, pro nobis et animabus antecessorum nostrorum, Deo et ecclesie sancte Marie et domui de Chatriz totam piscariam quam habemus in Horsewere cum pertinen-ciis sine aliquo retenemento, et totam piscariam quam habemus in Ethneswere^2 cum pertinenciis sine aliquo retenemento, et totam piscariam quam habemus in gordo de Redesteche cum pertinenciis sine aliquo retenemento, et totam piscari-am quam habemus in Newewere cum pertinenciis sine aliquo retenemento, tenendas et habendas libere et quiete imperpetuum. Et ego Andreas et Alicia

---

1 Heading *Chatriz piscarie.*
2 MS *Ethesneswere*, first *es* expunged.

uxor mea et heredes nostri warantizabimus predicte domui predictas piscarias cum pertinenciis contra omnes homines. Hiis testibus etc.

Note. For dating of Ralph Briston see nos. 19n and 23n.

87 *Grant by Robert de Insula to Chatteris abbey of 2 fisheries with specified rights and gift in free alms of the fee which Baldwin son of Augustine held of him in Upwell and Outwell (Cambs. and Norf.) for 10 sticks of eels, excepting Baldwin's tenement; with Alice, daughter of Richard Moler, his kinswoman.*
fos. 100v–101r [*s.* xii^4 × *s.* xiii^2]

Carta Roberti de Insula^1 de piscaria ut supra.

Omnibus etc. Robertus de Insula salutem. Sciatis me dedisse concessisse et hac presenti carta mea confirmasse Deo et ecclesie sancte Marie de Chatriz et monialibus ibidem Deo servientibus totam piscariam cum omnibus pertinenciis suis quam habui in Bradewere et Neustale, scilicet^2 unaquaque nocte quartam in una piscaria et unaquaque quartam^3 nocte in alia piscaria sine aliquo retinemento, et preterea totum feodum cum omnibus pertinenciis suis quod Baldewynus filius Augustini tenuit de me in villa de Welles per redditum decem stikkorum anguillarum, salvo tenemento ipsius Baldewini et heredum (fo. 101r)^4 suorum quamdiu ipse et heredes sui predictum servicium ecclesie de Chatriz fideliter reddiderunt, in puram et perpetuam elimosinam, liberam et quietam ab omni seculari servicio et exactione. Hanc autem donationem ⟨et⟩ concessionem^5 feci pro salute anime mee et Radulphi patris mei et Cassandre matris mee et heredum meorum, et insuper cum Alicia filia Ricardi Moler consanguinea mea que habitum religionis ad petitionem meam in eadem ecclesia suscepit. Hanc predictam elemosinam ego et heredes mei warantizabimus. Hiis testibus etc.

Note. Men called Robert de Insula occur in final concords in 3 John (1201–2), 19 Henry III (1234–5), 24 Henry III (1239–40), 45 Henry III (1260–1), and 1 Edw. I (1272–3) (*Cambs. Fines*, pp. 4, 20, 22, 39, 47). The language of this charter suggests that it was written between the late twelfth and the mid-thirteenth centuries.

---

1 *de Insula*, repeated.
2 MS *sicilicet*, first *i* expunged.
3 MS *quarta*.
4 Heading *Chatriz piscarie*.
5 Interlined.

88 *Grant by Ebrard, chaplain of Chatteris and son of Robert Briston, to Chatteris abbey of 4 fisheries [in Chatteris].*
fo. 101r [s. xiii$^{1-3}$]

Carta Ebrardi capellani de piscariis in Horsewere et Nuwewere et Redesteche et Hachenewere.

Sciant etc. quod ego Ebrard capellanus de Chatriz et filius Roberti Bricston' dedi etc. Deo et ecclesie sancte Marie de Chatriz et monialibus ibidem Deo servientibus totum jus quod habui vel habere potui in piscaria que dicitur Horsewere cum omnibus pertinenciis, et in piscaria de Newewere cum omnibus pertinenciis, et in piscaria que dicitur Redesteche cum pertinenciis, in piscaria que dicitur Hachenewere cum omnibus pertinenciis suis, habendas et tenendas imperpetuum sine aliquo retenemento in puram elemosinam, pro salute anime mee et pro salute antecessorum et successorum meorum. In cuius rei testimonium etc.

Note. For dating see occurrence of Ebrard, chaplain, in nos. 110 and 238.

89 *Exchange between Nigel, bishop of Ely, and Chatteris abbey of 20 sticks of eels each, and grant by Nigel to the abbey of an additional 10 sticks of eels, [from fisheries in Chatteris].*
fo. 101r–v [1 Oct. 1133 × 30 May 1169]

Donatio domini Nigelli de piscaria de Polwere et xxx^{ta} sticcis anguillarum.[1]

Nigellus Dei gracia Eliensis episcopus omnibus hominibus de honore sancte Etheldrede salutem. Universitati vestre notum facimus nos concessisse Deo et ecclesie sancte Marie de Chatriz et monialibus ibidem Deo servientibus in piscaria de Polwere, que solet reddere triginta sticcas anguillarum, viginti sticcas in excambio[2] pro decem sticcis quas solebant habere de piscaria de Egeswera de octava nocte, et pro quinque sticcis quas solebant habere de piscaria[3] de Segwere in Westfen, et pro quinque (fo. 101v)[4] sticcis quas solebant habere de piscaria de Northtdelf. Et decem sticcas que supersunt de Pow'[5] damus et concedimus et presenti carta nostra confirmamus prefate ecclesie in liberam et perpetuam

---

[1] *Et dimissionem ad firmam [eiu]sdem piscarie vide infra folio xxxvij°*, written in space after rubric and in margin.
[2] *ex* interlined.
[3] *de piscaria*, repeated.
[4] Heading *iij denarii in Heverhille*.
[5] Unfinished; followed by space, 6 mm.

elemosinam. Volumus ergo et firmiter precipimus ut[1] prenominata ecclesia et moniales prefatam piscariam cum omnibus pertinenciis et libertatibus suis libere quiete et honorifice, sicut nos illam unquam[2] melius et liberius tenuimus, habeant et tenendo possideant. Test' etc.

Note. Nigel was bishop of Ely 1 Oct. 1133–30 May 1169.

90 *Alleged sale and quitclaim by Alexander, son of Ingelram, steersman of the bishop of Ely, with the assent of his son John, to William of Ely, archdeacon of Cleveland, of: 3d. of rent from 1½ acres each of land and meadow [in Stuntney]; his rights and rent in a fishery at Upwell and Outwell (Cambs. and Norf.) and a rent of 3d. in Little Thetford, for 29s. 8d.*
fos. 101v–102r [1201 × 1222, ?date of forgery]

Quieta clamantia Alexandri ⟨filii Ingelrammi sturesmanni⟩ episcopi Eliensis Willelmo archidiachono Clevelandye de iij denariis in Heverhille.

Alexander filius Ingelrammi sturesmanni episcopi Elyensis omnibus Christi fidelibus presentem cartam visuris salutem in Domino. Sciatis me de assensu et voluntate Johannis filii mei et heredis vendidisse et quietum clamasse imperpetuum Willelmo Eliensi archidiacono Clyveland',[3] pro magna mea necessitate, servicium iij denariorum quod Margareta filia Walteri de Bereweye michi reddere debebat de una acra et dimidia terre que jacent in Hevereshille, et de una acra et dimidia prati pertinentibus ad eandem terram que jacent ibidem, quam terram et quod pratum magister Petrus de Stunteneye avunculus meus[4] dedit eidem[5] Margarete pro homagio et servicio suo et carta sua confirmavit, habenda et libere tenenda et hereditarie de se et heredibus suis pro sex denariis annuis, de quibus sex denariis tres denarii pertinent ad predictum archidiaconum et ad heredes suos, et de quibus sex denariis alii tres denarii pertinebant ad me antequam eos venderem. Vendidi etiam eidem Willelmo archidiacono et quietum clamavi de me et heredibus meis imperpetuum de assensu et voluntate predicti heredis mei, pro magna necessitate mea, totum jus et totum redditum (fo. 102r)[6] que[7] habui in piscaria apud Welle, que piscaria dicitur Tryllynge,

---

1 Interlined.
2 MS *umquam*, third minim of first *m* expunged.
3 MS *Clyeveland'*, first *e* expunged.
4 Recte *eius*: cf. no. 91
5 Followed by *magistro*, expunged.
6 Heading *Thetforth' Parva infra Insulam.*
7 MS *quod*, *d* expunged, *o* corr. to *e*.

cum pertinenciis suis, videlicet totam portionem meam quam habebam in eadem piscaria post partitionem factam redditus quem habuimus, ego videlicet et predictus archidiaconus et Radulphus de Ely filius Edelyne[1] amice mee,[2] in eadem pisscaria. Preterea vendidi ei archidiacono et quietum clamavi de me et heredibus meis imperpetuum, de assensu et voluntate predicti heredis mei, redditum iij denariorum in villa de Parva Thetford' qui ad me pertinebant per partitionem inter nos factam. Has autem omnes predictas venditiones, sicut determinatum est, memorato Willelmo feci pro viginti novem solidis et[3] octo denariis quos michi pacavit, que omnia tenementa habebit et tenebit, et que tanquam sua propria perquisita poterit dare vendere vel legare ubicumque vel cuicumque et quibuscumque voluerit. Ego autem et heredes mei debemus has venditiones eidem Willelmo, et illi vel illis quibus predicta tenementa dare vendere vel legare voluerit, contra omnes homines et feminas warantizare. Et ego Alexander hoc pro me et heredibus meis juravi tactis sacrosanctis evangeliis me et ipsos fideliter observaturos, et quod nullum nocumentum vel vexatio eidem Willelmo, vel eis ad quos predicta tenementa devenient, eveniet, unde ab ipsis tenementis elongentur vel vexentur. Et ut hec omnia firmius robur accipiant, presentem cartam ei feci et sigillo meo signavi. Hiis testibus.

> Note. This charter may be a forgery, based on no. 91 and produced to complement it. This
> would account for the misuse here of *meus* and *mee* for *eius* which seem to have been taken
> from no. 91. The document may possibly have been produced to replace an existing –
> perhaps damaged – original which would explain how the scribe knew that Alexander was
> the son of Ingelram. For dating see no. 91n. This document provides evidence of the parent-
> age of Ralph of Ely (see also nos. 72 and 91). Alice, here miscopied as Edelyna, is his mother.
> She must be the concubine of William of Ely and is referred to as his *amica*.

91 *Grant and gift in free alms by William of Ely, archdeacon of Cleveland, to Chatteris abbey, for the support of sick nuns in the infirmary, of: Richard de Bircham and his tenement in Bircham (Norf.), for an annual rent to the lord of the fee of a pair of gilt spurs, price 6d., or 6d.; 1½ acres each of land and meadow in Stuntney; 3d. of rent from this land which he bought from Alexander, steersman of the bishop of Ely; his portion of a fishery at Upwell and Outwell (Cambs. and Norf.) and a rent of 3d. in Little Thetford.*
fos. 102r–103r [1201 × 1222]

Carta Willelmi de Ely de Ricardo de Brecham cum tenemento suo in Brecham.

---

1 Recte *Aelicie*: cf. no. 91.
2 Recte *eius*: cf. no. 91.
3 *Parva The[t]ford']* marginated after *et*.

Sciant etc. quod ego Willelmus de Ely archidiaconus Clyveland' dedi etc., pro anima mea et patris et matris mee et pro animabus antecessorum et benefactorum meorum et omnium (fo. 102v)[1] fidelium defunctorum, in puram et perpetuam elemosinam Deo et ecclesie beate Marie de Chatriz et sanctimonialibus ibidem Deo servientibus, in auxilio ad sustentationem sanctimonialium in infirmaria egrotantium, Ricardum de Brecham hominem meum et totum tenementum suum quod de me[2] tenuit in Brecham, et omne jus quod in eo et suis habui, sicut carta Ricardi London' episcopi testatur, per quam idem episcopus michi confirmavit prefatum Ricardum cum predicto tenemento, salvo servicio quod debetur domino fuudi, sicut in carta continetur quam memoratus episcopus London' michi fecit, scilicet uno pari calcarum deauratorum precii vj denariorum vel pro sex denariis reddendis ad Pascha predicto domino et heredibus suis, pro omnibus serviciis et consuetudinibus ad ipsum dominum[3] vel heredes suos pertinentibus. Dedi etiam sanctimonialibus in[4] infirmaria egrotantibus totam terram cum pertinenciis quam emi de Margareta filia Walteri de Berquee in[5] campo de Stunteneye, quam terram magister Petrus avunculus meus dedit illi pro servicio suo, videlicet unam acram et dimidiam terre que jacent in Heverhille, et unam acram et dimidiam prati ad eandem terram pertinentes que jacent ibidem. Preterea dedi predictis sanctimonialibus servicium trium denariorum pertinens ad predictam terram, quod servicium emi de Alexandro esturesman episcopi Eliensis, et quod servicium memorata Margareta debuit solvere dicto Alexandro et heredibus suis singulis annis antequam servicium illud sepedictus Alexander michi vendidisset, sicut carta sua quam michi fecit testatur. Dedi etiam sepedictis monialibus totam[6] illam portionem piscarie apud Welle, que piscaria dicitur Tryllinge, cum pertinenciis suis, que portio contingebat dictum Alexandrum, per partitionem factam inter me et ipsum Alexandrum et Radulphum de Ely filium Aelicie[7] amice mee, antequam illam portionem (fo. 103r)[8] cum pertinenciis suis michi vendidisset. Preterea dedi prenominatis sanctimonialibus redditum trium denariorum in villa de Parva Thetford' qui pertinebat ad dictum Alexandrum, per partitionem

---

1 Heading *Briccham Stunteneye.*
2 *Briccham* marginated before *me.*
3 Followed by *h*, expunged.
4 Interlined.
5 *Stunteneye* marginated before *in.*
6 *Welle* marginated before *totam.*
7 MS damaged: possibly *Aeline.*
8 Heading *Ely.*

factam inter me et ipsum Alexandrum et Radulphum de Ely filium predicte[1]
Aelicie amice mee, antequam redditum illum michi vendidisset. Ut autem hec
mea donatio et concessio et carte mee confirmatio firma sit et stabilis, presenti
scripto sigillum meum apposui. Hiis testibus etc.

Note. No. 223 is another copy of the first part of this charter. William of Ely was archdeacon of Cleveland from 1201; he died in 1222 (C. T. Clay 'Notes on the Early Archdeacons in the Church of York' *Yorkshire Archaeological Journal* xxxvi (1947) part 144, pp.
429–30).

92 *Gift in free alms by Richard Muschet, with the assent of his wife, to the infirmary of Chatteris abbey of a messuage in Potter's Lane, Ely.*
fo. 103r [s. xiii[1-2]]

Carta Ricardi Muschet de jure quod habuit in quodam[2] mesuagio ad firmariam
pertinente.

Sciant presentes etc. quod ego Ricardus Muschet assensu et concilio uxoris mee
dedi et concessi etc. Deo et beate Marie[3] et infirmarie de Chatriz, pro salute
anime mee et uxoris mee et pro salute animarum et antecessorum nostrorum[4] et
successorum nostrorum, totum jus quod habui in mesuagio in Potterislane quod
fuit de feodo Gilberti carpentarii, quod mesuagium tenui de feodo Pagani
avunculi[5] mei in villa Eliensi cum omnibus pertinenciis, in puram et perpetuam
elemosinam quietum de me et heredibus meis imperpetuum. Et ut donatio mea
et concessio et huius presentis carte mee confirmatio rata et inconcussa permaneat, sigilli mei appositione hanc cartam roboravi. Hiis testibus etc.

Note. William of Ely, archdeacon of Cleveland, gave a messuage and croft in Potter's Lane,
Ely, to Richard Muschet, his nephew, for 18d. annually. Pain of Ely, brother of William and
uncle of Richard, confirmed William's gift (Cambridge UL, EDC 1/A/2, fo. 47r–v). For
dating of William of Ely, archdeacon of Cleveland, see no. 91n. See also no. 93.

93 *Gift by abbess A. de Rouen and the convent of Chatteris to Alan de Ely, gardener, and Alice his wife of a messuage in Potter's Lane, Ely, for 5s. and an annual
rent of 2s. 6d.*
fo. 103r–v [s. xiii[1-2]]

---

1 *Parva Thetford'* marginated after *predicte*.
2 *Ely* marginated in black after *quodam*.
3 *mesuagium infirmarie in Ely*, marginated after *Marie*.
4 Followed by *totum*, expunged.
5 MS *avungculi*, g expunged.

Conventio quedam inter abbatissam de Chatriz et quendam Alanum.

Notum sit omnibus quod ego A. de Rothomago humilis[1] ancilla de Chatriz et eiusdem domus conventus dedimus et concessimus et hac presenti carta nostra confirmavimus Alano de Ely gardinario[2] et Alie[3] uxori sue,[4] pro homagio et servicio suo, illud mesuagium in Potterislane in villa de Ely cum pertinenciis, quod mesuagium Gilbertus carpentarius tenuit de P[agano][5] filio Alexandri juxta mesuagium Johannis de I...,[6] tenendum (fo. 103v)[7] et habendum de nobis et successoribus nostris,[8] ⟨reddendo inde annuatim nobis et successoribus nostris⟩ duos solidos et sex denarios ad quatuor terminos anni usuales.[9] Et sciendum quod non licet predictis Alano et Alicie dare vendere nec invadiare predictum[10] mesuagium cum pertinenciis alicui domui religionis nisi tantum domui de Chatriz. Et si heredem aliquem inde facere voluerint, licet illis facere talem qui sit utilis et conveniens domui de Chatriz. Pro hac autem donatione et concessione carte nostre confirmatione, dedit nobis predictus Alanus v solidos in guersummam. Testibus hiis etc.

Note. This charter follows no. 92. A. de Rouen must precede Mabel de Bancis who was abbess *s.* xiii[2] × 28 Sept. 1265 (see no. 100n). She may also precede abbess I., who occurs in 1216 (no. 164), if the messuage in Potter's Lane passed rapidly through the hands of William of Ely, Richard Muschet and the abbey of Chatteris. It seems more likely, though, that A. de Rouen was a successor to abbess I.

94 *Grant by Geoffrey [Ridel], bishop of Ely, to Chatteris abbey of a prebend of 20s. annually in Fen Ditton.*
fo. 103v [6 Oct. 1174 × 21 Aug. 1189]

Donatio Galfridi de xx[ti] solidis in Ditton'.

1 *Ely* marginated after *humilis*.
2 Followed by *juxta mesuagium Johannis*, expunged.
3 Recte *Alicie*.
4 Corr. marg., *eius* expunged.
5 Hole 11 mm.
6 Damaged 13 mm.
7 Heading *Ditton'*.
8 The end of the *habendum* clause and the beginning of the *reddendo* clause have been omitted by the scribe. He probably made this error because of the recurrence of the phrase *nobis et successoribus nostris* in the original.
9 MS *usuales anni*, marked for transposition.
10 MS *predicta*.

Universis sancte matris ecclesie filiis ad quos littere presentes pervenerint Galfridus Dei gracia Elyensis episcopus salutem in Domino. Noverit universitas vestra nos, intuitu caritatis et necessitatis monialium de Chateriz, concessisse eis in perpetuam elimosinam prebendam illam viginti solidorum in Ditton' quam[1] Rogerus Niger consuevit habere, et volumus quod eedem moniales eandem prebendam ad sustentationem suam habeant, libere et quiete perpetuo possidendam toto tempore nostro et omnium successorum nostrorum, et accipiendam a firmariis eiusdem ville vel a balivis, si ipsa forte ad firmam non fuerit, ad quatuor terminos, ad festum sancti Andree v solidos, ad Pascha v solidos, ad festum sancti Johannis v solidos et ad festum sancti Michaelis v solidos. Et hoc eis presenti scripto et sigilli nostri appositione roboramus et confirmamus. Test' etc.

Note. Geoffrey Ridel was bishop of Ely 6 Oct. 1174–20 or 21 Aug. 1189. No. 95 proves that the bishop who made this grant was Geoffrey Ridel and not Geoffrey de Burgo.

95 *Notification by Hugh, bishop of Ely, to his stewards and bailiffs in his exchequer at Ely that he has granted to Chatteris abbey 36s. annually, of which the abbey had received 20s. annually from the time of bishop Geoffrey Ridel and Hugh has granted 16s. annually for their water-mill in Thriplow which they have given and quitclaimed to him.*
fos. 103v–104r [28 June 1243 × 6 Aug. 1254 *or* 14 Oct. 1257 × *c.* 16 June 1286]

Carta Hugonis de xxx[ta] solidis et sex de scaccario Eliensi pro molendino de Trippelowe.

Hugo Dei gracia Elyensis episcopus senescallis et quibuscumque aliis balivis suis sedentibus in scaccario suo Eliensi salutem in Domino. (fo. 104r)[2] Sciatis quod concessimus monialibus de Chatriz triginta et sex solidos sterlingorum annuatim percipiendos ad quatuor terminos usuales scaccarii nostri Elyensis imperpetuum, videlicet ad quemlibet terminum novem solidos equaliter. De quibus triginta et sex solidis receperunt viginti solidos a tempore bone memorie[3] Galfridi Rydel quondam episcopi Eliensis, et nos sexdecim solidos eis concessimus pro molendino suo de Tryppelowe aquatico, quod[4] nobis dederunt et quietum clamaverunt. Unde vobis mandamus quod, cum dicte moniales vel earum nuncius ad vos venerint pro dictis denariis, infra quartum diem cuiuslibet

1 *Ditton'* marginated before *quam*.
2 Heading *Ditton'*.
3 *i* interlined.
4 *nota xvj solidos pro molendino de Tryppelow[e]*, marginated after *quod*.

quatuor terminorum novem solidos eis liberari faciatis sine dilatione. In cuius rei testimonium has litteras nostras fieri fecimus patentes. Vale.[1]

> Note. The bishop in this notification could be Hugh de Northwold who was bishop of Ely 10 June 1229–6 Aug. 1254 or Hugh de Balsham who was bishop 14 Oct. 1257–c. 16 June 1286. Since Thriplow mill occurs in the privilege of pope Innocent IV (28 June 1243–7 Dec. 1254), which confirmed the possessions of Chatteris abbey, this document must post-date Innocent's privilege (no. 3).

96 *Inspeximus and confirmation by Hugh [de Balsham], bishop of Ely of no. 94.*
fo. 104r–v [14 Oct. 1257 × 6 Nov. 1280]

Confirmatio domini Hugonis episcopi Eliensis de donatione xx solidorum per cartam domini Galfridi episcopi Eliensis.

Omnibus hoc scriptum visuris vel audituris Hugo Dei gracia Elyensis episcopus salutem in Domino. Noveritis nos cartam bone memorie Galfridi quondam Eliensis episcopi predecessoris nostri[2] inspexisse in hec verba: Universis sancte matris ecclesie filiis ad quos littere presentes pervenerint Galfridus Dei gracia Elyensis episcopus salutem in Domino. Noverit universitas vestra nos, intuitu caritatis et necessitatis monialium de Chatriz, concessisse eis in perpetuam elemosinam prebendam illam viginti solidorum in Ditton' quam Rogerus Niger consuevit habere. Et volumus quod eedem moniales eandem prebendam[3] ad sustentationem suam habeant, libere et quiete perpetuo possidendam toto tempore nostro et omnium successorum nostrorum, et accipiendam a firmariis nostris eiusdem (fo. 104v)[4] ville vel a balivis, si ipsa forte ad firmam non fuerit, ad quatuor terminos, ad festum sancti Andree v solidos, ad Pascha v solidos, ad festum sancti Johannis v solidos et ad festum sancti Michaelis v solidos. Et hoc eis presenti scripto et sigilli nostri appositione roboramus et confirmamus. Hiis testibus etc. Nos autem plene intelligentes intentionem factum et propositum dicti predecessoris nostri laudabilia extitisse in hac parte, concedimus volumus et statuimus quod dicte moniales in scaccario Eliensi annuatim percipiant dictos viginti solidos terminis antedictis sine omni contradictione alicuius, sicut eos receperunt toto tempore nostro et temporibus predecessorum nostrorum, et totum tenorem dicte carte de verbo ad verbum quantum possumus pro nobis et

---

1 Followed by *n*, cancelled?
2 MS *nostris*, *s* expunged.
3 Followed by *successorum nostrorum*, expunged.
4 Heading *Chatriz Ditton'*.

successoribus nostris confirmamus. In cuius rei testimonium hanc cartam nostram dictis monialibus concessimus sigillo nostro signatam. Hiis testibus etc.

> Note. Hugh Balsham was bishop of Ely 14 Oct. 1257–*c.* 16 June 1286. This inspeximus must pre-date no. 97 which confirms it.

97 *Inspeximus and confirmation by prior John [de Hemmingestone] and the chapter of Ely, of no. 96.*
fos. 104v–105r   At Ely, 6 Nov. 1280

Confirmatio prioris et conventus de Ely supra prebenda xx solidorum in Ditton'.

Universis sancte matris ecclesie filiis ad quos presens scriptum pervenerit J(ohannes) prior Eliensis et eiusdem loci capitulum salutem in Domino sempiternam. Noverit universitas vestra nos cartam venerabilis patris nostri Hugonis Dei gracia Eliensis episcopi nostri, non cancellatam non abolitam nec in aliqua sui parte vitiatam, inspexisse in hec verba: Omnibus hoc scriptum visuris vel audituris Hugo Dei gracia Eliensis episcopus salutem in Domino. Noveritis nos[1] cartam bone memorie Galfridi quondam Eliensis episcopi predecessoris nostri inspexisse in hec verba: Universis sancte matris ecclesie filiis ad quos littere presentes pervenerint Galfridus Dei gracia Eliensis episcopus salutem in Domino. Noverit universitas vestra nos, intuitu caritatis et necessitatis monialium de Chatriz, concessisse eis in perpetuam elemosinam (fo. 105r)[2] prebendam illam viginti solidorum in Ditton' quam Rogerus Niger consuevit habere. Et volumus quod eedem moniales eandem prebendam ad sustentationem suam habeant, libere et quiete perpetuo possidendam toto tempore nostro et omnium successorum nostrorum, et accipiendam a firmariis nostris eiusdem ville vel a balivis, si ipsa forte ad firmam non fuerit, ad quatuor terminos, ad festum sancti Andree v solidos, ad Pascha v solidos et ad festum sancti Johannis Baptiste v solidos et ad festum sancti Michaelis v solidos. Et hoc eis presenti scripto et sigilli nostri appositione confirmamus. Test' etc. Nos vero intelligentes intentionem factum et propositum dicti predecessoris nostri laudabilia extitisse, in hac parte concedimus volumus et statuimus quod dicte moniales in scaccario Eliensi annuatim percipiant dictos viginti solidos terminis antedictis sine omni contradictione alicuius, sicut eos receperunt toto tempore nostro et temporibus

---

[1] Followed by *intuitu caritatis*, expunged.
[2] Heading *Elm.*

predecessorum nostrorum, et totum tenorem[1] dicte carte de verbo ad verbum quantum possumus pro nobis et successoribus nostris confirmamus. In cuius rei testimonium hanc cartam dictis monialibus concessimus sigillo nostro signatam. Hiis testibus etc. Nos vero dicti prior et capitulum, quod a[2] predicto venerabili patre nostro actum est ratum habentes, confirmamus et presenti scripto sigillum capituli nostri fecimus apponi. Datum apud Ely viij° idus novembris anno Domini M° ducentesimo octogesimo.

98 *Confirmation by Agnes de Roseby to Chatteris abbey of 5 acres of land in Elm given by Robert de Roseby, her father.*
fo. 105r–v [*s*. xiii[1] × 1290]

Confirmatio Agnetis de Rosbery de quinque acris terre in Pepirfyld'.

Sciant etc. quod ego Agnes de Roseby filia et heres Roberti de Roseby ratam et gratam habeo et hac carta mea confirmo Deo et ecclesie sancte Marie et omnium sanctorum de Chatriz et monialibus eiusdem loci donationem et concessionem quam predictus Robertus pater meus eis fecit [de quinque][3] acris terre in campo qui vocatur Pepyrfel[d] ...[4] (fo. 105v)[5] Elm.[6] Volo igitur quod predicta ecclesia de Chatriz et moniales memorate habeant et teneant et pacifice imperpetuum possideant totam predictam terram cum pertinenciis in liberam puram et perpetuam elemosinam, sicut carta prefati Roberti patris mei quam memorate moniales inde habent testatur, quietam et absolutam de me et heredibus meis imperpetuum. Et ego et heredes mei warantizabimus totam predictam terram prefate ecclesie de Chatriz et monialibus memoratis et acquietabimus de omnibus secularibus demandis serviciis et consuetudinibus, de residuo terre nostre in Elm, erga omnes homines imperpetuum. Et nec[7] ego vel heredes mei vel aliquis alius nomine meo in predicta terra cum pertinenciis aliquod jus vel clamium nobis de cetero vendicare possimus. Huic scripto sigillum meum apposui. Hiis testibus etc.

Note. See also no. 235, the charter of Robert de Roseby. For dating see no. 235n.

[1] MS *tenore*.
[2] Interlined.
[3] Hole 15 mm.
[4] Hole 20 mm.
[5] Heading *Ely*, preceded by *Chatriz*, expunged.
[6] *Elme* marginated before *Elm*.
[7] *c* interlined.

99 *Grant by Pain son of Alexander, clerk, of Ely to Chatteris abbey of a rent of 2s.
and 4 capons annually from a tenement in Potter's Lane, Ely, in exchange for land
in Stuntney which he was not able to warrant to the abbey.*
fo. 105v [*s.* xii^4 × *s.* xiii^2]

Carta Pagani de redditu duorum solidorum et iiij caponum.

Sciant etc. quod ego Paganus filius Alexandri clerici de Ely dedi et concessi et
hac presenti carta mea confirmavi Deo et ecclesie beate Marie de Chatriz et
monialibus ibidem Deo servientibus redditum duorum solidorum et quatuor
caponum[1] de tenemento quod Gilbertus carpentarius tenuit de antecessoribus
meis in Ely in Potterysslane, annuatim percipiendorum et imperpetuum possi-
dendorum libere quiete pacifice in puram et perpetuam elemosinam, pro salute
anime mee et pro salute animarum omnium antecessorum et successorum
meorum, in excambium cuiusdem terre in campis de Stunteneye' de feodo
monachorum Eliensium, quam prefatis monialibus warantizare non potui. Et in
huius rei testimonium et f[irm]itatem[2] hanc presentem cartam predicte ecclesie
[et predicti]s[3] monialibus de Chatriz feci et im[pressione sig]illi[4] mei roboravi.
Hiis testibus etc. (fo. 106r)[5]

   Note. The suggested dating is based on the occurrences of Pain son of Alexander in nos. 92–3.

100 *Release by abbess Mary de Sancto Claro and the convent of Chatteris to
Eustace son of William de Barrington of villein service in a messuage and land in
Barrington, held of Eustace by John son of Henry Broun, villein of Chatteris abbey.*
fo. 106r [*s.* xiii^2 × 28 Sept. 1265]

Quieta clamantia abbatisse de Chatriz de quodam mesuagio in Barenton'.

Omnibus etc. Maria de Sancto Claro permissione divina abbatissa de Chatriz
totusque eiusdem loci conventus salutem in Domino. Noverit universitas vestra
nos concessisse Eustachio filio Willelmi de Barenton' et heredibus suis quod
non exigemus nec clamabimus aliquid in uno mesuagio et tota terra cum pertinenciis suis in villa de Barenton' que Johannes filius Henrici Broun et heredes
sui tenent libere in feodo de dicto Eustachio et heredibus suis, ad tenendum in
dominico nostro ratione villenagii quod idem Johannes de nobis tenet in eadem

---

1 *vide aliam cartam de Ely supra folio iij°*, marginated before *caponum*.
2 Hole 7 mm.
3 Damaged 12 mm.
4 Hole 21 mm.
5 Heading *Barenton' Over'*; *Barenton'* preceded by O, expunged in black.

villa et eo quod nativus noster est, per quod dictus Eustachius et heredes sui amittere possent homagium wardam et relevium que eis de dicto libero tenemento libere accidere poterunt, dummodo dictus Eustachius et heredes sui formam et tenorem sue confirmationis quam dictus Johannes habet de dicto Eustachio secundum justiciam observaverint. Et in huius rei testimonium etc.

Note. Another copy of no. 123. Eustace son of William de Barrington occurs: in 37 Henry III (1252–3) in a final concord (*Cambs. Fines*, p. 32); on 16 Nov. 1275 (no. 124) and on 22 April 1277 (Cambridge, Trinity College Archives, Barrington 136). The precise chronology of the mid-thirteenth-century abbesses of Chatteris is unclear. Mary de Sancto Claro was probably abbess between Mabel de Bancis, who occurs as abbess before *c.* 29 Oct. 1247 (no. 139), and Emma de Somersham, who was abbess by 29 Sept. 1265 (no. 163). She could though have been abbess before both Mabel de Bancis and Emma de Somersham, but this alternative seems less likely. Nos. 51 and 231 suggest that Mary cannot have been abbess between Emma de Somersham and Amicia who was abbess by 16 Nov. 1275 (no. 124).

101 *Exchange between Roger de Seaton, rector of Over, and abbess Amicia and the convent of Chatteris of 2 tofts in Over, and grant by the abbess and convent to Roger of the right to close and appropriate a road in Over.*
fo. 106r–v   [9 July 1268 × Jan. 1280]

Donatio[1] rectoris de Overe unius tofti in excambium.

Omnibus presentes litteras visuris vel audituris Rogerus de Seyton' rector ecclesie de Overe salutem in Domino. Noverit universitas vestra me dedisse in excambium concessisse et hac presenti carta mea confirmasse domine Amicie Dei gracia abbatisse de Chateriz et eiusdem loci conventui toftum illum quem Juliana de Ketene tenere consuevit de feodo ecclesie de Overe integraliter, habendum et tenendum dictis abbatisse et conventui in liberam puram et perpetuam elemosinam. Et pro hac donatione concessione et presentis carte mee confirmatione, dicti abbatissa et conventus michi dederunt toftum que Petrus Pirun (fo. 106v)[2] de eisdem abbatissa et conventu tenebat in eadem villa de Overe, habendum et tenendum dicto Rogero et successoribus suis rectoribus in ecclesia de Overe in excambium, ut predictum est, libere quiete imperpetuum, sicut aliqua elemosina pura et perpetua liberius et quietius teneri poterit. Concesserunt etiam dicti abbatissa et conventus[3] eidem rectori, quantum in ipsis est, quod licite possit claudere chiminum quod tendit ad aquam inter curiam dicti rectoris et toftum Petri Pirun predictum et illud chiminum una cum tofto

---

[1] Preceded by *Barei*, expunged.
[2] Heading *Terre Chatriz et tenementa*, expunged in black.
[3] *v* interlined.

predicto sibi et suis successoribus appropriare et retinere imperpetuum. In cuius rei testimonium presenti scripto cirographato predicti Rogerus abbatissa et conventus alternatim sigilla sua apposuerunt. Hiis testibus etc.

> Note. Roger de Seaton occurs on 8 July 1268 in no. 178 when Emma de Somersham was still abbess. Roger de Seaton resigned the church of Seaton (Rutl.) in order to become an Augustinian canon, before 16 June 1280 (*Fasti 1066–1300* iii, p. 143). Agnes de Ely was abbess by Jan. 1280.

102 *Inspeximus and confirmation by abbot William [of Godmanchester] and the convent of Ramsey, patrons of the church of Over, of no. 101.*
fos. 106v–107r [9 July 1268 × 1285]

Confirmatio abbatis et conventus de Rameseya super excambio cuiusdam tofti[1] in Hovere inter abbatissam de Chatriz et rectorem.

Omnibus presentes litteras visuris vel audituris Willelmus Dei gracia abbas de Rameseya et conventus loci eiusdem patroni ecclesie de Overe salutem. Cartam dilectorum nobis in Christo magistri Rogeri de Seyton' rectoris ecclesie de Overe abbatisse et conventus de Chatriz inspeximus in hec verba: Omnibus presentes litteras visuris vel audituris Rogerus de Seyton' rector ecclesie de Overe salutem. Noverit universitas vestra me dedisse in excambium concessisse et hac presenti carta mea confirmasse domine Amicie Dei gracia abbatisse de Chatriz et eiusdem loci conventui toftum illum quem Juliana de Keten' tenere consuevit de feodo ecclesie de Overe integraliter, habendum et tenendum dictis abbatisse et conventui in liberam puram et perpetuam elemosinam. Et pro hac donatione concessione et presentis carte mee confirmatione, dicti abbatissa (fo. 107r)[2] et conventus michi dederunt toftum quem Petrus Piron' de eisdem abbatissa et conventu tenebat in eadem villa de Overe, habendum et tenendum dicto Rogero et successoribus suis rectoribus in[3] ecclesia de Overe in excambium, ut predictum est, libere quiete imperpetuum, sicut aliqua elimosina pura et perpetua liberius et quietius teneri poterit. Concesserunt dicti abbatissa et conventus eidem rectori, quantum in ipsis est, quod licite poterit claudere chiminum quod tendit ad aquam inter curiam dicti rectoris et toftum Petri Pirun' predictum et illud chiminum una cum tofto predicto sibi et suis successoribus appropriare et retinere imperpetuum. In cuius rei testimonium pre-

1 Preceded by c, expunged
2 Heading *Over'*.
3 Followed by *eadem*, expunged.

senti scripto cirographato[1] predicti Rogerus et abbatissa et conventus alternatim sigilla sua apposuerunt. Hiis testibus etc. Nos itaque presentes donationes et concessiones, quantum in nobis est, ratas et firmas habentes, ipsas approbamus et confirmamus pro nobis et successoribus nostris per presentes. In qua[rum][2] testimonium presentibus si[g]illa[3] nostra apposuimus etc.

Note. William of Godmanchester was abbot of Ramsey 3 March 1267–1285 (*Mon. Ang.* ii, p. 549). This confirmation follows no. 101: see no. 101n.

103 *Inspeximus and confirmation by Hugh [de Balsham], bishop of Ely, of no. 101.* fo. 107r–v [9 July 1268 × c. 16 June 1286]

Confirmatio domini Hugonis episcopi Eliensis super excambio inter abbatissam et rectorem de Overe.

Omnibus presentes litteras visuris vel audituris Hugo Dei gracia Eliensis episcopus salutem. Cartam dile[ct]orum[4] nobis in Christo magistri Rogeri de Seyto[n][5] rectoris ecclesie de Overe nostre diocesis abbatisse[6] et conventus de Chatriz inspeximus in hec verba: Omnibus presentes litteras visuris vel audituris Rogerus de Seyton' rector ecclesie de Overe salutem. Noverit universitas vestra me dedisse et in excambium concessisse et hac presenti carta mea confirmasse domine Amicie Dei gracia abbatisse de Chatriz et eiusdem loci conventui toftum illum quem Juliana (fo. 107v)[7] de Keten' tenere consuevit de feodo ecclesie de Overe integraliter, habendum et tenendum dictis abbatisse et conventui in liberam et perpetuam elemosinam. Et pro hac donatione et concessione et presentis carte mee confirmatione, dicti abbatissa et conventus michi dederunt toftum quod Petrus Pirun' de eisdem abbatissa et conventu tenebat in eadem villa de Overe, habendum et tenendum dicto Rogero et successoribus suis rectoribus in ecclesia de Overe in excambium, ut predictum est, libere quiete imperpetuum, sicut aliqua elemosina pura et perpetua liberius et quietius teneri poterit. Concesserunt etiam dicti abbatissa et conventus eidem rectori, quantum in ipsis est, quod licite possit claudere chiminum quod tendit ad aquam inter curiam dicti rectoris et toftum Petri Pyrun predictum et illud

---

1   *p* interlined; followed by *d*, expunged.
2   Hole 3 mm.
3   Hole 2 mm.
4   Hole 3 mm.
5   Hole 3 mm.
6   *i* written over *e*.
7   Heading *Cantabrig'*.

chiminum una cum tofto predicto sibi et suis successoribus appropriare et retinere imperpetuum. In cuius rei testimonium presenti scripto cyrographato[1] predicti Rogerus abbatissa et conventus alternatim sigilla sua apposuerunt. Hiis testibus etc. Nos itaque scriptas donationes et concessiones, quantum in nobis est, ratas et firmas habentes, ipsas approbamus et confirmamus[2] pro nobis et successoribus nostris per presentes. Date etc.

Note. Hugh de Balsham was bishop of Ely 14 Oct. 1257–c. 16 June 1286. This confirmation follows no. 101: see no. 101n.

104 *Grant by John son of Absolon de Cambridge to Chatteris abbey of ½ mark of quitrent annually from a messuage with buildings in Cambridge.*
fos. 107v–108r [s. xiii[1-2]]

Carta[3] Johannis filii Absolonis de dimidia marca quieti redditus in villa Cantabrig'.

Sciant presentes et futuri quod ego Johannes filius Absolonis de Cant' dedi concessi et presenti carta mea confirmavi, pro salute anime mee et animarum antecessorum meorum, in liberam puram et perpetuam elemosinam Deo et ecclesie beate Marie de Chatriz et sanctimonialibus ibidem (fo. 108r)[4] Deo servientibus dimidiam marcam[5] redditus quieti in villa de Cant' annuatim percipiendam de mesuagio cum edificiis eidem mesuagio pertinentibus quod teneo de feodo domini Eliensis episcopi, quod est inter mesuagium Walteri filii Walteri versus aquilonem et mesuagium quod Amicia soror mea michi dedit, quod est de feodo domini regis, habendam et tenendam et recipiendam de illo mesuagio, adeo libere et quiete sicut elemosina alicui domui religiose conferri potest, de me et heredibus meis imperpetuum ad duos terminos, scilicet ad festum sancti Michaelis xl denarios et ad Hokkeday xl denarios. Et ego et heredes mei warantizabimus predictam[6] dimidiam marcam[7] redditus predictis sanctimonialibus contra omnes homines et feminas in perpetuum. Et si ita contingat quod predictus redditus ad terminos statutos perpacatus non fuerit, bene liceat sanctimonialibus vel earum atturnatis in predicto mesuagio man-

1 Followed by *d*, expunged.
2 MS *confirmationes*, *-tiones* expunged, *-mus* interlined.
3 Followed by *filii*, expunged.
4 Heading *Cantabrig'*.
5 MS *marcatam*, *ca* expunged.
6 Followed by *terram*, expunged.
7 MS *marcatam*, *ca* expunged.

uum[1] capere et illud mesuagium secundum consuetudinem Cant' distringere pro predicto redditu donec plenarie persolvatur. Et ut hec mea donatio et concessio et huius presentis carte[2] confirmatio rata et stabilis permaneat, sigilli mei appositione hanc cartam corroboravi. Hiis testibus etc.

Note. No. 106 is the confirmation of this grant. For dating see no. 105n.

105 *Gift in alms by Cecilia Godsho and Amicia her sister to Chatteris abbey of land with buildings in the parish of St John [Zachary], Cambridge, from which land John, their brother, had previously granted to the abbey the right to receive 9s. of rent; for 1d. annually to them and their heirs and 1s. annually to the bishop of Ely.* fo. 108r–v [s. xiii[1-2]]

Carta Cecilie Godsho de quodam tenemento in parochia sancti Johannis Baptiste in Mylnestrete Cantabrig'.

Sciant etc. quod ego Cecilia Godsho et Amicia soror mea communi consilio et assensu nostro concessimus dedimus et hac presenti carta nostra confirmavimus, pro salute anime nostre et antecessorum nostrorum in perpetuam elemosinam, Deo et ecclesie beate Marie de Chatriz et sanctimonialibus ibidem perpetue Deo[3] servientibus totam illam ter[ram][4] nostram cum edificiis desuper existentibus et eius pertinenciis[5] (fo. 108v)[6] que jacet inter terram[7] que fuit Walteri Wymund' et terram nostram in qua Robertus de Ragenhulle solebat inhabitare in parochia sancti Johannis de Mylnestrate in Cantebr', salvo tamen jure sanctimonialium percipiendi novem solidorum redditum, quem Johannes frater noster ante confectionem istius carte, dum verus dominus et heres de predicta terra et eius pertinenciis erat, eis in libera potestate sua contulerat et carte sue robore confirmaverat, habendam et tenendam dictis sanctimonialibus de Chatriz ibidem Deo perpetue servientibus integre libere pacifice imperpetuum, reddendo inde annuatim nobis et heredibus nostris unum denarium ad Pascha et pro nobis et heredibus nostris domino episcopo Eliensi, qui pro tempore fuerit, annuatim sex denarios ad Hokkeday et sex denarios ad festum sancti Michaelis pro omnibus serviciis consuetudinibus et demandis. Et nos Cecilia et Amicia et

---

1 *-um* possibly erased.
2 Repeated and expunged.
3 MS *perpetueo*, with *de* written above *o*.
4 Hole 8 mm.
5 MS *pertisnenciis*, first *s* expunged.
6 Heading *Cantabrig'*.
7 Followed by *nostram in qua Robertus*, expunged.

heredes nostri warantizabimus defendemus et acquietabimus totam predictam terram cum suis pertinenciis dictis sanctimonialibus de Chatriz ibidem Deo servientibus perpetue contra omnes gentes per predictum servicium. Et ut hec nostra concessio donatio et presentis carte mee confirmatio et warantizatio perpetuo firmitatis robur optineat, presenti carte sigilla nostra apposuimus. Hiis testibus.

> Note. Entries in the hundred rolls in 1279 recording the previous holders of properties in Cambridge suggest that Cecilia and Amicia de Godsho lived in the first half of the thirteenth century (*Rot. Hund.* ii, pp. 371–2, 380, 385–6).

106 *Confirmation by Cecilia Godsho of Cambridge and Amicia her sister to Chatteris abbey of ½ mark of quitrent annually from a messuage with buildings in Cambridge, granted by their brother John son of Absolon de Cambridge, chaplain, and grant by Cecilia and Amicia to Chatteris abbey of 28d. annually from the increase of the quitrent from the messuage in Cambridge.*
fos. 108v–109v [s. xiii[1-2]]

Carta Cecilie Godsho de redditu quieto dimidie marce in villa de Cantabrig'.

Sciant etc. quod ego Cecilia Godsho[1] de Cantebr' in legitima viduitate mea et Amicia soror mea, sorores et heredes Johannis filii Absolonis capellani fratris nostri, unanimi concensu et mera voluntate nostra concessimus et hac presenti carta nostra confirmavimus, pro salute animarum (fo. 109r)[2] nostrarum et animarum antecessorum et successorum nostrorum in liberam puram et perpetuam elemosinam, Deo et ecclesie sancte Marie de Chatriz et sanctimonialibus ibidem Deo servientibus illam dimidiam marcam[3] redditus quieti in villa de Cantebr' quam predictus Johannes filius Absolonis de Cantebr' capellanus frater noster eisdem dedit, percipiendam annuatim de mesuagio illo cum edificiis eidem mesuagio pertinentibus quod tenemus de feodo domini Eliensis episcopi, quod est inter mesuagium Walteri filii Walteri versus aquilonem et mesuagium illud quod tenemus de feodo domini regis, habendam et percipiendam annuatim adeo libere et quiete ad duos terminos anni per equales partes sicut carta, quam de prefato Johanne fratre nostro habent, proportat et testatur. Dedimus etiam et concessimus et hac presenti carta nostra confirmavimus pro salute animarum nostrarum, sicut superius dictum est, in liberam puram et perpetuam elemosinam, Deo et ecclesie predicte beate Marie de Chatriz et monialibus ibidem

---

1　MS *Godsho Cecilia*, marked for transposition.
2　Heading *Cantabr'*.
3　MS *marcatam*, *ca* expunged.

Deo servientibus, de incremento viginti et octo denarios redditus quieti in villa de Cantebr'[1] percipiendos annuatim de mesuagio predicto cum edificiis, ut supradictum est, habendos tenendos et percipiendos de predicto mesuagio, adeo libere et quiete sicut elimosina alicui domui religiose conferri potest, de nobis et heredibus nostris imperpetuum ad duos terminos anni, scilicet ad festum sancti Michaelis quatuordecim denarios et ad Hokkeday quatuordecim denarios, simul cum predicta dimidia marca quam ad eosdem terminos per equales par[te]s[2] de nobis percipient annuatim, quam de dono Johannis filii Absolonis fratris nostri habent, ut supradictum est. Et nos et heredes nostri warantizabimus totum predictum redditum predictis sanctimonialibus contra omnes imperpetuum. Et si contingat quod predictus redditus ad terminos statutos perpacatus non fuerit, (fo. 109v)[3] bene liceat sanctimonialibus vel illarum attornatis in predicto mesuagio manuum capere et illud mesuagium secundum consuetudinem Cantebr' distringere pro predicto redditu donec plenarie persolvatur. Et ut hec nostra confirmatio et de predicto incremento donatio concessio et huius presentis carte nostre confirmatio rata et inconcussa[4] imperpetuum perseveret, eam sigillorum nostrorum appositione roboravimus. Hiis testibus etc.

Note. Confirmation of no. 104. For dating see no. 105n.

107 *Quitclaim by Simon to Chatteris abbey of a messuage in the parish of St John [Zachary], Cambridge.*
fo. 109v [s. xiii[1-3]]

Quieta clamantia de uno mesuagio in parochia sancti Johannis in Mylnestrete.

Omnibus Christi fidelibus ad quos presens scriptum pervenerit. Sciatis me Simonem[5] dedisse concessisse[6] nec non pro me et heredibus meis quietum clamasse abbatisse de Chatriz et conventui eiusdem domus et successoribus suis omne jus et clamium quod habeo vel habere potero in uno mesuagio cum pertinenciis in villa de Cantabr' in parochia sancti Johannis in Myllestrete, quod quidem mesuagium jacet inter terram Roberti Wymund' ex parte australi et terram que fuit quondam Roberti Huberd' ex parte occidentali, et abuttat ad unum caput super regiam viam que vocatur Myllestrete et ad aliud caput super

---

1   *in toto ix s.*, marginated after *Cantebr'*.
2   Hole 3 mm.
3   Heading *Cantabrig'*.
4   MS *incussa*.
5   Followed by space, 20 mm.
6   MS *concessesse*, with superscript *i* over second *e*.

mesuagium quod vocatur Heneye, quod quidem mesuagium Willelmus frater
meus quondam tenuit de predictis dominabus pro undecim solidis eis annuatim
reddendo, ita quod nec ego Simon nec heredes mei nec aliquis per nos aliquod
jus vel clamium in predicto mesuagio cum pertinenciis exigere vel vendicare
poterimus in futurum. In cuius rei testimonium presentibus sigillum meum
apposui. Hiis testibus etc.

Note. This quitclaim may be related to no. 105. For possible dating see no. 105n.

108 *Grant by John Percy, chaplain, to Chatteris abbey of 5s. of annual rent from a
tenement in the parish of Holy Trinity, Cambridge.*
fos. 109v–110r [s. xiii$^{2-4}$]

Carta Johannis Percy de uno mesuagio in parochia sancte Trinitatis Cant'.

Noverint universi per presentes et futuri quod ego Johannes capellanus filius
quondam Thome[1] Percy (fo. 110r)[2] de Cantebr' dedi concessi et hac presenti
carta mea confirmavi abbatisse et conventui monasterii beate virginis Dei genitricis Marie de Chatriz in puram et perpetuam elimosinam[3] quinque solidos
annui redditus in Cantebr', quos habui de dono et concessione quondam Rose
de Derislee, prout in carta eiusdem Rose plenius continetur, de tenemento quod
Johannes de Flocthorp tenuit in parochia sancte Trinitatis de Cantebr', habendos et tenendos de me et heredibus meis dictis abbatisse et conventui et earum
successoribus cum omnibus pertinenciis suis in puram et perpetuam elemosinam
libere et integre imperpetuum, sicuti ego dictum redditum liberius et plenius
unquam tenui. Et ad maiorem securitatem cartam quam habui de predicta Rosa
dictis abbatisse et conventui liberavi. In huius rei testimonium presentibus
sigillum meum apposui. Hiis testibus etc.

Note. Margaret daughter of John de Flocthorp occurs in 1279 (*Rot. Hund.* ii, p. 385).

109 *Confirmation by Richard [FitzNeal], archdeacon [of Ely], to Chatteris abbey of
1 hide of land in Madingley, given by Robert his brother.*
fo. 110r [c. 1159 × 30 May 1169]

Donatio[4] Ricardi archidiaconi de una hida terre in Madynglee.

1 Followed by *Petri*, expunged.
2 Heading *Maddynglee*.
3 Possibly corr. to *elemosinam*.
4 Preceded by *domino*, expunged.

Domino suo N(igello) Eliensi episcopo et Ricardus archidiaconus et[1] omnibus sancte matris ecclesie filiis tam presentibus quam futuris salutem. Sciatis me dedisse et in perpetuam elemosinam concessisse Deo et ecclesie sancte Marie de Chatriz et monialibus ibidem Deo servientibus unam idam terre in Maddynglee, quam Robertus frater meus eidem ecclesie dedit, libere sine aliqua exactione et omni seculari servicio preter[2] denegeldum et murdrum et vj denarios ad aux-ilium vicecomitis. Hiis[3] testibus domino Salamone priore de Ely et Hugone priore de Bernewelle et aliis. Ista carta registratur plenius in registro domini episcopi Eliensis.

> Note. Nigel was bishop of Ely 1 Oct. 1133–30 May 1169; Richard FitzNeal was archdeacon of Ely c. 1158–89 (*Fasti 1066–1300* ii, p. 50); Solomon was prior of Ely c. 1159 × 1163–1176 (*Fasti 1066–1300* ii, p. 48); Hugh Domesman was prior of Barnwell c. 1145 × 1149–c. 1165 × 1169 (D. Knowles, C. N. L. Brooke and V. C. M. London eds *The Heads of Religious Houses England and Wales 940–1216* (Cambridge, 1972) p. 150). No copy has been found in any of the extant records of the bishops of Ely.

110 *Gift in free alms by Aubrey son of Eustace de Madingley to Chatteris abbey of 1 acre of land in Madingley, for 7s. towards his pilgrimage to Jerusalem.*
fo. 110r–v [*s.* xiii[1–3]]

Carta Alberti filii Eustachii de una acra terre in Maddynglee.

Sciant presentes etc. quod ego Albericus filius Eustachi d[e][4] (fo. 110v)[5] Mad-dyngl' dedi in liberam et puram et perpetuam elemosinam Deo et ecclesie beate Marie de Chateriz et sanctimonialibus ibidem Deo servientibus unam acram terre de feodo meo in Maddynggel', scilicet acram illam que jacet juxta Berne-welledych, tenendam libere et quiete ab omni seculari servicio et exactione, ita quod ego et heredes mei acquietabimus et warantizabimus totam predictam terram et servicium iam dicte terre versus omnes homines et etiam versus dominum regem de aliis terris meis. Et pro hac donatione et warantizatione mea, dederunt michi predicte sanctimoniales de bonis eiusdem ecclesie septem solidos caritative ad iter meum Jerosolimitanum perficiendum. Et ut hec mea donatio et warantizatio stabilis et firma permaneat, eam presenti scripto et sigilli mei appositione confirmavi. Hiis testibus Eborardo, Alano, Rogero, capellanis;

---

1 Interlined; presumably added because of misplacement of *Ricardus archidiaconus* in sentence.
2 Followed by *de*, expunged.
3 *nota de vj denariis solvendis [ad] auxilium vicecomitis*, marginated after *Hiis*.
4 Hole 2 mm.
5 Heading *Kyngston'*.

Simone persona de Foxton', Thoma persona de Burewelle, Waltero persona de Haselingefeld', Hugone clerico de Bedeford', Willelmo Barnard', Jordano, Ricardo de Berle, Willelmo de Fleg' et aliis pluribus.

> Note. In 1279, John son of William owed scutage to the heirs of Aubrey son of Eustace for land in Madingley (*Rot. Hund.* ii, p. 447).

111 *Grant by William de Bancis to Jolanus de Bradehous of 40s. of rent in Kingston, Eversden and Wimpole as a marriage-portion with Beatrice his sister.*
fos. 110v–111r [*s.* xiii[1] × *c.* 1235]

Carta Willelmi de Bannz de quadraginta solidatis in Kyngston' Everesdon' et Wympol.

Sciant presentes et futuri quod ego Willelmus de Bannz dedi concessi et hac presenti carta mea confirmavi Jolano de Bradeho quadraginta solidatus redditus in libero maritagio cum Beatricia sorore mea in[1] Kynggestone Everisdone et Wynepol, scilicet de Simone janitore in Kynggeston viij solidos[2] pro dimidia virgata terre cum pertinenciis quam de eo libere tenet pro viij solidis per annum pro omni servicio seculari, salvo[3] forinceco servicio, quod faciet eidem Jolano et heredibus suis de predicta Beatricia [exeun]tibus,[4] et de Willelmo filio Osberti viij solidos per annum (fo. 111r)[5] pro dimidia virgata terre cum pertinenciis quam de eo simili modo tenet in Kynggeston', et de Basilia vidua iiij solidos pro xij acris terre cum pertinenciis quas de eo simili modo tenet in Kynggestone, et de Willelmo filio Aylmer' viij solidos pro xij acris terre cum pertinenciis quas simili modo de eo tenet, et de Johanne filio Wymari ij solidos per annum pro uno mesuagio cum crofto quam de eo simili modo tenet, tenenda et habenda libere etc. de me et heredibus meis eidem Jolano heredibus suis de predicta Beatricia exeuntibus, faciendo inde michi et heredibus meis forinsecum servicium quod ad predictum tenementum pertinet. Et ego et heredes mei warantizabimus predictos redditus cum pertinenciis predicto Jolano et heredibus suis de predicta Beatricia exeuntibus contra omnes homines. Et ut hec mea donatio et presentis carte mee confirmatio rata et inconcussa permaneat, huic presenti carte sigillum meum apposui. Hiis testibus.

---

1 Followed by *Kynstone*, expunged.
2 Followed by *d*, expunged.
3 Followed by *s*, expunged.
4 Hole 10 mm.
5 Heading *Barenton'*.

Note. Part of the charter seems to have been omitted by the scribe as only 30s. of rent are described and no rents in Eversden or Wimpole are listed. Eustace, father of William de Bancis, died *c.* 1175; William died after 1205 and his heir Eustace was dead by *c.* 1235 (*VCH Cambs.* v, pp. 113, 267). Jolanus de Bradehous and Beatrice his wife occur in 24 H III (1239–40) in a final concord (*Cambs. Fines*, p. 22); Beatrice occurs in another on 1 May 1250 as the former wife of Jolanus (*Final Concords of the County of Lincoln From the Feet of Fines Preserved in the Public Record Office A.D. 1244–1272* (Lincoln Record Society xvii, 1920) p. 59). See also no. 240.

112 *Tithe-suit heard by papal judges delegate commissioned by Innocent IV in which Robert Passelewe, archdeacon of Lewes, charged Chatteris abbey with with-holding the tithes from 1 carucate of their land in Barrington; the parties submitted to the jurisdiction of Hugh [de Northwold], bishop of Ely, who ordained that Robert should receive the tithes of corn and hay from the lands of the nuns in Barrington and that the nuns should retain the tithes of their mill and the lesser tithes.*
fos. 111r–112r   At Balsham, April 1249.

Delegatio sedis apostolice super quibusdam decimis in villa de Barenton'.

Omnibus sancte matris ecclesie filiis hoc presens scriptum visuris vel audituris sancte Trinitatis et sancti Bartholomei priores London' et archidiaconus Westm' London' diocesis, judices a domino papa delegati, salutem. Mandatum domini pape suscepimus in hec verba: Innocentius episcopus servus servorum Dei dilectis filiis sancte Trinitatis et sancti Bartholomei London' prioribus et archidiacono Westmon' London' diocesis salutem et apostolicam benedic-tionem. Dilectus filius archidiaconus Lewensis nobis conquerendo monstravit quod abbatissa et conventus de Chatriz, rector ecclesie de Stok', Ricardus de Swythesthorp miles et quidam alii London', Norwicen' et Eborac' civitatum et diocesum redditibus debitis et rebus aliis injuri[antur eis]dem.[1] Ideo[que dis-cret]ioni[2] (fo. 111v)[3] vestre per apostolica scripta mandamus quatinus partibus convocatis audiatis causam et appellatione remota usuris cessantibus fine debito decidatis, facientes quod decreveritis[4] per censuram ecclesiasticam firmiter observari. Testes autem qui fuerint nominati si se gracia odio vel timore sub-traxerint, per censuram eandem cessante appellatione conpellatis testimonium veritati perhibere quod si non omnes etc. Datum Lugd' ij nonas julii ponti-ficatus nostri anno quinto. Cuius auctoritate mandati, partibus in judicio coram

---

1 Hole 10 mm.
2 Hole 13 mm.
3 Heading *Barengton'*.
4 MS *decrementis*.

nobis constitutis, et cum parti ree a parte actrice in hunc modum esset editum. Dicit dominus Robertus[1] Passelewe archidiaconus Lewensis quod abbatissa et conventus de Chateriz injuste detinent decimas provenientes de una[2] terre caruca cum pertinenciis quam habent in Barenton' infra limites parochie sue de Barenton', unde petit dictam abbatissam compelli integre ad solutionem dictarum decimarum, cum damnis et interesse et expensis factis et faciendis ad arbitrium discreti judicis. Hec omnia dicit salvo sibi juris beneficio etc. Et ad istam editionem in hunc modum extitit contestatum. Dicit procurator abbatisse et conventus de Chatriz narrata in editione vera non esse prout narrantur, et ideo petita fieri non debere prout petantur, tandem cum esset in judicio tam super editione quam super contestatione et litteris papalibus altercatum, supposuerunt se partes ordinationi episcopi Eliensis qui in hunc modum inter dictas partes de consensu eorundem ordinavit: Universis Christi[3] fidelibus presens scriptum visuris vel audituris Hugo Dei gracia Eliensis episcopus salutem in Domino. N[ov]erit[4] universitas vestra quod, cum lis mota fuisset (fo. 112r)[5] inter dominum Robertum Passelewe archidiaconum Lewensem et moniales de Chatriz super quibusdam decimis in parochia de Barenton' nostre diocesis coram judicibus delegatis, tandem partes de consensu judicum super petitis ordinationi nostre se submiserunt. Nos vero inspectis hinc inde cause meritis et circumstanciis ita duximus ordinandum, scilicet quod dictus dominus Robertus nomine ecclesie sue de Barenton' recipiet integre omnes decimas garbarum et feni de terris dictarum monialium que sunt in parochia de Barenton', sive excolantur propriis manibus sive per manus aliorum. Dicte[6] vero moniales retinebunt sibi decimas unius molendini sui in eadem parochia et alias decimas minutas, scilicet de nutrimentis animalium et consimilibus. Et ut hec nostra ordinatio firma et stabilis imperpetuum perseveret, huic scripto sigillum nostrum fecimus apponi. Dat' apud Balesham mense aprili anno gracie M°CCxlix°.

113 *Exchange between abbess Agnes de Ely and the convent of Chatteris and John Waryn of Barrington, clerk, of a messuage and croft in Barrington for 3 selions of land in Barrington.*

---

1 Followed by Passewele, cancelled.
2 Followed by *carmata*, expunged.
3 *Universis Christi*, underlined.
4 Hole 4 mm.
5 Heading *Barenton'*.
6 *Decime molendini in Baryngton' et omnes decimas alias minutas pertinentes abbatisse de Chaterfiz]*, marginated after *Dicte*.

fo. 112r–v [17 Nov. 1275 × 1290]

Commutatio in excambium de¹ uno² mesuagio cum crofto et iij sellionibus.

Omnibus Christi fidelibus ad quos presentes littere pervenerint Agnes de Ely humilis abbatissa de Chatriz totusque eiusdem loci conventus salutem in Domino. Noveritis nos de communi assensu et voluntate totius capituli nostri dedisse et concessisse Johanni Waryn de Barenton' clerico unum mesuagium et croftum³ adjacentem cum pertinenciis in villa de Barenton', jacentes inter mesuagium et croftum dicti Johannis et stodum rectoris ecclesie de Barenton', in excambium tribus selionibus terre cum pertinenciis quas dictus Johannes nobis et successoribus nostris dedit et concessit, videlicet in campo occidentali unum selionem apud le Hakk' cum prato adjace[nt]e⁴ juxta terram nostram quam Willelmus Halwyne ...,⁵ (fo. 112v)⁶ et unum sellionem inter le Fordexis juxta terram nostramque dicti Willelmi Alveyne,⁷ et in campo orientali unum sellionem in Storkesdene juxta terram dicti Willelmi, tenendum et habendum pro nobis et successoribus nostris dictum mesuagium cum crofto cum pertin-enciis dicto Johanni heredibus suis vel suis assignatis per liberum excambium terre sue predicte libere quiete et hereditarie imperpetuum, ita videlicet quod nec nos nec successores nostri in predicto mesuagio et crofto cum pertinenciis de cetero nichil exigere vel vendicare poterimus imperpetuum, nec predictus Johannes in predictis tribus sellionibus terre de cetero nichil poterit vendicare. Et nos et successores nostri dictum mesuagium cum pertinenciis dicto Johanni et heredibus vel assignatis imperpetuum defendemus. In cuius rei testimonium presenti scripto,⁸ in modum cyrographi confecto, sigillum capituli nostri ap-posuimus et scripto penes nos residenti dictus Johannes sigillum suum apposuit. Hiis testibus etc.

> Note. Amicia, the abbess who preceded Agnes de Ely, occurs on 16 Nov. 1275 (no. 124). Abbess Agnes de Burwell occurs on 14 May 1293 (Cambridge, Trinity College Archives, Foxton 2, m. 2), but this exchange must date from before 1290 because the messuage and croft were to be held *pro nobis et successoribus nostris*.

---

1 Interlined.
2 MS *unum*, corr. to *uno*.
3 Followed by *dicti Johannis et*, expunged.
4 Damaged 4 mm.
5 Damaged 20 mm.
6 Heading *Barenton'*.
7 MS *Alveyene*, second *e* expunged.
8 Followed by *sigillum*, expunged.

114 *Grant by William son of Eustace de Barrington to Thomas de Bancis and Juliana his wife of the homage and the rent of 4s. annually which John Glenman and Henry son of Aveline each paid for their tenements in Barrington, for 8 marks in advance and 1d. annually.*
fos. 112v–113r [*s.* xiii$^{2-3}$]

Carta Willelmi filii Eustachii de homagio redditu et tenementis in Barenton'.

Sciant presentes etc. quod ego Willelmus filius Eustachii de Barenton' dedi etc. Thome de Bancis et Juliane uxori sue, pro octo marcis argenti quas michi dederunt pre manibus, totum homagium et redditum quod Johannes Glenman et Henricus filius Aveline michi solebant facere pro eorum tenementis que de me tenebant in villa de Barenton', scilicet de Johanne Glenman per annum ad festum sancti Michaelis duos solidos et ad Pascha duos solidos, et de Henrico filio Aveline ad festum sancti Michaelis duos solidos et ad Pascha duos solidos, et quicquid juris habui vel habere potui in ipsis et eorum tenementis et quicquid i[nd]e[1] michi et heredibus meis jure accidere possit, habenda et (fo. 113r)[2] tenenda de me et heredibus meis dicto Thome et Juliane uxori sue et heredibus eorum, et cuicumque dicta homagium et redditum dare assignare vendere vel legare voluerint, in lecto mortali et quando voluerint, libere quiete, reddendo inde annuatim michi et heredibus meis dictus Thomas et Juliana uxor sua et heredes eorum vel ipsorum assignati unum denarium ad Pascha pro omni servicio secta et seculari demanda. Et ego predictus Willelmus et heredes mei warantizabimus et defendemus totum homagium predictum et redditum predicto Thome et Juliane uxori sue et heredibus eorum et assignatis ipsorum contra omnes homines et feminas christianos et judeos per predictum servicium. Et ut hec mea donatio et concessio firma sit et stabilis imperpetuum, huic scripto sigillum meum apposui. Hiis testibus etc.

Note. Thomas de Bancis occurs in 1247 (no. 142) and in 1239 × *s.* xiii^3 (no. 240).

115 *Grant by Thomas de Bancis of Foxton to Chatteris abbey, for a light at the mass of St Mary and for the payment of a chaplain to celebrate the mass of St Mary there perpetually, of the homage and service of John Glenman, Henry son of Aveline and Elloria de la Lawe for the land which they hold of him in Barrington and Foxton.*
fo. 113r–v [*s.* xiii$^{2-3}$]

---

1 Hole 4 mm.
2 Heading *Barenton'*.

Carta Thome de Bancis de homagio Johannis le Glenman cum escaetis et wardis.

Sciant[1] presentes etc. quod ego Thomas de Bancis de Foxton' dedi etc. Deo et ecclesie beate Marie virginis et domine abbatisse de Chatriz et conventui eiusdem loci in puram et perpetuam elemosinam, pro anima mea et pro anima Juliane uxoris mee, homagium et servicium Johannis le Glenman et Henrici filii Aveline et Ellorie de la Lawe, quod michi fecerunt propter terram quam tenuerunt de me in villa de Barenton' et in villa de Foxton', cum omnibus pertinenciis et escaetis et wardis et omnimodis eventibus qui aliquo modo possent michi vel heredibus meis accidere, et quicquid juris habui vel habere potui in ipsis et eorum tenementis sine omni retinemento michi vel heredibus meis, ad luminare misse beate (fo. 113v)[2] Marie[3] et ad mercedem unius capellani ad celebrandum in eodem loco missam beate Marie imperpetuum. Et ego et heredes mei warantizabimus acquietabimus et defendemus dicte abbatisse de Chatriz et eiusdem loci conventus predicta servicia cum pertinenciis, sicut prenominatum est, contra omnes gentes imperpetuum. Et ut hec mea donatio sit imperpetuum stabilis, huic scripto sigillum meum apposui. Hiis testibus etc.

Note. Thomas de Bancis occurs in 1247 (no. 142) and in 1239 × s. xiii[3] (no. 240).

116 *Gift by William son of Eustace de Barrington to John son of Adam de Barrington of a messuage and 9 acres in Barrington, for 6 marks, ½ mark to Agatha his wife, 1 talent to his heir and an annual rent of 4s.*
fos. 113v–114r [s. xiii[1–3]]

Carta Willelmi filii Eustachii de uno mesuagio et ix acris terre.

Sciant presentes etc. quod ego Willelmus filius Eustachii de Barenton' dedi etc. Johanni filio Ade de Barenton' pro homagio et servicio suo totum mesuagium integrum quod Alanus filius Philippi tenuit, quod jacet inter mesuagia Alicie uxoris Humfridi et Estrild' uxoris Hugonis, et novem acras terre in campis de Barenton' cum pertinenciis pertinentes ad dictum mesuagium, habenda et tenenda de me et heredibus meis dicto Johanni et heredibus suis vel quibuscumque dare aut assignare voluerit, excepto loco religionis, libere quiete integre et[4] hereditarie, cum omnibus libertatibus et aysiamentis infra villam de Barenton'

1 MS *scient'*.
2 Heading *Barenton'*.
3 *vide mercedem capellani sancte Marie*, marginated before *Marie*.
4 Interlined.

et extra in pratis pascuis planis viis semitis communis ad predictam terram pertinentibus, reddendo inde annuatim dictus Johannes et heredes sui aut eius assignati michi et heredibus meis quatuor solidos, scilicet ad festum sancti Michaelis duos solidos et ad Pascha duos solidos, pro omni servicio consuetudine et demanda michi et heredibus meis pertinentibus, salvo servicio domini regis, scilicet quantum pertinet ad tantam terram eiusdem feodi in eadem villa. Et ego Willelmus et heredes mei warantizabimus et defendemus dictum mesuagium et totam dictam terram cum omnibus pertinenciis et libertatibus dicto Johanni et heredibus suis, aut quibuscumque dederit aut assignaverit, per predictum servicium contra omnes (fo. 114r)[1] homines et feminas imperpetuum. Pro hac autem donatione concessione carte mee confirmatione et warantizatione, dedit michi dictus Johannes sex marcas argenti in guersummam et Agathe uxori mee dimidiam marcam et heredi meo unum talentum. Et ut hec mea donatio concessio confirmatio et warantizatio rata et inconcussa futuris temporibus perseveret, hanc presentem cartam sigilli mei appositione roboravi. Hiis testibus etc.

Note. Another copy of no. 122. For dating of William son of Eustace de Barrington see no. 121n.

117 *Confirmation by Thomas de Bancis of Foxton to Henry son of John de Barrington of a messuage with buildings and croft and of land with meadow in Barrington, given by William son of Eustace de Barrington; for 4s. annually.*
fo. 114r–v [*s.* xiii$^{2-3}$]

Carta Thome de Bancis de uno mesuagio cum pratis et pertinenciis in Babenton'.

Sciant etc. quod ego Thomas de Bancis de Foxton' dedi etc. Henrico filio Johannis de Barenton' illud mesuagium cum edificiis et cum crofta adjacente et totam terram cum prato et omnibus pertinenciis suis in villa de Barenton', que scilicet Willelmus filius Eustacii de Barenton' dedit dicto Henrico pro homagio et servicio suo et carta sua confirmavit, habenda et tenenda de me et heredibus meis et assignatis dicto Henrico et heredibus suis, vel quibuscumque dare vel assignare vendere vel legare voluerit, excepta domo religionis, libere quiete bene et in pace integre et hereditarie, prout carta quam dictus Henricus habet de Willelmo filio Eustachii de Barenton' attestatur, reddendo inde annuatim michi et heredibus meis dictus Henricus et heredes sui vel eius assignati quatuor soli-

---

1 Heading *Barenton'*.

dos argenti, quos dictus Henricus predicto Willelmo filio Eustachii per annum reddere consuevit, videlicet ad festum sancti Michaelis duos solidos et ad festum Pasche duos solidos, pro omni servicio consuetudine et seculari exactione, salvo servicio domini regis, quantum pertinet ad tantam terram liberam eiusdem feodi in eadem villa. Ego vero dictus Thomas et heredes mei [et assignati][1] (fo. 114v)[2] warantizabimus et defendemus et acquietabimus dictum mesuagium et totam dictam terram cum prato et libertatibus et omnibus pertinenciis suis dicto Henrico et heredibus suis vel suis assignatis, ut dictum est, per predictum servicium contra omnes gentes imperpetuum. Pro hac autem concessione etc.

Note. Confirmation of no. 121. Thomas de Bancis occurs in 1247 (no. 142) and in 1239 × s. xiii[3] (no. 240).

118 *Agreement whereby Chatteris abbey leases to Warin de Barrington, miller, for his life, the mill of 'Theford' and a messuage in Barrington, for ½ mark and an annual rent of 44s.*
fos. 114v–115r [c. 1253 × c. 1307]

Locatio molendini de Barenton' Warino de Barenton' ad terminum vite.

Hec est conventio facta inter abbatissam[3] et conventum de Chatriz ex una parte et Warinum de Barenton'[4] molendinarium ex altera parte, scilicet quod predicte abbatissa et conventus concesserunt et dimiserunt[5] Warino dicto molendinum de Theford' ad totam suam vitam cum tota sequela sua et cum omnibus pertinenciis plenarie, sicut alii firmarii dictum molendinum tenuerunt, et unum mesuagium cum pertinenciis in Barenton' inter mesuagium Osberti Beyvin et mesuagium Alicie Gykeles super quod edificare debet, et pro dimidia marca argenti quam dictus Warinus dictis abbatisse et conventui dedit in guersummam, tenenda et habenda dicto Warino quamdiu vixerit libere quiete et honorifice, reddendo inde annuatim dicte abbatisse et conventui de Chatriz quadraginta quatuor solidos ad quatuor terminos anni, videlicet ad festum sancti Michaelis undecim solidos, ad Natale undecim solidos, ad Pascha undecim solidos et ad natale sancti Johannis Baptiste undecim solidos, pro omnibus serviciis consuetudinibus et exactionibus. Ad hanc autem conventionem fideliter observandam, dictus Warinus fidejussores invenit, scilicet Simonem West'

---

[1] Hole 18 mm.
[2] Heading *Barenton'*.
[3] Followed by *de Chatriz*, underlined for deletion.
[4] Followed by *ex*, cancelled.
[5] Followed by *de*, expunged.

et alios etc. Et dicte abbatissa et conventus warantizabunt et defendent dictum
molendinum cum omnibus pertinenciis suis et mesuagium predictum dicto
Warino ad totam vitam suam contra omnes homines et feminas per predictum
servicium. Et post decessum dicti Warini recipient dicte abbatissa et conventus[1]
(fo. 115r)[2] dictum molendinum cum pertinenciis et mesuagium prenominatum
cum edificiis solute et quiete sine contradictione alicuius. Et ut hec conventio et
concessio firma sit et stabilis, dicta abbatissa et conventus et Warinus predictus
huic scripto cirographato sigilla sua apposuerunt. Hiis testibus.

> Note. Warin de Barrington I fl. *c.* 1220; Warin de Barrington II held land in Barrington *c.*
> 1253–*c.* 1307 (*VCH Cambs.* v, p. 149). The language of this agreement suggests that the lessee
> is probably Warin de Barrington II.

119   *Grant in fee-farm by abbess Amicia and the convent of Chatteris to Warin de
Barrington of their half of a water-mill called 'le Estmelne' in Barrington and
Foxton and 2 pieces of meadow in Foxton towards the repair of the mill, excepting 9
villeins of Foxton who were accustomed to grind there and 7 roods of meadow in
Foxton; for 2s. annually.*
fo. 115r–v   [9 July 1268 × Jan 1280 *or* shortly before 8 July 1298 × 27 March
1306]

Carta abbatisse de Chatriz Warino de Barenton' de medietate unius molendini.

Sciant presentes et futuri quod nos Amicia abbatissa de Chatriz et ecclesie nostre
conventus unanimi assensu et voluntate dedimus concessimus et presenti carta
nostra confirmavimus Warino de Barenton' totam medietatem et totam partem
nostram quam habuimus et tenuimus in quodam[3] molendino aquatico, quod
vocatur le Estmelne, in villis de Barenton' et Foxton' cum Thoma filio Alexandri Atteaplue de Barenton' participe nostro, cum sitis eiusdem molendini cursu
aque et filo eiusdem stagnis exclusis gurgitibus piscariis viis semitis pasturis libertatibus liberis introitibus et exitibus predicte medietati nostre pertinentibus, et
etiam duas pecias prati jacentes in villa de Foxton' inter molendinum predictum
et pontem versus Foxton' ex utraque parte vie que ducit de Barenton' versus
Foxton', ad molendinum stagnum et exclusam predicta reparanda et emendanda
cum necesse fuerit, cum omnibus suis pertinenciis ad dictam medietatem et
partem nostram molendini predicti seu ad dictas pecias prati pred[icti][4] aliquo

---

1   Followed by catchwords, *dictum molendinum.*
2   Heading *Barenton'.*
3   MS probably *quodem.*
4   Unclear 5 mm.

modo seu jure[1] quocumque spectantibus, sine ullo retinemento sicut unquam nos seu predecessores nostri plenius vel liberius tenuimus, exceptis novem vill[a]nis[2] de Foxton' qui ad predictum molendinum molere con[sue]verunt,[3] et exceptis septem rodis[4] prati quondam ad predictum molendinum spectantibus in Foxton', habendas et tenendas totam predictam medietatem et partem nostram molendini predicti et etiam predictas pecias prati predicti cum o[mnibus][5] suis (fo. 115v)[6] pertinenciis, sicut predictum est, ad feodi firmam predicto Warino heredibus suis et assignatis, de capitalibus dominis feodi illius per servicia indebita et consueta, seu quibuscumque vel quandocumque dare vendere vel assignare voluerint, libere quiete bene et in pace et hereditarie imperpetuum, reddendo inde annuatim nobis et successoribus nostris seu assignatis predictus Warinus heredes sui seu assignati duos solidos sterlingorum pro[7] predicta feodi firma ad festum sancti Michaelis et ad Pascha pro equalibus portionibus, solvendos pro omnibus serviciis consuetudinibus sectis curie et omnibus aliis secularibus demandis de predictis tenementis nobis debitis vel consuetis. Et nos Amicia abbatissa de Chatriz et ecclesie nostre predicte conventus et successores nostri seu assignati predicto Warino heredibus suis et assignatis totam medietatem et partem nostram predictam molendini predicti et etiam predictas pecias prati predicti, exceptis novem villanis predictis et septem rodis prati, sicut predictum est, cum omnibus suis pertinenenciis warantizabimus et contra omnes gentes defendemus per predictum servicium imperpetuum. Et ut hec nostra donatio feodi firme concessio et presentis carte nostre confirmatio warantizatio et defensio rata et stabilis permaneant imperpetuum, huic presenti carte nostre sigillum comune domus nostre et sigillum predicti Warini imperpetuum huius rei testimonium alternatim apponi fecimus. Hiis testibus.

Note. This mill seems to be the half-mill in Foxton which occurs both in Domesday Book and in the privilege of Innocent IV which confirmed the possessions of Chatteris abbey (*Domesday Book*, i, fo. 193a; no. 3, fo. 74r). The abbess could be Amicia who was abbess 9 July 1268 × Jan. 1280 or Amicia de Cambridge who was abbess shortly before 8 July 1298 × 1306: see nos. 101n and 38n. Warin de Barrington held land in Barrington *c*. 1253–*c*. 1307 (*VCH Cambs*. v, p. 149).

---

1 MS four minims followed by *e*.
2 Unclear 3 mm.
3 Hole 4 mm.
4 Followed by *prad*, expunged.
5 Damaged 6 mm.
6 Heading *Baryngton*'.
7 MS *per*.

120 *Gift by abbess Agnes de Ely and the convent of Chatteris to Alice formerly wife of William de Fowlmere, carpenter, and James her son, clerk, of a croft called 'Brondescroft' with a messuage and meadow [in Barrington], for 2 marks in advance and 16d. annually.*
fos. 115v–116r [17 Nov. 1275 × 1290]

Carta abbatisse Alicie quondam uxori Willelmi carpentarii de j crofta.

Sciant etc. quod ego Agnes de Ely abbatissa de Chatriz et conventus illius domus dedimus concessimus et hac presenti carta confirmavimus Alicie quondam uxori Willelmi carpentarii de[1] Fulmere et Jacobo filio suo clerico, pro homagiis et serviciis suis et pro duabus marcis argenti quas nobis dederunt pre manibus in guersummam, unam croftam (fo. 116r)[2] que vocatur Brondescroft cum mesuagio et prato eidem adjacentibus, et jacet inter terram magistri Johannis le Sauser et domine Agnetis de Barenton', tenendam et habendam dictam croftam cum pertinenciis, ut predictum est, de nobis et successoribus nostris predictis Alicie et Jacobo et eorum heredibus vel assignatis, vel cuicumque vel quibuscumque vel quandocumque dictam croftam cum pertinenciis dare vendere legare invadiare vel assignare voluerint, libere quiete bene et in pace et imperpetuum, exceptis domo religionis et judaismo, reddendo inde annuatim sepedicti Alicia et Jacobus et eorum heredes vel assignati nobis et[3] successoribus nostris sexdecim denarios argenti ad quatuor anni terminos, videlicet ad festum sancti Johannis Baptiste quatuor denarios, ad festum sancti Michaelis quatuor denarios, ad festum Natalis Domini quatuor denarios et ad Pascha iiij denarios, pro omnibus serviciis consuetudinibus sectis curiarum et omnibus aliis secularibus demandis. Et ego predicte abbatissa et conventus et successores nostri dictam croftam cum pertinenciis predictis Alicie et Jacobo et eorum heredibus seu assignatis contra omnes gentes per predictum servicium warantizabimus defendemus et acquietabimus. Et ut hec autem nostra donatio concessio etc. Hiis testibus etc.

> Note. For dating of Agnes de Ely see no. 113n. This gift must date from before 1290 because the property is to be held *de nobis et heredibus nostris* and the gift reserves an annual rent.

121 *Gift by William son of Eustace de Barrington to Henry son of John de Barrington of a messuage with croft, land with meadow and other parcels of arable land*

---

1 Interlined above *ad*, expunged.
2 Heading *Barenton'*.
3 Followed *sus*, cancelled.

with two headlands of meadow in Barrington, for 5 marks, ½ mark to his wife, 2s. to his heir and an annual rent of 4s.
fos. 116r–117r [s. xiii$^{1-3}$]

Carta Willelmi filii Eustachii de Barenton' de uno mesuagio cum crofta et aliis.

Sciant presentes et futuri quod ego Willelmus filius Eustachii de Barenton' concessi dedi et hac presenti carta mea confirmavi Henrico filio Johannis de Barenton' pro homagio et servicio suo totum illud mesuagium cum crofta, quod jacet inter mesuagium Ade Bonegent et mesuagium Radulphi le taillur', et totam illam terram cum toto prato ad dictum mesuagium pertinentem in campo de Barenton' cum omnibus pertinenciis, quod scilicet mesuagium cum dicta terra Robertus filius Walteri et eius antecessores de me et de antecessoribus (fo. 116v)[1] meis quondam per servitutem tenuerunt, et quasdam alias particulas terre mee arabilis cum duabus foreris prati, quarum una particula jacet in campo occidentali, scilicet in le Cumbes, juxta terram Norman' filii Alani, et alia particula abuttat versus le Hakk' juxta terram dicti Norman', et quedam particula in le Mersh abuttans super Longeweye, et dimidia roda et tres pedes versus le Sik' juxta terram Ade Cuberd', et viginti pedes super Voxhelledon', et abuttat super fontem qui dicitur Blakewelle juxta terram Henrici militis et terram Thome juxta aquam, et una forera prati in le Sik' juxta predictum[2] pratum Ade filii Cuthbert, et alia forera prati in eodem Sik' juxta pratum Henrici le Fraunkeleyn, et in campo orientali una particula jacet desuper le Mylnestede juxta terram Thome Humfridi, et viginti pedes jacent super Wlmaresdong juxta terram Roberti filii Ricardi, et viginti pedes ad Whithakkis juxta terram Warini filii Sweyn, et dimidia roda ad Mamereswelle juxta terram domine abbatisse de Chatriz, et una roda super le Madwerescroft juxta terram dicti Henrici, in feudo et hereditate, tenenda et habenda de me et heredibus meis sibi vel heredibus suis vel cuicumque dare legare vendere vel assignare voluerit, excepta domo religionis, libere quiete bene et in pace integre et hereditarie, reddendo inde annuatim michi et heredibus meis dictus Henricus et heredes sui vel eorum assignati quatuor solidos, scilicet ad Pascha duos et ad festum sancti Michaelis duos solidos, pro omni servicio et consuetudine et seculari exactione, salvo servicio domini regis, scilicet tamen quantum pertinet ad tantam terram eiusdem feodi. Et ego predictus Willelmus et heredes mei warantizabimus et defendemus totum dictum mesuagium cum dicta crofta et totam terram prenominatam cum dicto

---

1 Heading *Baryngton'*.
2 *predi-* underlined, for deletion?

prato et cum omnibus pertinenciis dicto (fo. 117r)[1] Henrico et heredibus suis
vel eorum assignatis contra omnes gentes per predictum servicium. Pro hac
autem concessione dona[tione][2] et warantizatione et presentis carte confirmatione, dedit michi predictus Henricus quinque marcas sterlingorum in guersummam, uxori mee dimidiam marcam et heredi meo duos solidos pro suo assensu
et beneplacito. Et ut hec mea concessio donatio warantizatio et carte mee
confirmatio firmiter stabiles et inconcusse permaneant imperpetuum, presentem
cartam sigilli mei impressione roboravi. Hiis testibus etc.

> Note. This gift was later confirmed by Thomas de Bancis (no. 117). Thomas de Bancis occurs
> in 1247 (no. 142).

122 *Gift by William son of Eustace de Barrington to John son of Adam de Barrington of a messuage and 9 acres in Barrington, for 6 marks, ½ mark to Agatha his
wife, 1 talent to his heir and an annual rent of 4s.*
fo. 117r–v [*s.* xiii[1-3]]

Carta Willelmi filii Eustachii de uno mesuagio et novem acris.

Sciant etc. quod ego Willelmus filius Eustachii de Barenton' dedi etc. filio
Johanni Ade de Barenton' pro homagi[o][3] et servicio suo totum mesuagium
integrum quod Alanus filius Philippi tenuit, quod jacet inter mesuagia Alicie
uxoris Humfridi et Estrild' uxoris Hugonis, et novem acras terre in campis de
Barenton cum pertinenciis pertinentibus ad dictum mesuagium, habenda et
tenenda de me et heredibus meis dicto Johanni et heredibus suis vel quibuscumque dare aut assignare voluerit, excepto loco religionis, libere quiete integre et
hereditarie, cum omnibus libertatibus et aysiamentis infra villam de Barenton'
et extra in pratis pascuis planis viis semitis comunis ad predictam[4] terram
pertinentibus, reddendo inde annuatim dictus Johannes et heredes sui aut sui
assignati michi et heredibus meis quatuor solidos, scilicet ad festum sancti
Michaelis duos, ad Pascha duos solidos, pro omni servicio consuetudine et
demanda michi et heredibus meis pertinentibus, salvo servicio domini regis,
scilicet quantum pertinet ad tantam terram eiusdem feodi in eadem villa. Et ego
Willelmus et heredes mei warantizabimus defendemus dictum mesuagium et
totam dictam terram cum omnibus pertinenciis et libertatibus dicto Johanni et

1 Heading *Barenton'*.
2 Damaged 8 mm.
3 Hole 2 mm.
4 Followed by *viam*, expunged.

heredibus (fo. 117v)[1] suis, aut quibuscumque dederit aut assignaverit per predictum servicium contra omnes homines et feminas imperpetuum. Pro hac autem donatione concessione carte mee confirmatione et warantizatione, dedit michi dictus Johannes sex marcas argenti in guersummam et Agathe uxori[2] mee dimidiam marcam et heredi meo unum talentum. Et ut hec mea donatio concessio confirmatio et warantizatio rata et inconcussa futuris temporibus perseveret, hanc presentem cartam sigilli mei appositione roboravi. Hiis testibus etc.

Note. Another copy of no. 116. For dating of William son of Eustace de Barrington see no. 121n.

123 *Release by abbess Mary de Sancto Claro and the convent of Chatteris to Eustace son of William de Barrington of villein service in a messuage and land in Barrington, held of Eustace by John son of Henry Broun, villein of Chatteris abbey.* fo. 117v [*s.* xiii[2] × 28 Sept. 1265]

Relaxatio domine abbatisse et conventus de quodam messuagio et certa terra Eustachio.

Omnibus ad quos presens scriptum pervenerit Maria de Sancto Claro permissione divina abbatissa de Chatriz totusque eiusdem loci conventus salutem in Domino. Noverit universitas vestra nos concessisse Eustachio filio[3] Willelmi de Barenton' et heredibus suis quod non exigemus nec clamabimus aliquid in uno mesuagio et tota terra cum pertinenciis suis in villa de Barenton' que Johannes filius Henrici Broun et heredes sui tenent libere in feodo de dicto Eustachio et heredibus suis, ad tenendum in dominico nostro ratione villenagii quod idem Johannes de nobis tenet in eadem villa et eo quod nativus noster est, per quod dictus Eustachius et heredes sui amittere possent homagium wardam et relevium que eis de dicto tenemento libere accidere poterunt, dummodo dictus Eustachius et heredes sui formam et tenorem sue confirmationis quam dictus Johannes habet de dicto Eustachio secundum justiciam observaverint. Et in huius rei testimonium etc.

Note. Another copy of no. 100. For dating see no. 100n.

---

1 Heading *Baryngton'*.
2 Followed by *o*, expunged.
3 Followed by *Johanni*, expunged.

124 *Agreement between abbess Amicia and the convent of Chatteris and Eustace de Barrington that the suit of court at Foxton which the abbey was seeking from Eustace, on account of a tenement which he held of them in Barrington, was owed by Richard March because he held a capital messuage and part of the tenement by a lease of William de Barrington, father of Eustace; and that the abbey has remitted 2 of the 8 capons which Eustace owed annually for a meadow in Barrington.*
fos. 117v–118r   At Foxton, 16 Nov. 1275

Finalis concordia de redditu sex caponum. (fo. 118r)[1]

Anno regni regis Edwardi tertio die sancti Edmundi archiepiscopi apud Foxton', inter Amiciam abbatissam de Chatriz et eiusdem loci conventum ex parte una et Eustachium de Barenton' ex altera sic convenit, videlicet cum a parte dictorum abbatisse et conventus quedem secta curie, ratione tenementi quod idem Eustachius de eis tenet in villa de Barenton', ac octo capones annui redditus, ratione cuiusdam prati quod dicitur le Holm in eadem villa, ab eodem Eustachio peterentur, idem Eustachius dictam sectam de predicto tenemento debitam ad curiam dictarum abbatisse et conventus de Foxton' a Ricardo March' dicit debere fieri, ratione capitalis mesuagii et cuiusdam partis terre eiusdem tenementi que idem Ricardus tenet ex dimissione Willelmi de Barenton' patris Eustachii memorati, propter quod predicti abbatissa et conventus remiserunt eisdem Eustachio duos capones de predictis octo caponibus qui ab ipso prius[2] petebantur, et sic idem Eustachius obligavit se et heredes suos ad reddendum predictis abbatisse et conventui ad festum Natalis Domini sex capones competentes apud Foxton' de prato antedicto annuatim imperpetuum. Concessit etiam idem Eustachius pro se et heredibus suis quod predicti abbatissa et conventus per balivum suum possint distringere ipsos in predicto prato si predicti capones annuatim, ut predictum est, dicto termino non solvantur. Ad que omnia huic inde fideliter et sine fraude observanda, predicte partes huic scripto cirographato alternatim sigilla sua apposuerunt. Hiis testibus etc.

125 *Gift in free alms by Thomas de Bancis to Chatteris abbey of the land in Foxton given to him by Richard de la Lowe; for 2s. 6d. annually to Richard.*
fo. 118r–v   [s. xiii[2-3]]

[1] Heading *Barynton'*.
[2] *Redditus vj capo[nes] ad Natale Domini*, marginated after *prius*.

Carta Thome de Bancis abbatisse et conventui de tota terra quam habuit de dono Ricardi de la Lowe. (fo. 118v)[1]

Sciant etc. quod ego Thomas de Bancis dedi concessi et hac presenti carta mea confirmavi Deo et ecclesie sancte Marie de Chatriz et monialibus ibidem Deo servientibus, pro salute anime mee et animarum antecessorum meorum, totam terram quam habui in parochia de Foxton' de dono Ricardi de la Lowe cum pertinenciis omnibus sine aliquo retenemento, habendam et tenendam predictis monialibus in liberam et perpetuam elemosinam de predicto Ricardo et here-dibus suis[2] imperpetuum, reddendo inde annuatim prenominato Ricardo et heredibus suis duos solidos et sex denarios, scilicet ad festum sancti Michaelis quindecim denarios et ad Pascha quindecim denarios, pro omnibus serviciis consuetudinibus sectis et secularibus demandis. Et ut mea donatio concessio et presentis carte mee confirmatio robur optineat perpetuum, presenti carte mee sigillum meum appposui. Hiis testibus etc.

Note. No. 134 is the gift by Richard son of John de la Lowe to Thomas de Bancis of this land. Thomas de Bancis occurs in 1247 (no. 142) and in 1239 × s. xiii[3] (no. 240).

126 *Confirmation by Richard de la Lowe of the gift in free alms by Thomas de Bancis to Chatteris abbey of lands, rents and tenements in Foxton.*
fos. 118v–119r [s. xiii$^{2-3}$]

Confirmatio Ricardi le Lowe super donum Thome de Bancis abbatisse et conventui de Chatriz.

Sciant quod ego Ricardus de la Lowe concessi et hac presenti carta mea confirmavi donum et concessionem quam Thomas de Bancis fecit abbatisse et conventui sancte Marie de Chatriz, de omnibus terris redditibus et tenementis cum pertinenciis suis integre que dictus Thomas de Bancis tenuit de me in parochia de Foxton', habendis et tenendis predictis abbatisse et conventui de me et heredibus meis imperpetuum in liberam et perpetuam elemosinam, secundum quod carta predicti Thome de Bancis, quam diligenter inspexi, super predicto dono testatur, ita quod nec ego Ricardus nec aliquis heredum meorum nec aliquis per[3] me vel pro me contra predictam concessionem meam et confirmationem venire poterimus aut debemus. (fo. 119r)[4] Et ego Ricardus et heredes

---

1 Heading *Foxton'*.
2 Followed by *duos solidos et sex denarios*, expunged.
3 MS *pro*.
4 Heading *Foxton'*.

mei warantizabimus acquietabimus et defendemus predicta terras redditus et tenementa cum omnibus pertinenciis suis predictis abbatisse et conventui contra omnes mortales imperpetuum. Et ut hec mea concessio et presentis carte mee confirmatio robur optineat perpetuum, presenti carte sigillum meum apposui. Hiis testibus.

Note. See nos. 125 and 134. Thomas de Bancis occurs in 1247 (no. 142) and in 1239 × s. xiii[3] (no. 240).

127 *Gift in free alms by Adam Homo Dei of Heacham to Chatteris abbey of 3 acres of land in Foxton.*
fo. 119r [s. xii[4] × s. xiii[2]]

Carta Ade de Hecham iij acris terre in Foxton'.

Sciant etc. quod ego Adam Homo Dei de Hecham dedi etc. domui de Chatriz tres acras terre mee in villa de Foxton' de feodo Michaeli de Mora, scilicet in campo de Heydych unam rodam que abuttat ultra viam de Lythlowe inter terram Willelmi filii Edelmi et terram persone, in campo de Dreymere tres rodas in foresco juxta terram predicte domus, in campo de Ham duas acras que abuttant ultra viam de Barenton' inter terram predicte domus et terram Willelmi Manton', tenendas et habendas in puram et perpetuam elemosinam libere et quiete sine retenemento. Et ego Adam et heredes mei warantizabimus et defendemus predictam terram contra omnes homines. Hiis testibus etc.

Note. The dating is based solely on the language of the charter.

128 *Lease by abbess Agnes de Ely and the convent of Chatteris to Osbert Guthlac, Hawisia his wife and John their son of Foxton, for their lives, of a messuage with croft, 10 acres of arable land and 5 roods of meadow in Foxton, for an annual rent of 4s. and 6 capons and 2 suits of court annually.*
fos. 119r–120r [17 Nov. 1275 × 13 May 1293]

Concessio abbatisse de uno mesuagio ad terminum vite.

Omnibus Christi fidelibus Agnes de Ely abbatissa de Chatriz et totus conventus eiusdem loci salutem in Domino. Noveritis nos concessisse dedisse et hac presenti carta nostra communi consilio et assensu totius capituli confirmasse Osberto Guthlac, Hawisie uxori sue et Johanni filio eorundem de Foxton', ad terminum vite eorundem trium, totum mesuagium nostrum cum crofto idem[1]

1 MS *eidem.*

mesuagium adjacente quod quondam fuit Johannis Fraunceys de Foxton', adeo integre prout ille idem Johannes illud mesuagium cum crofto habuit et tenuit in villa de Foxton'[1] (fo. 119v)[2] predicta, quod jacet inter mesuagium Henrici le Knygth[3] ex una parte et terram ecclesie de Foxton' ex altera, et preterea decem acras[4] terre arabilis et quinque rodas prati prout jacent per particulas in campis et pratis de Foxton', tenenda et habenda de nobis et successoribus nostris omnia predicta mesuagium cum crofto, terram arabilem, pratum cum omnibus suis pertinenciis, adeo integre prout dictus Johannes eadem tenuit et habuit de nobis in vita sua, predictis Osberto, Hawisie uxori sue et Johanni filio eorundem, libere quiete bene et in pace ad terminum vite eorundem, reddendo inde annuatim nobis et nostris successoribus quatuor solidos argenti et sex capones, videlicet ad festum sancti Andree apostolici duodecim denarios, ad Pascha duodecim denarios, ad festum natalis sancti Johannis Baptiste duodecim den- arios et ad festum sancti Michaelis duodecim denarios et ad Natale Domini sex capones, pro omnibus serviciis consuetudinibus sectis curiarum et omnibus aliis secularibus exactionibus seu demandis, salvis tamen duabus sectis per annum ad curiam nostram quas predicti Osbertus, Hawisia uxor sua et Johannes filius eorundem facient, unam sectam videlicet ad proximam curiam nostram post Pascha et aliam sectam ad proximam curiam nostram post festum sancti Mich- aelis. Et nos predicte abbatissa et conventus predicti loci et nostri successores omnia predicta[5] mesuagium cum crofto et terram arabilem cum prato, sicut predictum est, cum omnibus suis prefatis Osberto et Hawisie uxori sue et Johanni filio eorundem contra omnes gentes warantizabimus acquietabimus et in omnibus defendemus per predictum servicium ad terminum vite eorundem. In cuius rei testimonium parti huius presentis carte indentate penes predictos Osbertum, Hawisiam uxorem suam et Johannem filium[6] eorundem residenti sigillum commune capituli nostri apposuimus, (fo. 120r)[7] et alteri parti penes nos remanenti predicti Osbertus, Hawisia et Johannes sigilla sua apposuerunt. Hiis testibus etc.

---

1 Followed by *ad terminum vite eorundem*, cancelled.
2 Heading *Foxton'*.
3 *g* interlined.
4 Corr. marg., *marcas* expunged.
5 MS *omni et predict'*: occurs as *omnia predicta* above; final *a* of *omnia* probably misread as Tironian *et*.
6 MS *filio*.
7 Heading *Foxton'*.

Note. Amicia, predecessor of Agnes de Ely, was abbess on 16 Nov. 1275 (no. 124); Agnes de Burwell was abbess on 14 May 1293 (Cambridge, Trinity College Archives, Foxton 2, m. 2). These lands and messuage were given to the abbey in no. 140.

129 *Confirmation by Geoffrey [?de Burgo], bishop of Ely, to Chatteris abbey, following a judgement by jurors, of 2 virgates and 9 acres of land, 3 messuages and a meadow in Foxton, which Simon, rector, was claiming belonged to the church of Foxton.*
fo. 120r–v   ?[29 June 1225 × 17 Dec. 1228]

Laudum episcopi Eliensis super certis terris et messuagiis cum prato.

Universis sancte matris ecclesie filiis ad quos littere presentes pervenerint Gaufridus Dei gracia Eliensis episcopus salutem in Domino. Noverit universitas vestra quod, cum Simon rector ecclesie de Foxton' querelam movisset sanctimonialibus de Catricia de duabus virgatis et novem[1] acris terre et tribus mesuagiis cum prato in Foxton, quas idem Simon de predio ecclesie de Foxton' esse asserebat, presertim cum duo predecessores eius proximi, scilicet Ricardus filius Ilberti et Petrus de Self', eas tenuissent, et prefate sanctimoniales ad dominicum ecclesie sue de Chatriz pertinere dicebant, partibus convocatis coram nobis et pluribus aliis viris discretis hoc modo veritatem didicimus, videlicet quod utraque pars in testimonium et juramentum xix hominum quos elegerunt spontanea voluntate compromiserunt, jurantes se stare testimonio et veritati quod super hoc ex ore ipsorum procederet.[2] Juratores autem sunt hii Willelmus de Bancis, Alanus de Seppree, Rogerus filius Osberti de Barenton', Henricus filius Willelmi filii[3] Alexandri de Trippelowe, Willelmus filius Isabelle, Willelmus filius Veiri, Willelmus filius Wluine, Osbertus filius Wlwine, Andreas Stephanus, Robertus Brine, Estach' de Barenton', Ricardus frater eius, Philippus d⟨e⟩ Foulmere, Ebrardus de Berlay, Osbertus filius Beatricis de Sepprea, Ricardus filius Stamardi de Sepprea. Et hii jurati dixerunt quod predicta due virgate et novem acre et tria mesuagia et pratum in Foxton' ad dominicum ecclesie de Chatriz pertinebant, et quod nec (fo. 120v)[4] Ricardus filius Ilberti nec Petrus de Siolf', qui prius erant rectores in ecclesia de Foxton', eas unquam tenuerunt nomine ecclesie sed nomine persone proprie. Nos itaque terras supra-

---

[1] Followed by *ar*, expunged.
[2] *c* written over *d*.
[3] MS *filius*.
[4] Heading *Foxton'*.

dictas, sicut monialibus[1] judicate[2] sunt, eis presenti carta confirmamus et sigilli nostri appositione roboramus. Hiis testibus etc.

> Note. Geoffrey de Burgo was bishop of Ely 29 June 1225–17 Dec. 1228. Eustace de Barrington was visor in an assize of last presentation in 1199 (*R. Cur. Reg.* i, p. 378). William de Bancis held the Foxton manor of Mortimers by the 1180s; he died after 1205 and his heir, William, died after 1228. Alan son of Alan de Shepreth held the de la Hayes manor in Foxton by 1200 (*VCH Cambs.* viii, pp. 167–8). If the juror called Alan de Shepreth in this document is not Alan son of Alan de Shepreth, but his father, the bishop here and in no. 130 could be Geoffrey Ridel (6 Oct. 1174–21 Aug. 1189). However, the use of testimony by jurors and the relatively complex language of the confirmation suggest that the bishop is Geoffrey de Burgo.

130 *Notification by Geoffrey [?de Burgo], bishop of Ely, of the agreement made between Chatteris abbey and Peter de Shelford, rector of Foxton, concerning 2 virgates and 9 acres of land, 3 messuages and a meadow in Foxton, which Peter acknowledged that he held of the demesne of the abbey for his life; for 1 gold coin annually.*
fo. 120v ?[29 June 1225 × 17 Dec. 1228]

Littera testimonialis episcopi Eliensis de finali concordia inter abbatissam et rectorem de Foxton'.

Universis sancte matris ecclesie filiis Gaufridus Eliensis episcopus salutem in Domino. Universitati vestre notum fieri volumus quod, de contraversia que erat inter moniales de Chatriz et Petrum clericum de Schelford', scilicet de duabus virgatis terre et novem acris et tribus mesuagiis in Foxton' et prato quod pertinet ad prescriptum tenementum, quod quidem tenementum prenominatus Petrus contendebat pertinere ad ecclesiam suam de Foxton', moniales vero asserebant esse de dominio suo, hoc modo inter eos convenit: predictus siquidem Petrus coram nobis et multis aliis confessus est[3] illud tenementum esse de dominico monialium,[4] ⟨tenendum⟩ de dictis monialibus tenementum predictum, solvendo eis inde annuatim unum aureum ad festum sancti Michaelis nostro nomine ecclesie sue de Foxton'. Et post recessum vel decessum ipsius revertetur terra[5] ad dominicum monialium. Test' etc.

[1] Followed by *jurate*, expunged.
[2] Interlined.
[3] Interlined.
[4] Followed by *tenedit*, expunged.
[5] Followed by *d*, expunged.

Note. Although the bishop in this document could be Geoffrey Ridel (1174–89), the description of the disputed lands is very similar to that in no. 129. This suggests that the bishop is Geoffrey de Burgo (1225–8). No. 131, in which the lands are described differently, probably preceded this agreement. For dating see also no. 129n.

131 *Agreement made between Chatteris abbey and Richard son of Ilbert, rector of Foxton, concerning 1 hide and 9 acres of disputed land in Foxton, held by Richard but claimed by the abbey, which Richard is to hold, for his life, for 1 talent of gold annually.*
fos. 120v–121r ?[*s.* xii[4] × *s.* xiii[1]]

Finalis concordia inter abbatissam et rectorem de Foxton' super una hida terre et ix acris.

Hec est compositio facta inter sanctimoniales de Chatriz et Ricardum filium Roberti[1] super controversia orta inter illos de terris quibusdam quas idem Ricardus tenebat, quas prefate sanctimoniales calumpniabantur velud ad[2] jus ecclesie sue de Chatriz specialiter (fo. 121r)[3] pertinentes, quas etiam e contra Ricardus allegabat ad ecclesiam suam de Foxton' pertinere, videlicet quod pretaxatus Ricardus supramemoratam ecclesiam de Foxton' toto tempore vite sue libere et[4] quiete tenebit, sicut antea tenebat, terram vero pro qua controversia similiter toto tempore vite sue tenebit, scilicet hidam et novem acras, reddendo inde ipsis sanctimonialibus pro ipsa terra annuum canonem, scilicet talentum unum auri, ita tamen quod nemo possit post decessum Ricardi, pro eo quod ipse eas tenuerit vel habuerit terras, aliquam in ipsa clamare successione juris, nisi ipse sanctimoniales huius compositionis. Testes sunt etc.

Note. This agreement pre-dates no. 129.

132 *Agreement whereby abbess Mabel de Bancis and the convent of Chatteris lease to Thomas de Bancis, for his life, a messuage and 12 acres of land in Foxton, 6 acres of which he formerly held of her at will; for 4s. annually.*
fo. 121r–v [*s.* xiii[2] × 28 Sept. 1265]

Dimissio abbatisse Thome de Bancis de uno mesuagio et vj acris terre.

---

[1] Recte *Ilberti*; cf. no. 129.
[2] Interlined.
[3] Heading *Foxton'*.
[4] Interlined.

Hec est conventio facta inter Mabiliam de Bancis dictam dominam de Chatriz et conventum eiusdem loci ex una parte et Thomam de Bancis ex altera, scilicet quod predicte domina et conventus dimiserunt et concesserunt predicto Thome de Bancis unum mesuagium et sex acras terre cum pertinenciis in Foxton', videlicet illud mesuagium quod Johannes Kithe tenuit quondam de predictis monialibus et predicte sex acre terre sic jacent, scilicet due acre in campo de[1] Heydych inter terras Willelmi de la Haye cum prato adjacente, et una acra in eodem campo juxta terram Roginaldi Binel, et una acra in campo de Caldewelle inter terram Willelmi de la Haye et terram Margerie que fuit uxor Andree filii Alani[2], et una acra in Douunfeld' inter terram Johannis prepositi et terram Agnetis uxoris Willelmi de Crawedane, et una (fo. 121v)[3] acra in eodem campo contra Wodewaye inter terram Roberti le Frie et Christiane sororis Alani le Fraunc[eys][4]. Preterea prenominata domina et conventus dimiserunt et concesserunt[5] Thome de Bancis sex acras terre in eadem villa, illas videlicet quas predictus Thomas prius tenuit de predicta domina ad voluntatem suam, habenda et tenenda dicto Thome et suis assignatis tota vita ipsius Thome libere quiete, reddendo inde annuatim predictis domine et conventui quatuor solidos ad quatuor terminos anni, ad Pascha duodecim denarios et ad festum sancti Johannis duodecim denarios et ad festum sancti Michaelis xij denarios et ad festum sancti Andree xij denarios pro omnibus serviciis consuetudinibus et secularibus demandis. Et sciendum est quod tota predicta terra cum mesuagio predicto et edificiis cum pertinenciis post obitum dicti Thome predictis domine et conventui sine alicuius contradictione quiete revertetur. Predicta vero domina et successores sui warantizabunt totam terram prenominatam cum mesuagio et aliis pertinenciis predicto Thome et suis assignatis quamdiu vixerit contra omnes mortales. Et ut hec conventio firma sit et stabilis, secundum quod predictum est, alter[6] alterius scripto cirographato sigillum suum apposuit. Hiis testibus etc.

Note. For dating of Mabel de Bancis see no. 100n. Thomas de Bancis occurs in 1247 (no. 142) and in 1239 × s. xiii[3] (no. 240).

[1] Followed by *Caldewelle inter terram Willelmi*, expunged.
[2] Followed by *le Fraunceys*, expunged.
[3] Heading *Foxton'*.
[4] Hole 7 mm.
[5] *et concesserunt*, ins. marg., MS *concessesserunt*.
[6] MS *alteri*.

133 *Surrender and quitclaim by Thomas de Bancis to Chatteris abbey of a messuage and 5 acres of land in Foxton, formerly belonging to Guy Babbe.*
fos. 121v–122r [Shortly after *c.* 29 Oct. 1247]

Quieta clamantia Thome de Bancis de uno mesuagio et quinque acris terre quondam Guidonis Babbe.

Sciant etc. quod ego Thomas de Bancis remisi de me et de heredibus meis omnino quietum clamavi totum jus et clamium quod habui vel habere potui in uno mesuagio et quinque acris terre cum pertinenciis in Foxton', que quondam fuerunt Wydonis (fo. 122r)[1] Babbe, Deo et beate Marie et sanctimonialibus de Chatriz ibidem Deo servientibus, ita quod nec ego Thomas nec aliquis heredum meorum nec aliquis per me vel pro me in predicto mesuagio et quinque acris terre prenominatis de cetero nullum juris clamium exigere clamare vendicare poterimus vel debemus. Et ut hec mea concessio et quieta clamatio futuris temporibus robur optineant, presenti carte sigillum meum apposui, et tradidi prenominatis sanctimonialibus cyrographum confectum coram justiciariis itinerantibus apud Cantabr', inter Hugonem filium Martini et Matill' uxorem eius et Aliciam sororem ipsius Matill' petentes et me tenentem, de predicto mesuagio et quinque acris prenominatis coram probis hominibus una cum mea remissione et quieta clamatione. Hiis testibus etc.

Note. The cartulary contains a copy of the final concord mentioned in this document (no. 142). This document is preceded by nos. 139 and 142 and followed by no. 148. For dating see no. 142n.

134 *Gift by Richard son of John de la Lowe of Foxton to Thomas de Bancis of all his land in Foxton, for 14 marks and an annual rent of 2s. 6d.*
fo. 122r–v [s. xiii$^{2-3}$]

Carta Ricardi de Foxton' Thome de Bancis.

Sciant presentes etc. quod ego Ricardus filius Johannis de la Lowe de parochia Foxton' dedi concessi et hac presenti carta mea confirmavi extra me et heredes meos Thome de Bancis, pro homagio et servicio suo et pro quatuordecim marcis argenti quas michi dedit in guersummam, totam terram meam quam habui in parochia de Foxtona cum pertinenciis omnibus sine retinemento, tenendam et habendam de me et heredibus meis sibi et heredibus suis vel cui dare vendere legare vel assignare voluerit, excepto loco religionis, libere quiete bene et in pace

---

[1] Heading *Foxton'*.

integre et hereditarie, reddendo inde annuatim michi et heredibus meis ille et
heredes sui[1] duos solidos et sex denarios, scilicet ad festum sancti Michaelis
quindecim denarios et ad Pascha quindecim denarios, pro omnibus serviciis
consuetudinibus exactionibus[2] sectis et de/mandis (fo. 122v).[3] Et ego Ricardus
et heredes mei warantizabimus defendemus et acquietabimus totam predictam
terram cum pertinenciis predicto Thome heredibus suis et suis assignatis per
predictum servicium contra omnes homines et feminas imperpetuum. Et ut hec
mea donatio rata et stabilis permaneat, presenti scripto sigillum meum apposui.
Hiis testibus etc.

> Note. Thomas de Bancis later gave this land to Chatteris abbey (no. 125). Thomas de Bancis
> occurs in 1247 (no. 142) and in 1239 × s. xiii[3] (no. 240).

135 *Surrender and quitclaim by Alan le Fraunceys of Foxton to Chatteris abbey of
8 acres of land in Foxton which he formerly held of the abbey at will.*
fos. 122v–123r [1246 × c. 1265]

Relaxatio Alani le[4] Fraunceys de viij acris cum pertinenciis in villa de Foxton'.

Sciant quod ego Alanus le Fraunceys de Foxton' reddidi remisi et de me et
heredibus meis omnino quietum clamavi Deo et ecclesie beate Marie de Chatriz
et monialibus ibidem Deo servientibus, pro salute anime mee et antecessorum
meorum, octo acras terre cum pertinenciis in Foxton', quas quidem de eisdem
prius tenui ad voluntatem earum, et quarum una acra et dimidia jacent inter
terram domini Roberti de Mortuo Mari et Jewedich', due acre in eodem campo
juxta terram ecclesie de Chatriz et terram Nicholai filii mei, una roda inter
⟨terras⟩ dicte ecclesie et[5] abuttat super viam de Barenton', una acra juxta terram
dicte ecclesie et terram Radulphi de Kareshe[6] et abuttat super Horsecroft, et in
campo de Caldewelle una acra juxta[7] terram Willelmi de la Haye et terram
quam Johannes de Rakeh' solebat tenere et abuttat super terram Margerie Ruffe,
j roda juxta terram persone de Foxton' et terram Rogeri Legat', una roda juxta
terram dicte ecclesie et terram Alicie Veiri et abuttat super fossatum de Jewedich', una roda ad Wodegate Howe juxta terram relicte Alani filii Andree et

---

[1] Followed by *duos solidos*, expunged.
[2] Followed by *d*, expunged.
[3] Heading *Foxton'*.
[4] MS *de*.
[5] Followed by *b*, cancelled.
[6] Final *e* may be *o*, cancelled.
[7] Followed by *a*, expunged.

terram dicte ecclesie, in Denefeld' dimidia acra juxta terram predicte ecclesie et
terram Alicie Veiri,[1] in eodem[2] (fo. 123r)[3] campo dimidia acra juxta terram
prenominate ecclesie et terram Rogeri fabri, et in Collande dimidia acra juxta
terram Andree Wynter et abuttat super regiam viam, ita quod nec ego dictus
Alanus nec aliquis heredum meorum nec aliquis pro nobis vel per nos in predictis octo acris terre cum pertinenciis de cetero nullum juris clamium exigere
clamare vel vendicare poterimus aut debemus. Et ut hec mea remissio et quieta
clamantia robur optineat perpetuum, presenti scripto sigillum meum apposui.
Hiis testibus etc.

> Note. William de la Haye was lord of de la Hayes manor in Foxton from *c.* 1250. Robert
> Mortimer was lord of Mortimers manor in Foxton 1246–*c.* 1265 (*VCH Cambs.* viii, pp. 167–
> 8). Alan le Frounceys occurs in *s.* xiii[2] × 28 Sept. 1265 in nos. 141 and 145.

136 *Agreement between Roger de Foxton, chaplain, and the abbess of Chatteris
concerning the cultivation of Roger's land which she received in exchange from him,
for his life; the abbess will sow half the land and will manure 3 acres of fallow-land
on condition that Roger will reap and gather the corn from all the land, will accept
half the costs and will receive half the corn from the land.*
fo. 123r   20 Nov. 1287 × 19 Nov. 1288

Conventio quod inter abbatissam et Rogerum de Foxton' de certis terris in
excambium.

Anno regni regis Edwardi sextodecimo convenit inter Rogerum de Foxton'
capellanum ex parte una et abbatissam de Chateriz ex altera, videlicet quod dicta
abbatissa totam terram dicti Rogeri, quam in excambium ab eo recepit, ad totam
vitam dicti Rogeri ad[4] medietatem fideliter seminabit et quolibet anno de terra
warrec[ta]ta[5] tres acras terre compostabit, ita videlicet quod dictus Rogerus in
autumpno bladum totius terre metet et colliget, et proportione sua medietatem
sumptus a predicta domina sine aliqua[6] contradictione recipiet, simul cum
medietate omnium bladorum in terris existentium. Et si predicta abbatissa vel
sui attornati hoc facere non curaverint, licebit ista convencione predicto Rogero
vel suis assignatis dictum bladum asportare et alienare ad libitum sue voluntatis

---

1 Or *Verri?*
2 Followed by catchwords, *campo dimidia acra.*
3 Heading *Foxton'.*
4 Followed by *s*, cancelled.
5 Hole 3 mm.
6 Followed by *proportione*, expunged.

ubicumque volueri[t],[1] sine aliqua contradictione ex parte dicte abbatisse. In cuius rei testimonium etc.

137 *Agreement between Chatteris abbey and John, carter, and Goditha his wife whereby the abbey grants to them, for their lives, ½ virgate of land which William son of Beatrice surrendered to the abbey, for the service performed by William and 1 mark; John becomes a villein of the abbey.*
fo. 123r–v   ?[*s.* xiii[1-3]]

Dimissio domine abbatisse dimidie virgate terre Johanni carectario qui devenit nativus domine. (fo. 123v)[2]

Hec est conventio facta inter dominam de Chatriz et conventum eiusdem loci ex una parte et Johannem carectarium et Goditham uxorem eius ex alia parte, videlicet quod predicte domina et conventus concesserunt Johanni et Godithe uxori eius toto tempore vite eorundem dimidiam virgatam terre quam Willelmus filius Beatricis reddidit quietam in curia predicte domine et conventus, habendam et tenendam pro simili servicio quod idem Willelmus filius Beatricis fecit. Et pro huius concessione sepedicti Johannes et Goditha dederunt unam marcam argenti predictis domine et conventui et ille Johannes[3] devenit nativus domine et conventus. Warantizabunt predictam[4] terram predictis Johanni et Godithe tota vita eorum. Et post decessum eorum redeat predicta terra soluta et quieta ad do[mu]m[5] de Chatriz. In huius rei testimonium signa sua ambe partes presentibus apposuerunt. Hiis testibus etc.

Note. Another copy of no. 75. This agreement shows a free man becoming a villein which suggests that it probably dates from before the late thirteenth century.

138 *Agreement whereby abbess M. and the convent of Chatteris lease to Alice daughter of Warin de Barrington, for her life, a messuage with croft in Foxton, for 12d. annually.*
fos. 123v–124r [*s.* xiii[2] × 28 Sept. 1265]

Concessio abbatisse Alicie filie Warini de j mesuagio cum crofta.

[1] Hole 2 mm.
[2] Heading *Foxton'*.
[3] Followed by *et Goditha*, expunged.
[4] Followed by *d*, expunged.
[5] Hole 6 mm.

Notum sit omnibus quod hec est conventio facta inter M. dictam dominam et
conventum de Chatriz et inter Aliciam filiam Warini de Barenton', scilicet
quod dicte domina et conventus concesserunt et dimiserunt dicte Alicie mesuagium cum crofta in villa de Foxton', quod Willelmus frater predicte Alicie ad
vitam suam tenuit tantum de eis, jacens inter terram Roginaldi le Fraunkelein et
inter terram Andree Wynter, et crofta que abuttat super croftam dictorum domine et conventus, tenendum et habendum de eis tota vita sua libere et quiete,
reddendo inde annuatim duodecim denarios, scilicet ad Pascha sex denarios et ad
festum sancti Michaelis [sex][1] denarios, pro omni servicio et seculari exactione.
(fo. 124r)[2] Et post decessum predicte Alicie redibit predictum mesuagium cum
dicta crofta domui de Chatriz solutum et quietum, sine clamio vel molestia
heredum[3] vel successorum suorum, cum omnibus edificiis. In huius rei testimonium sigillum suum presenti scripto appendi fecerunt. Hiis testibus etc.

> Note. Warin de Barrington I fl. *c.* 1220, Warin de Barrington II had an estate in Barrington *c.*
> 1253–*c.* 1307 and Andrew Wynter occurs in Foxton in 1246 × *c.* 1265 (*VCH Cambs.* v, p.
> 149; no. 135). Therefore this abbess is probably either Mabel de Bancis or Mary de Sancto
> Claro (for dating see no. 100n).

139 *Agreement whereby abbess Mabel de Bancis and the convent of Chatteris lease
to Thomas de Bancis, for his life, a messuage and 5 acres of arable land with 5 roods
of meadow in Foxton, for 3s. 6d. annually.*
fo. 124r–v [*s.* xiii[2], before *c.* 29 Oct. 1247]

Dimissio domine abbatisse de mesuagio v acris terre et 5 rodis prati.

Notum sit omnibus quod hec est conventio facta inter Mabiliam de Bancis
dictam dominam de Chatriz et conventum eiusdem loci et inter Thomam de
Bancis servientem eorum, scilicet quod predicte domina et conventus concesserunt et dederunt dicto Thome quoddam mesuagium in villa de Foxton', illud
scilicet quod Johannes Keche quondam tenuit de sanctimonialibus de Chatriz,
adjacens inter mesuagium G. de Bancis et Johannis Gold', et quinque acras terre
arabilis cum quinque rodis prati cum omnibus pertinenciis quas Wido Babbe et
Editha uxor sua tenuerunt de dictis monialibus in campis de Foxton', tenenda et
habenda de predictis domina et conventu tota vita sua libere quiete, pro tribus
solidis et sex denariis quos dictus Thomas persolvet annuatim dictis domine et
conventui ad quatuor terminos usuales, pro omni servicio seculari vel demanda.

[1] Hole 5 mm.
[2] Heading *Foxton'*.
[3] Followed by *meorum*, expunged.

Et sciendum quod omnes domorum plantationes vel emendationes facte per dictum Thomam in dicto mesuagio cum isto nominato mesuagio et cum predictis terra et prato post obitum dicti Thome salve et integre remanebunt dicto conventui de Chatriz, sine clamio vel molestia heredum vel successorum suorum. Et predicta domina et dictus conventus warantizabunt totam prefatam terram cum dicto prato sep[e]dic[to][1] (fo. 124v)[2] Thome usque ad finem vite sue contra omnes. Et ut hec concessio rata sit et stabilis, utrique eorum alterius scripto sigilla sua apposuerunt. Hiis testibus etc.

> Note. This agreement is followed by nos. 142, 133 and 148. G. de Bancis may be Geoffrey de Bancis who died in or shortly before 1250 (*Liber de Bernewelle* ed. Clark, p. 148). For dating of abbess Mabel de Bancis see no. 100n.

140 *Gift in free alms by Roger le Fraunceys of Foxton, chaplain, to Chatteris abbey of a messuage with croft and 10 acres and 5 roods of meadow in Foxton, which his predecessors had held of the abbey.*
fo. 124v [*s.* xiii^2 × 1290]

Carta Rogeri le Fraunceys de uno mesuagio et 5 rodis prati.

Sciant presentes etc. quod ego Rogerus le Fraunceys de Foxton' capellanus dedi concessi et hac presenti carta mea confirmavi ecclesie beate Marie de Chatriz et conventui eiusdem loci in puram et perpetuam elemosinam, pro salute anime mee et antecessorum meorum, totum mesuagium meum de Foxton' cum crofta jacente, simul cum decem acris et quinque rodis prati integre, sicut jacent cum omnibus suis pertinenciis in villa et in campis de Foxton', eo modo sicut plenius predecessores mei de predicta ecclesia per cartam tenuerunt, habenda et tenenda totum predictum mesuagium et terram cum prato in puram et perpetuam elemosinam, sicut predictum est, de me et heredibus meis libere quiete bene et in pace imperpetuum, quieta omnino sine clamio vel calumpnia, ita videlicet quod ego dictus Rogerus nec heredes mei molestiam vel gravamen predicte ecclesie de cetero inferre vel presumere possimus. In cuius rei testimonium huic presenti scripto sigillum meum apposui. Hiis testibus etc.

> Note. This gift follows no. 141 and precedes no. 128.

141 *Notification and exemplification by Alan le Fraunceys of the gift by abbess Mary de Sancto Claro and the convent of Chatteris to him of a messuage and 10*

---

1 Holes 2 mm and 4 mm.
2 Heading *Foxton'*.

acres of land in Foxton, which he and his father, Robert, formerly held of them at will; for an annual rent of 4s. 2d. and 6 hens.

fos. 124v–125r [*s.* xiii^2 × 28 Sept. 1265, date of gift]

Concessio domine abbatisse Alano[1] le Fr...nceys de x acris terre in Foxton'.

Omnibus Christi fidelibus presens scriptum visuris vel audituris Alanus le Frannceys salutem. Noverit universitas vestra me recepisse ex dono domine abbatisse de Chatriz et eiusdem loci conventus unum mesuagium et decem acras terre cum pertinenciis in Foxton' in hec verba: Omnibus hoc scriptum visuris vel audituris Maria de Sancto Claro abbatissa de Chatriz totusque eiusdem loci conventus (fo. 125r)[2] salutem in Domino. Noverit universitas vestra nos unanimi assensu dedisse concessisse et presenti carta nostra confirmasse Alano le Frannceys pro homagio et servicio suo unum mesuagium, quod jacet inter mesuagium persone de Foxton' et mesuagium Hemeri le Knyth, et decem acras terre cum pertinenciis in Foxton', quas quidem dictus Alanus et Robertus pater eius de nobis prius tenuerunt[3] ad voluntatem nostram, habenda et tenenda dicto Alano et heredibus suis de nobis et succestricibus nostris libere quiete et hereditarie in feodo imperpetuum, reddendo inde annuatim ille et heredes sui nobis et successtricibus nostris quatuor solidos et duos denarios ad quatuor anni terminos, videlicet ad festum sancti Michaelis xij denarios et obolum, ad festum sancti Andree xij denarios et obolum, ad Pascha xij et obolum et ad[4] festum sancti Johannis Baptiste xij denarios et obolum, et ad Natale Domini sex altilia,[5] pro omnibus serviciis consuetudinibus et secularibus demandis, salvo omni forinseco servicio.[6] Et nos vero et successtrices nostre warantizabimus totam predictam terram cum pertinenciis predicto Alano et heredibus suis contra omnes mortales imperpetuum per predictum servicium. Et ut hec nostra concessio et presentis carte confirmatio robur optineat perpetuum, presens scriptum sigillo capituli nostri fecimus muniri. Hiis testibus etc.

> Note. For dating of abbess Mary de Sancto Claro see no. 100n. Alan le Frannceys surrendered and quitclaimed 8 acres in Foxton in 1246 × c. 1265 (no. 135). Margaret, formerly wife of Robert le Frannceys, occurs in 12 Hen. III (1227–8) in a final concord (*Cambs. Fines*, p. 12). An Alan le Frannceys held a knight's fee in Badlingham, Cambs., in 1284–6, but this may be another Alan (*Feudal Aids* i, p. 136).

---

1 Followed by *de*, expunged.
2 Heading *Foxton'*.
3 MS *tenuererunt*.
4 *Redditus vj altilium ad Natale Domini*, marginated after *ad*.
5 MS *altailia*, middle *a* expunged.
6 Ins. marg.

142 *Final concord made at Cambridge between Hugh son of Martin, Matilda his wife and Alice sister of Matilda, plaintiffs, and Thomas de Bancis, defendant, concerning a messuage and 5 acres of land in Foxton, on a plea of mort d'ancestor, whereby the plaintiffs quitclaimed the property to the defendant, for 5 marks.*
fo. 125r–v At Cambridge, c. 29 Oct. 1247

Copy: (N) PRO CP 25/1/24/23, no. 29.

Concordia finalis inter Hugonem filium Martini et Thomam de Bancis de j mesuagio et 5 acris terre in Foxton'.

Hec est finalis concordia facta in curia domini regis apud Cantabr'g',[1] a die sancti Michaelis in unum mensem, anno regni regis Henrici filii regis Johannis tricesimo primo, coram Henrico de Bathonia, Alano de Wydgand',[2] Willelmo de Wylton'[3] et Roginaldo de Cobham[4] justiciariis itinerantibus et aliis domini regis fidelibus tunc (fo. 125v)[5] ibi presentibus, inter Hugonem filium Martini et Matill' uxorem eius et Aliciam sororem ipsius Matill' petentes, per Thomam de Fulmere positum loco ipsius Alicie ad lucrandum vel perdendum, et Thomam de Bancis tenentem, de uno mesuagio et quinque acris terre cum pertinenciis in Foxton', unde assisa mortis antecessoris submonita fuit inter eos in eadem curia, scilicet quod predicti Hugo et Matill' et Alicia remiserunt et quietum clamaverunt de se et heredibus ipsarum Matill' et Alicie predicto Thome et heredibus suis totum jus et clamium quod habuerunt in predictis mesuagio et terra cum pertinenciis imperpetuum. Et pro hac remissione quieta clamantia fine et concordia, idem Thomas dedit predictis Hugoni et Matill' et Alicie quinque marcas argenti.

Note. This final concord is preceded by no. 139 and followed by nos. 133 and 148.

143 *Gift in free alms by Guy son of Felka de Thriplow to Chatteris abbey of 5 acres of land and 5 roods of meadow in Foxton.*
fos. 125v–126r [*s.* xii[4] × *s.* xiii[2]]

Carta Wydonis de 5 acris terre in campo de Foxton'.

Sciant presentes et futuri quod ego Wydo filius Felke de Tryppelowe dedi etc. Deo et ecclesie beate Marie de Chatriz et sanctimonialibus ibidem Deo servi-

---

[1] N *Cantebr'*.
[2] N *Wadsand*.
[3] N *Wilton*.
[4] N *Reginaldo de Cobeham*.
[5] Heading *Foxton'*.

entibus in puram et perpetuam elemosinam, pro anima mea et pro animabus antecessorum meorum, quinque acras terre mee in campis de Foxton', scilicet apud Sik duas acras, et ad Bradeweye tres rodas juxta terram Ricardi filii Mabilie, et unam rodam apud Edeswelle juxta terram Radulphi cissoris, et in Cheldewellefeld' unam acram de forera juxta terram Alani Eustace, et in Dune Feld unam acram ultra unam de Fulmere juxta terram Alani Hyldemere, et quinque rodas prati ad molendinum Johannis de Hadfeld' juxta pratum Alani Eustace. Abjuravi etiam et affidavi in curia de Foxton' quod de cetero non querelam artem nec ingenium,[1] unde predicta ecclesia sit perdens aut in aliquo, (fo. 126r)[2] vexetur de predicto tenemento. Et ad majorem securitatem huic scripto sigillum meum apposui. Hiis testibus etc.

Note. The dating is based solely on the language of the charter.

144 *Agreement whereby abbess Mabel de Bancis and the convent of Chatteris lease to Roger, smith, and Roger his son ½ virgate of land in Foxton, which his father held of the abbey; for 40s., an annual rent of 4s. and other specified services.*
fo. 126r–v [*s.* xiii[2] × 28 Sept. 1265]

Dimissio domine abbatisse Rogero fabro de dimidia virgata terre in Foxton'.

Notum sit omnibus hoc scriptum visuris vel audituris quod hec est conventio facta inter M(abiliam) de Bancis dictam dominam de Chatriz et conventum eiusdem loci ex una parte et Rogerum fabrum et Rogerum filium suum ex altera parte, scilicet quod predicte M(abilia) domina et conventus concesserunt et dimiserunt predictis Rogero fabro et Rogero filio suo, et heredibus qui de se exibunt, unam dimidiam virgatam terre in territorio de Foxton' quam pater suus tenuit de domo nostra, reddendo inde annuatim nobis et successoribus nostris quatuor solidos ad quatuor anni terminos censuales, et tallagium custumabule aliquando plus aliquando minus, et guersummam pro filia sua, et unam aruram in hieme cum tot averiis quot habuerit in suam carucam, et unam aliam aruram in quadragesima absque cibo, et falcagium in Hoydych cum aliis ad cibum domine, et debet habere duos homines ad unam precariam in autumpno et tantundem ad aliam et ligare bladum quod metent et habebit cibum suum, et metet dimidiam acram frumenti et dimidiam acram avene et habebit quatuor panes, et debet cariare fenum cum aliis et habebit unum panem, et debet cariare bladum precarie cum aliis et habebit cibum suum et unam gallinam ad Natale

1 Verb such as *faciam* omitted.
2 Heading *Foxton'*.

Domini et sexdecim ova ad Pascha, et debet habere oves suas in caula domine et herrietum et scot et lot cum custumariis. Pro hac dimissione et concessione dedit nobis predictus Rogerus faber quadraginta (fo. 126v)[1] solidos. Et nos warantizabimus predictis Rogero fabro et Rogero filio suo et heredibus qui de eis exibunt predictum tenementum per predictum servicium et predictas consuetudines contra omnes gentes imperpetuum. Et ut hec concessio et dimissio et conventio stabilis permaneat, predicte M(abilia) et conventus et predictus Rogerus faber et predictus Rogerus filius suus sigillis suis hoc scriptum confirmaverunt, unde hoc scriptum modo cirographi est confectum. Hiis testibus etc.

> Note. Roger and his son seem to have been semi-free men. The servile dues of tallage and merchet suggest that they were villeins, but the labour services, which are specified in detail, are not substantial. Moreover, Roger and his son held the land in perpetuity and by charter, rather than for their lives by a copy of the court roll. For dating of abbess Mabel de Bancis see no. 100n.

145 *Exchange between Reginald Binel of Shepreth and abbess Mary de Sancto Claro and the convent of Chatteris of 5½ acres and 1 rood of land for a* cultura *called 'Brokstrate' and 2 acres of land [in Foxton].*
fos. 126v–127r   [*s. xiii*[2] × 28 Sept. 1265]

De terris receptis in excambium in villa de Scheperede[2] videlicet de 5 acris et dimidia et una roda.

Pateat universis quod ego Maria de Sancto Claro abbatissa de Chatriz et eiusdem loci conventus recepimus in excambium a Reginaldo Bynel de Scheper' quinque acras terre et dimidiam et unam rodam,[3] videlicet de feodo domini Eliensis episcopi, de quibus acris due jacent in Dunefeld' juxta croftam[4] de la Lawe et unum caput abuttat super Wodegate Herne et aliud caput super le Brokis, et una acra jacet juxta terram persone de Foxton' et abuttat super predictum Brokis, et una dimidia acra jacet in illa lancea terre juxta terram persone et lanceat ultra viam de Fulmere, et una roda jacet juxta[5] terram Johannis Leger' et abuttat super Wodeweye, et una dimidia acra jacet in eadem lancea juxta terram nostram et abuttat super unam lanceam que lanceat super Wodeweye, et tres dimidie acre jacent in campo de Caldewelle juxta terram Alani le Frounceys et

---

1 Heading *Sepereye*, expunged in black.
2 *Expunged* in black.
3 Followed by *videlicet*, expunged.
4 Followed by *super le Brokis*, expunged.
5 Followed by *illa lancea*, expunged.

abuttant super Marewye, habendas et tenendas nobis et successoribus nostris imperpetuum libere et quiete ab omni seculari servicio. Pro quibus quinque (fo. 127r)[1] acris et dimidia et una roda dedimus eidem Reginaldo, videlicet de feodo Britannie, culturam que vocatur Brokstrate extra murum de la Lawe inter terram que fuit Godardi le Cruser et Elloriam de la Lawe et unum caput abuttat super murum mesuagii de la Lawe et aliud caput super Wodeweyeherne, et unam acram que jacet in eodem campo inter terram dicti Edwardi[2] le Cruser et terram Radulphi de Kareseye et abuttat super[3] viam predictam, et unam acram in Calldewellefeld' que jacet juxta terram dicti Godardi et abuttat super Mere-weye, habendas et tenendas quiete et solute sibi et heredibus suis ab omni seculari servicio. Et ut hoc excambium firmum sit et stabile imperpetuum, scriptum dicto Reginaldo mansurum sigillo conventuali roboratur, scriptum vero similiter conventui mansurum sigillo Reginaldi confirmatur. Hiis testibus etc.

Note. For dating of Mary de Sancto Claro see no. 100n. For dating of Alan le Fraunceys see no. 141n. A Ralph de Kersey occurs in 1276 and 1295 and a John Leger in 1297 (Cambridge, Trinity College Archives, Foxton 1, rott. 1–3).

146 *Exchange between Alan son of Alan de Shepreth and abbess Agnes and the convent of Chatteris of 2* culture *called 'Pundefoldedole' and 'Appeltonesdole' for 1* cultura *called 'Briggedole' in Foxton.*
fo. 127r–v [*s.* xii[4] × *s.* xiii[1]]

De duabus culturis receptis in excambium in campo de Foxton'.

Sciant etc. quod ego Alanus filius Alani de Sepereya excambiavi cum Agnete dicta domina ecclesie sancte Marie de Chatriz et conventu eiusdem loci duas culturas terre mee in campo de Foxton', scilicet unam que jacet juxta viam de Barenton' et nominatur Pundefoldedole et habet in se quinque acras terre et unam perticatam, et aliam cuius unum caput tangit culturam[4] que fuit Willelmi de Bancis et nominatur Appeltonesdole et habet in se novem perticatas terre, pro una cultura terre sue in campo de Foxton' que nominatur Briggedole et habet in se septem acras terre et dimidiam, cuius unum caput tangit rivulum qui currit inter campum de Scheper' et campum de Foxton', et jacet juxta terram

---

1 Heading *Foxton'*.
2 Recte *Godardi*.
3 Followed by *totam*, expunged.
4 *tu* interlined.

persone de Foxton'. Et ut hoc (fo. 127v)[1] excambium firmum et stabile permaneat imperpetuum, ego Alanus pro me et heredibus meis hac illud presenti
carta mea confirmavi. Hiis testibus etc.

Note. The manor in Foxton later called de la Hayes was held by Alan son of Alan of
Shepreth in 1200 (*VCH Cambs.* viii, p. 168).

147 *Agreement between the prior and convent of Ely, proctors of Manuel de Bagnaria, rector of Foxton, and tenants at farm of the church of Foxton, and Chatteris
abbey concerning the pasturing of their cattle in Foxton.*
fos. 127v–128r   Dec. 1271

Cartulary copies: (H) BL Cotton MS Vesp. A. vi, fo. 118r; (J) Cambridge UL, EDC 1/A/2,
fo. 99v; (M) Cambridge UL, EDR G/3/28 ('Liber M'), pp. 564–5.

Finalis concordia inter abbatissam et Gamielem rectorem de Foxton' super pascendis avariis.

Pateat universis[2] ad quorum noticiam presens scriptum pervenerit quod,[3] inter
priorem et conventum Elienses, procuratores Gamyelis[4] de Bagnaria, rectoris
ecclesie sancti Laurencii de Foxton', dictam ecclesiam nomine dicti rectoris ad
firmam tenentes, ex una parte, et dominam abbatissam et conventum de Chatriz[5] ex altera, super pascendis averiis ad carucam ecclesie de Foxton' spectantibus, una cum averiis ipsius abbatisse et conventus sui in Foxton',[6] in propria et
separali pastura in villa predicta, ad ipsas spectantibus, suborta esset controversie
materia, tandem inter ipsas partes sic est amicabiliter compositum et conventum, videlicet quod predicta abbatissa, pro se et conventu suo, ob reverenciam
dictorum prioris et conventus,[7] pro bono pacis concessit quod tria averia ad
carucam dictorum prioris et conventus, excolentem terram ecclesie de Foxton',[8]
quam tenent cum averiis carucarum ipsius domine abbatisse in villa de Foxton',[9] in propria et separali pastura, sicut pasci consueverunt, spectantia in pace
et bono modo absque contradictione vel cavillatione aliqua pascantur, ita quod

1 Heading *Foxton'*.
2 Followed by *per presentes*, expunged.
3 HJM add *cum*.
4 HJM *Manuelis*.
5 HM *Chateryz*.
6 H *Foxtone*.
7 J *conventum*.
8 HM *Foxtone*.
9 H *Foxtone*.

dicta tria averia ingrediantur pasturam predictam, una cum averiis predicte abbatisse, et similiter egrediantur cum eisdem, excepto prato illo [quo]d[1] vocatur Heydyk,[2] quod commune est tantum dicte domine abbatisse et Willelmo de la[3] Haye. Promisit autem dicta[4] abbatissa, et[5] pro se et conventu suo,[6] per[7] presens scriptum se et conventum suum obligavit, quod, in grava/men (fo. 128r)[8] seu[9] dampnum dictorum prioris et conventus,[10] averia ad carucas[11] dicte abbatisse in dicta villa spectantia alibi[12] quam consueverunt pasci, de cetero non pascantur nec a pastura in qua solebant pasci in fraudem, de cetero subtrahantur.[13] Ut autem omnis discentionis materia ratione contentionis memorate perpetuo tollatur de medio, presens instrumentum dupplicatum ad instar cirographi, cui alternatim sigilla predictorum conventuum sunt apposita,[14] inter dictos priorem et conventum suum et ipsam abbatissam et conventum suum[15] est confectum, predicta compositione duratura, ac instrumento predicto in firma stabilitate permansuro, quamdiu dicti prior et conventus dictam ecclesiam de Foxton'[16] quocumque titulo tenuerint. Acta mense decembri anno Domini M^{mo} CC^{mo} septuagesimo primo.

Note. Manuel de Bagnaria was the last rector of Foxton: in 1275 bishop Hugh de Balsham appropriated the church to Ely (*VCH Cambs.* viii, p. 174).

148 *Surrender and quitclaim by Hugh son of Martin de Shepreth, Matilda his wife, Aubrey Chapel and Alice his wife to Chatteris abbey of a tenement [in Foxton], which they claimed from Thomas de Bancis of Foxton before the justices at Cambridge.*

1 Hole 6 mm.
2 M *Heydik*.
3 HJM omit.
4 HJM add *domina*.
5 J omits.
6 H adds, erroneously, *presens scriptum se et conventu suo*.
7 J omits.
8 Heading *Foxton'*.
9 J ins. marg., *et* expunged.
10 Followed by *ad*, expunged.
11 MS *caruescas, es* expunged.
12 HJ *aliqui*.
13 HJ *subtrahentur*, M *subtraentur*.
14 H *opposita*.
15 HJ omit *et ipsam ... suum*.
16 H *Foxtone*, M *Foxtun'*.

fo. 128r   [Shortly after *c.* 29 Oct. 1247]

Quieta clamantia Hugonis filii Martini de quoddam tenemento in Foxton'.

Omnibus Christi fidelibus presentes litteras visuris vel audituris Hugo filius
Martini de Scepere et Matill' uxor eius et Albredus de Capella et Alicia uxor
eius salutem. Sciatis nos dimisisse et quietum clamasse abbatisse et conventui de
Chatriz totum tenementum quod de Thoma de Banns de Foxton' pro jure
nostro clamavimus coram justiciariis apud Cantabr', et totum jus et clamium
quod habuimus vel habere poterimus de eodem tenemento aut de pertinenciis,
habendum sine aliqua contradictione de nobis vel de heredibus nostris vel de
aliquo alio ex consilio vel auxilio nostro vel heredum nostrorum proveniente.
In cuius rei testimonium sigilla nostra apposuimus huic scripto. Hiis testibus
etc.

Note. This document is preceded by nos. 139, 142 and 133. For dating see no. 142n.

149 *Gift in free alms by Simon son of Walter Martin of Shepreth to Chatteris*
abbey of 40 acres of land in Shepreth.
fos. 128r–129v   [*c.* 1250]

Carta Simonis filii Walteri Martin de Schepereye de quadraginta acris terre. (fo.
128v)[1]

Sciant etc. quod ego Simon filius Walteri Martin de Seph' dedi etc., pro salute
anime mee et antecessorum meorum, Deo et ecclesie sancte Marie de Chatriz et
monialibus ibidem Deo servientibus quadraginta acras terre mee, sicut jacent in
longitudine et in latitudinale cum forariis et aliis pertinenciis omnibus in villa[2]
de Scheper', quarum in campo versus Fulmere jacet una acra subter Caleberwe
juxta terram Reginaldi Burel, et una acra juxta terram Radulphi filii Radulphi,
et dimidia acra juxta terram Walteri de Seph', et una dimidia acra in le[3] Sladeweye juxta terram Willelmi Sewale, et una dimidia acra ad pontem de Foxton'
juxta terram Amphelise, et una dimidia acra in le Sladeweye juxta terram
predicti Radulphi que dicitur Forera, et una dimidia acra inter terram Ricardi
Wymart et viam que ducit versus Fulmere, et una acra ad caput del Reydole
juxta terram Radulphi predicti, et una dimidia acra super Mepus inter terram
Johannis fabri, et una acra versus le Crouch Madwe juxta terram Willelmi Suale,

---

1   Heading *Scheperey.*
2   *in villa* repeated and expunged.
3   Followed by *Swa*, expunged.

et una acra jacens ultra semitam que ducit versus Mepus; i[n][1] campo versus Milleree una acra et dimidia juxta terram Willelmi Persun, et una dimidia acra juxta terram Willelmi de la Haye, et una dimidia acra juxta terram Radulphi filii Radulphi que dicitur Forera, et una acra in Longelond' juxta [t]er[r]am[2] Ricardi Wymar', et una dimidia acra in Longel[ond][3] juxta terram dicti Ricardi, et una acra in eadem [quar]entena[4] juxta terram Radulphi predicti, et una dimidia acra a[buttans][5] super viam que ducit versus Mylleree juxta terram Cassandre, et una dimidia acra de terra Piteman, et una dimidia acra abuttans super viam pre-dictam (fo. 129r)[6] juxta terram Alani le Vavasour, et una dimidia acra in eadem quarentena juxta terram Seemode, et una acra et decem pedes ad caput crofte Hugonis le Knyth et juxta terram suam, et tres rode abuttantes super viam que ducit versus Archesford' juxta terram Walteri de Sceph', et una dimidia acra juxta terram predicti Radulphi, et una dimidia acra apud Wodesmanneshaveden' juxta terram Willelmi Wolmar, et una acra in Smalemadwe juxta terram Radulphi predicti, et una acra ad le Peth juxta terram Radulphi predicti, una dimidia acra in Smalemadwe que dicitur Forera, et una dimidia acra super le Blakelond juxta terram Seemod, et una acra aput Methlehowe juxta terram Avicie de Malketon', et una dimidia acra apud le Banches juxta terram Ade ad caput ville, et una dimidia acra juxta Babbyngeshaveden, et una dimidia acra super le Peselond juxta terram Radulphi predicti, et una dimidia acra super Irechemesaker, et una dimidia acra super le Fyshowes juxta terram Radulphi predicti, item le Brembaker; et in campo versus Barenton' una dimidia acra et decem pedes aput ostium molendini Willelmi de la Haye, et una dimidia acra juxta terram Avicie de Malketon', et una dimidia acra in eadem quarentena juxta terram Walteri ad Pontem, et una acra in le Hale juxta terram abbatisse de Chatriz, et tres rode subtus le Mere juxta terram Cassandre, et tres rode abut-tantes super le Mere juxta terram Reginaldi Burel, et una acra super le Mere juxta terram Walteri ad Po[ntem],[7] et una dimidia acra juxta terram Willelmi de la Haye, et una acra juxta terram Radulphi filii eiusdem, et una roda apud[8] Heyhaveden, et una acra dimidia pene in eodem loco juxta terram Reginaldi

---

1 Hole 3 mm.
2 Hole 3 mm.
3 Hole 7 mm.
4 Hole 6 mm.
5 Hole 13 mm.
6 Heading *Scheperey*.
7 Hole 8 mm.
8 Followed by *Hane*, expunged.

Burel, et (fo. 129v)[1] una dimidia acra in eadem quarentena juxta terram Walteri Uprey, et una dimidia acra in eadem quarentena juxta terram Wymart, et una acra ad capud dicte terre juxta terram Henrici Cateline, et una dimidia acra juxta stangnum molendini Willelmi de la Haye, et una dimidia acra super Litlehowe, et una dimidia acra juxta croftam Nicholai filii Roberti de Barenton', et una dimidia acra in Watelond' juxta terram Cassandre, et una dimidia acra in fossa molendini juxta terram dicte abbatisse, item longa forera, habendas et tenendas dicte ecclesie et monialibus superius memoratis et earum succestricibus imperpetuum, in liberam puram et perpetuam elemosinam, adeo libere et quiete sicut aliqua terra vel redditus alicui domui religiose liberius aut quietius dari possit vel assignari. Et ego Simon' et heredes mei warantizabimus acquietabimus et defendemus totam predictam terram cum pertinenciis omnibus, de residuo hereditatis nostre, predicte ecclesie et monialibus prenominatis contra omnes mortales imperpetuum, ab omni seculari servicio, ita quod nec ego Simon nec aliquis heredum meorum nec aliquis pro nobis vel per nos versus predictas moniales pro predicta terra nichil exigere poterimus aut debemus, nisi tantummodo orationes in Domino. Et ut hec mea donatio concessio et presentis carte mee confirmatio robur optineat imperpetuum, presenti carte sigillum meum apposui. Hiis testibus etc.

Note. The hundred rolls record in 1279 that Simon Martin had given 40 acres of land of the king's fee in free alms to the nuns of Chatteris 30 years previously (*Rot. Hund.* ii, p. 561).

150 *Gift in free alms by Philip de Insula to Chatteris abbey of 11 acres and 3 roods of land in 'Holmo', in Shepreth.*
fos. 129v–130r [*s.* xiii[2-3]]

Carta Philippi de Insula de xj acris terre et iij rodis.

Sciant presentes etc. quod ego Philippus de Insula concessi dedi et hac presenti carta mea confirmavi (fo. 130r)[2] Deo et dominabus Christo s[ervientibus] ...[3] in ecclesia beate Marie de Chatriz in puram et perp[etuam elem]osinam[4] undecim acras et tres rodas terre mee cum pertinenciis suis in villa de Schepere, scilicet in Holmo, quas habui de dono Symonis,[5] quarum tres acre jacent juxta croftam Gregorii, et due acre et dimidia ex opposito mesuagii Roberti Hardewyne juxta

1 Heading *Sepereye.*
2 Heading *Sepereye.*
3 Unclear 23 mm.
4 Unclear 20 mm.
5 Followed by *de Schepere*, expunged.

terram Willelmi de la Haye, et septem rode ex opposito mesuagii Alani ad
capud ville, pro Deo et anima mea et animabus antecessorum meorum, habendas et tenendas prenominatas terras cum pertinenciis suis predictis dominabus et
successoribus earum in puram et perpetuam elemosinam imperpetuum. Et ego
Philippus et heredes mei warantizabimus prenominatas terras cum pertinenciis
suis predictis dominabus et earum successoribus contra omnes mortales imperpetuum. Et ut hec mea concessio donatio warantizatio et carte mee confirmatio
perpetue firmitatis robur optineat, hoc scriptum eisdem feci impressione sigilli
mei roboratum. Hiis testibus etc.

> Note. Part of the description of the land has been omitted: only 7¼ of the 11¾ acres are
> described. No. 156 is the gift of this land by Simon son of Walter Martin to Philip de Insula.
> Philip de Insula had a fee in Impington *c.* 1235 and occurs in 45 Henry III (1260–1) in a final
> concord (*Liber de Bernewelle* ed. Clark, p. 241; *Cambs. Fines*, p. 39). William de la Haye
> occurs *c.* 1250 in no. 149. His grandson, also called William, occurs in the cartulary in Dec.
> 1271, in the hundred rolls in 1279 and he died in 1316 (no. 147; *Rot. Hund.* ii, p. 561; *CCR
> 1313–18*, p. 355).

151 *Lease by abbess Agnes and the convent of Chatteris to Robert son of Gorold de
Shepreth, for his life, of a messuage with croft and houses [in Shepreth], for 3½ marks
and an annual rent of 12d.*
fo. 130r–v [*s.* xii⁴ × *s.* xiii⁴]

Concessio abbatisse Roberto filio Goroldi de Schepereye de[1] mesuagio cum
crofto.

Sciant etc. quod ego Agnes abbatissa[2] et eiusdem loci conventus[3] de Chatriz
dedimus concessimus et hac presenti carta nostra confirmavimus Roberto filio
Goroldi de Schepere mesuagium cum crofto et domibus que fuerunt Willelmi
sacerdotis, tenenda et habenda de nobis sibi quamdiu vixerit libere quiete
honorifice, reddendo inde duodecim denarios per annum, scilicet ad festum
sancti Michaelis iij denarios, ad Natale iij denarios, ad Pascha iij denarios et ad
nativitatem sancti Johannis Baptiste iij denarios, pro omni servicio et consuetudine et exactione. Et ego predicta Agnes et totus conventus domos et
prefatum mesuagium cum (fo. 130v)[4] crofto predicto Rob[ert]o[5] tota vita sua
contra omnes homines et feminas warantizabimus. Pro hac autem donatione

---

1 Interlined.
2 Followed by *confirmavimus*, erroneously copied here.
3 *et ... conventus*, ins. marg.
4 Heading *Sepereye*.
5 Unclear 4 mm.

co[nc]essione[1] warantizatione, dedit nobis sepedictus Robertus tres marcas et dimidiam sterlyngorum. Hiis testibus etc.

> Note. This abbess Agnes could be Agnes de Ely or Agnes de Burwell, who were both late thirteenth-century abbesses of Chatteris, or Agnes de Rouen who occurs in the first half of the thirteenth century (no. 93); she could also be the abbess Agnes who occurs in *s*. xii[4] × *s*. xiii[1] (no. 146) and in *s*. xiii[1] × 1233 (no. 281), or the abbess A. who occurs in *c*. 1190 × *c*. 1198 (no. 186).

152 *Gift in free alms by Alan son of Robert de Shepreth to Chatteris abbey of 15 roods and 2 acres of land in Shepreth, 5 acres in Foxton, a croft in 'Hulmo' [in Shepreth], 1 acre of meadow, and a messuage in Cambridge, with Agatha his daughter.*
fo. 130v [*s*. xiii[1-3]]

Carta Alani filii Roberti de Sephereya de xv rodis et ij acris terre.

Sciant presentes etc. quod ego Alanus filius Roberti de Seperey dedi concessi ecclesie sancte Marie de Chatrich, una cum Agatha filia mea quam ibi Deo sanctimonialem optulit, quindecim rodas et duas acras terre in Sepereya, scilicet in Westfeld', et in campis de Foxton' quinque acras, duas acras in campo de Heydych', scilicet juxta acram quam pater meus dedit ecclesie de Chatriz, et in campo Donefeld unam acram et dimidiam juxta acram quam pater meus dedit eidem ecclesie, et acram et dimidiam in campo de Drunefeld' juxta acram quam pater meus dedit eidem ecclesie, et croftam quam Go[ro]ldus[2] tenuit in Hulmo juxta domum Hardwini, et unam acram prati quam[3] Friso tenuit, scilicet tres rodas ad Wymundeshoga et una roda in Oslacunlue...,[4] et in Cantabr' unum mesuagium quod Reginaldus filius[5] Osberti tenuit. Hanc concessionem et donationem e[g]o[6] Alanus et uxor mea et heredes mei dedimus et con-c[es]simus[7] predicte ecclesie de Chatriz, imperpetuum et in liberam et quietam elemosinam ab omni seculari servicio habendam et possidendam, et[8] hoc fecimus pro animabus patrum nostrorum et matrum nostrorum et antecessorum nostrorum. Et ut hec nostra donatio firma et inconcussa permaneat, presentam

1 Unclear 4 mm.
2 Unclear 4 mm.
3 Ins. marg.
4 Unclear 7 mm.
5 *nota mesuagium in Cantabr'*, marginated before *filius*.
6 Hole 2 mm.
7 Hole 3 mm.
8 Interlined.

cartam[1] nostri sigilli attestatione confirmamus et corroborarmus. Hiis testibus etc.[2] (fo. 131r)[3]

Note. The dating is based solely on the language of the charter.

153 *Quitclaim by Ralph son of Ralph son of Fulk de Shepreth to Chatteris abbey of a messuage and land in Shepreth, formerly of Robert son of Bartholomew son of Auger, which William son of Robert surrendered and quitclaimed to the abbey.* fo. 131r [1251 × c. 1302]

Quieta clamantia domini Radulphi de uno mesuagio et certis terris.

Omnibus Christi fidelibus ad quos presens scriptum per[ven]erit[4] dominus Radulphus filius Radulphi filii Fulconis de Scepere salutem in Domino. Noverit universitas vestra me concessisse remisisse et omnino pro me et heredibus meis imperpetuum quietum clamasse Deo et beate Marie de Chatriz et monialibus ibidem Deo servientibus et eorum successoribus totum jus et clamium quod habui vel aliquo modo habere potui in mesuagio et terra cum pertinenciis, que quondam fuit Roberti filii Bartholomei filii Augeri in villa de Scheper', et quod mesuagium et terram Willelmus filius predicti Roberti predictis monialibus dimisit et quietum clamavit, ita quod nec ego dictus Radulphus nec heredes mei nec aliquis per nos vel ex parte nostra aliquod jus vel clamium in predicto mesuagio et terra cum pertinenciis in parte vel in toto de cetero possimus exigere vel vendicare. In cuius rei testimonium huic presenti scripto sigillum meum apposui. Hiis testibus etc.

Note. In 1251 Geoffrey de Scalars held the wardship of Ralph son of Ralph son of Fulk de Broadfield (*VCH Cambs.* v, p. 256). Ralph occurs in a deed dated 16 March 1301 (Oxford, Bodl. MS Rawl. B 278, fo. 132v). His lands were held by his brother, William son of Ralph, by 1303 (*VCH Herts.* iii, p. 210; *VCH Cambs.* v, p. 256). William son of Robert son of Bartholomew son of Auger may be William son of Robert de Shepreth in no. 154.

154 *Surrender and quitclaim by William son of Robert de Shepreth to Chatteris abbey of a tenement in Shepreth which he bought from them; for 40s. in advance.* fo. 131r–v ?[1251 × c. 1302]

Carta Willelmi filii Roberti de Schepere de uno tenemento cum pertinenciis.

---

1 Followed by *nostram*, expunged.
2 Followed by catchwords, *quieta clamantia*.
3 Heading *Scheper'*.
4 Hole 6 mm.

Sciant presentes etc. quod ego Willelmus filius Roberti de Schepereche reddidi remisi et de me et heredibus meis omnino quietum clamavi Deo et ecclesie beate Marie de Chatriz et sanctimonialibus ibidem Deo servientibus, pro salute anime mee et pro quadraginta solidis quos michi dederunt pre manibus, totum tenementum cum pertinenciis quod de eis emi in villa de Schepereche, sine aliquo retinemento, habendum et tenendum dictis monialibus imperpetuum, ita quod nec ego Willelmus nec aliquis heredum meorum vel aliquis per nos vel pro nobis de cetero nullum juris clamium in predicto tenemento cum pertinenciis exigere poterimus (fo. 131v)[1] aut debemus. Et ut hec mea remissio et quieta clama[tio][2] futuris temporibus robur optineat perpetuum, presenti carte sigillum meum apposui. Hiis testibus etc.

> Note. William son of Robert de Shepreth may be William son of Robert son of Bartholomew son of Auger in no. 153. For possible dating see no. 153n.

155 *Gift by Basilia daughter of Bartholomew, clerk of Shepreth, to Ralph son of Fulk [de Broadfield] of a messuage and tenement in Shepreth and grant of the farm which Helen and Isolda, sisters of Basilia, paid to her; for an annual rent of 2s. and a pair of gloves, price 1s.*
fo. 131v [s. xiii[1] × c. 1235]

Carta Basilie unius mesuagii cum terris, pasturis etc.

Sciant etc. quod ego Basilia filia Bartholomei clerici de Sepere dedi et hac presenti carta mea confirmavi domino Radulpho filio Fulconis, pro homagio et servicio suo, unum mesuagium cum omnibus pertinenciis in eadem villa, jacens juxta mesuagium Arnoldi molendini, de feodo domini Roberti Martin, et totum tenementum tam in viis quam in semitis pratis et pascuis et aliis eschaetis quod ad me de j[u]re per heredem patris mei Bartholomei poterunt accidere, sine aliquo retinemento vel diminutione. Preterea concessi domino Radulpho et heredibus suis totam firmam Ellorie et Isodie sororum mearum, sicut michi solvere solebant, tenenda et habenda de me et heredibus meis sibi et heredibus suis, vel cuicumque dare vendere vel assignare voluit, bene et in pace plene hereditarie, reddendo inde annuatim abbatisse et conventui de Chatriz duos solidos ad quatuor terminos anni, scilicet ad festum sancti Michaelis sex denarios, ad festum sancti Andree sex denarios, ad Pascha sex denarios et ad festum sancti Johannis Babtiste sex denarios, et michi unum par cirotecarum precii solidi ad

1 Heading *Sepereye*.
2 Hole 4 mm.

Pascha, pro omnibus serviciis sectis et demandis et consuetudinibus. Et ego
Basilia et heredes mei warantizabimus et defendemus etc. Et ut hec etc. Hiis
testibus etc.

> Note. Robert Martin inherited half a knight's fee in Shepreth before 1200 and was succeeded
> by Simon Martin in 1214 × c. 1235 (*VCH Cambs.* v, p. 256; *Cur. Reg. R.* vii, p. 302; *Liber de
> Bernewelle* ed. Clark, p. 251). Ralph son of Fulk de Broadfield inherited his father's lands in
> 1221 and levied a fine in 1222. He was dead by 1251 when Geoffrey de Scalars had the ward-
> ship of his land and heir (*VCH Herts.* iii, p. 210).

156 *Gift by Simon son of Walter Martin of Shepreth to Philip de Insula of 11 acres
and 3 roods of land in 'Holmo' in Shepreth, excepting 2 messuages sited in the same
fee, for 22 marks and an annual rent of a clove.*
fos. 131v–132r [s. xiii²⁻³]

Carta Simonis Martin Philippo de Insula de xj acris[1] terre et tribus rodis in
Sepereye.

Sciant etc. quod ego Simon filius Walteri Martin (fo. 132r)[2] de Scepereya dedi
etc. domino Philippo de Insula, pro servicio suo et pro viginti et duabus marcis
argenti quas michi dedit in guersummam, undecim acras et tres rodas terre mee
in villa de Seperch' cum pertinenciis suis que jacent in Holmo, exceptis duobus
mesuagiis sitis in eodem feodo, videlicet illis in quibus Walterus le Wyld' et
Juliana filia Roberti Guchmund' manserunt, quarum undecim acrarum et trium
rodarum, tres acre jacent juxta croftam Gregorii, et due acre et dimidia juxta
terram Hugonis Martin jacent, et due acre apud la Howe, et due acre et dimidia
ex opposito mesuagii Roberti Hardwyne juxta terram Willelmi de la Haye, et
septem rode ex opposito Alani ad capud ville, tenendas et habendas de me et
heredibus meis sibi et heredibus suis, [vel cuicumque][3] et quando dictas undecim acras et tres [rodas terre cum][4] pertinenciis dare legare vendere vel
[assignare voluerit, im]perpetum[5] libere quiete bene et in [pace, reddend]o[6]
in[d]e[7] annuatim dictus dominus Philippus et heredes sui vel assignati michi et
heredibus meis unum clavum gariofili ad Pascha, pro omnibus serviciis consuetudinibus sectis curie et secularibus demandis. Et ego Simon et heredes mei

---

1 Interlined above *rodis*, expunged.
2 Heading *Scheperey*.
3 Hole 18 mm.
4 Hole 22 mm.
5 Hole 38 mm.
6 Hole 30 mm.
7 Hole 2 mm.

warantizabimus defen[demus et acq]uietabimus[1] undecim acras terre predictas cum per[tinenciis suis predict]o[2] Philippo et heredibus suis vel suis assignatis contra omnes gentes per predictum servicium imperpetuum. Ut autem hec mea donatio concessio et presentis carte mee confirmatio robur optineat perpetuum, presenti carte sigillum meum apposui. Hiis testibus etc.

Note. Philip de Insula subsequently gave this land to Chatteris abbey (no. 150). Simon son of Walter Martin was tenant of half a knight's fee in Shepreth *c.* 1235 and gave 40 acres to Chatteris abbey *c.* 1250 (*Liber de Bernewelle* ed. Clark, p. 251; no. 149). For dating see also no. 150n.

157 *Gift in free alms by William son of Robert de Shepreth to Chatteris abbey of all his land with a messuage in Shepreth.*
fo. 132r–v ?[*s.* xiii[2] × *s.* xiv[1]]

Carta Willelmi filii[3] Roberti de terris et mesuagio in Schepere. (fo. 132v)[4]

Sciant presentes etc. quod ego Willelmus filius Roberti de Schepere dedi etc. Deo et ecclesie beate Marie de Chatriz et sanctimonialibus ibidem Deo servientibus in puram et perpetuam elemosinam, pro salute anime mee et antecessorum meorum, totam terram quam habui cum mesuagio et aliis pertinenciis in villa de Scheperech' sine aliquo retinemento. Et ego Willelmus et heredes mei warantizabimus predictam terram cum mesuagio et aliis pertinenciis predicte ecclesie et sanctimonialibus ibidem Deo servientibus contra omnes gentes. Et ut hec mea donatio et presentis carte mee confirmatio rata et stabilis permaneat imperpetuum, huic scripto sigillum meum apposui. Hiis testibus etc.

Note. For possible dating see nos. 153n and 154n.

158 *Confirmation by Basilia, Isolda and Helen de Shepreth to Chatteris abbey of ½ acre of land in Shepreth, given by Robert their brother.*
fo. 132v [*s.* xiii[1–2]]

Carta Basilie, Isolde et Elene domine abbatisse de dimidia acra terre.

Sciant presentes etc. quod ego Basilia de Sepereya et ego Isolda de S[epereya][5] et ego Helena de Sepereyha conce[ssimus et presenti][6] carta nostra confirmavimus

1 Hole 20 mm.
2 Hole 25 mm.
3 Followed by *F.*
4 Heading *Sepereye.*
5 Hole 14 mm.

Deo et ecclesie beate [Marie de Chatriz][1] et sanctimonialibus ibidem Deo[2]
servien[tibus illam dona]ationem[3] quam Robertus frater noster illis fecit et
incartavit, de illa dimidia acra[4] terre que jacet in campo de Sepereya versus
Melie inter terram Reginaldi filii Johannis et terram nostram. Et warantizabimus istam donationem d[ictis sanctim]onialibus[5] contra omnes gentes et
heredes [nostri] ... ...s[6] imperpetuum. Et ut hoc firmum et stabile imperpetuum
permaneat, huic carte sigilla nostra apposuimus. Hiis testibus etc.

   Note. For dating see no. 155n.

159 *Grant by Ralph, knight, son of Ralph son of Fulk de Broadfield to Chatteris*
abbey of the power to cleanse their mill-pond and to extend it by 4 feet upon the croft
of his meadow in Shepreth.
fos. 132v–133r [1251 × c. 1302]

Carta Radulphi militis de licentia purgandi stagnum molendini aput Schepere.

Omnibus Christi fidelibus presens scriptum visuris vel audituris Radulphus
miles filius domini Radulphi filii Fulconis de Bradefeld' salutem in Domino.
Noverit universitas (fo. 133r)[7] vestra me concessisse et hac presenti carta mea
confirmasse Deo et ecclesie beate Marie de Chatriz et abbatisse et monialibus
eiusdem loci ibidem Deo servientibus liberam potes[tatem][8] stagnum suum purgandi et s⟨tagnum⟩[9] predictum ...[10] proiciendi super croftam prati mei quatuor
pedum latitudine et longo in longum, dummodo solum proprium non habent
ex opposito predicti prati, quod pratum recepi de dono predictarum monialium
in villa de Sepere quod vocatur Niwemade, sine aliqua contradictione mei vel
alicuius heredum meorum. Et ego predictus Radulphus et heredes mei meam
predictam concessionem predicte libere potestatis predictis monialibus contra
omnes warantizabimus et defendemus. Et ut hec mea concessio firma sit et
stabilis, huic presenti scripto sigillum meum apposui. Hiis testibus etc.

---

6 Hole 22 mm.
1 Hole 35 mm.
2 Followed by *d*, expunged.
3 Hole 25 mm.
4 Followed by *d*, expunged.
5 Hole 20 mm.
6 Hole 21 mm.
7 Heading *Sepereye*.
8 Hole 9 mm.
9 Space, 10 mm.
10 Hole 14 mm.

Note. For dating see no. 153n.

160 *Appropriation by Eustace, bishop of Ely, to Chatteris abbey of Shepreth church.*
fo. 133r [8 March 1198 × 3 Feb. 1215]

Carta appropriationis ecclesie de Sepereye ex dono Eustacii Eliensis episcopi.

Universis sancte matris ecclesie filiis presentibus et futuris Eustachius Dei gracia
Eliensis episcopus salutem in Domino. Noverit universitas vestra nos divine
pietatis intuitu dedisse concessisse et presenti carta confirmasse monialibus de
Chatriz ecclesiam de Sepereyha cum omnibus pertinenciis suis, habendam in
usus proprios et perpetuo possidendam, salvo jure episcopali. Hiis testibus etc.

> Note. Eustace was bishop of Ely 8 March 1198–3 Feb. 1215. In 1214 Robert Martin tried un-
> successfully to claim the advowson of Shepreth church from Chatteris abbey (*Cur. Reg. R.*
> vii, pp. 246, 248, 303), but neither the entries on the Curia Regis rolls nor this charter reveal
> whether Martin made his claim before or after the church was appropriated to the abbey.
> The appropriation is unlikely to have been made during the papal Interdict of 23 March
> 1208–2 July 1214.

161 *Notification by Hugh [de Balsham], bishop of Ely, of the settlement of the
dispute between the vicar of Shepreth and Chatteris abbey concerning the augmentation of the vicarage. Hugh arranged, after an inquisition into the value of their
portions in the church, that the vicar should have 5 acres of arable land, hitherto
held by the abbey, all the lesser tithes and 20s. annually from the abbey, whilst the
abbey should have the tithe of corn and should retain a villein and croft from the 5
acres; the vicar and his successors should pay no pension to the abbey, should live in
the house then inhabited by the vicar and should bear episcopal and archidiaconal
expenses.*
fos. 133r–134r At Hadham, 14 Aug. 1269

Compositio vicarii et vicarie de Sepereye.

Universis presentes litteras inspecturis H(ugo) permissione divina episcopus
Eliensis salutem in auctore salutis. Universitati vestre tenore presentium notum
fiat quod, cum perpetuus[1] vicarius de Sepereya contra abbatissam et conventum
de Chatriz a venerabili patre O(ttobono) Dei gracia sancti Adriani diacono
cardinale, quondam in Anglia apostolice sedis legato, super (fo. 133v)[2] augmentatione vicarie sue ad priorem sancte Trinitatis de Gypwico litteras impetrasset,

---

1 Final minim interlined.
2 Heading *Scheperede*.

et ipsas ad ...[1] d...[2] et locum per eundem priorem fecisset ad judicium evocari ad nostram instanciam, idem vicarius renunciavit litteris et liti mote predictis, ita quod nos faceremus inquisitionem super valore portionum quas tam dicte abbatissa et conventus quam ipse vicarius percipiunt in ecclesia vel de ecclesia supradicta, et quod nos secundum illam inquisitionem ordinaremus super augmentatione dicte vicarie, prout nobis videretur equitati et justicie convenire, quibus scilicet inquisitioni et ordinationi faciendis dicta abbatissa et conventus unanimiter consenserunt. Nos itaque, factam de consensu partium earundem per mandatum nostrum speciale inquisitionem sequentes, statuimus et etiam ordinamus quod dictus vicarius et sui successores imperpetuum quinque acras terre arabilis pertinentes ad dictam ecclesiam habeant, quas dicte moniales hactenus habuerunt, villanus autem cum crofto remaneat dominabus eisdem. Item statuimus quod iidem vicarii habeant omnes minutas decimas et alia ad dictam ecclesiam spectantia, excepta decima garbarum bladi quam ipse moniales in proprios usus iam dudum habuerunt et habebunt imperpetuum. Item statuimus et ordinamus quod dicta abbatissa et conventus annuos viginti solidos solvant dicto vicario et suis successoribus imperpetuum in ecclesia de Schepere terminis infra scriptis, videlicet in festo[3] sancti Michaelis quinque solidos et in festo Natalis Domini quinque solidos et in festo Resurrectionis Dominice quinque solidos et in festo nativitatis (fo. 134r)[4] sancti Johannis Baptiste quinque solidos, ad quam solutionem dictis terminis faciendam una cum dampnis et expensis, que vel quas dictus vicarius vel sui successores propter defectum solutionis alicuius vel aliquarum incurrent vel fecerint, per censuram ecclesiasticam in abbatissam et aliquas maiores de dicta domo et senescallos et ballivos suos de Sepere et de Foxton' per nos et officiales nostros successores nostros et officiales ipsorum excercendam, ad requisitionem dicti vicarii et successorum suorum, compelli poterunt et debebunt. Item statuimus et ordinamus quod dictus vicarius et successores sui nullam pentionem[5] eis solvere debeant, tam pro tempore preterito quam futuro, et quod omnes imperpetuum habeant mansum in quo dictus vicarius modo habitat liberum et quietum. Item statuimus et ordinamus quod dictus vicarius et sui successores omnia onera episcopalia et archidiaconalia[6] debita et consueta sustineant et agnoscant. In cuius

---

[1] Hole 10 mm.
[2] Damaged 7 mm.
[3] Followed by *Resurrectionis Dominice*, expunged.
[4] Heading *Sepereye*.
[5] MS *pentitionem*, first *ti* expunged.
[6] MS *archiadiaconalia*, second *a* expunged.

rei testimonium presentem paginam sigilli nostri munimine[1] fecimus roboravi. Dat' apud Hadham in vigilia Assumptionis beate Marie[2] virginis anno Domini M°CC°lxix° et pontificatus nostri anno duodecimo.

162 *Confirmation by abbess Agnes and the convent of Chatteris to William de la Haye, knight, of a chantry in his chapel in the manor of Shepreth, provided that Shepreth church will lose nothing and that all obventions from the chapel will be paid to it, for 1 pound of wax annually to Shepreth church.*
fo. 134r–v [*c.* 1265 × 1297]

> Copy: (W) Oxford, Bodl. MS Rawl. B. 278, fo. 132: transcript of original, now lost, by John Layer.
> Transcript by John Layer printed, without witness-list, in W. M. Palmer *John Layer (1586–1640) of Shepreth, Cambridgeshire. A Seventeenth-century Local Historian* (Cambridge Antiquarian Society, octavo ser. liii, 1935) p. 43.

Carta licencie abbatisse et conventus domino Willelmo de la Haye militi de oratorio in Sepereye.

Universis sancte matris ecclesie filiis ad quos presens carta pervenerit[3] Agnes permissione divina[4] abbatissa de Chatriz[5] et eiusdem[6] loci conventus salutem in Domino. Noverit universitas vestra nos unanimi assensu totius capituli nostri concessisse et hac presenti carta nostra confirmasse, pro nobis et successtricibus[7] nostris imperpetuum, domino Willelmo de la Haye militi et heredibus (fo. 134v)[8] suis ex suo genere provenientibus[9] cantariam in capella sua sita in manerio[10] de Scheper',[11] ita videlicet quod matrix ecclesia[12] de Scheper' ratione dicte capelle nichil amittet. Capellanus vero, qui pro tempore fuerit in dicta capella ministrans, inspectis sacrosanctis evangliis,[13] jurabit quod omnes obventiones ad dictam capellam venientes dicte matrici ecclesie de Scheper' fideliter

1 15 minims.
2 *i* written over *e*.
3 MS *perverenerit*.
4 W adds *humilis*.
5 W *Chateris*.
6 W *eidem*.
7 W *successoribus*.
8 Heading *Sepereye*.
9 W *genere suo provenientibus*.
10 W adds *suo*.
11 W *Shepere* throughout document.
12 W *ecclesie*.
13 W *evangeliis*.

persolvet. Si vero dicta matrix ecclesia de Scheper' aliquod dampnum per dictam[1] capellam incurrerit, aut dictus capellanus contra sacramentum suum aliquo modo venire presumpserit, quod absit, licebit vicario loci, qui pro tempore fuerit, auctoritate domini Eliensis[2] episcopi, dictam capellam a celebratione divinorum suspendere, quousque matrici ecclesie inde fuerit satisfactum. Pro hac autem concessione et presentis carte nostre confirmatione, dictus dominus Willelmus[3] et heredes sui predicti annuatim dabunt dicte matrici ecclesie unam libram cere die Pasche. Et si in solutione dicto[4] termino statuto cessaverit, concedit pro se et heredibus suis predictis quod dicta capella per dictum vicarium suspendatur, quousque dicta libra cere in duplo predicte ecclesie restituatur. In cuius rei testimonium hanc presentem cartam, in modum cirographi confectam, prefate partes inter se diviserunt,[5] et ad majorem securitatem predictus dominus Willelmus huic parti sigillum suum apposuit.[6] Hiis testibus etc.[7]

Note. *VCH Cambs.* v, p. 254 dates this document *c.* 1280, but this is probably based on the assumption that this abbess Agnes is Agnes de Ely, who occurs in 1280 in no. 172. The abbess could also be Agnes de Burwell who occurs on 14 May 1293 (Cambridge, Trinity College Archives, Foxton 2, m. 2). William de la Haye occurs in Dec. 1271 and 1279; he died in 1316 (no. 147; *Rot. Hund.* ii, p. 561; *CCR 1313–18*, p. 355). Sir William de Mortimer was lord of Mortimers manor in Foxton *c.* 1265–1297 (*VCH Cambs.* viii, p. 167). Warin de Barrington had an estate in Barrington *c.* 1253–*c.* 1307 (*VCH Cambs.* v, p. 149). The dating shows that the witness Ralph son of Fulk must really be Ralph son of Ralph son of Fulk, since the elder Ralph was dead by 1251 (*VCH Cambs.* v, p. 256).

163 *Agreement whereby abbess Emma de Somersham and the convent of Chatteris lease to William de Fowlmere, carpenter, the mill called 'Mepus' in Shepreth with 1 rood of arable land, all the multure of the abbey's court in Foxton and the suit of all their tenantry within Foxton and Shepreth, for 10 years for 40s. annually.*
fos. 134v–135v   29 Sept. 1265

Dimissio molendini de Mepus in Schepereye ad firmam.

---

1 W *predictam.*
2 W *Elyensis.*
3 W adds *de la Haye.*
4 W omits *dicto*, adds *dicte libre cere.*
5 MS *dimiserunt*, second minim expunged; W *dimiserunt.*
6 W omits *predictus ... apposuit*, adds *predicta domina abbatissa et conventus sigillum capituli sui huic parti apposuerunt.*
7 W omits *etc.*, adds *domino Willelmo de Mortuo Mari, domino Radulpho filio ⟨Fulconis filii⟩ Fulconis, militibus, Rogero de Thorunton, Phillippo de Sancto Claro, Warino de Barenton, Waltero Martin de Shepere, Ricardo ad Ecclesiam de Harleston' et aliis.*

Hec est conventio facta ad festum sancti Michaelis, anno regni regis Henrici xlix° in fine, inter dominam Emmam de Someresham (fo. 135r)[1] abbatissam de Chatriz et eiusdem loci conventus ex una parte et magistrum Willelmum de Fulmere carpentarium ex altera, videlicet quod dicte domine dimiserunt dicto Willelmo ad firmam molendinum suum, quod vocatur Mepus, integre cum omnibus pertinenciis, scilicet cum stagno et cum introitu et exitu totius aque provenientis a molendino de Fulmere, et cum illa roda terre arabilis eidem pertinente, que jacet juxta regale[2] chiminum, et cum tota multura curie dictarum dominarum in Foxton', et cum tota sequela totius homagii sui infra Foxton' et Schepere sectam ibidem debentis, scilicet de Rogero fabro, de uxore Werry et de Roberto Haylston' et de omnibus aliis hominibus suis in dictis villis plus vel minus tenentibus et sectam debentibus, ita scilicet plenarie sicut Henricus molendinarius iddem molendinum ad firmam prius tenuit, habendum et tenendum dicto Willelmo carpentario vel cuicumque assignare voluerit, exceptis viris religiosis et magnatibus per quos dicte domine exheredari vel elongari a jure suo, per decem annos sequentes et integre completos, pro quadraginta solidis annuatim ad quatuor terminos solvendis,[3] scilicet ad festum sancti Andree quando primam firmam solvere incipiet decem solidis, ad Pascha decem solidis, ad festum sancti Johannis Baptiste decem solidis, ad festum sancti Michaelis decem solidis, pro omnibus serviciis et demandis. Dicte vero domine, cum fuerit necesse, invenient dicto Willelmo vel assignatis suis homagium suum totiens ad dictum molendinum mundandum et curandum, scilicet stagium molendini, quotiens dictus Henricus molendinarius dictum homagium pro eodem negotio habuit. Finitis autem dictis decem annis et (fo. 135v)[4] integre completis, recipient dicte domine dictum molendinum ad ultimum festum sancti Michaelis, quando ultima firma persolvetur, quietum, scilicet de eodem predicto quo fuit cum pertinenciis dicto termino principio, ita scilicet quod mola superior sit spissitudinis septem unciarum et mola inferior spissitudinis unius uncie. Si vero minoris precii fuerit, predictus Willelmus vel sui assignati satisfacient dominabus per visum proborum hominum, et si precii majoris fuerit, dicto modo satisfacient dicte domine dicto Willelmo vel suis assignatis. Et idem ordo teneatur de dicto molendino quod totum appreciatur, cum omnibus pertinenciis meremii infra terram vel aquam vel extra stantis, pro quindecim solidis argenti. Ut hec autem conventio fideliter et absque fraude teneatur, scriptum domino

1 Heading *Scheperey.*
2 g written over *l.*
3 MS *solvendos.*
4 Heading *Pro capella de Honneye.*

Willelmo mansurum sigillo conventuali roboratur. Scriptum vero conventui mansurum sigillo[1] Willelmi similiter, cum fidei sue appositione, confirmatur ad majorem etc.

164 *Remission by prior Hugh [Foliot] and the convent of Ramsey to I. abbess of Chatteris, following a complaint made by her to the lord treasurer, of all disputes between them until the election of an abbot, and assurance that the abbess shall have all oblations and tithes pertaining to the chapel of Honey Hill (par. Chatteris) and that, when Ramsey has an abbot, he will make any compensation necessary.*
fo. 135v [1216, before 14 June]

Littera pro capella de Honneye.

I.[2] Dei gracia domine de Chatriz frater Hugo prior Rams' et eiusdem loci conventus salutem in Domino. Ex relatione quorundam monachorum nostrorum, comparimus dominum thesaurarium plurimum adversus nos commotum pro querela quam vos ei fecistis de nobis, super causa capelle de Honneye et aliis controversiis inter nos nuper exortis, unde ad petitionem ipsius, ut cum propitium habere mereamur, omnes predictas controversias et querelas remittimus usque ad creationem abbatis, et sustinebimus ut bene et in pace habeatis oblationes et decimas ad predictam capellam pertinentes, et cum abbatem habuerimus, tantum pro amore domini thesaurarii, vobis faciemus, sive in escambio seu alio modo, quod ipse ad graciarum vobis tenetur actiones. Rogamus ergo dilectionem[3] vestram quatinus ista significetis domino thesaurario, et rogetis ut iram suam avertat a nobis, et in agendis vestris nobis asserit propitius. Valete in Domino. (fo. 136r)[4]

> Note. This document dates from the vacancy between the death of abbot Richard and the election of prior Hugh Foliot as abbot. Richard seems to have died in 1216 and royal assent to the election of Hugh Foliot was given on 14 June (D. Knowles, C. N. L. Brooke and V. C. M. London eds *The Heads of Religious Houses England and Wales 940–1216* (Cambridge, 1972) p. 63).

165 *Confirmation by Nigel, bishop of Ely, of the gift by William de Lavington, archdeacon [of Ely], to Richard [de Stuntney], his clerk, for 6s. annually from Rich-*

---

1 Followed by *communi*, expunged.
2 Or *J*.
3 MS *dilctionem*.
4 Heading *Trippelowe*.

ard to Nigel, of land with a mill in Thriplow, held of Nigel, which William had
bought from Robert son of Folcold.
fo. 136r [*c.* 1150 × *c.* 1158]

Carta Nigelli de terra et molendino in Trippelowe.

Nigellus[1] Dei gracia Eliensis episcopus omnibus hominibus de honore sancte
Etheldrede salutem. Sciatis quod Willelmus de Laventon' archidiaconus, mea
consessione et licencia, emit de Roberto filio Folcoldi terram cum molendino
quam tenebat de me in manerio de Trippelowe. Eandem tamen terram cum
molendino dedit postea ipse archidiaconus, me concedente et in presentia mea,
Ricardo clerico suo pro suo servicio, hereditarie possidendam, salvo servicio
meo, videlicet pro terra cum molendino sex solidis per annum, pro omnibus
serviciis et consuetudinibus. Volo igitur et firmiter precipio quod idem Ricardus
et heredes eius post ipsum terram illam cum molendino, ita bene et in pace et
libere et honorifice et plenarie sicut predictus Robertus vel archidiaconus eam
unquam melius vel plenius tenuerunt, teneant predictum faciendo servicium.
Test' etc.

> Note. William of Lavington, archdeacon of Ely, *c.* 1150–*c.* 1158 (*Fasti 1066–1300* ii, p. 50).
> Nigel was bishop of Ely 1 Oct. 1133–30 May 1169.

166 *Gift in alms by Nigel, bishop of Ely, at the request of Richard de Stuntney, to*
Chatteris abbey of the land with a mill in Thriplow which William de Lavington,
archdeacon [of Ely], bought from Robert brother of Alan [son of Folcold] and gave to
Richard, his clerk; for 6s. annually. In addition, Robert, servant of Richard, clerk, is
to hold 9 acres of the land and half a house, for 2s. annually to Chatteris abbey.
fo. 136r–v [*c.* 1150 × *c.* 1158]

Donatio seu carta domini Nigelli[2] abbatisse et conventui de terra et molendino.

Nigellus Dei gracia Eliensis episcopus omnibus hominibus de honore sancte
Etheldrede salutem. Sciatis me dedisse concessisse ecclesie de Chatriz in perpetuam elimosinam terram illam de Trippelowe quam Willelmus de Laventon'
archidiaconus meus assensu meo emit de Roberto fratre Alani et quam idem
archidiaconus similiter assensu meo dedit[3] Ricardo de Tunteneya[4] clerico suo.

---

1 The scribe has copied *Nigellus* in full, complete with its initial *N*, failing to allow for the subsequent addition of a decorated initial *N* in the margin.
2 Followed by *E*, expunged.
3 Corr. marg., *dabit* expunged.
4 Recte *Stunteneya*.

Hanc itaque terram cum molendino et omnibus pertinenciis suis, petitione ipsius Ricardi et assensu archidiaconi, dedi ego et concessi predicte ecclesie de Chatriz, salvo servicio meo, videlicet sex solidis annuatim reddendis (fo. 136v)[1] pro omnibus serviciis et consuetudinibus. Hoc tamen apposito, quod Robertus serviens Ricardi clerici teneat de eadem terra novem acras terre et dimidiam mansure, pro duobus solidis annuatim reddendis supramemorate [eccles]ie[2] de Chatriz. Test' etc.

> Note. For dating see no. 165n.

167 *Confirmation by Nigel, bishop of Ely, to Chatteris abbey of the land with a mill in Thriplow given in no. 166, with grant that it is to be free from all secular service except danegeld and murder-fine; and grant that the abbey may have its sheep-fold upon the land with the sheep of its men.*
fo. 136v [c. 1150 × c. 1158]

Carta domini Nigelli de terra et molendino in Trippelowe.

Nigellus Dei gracia episcopus[3] Eliensis omnibus hominibus de honore sancte Etheldrede salutem. Sciatis me dedisse et concessisse et presenti carta mea confirmasse ecclesie de Chatriz in perpetuam elemosinam terram illam de Trippelowe quam Willelmus archidiaconus meus assensu meo emit de Roberto filio[4] Alani et quam idem archidiaconus similiter assensu meo dedit Ricardo de Stunteneya clerico suo. Hanc itaque terram cum molendino et omnibus pertinenciis suis, petitione[5] ipsius Ricardi et assensu predicti archidiaconi, dedi et concessi predicte ecclesie de Chatriz, liberam et quietam ab omni seculari servicio preter denegeldum et murdrum. Et preterea concedo eidem ecclesie et sanctimonialibus ibidem Deo servientibus ut[6] habeant ovile suum super ipsam terram cum ovibus hominum suorum. Hiis testibus etc.

> Note. For dating see no. 165n.

---

1 Heading *Trippelowe*.
2 Hole 6 mm.
3 Interlined.
4 Recte *fratre*? cf. no. 166.
5 Followed by *ipus*, cancelled.
6 *nota pro ovili in Treplowe*, marginated before *ut*.

168 *Grant in fee-farm by abbess Agnes and the convent of Chatteris to John Marvin of Thriplow, of a messuage in Thriplow called 'Motlowe' with arable land, pasture and 'dambote', for ½ mark annually, with warranty for the life of John.*
fos. 136v–137r [s. xiii$^{2-4}$]

Feodi firma domine abbatisse Johanni Martyn de Tryppelowe.

Omnibus Christi fidelibus ad quos presens scriptum pervenerit domina Agnes abbatissa de Chatriz et conventus eiusdem loci salutem in Domino. Noverit universitas vestra nos concessisse et ad feodi firmam tradidisse Johanni Marvin de Trippelowe ⟨unum mesuagium⟩, quod vocatur Motlowe, cum tota terra arabili et cum tota pastura inclusa et extra et cum dambote, sicut mete et bunde condonant, et aliis pertinenciis, prout jacet inter terram domini episcopi (fo. 137r)^1 Eliensis ex una parte et filum aque currentis inter villam de Witlesford et Trippelowe ex altera, unde unum caput abuttat super pasturam domini episcopi Eliensis et aliud caput abuttat super^2 terram Willelmi filii Thome, habendum et tenendum de nobis libere quiete bene et in pace, reddendo inde annuatim nobis dimidiam marcam^3 ad duos anni terminos, videlicet ad Pascha quadraginta denarios et ad festum sancti Michaelis quadraginta denarios, pro omnibus serviciis sectis curie et secularibus demandis. Et nos predicte abbatissa et conventus warantizabimus et acquietabimus et defendemus predictum tenementum cum pertinenciis predicto Johanni Marvin ad terminum vite sue contra omnes gentes. Et ad maiorem securitatem sunt duo scripta ad modum cirographi inter nos et predictum Johannem facta, quorum unum residet penes predictum Johannem sigillo capituli nostri signatum et aliud penes nos sigillo predicti Johannis signatum. Hiis testibus etc.

Note. The dating is based partly on the language of the charter. In addition, there are no known fourteenth century abbesses called Agnes.

169 *Grant by abbess Albreda and the convent of Chatteris to William son of Hugh, reeve of Doddington, of a fishery called 'Polwere' and all the water between 'Polwere' and 'Echinewere' [in Chatteris] with all its fisheries, for 40 sticks of eels and 2s. annually.*
fo. 137r–v [s. xii^3 × s. xiii^2]

---

1 Heading *Dodyngton'*.
2 Followed by *pasturam domini episcopi*, expunged.
3 Followed by *nobis*, expunged.

Concessio abbatisse de quadam piscaria vocata Polwere.[1]

Notum sit tam presentibus quam futuris quod ego Albreda Dei gracia abbatissa
de Chatriz et totus conventus eiusdem loci dedimus et concessimus Willelmo
filio Hugonis prepositi de Dudyngtone piscaturam quamdam, scilicet Polwere,
et totam aquam que est inter Polwere et Echinewere et cum omnibus prefatis
piscaturis pertinentibus, illi et heredibus suis tenendas de nobis libere quiete et
hereditarie pro omni servicio, reddendo annuatim quadraginta[2] stikkas anguillarum[3] in prima die lune quadragesime et duos solidos sterlingorum reddendos
ad iiij[or] terminos, scilicet ad Pascha vj denarios, ad Assumptionem beate Marie
vj denarios, ad Natale vj denarios et ad Pentecosten' (fo. 137v)[4] vj denarios, vel
ad unumquemque istorum terminorum unum presentum s[e]x[5] denariorum.
Willelmus anteprefatus se censum ad terminos prenominatos fideliter fore sol-
iturum, fide mediante, sacramentum prestitit corporaliter. Et ut hec nostra
donatio et concessio rata sit et inconcussa, presenti scripto piscaturam prefatam
cum pertinenciis ei confirmavimus et sigilli nostri appositione roboravimus.
Hiis testibus etc.

> Note. Albreda, who occurs only in this grant, must have been abbess either in the later
> twelfth century or in the thirteenth century before the string of datable later thirteenth-
> century abbesses.

170 *Grant by Richard de Columbers, with the consent of Peter his heir, to Chatteris abbey, in which his daughters, Rose and Margaret, were received as nuns, of a
weight of marketable cheese annually at Dunstable (Beds.).*
fos. 137v–138r [*s.* xii[4] × *s.* xiii[2]]

Carta Ricardi de Columbers de penso casii pacabilis apud Dunstapyl.

Universis etc. ad quos presens scriptum pervenerit Ricardus de Columbers salutem in Domino. Noverit universitas vestra me dedisse et concessisse et presenti
carta mea confirmasse in perpetuam elimosinam ecclesie beate Marie de Chatriz,
in qua due filie mee velum sanctimoniale susceperunt, videlicet Roisia et Margareta, unum pensum casei pacabilis usque ad Dunstaple a me et heredibus meis ad
vincula sancti Petri annuatim, sumptibus propriis transmittendum et ibidem a

---

1 *Donationem istius piscarie vide supra folio xxxvij°*, marginated after *Polwere*.
2 Followed by *denarios*, expunged.
3 First *l* written over *s*.
4 Heading *Dunstapyl*.
5 Hole 2 mm.

nunciis sanctimonialium de Chatriz percipiendum. Hanc autem concessionem feci consensu Petri proximi heredis mei, qui hoc idem carta sua confirmabit vel quicumque de progenie mea heres meus[1] sit. Quare volo et precipio ut predicta ecclesia de Chatriz libere et quiete a me et heredibus meis hanc elimosinam imperpetuum percipiat, ob salutem anime mee et omnium successorum (fo. 138r)[2] meorum et benefactorum nostrorum. Hiis testibus etc.

Note. The dating is based solely on the language of the charter.

171 *Notification by Richard de Myldebourn' that he is bound to Chatteris abbey, in 10 marks received from the abbey in the name of Richard his son for the quit-claim made by his son of lands and tenements [in Barley, (Herts.)] formerly of John de Beauchamp, to warrant the lands; and grant that if the abbey should incur loss through the failure of the warranty, the abbey may recover the 10 marks with damages and bar Richard and his heirs from further claim.*
fo. 138r–v   At Barley (Herts.), 17 Jan. 1280

Carta Ricardi de Myldeburn' abbatisse et conventui cum clausula warantie.

Omnibus Christi fidelibus ad quos presens scriptum pervenerit Ricardus de Myldebourn' in Berle salutem in Domino. Noverit universitas vestra me concessisse et omnino me et heredes meos obligasse abbatisse de Chatriz et conventui eiusdem loci pro decem marcis argenti, quas ab eisdem recepi nomine Ricardi filii et heredis mei, pro quieta clamatione facta per dictum Ricartum filium meum, pro terris et tenementis que fuerunt Johannis de Beauchaunp', dicto Ricardo filio meo per warentum vocatum de terris dicte abbatisse, extentam et valorem pro portione sua sibi adjudicatam,[3] ita scilicet quod si dicte abbatissa et conventus per aliquem in placitum trahuntur ratione terrarum predictarum personam suam tangentium, ego dictus Ricardus et heredes mei vel mei assignati[4] warantizabimus defendemus et omnino acquietabimus dictas abbatissam et conventum contra omnes gentes imperpetuum, secundum quod decet[5] pro portione dicti Ricardi filii mei. Item concedo pro me et heredibus meis, si dicte abbatissa et conventus dampnum incurrant[6] pro defectu warantizationis, quod versus me et heredes meos dictas decem marcas simul cum

---

1   Followed by one cancelled letter.
2   Heading *Berle*.
3   Some words apparently omitted in passage *dicto Ricardo ... adjudicatam*; cf. no. 172.
4   *vel mei assignati*, repeated and expunged.
5   MS *dedcet*, second *d*, expunged.
6   MS *incurrat*.

dampnis suis possint sine aliqua calumpnia recuperare, (fo. 138v)[1] et ea occasione me et heredes meos ab omni actione petendi extentam et valorem dicto Ricardo filio meo adjudicatam, sicut predictum est, pro terris Johannis de Beauchaunp omnino expellere. In cuius rei testimonium has litteras meas eisdem fieri fecimus patentes. Dat' apud Berle die mercurii proximo post festum sancti Hillarii anno regni regis Edwardi filii regis Henrici octavo.

172 *Gift and quitclaim by Richard son of Richard de Myldeborn' to abbess Agnes de Ely and the convent of Chatteris of the lands, tenements, meadows and pastures formerly of John de Beauchaump in Barley (Herts.), which he recovered before the justices in eyre at Hertford; for 10 marks in advance.*
fos. 138v–139r [Shortly before 17 Jan. 1280]

Quieta clamantia Ricardi de Myldeborn' de terris et pratis.

Omnibus Christi fidelibus ad quos presens scriptum pervenerit Ricardus filius Ricardi de Myldeborn' in Berlee salutem in Domino. Noverit universitas vestra me concessisse dedisse et omnino pro me et heredibus meis imperpetuum quietum clamasse Agneti de Ely abbatisse de Chatriz et conventui eiusdem loci Deo servientibus totum jus meum et clamium, quod unquam habui vel habere potui jure hereditationis, in terris tenementis pratis pasturis et rebus aliis que fuerunt Johannis de Beauchaump in Berlee, videlicet in illis terris et tenementis que recuperavi simul cum percenariis meis coram justiciariis itinerantibus aput Hertford et michi adjudicatis pro portione mea per warentum vocatum, ita quod nec ego[2] dictus Ricardus nec heredes mei nec aliquis per me aliquod jus vel clamium in dictis terris et tenementis per warentum vocatum super dictas abbatissam et conventum de cetero poterimus vendicare, set omnino simus exclusi ab omni actione petendi extentam et valorem terrarum et tenementorum dicti Johannis de Beauchaump, sicut adjudicatum fuit coram Johanne de Beigate[3] et sociis suis justiciariis itinerantibus. Pro hac autem donatione concessione et quieta clamatione, dederunt michi dicte abbatissa et[4] (fo. 139r)[5] conventus decem marcas argenti pre manibus. In cuius rei testimonium huic presenti scripto sigillum meum apposui. Hiis testibus etc.

---

[1] Heading *Berlee.*
[2] Interlined.
[3] Recte *Reigate.*
[4] Repeated on next folio; followed by catchwords, *conventus decem.*
[5] Heading *Berlee.*

Note. For dating see no. 171. The recovery by Richard son of Richard de Myldeborn' of lands in Barley is not recorded in the assize rolls for the Hertfordshire eyre of 1278 (PRO JUST 1/323–4). The last eyre in Hertfordshire before 1278 was held in 1262.

173 *Quitclaim by Eldreda daughter of John de Beauchaump to Chatteris abbey of the lands and tenements formerly of John her father in Barley (Herts.) and grant of her right, by reason of the lands surrendered before the justices at Hertford, to claim the title awarded to her; for 100s. in advance.*
fo. 139r [After 17 Jan. 1280]

Quieta clamantia Eldrede filie Johannis erga abbatissam.

Omnibus Christi fidelibus ad quos presens scriptum pervenerit Eldreda filia Johannis de Beauchaump salutem in Domino. Noverint universi me concessisse dedisse et in pura virginitate mea pro me et heredibus meis imperpetuum quietum clamasse abbatisse de Chatriz et conventui eiusdem loci totum jus meum et clamium, quod umquam habui vel habere potui ratione hereditationis, in terris et tenementis et rebus aliis que quondam fuerunt predicti Johannis patris mei in villa de Berlee. Concedo etiam predictis abbatisse et conventui pro me et heredibus meis totum jus meum et clamium, quod habui ratione predictarum terrarum coram justiciariis domini regis apud Hertford' amissarum, ad petendum extentam et valorem secundum quod michi adjudicatum fuit per predictos justiciarios, ita quod nullo modo per predictas rationes aliquod jus vel clamium versus predictas abbatissam et conventum de cetero potero vendicare. Pro hac autem concessione donatione et quieta clamatione, dederunt michi dicte abbatissa et conventus centum solidos pre manibus. In cuius rei testimonium huic presenti scripto sigillum meum apposui. Hiis testibus etc.

Note. For dating see no. 171.

174 *Confirmation by Ralph de Barley to Chatteris abbey of the quitclaim by Richard his father and Godfrey his uncle of 240 acres of land in Barley (Herts.).*
fo. 139r–v [s. xiii$^{1-3}$]

Quieta clamantia Radulphi de Berlee de CC^{tis} acris terre et xl.

Sciant quod ego Radulphus de Berle filius Ricardi concessi et hac presenti carta mea confirmavi Deo et ecclesie beate Marie[1] de Chatriz et monialibus ibidem

---

[1] Followed by *et ecclesie*, expunged.

Deo servientibus concessionem ab[jura]tionem[1] et quietam clamantiam quam Ricardus p[ater][2] meus (fo. 139v)[3] ⟨et⟩ Godfridus avunculus meus fecerint predicte ecclesie et monialibus prenominatis de terris tenementis, scilicet de ducentis et quadraginta acris terre cum omnibus pertinenciis in Berle, per cartam suam quiete clamantie quam diligenter inspexi, ita quod nec ego Radulphus nec aliquis heredum meorum nec aliquis per nos vel pro nobis de cetero nullum juris clamium in predictis terris et tenementis cum omnibus suis pertinenciis exigere clamare vel vendicare poterimus aut debemus. Et ut hec mea concessio remissio et quieta clamantia futuris temporibus robur optineat perpetuum, presenti carte sigillum meum apposui. Hiis testibus etc.

Note. Ralph de Barley is a witness in 1239 × *s*. xiii[3] and occurs *s*. xiii[1] × 6 Aug. 1254 and *s*. xiii[2] × 28 Sept. 1265 (nos. 240, 17 and 74).

175 *Gift by John son of John Pompun of Barley (Herts.) to Chatteris abbey of 4 acres of land in Barley, for 1 mark in advance and 2d. annually.*
fos. 139v–140r [*s*. xiii[1–3]]

Carta Johannis Pompun de quatuor acris terre.

Sciant etc. quod ego Johannes filius Johannis Pompun de Berle dedi etc. abbatisse et conventui de Chatriz quatuor acras terre mee jacentes in campis de Berle, videlicet tres acras jacentes in Holecroft juxta terram dicte abbatisse, item unam acram jacentem sub Wycheney juxta terram Radulphi de Berle, habendam et tenendam totam predictam terram cum pertinenciis predictis abbatisse et conventui et earum successoribus de me et heredibus meis vel meis assignatis, libere quiete bene et in pace et hereditarie imperpetuum, reddendo inde annuatim michi et heredibus meis vel meis assignatis duos denarios ad duos anni terminos, videlicet unum denarium ad Pascha et unum denarium ad festum sancti Michaelis, pro omnibus serviciis consuetudinibus et demandis. Et ego predictus Johannes et heredes mei vel mei assignati warantizabimus defendemus et omnino acquietabimus totam predictam terram cum pertinenciis predictis abbatisse et conventui et earum successoribus, vel c[uicu]mque[4] dare vendere legare vel assignare voluerit, per p[redic]tum[5] servicium contra omnes homines

---

1 Hole 6 mm.
2 Hole 5 mm.
3 Heading *Berlee*.
4 Hole 6 mm.
5 Hole 6 mm.

imperpetuum. Pro hac (fo. 140r)[1] autem donatione et huius scripti confirmatione, dederunt michi predicte abbatisssa et conventus unam marcam pre manibus. In cuius rei testimonium huic presenti scripto sigillum meum apposui. Hiis testibus etc.

Note. For dating see no. 174n.

176 *Grant in fee-farm by abbess Agnes de Ely and the convent of Chatteris to John de Acle of Barley (Herts.), for his life, of a parcel of land with 3 roods of land [in Barley], for 18d. annually.*
fo. 140r [17 Nov. 1275 × 13 May 1293]

Dimissio abbatisse cuiusdem terre ad feodi firmam in Berlee.

Omnibus Christi fidelibus ad quos presens scriptum pervenerit Agnes de Ely abbatissa de Chatriz totusque conventus eiusdem loci salutem in Domino. Noveritis nos unanimi assensu et voluntate capituli nostri concessisse et ad feodi firmam dimississe Johanni de Acle de Berle quandam particulam terre nostre jacentem in campo le Eldebery, abuttantem super regalem viam, ex opposito porte dicti Johannis de Acle, simul cum tribus rodis terre jacentibus sub Chalkyhil, habendam et tenendam totam predictam terram cum suis pertinenciis de nobis et successoribus nostris usque ad totam vitam[2] predicti Johannis, reddendo inde annuatim nobis et successoribus nostris decem et octo denarios ad quatuor terminos usuales pro omnibus serviciis consuetudinibus et demandis, ita videlicet quod predicta terra, post mortem dicti Johannis, nobis et successoribus nostris salva et quieta plenarie revertatur, sine aliqua calumpnia dicti Johannis vel heredum suorum. In cuius rei testimonium huic presenti scripto sigillum meum apposui. Datum etc.

Note. For dating of abbess Agnes de Ely see no. 128n.

177 *Gift in free alms by Ralph, knight, son of Ralph son of Fulk de Broadfield to abbess Emma de Somersham and the nuns of Chatteris of 3 acres and 3 roods of arable land in Barley (Herts.) and grant of the advowson of the church.*
fos. 140r–141r [c. 8 July 1268]

Carta Radulphi militis de tribus acris et tribus rodis cum advocatione ecclesie de Berlee.

---

1 Heading *Berlee.*
2 Followed by *suam*, expunged.

Sciant presentes et futuri quod ego Radulphus miles filius domini Radulphi filii
Fulconis de Bradefeld dedi concessi[1] et hac presenti carta mea confirmavi Deo
et ecclesie sancte Marie de Chatriz et Emme de Someresham abbatisse et monialibus loci eiusdem ibidem (fo. 140v)[2] Deo servientibus, pro salute anime mee et
Radulphi patris mei et Petronelle matris mee et antecessorum meorum, tres
acras et tres rodas terre mee arabilis cum pertinenciis suis in campis de Berlee et
cum advocatione ecclesie de Berle, in liberam puram et perpetuam elemosinam,
solute et quiete et adeo libere sicut aliqua terra vel aliqua advocatio alicuius
ecclesie dari poterit, quarum due acre jacent inter terram domine Alicie de Sales
et terram Castayne de Berle et unum caput abuttat super Blerestrate et aliud
super terram predicte domine Alicie, et una acra et tres rode jacent apud
Bradehepedelle inter terram Johannis de Gledeseye et terram Ade messoris et
utrumque caput abuttat super terram Theobaldi de Broel, habendas et tenendas
predicte ecclesie[3] sancte Marie de Chatriz et Emme abbatisse et monialibus loci
eiusdem et suis successricibus, et cuicumque dare vendere aut assignare voluerint, libere bene et in pace, solute et quiete ab seculari servicio imperpetuum.
Et ego predictus Radulphus et heredes mei warantizabimus defendemus et
acquietabimus totam predictam terram cum suis pertinenciis et cum advocatione predicte ecclesie de Berlee ecclesie prenominate de Chatriz et Emme
abbatisse et monialibus loci eiusdem et suis successricibus, tanquam liberam
puram et perpetuam elemosinam nostram contra omnes gentes imperpetuum,
ita quod nec ego Radulphus nec heredes mei nec aliquis per nos vel pro nobis
aliquod jus vel clamium in predicta terra nec in predicta advocatione ecclesie de
Berlee, nisi tantum orationes in Domino, de cetero exigere vel vendicare poterimus. Et ut hec mea donatio concessio et carte mee confirmatio robur optineat
perpetuum, (fo. 141r)[4] presens scriptum sigilli mei impressione roboravi. Hiis
testibus etc.

Note. For dating see no. 178, the final concord associated with this gift.

178 *Final concord made at Westminster between Emma [de Somersham], abbess of
Chatteris, querent, and Ralph son of Ralph son of Fulk [de Broadfield], defendant,
concerning 3 acres and 3 roods of land in Barley (Herts.) and the advowson of the*

---

[1] Followed by *co*, expunged.
[2] Heading *Berlee*.
[3] Repeated and expunged.
[4] Heading *Berlee*.

church, on a plea of charter of warranty, for the reception of Ralph and his heirs into the benefits and prayers of the abbey.

fo. 141r–v   At Westminster, *c.* 8 July 1268

Copy: (P) PRO CP 25/1/85/31, no. 594.

Finalis concordia de iij acris et tribus rodis cum ecclesie advocatione.

Hec est finalis concordia facta in curia domini regis apud Westm', a die sancti Johannis Baptiste in quindecim dies, anno regni regis Henrici filii regis Johannis quinquagesimo secundo, coram Martino de Lytlebur',[1] magistro Rogero de Seyton' et Johanne de Cobham[2] justiciariis et aliis domini regis fidelibus tunc ibi presentibus, inter Emmam abbatissam de Chatriz[3] querentem, per Alexandrum de Chyrdyrleye[4] capellanum positum loco suo ad lucrandum vel perdendum, et Radulphum filium Radulphi filii Fulconis impedientem, de tribus acris et tribus rodis terre cum pertinenciis in Berlee[5] et advocatione[6] ecclesie eiusdem ville, unde placitum warantie carte summonitum fuit inter eos in eadem curia, scilicet quod predictus Radulphus recognovit predictam terram et advocationem dicte[7] ecclesie cum pertinenciis esse jus ipsius abbatisse et ecclesie sue de Chatriz,[8] ut illas quas ipsa abbatissa et ecclesia sua predicta habent de dono predicti Radulphi, habendas et tenendas eidem abbatisse, et[9] aliis abbatissis que ei succedent, et ecclesie sue predicte, de predicto Radulpho et heredibus suis in puram et perpetuam elemosinam, liberam et quietam ab omni servili[10] servicio et exactione imperpetuum. Et predictus Radulphus et heredes sui warantizabunt acquietabunt et defendent eidem abbatisse, et aliis abbatissis que ei succedent, et ecclesie sue predicte predictam terram et advocationem predicte ecclesie cum pertinenciis ut liberam puram et perpetuam elemosinam suam, absque aliquo servicio inde faciendo, contra omnes homines imperpetuum. Et ipsa abbatissa recepit predictum Radulphum et heredes suos in singulis ...is[11]

---

[1]   P *Litlebir'*.

[2]   P *Cobbeham*.

[3]   P *Chateryz*.

[4]   P *Childerlegh'*.

[5]   P *Berle*.

[6]   MS *advocationem*.

[7]   P *predicte*.

[8]   P *Chateriz*.

[9]   Followed by *aliis*, expunged.

[10]   P *seculari*.

[11]   Damaged 5 mm: seems to be a word ending *-is*, perhaps cancelled since nothing is added in P.

benefactis (fo. 141v)[1] et orationibus que de cetero fient in ecclesia sua predicta imperpetuum.

179 *Acquittance by Ralph [son of Ralph] son of Fulk [de Broadfield] to the abbess of Chatteris of 40s. for the release of his claim in the advowson of the church of Barley (Herts.), at that time vacant.*
fo. 141v   10 Nov. 1281

Acquietancia domine abbatisse pro advocatione ecclesie de Berlee de Radulpho filio Fulconis.

Universis Christi fidelibus presens scriptum visuris vel audituris Radulphus filius Fulconis salutem in Domino sempiternam. Noveritis me recepisse de abbatissa de Chatriz, per manum Johannis But in aula Westm', die lune proximo ante festum sancti Martini anno regni regis Edwardi filii regis Henrici nono, quadraginta solidos in quibus michi tenebatur[2] pro relaxatione clamii quam posui in advocatione ecclesie de Berlee London' diocesis tunc temporis vacantis, unde prius inde cartam meam feci et finis in curia regis levatus est[3] inter Emmam de Someresham querentem et[4] meipsum impedientem, quos quidem quadraginda solidos plene michi solutos fore cognosco et predictam abbatissam de predicta solutione esse quietam. In cuius rei testimonium sigillum meum presenti scripto est appensum.

180 *Settlement of the dispute between Osbert, rector of Barley (Herts.), and Chatteris abbey concerning certain tithes in the parish of Barley which had been acquired by the abbey during the war but were claimed by Osbert; the tithes from the lands which the nuns had held in their demesne in the time of Henry I were to remain to the nuns and the tithes from all the other lands in Barley were to remain to the church, but Osbert and the nuns exchanged the tithes from two parcels of 11½ acres and from two half virgates.*
fos. 141v–142r [*temp.* Henry II]

---

1   Heading *Berlee.*
2   MS *tenebantur,* second *n* expunged.
3   MS *levavit.*
4   Interlined.

Concordia finalis inter abbatissam de Chatriz et rectorem de Berlee super decimis eiusdem ecclesie.[1]

Jubente Domino pacem et veritatem diligere pro[2] bono pacis in posterum presenti cautione providemus, ne lites semel sopite tractu temporis revocentur, Osbertus persona ecclesie de Berleya adversus conventum sanctimonialium de Chatriz nomine ecclesie sue quasdam decimas parochiali jure petebat, et de possessione earum habita tempore Henrici regis primi testes plurimos producebat, sed eas ecclesia sua defuerat[3] possidere occasione guerre, disparsis pro guerra colonis et vacantibus agris ad dominium de Chatriz congregatis (fo. 142r)[4] sanctimonialibus, ⟨que⟩[5] decimas illas detineban[t] ... ...es[6] et libere a prestatione decimarum de dominicis suis culturis provenientium. Lis illa hac compositione inter ecclesias solemniter et in capitulo facta conquievit, de culturis illis quas sanctimoniales predicte tempore prefati regis Henrici in dominio habuerunt, sue sanctimonialibus remanent decime. Cetere omnes de omnibus terris earum in Berle remanent ecclesie de Berlee, exceptis de[7] crofta Walteri Boggari continente undecim acras et dimidiam decimis, quas sanctimoniales habebunt quia croftam illam[8] in dominio retinent, et pro decimis illis in excambium donant aliarum undecim acrarum et dimidie decimas secus antiquam earum mansionem. Et alia similiter commutatio facta est decimarum dimidie virgate Ordgari que remanent sanctimonialibus, et ecclesia[9] de Berleye habebit decimas dimidie virgate Hugonis prepositi de essartis de Wydiheya. Testibus hiis etc.

181 *Tithe-suit heard by papal judges delegate commissioned by Innocent IV in which Richard, rector of Barley (Herts.), charged Chatteris abbey with the loss allegedly caused to his church by a tithe settlement made between Herbert, a previous rector, and Chatteris abbey; the judges delegate confirmed the settlement, which Richard swore to observe, and the nuns paid 12 marks to him to buy properties for the benefit and improvement of the church.*

1 MS *ecclesiis*.
2 Ins. marg.
3 MS *desierat*.
4 Heading *Berlee*.
5 Space 5 mm.
6 Damaged 19 mm.
7 Followed by single letter, perhaps *r*.
8 Followed by *d*, cancelled.
9 MS *ecclesie*.

fos. 142r–143v   2 April 1246 (date of mandate)

Delegatio sedis apostolice super decimis de Berlee.

Omnibus sancte matris ecclesie filiis hoc presens scriptum audituris vel visuris de Cruce Roesia et de Lega priores salutem in Domino. Mandatum domini pape recepimus[1] in hec verba: Innocentius episcopus servus servorum Dei dilectis filiis de Cruce Rois et de Lega London'[2] diocesis prioribus salutem et apostolicam benedictionem. Dilectus filius Ricardus rector ecclesie de Berleia sua nobis petitione monstravit quod, cum olim inter Herbertum rectorem ipsius ecclesie predecessorem eius ex una parte et abbatissam et conventum de Chatriz Eliensis diocesis e[x al]tera,[3] super quibusdam decimis ad eandem ecclesiam de jure spectantibus, coram archidiacono London' et conjudicibus suis auctoritate apostolica questio agitata fuisset, tandem (fo. 142v)[4] dictus predecessor cum eisdem abbatissa et conventu quamdam compositionem inire presumpsit, per quam ecclesia ipsa noscitur enormiter fore lesa, quam etiam compositionem dicte abbatissa et conventus per bone memorie Rogerum episcopum diocesis loci et dilectos filios capitulum London' optinuerunt, sicut dicitur confirmari. Quare dictus rector nobis humiliter supplicavit ut indempnitati eiusdem providere misericorditer curaremus, quo circa discretioni vestre per apostolica scripta mandamus quatinus, vocatis qui fuerunt evocandi et auditis hinc inde propositis, quod visum fuerit oportunum appellatione remota statuatis, facientes quod decreveritis per censuram ecclesiasticam firmiter observari. Testes autem qui fuerunt nominati si se gracia, odio vel timore subtraxerint, per tenuram eandem appellatione cessante cogatis veritati testimonium perhibere. Datum Lugd' iiij[to] nonas aprilis pontificatus nostri anno tertio. Huius igitur auctoritate mandati dictas moniales coram nobis fecimus evocari et proposita intentione dicti rectoris in hec verba: Hec est intentio rectoris ecclesie de Berleya contra moniales de Chatriz. Dicit quod, cum ecclesia sua de Berleya per compositionem factam inter predictas moniales ex una parte et Herbertum predecessorem predicti Ricardi ex [a]ltera,[5] super decimis tam majoribus quam minoribus de dominico earundem promoventibus infra terminos parochie s[ue][6] de Berleya et ad ipsum de jure spectantibus, coram archidiacono London' et suis conjudicibus

---

1 MS *rececpimus.*
2 Followed by *c,* expunged.
3 Hole 9 mm.
4 Heading *Berlee.*
5 Hole 3 mm.
6 Hole 4 mm.

auctoritate apostolica de causa cognoscentibus enormiter lesa est, unde petit idem rector per vos domini judices, non obstante confirmatione bone memorie Rogeri (fo. 143r)[1] London' episcopi et capituli beati Pauli London' que superdicitur, intervenisse pronuntiari, legitima discuscione prehabita, ipsam compositionem enormem fuisse, et per eam ecclesiam de Berleya lesam esse enormiter, et per vos predictum enormitatem excessum ad debitam juris formam reduci, et partem adversam super hoc sibi nomine ecclesie de Berleya sententialiter condempnari. Hoc[2] dicit salvo sibi jure etc. Et cum super eadem coram nobis diutius esset altercatum,[3] tandem lis inter partes mota hac amicabili compositione conquievit, videlicet quod, restitutis dictis monialibus litteris apostolicis et omnibus aliis instrumentis dictam causam contingentibus, et partibus simpliciter et absolute se voluntati et dispositioni nostre subicientibus sine appelationis remedio, ad petitionem partium prefatam compositionem coram venerabili patre Rogero[4] episcopo London' factam et a loci capitulo acceptatam inspeximus et diligenter examinavimus, per quam nobis evidenter constabat sex acras terre frugifere ecclesie de Berleya pretextu dicte compositionis[5] inite fuisse a dictis monialibus collatas. Insuper etiam inspeximus litteram apostolicam ad dictam compositionem infirmandam impetratam, in quam continebatur ecclesiam de Berleia enormiter fuisse lesam per compositionem memoratam, et ex assertione partium recepimus eas dictas decimas super quibus facta fuit compositio antea ab antiquo percepisse, propter quod, hiis cognitis et intellectis nec non et aliis dictam compositionem contingentibus, de consilio jurisperitorum eandem compositionem auctoritate apostolica confirmavimus de consensu partium, reservantes nobis ac successoribus nostris coertionem ac jurisdictionem ad compellendam partem (fo. 143v)[6] renitentem dictam compositionem observare. Insuper etiam ad securitatem perpetuam habendam, dicte moniales duodecim marcas argenti dicto rectori numerabant, ad emenda terras vel possessiones seu redditus ad opus et ad utilitatem et meliorationem ecclesie de Berleya, dicto rectore corporale sacramentum prestando se dictam compositionem observare nec se contra eandem venturum. Procurator vero monialium, habens speciale mandatum ad jurandum[7] in animas monialium, consimile pre-

---

1 Heading *Berlee*.
2 Followed by *s*, expunged.
3 MS *alteratum*.
4 Followed by *nostro*, expunged.
5 Followed by *iite*, expunged.
6 Heading *Berlee*.
7 Followed by *moniales*, expunged.

stitit juramentum. Et in huius rei testimonium, in signum probationis perpetue, tam dominus episcopus London' quam episcopus Eliensis signa sua apposuerunt una cum signis nostris. Hiis testibus etc.

182 *Confirmation by dean Geoffrey de Lucy and the chapter of St Paul's, London, of the settlement agreed between Herbert, rector of Barley (Herts.) and Chatteris abbey, before papal judges delegate, concerning the ownership of lesser and greater tithes in Barley.*
fos. 143v–144r   1 × 16 July 1238

Compositio de decimis in Berlee inter abbatissam de Chatriz et rectorem de Berlee.

Omnibus Christi fidelibus has litteras visuris vel audituris G(alfridus) de Lucy decanus sancti Pauli London' et eiusdem loci capitulum salutem. Ad notitiam vestram volumus pervenire quod, cum Herbertus rector ecclesie de Berle et sanctimoniales de Chatriz Eliensis diocesis coram judicibus delegatis auctoritate apostolica London' convenissent, super decimis minutis de dominico earundem et omnibus majoribus de terris earum quas excolunt propriis sumptibus in villa de Berle provenientibus, et de intentione decimarum majorum provenientium ex viginti septem acris terre in eadem villa, quas homines predictarum monialium excolunt et tenent de dominico predicto, eo quod de jure communi spectabant ad ecclesiam suam de Berle ut dicebat, et cum inter partes super proprietate dictarum decimarum diutius fuisset altercatum,[1] tandem, dicto Herberto (fo. 144r)[2] litteris apostolicis renunciante impetratis, lis inter eos mota amicabili compositione conquievit,[3] quam per venerabilem patrem nostrum R(ogerum) Dei gracia episcopum London' inspeximus improbatam et auctoritate diocesana confirmatam, prout in litteris suis patentibus super hoc confectis et sigilli sui munimine[4] corroboratis plenius et expressius continetur. Nos vero dictam compositionem, acceptantes et ratam habentes eam quantum ad nos pertinet, sicut in litteris supradicti episcopi expresse continetur approbantes, communi assensu nostro confirmavimus et sigilli nostri munimine[5] corroboravimus. Hiis testibus Deo et capitulo nostro. Anno ab incarnatione Domini M°CCxxxviij intrante mense julii.

---

[1] *c* interlined.
[2] Heading *Keresey*.
[3] *con* interlined.
[4] 15 minims.
[5] 15 minims.

Note. The bishop of London is Roger Niger (1229–41).

183 *Opening words of narrative concerning Eadnoth: see no. 2.*
fo. 144r

Ednodus vir in Christo famosus etc. Vide hanc cronicam in principio libri.[1]

184 *Opening words of bull of Innocent IV: see no. 3.*
fo. 144r

Inocentius episcopus servus servorum Dei etc. Vide hanc bullam in principio libri.[2]

185 *Notification by Nigel, bishop of Ely, that Robert son of Auger has quitclaimed in his court the lands in Shepreth, Barrington, Foxton and Kersey (Suff.), which he was claiming against Chatteris abbey, and Nigel gave him 1 virgate and 5 acres in Shepreth, for his life, to be relinquished to Chatteris abbey after his death.*
fo. 144r–v [1 Oct. 1133 × 30 May 1169]

Confirmatio domini Nigelli episcopi Eliensis super quadam concordia.

Nigellus Dei gracia Eliensis episcopus omnibus hominibus de honore sancte Etheldrede salutem. Sciatis quod[3] Robertus filius Augeri quietas clamavit in curia mea et ab eo et heredibus suis abjuravit terras quas calumpniabat versus moniales de Chatriz, videlicet (fo. 144v)[4] in Sepereia unam hidam et dimidiam virgatam et novem acras, et in Barenton' unam virgatam, et Foxton' dimidiam virgatam, et Kareseya dimidiam hidam, et ego dedi ei unam virgatam terre et v acras in Sepereya pro masagio suo tantum in vita sua tenendas, de ⟨quibus⟩ quidem ⟨terris⟩ idem Robertus juravit quod eas post mortem suam quietas a se et heredibus suis relinqueret ecclesie de Chatriz, et quod predictas terras warantizaret si quis de eis versus moniales de Chatriz vellet monere calumpniam. Hiis testibus etc.

Note. Nigel was bishop of Ely 1 Oct. 1133–30 May 1169.

---

1 In black; *Vide ... libri*, underlined in red.
2 In black; *Vide ... libri*, underlined in red.
3 Followed by *ego*, expunged.
4 Heading *Kerseye*.

186 *Confirmation by abbess A. and the convent of Chatteris to Adam son of Robert de Cockfield of the manor of Kersey (Suff.), to be held in fee-farm for £10 annually, which manor Nigel, bishop of Ely, and Hadewisa, prioress of Chatteris, had granted and confirmed to Adam de Cockfield, grandfather of Adam.*
fo. 144v [c. 1191 × c. 1198]

Dimissio manerii de Kerseye ad feodi firmam Ade de Cokefeld'.

A. dicta domina ecclesie beate Marie de Chatriz et conventus eiusdem loci baronibus vavassatoribus et omnibus hominibus et fidelibus sancte ecclesie Francis et Anglis salutem. Sciatis nos concessisse et presenti carta confirmasse Ade filio Roberti de Cokefeld' et heredibus suis manerium de Kerseye de feodo sancte Marie et nostro, tenere de eadem ecclesia et de nobis in feodi firmam, decem libras reddendo[1] michi per annum quatuor terminis subscriptis, videlicet in festo sancti Nicholai quinquaginta solidos et in Ramis Palmarum quinquaginta solidos et in octo dies ante festum beate Johannis Baptiste[2] quinquaginta solidos et in festo sancti Michaelis quinquaginta solidos. Et volumus et concedimus ut manerium illud bene et honorifice teneat, in hominibus et bosco et plano et pratis et pasturis et omnibus aliis consuetudinibus eidem manerio juste pertinentibus, sicut episcopus Nigellus Eliensis ecclesie et Hadewisa quondam priorissa ecclesie nostre et conventus concesserunt Ade de Cokefeld' avo predicti Ade et heredibus suis et cartis suis confirmaverunt. Hiis testibus etc.

Note. Robert de Cockfield died c. 1191 and Adam, his son, was dead by 1198 (Farrer *Honors* iii, pp. 361–2).

187 *Acknowledgement by Philip Basset to Chatteris abbey of £10 of rent owed for the manor of Kersey (Suff.) and of 2s. owed by his tenants if they shall have refused to bring the rent to the abbey at the four terms of the year.*
fos. 144v–145r [20 April 1243 × 29 Oct. 1271]

Carta recognitionis Philippi Basset de feodi firma in Keresey. (fo. 145r)[3]

Omnibus ad quos presens scriptum pervenerit Philippus Basset salutem in Domino. Sciatis quod, cum religiose domine abbatissa et moniales de Chatriz percipere debeant annuatim de manerio nostro de Kerseye decem libras annui redditus ad quatuor terminos anni, quas quidem decem libras tenentes nostri de Kerseye periculo et sumptibus suis propriis ad abbatiam suam de Chatriz ad

1 Followed by *inde*, expunged.
2 MS *Beaptiste*, first *e* expunged.
3 Heading *Keresey*.

quatuor anni terminos debent deferre, et[1] nisi fecerint dicti tenentes nostri manerii nostri predicti in duobus solidis argenti dictis abbatisse et monialibus teneantur, prout in carta dictarum abbatisse et monialium plenius continetur, volumus et concedimus pro nobis vel heredibus vel assignatis nostris quibuscumque quod abbatissa et moniales predicte dictum redditum habeant et teneant, adeo libere sicut umquam liberius habere et tenere consueverunt. Et si dicti tenentes nostri de Kereseye dictum redditum suum ad abbatiam predictam ad quatuor anni terminos, ut predictum est, deferre recusaverint, dicti tenentes nostri dictis abbatisse et monialibus pro dictis anni quatuor terminis non observatis in duobus solidis argenti teneantur, scilicet in sex denariis pro quolibet termino dictorum quatuor terminorum anni non observato. In cuius rei testimonium etc.

Note. Henry III gave the manor of Kersey to Philip Basset on 20 April 1243 (*CPR 1232–47*, p. 374; Philip Basset died 29 Oct. 1271 (*Cal. IPM* i, pp. 272–3, no. 807). See also no. 189.

188 *Grant by Adam son of Robert de Cockfield to Chatteris abbey of an annual rent of 40s. from the first church in his gift to fall vacant, excepting the church of Kersey and the chapel of Lindsey (Suff.), meanwhile giving to the abbey 1 mark annually.*
fo. 145r–v [*c.* 1191 × *c.* 1198]

Carta[2] Ade de Cokefeld' de redditu quadraginta solidorum.

Universis sancte matris ecclesie filiis Adam filius Roberti de Cokefeld' salutem. Noverit universitas vestra me dedisse et hac carta mea confirmasse in perpetuam elemosinam monialibus Deo et sancte Marie in ecclesia de Chatriz servientibus, pro anima patris mei et predecessorum meorum et salute propria, redditum annuum quadraginta[3] solidorum in prima ecclesia vacante que sit de donatione mea, excepta ecclesia de Kereseye (fo. 145v)[4] et capella de Lelseia.[5] Et interim dabo eis unam marcam argenti annuatim, videlicet quadraginta denarios in festo sancti Nicholai et quadraginta denarios in Ramis Palmarum et octo diebus ante festum sancti Johannis Babtiste quadraginta denarios et ad festum sancti Michaelis xl denarios, quousque redditum predictorum xl solidorum annuatim in ecclesia que prima michi vacaverit, cum exceptione premissa, illis determinate

1 Followed by *s*, cancelled.
2 Followed by *domini*, expunged.
3 MS *quadragindta*, second *d* expunged.
4 Heading *Kerseye*.
5 Corr. from *Kerseia*.

assignaverim in perpetuam elemosinam et carta mea confirmaverim. Hanc autem donationem ego et heredes mei eis warantizabimus. Hiis testibus etc.

> Note. Another copy of no. 73. See also no. 204, a confirmation of this grant. For dating see no. 186n.

189 *Presentment before justices in eyre of the half-hundred of Cosford (Suff.) concerning the tenants of the manor of Kersey and their tenure, followed by a statement by the justices concerning the services relating to the manor.*
fos. 145v–146r [20 April 1243 × 29 Oct. 1271]

Veredictum coram justiciis itinerantibus tempore regis Henrici seu Johannis pro manerio de Kerseye.

In veredicto dimidii hundredi de Coresford' coram justiciis itinerantibus continetur quod Nesta de Cokefeld' tenuit Kerseye pro[1] x libris de dominabus de Chatriz et domino episcopo Eliensi, et postea Matheus de Leyham et predicta Nesta dederunt Kersey Huberto de Ruly. Hubertus de Ruly reddidit Kersey domino regi et dominus rex Henricus deinde feoffavit Philippum Basset pro servicio unius paris calcarum deauratorum precii[2] vj denariorum. Et clamat habere omnes libertates, videlicet warenum, furcam, tripechett', tumberellum, amerciamentum tenentium suorum, visum franciplegii, catalla felonum. Istud veredictum est sigillatum cum vj sigillis, videlicet H. de Batesford', Arnulphi de Lepham, Alardi de Graveney, Radulphi de Watesford', Jacobi clerici de Kersey, Ade de Waleys de Kerseye, tempore Johannis regis vel Henrici tertii filii sui. Et dicunt[3] jurisperiti Anglie quod, citra illud tempus quo per regem Henricum supradictus Philippus (fo. 146r)[4] Basset erat feoffatus de dicto manerio, tenuerunt supradicti[5] Matheus, Nesta et Hubertus idem manerium per servicium vocatum petit cariante, et sic est de feodo socage et non de feodo militari, nec rex habebit durantem non etatem cuiuscumque heredis eiusdem manerii, et quantum ad redditum dominarum de Chatriz, non erat redditus servicii citra tempus quo rex erat feoffatus de dicto manerio, sed ut quidam dicunt vertitur in redditum vocatum rentt seke, pro quo non possunt dicte domine distringere in quorumcumque manibus fuerit dictum manerium, sed quotiens a retro fuerit

---

1 Followed by Tironian *et.*
2 Followed by Tironian *et.*
3 Followed by *jus*, expunged.
4 Heading *Kereseye.*
5 Followed by *Philippus*, expunged.

dictas dominas oportet[1] prosequi assisam, nisi quatenus dicte domine et earum predecessores sint et fuerint in possessione distringendi a tempore cuius contrarii memoria hominum non existit.

Note. No copy was found at the PRO owing to the lack of a precise date. Nesta de Cockfield, daughter of the Adam de Cokefield in no. 186, married Matthew de Layham *c.* 1242 (Farrer *Honors* iii, p. 362). Hubert de Ruly gave the manor to Henry III before 20 April 1243 following a trespass against the peace (*CPR 1232–1247*, p. 374). See also no. 187n for dating. Petit cariante is carriage-service; rent-seck is a rent reserved by deed without a clause of distress in case of arrears.

190 *Commission by Edward III to John de Cambridge and Nicholas de Cambridge to hold an inquisition into whether Hugh le Despenser junior held the manor of Kersey (Suff.) from the abbess of Chatteris for £10 annually and whether the abbess is owed rent, because the abbess has petitioned the king concerning arrears of rent since the manor came into his hands.*
fos. 146r–147r At Westminster, 10 March 1327

Supplicatio abbatisse penes dominum regem pro manerio de Kerseye.

Edwardus Dei gracia rex Anglie dominus Hibernie et dux Aquietannie dilectis et fidelibus suis Johanni de Cantebrig' et Nicholao de Cantabrigg' salutem. Supplicavit nobis abbatissa de Chatriz per petitionem [su]am[2] coram nobis et consilio nostro exhibitam ut, cum Hugo le Spenser junior nuper tenuerit manerium de Kerseye in comitatu Suff' de predicta abbatissa per servicium decem librarum per annum, et de quibus decem libris annuis eadem abbatissa et predecessores sue abbatisse loci predicti per manus predicti Hugonis et aliorum qui manerium predictum pro tempore tenuerunt seisite fuerunt, ut de jure ecclesie sue de Chatriz, quousque manerium predictum ad manum nostram per forisfactum eiusdem [Hugon]is[3] devenit, et adhuc in manu nos[tra] ...[4] (fo. 146v)[5] eidem abbatisse de eo quod a retro est de predictis decem libris de tempore quo manerium predictum in manu nostra devenit, debitam solutionem fieri ac predictas decem libras annuas ex tunc solvi jubere. Nos, supplicationi eiusdem abbatisse annuentes in hac parte, assignavimus vos ad inquirendum per sacramentum proborum et legalium hominum de comitatu predicto, per quos

---

[1] Ins. marg.
[2] Hole 3 mm.
[3] Hole 14 mm.
[4] Hole 35 mm.
[5] Heading *Kerisey*.

rei veritas melius sciri poterit, in presentia custodis nostri manerii predicti, per vos super hoc premuniendis utrum predictus Hugo tenuerit manerium predictum de predicta abbatissa per servicium decem librarum per annum sicut predictum est necne, et si sic tunc qualiter et quomodo, et si de alio tunc de quo vel de quibus et per quod servicium et qualiter et quomodo, et si predicta abbatissa et predecessores sue abbatisse loci predicti seisite fuerint ut de[1] jure ecclesie sue predicte, per manus predicti Hugonis et aliorum qui manerium predictum pro tempore tenuerunt, de predictis decem libris annuis sicut predictum est necne, et si sic tunc a quo tempore et quando et qualiter et quomodo et qualiter manerium predictum in manu nostra existit, et si predicta abbatissa jus q[u]od[2] habuit in predictis decem libris annuis prefato Hugoni in seisina sua remiserit vel alium statum ei vel alicui alteri inde fecerit necne, et si sic tunc quem statum et cui et quando et qualiter et quomodo et quantum predictum manerium valeat per annum in omnibus exitibus, et de aliis circumstanciis premissa contingentibus plenius veritatem. Et ideo vobis mandamus quod, ad certos diem et locum quos adhuc provideritis, inquisitionem super premissis faciatis et eandem distincte et aperte factam nobis, sub si[gillis vestris][3] et [si]gillis[4] eorum per quos facta fuerit, s[ine dilatione mittas et][5] hoc breve. Mandamus eti[am][6] (fo. 147r)[7] vicecomiti nostro comitatus predicti quod, ad certos diem et locum quos ei scire feceritis,[8] venire faciat[9] coram vobis tot et tales probos et legales homines de baliva sua per quos rei veritas in premissis melius scire poterit et inquiri. In cuius rei testimonium has litteras nostras fieri fecimus patentes. Teste meipso apud Westm' x die marcii anno regni nostri primo.

Note. This commission is not enrolled on the patent rolls. The John de Cambridge in this document may possibly be the steward recorded in the manorial court rolls of the abbey's manor of Foxton, 1305–20 (Cambridge, Trinity College Archives, Foxton 1 and 4–5).

[1] Followed by *ec*, expunged.
[2] Hole 2 mm.
[3] Hole 20 mm.
[4] Hole 3 mm.
[5] Hole 35 mm.
[6] Unclear 10 mm: *vic'* visible at end of line under ultra-violet light only; repeated at top of fo. 147r, but omitted from catchwords, *nostro comitatus predicti*.
[7] Heading *Kerseye*.
[8] MS *fac'*.
[9] MS *facit*.

191 *Inquisition which finds that Hugh le Despenser junior held the manor of Kersey (Suff.) by the gift of Hugh le Despenser, the late earl of Winchester; and an extent of the manor which is held in fee-farm of Chatteris abbey for £10 annually.*
fo. 147r–v   10 March 1327 × 24 Jan. 1328

Partial transcript: Oxford, Bodl. MS Dodsworth 105, fo. 85r.

Extenta facta per probos et legales homines anno regni regis Edwardi tertii ut patet infra in nigro et in rotulis scaccarii.

Inquisitio capta coram excaetore et exten[ta fa]cta^1 de manerio de Kerseye in comitatu Suffolch', anno regni regis Edwardi tertii post conquestum primo, et returnatis in scaccario eodem anno, ut patet in rotulis memorandorum eiusdem scaccarii, videlicet juratores dicunt quod Hugo le Despenser junior tenuit manerium de Kerseye in comitatu predicto, ex dono Hugonis nuper comitis Wyntonie, et capitale mesuagium ibidem cum gardinis continens in se unam acram et dimidiam, et nichil valet ultra reprisas domorum. Item sunt ibidem ij^C xxxviij acre et dimidia terre lucrabilis per numus^2 tente et valet per annum iiij li. vj s. et ij d., precii acre iiij d. Sunt ibidem de terris dimissis ad firmam lx s. Sunt ibidem de pastura separale x acre et valent per annum xv s., precii acre^3 xviij d. Item dimidia acra pasture que valet vj d. Est ibidem quoddam molendinum ...^{4} valet ultra reprisas per annum xiij^5 s. ... [Sun]t^6 ibidem de redditu assiso per annum [i]x^7 li. Et ...^{8} quoddam mercatum diem ve[neris] ...p...^{9} per annum x marcas. Et sunt [ibidem opera]^{10} (fo. 147v)^{11} hiemalia et estivalia^{12} viij^{xx} que valent per annum dimidiam marcam,^{13} precium operis obolum. Sunt ibidem placita et perquisitiones curie que valent per annum v s. Et sciendum quod predictum

---

1 Damaged 8 mm.
2 6 minims before *us* abbreviation.
3 MS *acras.*
4 Damaged 20 mm.
5 MS *xiiij*, first *i* expunged.
6 Hole 17 mm.
7 Unclear 2 mm; *lacuna* supplied from partial transcript in Oxford, Bodl. MS Dodsworth 105, fo. 85r.
8 Hole 10 mm.
9 Damaged 25 mm.
10 Two holes 13 mm and 12 mm; MS perhaps, wrongly, *ibidem de operibus hiemalibus et estivalibus*, anticipating sum of money following rather than number of works.
11 Heading *Kereseye.*
12 MS *hiemalis et estivalis*, with a bar abbreviation mark through each *l*; followed by *xx* which seems to have been added incorrectly as part of the following numeral.
13 MS *dimidia marcas.*

manerium tenetur de monialibus de Chatriz ad feodi firmam, reddendo inde eisdem per annum x li. Item redduntur priori Cantuariensi ad manerium suum de Hadelegh viij d. de redditu assiso per annum.

> Note. The memoranda roll for Michaelmas term 1326 includes the following entry: Order to Ralph de Bockyng, knight, and John de Garbotesham to extend Barwe, Suffolk (to which are later added Leyham and Kerseye, because they too are in Suffolk). *Postea omnes extente predicte retornantur et mittantur in Cancellariam.* (*Calendar of Memoranda Rolls (Exchequer) Preserved in the Public Record Office. Michaelmas 1326–Michaelmas 1327* (PRO Texts and Calendars, 1968) pp. 16–17, no. 68.) No copy of this inquisition and extent has been found at the PRO.

192 *Acquittance by Margaret Hotot, abbess of Chatteris, to Edward, prince of Wales, of 50s. of rent from the manor of Kersey (Suff.).*
fo. 147v   At Chatteris, 30 Sept. 1368 × 5 Dec. 1368

Acquietancia domine Margarete Hotot abbatisse metuendissimo domino Edwardo ut infra.

Pateat universis per presentes quod nos Margareta Hotot permissione divina abbatissa de Chatriz recepimus de venerabili domino domino Edwardo filio domini nostri regis Anglie, principe Wallie et comite Kant' quinquaginta solidos argenti de quodam anno redditus de manerio de Kerseye pro termino sancti Michaelis ultimo preterito ante diem confectionis presentium, de quibus vero quinquaginta solidis simul cum omnibus arreragiis de toto tempore preterito fatemur nos plenarie esse solutas et predictum dominum principem heredes et exequutores suos inde fore quietos per presentes. In cuius rei testimonium hiis litteris acquietancie sigillum nostrum apposuimus. Date apud Chatriz tali die anno regni regis Edwardi t[ert]ii[1] post conquestum quadragesimo secundo.

> Note. The year 42 Edward III was 25 Jan. 1368–24 Jan. 1369. Since the next payment of rent after Michaelmas was due at the feast of St Nicholas (see no. 186), this acquittance must be dated 30 Sept. 1368 × 5 Dec. 1368.

193 *Order by Joan, countess of Kent, to her bailiff of Kersey (Suff.) to pay to Chatteris abbey £10 of rent owed for the manor of Kersey.*
fos. 147v–148r   At Berkhamsted (Herts.), 19 Nov. 1377

Littera venerabilis domine Johanne comitisse de le Kent.

---

[1] Hole 5 mm.

Johanne etc. a nostre baillif ou fermour de Kerseye s[a]lu[tz. Com]e[1] noz chiers en Dieu labbesse et covent de Chatriz nous ount compleynez coment ...[2] leur predecessours ont este[3] seisiez de [temps dount][4] memoire ne court de dix livres (fo. 148r)[5] per an a prendre de nostre dit manoir as quatre[6] termes[7] del an, et vous, quant ils en voient pur ycelle les taliez de leur dit paiement fere per trois jours ou quatre agraunt damage de euy la quele chose, nous valons et fermement vous mandons qas dites abbesse et covent en quanque en vous est vous le facez amender dolore enavaunt et saennes deviers des dites dix livres leur soient deves venes cestes vous les paiez saunz de ley, sique nous veions autrement nul pleynt en ce que. Donne per tesmoigne de nostre seal a Berkehamsted', le xix jou de novembre lan du reigne de nostre treshonere filz le roi Richard primer.

194 *Acquittance by abbess Alice de Shropham and the convent of Chatteris to the countess of Kent of 50s. of rent from the manor of Kersey (Suff.).*
fo. 148r [1331 × 12 Oct. 1347]

Acquietancie exemplar domine abbatisse venerande domine comitisse de le Kent.

Pateat universis per presentes nos A(lice) de S(hropham) permissione divina abbatissam de Chatriz et eiusdem loci conventum recepisse de venerabili domina comitissa de Kent quinquaginta solidos argenti annui redditus de manerio de Kereseye pro termino sancti Johannis Baptiste nunc proximo preterito, de quibus vero quinquaginta solidis fatemur nos bene et fideliter esse solutas et[8] predictam dominam heredes ac exequtores suos esse quietos per presentes. In cuius rei testimonium presentibus litteris etc. Date etc.

> Note. The countess of Kent is Margaret, widow of Edmund of Woodstock who was executed on 19 March 1330. Her infant son, Edmund, was restored on 7 Dec. 1330 but he died before 5 Oct. 1331. His brother, John, born on 7 April 1330, succeeded him but did not have livery of his lands until 10 April 1351. Margaret had livery of her dower in Feb. 1331 and died on 29 Sept. 1349 (*The Complete Peerage* eds V. Gibbs, H. A. Doubleday and Lord Howard de Walden, vii (London, 1929) pp. 146–8). Alice de Shropham's successor, Matilda

---

1 Hole 17 mm.
2 Damaged 5 mm.
3 Followed by *sey*, cancelled.
4 2 holes, 27 mm in total.
5 Heading *Kereseye*.
6 MS *quatere*, first *e* expunged.
7 Followed by *al*, expunged.
8 Interlined.

Bernard, was elected on 13 Oct. 1347 (Cambridge UL, EDR G/1/1 de Lisle register, fos. 51r–52r).

195 *Petition by Chatteris abbey to Edmund [Mortimer], earl of March and Ulster, for the fee-farm of £10 owed from the manor of Kersey (Suff.) which is 3 years in arrears.*
fo. 148r–v [9 June 1413 × 18 Jan. 1425]

Supplicatio domine abbatisse venerabili domino comiti March'.

Suo graciosissimo domino Edmundo domino comiti Marc' et Ulton', domino de Wygmor' et de Clare[1] supplicant[2] humilime vestre devote oratrices abbatissa et conventus de Chatriz quod, cum eedem abbatissa et conventus et predecessores sue abbatisse et (fo. 148v)[3] conventus monasterii de Chatriz suam feodi firmam, videlicet x libras de redditibus manerii de Kereseye, per manus balivi eiusdem manerii a tempore cuius contrarii memoria hominum non existit, eis jure ecclesie sue debitam, singulis annis perceperunt, et in cuius feodi firme perceptione dicte abbatissa et conventus et earum predecessores abbatisse et conventus dicti monasterii pro tempore existentes a tempore predicto continue extiterunt, exceptis tribus annis ultimo elapsis, quatinus placeat dominationi vestre graciose pie considerare, quod non solutio feodi firme supradicte in magnum cedit dicti monasterii detrimentum, et quod summe pietatis opus est jura religiosarum domorum conservare illesa, et sic gracosius percipere et mandare balivo manerii vestri supradicti ut feodi firmam supradictam a retro ut permittitur existentem prefatis abbatisse et conventui plenarie absque difficultate persolvat, et hoc intuitu caritatis.

> Note. Two Edmund Mortimers were earl of March and Ulster: this earl must be the later Edmund who was earl 9 June 1413–18 Jan. 1425 and who also occurs in nos. 196–7. It cannot be the earlier Edmund – who was earl 24 Aug. 1369–27 Dec. 1381 – because Edward, prince of Wales, and his widow Joan, countess of Kent, held the manor of Kersey then (nos. 192–3).

196 *Order by Edmund [Mortimer], earl of March and Ulster, to his bailiff of Kersey (Suff.) to pay to Chatteris abbey £10 annually owed for the manor of Kersey.*
fos. 148v–149r At London, 1 Jan. 1423

---

1 *Suo ... Clare*, underlined in red; initial *s* of *suo* not decorated.
2 Initial *s* decorated.
3 Heading *Kereseye*.

Littera domini Edmundi comitis March' que vocatur le Dormaunt' suo balivo etc. ut infra in nigro.

Esmon' count de la Marche et Duluestre, seniour de Weggemore et de Clare a[1] nostre bailliff de Kerseye quore est ou que pour le temps serra salutz. Et pour cee que nous sumes en debtez envers les nonaynes de la monasterie de Chatriz pone nostre[2] manoire de Kerseie, quest tenuez de les dytz nonaynes par la feerme de dys livers par an, vollons et vous chargeons que defere en avant vous facez paiere as ditz nonaynes les avant ditz dys livers annuelment (fo. 149r)[3] as termes usuelles sanz ent failer per ascune voie et cestez noz lettres vos ent serront garantz. Done a Londres le primer jour de januar' lan du regne nostre seigneur le roy Henry sext puis le conquest primer.

A nostre baillif de nostre ville de Kerseye quest ou que pour le temps serra.[4]

197 *Acquittance by abbess Agnes Ashfield and the convent of Chatteris to Edmund [Mortimer], earl of March and Ulster, of 100s. for the fee-farm of the vill of Kersey (Suff.).*
fo. 149r [9 June 1413 × 18 Jan. 1425]

Acquietancia domine Agnetis Aschfeld' abbatisse quondam de Chatriz venerabili domino comiti March' eiusque balivo.

Noverint universi per presentes nos Agnetem abbatissam de Chatriz et eiusdem loci conventum recepisse et habuisse d[ie][5] confectionis presentium de metuendo domino domino Edmundo comite Marchie et Ultonie centum solidos sterlingorum per manus Johannis Skeet balivi sui apud Kerseye, denarios solventes pro feodi firma dicte ville de Kerseie nobis per ipsum dominum comitem debita de terminis Natalis Domini et Pasche ultimo preteritis, de quibus quidem centum solidis fatemur nos bene et fideliter fore solutas, prefatum vero dominum comitem eiusque ballivum inde acquietamus per presentes sigillo nostro signatas. Date etc.

Note. Edmund Mortimer received livery of his lands on 9 June 1413 and died on 18 Jan. 1425. Agnes Ashfield occurs in dated documents between Sept. 1415 (no. 259) and 20 July 1437 (no. 276).

---

1 Followed by *no*, expunged.
2 Followed by *bai*, expunged.
3 Heading *Kereseye*.
4 *A … serra*, underlined in red.
5 Hole 3 mm.

198 *Acquittance by abbess Agnes Ashfield and the convent of Chatteris to William Sugge, bailiff, of 100s. of rent from the manor of Kersey (Suff.).*
fo. 149r–v [21 July 1398 × 8 June 1413]

Acquietancia domine Agnetis Aschefeld' domino regi eiusque balivo.

Noverint universi per presentes nos Agnetem abbatissam de Chatriz et eiusdem loci conventum recepisse et habuisse die confectionis presentium de Willelmo Sug balivo manerii de Kereseye in comutatu Suffolchie centum solidos sterlingorum de quodam annuo redditu decem librarum nobis et ecclesie nostre beate Marie de Chatriz de manerio predicto a tempore cuius contrarii memoria hominum non existit, et nobis ut in jure ecclesie nostre predicte debito, exeunte, videlicet pro terminis natalis sancti Johannis Baptiste et Michaelis ultimo preteritis ante datam presentium, de quibus (fo. 149v)[1] quidem centum solidis in forma predicta fatemur nos esse solutas, dictum vero Willelmum Sugge heredes et exequtores suos tam erga dominum regem quam quoscumque alios inde esse quietos per presentes sigillo nostro signatas. Date etc.

> Note. This acquittance probably dates from the period between the death of Roger Mortimer, earl of March and Ulster, on 20 July 1398, and the receipt by his son and heir, Edmund Mortimer, of livery of his lands on 9 June 1413. Agnes Ashfield occurs in dated documents as abbess from Sept. 1415 (no. 259) to 20 July 1437 (no. 276); William Sugge occurs in 1426 (no. 209).

199 *Acquittance by abbess Agnes Ashfield and the convent of Chatteris to Anne, countess of March, of £10 for the fee-farm of the vill of Kersey (Suff.).*
fo. 149v [18 Jan. 1425 × 5 March 1427]

Acquietancia domine Agnetis Aschefeld' venerabili domine Anne comitisse March'.

Noverint universi per presentes nos Agnetem abbatissam de Chatriz et eiusdem loci conventum recepisse et habuisse die [con]fectionis[2] presentium de venerabili domina domina [Anna][3] comitissa March' decem libras per manus Willelmi Sugge balivi sui apud Kerseye in plenam solutionem decem librarum feodi firme nostre dicte ville de Kerseye, de terminis Natalis Domini, Pasche, natalis sancti Johannis Baptiste et Michaelis ultimo preteritis, nobis per ipsam venerabilem dominam debite, de quibus quidem decem libris fatemur nos bene et fideliter

[1] Heading *Kereseye.*
[2] Hole 6 mm.
[3] Damaged 10 mm.

fore solutas, prefatam vero dominam comitissam eiusque balivum inde acquietamus per presentes nostro sigillo signatas. Date etc.

> Note. Anne countess of March married: (i) Edmund Mortimer, earl of March and Ulster (d.
> 18 Jan. 1425); (ii) John Holand, earl of Huntingdon, before 6 March 1427; she died on 20 or
> 24 Sept. 1432.

200 *Petition by Chatteris abbey to John Holand, earl of Huntingdon, for the fee-*
farm of £10 owed from the vill of Kersey (Suff.) which is 1 year in arrears.
fos. 149v–150r [15 Oct.1429 × 5 Aug. 1447]

Supplicatio domine abbatisse per Henricum Bucworth domino Johanni Holond
comiti Huntidonie.

Suo domino graciosissimo domino Johanni Holond' comiti Huntidonie[1] supplicant[2] humilime vestre devote oratrices abbatissa et conventus de Chatriz
quod, cum eedem abbatissa et conventus et predecessores sue abbatisse[3] et
conventus de Chatriz sunt et fuerunt in continua et pacifica possessione percipiendi suam feodi firmam, videlicet decem libras de redditibus ville de Kereseye,
per manus balivi eiusdem ville a tempore cuius contrarii memoria hominum
non existit, eis ut in jure (fo. 150r)[4] ecclesie sue debitam, singulis annis ad
quatuor a[n]ni[5] terminos per equales portiones, videlicet Natalis Domini,
Ramis Palmarum, natalis sancti Johannis Baptiste et Michaelis, quatinus placeat
vestre dominationi[6] graciose pie considerare, quod non solutio feodi firme
supradicte in magnum posset detrimentum cedere monasterii antedicti, et quod
summe pietatis opus est jura religiosarum domorum conservare illesa, et sic
graciosius vestro balivo ville supradicte percipere et mandare ut sepedictam
feodi firmam a retro per unum annum existentem prefatis abbatisse et conventui
plenarie absque[7] difficultate persolvat, et hoc intuitu caritatis.

> Note. Henry Buckworth was admitted vicar of Chatteris on 15 Oct. 1429 (Cambridge UL,
> Add. MS 6394, fo. 3v); he died before 29 April 1456 when Thomas Holand became the next
> vicar of Chatteris (Cambridge UL, EDR G/1/5 Grey register, fo. 14r). John Holand became
> earl of Huntingdon *c.* 1417, was created duke of Exeter on 6 Jan. 1444 and died on 5 Aug.

---

1 *Suo ... Huntidonie*, underlined in red.
2 Initial *s* decorated.
3 MS *abbatissa*.
4 Heading *Kereseye*.
5 Hole 2 mm.
6 Followed by single letter, cancelled.
7 Followed by *cum*, expunged.

1447. The inclusion of Buckworth's name in the rubricated heading, despite its absence from the text of the petition, suggests that Buckworth may have been the scribe of the manuscript.

201 *Presentment at the court of John Holand, earl of Huntingdon, held at Kersey (Suff.) concerning the tenure of the vill of Kersey.*
fo. 150r   3 Sept. 1427

Veredictum tenentium ville de Kereseye in curia tenta apud Kereseye anno et die ut infra.

Ad curiam venerabilis domini domini comitis Huntidonie, videlicet domini J(ohannis) Holond', tentam apud Kerseye tertio die mensis Septembris anno regni regis Henrici sexti post conquestum sexto per Edmundum Wynter, sineschallum dicti venerabilis domini comitis, Johannes Millere, Johannes Skete et alii juratores dicunt super sacramentum suum quod dicta villa de Kereseye tenetur in feodi firmam de religiosis monialibus abbatissa de Chatriz et eiusdem loci conventu, reddendo annuatim decem libras ad terminos usuales. Dicunt etiam iidem juratores quod dicte abbatissa et conventus et omnes predecessores eorum abbatisse et conventus de Chatriz sunt et fuerunt in continua possessione percipiendi supradictam feodi firmam, videlicet decem libras, a tempore cuius contrarii memoria hominum non existit.

202 *Order by John Holand, earl of Huntingdon, to his bailiff to pay to Chatteris abbey the fee-farm of £10 owed for the vill of Kersey (Suff.), which is 1 year in arrears, and to pay it annually to the abbey in advance during the life of Anne, his wife.*
fo. 150r–v   2 Oct. 1427

Littera J(ohannis) Holond' comitis Huntidonie que vocatur le dormaunt. (fo. 150v)[1]

[Jo]han[2] counte de Huntidonie a nostre baillif de nostre vill de Kerseye est tenuz de lez monialz de la monasterie de Chatriz par le feferme de dys livrez par an, les qux[3] dis livrez sount[4] duez et aderere[5] as ditz monialx par un an entier

---

1 Heading *Kereseye.*
2 Guide-letter for initial *J* present, but no decorated initial; hole 2 mm, *o* lacking.
3 Followed by *s*, expunged.
4 Followed by *diez*, expunged.
5 MS *arderere*, first *r* expunged.

al fest de Sent Michel darrein passe, volons et vous chargeons que de lez[1] issuez et profitz de nostre dit manoir vous paiez ou facez paier as ditz monialx lez diz liverez susditz ensi a eux duez a le dit fest, et auxi paiez ou facez paier as ditz monialx desore[2] en avant le dit feferme de dis liveres annuelment astermes illeoques usuelx durant la vie de Anne nostre compaigne,[3] pregnant de vers vous de les ditz monials lettres dacquitance tesmongauntz chescun paiement qe vous et eux ensi ferrez pur nostre descharge celle partie, par lez quelx et par icestez nous volouns qe vous evayez due alloaunce en vostre[4] accompte. Donez soubz nostre seal, le secounnde jour doctobre lan du regne tressoveraigne seigneur le roy Henry sisme puis le conquest le sisme.

203 *Acquittance by abbess Agnes Ashfield and the convent of Chatteris to John Holand, earl of Huntingdon, of £10 from the manor of Kersey (Suff.).*
fos. 150v–151r   At Chatteris, 9 May 1428

Acquietancia domine Agnetis Aschefeld' abbatisse domino Johanni comiti Huntidonie eiusque balivo.

Noverint universi per presentes nos Agnetem abbatissam de Chatriz et eiusdem loci conventum recepisse et habuisse die confectionis presentium de metuendo domino domino Johanne Holand' comite Huntidonie decem libras sterlingorum per manus Johannis Skete balivi sui apud Kerseye, nobis per ipsum dominum comitem debitas, pro terminis Natalis Domini, dominice in Ramis Palmarum, natalis sancti Johannis Baptiste et Michaelis ultimo preteritis (fo. 151r)[5] post datam presentium, de quibus quidem decem libris fatemur nos bene et fideliter fore solutas, prefatum vero dominum comitem eiusque balivum inde acquietamus per presentes nostro sigillo signatas. Date apud Chatriz nono die mensis maii anno regni regis Henrici sexti post conquestum sexto.

204 *Confirmation by Thomas son of Henry de Burgo to Chatteris abbey of the grant by Adam son of Robert de Cockfield of an annual rent of 40s. from the first church in his gift to fall vacant, excepting the church of Kersey and the chapel of Lindsey (Suff.), meanwhile giving to the abbey 1 mark annually.*

1 Followed by *v*, expunged.
2 Followed by *ai*, expunged.
3 MS *compaigene*, first *e* expunged.
4 MS *vostere*, first *e* expunged.
5 Heading *Kereseye*.

fo. 151r–v [*c.* 1198 × *c.* 1240]

Carta Thome de Burgo de quadraginta solidis annui redditus quousque etc. ut in nigro.

Universis sancte matris ecclesie filiis presentem paginam inspecturis Thomas filius Henrici de Burgo salutem. Noverit universitas vestra me hac presenti carta mea confirmasse in puram et perpetuam elemosinam monialibus Deo et sancte Marie in ecclesia de Chatriz servientibus, pro anima patris mei et predecessorum meorum et salute propria, redditum annuum quadraginta solidorum in prima ecclesia vacante que sit de donatione mea, excepta ecclesia de Karesheia et cap-ella de[1] Lesseya. Et interim dabo eis unam marcam argenti annuatim, videlicet[2] xl denarios in festo sancti Nicholai et xl denarios in Ramis Palmarum et octo diebus ante festum sancti Johannis Baptiste xl denarios et ad festum sancti Michaelis xl denarios, quousque redditum predictorum xl solidorum annuatim in ecclesia que prima michi vacaverit cum exceptione premissa illis determinate assignaverim et carta mea in perpetuam elemosinam confirmaverim, sicut in carta Ade[3] filii Roberti de Kokefeld' quam eisdem monialibus fecit continetur. Ego autem et heredes mei hanc confirmationem predictis monialibus contra omnes homines warantizabimus. Hiis testibus magistro Nicholao capellano, Alexandro capellano archidiaconi Norwicensis, Willelmo (fo. 151v)[4] capellano sancte Marie, Nicholao capellano de cruce, Amiano clerico, Simone clerico, magistro Willelmo de Tilneia, Ricardo de Fresingefeld', Willelmo de Waldynge-feld',[5] Reinaldo mareschallo, Mauricio janitore et multis aliis.

Note. Confirmation of nos. 73 and 188 (grant copied twice). Adam de Cockfield died *c.* 1198 leaving an infant heir, Margaret *alias* Nesta. Thomas de Burgo acquired the wardship before 1201 and subsequently became the first of Nesta's three husbands. She married her second before 1240 (Farrer *Honors* iii, p. 362).

205 *Form of acquittance by the abbess of Chatteris to the bailiff of the manor of Kersey (Suff.) of an annual rent of £10 from the manor.*
fo. 151v At Chatteris, 30 June 1441

Noverint universi per presentes nos N. abbatissam de Chateriz et eiusdem loci conventum recepisse et habuisse die confectionis presentium de N. ballivo

1 Followed by *Lesseya*, expunged.
2 Followed by *v*, expunged.
3 Interlined.
4 Heading *Kersey*, in black.
5 MS *Waldefeldyngefeld'*, *defel* expunged.

manerii de Kersey in comitatu Suffolc' x libras sterlingorum de quodam annuo
redditu decem librarum nobis et ecclesie nostre beate Marie de Chateriz predicta
de manerio antedicto ad terminos natalis sancti Nicholai episcopi et confessoris,
diei dominice in Ramis Palmarum, nativitatis sancti Johannis Baptiste et sancti
Michaelis archangeli a tempore cuius contrarii memoria hominum non existit,
in jure ecclesie nostre predicte annuatim debito, exeunte, de quibus vero decem
libris, ut pro uno anno integro ultimo preterito ante primum diem octobris in
anno regni regis nunc decimo nono, fatemur nos esse solutas dictumque ballivum inde acquietamus per presentes sigillo nostro consignatas. Date apud Chateriz predictam ultimo die junii anno regni regis Henrici sexti post conquestum
anno decimo nono.

206 *Paraphrase of a passage from St Augustine's exposition of Psalm 91.*
fo. 151v

> Si[1] bene loqueris tantum, canticum est sine cithara,
> Si operaris et non loqueris, cithara est sine cantico,
> Idio et bene loquere et bene fac etc.

Note. cf. St Augustine, bishop of Hippo *Enarratio in Psalmum XCI*, 5 (*Patrologiae Cursus Completus, Series Latina* ed. J.-P. Migne, xxxvii, 1174): 'Si verba sola dicis, quasi canticum solum habes, citharam non habes; si operaris et non loqueris, quasi solam citharam habes. Propter hoc et loquere bene et fac bene, si vis habere canticum cum cithara.'

207 *Quotation from 'The Mirror of Simple Souls', a French, mystical tract by Margaret Porete, translated into English by 'M. N.'.*
fo. 151v [s. xiii[4] × s. xiv[1]; translated into English s. xiv[2-4]]

> Sigh and sorowe deeply,
> Wepe[2] and moorne inwardly,
> Prey and thynk devoutly,
> Love and long contynuelly. (fo. 152r)[3]

Note. See M. Doiron ed. 'Margaret Porete: "The Mirror of Simple Souls". A Middle English Translation' *Archivio Italiano per la Storia della Pietà* v (1968) pp. 241-355. See also C. Brown and R. H. Robbins *The Index of Middle English Verse* (New York, 1943) p. 493, no. 3102, and R. H. Robbins and J. L. Cutler *Supplement to the Index of Middle English Verse* (Lexington, 1965) p. 341, no. 3102.

1 *Augustine* marginated before *si*.
2 *nota bene* marginated before *Wepe*.
3 Heading *Kersey*, in black.

208 *Order by Henry Gray, earl of Tankerville, to all his officials of the manor of Kersey (Suff.) to pay to Chatteris abbey both the annual rent of £10 from the manor in the future and the arrears owed.*
fo. 152r   16 July 1443

Copia dormandi Henrici Grey domini de Kersey.

Henricus Gray comes de Tancarvill' dominus de Powys et Tylly camerarius hereditarius de Normannia universis et singulis senescallis auditoribus receptoribus ballivis et aliis ministris quibuscumque manerii sive dominii nostri de Kersey in comitatu Suff' salutem. Cum abbatissa de Chateris in comitatu Cant' et predecessores sue, per tempus cuius contrarii memoria hominum non existit, seisite fuerint in dominico suo, ut de feodo ut in jure ecclesie sue de Chateris predicte, de quodam annuo redditu decem librarum, exeunte de manerio sive dominio predicto, solvendo annuatim, videlicet in festo sancti Nicholai quinquaginta solidos et in dominica in Ramis Palmarum quinquaginta solidos et infra octo dies ante festum nativitatis sancti Johannis Baptiste quinquaginta solidos imperpetuum, pro cuius arreragiis licite distringere consueverint a tempore predicto in manerio sive dominio antedicto, vobis et cuilibet vestrum precipimus quod abbatisse predicte et successoribus suis plenam et celerem solutionem faciatis de redditu predicto et arreragiis eiusdem, a dominica in Ramis Palmarum anno regni domini regis nunc vicesimo exclusive et deinceps perpetuis temporibus futuris. In cuius rei testimonium sigillum armorum nostrorum presentibus est appensum. Date sextodecimo die mensis julii anno regni regis Henrici sexti post conquestum Anglie vicesimo primo.

209 *Lease by John Talbot, Robert Illary and William Sugge of Hadleigh (Suff.) and John Waryn of Kersey (Suff.) to Robert Pery of Kersey, Agnes his wife, John Colman of Offton (Suff.) and John Gibbes, John Pusk and John Skeet of Kersey, of a tenement in Kersey, given to the lessors by Thomas Meller and Richard Halden of Kersey and Hamo atte Ston' of Hadleigh.*
fo. 152r–v   At Kersey (Suff.), 27 May 1426

Carta de quodam tenemento in Kersey quondam Nicholai Webbe postea Roberti Pery de Kersey predicta.

Sciant presentes et futuri quod nos Johannes Talbot de (fo. 152v)[1] Hadlegh', Robertus Illary, Willelmus Sugge de eadem et Johannes Waryn' de Kersey con-

---

1 Heading *Kersey*, in black.

cessimus dimisimus et hac presenti carta nostra confirmavimus Roberto Pyrye de Kersey, Agneti uxori eius, Johanni Colman' de Ofton', Johanni Gybbes de Kersey, Johanni Pusk et Johanni Skeet de eadem totum illud tenementum cum omnibus suis pertinenciis quondam Nicholai Webbe de Kersey, prout situatur in villa de Kersey, inter mesuagium nuper Johannis Ku ex parte una et quoddam mesuagium prioris et conventus de Kersey ex parte altera, uno capite abuttante super viam ducentem de Kersey Brigge versus ecclesiam eiusdem ville, quod quidem tenementum cum pertinenciis nuper habuimus ex dono et feoffamento Thome Meller' de Kersey, Ricardi Halden' de eadem et Hamonis atte Ston' de Hadlegh', habendum et tenendum totum illud predictum tenementum cum omnibus suis pertinenciis prefatis Roberto Pyrye, Agneti uxori eius, Johanni Colman', Johanni Gibbes, Johanni Pusk et Johanni Skeet, heredibus et assignatis eorundem Roberti Pyrye, Johannis Colman', Johannis Gybbes, Johannis Pusk et Johannis Skeet, de capitalibus dominis feodi per servicia inde de jure debita et consueta imperpetuum. In cuius rei testimonium presenti carte sigilla nostra apposuimus. Hiis testibus Willelmo Goodwen', Jacobo Pusk, Johanne Sybry, Johanne Meller, Willelmo Polsted' et aliis. Data apud Kersey die lune proximo post festum sancte Trinitatis anno regni regis Henrici sexti post conquestum quarto.

Note. Although the verb *dimisimus* is used to describe this transaction, the document states that the tenement is to be held *imperpetuum*. No. 210 shows that not all the beneficiaries acquired a perpetual right in the tenement; rather they held it jointly for their lives and only the longest liver held it perpetually. Therefore, the document granted a life-interest only in the tenement to all but the surviving recipient, for whom the document was in effect a gift.

210 *Lease by John Pusk of Kersey (Suff.) to Meliora, formerly wife of Robert Pery of Kersey, for her life, of a tenement in Kersey which he lately held with Robert Pery, Agnes his wife, John Colman of Offton (Suff.), John Gibbes and John Skeet, all now dead, and which will remain to William Wolflete, dean of the college of Stoke, and others named.*
fos. 152v–153r   At Kersey (Suff.), 2 June 1456

Carta Johannis Pusk de tenemento in Kersey nuper Ricardi Pyry.

Sciant presentes et futuri quod ego Johannes Pusk de Kersey in comitatu Suff' dimisi tradidi liberavi et hac presenti carta mea indentata confirmavi Meliore que fuit uxor (fo. 153r)[1] Roberti Pery de Kersey predicta unum tenementum meum edificatum cum suis pertinenciis in Kersey predicta, situatum in villa de

---

[1] Heading *Kersey*, in black.

Kersey inter mesuagium nuper Johannis Ku postea Johannis Gibbes ex una
parte et quoddam mesuagium nuper prioris et conventus de Kersey ex altera
parte, uno capite abuttante super viam ducentem de Kersey Brigge versus ecclesiam eiusdem ville, quod quidem tenementum cum suis pertinenciis nuper
habui simul cum Roberto Pery predicto, Agnete uxore eius, Johanne Colman'
de Ofton', Johanne Gibbes et Johanne Skeet iam defunctis ex dono et feoffamento Johannis Talbot de Hadlegh', Roberto Illary, Willelmi Sugge et Johannis
Waryn', ut in una carta inde nobis confecta plene apparet, habendum et tenendum totum predictum tenementum cum omnibus suis pertinenciis prefate
Meliore ad terminum vite sue, et post decessum dicte Meliore quod totum
predictum tenementum cum omnibus suis pertinenciis integre remanebit Willelmo Wolflete decano collegii de Stoke, Johanni Clopton', Johanni Denston',
armigeris, Johanni Ansty seniori, Johanni Batysford', Johanni Aleyn', Willelmo
Wyghton et Johanni Bonyard' heredibus et eorum assignatis imperpetuum, de
capitalibus dominis feodi[1] illius per servicia inde debita et de jure consueta. In
cuius rei testimonium huic presenti carte mee indentate sigillum meum apposui.
Hiis testibus Johanne Lovetopp', Edmundo Freman', clericis, Willelmo Lovetopp', Johanne Howardyn', Ricardo Ambrose, Roberto Cook, Willelmo Wylford' et aliis. Data apud Kersey predictam secundo die mensis junii anno regni
regis Henrici sexti post conquestum tricesimo quarto.

Sequitur irrotulamentum cuiusdem curie tente ibidem etc. de xv acris terre
nuper Roberti Pery de Kersey predicta. (fo. 153v)

Note. See no. 209n.

211 *Grant by Ralph Briston, Azo Noreis and John Fithien of Chatteris to Chatteris
abbey of a fishery with meadow [in Chatteris].*
fos. 153v–154r   ?[*s.* xiii[3] × *s.* xiv[1]]

Sciant presentes et futuri quod nos Radulphus Braxton, Azotis Noreys et Johannes Fechien de Chateriz dedimus et concessimus et hac presenti carta nostra
confirmavimus Deo et ecclesie beate Marie de Chateriz et sanctimonialibus
ibidem Deo servientibus quandam piscariam vocatam Myle Water' cum prato
ibidem[2] jacente, continentem[3] in latitudine ad finem inferiorem tendentem ad

---

1 Repeated.
2 MS *ibadem.*
3 MS *continente,* but the boundary description seems to refer to the fishery rather than the
   meadow.

partem borialem viij virgas et dimidiam, et sic a marisco usque ad mariscum, ad communem usque ad lacum nominatum Pamplake, ibi habituram a propria aqua, videlicet Severyll Water', xvj virgas in longitudine[1] et quatuordecim pedes in latitudine ad minandam vel ducendam, et etiam a marisco ad mariscum et ad mariscum etiam et ultra mariscum ad lacum vocatum Ipyslake, et tunc ab aqua Severilla tendente ad orientem continentem lj virgas, et etiam a propria aqua usque ad finem xxxviij virgarum illarum lj virgarum predictarum juxta communem, a communi de latere australi tendente ad bariam continentem xxiij virgas in latitudine, et ad finem orientalem ipsarum lj virgarum continentem sex virgas in latitudine, tenendam et habendam predictis monialibus libere bene quiete et in pace in liberam puram et perpetuam elimosinam, adeo liberius et quietius sicuti aliqua elimosina aliquibus mulieribus religiosis dari potest vel conferri. Et nos Radulphus Brixton, Azotis et Johannes Fechien predicti warantizabimus defendemus et aquietabimus totam predictam piscariam, cum predicto prato ad predictam piscariam pertinente, predictis monialibus contra (fo. 154r) omnes gentes tam christianos quam judeos imperpetuum. Et ut hec nostra donatio et presentis carte nostre confirmatio rata et stabilis permaneat imperpetuum, huic scripto sigilla nostra apposuimus.[2] Hiis testibus. (fo. 154v)

Note. The detail in the boundary descriptions suggests that this charter does not date from the earlier part of the thirteenth century. The language of the charter is consistent with the dates of the John Fithien who occurs in 1289 and shortly before 8 July 1298 × 27 March 1306 (Ault ed. *Ramsey Court Rolls*, pp. 278–9; nos. 38 and 63). The Ralph Briston, who occurs in nos. 19 and 23, and the Azo le Noreis, who occurs in nos. 25/41, 27/40, 32/37, 33 and 67, seem therefore to be different from their namesakes in this charter. This Azo may possibly be a son of Emma daughter of Azo le Noreis who occurs in nos. 52, 54, 61 and 81.

212 *Inquisition post mortem held at Kersey (Suff.) before John Fox, escheator, concerning Henry Gray, knight, who held the manor of Kersey and a third part of the manor of Layham (Suff.).*
fo. 154v   At Kersey, 1 Oct. 1450

Copy: (U) PRO C 139/140/30.

In[3] baga de particulis compoti Johannis Fox' nuper escaetoris regis in custodia remembrancarii regis remanente inter alia continetur sic.[4]

---

1   MS *longitidine*.
2   5 minims for *-uim-*.
3   *Suff'* marginated before *In*.
4   *In baga … sic*, in black.

Inquisitio capta apud Kersey in comitatu Suff' die jovis proximo post festum
sancti Michaelis archangeli anno regni regis Henrici sexti post conquestum
vicesimo nono coram Johanne Fox' escaetore domini regis in comitatu predicto,
virtute cuiusdam brevis dicti domini regis eidem escaetori directi et huic inquisitioni consuti, per sacramentum etc.[1] Qui dicunt super sacramentum suum
quod Henricus Gray miles in dicto brevi nominatus, qui diem suum clausit
extremum, tenuit die quo obiit in dominico suo ut de feodo manerium de
Kersey cum suis pertinenciis in comitatu predicto de domino rege per servicium
militare, set de quantitate eiusdem servicii juratores supradicti ad presens penitus ignorant. Et quod dictum manerium cum suis pertinenciis valet per annum
in omnibus exitibus ultra reprisas xj libras et ultra quendam annualem redditum
decem librarum, de quo abbatissa et conventus ecclesie beate Marie de Chaterise
et omnes predecessores sue[2] abbatisse loci predicti seisite fuerunt, et ipsum
redditum annuatim perceperunt de et in manerio predicto cum suis pertinenciis
a tempore cuius contrarii memoria hominum non existit ad quatuor anni terminos, videlicet ad festa sancti Michaelis archangeli, Natalis Domini, Annunciationis beate Marie et natalis sancti Johannis Baptiste per equales portiones. Et
dicunt quod dictus Henricus tenuit, dicto die quo obiit, in dominico suo ut de
feodo tertiam partem manerii de Leyham cum suis pertinenciis in comitatu predicto similiter de domino rege per servicium militare, set de quantitate servicii
juratores supradicti similiter penitus ignorant. Et quod dicta[3] pars valet per
annum ij marcas ultra x marcas Ricardo Pemberton' durante vita sua resol-
vendas de eadem tertia parte. Et dicunt quod idem Henricus Gray nulla alia
terras seu tenementa in comitatu predicto tenuit de domino rege nec de aliquo
alio predicto die quo obiit. Et quod dictus Henricus Gray obiit in festo sancti
Hillarii episcopi ultimo preterito. Et dicunt quod Ricardus Gray filius dicti
Henrici Gray est heres eius inde propinquior et etatis xiiij[cim] annorum. In cuius
rei testimonium huic inquisitioni juratores supradicti sigilla sua apposuerunt.
Data die loco et anno supradictis. (fo. 155r)[4]

---

[1] U omits, adds *Roberti Prylle, Willelmi Turnour', Thome Holbroke, Maricii Lovell, Johannis
Holbroke, Johannis Puske, Alexandri Marchaunt, Roberti Perye, Simonis Waylond, Johannis
Hawarden, Thome Smyth et Johannis Ma....*

[2] MS *sui*.

[3] U adds *tertia*.

[4] Heading *Leen*.

213 *Confirmation by William, cordwainer, son of Elwin, cordwainer, of Lynn (Norf.) to William son of Wluric de Wootton of the land in Lynn given by Elwin, his father; for 3 marks.*
fo. 155r [*s.* xii^4 × *s.* xiii^1]

Carta Willelmi cordewanerii Willelmo filio Wlurici versus cimiterium ecclesie sancte Margarete in Lenna.

Sciant presentes et futuri quod ego Willelmus cordewanerius filius Elwyni cordewaner de Lennia concessi et hac presenti carta mea confirmavi Willelmo filio Wlurici de Wotton' et heredibus suis donum et concessionem quam Elwynus pater meus fecit eis, scilicet de tota medietate terre illius in Lennia versus orientem que jacet inter terram que quondam fuit Simonis filii Arnaldi et terram Aluredi de Walton' et Willelmi et Henrici fratrum suorum, in latitudine et longitudine quatrer viginti et sesdecim pedes terre, a terra quam teneo de Elwyno patre meo versus cimiterium sancte Margarete, tenendam eadem libertate et eodem servicio quod continetur in carta predicti Elwini patris mei et prout eadem carta testatur. Pro hac concessione et istius carte mee confirmatione predictus Willelmus dedit michi tres marcas argenti. Hiis testibus etc.

Note. For dating see no. 214n. This confirmation follows no. 214 and precedes nos. 216, 217 and 218.

214 *Gift by Elwin, cordwainer, of Lynn (Norf.) to William son of Wluric de Wootton of half of his land in Lynn; for 11 marks, 2s. for a cloak for Alice his wife and an annual rent of 6d.*
fo. 155r–v [*s.* xii^4 × *s.* xiii^2]

Carta Elwini Willelmo filio Wulrici de Wotton' de eodem tenemento.

Sciant presentes et futuri quod ego Elwynus cordewarnerius de Lenna concessi et dedi et hac mea carta confirmavi Willelmo filio Wlurici de Wotton' et heredibus suis totam medietatem totius terre mee in Lenna versus orientem que jacet inter terram que fuit Simonis filii Arnaldi et terram[1] Aluredi de Walton' et Willelmi et Henrici fratrum suorum, in latitudine et longitudine quater viginti et sesdecim pedes terre, a terra quam Willelmus filius meus tenet de me versus cimiterium sancte Margarete, (fo. 155v)[2] pro homagio suo quod michi fecit de feodo, et pro undecim[3] marcis argenti quas michi dedit in guersumma et duos

1 Followed by *Alerudi*, expunged.
2 Heading *Lenna*.
3 MS *undecimo, o* expunged.

solidos ad unum pallium ad opus Alicie uxoris mee, tenendam de me et heredibus meis in feodo et hereditate, reddendo inde annuatim michi et heredibus
meis sex denarios de[1] censu, scilicet ad festum sancti Andree tres obolos et ad
Annunciationem sancte Marie tres obolos et ad nativitatem sancti Johannis
Baptiste tres obolos et ad festum sancti Michaelis tres obolos, libere et quiete et
pacifice pro omnibus serviciis et consuetudinibus et exactionibus. Hiis testibus
etc.

> Note. The English names Elwin, Wluric and Alfred in this charter suggest that its date may
> be as early as the end of the twelfth century. Nos. 213, 215, 216, 217 and 218 follow this
> charter. D. M. Owen assigns no. 217 to the early thirteenth century (D. M. Owen ed. *The
> Making of King's Lynn. A Documentary Survey* (London, 1984) p. 81, no. 32).

215 *Confirmation by Walter, cordwainer, son of Elwin, cordwainer, of Lynn
(Norf.) to William son of Wluric de Wootton of the land in Lynn given by Elwin,
his father; for 2 marks.*
fos. 155v–156r [*s.* xii[4] × *s.* xiii[2]]

Carta Walteri cordewanerii Willelmo filio Wlurici de Wotton' de medietate ut
supra.

Sciant presentes et futuri quod ego Walterus cordewanerius filius Elwini cordewanerii de Lenna concessi et hac mea carta confirmavi Willelmo filio Wlurici de
Wotton' et heredibus suis donum et concessionem quam Elwynus pater meus
fecit eis, scilicet de tota medietate totius terre illius in Lenna versus orientem
que jacet inter terram que fuit Simonis filii[2] Arnaldi et terram Aluredi de
Walton' et Willelmi et Henrici fratrum suorum, in latitudine et longitudine
quater viginti et sesdecim pedes terre, a terra quam Willelmus frater meus tenet
de Elwyno patre meo versus cimiterium sancte Margarete, tenendam eadem
libertate et eodem servicio quod continetur in carta predicti[3] Elwini patris mei
et prout eadem carta testatur. Pro hac autem concessione et istius carte mee
confirmatione predictus (fo. 156r)[4] Willelmus dedit michi duas marcas argenti.
Hiis testibus etc.

> Note. For dating see no. 214n. This confirmation follows no. 214 and precedes nos. 216, 217
> and 218.

1 Followed by *s*, cancelled.
2 MS *filius*.
3 Followed by *Willelmi*, expunged.
4 Heading *Lenna*.

216 *Confirmation by Laurence son of William, cordwainer, of Lynn (Norf.) to William son of Wluric de Wootton of the land with buildings in Lynn given by Elwin, his grandfather; for 2 talents.*
fo. 156r [s. xiii$^{1-2}$]

Carta Laurencii filii Willelmi cordwaner Willelmo filio Wlurici de Wotton'.

Sciant presentes et futuri quod ego Laurencius filius Willelmi cordewanerii de Lenna concessi et hac carta mea confirmavi Willelmo filio Wlurici de Wotton' et heredibus suis concessionem et donationem quam Elwynus avus meus et Willelmus pater meus eis fecerunt de tota medietate terre que fuit Elwyny avi mei in Lenna cum edificiis que abuttat super cimiterium beate Margarete, scilicet de illa medietate versus orientem, tenendam eadem libertate et eodem servicio quod^1 continetur in carta predicti Elwini avi mei quam predictus Willelmus inde habet et prout eadem carta testatur. Pro hac autem concessione et huius carte mee confirmatione predictus Willelmus dedit michi duo talenta auri. Hiis testibus etc.

> Note. For dating of the gift confirmed see no. 214n. This confirmation follows nos. 214, 213 and 215 and precedes nos. 217 and 218.

217 *Gift in alms by William son of Wluric de Wootton to Chatteris abbey of the land with buildings in Lynn (Norf.) which he bought from Elwin, cordwainer, for 6d. annually.*
fo. 156r–v [s. xiii$^{1-2}$]

> Extracts, taken from this cartulary, printed in D. M. Owen ed. *The Making of King's Lynn. A Documentary Survey* (London, 1984) p. 81, no. 32.

Carta Willelmi filii Wlurici de Wotton' Deo et sancte Marie de Chatriz et monialibus ibidem Deo servientibus.

Omnibus Christi fidelibus ad quos presens scriptum pervenerit Willelmus filius Wlurici de Wotton' salutem. Notum vobis facio me dedisse et concessisse et presenti carta mea confirmasse Deo et sancte Marie de Chatriz et monialibus ibidem Deo servientibus, pro salute anime mee et uxoris mee et predecessorum meorum, totam illam medietatem terre in Lenna cum edificiis tam lapideis quam ligneis quam de Alwino cordewanerio peccunia mea [adqui]sivi^2 [in]^3

---

1 Followed by *in*, expunged.
2 Hole 9 mm.
3 Damaged 4 mm.

puram et perpetuam elemosinam, [que scilicet antedicta][1] (fo. 156v)[2] terra habet
in latitudine sesdecim pedes et in longitudine quater viginti pedes, salvo michi et
heredibus meis redditu sex denariorum a predictis monialibus de eadem terra
annuatim reddendorum pro omni servicio consuetudine et exactione, quibus sex
denariis annuis ego et heredes mei erga heredes predicti Alwini acquietabimus et
predictam terram contra omnes homines ecclesie sancte Marie de Chatriz et
monialibus eiusdem loci warantizabimus. Terra autem predicta jacet inter terram que fuit Simonis filii Arnaldi et terram Aluredi de Walton' et Willelmi et
Henrici fratrum eius juxta cimiterium sancte Margarete in boreali parte. Et ut
hec omnia predicta rata imperpetuum permaneant, huic scripto sigillum meum
apposui. Hiis testibus etc.

> Note. D. M. Owen assigns this charter to the early thirteenth century. It follows nos. 214,
> 213, 215 and 216 and precedes no. 218.

218 *Notification by Warin son of Gilbert de Lynn that he is bound to Chatteris
abbey in 1 mark of annual rent for a messuage in Lynn (Norf.).*
fos. 156v–157r [s. xiii[1-2]]

> Extract, taken from this cartulary, printed in D. M. Owen ed. *The Making of King's Lynn. A
> Documentary Survey* (London, 1984) pp. 81–2, no. 33.

Carta Warini filii Gilberti de Lenna seu obligatio domine abbatisse et conventui
de una marca.

Universis Christi fidelibus presentes litteras visuris vel audituris Warinus filius
Gilberti de Lenna salutem in Domino. Noverit universitas me et heredes meos
teneri abbatisse de Chatriz et conventui eiusdem loci in unam marcam argenti
annuatim solvendam de annuali redditu ad quatuor anni terminos pro quodam
mesuagio proximo jacente meo capitali mesuagio ex parte occidentali, ex opposito ecclesie beate Margarete a parte boreali, quod mesuagium in latitudine
continet sesdecim pedes et in longitudine quater viginti pedes, videlicet[3] ad
Natale Domini quadraginta denarios et ad Pascha xl denarios et ad festum
nativitatis sancti Johannis Baptiste xl denarios et [ad festum sancti][4] Michaelis
quadraginta denarios. Et (fo. 157r)[5] si contingat me in solutione dicte peccunie
alicuius termini deficere, concedo et obligo me et heredes meos et dictum

---

1 Hole 37 mm.
2 Heading *Lenna*.
3 Interlined.
4 Hole 32 mm; MS probably *...is* before *Michaelis*.
5 Heading *Lenna*.

mesuagium districtioni predictarum abbatisse et conventus predicti loci, ita scilicet quod predicte abbatissa et conventus et earum certus attornatus plenam et liberam potestatem habeant distringendi dictum mesuagium per medium infra et extra, in longum et latum, sine aliqua contradictione mei vel heredum meorum omni occasione tam alicuius libertatis quam cause vel previlegii postposita. In cuius rei testimonium presens scriptum in modum obligationis confectum sigilli mei impressione roboravi. Hiis testibus etc.

Note. D. M. Owen assigns this charter to the early thirteenth century. It follows nos. 214, 213, 215, 216 and 217.

219 *Agreement between abbess Amicia de Cambridge and the convent of Chatteris and Alexander, butcher, of Lynn (Norf.), whereby they released and acquitted him from all the arrears owed for 1 mark of annual rent from a piece of land with buildings in Lynn, and he agreed to pay the rent in future.*
fo. 157r–v [Shortly after 29 Sept. 1300]

Conventio quedam inter dominam abbatissam et Alexandrem carnificem de Lenna super dicto tenemento in Lenna.

Pateat universis per presentes quod ita convenit inter Amiciam de Cantebr' abbatissam de Chatriz et eiusdem loci conventum ex una parte et Alexandrem carnificem de Lenna ex parte altera, videlicet quod predicti abbatissa et conventus concesserunt relaxaverunt et omnino de se et successoribus suis quietum clamaverunt imperpetuum predicto Alexandro omnia arreragia debita ac vendicanda de omni tempore preterito usque ad festum sancti Michaelis anno regni regis Edwardi filii regis Henrici vicesimo octavo, de una marca annualis redditus quam iidem abbatissa et conventus clamaverunt recepisse de una placea terre cum edificiis jacente in villa Lenn' Episcopi, scilicet prope ecclesiam sancte Margarete, inter terram Johannis filii Gilberti ex parte orientali et terram Petri carnificis ex parte occidentali in latitudine, et se extendit in longitudine a communi via (fo. 157v)[1] versus austrum usque ad terram Thome Astyn versus aquilonem, ita quod nec iidem abbatissa et conventus nec aliquis per eos seu pro eis de dictis arreragiis aliquid juris vel clamii exigere vel vendicare poterunt in posterum. Et predictus Alexander concedit pro se et heredibus suis vel suis assignatis solvere pro predicta placea terre ac distringi in predicta placea terre cum edificiis, tam infra domum quam extra, pro una marca annualis redditus recipienda de predicta placea terre per predictos abbatissam et conventum ac

---

[1] Heading *Leen.*

successores[1] eorum vel eorum certum attornatum ad quatuor anni terminos, scilicet ad Natale Domini tres solidos et quatuor denarios et ad festum Pasche tres solidos et quatuor denarios et ad nativitatem sancti Johannis Baptiste tres solidos et quatuor denarios et ad festum sancti Michaelis tres solidos et quatuor denarios, a tempore confectionis istius scripti usque ad finem mundi. In cuius rei testimonium huic scripto indentato partes alternatim sigilla sua apposuerunt. Hiis testibus etc.

220 *Acquittance by abbess Agnes [Ashfield] and the convent of Chatteris to the mayor and corporation of Lynn (Norf.) of 13s. 4d. (1 mark) of annual rent from their tenement in Lynn.*
fos. 157v–158r [Shortly after 29 Sept. 1425]

Acquietancia domine abbatisse maiori[2] et comunitati de Lenna per manus Johannis Kopnote.

Noverint universi per presentes nos Agnetem abbatissam monasterii de Chateriz et eiusdem loci conventum recepisse de maiore et communitate ville de Lenna, per manus Johannis Copnote burgencis Lenne predicte, tresdecim solidos et quatuor denarios sterlingorum in plenam solutionem cuiusdam annui redditus exeuntis[3] de tenemento dictorum maioris et communitatis in Lenna predicta quondam Hugonis (fo. 158r)[4] Folkard', de quibus quidem tresdecim[5] solidis et quatuor denariis pro anno elapso, videlicet a festo sancti Michaelis anno regni regis Henrici sexti tertio usque idem festum anno dicti regis quarto, fatemur nos esse solutos dictosque maiorem et communitatem inde fore quietos per presentes sigillo nostro ad causas assignato signatas. Date etc.

221 *Confirmation by Hubert de Rye to Ralph, merchant, son of Agnes de Bircham of 40 acres of land with 3 crofts and foldage [in Bircham, (Norf.)], formerly held of Henry de Rye, father of Hubert; for 5s. 2d. annually and an aid of 1 mark 7½d.*
fo. 158r [c. 1162 × c. 1171]

---

1 MS *successessores*.
2 MS *mariori*.
3 *i* written over *e*.
4 Heading *Brecham*.
5 Followed by *s*, erased.

Carta Huberti de Ria Radulpho mercatori de quadraginta acris terre et tribus[1] croftis cum foldagia.

Hubertus de Rya omnibus hominibus Francis et Anglicis salutem. Sciant tam presentes quam futuri quod ego Hubertus de Rya dedi concessi huic[2] Radulpho[3] mercatori filio Agnetis de Brecham totam terram quam tenuit eo die quo Henricus de Rya pater meus fuit vivus et mortuus, xl[a] acras terre cum tribus croftis et cum[4] faldagia sua, reddendo inde annuatim pro libero servicio suo quinque solidos et ij denarios et ad auxilia ad marcam vij denarios et obolum pro omnibus consuetudinibus. Inde est quod volo et jubeo ut idem Radulphus et heredes sui totam terram predictam cum faldagia sua teneat de ⟨me⟩ et heredibus meis pro servicio prenominato, libere et honorifice et quiete sine calumpnia. Hii sunt testes Roginaldus de Toftes, Henricus clericus cum aliis etc.

Note. Henry de Rye died *c.* 1162; Hubert died *c.* 1171 (*Pipe R.* 7 Hen. II, p. 4; 8 Hen. II, p. 65; 18 Hen. II, p. 30; I. J. Sanders *English Baronies. A Study of their Origin and Descent* (Oxford, 1960) p. 53).

222 *Grant by Hubert de Rye to Richard [FitzNeal], archdeacon of Ely and treasurer, of Ralph de Bircham and gift of his tenement in Bircham (Norf.), for 1 gold coin and an annual rent of a pair of gilt spurs, price 6d., or 6d.*
fo. 158r–v [*c.* 1162 × 1188]

Carta Huberti de Rya Ricardo archidiacono Eliensi.

Hubertus de Rya omnibus hominibus suis Francis et Anglicis tam presentibus quam futuris s[alute]m.[5] Sciatis me dedisse et presenti carta mea con[firmass]e[6] Ricardo Eliensi archidiacono et d[omini regis the]saurario[7] Radulphum de Brecham hominem meum et totum (fo. 158v)[8] tenementum suum quod de me tenuit in Brecham, et omne jus quod in eo et in suis habui, de me et de heredibus meis[9] sibi et cui[10] in heredem facere voluerit hereditario jure tenenda,

---

1 Followed by *rodis*, expunged.
2 Followed by *adverso*, expunged.
3 Followed by large, black and red *B* on edge of outer margin.
4 Followed by *fadldach'*, expunged.
5 Hole 12 mm.
6 Hole 12 mm.
7 Hole 23 mm.
8 Heading *Brecham*.
9 Followed by *et*, expunged.

reddendo michi et heredibus[1] meis per annum unum par calcarum deauratorum precii sex denariorum vel sex denarios ad Pascha, pro omnibus serviciis et consuetudinibus ad me pertinentibus. Hanc autem[2] donationem et concessionem feci ei pro servicio et pro uno aureo quem michi dedit. Et ego affidavi ei, et Gerardus de Wechesham et Robertus de Hengham homines mei similiter affidaverunt precepto meo, quod ego hanc meam donationem firmiter tenebo. Quare volo quod predictus thesaurarius, et ille quem ipse de predicto tenemento heredem facere voluerit, libere honorifice et hereditarie predictam tenuram per prenominatum servicium teneant et possideant. Test' etc.

> Note. Richard FitzNeal was archdeacon of Ely from *c.* 1158–Dec. 1189 (*Fasti 1066–1300* ii, p. 50). He was also a canon of St Paul's and dean of Lincoln from 1184 until Dec. 1189 when he became bishop of London; he was treasurer from *c.* 1158–1196. This Hubert de Rye may be the Hubert in no. 221 or his son who came of age *c.* 1174 and died in 1187–8 (*Pipe R.* 20 Hen. II, p. 44; 34 Hen. II, p. 55).

223 *Grant by William of Ely, archdeacon of Cleveland, to Chatteris abbey, for the support of sick nuns in the infirmary, of Richard de Bircham and gift in free alms of his tenement in Bircham (Norf.), for an annual rent to the lord of the fee of a pair of gilt spurs, price 6d., or 6d.*
fos. 158v–159r [1201 × 1222]

Carta Willelmi de Ely abbatisse de Chatriz ad sustentationem etc.

Sciant etc. quod ego Willelmus de Ely archidiaconus Cliveland' dedi etc., pro anima mea et patris et matris mee et pro animabus antecessorum meorum et benefactorum et omnium fidelium defunctorum, in puram et perpetuam elemosinam Deo et ecclesie beate Marie de Chatriz et sanctimonialibus ibidem Deo servientibus, in auxilio ad sustentationem sanctimonialium in firmaria egrotantium, Ricardum de Brecham hominem meum et totum tenementum suum quod de [me tenu]it[3] in Brecham, et omne jus quod in eo [et suis habui],[4] sicut carta Ricardi London' episcopi testatur, per q[uam][5] idem episcopus michi confirmavit prefatum (fo. 159r)[6] Ricardum cum predicto tenemento, salvo servicio quod debetur domino fuudi, sicut in carta continetur quam memoratus episcopus

10 MS *quem*.
1 MS *hedredibus*, first *d* expunged.
2 Followed by *et*, expunged.
3 Hole 12 mm.
4 Hole 25 mm; supplied from no. 91, the other copy of the charter.
5 Damaged 3 mm.
6 Heading *Brecham*.

London' michi fecit, scilicet uno pari calcarum deauratorum precii vj denariorum vel pro sex denariis reddendis ad Pascha predicto domino et heredibus suis, pro omnibus se[rv]iciis[1] et consuetudinibus ad ipsum dominum vel heredes suos per[tin]entibus[2] etc. ut supra in carta domini Willelmi de Ely.

Note. Another copy of part of no. 91. For dating see no. 91n.

224 *Grant by Richard [FitzNeal], bishop of London, to William of Ely, treasurer, of Ralph de Bircham and gift of his tenement in Bircham (Norf.), for an annual rent to the chief lord of the fee of a pair of gilt spurs, price 6d., or 6d.*
fo. 159r–v [1196 × 10 Sept. 1198]

Carta domini Ricardi London' episcopi Willelmo de Ely domini regis thesaurario de Ricardo de Brecham etc.

Ricardus Dei gracia London' episcopus omnibus hominibus suis Francis et Anglicis tam presentibus quam futuris salutem in Domino. Sciatis nos dedisse et presenti carta mea confirmasse Willelmo de Ely domini regis thesaurario, pro servicio et homagio suo, Radulphum de Brecham hominem nostrum et totum tenementum suum quod de nobis tenuit in Brecham, et omne jus quod in eo et in suis habui, sicut carta Huberti de Ria testatur, per quam idem Hubertus nobis confirmavit prefatum Radulphum cum predicto tenemento, salvo servicio quod debetur capitali domino fuudi quod idem Hubertus constituit, sicut in prefata carta continetur, scilicet uno pari calcarum deauratorum precii vj denariorum vel pro sex denariis reddendis ad Pascha predicto domino et heredibus suis, pro omnibus serviciis et consuetudinibus ad ipsum dominum vel heredes suos pertinentibus. Tenebit itaque predictus Willelmus thesaurarius prefatum Radulphum cum tenemento predicto et heredes suos per prefatum servicium tota vita sua, et post decessum suum prefatum Radulphum cum heredibus suis et predicto tenemento donabit vel legabit cui vel quibus voluer[it] ...[3] tenendum jure hereditario. Et ut hec nostra [donatio][4] (fo. 159v)[5] robur optineat imposterum, eam presentis pagine testimonio et sigilli nostri munimene roboravimus. Hiis tesibus etc.

[1] Hole 4 mm.
[2] Hole 4 mm.
[3] Hole 10 mm.
[4] Hole 20 mm.
[5] Heading *Brecham*.

Note. Richard FitzNeal was bishop of London, 31 Dec. 1189–10 Sept. 1198; William of Ely was treasurer, 1196–1215.

225 *Agreement between abbess Mary de Shouldham and the convent of Chatteris and William Wimar, burgess of Lynn (Norf.), and Agnes his wife and William Chaumppaygne, burgess of Norwich (Norf.), and Joan his wife, whereby the abbess and convent acquitted them of the arrears of 5s. of annual rent from the lands and tenements formerly of Nicholas de Bircham in Bircham (Norf.), and they agreed that they and their heirs would pay the rent perpetually to the abbess and convent.*
fos. 159v–160r   At Chatteris, [Shortly after 29 Sept. 1317]

Quieta clamantia domine abbatisse super quibusdam arreragiis de tenemento quondam Nicholai Brecham.

Pateat universis per presentes quod ita convenit inter Mariam de Schuldam abbatissam de Chatriz et eiusdem loci conventum ex parte una, et Willelmum Wimar et Agnetem uxorem eius burgensem de Lenn' et Willelmum Chaump-paygne et Johannam uxorem eius burgensem[1] Norwyci ex parte altera, videlicet quod predicta abbatissa et conventus concesserunt relaxaverunt et omnino de se et successoribus suis quietum clamaverunt predictis Willelmo et Agneti uxori eius et Willelmo et Johanne uxori eius et eorum heredibus omnia arreragia debitaque quomodo vendicanda, de omni tempore preterito usque ad festum sancti Michaelis anno regni regis Edwardi filii regis Edwardi undecimo, de quinque solidatis annualis redditus quos eedem abbatissa et conventus clamav-erunt recepisse de omnibus terris et tenementis que quondam fuerunt Nicholai[2] de Brecham in Brecham, et que idem Nicholaus dictas[3] terras et tenementa per servicium prenominatum dictis abbatisse et conventui annuatim faciendum tenuit sibi et heredibus suis, ita quod eedem abbatissa et conventus nec aliquis per eos seu pro eis de predictis arreragiis aliquid juris vel clamii exigere vel vendicare poterunt in [poste]rum,[4] et predicti Willelmus et Agnes uxor [eius et Willelmus][5] et Johanna uxor eius concedunt, (fo. 160r)[6] pro se et heredibus suis vel suis assignatis, solvere predictos quinque solidos pro terris et tenementis supradictis predictis abbatisse et conventui et earum successoribus imperpet-

---

1 *Northwici* marginated before -*gensem*.
2 Final *i* written above expunged *o*.
3 MS *dicas*.
4 Hole 12 mm.
5 Hole 27 mm.
6 Heading *Pynchebec*.

uum, videlicet medietatem ad festum sancti Michaelis et aliam medietatem ad festum Pasche. Et si necesse fuerit per se vel per atturnatos suos in omnibus terris[1] et tenementis predictis distringere et districtiones captas retinere, contra vadium et plegium, quousque eisdem abbatisse et conventui vel earum successoribus satisfactum fuerit de predicto annuali redditu. In cuius rei testimonium huic scripto indentato partes alternatim sigilla sua apposuerunt. Dat' apud Chatriz etc.

226 *Grant by John son of Hugh de Bradehous to abbess Mabel [de Bancis] and the convent of Chatteris of an annual rent of 9s. 4d. owed by John son of Lambert de Bradhous for land in Pinchbeck (Lincs.), an annual rent of 6d. owed by Simon son of Joyce de Pekkesbregg' and an annual rent of 2d. owed by Reginald son of John Joyce of Fulney (Lincs.).*
fo. 160r–v [*s.* xiii² × 28 Sept. 1265]

Carta Johannis de Bradehowes de redditu ix solidorum et quatuor denariorum.

Omnibus Christi fidelibus ad quos presens scriptum pervenerit Johannes filius Hugonis de Bradehowes salutem. Noverit universitas vestra me dedisse concessisse et hac presenti carta mea confirmasse Deo et sancte Marie et domine Mabilie moniali de Chatriz et eiusdem loci conventui,[2] vel cui assignare voluerint, pro salute anime mee et antecessorum meorum in puram et perpetuam elemosinam redditum novem solidorum et quatuor denariorum, quem Johannes filius Lamberti de Bradehowes michi debuit per annum pro terra illa quam tenuit de me in Pincebec, scilicet ad festum sancti Michaelis duos solidos[3] et quatuor denarios, ad festum sancti Nicholai duos solidos et quatuor denarios, ad Pascha duos solidos et quatuor denarios et ad festum sancti Botolphi duos solidos et quatuor denarios, et redditum sex denariorum quem Simon filius [J]oecei[4] de Pekkesbregg' michi debuit per annum (fo. 160v),[5] scilicet ad festum sancti Nicholai,[6] et redditum duorum denariorum quem Roginaldus filius Johannis Jocei de Fulneyne michi debuit per annum, scilicet ad festum sancti Botolphi, tenendos et habendos de me et heredibus meis bene et in pace. Et ego

1 MS *terre.*
2 *i* interlined.
3 Interlined.
4 Hole 2 mm; first *e* unclear.
5 Heading *Lincolnie.*
6 MS *Nichs'*: the scribe may have miscopied *Michaelis.*

Johannes[1] et heredes mei warantizabimus defendemus et acquietabimus totum predictum redditum predicte domine Mabilie monialium de Chatriz et eiusdem loci conventui vel earum assignatis contra omnes homines imperpetuum. In huius rei testimonium presenti scripto sigillum meum apposui. Hiis testibus etc.

Note. For dating of abbess Mabel de Bancis see no. 100n.

227 *Grant by Hugh de Cranwell to Chatteris abbey of 10s. of rent in Lincoln, from the houses held by David son of Eilsus de Lincoln, on condition that Adelicia his daughter, a nun of Chatteris, should have this rent for her life and that her prebend should not be reduced on account of it; after her death it will remain to the abbey.*
fos. 160v–161r [*s.* xii[3] × 1188]

Carta Hugonis de Cornewellia abbatisse et conventui de Chateriz de redditu decem solidorum de certis domibus et dicitur quod fratres predicatores occupant domos illas.

Omnibus amicis suis et omnibus sancte matris ecclesie fidelibus tam presentibus quam futuris Hugo de Cranewellia salutem. Noverit universitas vestra me dedisse et concessisse Deo et sancte Marie et omnibus sanctis et ecclesie de Chatriz et monialibus ibidem Deo servientibus decem solidatos redditus in civitate Lincoln', scilicet domos illas quas David filius Eilsi de Lincoln' de me tenuit, ita dico quod Idelicia filia mea, que monialis est in predicta domo, hunc redditum habeat et teneat quamdiu vixerit, ut inde faciat quod voluerit. Et eo modo hunc redditum Adelicie filie mee in vita sua concessi, ut prebenda sua quam habet in domo de Chatriz in nullo propter hunc redditum ei comminuatur. Et[2] post obitum Adelicie ipsius volo ut iste redditus remaneat predictis monialibus in elimosinam perp[et]uam[3] liberam et solutam et quietam ab omni seculari servicio et exactione, pro salute anime mee et pro [re]medio[4] omnium peccatorum meorum, et ut consors et particeps (fo. 161r)[5] efficiar omnium beneficiorum et earum que fuerint in domo de Chatriz. Et dominos meos fratres de Templo precor quatinus pro amore Dei istam elemosinam meam manuteneant et ratam esse faciant huius donationis mee, et testes sunt frater Henricus de Aren[is],[6] frater

---

[1] *e* interlined.
[2] MS *E*.
[3] Hole 3 mm.
[4] Damaged 3 mm.
[5] Heading *Lincoln' Huntyngdon'*.
[6] Unclear 3 mm.

Robertus filius[1] Ricardi, frater Gilbertus de Ogeresta[n],[2] frater [Ba]ldewinus Augustinus sacerdos de Scapewic, Turstanus clericus de Templo qui hanc cartam scripsit, cum multis aliis.

> Note. Gilbert de Oggerston was present at the making of a composition on 29 Aug. 1176 and he was a member of the chapter of the London Temple *c.* 1165–80. In all likelihood this grant was made before 1188 because in 1188 Gilbert confessed to embezzling money from the tithe he was collecting for the crusade and was punished by the master of the London Temple (*Records of the Templars in England in the Twelfth Century* ed. B. A. Lees (British Academy, 1935) pp. lviii–lix, 224–5, 246–7).

228 *Power of attorney from abbess Mabel de Bancis and the convent of Chatteris appointing Jocelin, their serjeant, to manage and collect their rent in Lincoln.*
fo. 161r [*s.* xiii^2 × 28 Sept. 1265]

Littera atturnata abbatisse et conventus pro redditu in Lincoln'.

Omnibus ad quos presens scriptum per[venerit]^3 M(abel) de B(ancis) divina permissione abbatissa de Chatriz et eiusdem loci conventus salutem eternam in Domino. Noveritis nos constituisse Jocelinum dilectum et fidelem servientem nostrum procura[tor]em^4 et attornatum nostrum ad ordinandum et disponendum de redditu nostro quem habemus Lincoln', prout viderit melius expedire et ad utilitatem domus nostre cedere, et ad pentionem dicti redditus nomine nostro percipiendam, ratum et gratum habiturum quicquid super predictis predecessor nostra^5 duxerit faciendum. In huius rei testimonium sigilla nostra presenti scripto patenti fecimus etc.

> Note. Jocelin also occurs as a witness in no. 240, dated 1239 × *s.* xiii^3, therefore this abbess is probably either Mary de Sancto Claro or Mabel de Bancis (for dating see no. 100n).

229 *Confirmation by abbess Mary de Shouldham and the convent of Chatteris to Richard, cobbler, of Huntingdon of the croft in Huntingdon given to him by Robert son of Hamo and held of the abbey for 6d. annually.*
fo. 161r–v [30 Sept. 1300 × 1347]

---

1 Followed by *Ricri'*, cancelled.
2 MS unclear 2 mm.
3 Unclear 10 mm.
4 Unclear 5 mm.
5 MS unclear: seems to read *predec' nr'*.

Carta abbatisse de uno[1] crofto cum pertinenciis in Huntyngdon.

Notum sit omnibus quod nos Maria de Schuldam abbatissa de Chatriz et totus conventus noster inspeximus cartam feaffmenti quam Robertus filius Hamonis fecerunt[2] Ricardo le cobeler' de Huntyngdon' de uno͑ crofto cum pertinenciis in villa de Huntyngdon' in parochia sancti Andree, quod jacet inter terram quondam Matill' Fyn' ex una parte et terram Johannis Stertelowe ex altera, tenendum sibi et heredibus suis et[3] assignatis de nobis et successoribus nostris, per servicium sex denariorum per annum (fo. 161v)[4] nobis reddendorum, quod donum nos dicti abbatissa et conventus noster pro nobis et successoribus nostris predicto Ricardo et heredibus[5] suis assignatis confirmamus imperpetuum. In cuius rei testimonium parti penes dictum Ricardum residenti sigillum suum commune capituli nostri et isti parti penes nos residenti sigillum dicti Ricardi est appensum.

Note. For dating of Mary de Shouldham see no. 66n. Matilda Fyn occurs in 14 Edward II (1320–1) in a final concord (*Hunts. Fines*, p. 43).

230 *Agreement between abbess Mary de Shouldham and the convent of Chatteris and Robert Fin of Huntingdon, following a plea before the court of common pleas, whereby Robert acknowledges that he holds 3 tofts in Huntingdon of the abbey for 30d. annually, for which acknowledgement the abbey granted to him 18d. of rent from a toft in Huntingdon; Robert has paid the rent of 30d. with the arrears.*
fos. 161v–162r   At Chatteris, 28 March 1306.

Finalis concordia inter abbatissam de Chatriz et Robertum Fyn de tribus toftis.

Notum sit omnibus quod, cum placitum fuit inter dominam Mariam de Schuldam abbatissam de Chatriz et me Robertum Fyn de Huntyngdon' de tribus toftis cum pertinenciis in villa predicta, coram Radulpho de Hengham et sociis suis justiciariis de banco, per breve domini regis, per quod dicta abbatissa et eiusdem loci conventus predictas tres toftas ut jus suum et ecclesie sue petierunt, per formam statuti inde provisi, eo quod dictus Robertus in faciendo servicia inde debita et consueta dicte abbatisse et conventui eiusdem ante confectionem istius scripti per biennium cessavi, unde ad dictum placitum ad nichillandum

[1] Followed by *co*, expunged.
[2] Plural verb; name omitted?
[3] Followed by *suis*, expunged.
[4] Heading *Huntyndon'*.
[5] Followed by *et*, expunged.

inter dictam abbatissam et eiusdem loci conventum ex parte una et me dictum
Robertum Fin ex altera parte, ita convenit scilicet quod ego dictus Robertus
cognosco me esse tenentem dictarum abbatisse et conventus de predictis tribus
toftis, de quibus una placea jacet in vico pontis que dudum vocari solebat Aula
Teculata et jacet juxta domum Rogeri le Lestere, et secunda placea jacet ad
oppositum carceris inter terram quondam Margerie Aryng' de eodem feodo et
terram dicti Roberti Fyn, et tertia placea jacet ad parvum pontem juxta feodum
vestrum quod Ricardus le cobeler' de vobis tenet, faciendo (fo. 162r)[1] inde per
annum antedictis abbatisse et conventui ego et heredes mei vel mei assignati pro
predictis tribus toftis pacifice et sine calumpnia de eisdem tenendis servicium
triginta denariorum ad terminos censuales. Pro hac autem recognitione dicte
abbatissa et conventus michi remiserunt decem et octo denarios redditus quos
recipere solebant et debebant de tofto illo jacente ex opposito carceris, ut patet
supra, ultra redditum triginta denariorum antedictorum. Et ego dictus Robertus
in confectione istius scripti redditum triginta denariorum, una cum arreragiis a
retro existentibus, antedictis abbatisse et conventui plenarie persolvi. Et volo
pro me et heredibus meis seu pro assignatis quod quandocumque dictus redditus
amodo ob defectum heredum meorum vel successorum incurratur, quod ex
tunc predicte abbatissa et conventus me heredes seu assignatos distringant ubicumque voluerint in predictis tribus toftis donec de predictis triginta denariis
eisdem plenarie satisfiat. In cuius rei testimonium huic scripto[2] in modum
cirographi confecto tam dicta domina abbatissa quam ego Robertus antedictus
alternatim sigilla nostra apposuimus. Datum aput Chatriz die lune in crastino
Palmarum anno regni regis Edwardi filii regis Henrici tricesimo quarto.

Note. Ralph de Hengham was chief justice of the court of common pleas from 1301–1309.

231 *Notification and exemplification by Roger son of Basilia de Hemingford of the
gift by abbess Mary de Sancto Claro and the convent of Chatteris to him of all their
land in Hemingford Grey (Hunts.), for 1 mark annually and scutage of 40s.*
fos. 162r–163r [s. xiii² × 28 Sept. 1265, date of gift]

Dimissio domine abbatisse de certa terra in Hemyngford'.

Omnibus Christi fidelibus hoc scriptum visuris vel audituris Rogerus filius
Basil' de Hemyngford' salutem in Domino. Noverit universitas vestra me re-

---

1 Heading *Hemyngford'*.
2 Followed by *sigillum*, expunged.

cepisse de abbatissa et conventu de Chatriz totam terram cum[1] pertinenciis
quam habuerunt in Estmingford' in hec verba: Omnibus Christi fidelibus ad
quos presens scriptum pervenerit Maria de Sancto Claro abbatissa de Chatriz
totusque eiusdem loci conventus salutem in Domino. Noverit (fo. 162v)[2] universitas vestra nos unanimi assensu dedisse concessisse et hac presenti carta mea
confirmasse Rogero filio Basil' de Hemyngford' pro homagio et servicio suo
totam terram cum pertinenciis quam habuimus in Esthemnygford', habendam
et tenendam predicto Rogero et heredibus suis de se et uxore sua sibi desponsata
venientibus de nobis et succestricibus nostris in feodo imperpetuum, excepta
domo religiosa alia quam nostra, libere quiete bene et in pace, reddendo inde
annuatim nobis et succestricibus nostris unam marcam sterlingorum, videlicet
ad Pascha quadraginta denarios, ad nativitatem sancti Johannis Baptiste xl[a]
denarios, ad festum sancti Michaelis xl denarios et ad festum sancti Andree
quadraginta denarios, pro omnibus serviciis consuetudinibus exactionibus et
demandis nobis et ecclesie nostre de Chatriz spectantibus, salvo servicio domini
regis, scilicet ad scutagium quadraginta solidorum[3] ad plus plus ad minus minus.
Predictus etiam Rogerus et heredes sui acquietabunt et defendent propriis sumptibus predictam terram cum omnibus[4] de[5] serviciis,[6] de sectis, auxiliis, turnis
vicecometum et dominorum et de omnibus aliis quacunque de causa pervenerint
contra omnes mortales imperpetuum. Nos vero et succestrices nostre totam
predictam terram cum pertinenciis predicto Rogero et heredibus suis de se et
uxore sua sibi desponsata venientibus warantizabimus contra omnes gentes
imperpetuum per predictum servicium, excepta domo religiosa alia quam
nostra. Et si forte contingat quod ego Rogerus vel heredes mei predictum
redditum in aliquo termino predictis monialibus non solverimus, bene liceat
predictis abbatisse et conventui per balivos suos me et heredes[7] (fo. 163r)[8] meos
distringere per averia nostra in feodo suo in Hemmyngford' inventa, et ea
fugare quo voluerint et tenere quousque illis de arreragiis redditus sui plenarie
satisfecerimus. Et ne ego Rogerus vel aliquis heredum meorum contra hanc

---

[1] Interlined.
[2] Heading *Hemyngford'*.
[3] Followed by space, 43 mm.
[4] Followed by *pertinenciis*, cancelled.
[5] Ins. marg.
[6] Followed by space, 17 mm.
[7] Followed by catchwords, *meos distringere*.
[8] Heading *Chatriz*.

formam prescriptam in aliquo tempore[1] venire poterimus, presenti scripto pro
me et pro heredibus meis sigillum meum apposui. Hiis testibus domino Philippo, Hugone de Empigton', Michaele Basset de eadem et multis aliis.

> Note. Hugh de Impington occurs in a final concord in 35 Henry III (1250–1) and Michael
> Basset occurs in another in 37 Henry III (1252–3) (*Cambs. Fines*, pp. 32–3). For the dating of
> abbess Mary de Sancto Claro see no. 100n.

232 *Confirmation by abbess M. and the convent of Chatteris, through the inter-*
cession of Ralph de Barley, of the rent of 5s. annually in Hemingford (Hunts.) which
Agnes, a former abbess, had assigned to the alms-house, namely half of the 10s.
annually which Isabel de Indyngword' had given to the abbey; for which Ralph gave
and quitclaimed to the abbey 10 acres of land which he held of them in Foxton and
Barrington.
fo. 163r [*s.* xiii[2] × 28 Sept. 1265]

Conventio abbatisse et conventus de Chatrix de quinque solidis elemosinarie.

Omnibus Christi fidelibus ad quos presens scriptum pervenerit[2] M. dicta domina de Chatriz totusque eiusdem loci conventus salutem in Domino. Noveritis
nos concessisse et hac presenti carta[3] nostra confirmasse, per intercessionem
Radulphi de Berlee et pro salute anime sue, domui elimosina[rie] nostre de
Chatriz [reddi]tum quinque so[lidorum quem] Agnes quondam d[omina de]
Chatriz antecessor [nostri] dicte[4] domui elimosinarie assignavit, scilicet medietatem decem solidorum quos annuatim percepimus in Hemyngford' de dono
domine Isabelle de Indyngword',[5] tenendam et habendam imperpetuum et
dictos quinque solidos ad quatuor terminos anni usuales percipiendos annuatim.
Pro hac autem concessione et carte mee confirmatione, dedit nobis et quietum
clamavit dictus Radulphus de Berlee decem acras terre quas de nobis tenuit in
campis de Foxton' et de Barenton'. Et ut hec concessio rata et inconcussa permaneat, presens scriptum sigilli nostri conventualis appositione roboravimus.
Hiis testibus etc.

---

1 *vide aliam cartam pro Hemyngford infra folio xx[f°]*, marginated after *tempore*; edge of folio
  lacking.
2 MS *perverenerint.*
3 Followed by *mea*, expunged.
4 *d[om]ui ... dicte*, ins. marg.; words and letters have been supplied where the edge of the folio
  is lacking.
5 Or possibly *Judyngword'.*

Note. Ralph de Barley occurs in 1239 × *s.* xiii[3] (no. 240) and in *s.* xiii[1] × 6 Aug. 1254 (no. 17); he also occurs with abbess Mabel de Bancis *s.* xiii[2] × 28 Sept. 1265 (no. 74). The abbess in this confirmation is probably either Mabel de Bancis or Mary de Sancto Claro (see no. 100n).

233 *Quitclaim by John Vivien of Chatteris to Alexander de Barley and Hamo his brother of 2 butts of land and a meadow [in Chatteris].*
fo. 163r–v [*s.* xiii[2–3]]

Quieta clamantia Johannis Vivien de una butta terre cum pertinenciis.

Noverint universi presens scriptum visuris vel audituris quod ego Johannes Vivien de Chatriz concessi et (fo. 163v)[1] quietum clamavi pro me et heredibus meis Alexandro de Berle et Hamoni fratri suo et heredibus eorum omne jus et clamium quod habeo vel habere potui in una butta terre cum pertinenciis que jacet in fossa de Elmene juxta terram Rodulphi[2] de Berlee, que data fuit eidem Rodulpho in excambiis pro una alia butta que jacet in Elmene, que abuttat super terram Katerine de Coveneye[3] ex una parte et terram Custancie Bleysie ex altera parte, et in toto prato quod pertinebat Henrico patri meo in Toft' prout in carta ab Henrico patre meo eidem Rodulpho concessa continetur, et[4] in[5] una butta terre cum pertinenciis in campo de Elmene quam dictus Rodulphus dedit Henrico Vivien patri meo in excambiis, quam dictus Henricus Vivien pater meus dedit et concessit Cistillie[6] uxori predicti Rodulphi de Berlee, reddendo inde annuatim predicta Cistilia et heredes sui dicto Henrico Vivien et heredibus suis vel assignatis unum quadrantem annuatim ad festum sancti Michaelis pro omni servicio, seculari servicio et demanda, prout in carta a dicto Henrico patri meo dicte Cistillie concessa continetur. In cuius rei testimonium presens scriptum quiete clamationis sigilli mei[7] munimine roboravi. Hiis testibus domino Rodulpho vicario, Rodulpho de Karysseye, Gilberto de Linton', Johanni de Witcham, Johanni Broun et multis aliis.

Note. John Vivien, son of Henry, occurs in *s.* xiii[2] × 1291 (no. 275). Ralph de Barley is a witness in 1239 × *s.* xiii[3] (no. 240) and occurs *s.* xiii[1] × 6 Aug. 1254 (no. 17); Katherine de Coveney occurs *s.* xiii[2–3] (no. 24).

1 Heading *Chatriz*.
2 Corr. marg., MS *Roberti*.
3 *ve* interlined.
4 Followed by *sc*, expunged and cancelled.
5 MS *a'*.
6 Corr. marg., MS *Eistillie*.
7 Followed by *impressione*, expunged.

234 *Gift by Robert Baldock of Chatteris and Alice his wife to Gilbert son of Gil-*
bert de Litton of Chatteris and Agnes his wife of 4 selions of land with headlands of
meadow and 1 acre of meadow in Chatteris, for 30s. in advance.
fos. 163v–164v [1290 × s. xiv[1]]

Carta Roberti Baldok de iiij selionibus et una acra prati cum capitibus prati.

Sciant presentes et futuri quod ego Robertus Baldolk de Chatriz et Alicia uxor
mea dedimus concessimus et hac p[res]enti[1] carta nostra confirmavimus Gilberto filio G[ilber]ti[2] de Littone de Chatriz et Agneti (fo. 164r)[3] uxori eius et
heredibus ipsius Gilberti quatuor selliones terre cum capitibus prati ad eandem
terram adjacentibus et unam acram prati cum pertinenciis in villo et territorio
de Chatriz, unde tres selliones terre cum capitibus prati adjacentibus jacent in
campo qui vocatur Horingslade inter terram predicti Gilberti ex utraque parte,
et una cellio terre jacet in campo qui vocatur Horsethefeld' inter terram quondam Warini de Insula et pratum dicti Gilberti, et tres rode prati jacent super
Wenneye inter pratum dicti Gilberti et pratum quondam Warini de Insula, et
una roda prati jacet super Wenneye inter pratum abbatis de Rameseye et pratum
abbatisse de Ch[atriz][4] quod fuit Roberti le Noreys et unum caput ab[uttat][5]
super Cotestede Henrici de Contennham, h[abendas][6] et ten[endas][7] dictis
Gilberto et Agneti et heredibus ipsius Gilberti et assigna[tis],[8] et cuicumque
predictas quatuor seliones terre cum capitibus prati adjacentibus et predictam
acram prati cum omnibus pertinenciis suis dare vendere[9] legare vel assignare
voluerit, libere quiete in feodo et hereditarie, faciendo inde capitalibus dominis
feodi servicia debita et consueta. Et ego predictus Robertus et Alicia uxor mea et
heredes nostri warantizabimus et defendemus predictas quatuor seliones terre
cum capitibus prati adjacentibus et predictam acram prati [cum][10] omnibus
pertinenciis suis dictis Gilberto et Agnetis et heredibus ipsius G[ilber]ti[11] et

---

1 Damaged 4 mm.
2 Damaged 9 mm.
3 Heading *Chateriz.*
4 Hole 7 mm.
5 Hole at right hand side of folio.
6 Damaged 7 mm.
7 Unclear 4 mm; followed by hole at right hand side of folio.
8 Hole at right hand side of folio.
9 Repeated and expunged.
10 Unclear 5 mm.
11 Damaged 5 mm.

assignatis, sicut supradictum est, contra om[nes] ...[1] gente[s][2] imperpetuum. Pro hac autem concessione donatione et presentis carte nostre confirmatione, dederunt nobis dicti Gilbertus et Agnes[3] triginta solidos sterlingorum premanibus. Et ut hec nostra donatio concessio et presentis carte nostre confirmatio perpetue firmitatis robur optineat, (fo. 164v)[4] presentem cartam sigilli nostri munumine roboravimus. Hiis testibus Henrico de Cotenham, Alexandro de Horseheth' de Chatriz, Radulpho de Kareseye de eadem, Petro de Novo Foro et multis aliis.

Note. Robert Baldock occurs in 1272 and Alexander de Horseheath in 1271 and 1289 (Ault ed. *Ramsey Court Rolls*, pp. 263, 267, 279); Ralph de Kersey occurs in 1276 and 1294 (Cambridge, Trinity College Archives, Foxton 1, rott. 1–2).

235 *Gift in free alms by Robert de Roseby to Chatteris abbey of 5 acres of land in Elm.*
fo. 164v [s. xiii[1-3]]

Carta Roberti de Rosebi de quinque acris terre in Pepirfeld'.

Sciant[5] presentes et futuri quod ego Robertus de Boseby[6] dedi concessi et presenti carta mea confirmavi Deo et ecclesie sancte Marie et omnium sanctorum de Chatriz et eiusdem loci monialibus, pro salute anime mee et anime Chastanee uxoris mee et omnium antecessorum meorum, quinque acras terre in campo qui vocatur Pepyrfeld' in villa de Elm, habendas [et t]enendas[7] in liberam puram et perpetuam elemosinam [q]uietas[8] et absolutas de me et heredibus meis imperpetuum. Et ego et heredes mei warantizabimus totam predictam terram cum pertinenciis predicte ecclesie de Chatriz et monialibus memoratis et acquietabimus[9] de omnibus secularibus serviciis consuetudinibus et demandis erga omnes homines et feminas imperpetuum de residuo terre nostre in Elm. Et ut hec mea donatio concessio et carte mee confirmatio sit firma[10] et stabilis imperpetuum, huic scripto sigillum meum apposui. Hiis testibus Stephano de

1 Hole 12 mm.
2 Hole 2 mm.
3 MS *Agnet'*.
4 Heading *Elm Burewelle*.
5 *[E]lm* marginated before *Sciant*.
6 Recte *Roseby*: see no. 98.
7 Hole 3 mm.
8 Hole in left hand side of folio.
9 Corr. from *acquietatabimus*; *-mus* interlined.
10 Ins. marg.

Marisco, Henrico de Walpol, Matheo Christiani, Ricardo de Melkesham, Willelmo de Sculham et multis aliis.

Note. See also no. 98, the confirmation of this gift by Agnes de Roseby, daughter of Robert. Richard de Melksham and William de Sculham occur in final concords in 14 Henry III (1229–30) and 18 Henry III (1233–4) respectively (*Cambs. Fines*, pp. 14, 17).

236 *Surrender by Simon, parson of Cranfield (Beds.), to Chatteris abbey of all the land he held with men and with all his rights in Burwell.*
fos. 164v–165r [*s.* xii[4] × *s.* xiii[2]]

Sciant[1] omnes homines[2] ad quos presens scriptum pervenerit quod ego Si[m]on[3] persona de Cramfeud' divine caritatis [intuitu][4] reddidi domui de Chatriz totam terram quam tenui[5] in[6] villa de Burewelle cum hominibus et aliis pertinenciis, similiter cum omni jure meo in eadem villa. Et ut hec donatio in posterum nulla fraudis interventione per me vel per meos posset revoca/ri (fo. 165r)[7] in irritum, sigilli mei impressionem huic resignationi in testimonium apposui. Hiis testibus etc.

Note. The dating is based solely on the language of the document.

237 *Gift by Henry son of Walter de Barrington to Warin his younger brother of all his land with a messuage in Barrington, held of the abbess of Chatteris, for 4s. annually to the abbess of Chatteris.*
fo. 165r [*c.* 1253 × 1290]

Carta Henrici filii Walteri Warino fratri[8] suo de certa terra.

Sciant presentes[9] et futuri quod ego Henricus filius Walteri de Barenton' dedi concessi et hac presenti carta mea confirmavi Warino[10] meo fratri juniori totam

---

1 The text begins on the line immediately following the last line of the previous charter; there is no rubricated heading.
2 *omnes homines* ins. marg.
3 Hole 3 mm.
4 Hole 13 mm.
5 *Burewelle*, in red, marginated before *tenui*.
6 Followed by *villa domo in*, expunged.
7 Heading *Barenton'*.
8 MS *fatri*.
9 Corr. from *presenti*.
10 Followed by *filio*, expunged.

illam terram[1] quam teneo in villa de Barenton' et campis, cum mesuagio dicte terre pertinente, de abbatissa de Chatriz pro homagio et servicio suo, tenendam et habendam totam terram prenominatam cum mesuagio et cum omnibus suis pertinenciis de me et heredibus meis et assignatis sibi et heredibus suis et suis assignatis, et cuicumque vel quibuscumque et quandocumque totam prenomin- atam terram dare legare vendere vel assignare voluerit, libere quiete bene et in pace et hereditarie, excepto loco religioso et judaismo, reddendo inde annuatim abbatisse de Chatriz et successoribus suis ipse et heredes sui et sui assignati quatuor solidos argenti ad quatuor anni terminos, videlicet ad festum sancti Michaelis xij denarios,[2] ad Natale Domini xij denarios et ad Pascha xij denarios et ad festum natale sancti Johannis Baptiste xij denarios, pro omnibus secul- aribus serviciis consuetudinibus exactionibus et demandis, salvo servicio domini regis, quantum pertinet ad tantam[3] terram de feodo eodem in eadem villa. Ego autem predictus Henricus et heredes mei et mei assignati warantizabimus ac- quietabimus et defendemus totam prenominatam terram cum omnibus suis pertinenciis dicto Warino et heredibus suis et suis assignatis, sicut predictum est, contra omnes mortales imperpetuum. Et ut hec mea donatio et warantizatio et c[arte][4] mee confirmatio rata et stabilis permaneat, huic p[res]enti[5] scripto sigil- lum meum apposui. Hiis testibus etc. (fo. 165v)[6]

> Note. Warin de Barrington I fl. *c.* 1220; Warin de Barrington II held land in Barrington *c.* 1253–*c.* 1307 (*VCH Cambs.* v, p. 149). The language of this gift suggests that the recipient is probably Warin de Barrington II.

238 *Gift in free alms by Aubrey son of Eustace de Madingley to Chatteris abbey of 8 selions of land and 1 rood of meadow in Madingley, for 40s.*
fo. 165v [*s.* xiii[1-3]]

Carta Albrici filii Eustachii de viij ⟨seliones⟩ terre et una roda.

Sciant presentes et futuri quod ego Albrig' filius Eustachii de Maddyngle dedi in liberam et perpetuam et puram elemosinam sancte Marie ecclesie de Chatriz et sanctis monialibus ibidem Deo servientibus, pro salute anime mee et anteces- sorum meorum, viij seliones terre de feodo meo in Maddynglee et unam rodam

---

1 Ins. marg.
2 Followed by *solidos*, expunged.
3 Corr. marg., *totam* expunged.
4 Damaged 5 mm.
5 Hole 2 mm.
6 Heading *Maddynglee*.

prati, scilicet vij seliones juxta terram prioris de Bernewelle ad Sigares Broke, et unum seillium ad Litlebureshenet juxta terram Alicie filie Rogeri senescalli, et unam rodam prati juxta pratum Rogeri,[1] tenenda libere et quiete ab omni seculari servicio et exactione, ita quod cetere terre mee acquietabunt illas terras tam versus regem quam versus dominos in omnibus serviciis, et[2] ego et heredes mei warantizabimus predictam terram predicte ecclesie contra omnes homines. Et pro hac donatione et warantizatione mea dedit michi iam dictus conventus xl solidos[3] de bonis eiusdem ecclesie. Et ut hec mea donatio et concessio firma et stabilis imperpetuum permaneat, hoc scriptum sigilli mei appositione communivi. Testibus Ewarardo, Rogero, Radulpho, capellanis de Chatriz; Thoma persona de Burwelle, Waltero persona de Haslyngfeld' et aliis.

Note. In 1279, John son of William owed scutage to the heirs of Aubrey son of Eustace for land in Madingley (*Rot. Hund.* ii, p. 447).

239 *Gift in free alms by R. to Chatteris abbey of 5 acres of land and ½ acre of meadow in Madingley.*
fos. 165v–166r [1196 × Aug. 1215]

Carta alia de 5 acris et dimidia acra prati.

Sciant presentes et futuri quod ego R.[4] dedi concessi et hac carta mea confirmavi Deo[5] ecclesie beate Marie de Chatriz et monialibus ibidem Deo servientibus intuitu [c]a[rita]tis,[6] pro animabus patris mei et matris mee[7] et [omnium ante]cessorum[8] meorum et pro salute anime mee, quinque [acras terr]e[9] et dimidiam acram prati cum omnibus pertinenciis suis [in vi]lla[10] de Maddynglee, scilicet quinque rodas terre (fo. 166r)[11] in[12] dominica crofta mea juxta terram J. filii Roberti, et unam acram in Morolwesdale juxta terram que[13] fuit Hugonis filii

---

1 Followed by space, 18 mm.
2 Followed by *her'*, an error apparently arising through *et heredes* later in the sentence.
3 Interlined.
4 Followed by space, 17 mm.
5 Followed by *et*, cancelled.
6 Unclear 10 mm.
7 Corr. from *mei*.
8 Hole 12 mm.
9 Damaged 11 mm.
10 Damaged 7 mm.
11 Heading *Kyngeston*.
12 Preceded by *te*, expunged.
13 MS *qui*.

Rogeri, et unam rodam que tendit versus pratum juxta terram que fuit Eustachii filii Willelmi, et unam dimidiam acram que vocatur F. Pockedeha...ke[1] juxta terram Eustachii filii Willelmi, et unam rodam que tendit versus Bernolues-dychs[2] juxta terram Eustachii filii Willelmi, et unam dimidiam acram que est in Musemere[3] juxta terram que fuit Gunware, et unam rodam que tendit versus Aschwieshevvedland juxta terram Ricardi Haked, et unam dimidiam acram que tendit versus Litlewellebrot' juxta terram Yvonis de Cantabrig', et unam dimidiam acram super montem qui vocatur Clynt[4] juxta terram prioris de Berne-welle, et unam dimidiam acram prati que est in Mersse propinquiore[5] ville de Maddynglee, que jacet inter prata Gilleberti filii Ricardi et Yvonis de Cantabr', tenendas et habendas in puram et perpetuam elemosinam, liberas et quietas imperpetuum ab omni seculari servicio et exactione. Has vero terras ego et heredes mei tenemur warantizare predicte ecclesie contra omnes homines et omnes feminas. His testibus Willelmo domini regis thesaurario, Alano de Sche-pereya, Warino de Barenton' et aliis.

> Note. Warin de Barrington fl. *c.* 1220; Alan son of Alan de Shepreth held the manor of de la Hayes in Foxton by 1200 (*VCH Cambs.* v, p. 149; viii, p. 168). William of Ely was treasurer 1196–Aug. 1215.

240 *Grant by Beatrice formerly wife of Jolanus de Bradhous to Chatteris abbey, for the maintenance of a candle in Chatteris at the mass of St Mary, of 4s. of annual rent in Kingston, collected from John son of Jordan.*
fo. 166r–v [1239 × s. xiii[3]]

Carta Beatricis de redditu quatuor solidorum.

Sciant presentes et futuri quod ego Beatriz, que quon[dam][6] fui uxor Jollani de Bradehouus, in lib[era v]iduet[ate][7] mea constituta, dedi concessi et hac pre[senti carta][8] mea confirmavi Deo et beate Marie et monialibus de Chatriz ibidem Deo servientibus, pro salute anime (fo. 166v)[9] mee et antecessorum meorum, quatuor solidatas annui redditus cum pertinenciis in Kyngestun', anuatim per-

---

1 Hole 7 mm.
2 Second *b* in *Bernoluesbychs* corr. marg. to *d.*
3 MS has five minims before -*semere*; *Musemere* is only one of several possible readings.
4 Corr. marg., MS *Elent.*
5 Final *i* corr. to *e.*
6 Damaged 5 mm.
7 Damaged 20 mm.
8 Hole 18 mm.
9 Heading *Foxton'.*

cipiendas de Johanne filio Jordanis et heredibus suis, cum homagio ipsius Johannis et heredum suorum et cum omnibus que ad predictum homagium pertinere poterunt aut debeant in releviis escaetis wardis, sine ullo retenemento ad me vel ad heredes meos pertinente, ad duos terminos, scilicet ad festum sancti Michaelis duos solidos et ad Pascha duos solidos, habendas et tenendas predictis monialibus et earum successricibus de me et heredibus meis imperpetuum in liberam puram et perpetuam elemosinam, ad sustentationem unius cerei in Chatriz ad missam beate Marie. Et ego Beatriz et heredes mei warantizabimus acquietabimus et defendemus predictas quatuor solidatas annui redditus cum omnibus pertinenciis, ut supradictum est, predictis monialibus et earum successricibus contra omnes mortales imperpetuum. Et ut hec mea donatio concessio et presentis carte mee confirmatio robur optineat perpetuum, presenti carte sigillum meum apposui. Hiis testibus Hugone de Impetun' tunc senescallo domus de Chatriz, Thoma de Bancis, Gilberto[1] de Hardlestune, Eustachio de Bancis, Gocelin' tunc serviente domus de Chatriz, Alano le Fraunceys, Rogero Luvel, Radulpho de Berlee, Radulpho filio suo, Willelmo de Foresta et aliis.

Note. Beatrice occurs with her husband, Jolanus de Bradehous, in a final concord in 24 H III (1239–40) (*Cambs. Fines*, p. 22); she occurs in another on 1 May 1250 as the former wife of Jolanus (*Final Concords of the County of Lincoln From the Feet of Fines Preserved in the Public Record Office A.D. 1244–1272* (Lincoln Record Society xvii, 1920) p. 59). See also no. 111.

241 *Gift by Richard de Sprotford of Kingston to Ralph de Cardington, parson of Barley (Herts.), Gilbert Bernard and Edmund Dreng ('Breng'') of all his lands and tenements in Foxton and Shepreth, formerly of J., smith, of Foxton.*
fos. 166v–167r At Foxton, 22 Aug. 1355

Carta Ricardi de Sprotford de terris suis in Foxton' et Scheperede.

[Sciant][2] presentes et futuri quod ego Ricardus de Sprot[ford d]e[3] Kyngeston' dedi concessi et hac presenti carta mea confirmavi domino Radulpho de Carleton' persone ecclesie de Berlee, Gilberto Bernard' (fo. 167r)[4] et Edmundo Breng' omnia terras et tenementa mea in villa[5] et in campis de Foxton' et Scheper' que quondam fuerunt J. le smyth' de Foxton', habenda et tenenda omnia predicta terras et tenementa cum omnibus suis pertinenciis prefatis

1 MS *Gilbrerto*, first *r* expunged.
2 Hole 19 mm.
3 Hole 13 mm.
4 Heading *Berlee*.
5 Followed by *d*, expunged.

domino Radulpho, Gilberto et Edmundo heredibus et assignatis eorum de capitalibus dominis feodi, per servicia inde debita et consueta imperpetuum. Et
predictus Ricardus et heredes mei omnia predicta terras et tenementa cum
omnibus suis pertinenciis predicto domino Radulpho, Gilberto et Edmundo
heredibus et assignatis eorum contra omnes gentes warantizabimus imperpetuum. In cuius rei testimonium huic presenti carte sigillum meum apposui. Hiis
testibus J. Stacy, W. Goudlok, Ricardo Ingelond', Roginaldo Burel, J. Goudlok
et aliis. Data apud Foxton' die sabbati proximo post festum Assumptionis beate
Marie virginis anno regni regis Edwardi tertii post conquestum vicesimo nono.

242 *Confirmation by Theobald son of Fulk to Alan his son of the land in Barley
(Herts.), formerly of Theobald, Alan's brother, with the advowson of the church, for
the service of a half and a sixth of a knight.*
fo. 167r–v [s. xii[4]]

Carta Theobaldi de certa terra cum advocatione ecclesie de Berlee.

Theobaldus filius Fulconis[1] omnibus hanc cartam inspecturis salutem. Sciatis
me concessisse et hac presenti carta mea confirmasse Alano filio meo pro servicio et homagio suo totam terram de Berleia que fuit Theobaldi fratris sui, et
de qua Fulco filius meus et heres cepit homagium ipsius Theobaldi, simul cum
advocatione ecclesie eiusdem villa, habendam et tenendam sibi et heredibus suis
de me et heredibus meis libere quiete et honorifice, per servicium dimidi militis
et sexte partis unius militis, pro omni servicio michi et heredibus meis pertinente. Quare volo quod[2] predictus Alanus et heredes [sui post][3] ipsum habeant
et teneant predictam terram integre cum advocatione ecclesie et cum omnibus
aliis suis pertinenciis (fo. 167v)[4] et libertatibus, secundum quod continetur in
carta quam feci prefato Theobaldo filio meo, a quo iam dicta terra ipsi Alano
descendit. Hiis testibus.

> Note. Fulk had succeeded to the lands of his father, Theobald son of Fulk, by 1198–9 (*VCH
> Herts.* iii, p. 210). Alan was still living in 1222 (*VCH Herts.* iv, p. 39).

1 Corr. marg., MS *Fulconis*.
2 Followed by *ecclesie*, expunged.
3 Hole 12 mm.
4 Heading *Dodyngton'*.

243 *Gift by Alexander Polwere of Doddington to Henry Dery and Eleanor his wife, of a piece of meadow in the marsh [of Doddington], for a sum of money in advance and ½d. annually.*
fo. 167v [*s.* xiii³ × 1290]

Carta Alexandri Polwere de una pecia prati in marisco.

Sciant presentes et futuri quod ego Alexander Polwere de[1] Dodyngton' dedi concessi ac presenti carta mea confirmavi Henrico Dery et Elyanore uxori sue et eorum heredibus de se legitime procreatis, pro homagio et servicio suo et pro quadam summa peccunie quam michi dederunt pre manibus in guersummam, unam peciam prati mei in marisco quod vocatur Hilsingges,[2] et continet in latitudine duodecim rodas, et jacet inter pratum predicti Alexandri ex parte australi et pratum Henrici filii Augustini ex parte aquilonali, et abuttat ad unum caputt super alteram ripam et aliud caput super mariscum communem, habendam et tenendam de me et heredibus meis predictis Henrico et Elianore uxori sue et eorum heredibus, vel cuicumque dare vendere legare vel assignare voluerint, libere quiete bene et hereditarie imperpetuum, reddendo inde annuatim michi et heredibus vel assignatis unum obolum ad festum sancti Michaelis, pro omnibus serviciis consuetudinibus sectis curie vel hundredi. Et ego predictus Alexander et heredes mei vel assignati warantizabimus et defendemus predicto Henrico et Elianore et eorum heredibus vel assignatis predictam peciam prati, ut supradictum est, per predictum servicium contra omnes gentes imperpetuum. In cuius rei testimonium[3] sigillum meum est appensum. His testibus Corwersham ...erun',[4] Philippo filio Adon', Waltero filio Ranulfi, ...ng',[5] Waltero filio et multis aliis.

> Note. This gift must date from before 1290 because the property is to be held *de me et heredibus meis*, but it must be a later thirteenth-century document since Henry Dery and Eleanor, his wife, also occur in no. 244, which is a post-1290 gift.

244 *Gift by Walter son of Richard de Doddington and Joan his wife to Henry Dery and Eleanor his wife of ½ rood of land in Doddington, for 1 clove annually.*
fos. 167v–168r [1290 × *s.* xiv²]

---

1 Followed by *dog*, expunged.
2 Probably *recte* Bilsingges: cf. no. 279.
3 Followed by single cancelled minim.
4 Damaged 12 mm.
5 Hole 12 mm.

Carta de una dimidia roda terre in Dundyton'. (fo. 168r)[1]

Sciant etc. quod ego Walterus filius Ricardi de Dodygton' et Johanna uxor mea
dedimus et concessimus et hac presenti carta nostra confirmavimus Henrico
Dony et Elianore uxori eius et heredibus predicti Henrici unam dimidiam
rodam terre cum pertinenciis jacentem in campo de Dodyngton' quod vocatur
le Hil, inter terram que fuit Baldewini prepositi ex parte aquilonali et terram
Willelmi Kille ex parte australi, et abuttat ad unum caput super commune
mariscum versus occidentem et ad aliud caput super terram predicti Willelmi
Kylle versus orientem, habendam et tenendam predictam dimidiam rodam terre
cum suis pertinenciis de capitali domino feodi illius predictis Henrico et
Elianore et dicti Henrici heredibus vel suis assignatis libere quiete bene et in
pace imperpetuum, reddendo inde annuatim capitali domino unam clavem
gelofre ad festum Nativitatis Domini pro omnibus serviciis consuetudinibus et
aliis secularibus demandis. Et preterea ego Walterus predictus et Johanna uxor
mea et heredes mei seu assignati mei predictam dimidiam rodam terre cum
omnibus pertinenciis predictis Henrico Elianore et dicti Henrici heredibus vel
suis assignatis warantizabimus acquietabimus et defendemus per predictum servicium contra omnes gentes imperpetuum. In cuius rei testimonium huic presenti
carte sigillum nostrum est appensum. Hiis testibus. Data etc.

> Note. This gift dates from after 1290 because the property is to be held *de capitali domino
> feodi illius*, but it cannot have been made after the early fourteenth century since Henry
> Dery and Eleanor, his wife, also occur in no. 243, which is a pre-1290 gift.

245 *Gift by John Balsham of Wimblington to Robert Penw... of Doddington of 2
roods of land in Wimblington.*
fo. 168r–v   At Doddington, [1290 × s. xiv]

Carta Johannis Balsham de duabus rodis terre in Wymlyngton'.

Sciant presentes et futuri quod ego Johannes Balsham de Wymlyngton' dedi
concessi et hac presenti carta mea confirmavi Roberto Penw...[2] de Dodyngton'
duas rodas terre [ja]ce[ntes in cam]pis[3] de Wymlyngton' cum pertinenciis, q[ua-
rum][4] una roda jacet apud Coniwode et es...[5] (fo. 168v)[6] forera et abuttat ad

---

1 Heading *Wymlygton'*.
2 Damaged 5 mm.
3 Damaged 4 mm and 16 mm.
4 Unclear 7 mm.
5 Damaged 13 mm.
6 Heading *Dodynton'*.

unum caput super terram Willelmi filii Ade Mody versus boream et ad aliud super terram Ade Austyn versus austrum, et altera roda jacet super Bradforlong' inter terram Alexandri le boteler' ex una parte et terram Johannis Baltewene junioris ex altera parte, et abuttat ad unum caput super terram Willelmi filii Ade Mody versus austrum, habendas et tenendas predictas duas rodas terre cum omnibus suis pertinenciis dicto Roberto et heredibus suis vel assignatis de capitali domino feodi illius, libere integre jure et hereditarie in feodo et[1] imperpetuum, per servicia inde debita et de jure consueta. Et ego dictus Johannes et heredes mei predictas duas rodas terre cum omnibus suis pertinenciis dicto Roberto et heredibus suis vel assignatis contra omnes gentes warantizabimus imperpetuum. In cuius rei testimonium huic presenti carte mee sigillum meum apposui. Hiis testibus etc. Data aput Codygton'[2] etc.

Note. This gift must date from after 1290 because the land is to be held *de capitali domino feodi illius*.

246 *Gift by Ralph [de Walpole], bishop of Ely, to John de Stockton, his marshall, of a messuage with croft in Doddington, which had escheated to him through the death of Humphrey de Balsham; for 12d. annually.*
fos. 168v–169r [5 June 1299 × 20 March 1302]

Donatio Radulphi episcopi Eliensis Johanni de Stokston de quodam mesuagio cum crofto adjacente.

Sciant presentes et futuri quod nos Radulphus permissione divina Eliensis episcopus dedimus concessimus et hac presenti carta nostra confirmavimus Johanni de Stokton' marescallo nostro unum mesuagium cum crofta adjacente in villa de Dudyngton', cum omnibus pascuis et pasturis et aliis pertinenciis ad dictum mesuagium spectantibus, quod quidem mesuagium nobis accidit in escaeta per mortem quondam Humfridi de Balsham,[3] habendum et tenendum[4] de nobis et successoribus nostris[5] sibi heredibus et assignatis suis, aut cuicumque vel quandocumque dare vendere vel assignare voluerit, (fo. 169r)[6] libere quiete bene et in pace et hereditarie imperpetuum, reddendo inde nobis et successoribus nostris annuatim duodecim denarios pro omni servicio consuetudine sectis curie et aliis

---

1 Interlined.
2 Presumably recte *Dodygton'*.
3 Corr. from *Bassham*.
4 Followed by space, 12 mm.
5 Left hand side of last three lines of page left blank, 30–25 mm.
6 Heading *Dudyngton*.

demandis. In cuius rei testimonium huic carte sigillum nostrum apponi fecimus. Hiis testibus. Data etc. etc.

Note. Ralph de Walpole was bishop of Ely 5 June 1299–20 March 1302.

247 *Gift by Robert de Harpswell, clerk, to John de Ousthorp, clerk, of a messuage with croft and all his other lands and meadows in Doddington.*
fo. 169r [1290 × s. xiv²]

Carta Roberti de Harpeswelle de uno mesuagio cum crofto adjacente.

Sciant presentes et futuri quod ego Robertus de Harpeswelle clericus dedi concessi et hac presenti carta mea confirmavi domino Johanni de Ousthorp clerico heredibus suis et suis assingnatis unum mesuagium cum crofto adjacente, una cum omnibus aliis terris et pratis quas umquam habui in villa et in campis de Dudyngton' cum pascuis pasturis et omnibus aliis pertinenciis, habendum et tenendum dictum mesuagium cum omnibus predictis pertinenciis dicto domino Johanni heredibus suis et suis assignatis libere quiete bene et in pace imperpetuum, reddendo inde annuatim capitalibus dominis feodi illius debita servicia et jure consueta. Et ego dictus Robertus et heredes mei et mei assignati dicta mesuagium croftum cum terris et omnibus aliis pertinenciis dicto domino Johanni heredibus suis et suis assignatis contra omnes homines warantizabimus imperpetuum. In cuius rei testimonium huic presenti carte sigillum meum apposui. Hiis testibus. Data etc.

Note. John de Ousthorp, clerk, occurs in final concords in 11 and 20 Edward II (1317–18 and 1326–7) (*Hunts. Fines*, pp. 60, 65).

248 *Gift by Philip son of William Ace of Doddington to Geoffrey, potter, of Doddington of a piece of arable land with a yard [in Doddington].*
fo. 169r–v [1290 × s. xiv³]

Carta Philippi filii Willelmi Ace de una pecia terre cum pertinenciis.

Sciant presentes et futuri quod ego Philippus filius Willelmi Ace de Dudyngtun' dedi concessi et hac presenti carta mea [confi]rmavi[1] Galfrido le pottere de Est...[2] in Dudyngtun' unam peciam terre arabilis cum per[t]inenciis[3] et cum

[1] Hole 8 mm.
[2] Hole 26 mm.
[3] Hole 2 mm.

curtilagio, que jacet in campo qui¹ vocatur (fo. 169v)² le Hyl et continet in latitudine xlviij pedes, et abuttat ad unum caput super mesuagium Alexandri le boteler' et aliud caput super communem mariscum, et terram domini episcopi ex una parte et terram dicti Philippi ex altera, habendam et tenendam predictam terram cum pertinenciis et cum curtilagio predicto Galfrido et heredibus suis et suis assignatis de capitali domino feodi illius, per servicia inde debita et de jure consueta, libere quiete bene et hereditarie imperpetuum. Et ego predictus Philippus et heredes mei predictam terram cum pertinenciis et cum curtilagio predicto Galfrido et heredibus suis et suis assignatis warantizabimus contra omnes gentes imperpetuum. In cuius rei testimonium huic presenti scripto sigillum meum apposui. Hiis testibus etc. Dat' etc.

> Note. This gift must date from after 1290 because the land is to be held *de capitali domino feodi illius*. In no. 251 Geoffrey, potter, gave property in Doddington to Henry son of Robert de Coveney who, in no. 252, gave property to Ralph de Cardington, rector of Barley (Herts.), and others. Ralph de Cardington was rector of Barley 1329–1359 (see no. 252n).

249 *Gift by Philip son of William Ace of Doddington to Henry son of Robert de Coveney of his part of a messuage with buildings and 6 feet of land in Doddington, with his claim in the messuage through his mother's dower.*
fos. 169v–170r [1290 × s. xiv³]

Carta³ Philippi Ace⁴ de particula unius mesuagii.

Sciant presentes et futuri quod ego Philippus filius Willelmi Ace de Dodyngton' dedi concessi et hac presenti carta mea confirmavi Henrico filio Roberti de⁵ Covenye⁶ et heredibus suis vel suis assignatis totam meam partem unius mesuagii cum edificiis et sex pedibus terre in latitudine versus dictum mesuagium ex parte boreali, cum toto jure et juris clameo quod habeo vel aliquo modo habere potero in⁷ toto dicto mesuagio, videlicet in dote matris mee, cum omnibus aliis pertinenciis in villa de Dodyngton', jacentem juxta Suthfen de Dodyngton', inter [terr]am⁸ Galfridi le pottere, quam emit a dicto P[hilippo, ex]⁹ parte ori-

---

1 MS *que*.
2 Heading *Dodyngton'*.
3 Followed by *Willelmi*, expunged.
4 MS *Ace Philippi*, marked for transposition.
5 MS *le*.
6 *n* interlined.
7 Followed by *d*, expunged.
8 Unclear 4 mm.
9 Damaged 12 mm.

entali et terram Thome le clerk et ... [ex]¹ parte occidentali, et abuttat [ad unum
ca]put² versus communem mariscum et ad [a]liud³ caput versus terram dicti
Philippi filii Willelmi Ace, habendam et tenendam predictam partem mesuagii,
cum (fo. 170r)⁴ toto jure et juris clameo ad dictum Philippum spectantem, prefato Henrico et heredibus suis vel assignatis de capitalibus dominis feodi illius,
libere integre bene et in pace in feodo et imperpetuum, per servicia indebita et
de jure consueta. Et ego predictus Philippus⁵ filius Willelmi Ace et heredes mei
prefatam partem mesuagii cum toto jure et juris clameo prefato Henrico
Coveneye heredibus suis vel assignatis contra omnes gentes warantizabimus
imperpetuum. In cuius rei testimonium huic presenti carte mee sigillum meum
apposui. Hiis testibus. Data etc.

> Note. This gift must date from after 1290 because the land is to be held *de capitali domino
> feodi illius*. In no. 252 Henry son of Robert de Coveney gave property in Doddington to
> Ralph de Cardington, rector of Barley (Herts.), and others. Ralph de Cardington was rector
> of Barley 1329–1359 (see no. 252n).

250 *Gift by Philip son of William Ace of Doddington to Henry son of Robert de
Coveney and Matilda his wife of his land in 'le Hyl', Doddington, which he had by
paternal inheritance, and grant of his claim in the land in 'le Hyl' belonging to his
mother's dower, for a certain sum of money.*
fo. 170r–v [1290 × s. xiv³]

Carta Philippi filii Willelmi Ace de certa terra vocatur le Hyl in Dodyngton'.

Sciant etc. quod ego Philippus filius Willelmi Ace de Dodyngton' dedi concessi
et hac presenti⁶ carta mea confirmavi Henrico filio Roberti⁷ de Coveneye et
Matild' uxori eius, pro quadam summa peccunie quam michi dederunt, totam
terram meam jacentem in campo de Dodyngton' vocato le Hyl quam habui de
hereditate paterna, et totum jus meum et juris clamium quod habeo vel aliquo
modo habere potero in tota terra in eodem campo jacente ad dotem matris mee
spectante cum pertinenciis, habendam et tenendam totam predictam terram
meam in predicto campo jacentem, et totum jus meum et juris clameum quod

---

¹ Hole 23 mm.
² Damaged 19 mm.
³ Hole 2 mm.
⁴ Heading *Dodyngton'*.
⁵ MS perhaps, incorrectly, *Johannes*.
⁶ MS *pesenti*.
⁷ Ins. marg.

ibidem habeo in dote matris mee quando accederit cum per[tinenciis],[1] predictis Henrico de Coveneye et Matilld' [uxori eius et heredibus][2] vel assignatis suis de capita[libus dominis feodi][3] illius, libere quiete bene et in pace in feodo et [im]per[pet]uum,[4] per servicia inde debita et de jure [con]sueta.[5] Et ego predictus Philippus filius Willelmi Ace et heredes mei totam predictam terram in predicto campo jacentem et totum (fo. 170v)[6] jus meum et juris clamium quod ibidem habeo vel habere aliquo modo potero in futuro, videlicet in dote matris mee quando acciderit, predictis Henrico Coveneye et Matild' uxori eius et heredibus vel assignatis suis contra omnes gentes warantizabimus imperpetuum. In cuius rei testimonium huic presenti carte mee sigillum apposui. Hiis testibus. Data etc.

Note. For dating see no. 249n.

251 *Gift by Geoffrey, potter, of Doddington to Henry son of Robert de Coveney of his part of a messuage with land in Doddington, which he bought from Philip son of William Ace of Doddington.*
fos. 170v–171r [1290 × s. xiv[3]]

Carta Galfridi le pottere de parte unius mesuagii cum terra in crofto adjacente.

Sciant presentes et futuri quod ego Galfridus le pottere de Dodyngton' dedi concessi et hac presenti carta mea confirmavi Henrico filio Roberti de Coveneye et heredibus vel assignatis suis totam meam partem unius mesuagii cum terra in crufta adjacente jacentem in villa et in campis de Dodyngton' cum suis pertinenciis, quam quidem partem mesuagii cum terra adjacente emi e Philippo filio Willelmi Ace de eadem, et jacent[7] linealiter inter terram et mesuagium euisdem Henrici ex parte una et terram domini[8] episcopi ex parte altera, et abuttat ad unum caput versus communem mariscum ex[9] parte australi et mesuagium Alexandri le boteler' ex parte boreali, habendas et tenendas totam meam partem dicti mesuagii et terram adjacentem cum omnibus suis pertinenciis

---

1 Unclear 7 mm.
2 Unclear 24 mm.
3 Unclear 25 mm.
4 Unclear 10 mm.
5 Unclear 5 mm.
6 Heading *Dodyngton'*.
7 Followed by *inter*, cancelled.
8 Followed by *M*, expunged.
9 Repeated and expunged.

predicto Henrico et heredibus et suis assignatis de capitalibus dominis feodi illius, libere integre bene et in pace in feodo et imperpetuum, per servicia inde debita et de jure consueta. Et ego Galfridus le pottere et heredes mei prefatam totam meam partem dicti mesuagii et terram adjacentem cum omnibus suis pertinenciis [pre]dicto[1] Henrico filio Roberti de Coveneye et heredibus vel assignatis suis warantizabimus imperpetuum.[2] (fo. 171r)[3] In cuius rei testimonium sigillum meum apposui. Hiis testibus.

Note. For dating see nos. 248n and 252n.

252 *Gift by Henry son of Robert de Coveney to Ralph [de Cardington], rector of Barley (Herts.), Thomas de Lansill, chaplain, Robert John, chaplain, John Fithien, Edmund Chipman and John Broun of a messuage in Doddington called 'le Fenhous' with croft, which he acquired from Philip son of William Ace, with the reversion of his mother's dower.*
fo. 171r [5 March 1329 × 1359]

Carta Henrici filii Roberti de Coveneye Radulpho persone de Berle et aliis de uno mesuagio cum crofto.

Sciant presentes et futuri quod ego Henricus filius Roberti de Coveneye dedi concessi et hac presenti carta mea confirmavi Radulpho rectori ecclesie de Berlee, Thome de Lansill' capellano, Roberto Johanne capellano, Johanni Fechyon', Edmundo Chipman et Johanni Broun unum mesuagium in Dudyngton' cum pertinenciis, et vocatur le Fenhous, cum crofta adjacente, quod quidem perquisivi de Philippo filio Willelmi Ace, cum reversione dotis matris mee ad se spectante, habendum et tenendum predictum mesuagium cum crofta adjacente cum omnibus suis pertinenciis predictis Radulpho, Thome, Roberto, Johanni, Edmundo et Johanni heredibus et assignatis suis, libere int[eg]r[e][4] jure et hereditarie in feodo et[5] imperpetuum, de capitalibus dominis feodi ill[ius][6] per servicia inde debita et de jure consueta. Et ego dictus Henricus et heredes mei predictum mesu[a]gium[7] cum crofta adjacente cum omnibus suis per[tinenciis][8]

1 Unclear 3 mm.
2 Followed by catchwords, *In cuius rei testimonium.*
3 Heading *Dodyngton'.*
4 Holes 3 mm and 1 mm.
5 Interlined.
6 Hole 2 mm.
7 Hole 2 mm.
8 Hole 11 mm.

pre[fat]is[1] Radulpho, Thome, Roberto, Johanni, Edmundo et Johanni, heredibus et assignatis suis, contra omnes gentes warantizabimus imperpetuum. In cuius rei testimonium h[u]ic[2] p[re]s[ent]i[3] carte mee sigillum meum apposui. Hiis t[estibus][4] etc. Da[ta][5] etc.

Note. Ralph de Cardington (Kerdington), rector of Barley (Herts.), was instituted on 5 March 1329 (*Reg. Gravesend*, p. 284). He occurs on 13 Oct. 1347 at the election of abbess Matilda Bernard, successor to Alice de Shropham (Cambridge UL, EDR G/1/1, de Lisle register, fo. 51v), and on 22 Aug. 1355 (no. 241). He was master of Clare Hall, Cambridge 1342–59 (A. B. Emden *A Biographical Register of the University of Cambridge to 1500* (Cambridge, 1963) p. 336).

253 *Gift by Henry son of Robert de Coveney to Walter son of William, potter, and Agnes his wife of ½ acre of land in Doddington.*
fo. 171r–v [1290 × s. xiv[3]]

Alia carta eiusdem Henrici de dimidia acra terre cum pertinenciis.

Sciant etc. quod ego Henricus filius Ro[berti][6] de Coveneye dedi concessi et hac presenti carta mea [con]fir[ma]vi[7] Waltero filio Willelmi le pottere de ...we-...ich'[8] et Agneti [uxori][9] eius unam dimidiam acram terre mee in Dudyngton' [cum pertinen]ciis[10] j[acen]tem[11] [in quo]dam[12] loco voc[at]o[13] le Hyl, inter t[er]ram[14] dicti Walt[eri][15] quam tenet de [domino][16] episcopo (fo. 171v)[17] et terram domini Henrici ex parte occidentali, et caput boreale abuttat super[18] mesuagium abbatisse de Chatriz et conventus ibidem, et caput australe abuttat

---

1 Hole 5 mm.
2 Hole 2 mm.
3 Hole 9 mm.
4 Hole 7 mm.
5 Hole 5 mm.
6 Damaged 4 mm.
7 Hole 4 mm and unclear 5 mm.
8 Damaged 7 mm and 2 mm.
9 Hole 5 mm.
10 Hole 14 mm.
11 Hole 7 mm.
12 Hole 10 mm.
13 Hole 3 mm.
14 Hole 2 mm.
15 Hole 3 mm.
16 Hole 6 mm.
17 Heading *Chatriz Dodyngton'*.
18 Followed by *boreale abuttat super* repeated, *abuttat* expunged.

super terram dicti Henrici, habendam et tenendam dictam dimidiam acram terre cum omnibus suis pertinenciis prefatis Waltero et Agneti uxori eius et heredibus suis vel assignatis, libere integre[1] jure et hereditarie in feodo imperpetuum, de capitali domino feodi illius per servicia inde debita et de jure consueta. Et ego dictus Henricus et heredes[2] mei predictam dimidiam acram terre cum pertinenciis omnibus suis predictis Waltero Agneti et heredibus suis vel assignatis contra omnes gentes warantizabimus imperpetuum. In cuius rei testimonium huic presenti carte mee sigillum meum apposui. Hiis testibus. Data apud etc.

> Note. This gift must date from after 1290 because the land is to be held *de capitali domino feodi illius*. In no. 252 Henry son of Robert de Coveney gave property to Ralph de Cardington, rector of Barley (Herts.), and others. Ralph de Cardington was rector of Barley 1329–1359 (see no. 252n). There is no evidence in the cartulary that William and Agnes subsequently gave this ½ acre to Ralph de Cardington before no. 254.

254 *Surrender and quitclaim by Ralph [de Cardington], parson of Barley (Herts.), to abbess Batill' de Woveton' and the convent of Chatteris of all the lands and tenements which he had acquired in Chatteris and Doddington.*
fo. 171v [5 March 1329 × 1347 *or* 1347 × 1359]

Quieta clamantia Radulphi persone de Berlee de diversis terris et tenementis.

Pateat universis per presentes quod ego Radulphus persona ecclesie de Berlee remisi et omnino de me et heredibus [meis][3] quietum clamavi domine Batill' de Woveton' abbatisse de Chatriz et conventui eiusdem loci et eorum successoribus imperpetuum totum jus et clameum q[uod][4] habui vel aliquo modo habere potui in omnibus terris et [te]nementis[5] que adquisivi in villis de Chatriz et Dodyngton', ita quod nec dictus Radulphus nec heredes mei nec aliquis in nomine meo in pred[ic]tis[6] terris et tenementis cum pertinenciis aliquid [jur]is[7] vel clamei amodo exigere vel vendicare poterimus imperpetuum. In cuius rei testimonium h[uic pr]esenti[8] facto si[gill]um[9] m[eum apposui].[10] [Hii]s[11] testibus ctc. Dat' etc. (fo. 172r)[12]

1 Followed by *et*, expunged.
2 MS *Henr'*, *n* expunged.
3 Hole 8 mm.
4 Hole 7 mm.
5 Hole 4 mm.
6 Hole 3 mm.
7 Hole 3 mm.
8 Damaged 10 mm.

Note. The position of abbess Batill' de Woveton' in the chronology of the abbesses of Chatteris is not certain. This document contains the only known reference to her. In 1347, Matilda Bernard was elected abbess following the resignation of Alice de Shropham (Cambridge UL, EDR G/1/1, de Lisle register, fos. 51r–52r). Woveton' may have been abbess between Mary de Shouldham and Agnes de Shropham, or between Matilda Bernard – Shropham's successor – and Margaret Hotot. The last dated occurrence of Mary de Shouldham is shortly after 29 Sept. 1317 (no. 225). Alice de Shropham resigned on 13 Oct. 1347 when Matilda Bernard was elected to succeed her (Cambridge UL, EDR G/1/1 de Lisle register, fos. 51r–52r). The first datable occurrence of Margaret Hotot is 30 Sept. 1368 × 24 Jan. 1369 (no. 192). For dating see also no. 252n.

255 *Grant by Edward III to Chatteris abbey of a licence to acquire property to the value of £10 annually, notwithstanding the statute of mortmain.*
fo. 172r At Westminster, 27 Jan. 1332

Copy: (R) PRO C 66 178, m. 29.

Carta licencie ad manum mortuam ad valorem x librarum.

Edwardus Dei gracia rex Anglie dominus Hibernie et dux Aquitannie omnibus ad quos presentes littere pervenerint salutem.[1] Sciatis quod de nostra gracia[2] speciali concessimus et licenciam dedimus pro nobis et heredibus nostris, quantum in nobis est, dilectis nobis in Christo abbatisse et conventui de Chatriz[3] quod ipsi terras tenementa et redditus cum pertinenciis ad valentia decem librarum per annum juxta verum valorem eorundem, tam de feodo suo proprio quam alieno, exceptis terris tenementis et redditibus que de nobis tenentur in capite, adquirere possint, habenda et tenenda sibi et successoribus suis imperpetuuum, statuto de terris et tenementis a[d m]anum[4] mortuam non ponendis edito non obstante. Dum tamen per inquisitiones inde in forma debita faciendas, et in cancellaria nostra vel heredum nostrorum rite retornandas, compertum sit quod id fieri poterit absque dampno et prejudicio nostro et heredum nostrorum ac alterius cuiuscumque. In cuius rei testimonium has litteras nostras fieri fecimus

[9] Hole 9 mm.
[10] Hole 22 mm.
[11] Hole 4 mm.
[12] Heading *Carte Edwardi et Ricardi regum.*
[1] R begins *Rex omnibus ad quos etc. salutem.*
[2] R *gracia nostra.*
[3] R *Chaterice.*
[4] Hole 7 mm.

patentes.[1] Teste meipso[2] apud Westm' vicesimo septimo die januarii anno regni nostri sexto. Rasen.[3] Per breve de privato sigillo.

Note. Another copy of no. 8.

256 *Writ of Richard II to Thomas More of Balsham, his escheator in Cambs., for an inquisition* ad quod damnum *into the gift by John Dreng ('Brenge'), baxster, to Chatteris abbey of 15 messuages, 1 toft, 21 acres and 1½ roods of land, 9 acres and 1 rood of meadow and 2s. 2d. of rent in Chatteris, Doddington and Wimblington in partial satisfaction of £10 of property annually which Edward III licenced it to acquire.*
fos. 172r–173r At Westminster, 12 April 1387

Copy: (S) PRO C 143/405/10.

Carta domini regis pro inquisitione ad manum mortuam.

Ricardus Dei gracia[4] rex Anglie et Francie dominus Hibernie dilecto sibi Thome Mor'[5] de Balsham escaetori[6] suo in comitatu Cant'[7] salutem. Precip-imus[8] quod per sacramentum proborum et legalium hominum de ba[lliv]a[9] tua, per [q]uos[10] rei veritas melius[11] sciri poter[it],[12] diligenter i[nqu]ir[a]s[13] si sit ad prejudicium vel dampnum[14] nostrum (fo. 172v) aut aliorum si concedamus[15] Johanni Brenge[16] baxstere quod ipse xv mesuagia, j toftum, viginti et unam acras terre[17] et unam rodam et dimidiam, novem acras et unam rodam prati,

---

1 R omits *rei ... patentes,* adds *etc.*
2 R *rege.*
3 R omits *anno ... Rasen.*
4 S omits *Ricardus dei gracia.*
5 S *More.*
6 *-ri* interlined.
7 S *Cantebr'.*
8 S adds *tibi.*
9 Damaged 4 mm.
10 Hole 2 mm.
11 S omits.
12 Damaged 3 mm.
13 Holes 7 mm and 3 mm.
14 S *dampnum vel prejudicium.*
15 Interlined.
16 S *Dreng.*
17 S omits.

duas solidatas et duas denaratas redditus, imperpetuum[1] in Chatriz[2] Dudyngton' Wylmyngton'[3] dare possit[4] et assignare dilectis nobis in Christo abbatisse
et conventui de Chatriz,[5] habenda et tenenda sibi et successoribus suis imperpetuum in partem satisfactionis decem librarum terre[6] et tenementorum et
redditus per annum, quas dominus Edwardus[7] rex Anglie avus noster per
litteras suas patentes eisdem abbatisse et conventui[8] de feodo suo proprio quam
alieno, exceptis terris et tenementis que de ipso avo nostro tenebantur[9] in
capite, concessit adin[qui]rendas[10] necne. Et si sit ad dampnum vel prejudicium
nostrum, et[11] ad quod dampnum et ad[12] quod prejudicium aliorum et quorum
et qualiter et quomodo, et de quo et[13] de quibus predicta mesuagia toftum terra
pra[tum][14] precium et redditus teneantur, et[15] quod servicium et qualiter et
quomodo, et quantum valeant per annum in omnibus exitibus juxta verum valorem eorundem, et qui quotquot[16] sunt medii inter nos et prefatum Johannem
de mesuagiis tofto terra et tenementis prato et redditu predictis, et que terre et
que tenementa eidem Johanni ultra donationem et assingnationem predictas
remaneant, et ubi et de quo vel de quibus teneantur, et per quod servicium et
qualiter et quomodo, et qualiter valeantur[17] per annum in omnibus ex[it]ibus.[18]
Et si terre et tenementa eidem Johanni remanentia ultra dona[tio]nem[19] et
assignationem predictas sufficiant ad consuetudines et servicia, tam de predictis
mesuagiis tofto terra prato et redditu sicut ⟨datis⟩[20] quam de aliis terris[21]

1 S *cum pertinenciis.*
2 S *Chaterice.*
3 S *Wilmyngton.*
4 MS *possunt.*
5 S *Chaterice.*
6 S *libratarum terrarum.*
7 S adds *nuper.*
8 S adds *tam.*
9 MS *cenelantur.*
10 Hole 6 mm.
11 S omits, adds *aut aliorum tunc.*
12 S omits.
13 S *vel.*
14 Hole 4 mm.
15 S adds *per.*
16 S *et quot.*
17 S *quantum valeant.*
18 Damaged 3 mm.
19 Hole 5 mm.
20 Space, 10 mm.
21 S adds *et.*

tenementis sibi ret[ent]is,[1] d[e]bita[2] facienda, et ad omnia alia onera (fo. 173r)[3] que sustinuit[4] et sustinere consuevit, ut in sectis visibus franciplegii auxiliis tallagiis vigiliis finibus re[de]mptionibus[5] amerciamentis contributionibus et aliis quibuscumque[6] oneribus emergentibus sustinendis. Et quod idem Johannes in assisis juratis et aliis recognitionibus quibuscumque poni possit,[7] proinde[8] ante donationem et assignationem predictas poni[9] consuevit, ita quod patria per donationem et assignationem predictas in ipsius Johannis defectum magis solito non oneretur seu gravetur. Et inquisitionem[10] inde distincte et aperte factam nobis in cancellariam nostram, sub sigillo tuo et sigillis eorum per quos facta fuerit, sine dilatione mittas et hoc breve. Teste meipso aput Westm' xij° die aprilis anno regni nostri decimo.[11]

257 *Inquisition* ad quod damnum *held at Cambridge before Thomas More of Balsham, escheator, which found that the gift by John Dreng ('Brenge'), baxster, to Chatteris abbey of 15 messuages, 1 toft, 21 acres and 1½ roods of land, 9 acres and 1 rood of meadow and 2s. 2d. of rent in Chatteris, Doddington and Wimblington, held of the bishop of Ely and the abbess of Chatteris, would not cause damage to the king or others.*
fos. 173r–174r   At Cambridge, 20 April 1387

Copy: (S) PRO C 143/405/10.

Certificatio inquisitionis capta ad manum mortuam super sacramentum proborum et legalium hominum.

Inquisitio capta apud Cant' die sabbati proximo ante festum[12] Georgii martiris anno regni regis Ricardi secundi decimo, coram Thoma Mor[13] de Balsham escaetore dicti domini regis in comitatu predicto, virtute cuiusdam brevis dicti

1 Unclear 3 mm.
2 Hole 2 mm.
3 Heading *Certificatio inquisitionis*, MS *inquisionis*.
4 MS *sustinent*.
5 Hole 4 mm.
6 MS *quibusque*.
7 MS *possunt*.
8 S *prout*.
9 MS *qui*.
10 MS *inquisisstionem*.
11 S adds *Burton'*.
12 S adds *sancti*.
13 S *Moor*.

domini regis eidem escaetori directi et huic inquisitioni consuti, per sacramentum Johannis Vycary, Johannis Frere, Johannis Lolleworth',[1] Johannis Prykke,
Willelmi Kos,[2] Johannis Eoydon',[3] Johannis Salman, Willelmi Halsteyn,
Henrici Elankpayn,[4] Ricardi Sped',[5] Hugonis Warde,[6] Johannis talliour[7] juratorum, qui dicunt super sacramentum suum quod non est ad dampnum domini
regis nec aliorum licet dominus rex concedat Johanni Brenge[8] baxstere quod
ipse quindecim mesuagia,[9] unum toftum, viginti et unam acras terre unam
r[odam][10] (fo. 173v)[11] et dimidiam, novem acras et unam rodam prati, duas
solidatas et duas denaretatas[12] redditus[13] cum pertinenciis in Chatriz[14] Dudyngton' et Wylmyngton' dare possit et assignare abbatisse et conventui de Chatriz,
habenda et tenenda sibi et successoribus suis imperpetuum. Et dicunt quod
duodecim mesuagia de mesuagiis predictis et unum toftum, octodecim acre terre
due rode et dimidia de terris predictis, novem acre et una roda prati et quatuor
denarate redditus de redditu predicto cum pertinenciis in Chateriz Dudyngton'
et Wylmyngton' tenentur de episcopo Eliensi, per servicia portandi virgam dicti
episcopi infra villatam de Chatriz, et sectandi[15] curiam palacii Eliensis de tribus
septimanis in tres septimanas, et sectandi hundredum de Wych'[16] de tribus
septimanis in tres septimanas, et reddendi ad manerium dicti episcopi in Dudyngton' unum denarium per annum. Et dicunt quod dictus episcopus ea ultra
tenet de domino rege[17] in capite. Et dicunt quod tria alia mesuagia de mesuagiis
predictis, due alie acre et tres rode terre de predict[i]s[18] ter[ris][19] et viginti due

---

1 S *Lolleworthe*.
2 S *Koo*.
3 S *Boydon'*.
4 S *Blankpayn*.
5 S *Speed*.
6 S adds *et*.
7 S *taylour*.
8 S *Dreng*.
9 Followed by *ut...*, cancelled? Damaged 3 mm.
10 Hole 6 mm.
11 Heading *Certificatio*.
12 First *t* interlined.
13 MS *reddend'*.
14 S *Chaterice* throughout document.
15 MS *vitandi*.
16 S *Wich'*.
17 *de domino rege*, repeated.
18 Hole 2 mm.
19 Hole 4 mm; S *terris predictis*.

denarate redditus de redditu predicto cum pertinenciis in predicta[1] villa de Chatriz tenentur de abbatissa de Chatriz, per servicia viginti denariorum obuli[2] per annum. Et dicunt quod dicta abbatissa ea ult[ra][3] tenet de episcopo Eliensi, et[4] episcopus ea ultra tenet de domino rege in capite. Et dicunt quod predicta quindecim mesuagia, unum toftum, viginti et una acre[5] terre et u[na ro]d[a et][6] dimidia, novem acre[7] et una roda prati, due[8] soli[date et] d[ue][9] denariate[10] cum pertinenciis in dicta willa de [Chatriz][11] Dudyngton' et[12] Wyllmyngton'[13] [valent][14] per a[nnum][15] in omnibus e[xiti]bus[16] juxta v[er]um[17] va/lorem (fo. 174r)[18] eorundem ultra reprisas x s. Et dicunt quod [remanent][19] dicto Johanni ultra donationem et assignationem istam [unum][20] mesuagium et tres acre terre in dicta villa de [Chat]riz,[21] que tenentur de episcopo Eliensi per servicium [portandi][22] virgam in eadem villa, et valent per annum in [omni]bus[23] exitibus juxta verum valorem[24] ultra reprisas iij s. iiij d. Et dicunt quod terre et tenementa eidem Johanni remane[ntia][25] ultra donationem et assignationem istam sufficiunt[26] ad consuetudines et servicia, tam de predictis mesuagiis tofto terra[27]

---

1 S *dicta*.
2 MS *obulum*.
3 Unclear 2 mm.
4 S adds *quod*.
5 MS *acras*.
6 Damaged 19 mm.
7 MS *acras*.
8 Corr. from *duas* by *e* ins. marg.
9 Damaged 18 mm.
10 MS *denarite*.
11 Damaged 13 mm.
12 Followed by *Wyllyngt'*, cancelled?
13 S *Wylmyngton'*.
14 Hole 11 mm.
15 Damaged 7 mm.
16 Hole 9 mm.
17 Damaged 4 mm.
18 Heading *Carta confirmationis*.
19 Hole 7 mm.
20 Hole 7 mm.
21 Hole 8 mm.
22 Hole 13 mm.
23 Damaged 8 mm.
24 S adds *eorundem*.
25 Damaged 4 mm.
26 MS *sufficit*.
27 MS *terre*.

prato et redditu sic datis quam de aliis terris et tenementis sibi retentis, debita[1]
facienda, et ad omnia alia onera que sustinere consuevit, ut in sectis visibus
franciplegii au[xi]liis[2] tallagiis vigilliis finibus redemptionibus amerciamentis
cont[rib]utionibus[3] et aliis quibuscumque[4] oneribus emergentibus sustinendis.
Et dicunt quod idem Johannes in assisis juratis et aliis[5] recognitionibus quibuscumque [pon]i[6] possit, pro ut ante donationem et assignationem [ist]am[7] poni
consuevit, ita quod patria per donationem et a[ssig]nationem[8] istam in ipsius
Johannis defectum magis so[lito][9] non oneretur seu gravetur. In cuius rei
testimonium predicti juratores[10] inquisitioni sigilla sua apposuerunt. Data die
loco et anno supradictis.

Note. The court of the palace of Ely was probably a survival from the time when the two
hundreds of Ely and Witchford had not been clearly separated and had only one court. From
the thirteenth century, the two hundreds were distinct and held their own courts; the court
of the palace of Ely seems to have exercised, in the later medieval period, only a trace of the
jurisdiction formerly belonging to the court of the two hundreds. (*VCH Cambs.* iv, p. 11 and
Miller *Abbey and Bishopric of Ely*, pp. 221–5.)

258 *Licence by Richard II to John Dreng, baxster, to give, and to Chatteris abbey
to receive, 15 messuages, 1 toft, 21 acres and 1½ roods of land, 9 acres and 1 rood of
meadow and 2s. 2d. of rent in Chatteris, Doddington and Wimblington, in accord-
ance with the licence, granted to the abbey by Edward III, to acquire £10 of property
annually, notwithstanding the statute of mortmain.*
fos. 174r–175r   At Westminster, 3 May 1387

Copy: (T) PRO C 66/323, m. 11.

Carta confirmationis super inquisitionem captam ad manum mortuam ad valorem[11] l solidorum.

---

1 MS *debitum*.
2 Hole 3 mm.
3 Hole 4 mm.
4 Followed by *poni possit*, expunged.
5 Followed by *reg*, expunged.
6 Hole 12 mm.
7 Hole 5 mm.
8 Hole 7 mm.
9 Damaged 7 mm.
10 S adds *huic*.
11 Followed by *xx*, expunged.

Ricardus Dei gracia[1] rex Anglie[2] et Francie domi[nus][3] Hibernie omnibus ad quos presentes [littere pervenerint s]alutem.[4] Sciatis quod, cum dominus E[d-wardus nuper rex][5] Anglie [a]vus[6] [noster][7] per suas litteras[8] patentes [de gracia sua speciali][9] concessisse et[10] licenciam [dedisse pro se et heredibus][11] suis, quantum in ipso fuit, [dilectis sibi in][12] Christo [abbati]sse[13] et conventui de Ch[atr]iz,[14] [quod][15] ipsi (fo. 174v)[16] [terras][17] et tenementa et redditus cum pertinenciis ad valentiam decem librarum per annum juxta verum valorem eorundem [ta]m[18] de feodo suo proprio quam alieno, exceptis terris tenementis [et re]dditibus[19] que de ipso avo nostro tenebantur in capite, adquirere possent, habenda et tenenda sibi et successoribus suis imperpetuum, statuto de terris et tenementis ad manum mortuam non ponendis edito non obstante, prout in eisdem litteris plenius continetur, nos, volentes dictam concessionem prefati avi nostri effectui debito mancipari, concessimus et licenciam dedimus pro nobis et heredibus nostris, quantum in nobis est, dilecto nobis Johanni Dreng' baxstere quod ipse quindecim mesuagia, unum toftum, viginti et unam acras et unam rodam terre et dimidiam, novem acras et unam rodam prati, duas solidatas et duas denaratas redditus cum pertinenciis in Chatriz[20] Dudyngton' et Wylmyng-ton',[21] que de nobis non tenentur et que valent per annum in omnibus exitibus juxta verum valorem eorundem decem solidos, [si]cut[22] per inquisitionem inde

1 T omits *Ricardus Dei gracia.*
2 T omits *Anglie ... pervenerint*, adds *etc.*
3 Damaged 5 mm.
4 Damaged 27 mm; *lacunae* supplied from T.
5 Damaged 22 mm.
6 Hole 2 mm.
7 Unclear 5 mm.
8 T *litteras suas.*
9 Holes 21 mm and 10 mm.
10 Followed by *d*, expunged.
11 Holes 22 mm and 4 mm; then unclear 8 mm.
12 Hole 25 mm.
13 Hole 7 mm.
14 Hole 7 mm; T *Chaterice.*
15 Hole 3 mm.
16 Heading *Carta confirmationis.*
17 Hole 8 mm.
18 Hole 4 mm.
19 Hole 6 mm; MS *redditus*; followed by *cum pertinenciis*, expunged.
20 T *Chaterice.*
21 T *Wilmyngton'.*
22 Hole 3 mm.

per dilectum nobis Thomam More de Balsham escaetorem nostrum in comitatu Cantebr' de mandato nostro captam et in cancellaria nostra retornatam est compertum, dare possit et assignare prefatis abbatisse et conventui, habenda et tenenda sibi et successoribus suis, in valorem qu[inq]uaginta[1] solidorum in partem satisfactionis de[ce]m[2] libratarum[3] terrarum tenementorum et reddituum predictorum, imperpetuum. Et [eisdem][4] abbatisse et conventui, quod ipse dicta [mesuagia to]ftum[5] terram pratum et redditum a prefato [Johanne recipere][6] possint et tenere prefatis abbatiss[e et conventui][7] et successoribus suis imperpetuum, sicut (fo. 175r)[8] predictum est, tenore presentium similiter licenciam dedimus specialem, statuto predicto non obstante. Ac[9] nolentes quod idem Johannes vel heredes sui aut pre[fate abbat]issa[10] et conventus vel earum successores ratione statuti predicti per nos vel heredes nostros justiciarios escaeto[r]es[11] vicecomites aut alios balivos seu ministros nostros quoscumque inde occasionentur molestentur in aliquo seu graventur, salvis tamen capitalibus dominis feodi illius serviciis inde debitis et consuetis. In cuius rei testimonium has litteras nostras fieri fecimus patentes.[12] Teste meipso[13] apud Westm' tertio die maii anno regni nostri decimo.[14]

259 *Pardon by Henry V to abbess Agnes [Ashfield] and the convent of Chatteris of whichever of the many offences listed they had committed.*
fos. 175r–176v   At Westminster, Sept. 1415

Perdonatio domini regis Henrici quarti[15] super diversis articulis et adquisitione ad manum mortuam.

---

1 Hole 5 mm.
2 Hole 5 mm.
3 *ta* interlined.
4 Hole 9 mm.
5 Hole 21 mm.
6 Hole 21 mm.
7 Holes 4 mm and 22 mm.
8 Heading *Perdonatio regis Henrici iiij*[ti].
9 T omits.
10 Damaged 17 mm.
11 Hole 7 mm.
12 T omits *rei … patentes*, adds etc.
13 T *rege*.
14 T omits *anno … decimo*.
15 Recte *quinti*.

Henricus Dei gracia rex Anglie et Francie et dominus Hibernie omnibus ballivis et fidelibus suis ad quos presentes littere pervenerint salutem. Sciatis quod, de gracia nostra speciali, de assensu dominorum spiritualium et temporalium ac ad requisitionem communitatum regni nostri Anglie in ultimo parliamento nostro existentium, perdonavimus et relaxavimus Agneti abbatisse de Chateriz et eiusdem loci conventui, quibuscumque nominibus censeantur, omnimodas transgressiones mesprisiones comtemptus et impetitiones per ipsas ante octavum diem decembris ultimo preteritum contra formam statutorum de liberatis pannorum et capitiorum facta sive perpetrata, unde punitio caderet in finem et redemptionem aut in alias penas pecuniareas [s]eu[1] imprisonamenta, statutis predictis non obstan[tib]us,[2] ita tam[e]n[3] quod presentes perdonatio et relax[ati]o[4] [non cedant in][5] in dampnum p[rejudicium vel de]rogationem[6] (fo. 175v)[7] ali[cu]ius[8] [pe]rsone[9] quam nostre dumtaxat. Et insuper ex [mero motu][10] nostro, ob reverenciam Dei et caritatis[11] [intuitu, per]donavimus[12] eisdem abbatisse et conventui sectam pacis n[ostre qu]e[13] ad nos versus ipsas pertinet pro omnimodis pro[ditioni]bus[14] murdris raptibus mulierum rebellionibus in[surrectio]nibus[15] feloniis conspirationibus ac aliis [trans]gressionibus[16] offensis negligenciis extorsionibus mesprisionibus ignoranciis contemptibus[17] concelamentis [et][18] deceptionibus per ipsas ante octavum diem decembris qualitercumque factis sive perpetratis, murdris per ipsas post decimum novum diem novembris ultimo preteritum perpetratis sique fuerint exceptis, unde indicate

---

1 Hole 3 mm.
2 Hole 5 mm.
3 Hole 2 mm.
4 Hole 3 mm.
5 Hole 15 mm; *lacunae* supplied from similar pardon enrolled on the patent roll for 4 Henry V (PRO C 66/399, m. 39).
6 Hole 29 mm.
7 Heading *Perdonatio regis Henrici iiij.ti*.
8 Hole 3 mm.
9 Damaged 12 mm; preceded by expunged word.
10 Damaged 20 mm.
11 *et caritatis* repeated.
12 Damaged 18 mm.
13 Damaged 15 mm.
14 Damaged 17 mm.
15 Damaged 20 mm.
16 Damaged 10 mm.
17 MS *comtemptibus*, third minim of first *m* expunged.
18 Hole 2 mm.

rectate vel appellate existant, acetiam waiviare sique in ipsas hiis occasionibus
fuerint promulgate, et firmam pacem nostram eis inde concedimus, dum tamen
eedem[1] abbatissa et conventus controfactrices mistere monete et [cun]agii,[2]
multiplicatrices et lotrices auri et argenti cum cuneo nostro cunatorum et tons-
atrices monete nostre, probatrices communes et notorie latrones seu felones que
abjurationes fecerant non existant, ita tamen quod stent recto in curia nostra
siquis[3] versus eas loqui voluerit de premissis vel aliquo premissorum. Et ulterius
de uberiori gracia nostra perdonavimus et relaxavimus eisdem abbatisse et conventui omnimoda escapia felonum et catalla felonum, et fugitiorum [ca]talla[4]
utlagatorum et felonum de se, deodanda, [va]sta,[5] impetitiones ac omnimodos
articulos [itineri]s,[6] d[is]trinctiones[7] et transgressiones de v[ir]idi[8] [vel ven-
atione],[9] venditionem boscorum infra forestas ac [extra, et aliarum rerum
quarumcum]que[10] [ante eundem][11] octavum (fo. 176r)[12] diem decembris infra
regnum nostrum Anglie et partes Wallie emersa et eventa, unde punitio caderet
in demandam debitum seu in finem et redemptionem aut in alias penas pecun-
iarias, seu in forisf[actur]am[13] bonorum et catallorum aut imprisionamenta seu
amerciamenta communitatum villarum vel singularum personarum, vel in
onerationem liberi tenementi eorum qui unquam transgressi fuerint ut heredum
exequutorum, vel terre tenentium escaetorum vicecomitum coronatorum et
aliorum huiusmodi, et omne id quod ad nos versus ipsas pertinet vel pertinere
posset ex causis supradictis, acetiam omnimodas donationes alienationes et
perquisitiones per ipsas de terris et tenementis de nobis vel progenitoribus
nostris quondam regibus Anglie in capite tentas, acetiam donationes alienationes
et perquisitiones ad manum mortuum factas et habitas absque licencia regia,
necnon omnimodas intrusiones et ingressus per ipsas in hereditatem suam in
parte vel in toto post mortem antecessorum suorum absque debita prosequut-

---

1 MS *eeadem*, *a* cancelled.
2 Hole 6 mm.
3 Followed by *eas*, expunged.
4 Hole 3 mm.
5 Damaged 5 mm.
6 Damaged 7 mm.
7 Damaged 3 mm.
8 Hole 4 mm.
9 Damaged 24 mm.
10 Hole 50 mm.
11 Hole 14 mm.
12 Heading *Perdonatio regis Henrici iiij^{ti}*.
13 Unclear 6 mm.

ione eiusdem extra manum[1] regiam ante eundem octavum diem decembris facta, una cum exitibus et profituis inde medio tempore perceptis, acetiam perdonavimus et relaxavimus prefatis abbatisse et conventui omnimodas fines adjudicates amerciamenta exitus forisfactiones relevia scutagia ac omnimoda debita compota prestita arreragia firmarum et com[poto]rum[2] nobis vicesimo primo die marciis anno regni nostri primo qualitercumque debita et per[ti-nencia, ne]cnon[3] omnimodas actiones et de[mandas quas nos]4 sol[us versus ipsas]5 vel nos con[junctim cum aliis]6 personis (fo. 176v)7 seu persona habemus seu habere poterimus, acetiam waiviare in ipsas promulgatas pro aliqua causa-rum supradictarum. Et insuper perdonavimus et relaxavimus eisdem abbatisse et conventui omnimodas penas ante eundem octavum diem decembris forisfactas coram nobis seu consilio nostro cancellario thesaurario seu aliquo judicum nostrorum pro aliqua causa et omnes alias penas, tam nobis quam carissimo patre nostro defuncto, per ipsas pro aliqua causa ante eundem octavum diem decembris forisfactas et ad opus nostrum levandum, ac omnimodas securitates pacis ante illum diem octavum similiter forisfactas, ita quod presens perdonatio nostra quo ad premissa seu aliquod premissorum non cedat in dampnum prejudicium vel derogationem alicuius alterius persone quam persone nostre dumtaxat. In cuius rei testimonium has litteras nostras fieri fecimus patentes. Teste Johanne duce Bedford' custode Anglie aput Westm'8 die Septembris anno regni nostri tertio. Per ipsum regem. Prestwik.

> Note. Contrary to the rubric and running heading, this document must date from the reign of Henry V, because John, duke of Bedford, was keeper (*custos*) of England in 1415. This pardon is not enrolled on the patent rolls.

260 *Exchequer plea concerning the ninths owed in Barley (Herts.) by the the prior of Anglesey and the abbess of Chatteris, who are judged to be quit by reason of 8s. 4d. exacted from the prior and 20s. exacted from the abbess, since all their temporalities in Barley are annexed to their spiritualities and were taxed at a tenth with the clergy both in 1291 and hitherto.*

---

1 Followed by *mortuam*, expunged.
2 Hole 10 mm.
3 Holes 11 mm and 3 mm.
4 Unclear 26 mm.
5 Holes 29 mm.
6 Damaged 28 mm.
7 Heading *Placita in scaccario*.
8 Ordinal number omitted.

fos. 176v–177v   13 Nov. 1353–*c.* 13 Oct. 1356

   Copy: (V) PRO E 13/79, rot. 42.

Placita coram baronibus de scaccario de termino sancti Michaelis anno regni regis Edwardi tertii vicesimo octavo[1] pro priore de Angleseye et abbatissa de Chatriz.

Dominus rex mandavit[2] breve suum de magno sigillo suo quod est inter communia de hoc anno, termino videlicet sancti Michaelis, in hec verba: Edwardus Dei gracia etc. Et[3] aliud breve[4] de dicto[5] magno sigillo[6] quod est inter

---

[1] Recte *septimo.*

[2] V adds *hic.*

[3] V omits *etc. Et,* adds *rex Anglie et Francie et dominus Hibernie thesaurario et baronibus suis de scaccario salutem. Cum nos nuper, ex parte religiosorum et aliorum virorum ecclesiasticorum regni nostri Anglie, qui ad parliamentum nostrum apud Westm' ad diem mercurii proximum post diem dominicam in medio quadragesime anno regni nostri Anglie xiiij° tentum, ubi prelati comites barones et communitates eiusdem regni ad idem parliamentum personaliter summoniti nonam garbam, nonum vellus et nonum agnum nobis pro expeditione quorundam arduorum negotiorum nostrorum in partibus transmarinis concesserunt, summoniti non fuerunt, per petitionem suam coram nobis et consilio nostro in parliamento nostro exhibitam accipientes quod, cum ipsi quandam decimam anualem nobis ultra decimas anualem et triennalem prius pro ipsos concessas de spiritualibus suis et temporalibus spiritualibus illis annexis, de quibus decimas huiusmodi dare et solvere consueverunt, concesserint, et licet iidem religiosi et alii viri ecclesiastici portiones ipsos de decima huiusmodi nobis ad terminos tunc elapsos contingentes solverint, et residuum inde ad terminum tunc constitutum solvere fuerunt parati, assessores tamen et venditores none predicte ipsos religiosos et alios viros ecclesiasticos ad dictam nonam nobis de temporalibus suis predictis solvendam, ac si nonam predictam concesserint cum non fecerint, distrinxerunt, per quod postmodum in parliamento nostro super premissis concordatum extiterat quod dicti religiosi et alii viri ecclesiastici, qui ad dictum parliamentum ad dictum diem mercurii summoniti non fuerunt, nec huiusmodi nonam nobis concesserunt, et qui decimas nobis per eos sic concessas de temporalibus spiritualibus suis annexis que ad decimam inter spiritualia anno regni domini Edwardi quondam regis Anglie avi nostri vicesimo taxata fuerunt solverunt, de solutione none predicte pro predictis temporalibus sic ad decimam taxatis penitus exonerarentur, quodque de terris et tenementis per ipsos religiosos et alios viros ecclesiasticos post dictum annum vicesimum adquisitis eadem nona levaretur ad opus nostrum. Vobis mandamus quod demande quam per summonitionem scaccarii predicti dilecto nobis in Christo priori de Angleseye, qui ad dictum parliamentum nostrum summonitus non fuit, sicut per inspectionem rotulorum cancellarie nostre nobis constat, pro dicta nona garbarum vellerum et agnorum de temporalibus eiusdem prioris spiritualibus suis annexis, si ad decimam inter eadem spiritualia dicto anno xx° taxata fuerint nobis solvendam fieri facitis omnino supersederi et ipsum coram vobis in scaccario predicto exonerari et quietum esse faciatis. Proviso quod eadem nona de terris et tenementis si que per ipsum priorem vel predecessores suos post dictum annum vicesimum adquisita fuerint ad opus nostrum levetur ut est justum. Teste meipso apud Westm' xx° die novembris anno regni nostri Anglie vicesimo septimo, regni vero nostri Francie quartodecimo. Mandavit etiam idem rex quoddam.*

communia de hoc termino in hec verba: Edwardus Dei gracia etc.[1] Et modo ad xv^{am} sancti Martini venerunt predictus[2] prior de Angleseye et a[bbatissa][3] de Chatriz per[4] attornatum suum[5] et dicunt ipsos graviter district[os e]sse[6] per vicecomitem Hertf' pro nona predicta.[7] Et petunt sibi f[ieri][8] in premissis quod etc. secundum tenorem [mandatorum regis][9] su[pra]dictorum.[10] (fo. 177r)[11] Et super hoc scrutatis rotulis[12] compertum est in magno[13] rotulo examinato[14] in Hertf' quod viij s. iiij d. exiguntur de prefato priore[15] de nona garbarum[16] vellerum et agnorum regi anno xiiij° concessa pro temporalibus suis in[17] Berle, sicut continetur in dicto[18] rotulo etc.[19] Exiguntur etiam de prefata abbatissa in

---

4   V adds *suum*.

5   V omits.

6   V adds *suo pro abbatissa de Chateriz*.

1   V omits, adds *rex Anglie et Francie et dominus Hibernie ... ad opus nostrum* (see note 3 above). *Vobis mandamus quod demande quam per summonitionem scaccarii predicti dilecte nobis in Christo abbatisse de Chateriz pro dicta nona garbarum vellerum et agnorum de temporalibus eiusdem abbatisse spiritualibus suis annexis, si ad decimam inter eadem spiritualia dicto anno vicesimo taxata fuerint nobis solvendam fieri facitis omnino supersederi et ipsam coram vobis in scaccario predicto exonerari et quietam esse faciatis. Proviso quod eadem nona de terris et tenementis si que per ipsam abbatissam vel predecessores suos post dictum annum vicesimum adquisita fuerint ad opus nostrum levetur ut est justum. Teste meipso apud Westm' xiij° die Novembris anno regni nostri Anglie vicesimo septimo, regni vero nostri Francie quartodecimo.*

2   V *venerunt hic predicti*.

3   Hole 9 mm.

4   V adds *Simonem de Charwelton' eorum*.

5   V omits.

6   Hole 4 mm.

7   V adds *ac si temporalia sua spiritualibus suis non forent annexa*.

8   Hole 4 mm.

9   Hole 20 mm.

10   Hole 2 mm.

11   Heading *Placita in scaccario*.

12   V adds *etc*.

13   V omits.

14   MS *examio*.

15   V adds *de Angleseye*.

16   MS *garba*.

17   V adds *parochia de*.

18   V *magno*.

19   V omits, adds *de anno xv° in Hertford' et in rotulis de particulis computorum Hugonis Fitz-Simond', Johannis Blomvyll' prioris de Donemawe, Roberti de Geddeworth, Ricardi de Kelleshull' et Willelmi de Teye, assessorum et venditorum none predicte in dicto comitatu Hertford', hic in thesauro existentis.*

dicto rotulo examinato xx s. de nona predicta pro temporalibus suis ibidem,[1]
sicut continetur in dicto[2] rotulo examinato.[3] Compertum est etiam in rotulis
de particulis taxationis temporalium cleri in diocese London', archidiaconatu
videlicet Midd', decanatu de Brakkyng', que taxatio facta fuit anno xx° regis
Edwardi avi regis nunc, quod[4] temporalia dicti prioris[5] in dicto decanatu[6] ad
iiij li. xix s. iiij d. et temporalia dicte abbatisse[7] ad x li. ij s. x d. in universo ad
x^{am} cum clero taxantur[8] etc. Et super hoc quesitum est a prefatis priore et
abbatissa si sciant informare curiam de particulari taxatione temporalium suorum predictorum. Dicunt quod non, sed dicunt quod omnia temporalia sua in
Berle ubi assidentur ad nonam predictam[9] comprehenduntur et taxantur sub
taxationibus predictis ad x^{am} cum clero ipsius, videlicet prioris sub predicta
taxatione iiij li. xix s. iiij d. et prefate abbatisse sub prefata taxatione x li. ij s. x
d., et sunt parcella eorundem temporalium.[10] Et dicunt ulterius quod omnia[11]
terre et tenementa sua in Berle spiritualibus suis sunt annexa et fuerunt de
possessione domorum suarum predicto anno xx° avi et eodem anno ad x^{am} cum
clero taxata fuerunt,[12] et quod[13] ipsi et predecessores[14] sui in singulis conces-
sionibus x^{arum} cleri a predicto anno xx° hucusque solverunt x^{as} et alias quo[tas
cum][15] clero quotiens et quando etc.[16] Adiciendo [ipso]s[17] seu predecessores[18]
suos aliqua terre et[19] tenementi in dicta [villa][20] de Berle[21] (fo. 177v)[22] post

---

1 V omits *de nona predicta pro temporalibus suis ibidem*, adds *pro temporalibus suis in dicta par-*
   ochia de Berle de nona supradicta.

2 V *magno*.

3 V omits, adds *de anno xv° predicto et in rotulis de particulis computorum assessorum et vendi-*
   torum predictorum in comitatu predicto hic in thesauro existentis.

4 Followed by *d*, expunged.

5 V omits *dicti*, adds *de Angleseye* after *prioris*.

6 V adds *de Brakkyng*.

7 V omits *dicte*, adds *de Chateriz* after *abbatisse*.

8 V adds *juxta quas taxas iidem prior et abbatissa et predecessores sui solverunt x^{as} et alias quotas*
   cum clero quotiens et quando.

9 V adds *ut premittitur*.

10 V adds *sic ad x^{am} cum clero taxantur*.

11 Followed by *re*, cancelled.

12 V omits.

13 V omits.

14 MS *predic'*.

15 Hole 12 mm.

16 V omits *quotiens ... etc.*, adds *pro temporalibus suis ibidem*.

17 Hole 10 mm.

18 MS *predic'*.

19 V *seu*.

dictum annum xx[m] non adquisivisse nec aliqua bona seu catalla[1] dicto anno xiiij° ibidem[2] habuisse, alia quam de terris et tenementis illis sic spiritualibus suis annexis exeuntia, et hec omnia pretendunt verificare etc. Et preceptum est[3] vicecomiti quod venire faciat hic a die sancti Hillarii in xv dies xij etc. de usu de Berle quorum quilibet etc. per quos etc. qui nec etc. ad recognitionem etc. Postea ad xv[am] sancti Michaelis anno xxx° dicti regis nunc[4] Robertus de Chirwelton'[5] clericus placitorum huius scaccarii[6] liberavit hic[7] inquisitionem captam super premissis[8] aput Berqweweye[9] etc.[10] per sacramentum Willelmi Grimbald',[11] Roberti Bassett[12] et aliorum juratorum etc.[13] qui dicunt super sacramentum suum quod omnia temporalia dictorum prioris et abbatisse, pro quibus ipsi assidentur ad nonam predictam in villa de Berle, spiritualibus suis

---

[20] Hole 9 mm.

[21] V *Berleye.*

[22] Heading *Placita.*

[1] V adds *ibidem.*

[2] V omits.

[3] MS *s'.*

[4] V omits *Postea ... nunc,* adds *Et quod premunire faciat prefatos assessores et venditores quod interfuit captioni inquisitionis predicte si sibi viderint expedire. Et idem dies datus est prefatis priori et abbatisse et interim respitium. Et continuato processu isto usque a die sancte Trinitatis in xv dies anno xxix[no], sicut continetur alibi in hoc rotulo inter placita de termino sancti Hillarii. Et similiter in rotulo placitorum huius scaccarii de dicto anno xxix[no] inter placita de termino sancti Michaelis. Quo die prefati prior et abbatissa per dictum attornatum suum venerunt. Et vicecomes non retornavit breve. Ideo datus est dies prefatis priori et abbatisse ulterius usque a die sancti Michaelis in xv dies. Et preceptum est vicecomiti sicut pluries quod distringat juratores etc. Et preter illos octo tales etc. Et quod premunire faciat prefatos assessores etc. Ita etc. ad eundem diem vel interim coram Roberto de Charwelton', clerico placitorum huius scaccarii, assignato per litteras regis patentes ad inquisitionem illam capiendam ad certos diem et locum quos etc. Ita quod inquisitionem illam habeat hic ad predictam xv[am] sancti Michaelis. Ad quem diem predicti prior et abbatissa venerunt per dictum attornatum suum. Et predictus.*

[5] V *Charwelton'.*

[6] V omits *clericus ... scaccarii.*

[7] V adds *quandam.*

[8] V omits *captam super premissis,* adds *coram eo.*

[9] V *Berkwey.*

[10] V omits, adds *die veneris proximo post festum sancte Marie Magdalene predicto anno xxix[no], in presentia predictorum prioris et abbatisse ibidem per Gilbertum Bernard' eorum attornatum comperentium captam, prefatis assessoribus et venditoribus dicte none in eodem comitatu pluries vocatis et non comperentibus.*

[11] V *Grymbaud'.*

[12] V *Basset.*

[13] V omits, adds *quorum nomina annotantur in panello brevis.*

sunt annexa et fuerunt de possessione domorum suarum[1] predicto anno xx°
predicti avi regis nunc, et eodem anno ad x[am] cum clero taxata fuerunt, et
semper hucusque quando decime cleri currebant, [et][2] non cum laicis, et quod
ipsi nec eorum alter aliqua terre seu tenementi in parochia de Berle predicta[3]
post dictum annum xx[m] adquisiverunt,[4] nec aliqua bona mobilia ibidem dicto
anno octavo[5] habuerunt alia quam de terris et tenementis illis sic spiritualibus
suis[6] exeuntia. Item dicunt quod omnia temporalia ipsius prioris apud dictam
villam de Berle sub iiij li. ix s. et iiij d.[7] et prefate abbatisse sub x[cem8] libris[9] ij s.
et[10] x d. predictis comprehenduntur et taxantur et sunt parcella earundem
summarum. Ideo consideratum est [quod][11] predictus prior de octo solidis et[12]
quatuor denariis ...[13] et predicta abbatissa de predictis xx[ti] solidis, ab e[is][14]
seper[atim][15] exactis, de eadem nona exhone[rentur et quieti existant][16] pretextu
premissorum. (fo. 178r)[17]

261 *Exchequer plea concerning the ninth owed by the prior of Anglesey in Litlington, Haslingfield, Stow cum Quy, Little Wilbraham, Bottisham and Swaffham
Prior, and the ninth owed by the abbess of Chatteris in Shepreth, Barrington and
Foxton. Since all their temporalities in each place are annexed to their spiritualities
and were taxed at a tenth with the clergy both in 1291 and hitherto, the prior and
abbess are judged to be quit by reason of £4 7s. 11d. exacted from the prior and £4
13s. ¼d. exacted from the abbess.*
fos. 178r–179r   *c.* 3 Nov. 1354–*c.* 13 Oct. 1355

1 V adds *de Angleseye et Chateriz.*
2 Damaged 3 mm.
3 V *predicta de Berle.*
4 MS *adquisierunt.*
5 V *xiiij°.*
6 V adds *annexis.*
7 V *iiij li. xix s. iiij d.*
8 V *ix.*
9 Followed by hole 3 mm; appears to be something lacking, but nothing added in V.
10 V omits.
11 Damaged 8 mm; V adds *tam.*
12 V omits.
13 Hole 14 mm.
14 Hole 5 mm.
15 Damaged 7 mm. V omits *et predicta ... seperatim*, adds *ab eo exactis de nona predicta, quam
prefata abbatissa de xx s. ab ea.*
16 Damaged 43 mm.
17 Heading *In scaccario.*

Placita coram baronibus de scaccario super taxam temporalium villarum de Berlee et Scheperey pro priore de Angleseye et abbatissa de Chateriz.

Dominus rex mandavit breve suum etc. q[uod est][1] inter communia de anno xx° viij°, termino videlicet sancti Michaelis, in hec [verba]:[2] Edwardus etc. Mandavit etiam q[uoddam ali]ud[3] breve quod est ibidem in hec verba etc.: Edwar[dus][4] etc. Et [modo][5] ad crastinum Animarum venerunt hic predicti [pri]or[6] et abbatissa [per atturnatum][7] suum et dicunt ipsos graviter d[istrictos][8] esse per vicecomitem Cantabr' pro nona predicta [ac][9] si temporalia sua spiritualibus suis non for[ent annexa].[10] Et petunt sibi fieri in premissis quo[d][11] etc. secundum [tenorem][12] mandatorum regis [sup]radictorum.[13] Et [su]per[14] hoc scrutatis rotulis etc. Compertum est in rotulo examinato in Cantabr' quod iiij li. vij s. xj d. exiguntur de priore de Angleseye de nona garbarum etc., videlicet x s. in Littyngton', vj s. et viij d. in Haselyngfeld', ij s. in Stowe cum Qweia, ix s. et iij d. in Wylberam Parva, xlviij s. in Botkysham et xij s. in Swafham Prioris, sicut continetur etc. Exiguntur etiam de prefata abbatis[sa][15] in dicto rotulo examinato in Cantabr' iiij li. xiij s.[16] qu. de nona predicta, unde xv s. in Scheperede, xvj s. in Barenton' et l s. j d. qu. in Foxton', sicut continetur ibidem etc. Compertum est etiam in particulis de taxatione temporalium cleri in diocese Eliensi, que taxatio facta fuit anno xx° regis Edwardi avi nostri regis nunc, quod tem[porli]a[17] prefati prioris apud Littyngton' ad[18] l[xvj][19] s. [viij][20] d.,

1 Hole 9 mm.
2 Hole 5 mm.
3 Damaged 18 mm.
4 Hole 5 mm.
5 Hole 8 mm.
6 Hole 5 mm.
7 Hole 23 mm.
8 Hole 17 mm.
9 Hole 5 mm.
10 Hole 22 mm, MS very distorted.
11 Hole 9 mm, MS very distorted.
12 Hole 10 mm.
13 Hole 4 mm.
14 Hole 4 mm.
15 Hole 2 mm.
16 Followed by *quam*, cancelled.
17 Hole 7 mm.
18 Followed by *xl*, cancelled.

apud Haselinfeld' ad lxxiiij s., apud Stowe ad xl ⟨s.⟩, apud Queye ad xl ⟨s.⟩ v d., aput Wylberham Parva ad vij li. xij s. iiij d. et apud Swafham Prioris ad iiij li. iiij s. separatim taxantur. Compertum (fo. 178v)[1] est etiam in eisdem rotulis quia temporalia prefate abbatisse apud Barenton' ad xj li. xiiij[2] s. j d. et apud Foxton' ad xxv [li.] [x]ij[3] s. ij d. taxantur. Et quia non ap[ar]et[4] per premissa si predictus prior in Bokesham et prefa[ta ab]batissa[5] in Scheperethe ...[6] ad aliquam[7] quotam cum clero t[axan]tur,[8] quesitum est a[b][9] eis quare particule none ibidem super istas assessas de ipsis levare non debet, ad quod idem p[rior][10] dicit quod Angleseye, ubi prioratus[11] predictus situatur infra parochiam de B[okesham],[12] et temporalia sua ibidem cum clero taxantur ad ...ndum[13] tempo[ra]lia[14] sic cum clero taxata sunt illa [sed][15] eadem temporalia pro ...bus.[16] Idem prior assessus fuit ad nonam predictam in Betekesham et non alia. Et quo ad Scheperede ubi predicta abbatissa dicit quod ipsa predicto anno xiiij° aliqua terre et tenementi non habuit ibidem, nisi ecclesiam eiusdem ville quam ipsa tenet in proprios usus et terras[17] et tenementa de dote eiusdem[18] ecclesie etc. Et dicit ulterius quod omnia temporalia sua in singulis villis et locis predictis spiritualibus suis sunt annexa et ad x^am cum clero taxata, ut infra in placito de comitatu Hertf'. Postea ad xv^am sancti Michaelis anno xxix° regis nunc Robertus de Carwelton' clericus etc. liberavit hic quandam inquisitionem

---

19 Unclear 5 mm; illegible sums for prior supplied from *Taxatio Ecclesiastica Angliae et Walliae Auctoritate Nicholai IV circa A.D. 1291* [ed. T. Astle et al.] (Record Commission, 1802) p. 269.

20 Unclear 5 mm.

1 Heading *Placita in scaccario*.

2 Recte *iij*; cf. *Taxatio Ecclesiastica Nicholai IV*, p. 268.

3 Hole 9 mm; supplied from *Taxatio Ecclesiastica Nicholai IV*, p. 268.

4 Unclear 3 mm.

5 Hole 8 mm.

6 Hole 5 mm.

7 MS *aliqua*.

8 Hole 9 mm.

9 Hole 6 mm.

10 Hole 9 mm.

11 MS *prio ad...nd' te... ...lis ratus; ad...nd' te... ...lis* expunged; holes 12 mm and 10 mm.

12 Hole 19 mm.

13 Hole 11 mm.

14 Hole 9 mm, MS very distorted.

15 Hole 2 mm.

16 Hole 7 mm.

17 MS *terre*.

18 Followed by *l*, expunged.

coram eo captam super premissis apud Cantabr', die sabbati proximo post festum sancte Marie Magdalene anno xxix° predicto, per sacramentum suum Hugonis Oressy et aliorum juratorum etc. qui dicunt ...um[1] pro parte prout iidem prior et abbatissa placitaverunt. Ideo consideratum est quod tam dictus prior[2] de predictis iiij li. vij s.[3] xj d. quam prefata abbatissa de predictis iiij li. xiij s. qu., ab eis separatim ut premittitur exactis, exhonerentur et quieti existant (fo. 179r) pretextu premissorum. Et quod predictus ⟨prior⟩ venit hic ad ostendendum siquidem pro se habeat vel[4] dicere sciat quare dicta terra et tenementa de novo adquisita in manum regis seisiri non debe[nt],[5] videlicet xlj acre terre.

Note. The exchequer plea roll for 28 & 29 Edward III is lacking.

262 *Statement of the amounts owed by the abbess of Chatteris for the ninth and that she should not thence be summoned by the royal writ enrolled in the memoranda rolls.*
fo. 179r   [In or after October 1354]

Extenta monasterii de Chateriz.

Abbatissa de Chatriz debet[6] iiij li. xiij d. qu. de pred[icta][7] nona pro bonis suis in villis[8] de Schep... [Barenton][9] et Foxton', sicut continetur in dicto rotulo exannali in Cant', et xx s. de eadem nona in villa de Berle, sicut continetur in dicto rotulo exannali in Essex'. Summa Cj s. j d. qu. Sed non debet inde summoniri per breve regis irrotulatum in memorandis de anno xxviij° regis huius termino Michaelis et per considerationem baronis annotatam in rotulis predictis et ... [p]re[d]ictis.[10]

263 *Memorandum of the payments made by the abbess of Chatteris for procuration for a cardinal from her income in the dioceses of Ely and Norwich.*
fo. 179r

1 Hole 6 mm.
2 Followed by *venit hic ad ostendendum*, expunged.
3 Followed by *vj*, expunged.
4 Interlined.
5 Hole 2 mm.
6 Followed by *x*, expunged.
7 Hole 3 mm.
8 MS *villa, a* expunged, abbreviation mark added.
9 Hole 31 mm.
10 Hole 13 mm.

Procuratio monasterii de Chateriz cuidam cardinali.

Memorandum quod abbatissa de Chatriz solvit pro procuratione cardinali de bonis suis in diocese Eliensi iiij li. vij s. j d.,[1] s. de marca viij d. Et pro moderatis expensis iij s. iiij d. ob. de libra per acquietanciam.

Item solvit pro eodem in diocese Norwicensi xj s. ix d. ob. per acquietanciam.

264 *Valuation of the temporalities of Chatteris abbey [for the taxation of pope Nicholas IV, 1291].*
fo. 179r

Bona temporalia abbathie de Chatriz ad taxam.

In Chatriz summa bonorum xvj li.[2] iiij s. v d.
In Kyngeston' summa bonorum xiiij s.
In Foxton' summa bonorum xxv li. xij s. ij d.
In Barenton' summa bonorum xj li. iij s. j d.
In Over'[3] summa bonorum xlviij s.
In Maddynglee summa bonorum xx s.
In Wilberton' summa bonorum vj d.
Summa omnium bonorum lvij li. ij s. [ij d. Inde][4] decima Cxiiij s. iij d.

265 *Valuation of the spiritualities of Chatteris abbey [for the taxation of pope Nicholas IV, 1291].*
fo. 179r–v

Bona spiritualia abbathie de Chatriz ad taxam. (fo. 179v)[5]

Ecclesia de Chatriz xvj li. xiij s. iiij d.
Inde decima xxxiij s. iiij d.
Ecclesia de Schepereye xiij li. vj s. viij[6] d.
Inde decima xxvj s. viij d.

---

[1] Followed by space, 10 mm.
[2] Preceded by *s.*, expunged.
[3] MS *Quer'*.
[4] Hole 18 mm; *ij d.* supplied from *Taxatio Ecclesiastica Nicholai IV*, p. 268.
[5] Heading *Berle*.
[6] *v* seems to be expunged, but the sum is £8 6s. 8d. in *Taxatio Ecclesiastica Nicholai IV*, p. 267.

266 *Form of presentation by Chatteris abbey of a chaplain to the rectory of Barley (Herts.), for admission and institution by John [Kempe], bishop of London.*
fo. 179v In the chapter-house at Chatteris abbey, [22 May 1422 × 20 July 1425]

Presentatio ecclesie de Berle quando vacaverit per dominam abbatissam et conventum de Chatriz.

[Reverendo in Ch]risto[1] patri et domino domino J(ohanni) Dei gracia episcopo London' vestre humiles et devote filie abbatissa et conventus de Chatriz[2] omnimodam reverenciam tanto patri debitam cum honore. Ad perpetuam[3] rectoriam ecclesie parochialis beate Marie de Berle, per mortem domini B. de D. ultimi rectoris ibidem vacantem et ad nostram[4] presentationem spe[ctantem],[5] dilectum nobis in Christo dominum J.[6] de F. capellanum paternitati vestre reverende [pr]esen[tamus],[7] intuitu caritatis humiliter supplicantes [et][8] devo[te][9] quatinus dominum eundem J. ad rectoriam predictam admittere et ipsum instituere canonice in eadem ⟨et⟩ cetera que vestro pastorali incumbunt officio in hac parte peragere dig[nemini][10] graciose. In cuius rei testimonium sigillum nostrum commune presentibus est appensum. Date in domo nostra capitulari de Chatriz predicta quarto die mensis etc. anno Domini etc.

Note. Bishop John Kempe was translated from Chichester to London on 17 Nov. 1421 but did not receive his spiritualities until 22 May 1422 (*Fasti 1300-1541* v, p. 3); he was translated to York on 20 July 1425.

267 *Form of presentation by Chatteris abbey to the vicarage of Chatteris [for admission and institution by Philip Morgan, bishop of Ely].*
fos. 179v–180r [27 Feb. 1426 × 25 Oct. 1435]

1 Hole 33 mm.
2 Followed by *omnimd*, expunged.
3 Followed by *vicar'*, expunged.
4 Followed by *vacatio*, expunged.
5 Hole 13 mm.
6 Unclear; possibly *N.* but chaplain is called *J.* below.
7 Holes 3 mm and 9 mm.
8 Hole 1 mm.
9 Hole 4 mm.
10 Hole 4 mm.

Presentatio ad vicariam ecclesie de Chatriz cum vac[av]erit[1] ut supra terminis mutatis.

Reverendo in Christo patre et domino domino Philippo Dei gracia Eliensi episcopo vestre humiles et devote abbatis[sa][2] et conventus de Chatriz vestre diocesis obedien[tiam et][3] reverenciam [tanto][4] patri debitas cum honore. [Ad][5] perpetuam vicariam ecclesie parochialis sancti Petri de (fo. 180r)[6] Chatriz, per mortem domini B. de D. ultimi vicarii ibidem vacantem etc. ut supra.

Note. Philip Morgan was bishop of Ely 27 Feb. 1426–25 Oct. 1435.

268 *Form of presentation by Chatteris abbey to the vicarage of Shepreth.*
fo. 180r

Item ad perpetuam vicariam ecclesie parochialis omnium sanctorum[7] de Scheperede per mortem domini B. etc. ut supra.[8]

269 *Privilege 'Ex commisso nobis' of pope Lucius II to Nigel, bishop of Ely, confirming the possessions of the church of Ely, including Chatteris abbey.*
fos. 180r–182v [At the Lateran, Rome, 24 May 1144]

> Cartulary copies: (C) Cambridge, Trinity College MS O. 2. 41, pp. 146–53; (D) BL Cotton MS Tib. A. vi, fos. 114v–116r; (E) Cambridge, Trinity College MS O. 2. 1, fos. 148r–149r; (F) Cambridge UL, EDC 1, fos. 152r–153v; (G) BL Cotton MS Titus A. i, fos. 39r–40v; (M) Cambridge UL, EDR G/3/28 'Liber M', pp. 5–8; (O) Oxford, Bodl. MS Laud. Misc. 647, fo. 90r–v.
> Printed in *Papsturkunden in England* ii, pp. 181–5, no. 35 and *Liber Eliensis* ed. Blake, pp. 330–2.

Lucius episcopus servus servorum Dei venerabili fratri Nigello Eliensi episcopo eiusque successoribus canonice substituendis inperpetuum. Ex commisso nobis a Deo apostolatus officio fratribus nostris tam vicinis quam longe positis paterna nos convenit provicione consulere et[9] ecclesiis, in quibus Domino militare

---

1 Unclear 3 mm.
2 Hole 3 mm.
3 Damaged 6 mm.
4 Hole 10 mm.
5 Damaged 4 mm.
6 Heading *Presentatio.*
7 *Presentatio*, marginated in red, after *sanctorum.*
8 *Item ... supra*: in black, underlined in red.
9 MS *in*: misreading of ampersand.

noscuntur, suam justiciam conservare, ut quemadmodum disponente Domino patres vocamur in nomine, ita nichillominus comprobemur[1] in opere. Proinde, venerabilis frater Nigelle episcope, tuis justis desideriis paterna benignitate annuentes Eliensem ecclesiam, cui Deo auctore presides, sub beati Petri et nostra protectione suscipimus et presentis scripti privilegio communimus. Statuentes, ut quascumque possessiones, quecumque bona inpresentiarum juste et legitime[2] possides aut in futurum largitione regum vel principum, oblatione fidelium seu aliis justis modis D[eo prop]itio[3] eadem ecclesia poterit adip[isci],[4] firma tibi tuisque successoribus et illibata per/maneant. (fo. 180v) In quibus hec nominatim[5] duximus annotanda: quecumque silicet rex Henricus recordationis egregie [ei]dem[6] ecclesie pro sua devotione tradidit et concessit, relaxationem silicet servicii[7] militum episcopatus Eliensis, quod in castello de Northwyc[8] fieri consuevit, remissionem quoque viginti quinque solidorum et quinque denariorum et unius oboli, qui per singulos annos dabantur vigili ipsius castri, relaxationem in super totius servicii et[9] operationum quas homines Eliensis ecclesie facere in predicto castello solebant, remissionem etiam quatraginta librarum de scutagio, pro ut ab eodem[10] noscitur institutum et scripto firmatum. Preterea abbatiam de Chateriz[11] cum omnibus suis pertinenciis[12] Eliensi ecclesie nichilominus confirmamus, ita tamen quod sanctimoniales, que ibi sunt aut in antea fuerint, juxta institutionem[13] beati Benedicti regulariter vivant. Remissionem quoque de wardpeni in omnibus terris eiusdem Eliensis ecclesie et ecclesie de Chateriz[14] necnon restitutiones terrarum, libertatum ac dignitatum ab illustri viro rege Stephano factas firmas et inconvulsas[15] vobis[16] inperpetuum servari precipimus.

1   O *complemur.*
2   EFGO *religiose.*
3   Hole 11 mm.
4   Hole 4 mm.
5   O *nominatim hec.*
6   Hole 4 mm.
7   MS and CEFGO *servicium.*
8   C *Northwic,* D *Nortwic,* EFO *Norwic,* G *Norwich,* M *Northwico.*
9   MS *in*: misreading of ampersand.
10 DM add *rege* (D ins. marg.).
11 C *Catheriz,* D *Chatriz,* E *Cateriz,* F *Chateric,* G *Caterit.*
12 G *pertinenciis suis.*
13 FO *constitutionem.*
14 CDE *Catheriz,* F *Cateric.*
15 MS *inconvullas.*
16 MS *nobis.*

Simili etiam modo possessiones,[1] libertates ac dignitates a reliquis Anglorum regibus atque[2] principibus ecclesie tue collatas et[3] predecessore nostro Victore papa bone memorie confirmatas[4] tibi tuisque successoribus et per vos[5] eidem ecclesie confirmamus. Porro quecumque bona monachis ipsius ecclesie conservande religionis et sectande hospitalitatis intuitu contulisti, eidem illibata manere sanctimus,[6] ita tamen ut de hiis, que habent idem mona/chi (fo. 181r) seu etiam que episcopalibus usibus[7] reservasti, tibi vel successoribus tuis vel etiam eisdem monachis distrahere aliqua vel militari officio deputare non liceat, quin potius ea que distracta sunt recuperare et que recuperata sunt[8] in jure ac dicione tue ecclesie retinere liberam habeas facultatem. Monachis autem ipsis terras suas alicui hereditario jure tenendas concedere omnimodis[9] prohibemus. Nomina vero terrarum et possessionum, quas eisdem monachis tam in villis quam earundem ecclesiis ipsarumque omnimodis appendiciis concessisti, sunt[10] hec: infra Insulam Suttuna,[11] Wycheham,[12] Wycheford,[13] Lyteltieford,[14] Wyntwortha,[15] Tydbrytesya,[16] Wytleseya,[17] Stunten[e]ya[18] cum viginti tribus milibus anguillarum, que capiuntur in paludibus et aquis, que adjacent manerio illi, et omnes apportatus et oblationes altarium matris ecclesie ad sustentandas eiusdem ecclesie necessitates,[19] ecclesia[20] sancte Marie[21] de Eli[22] cum terris et

---

1   O adds *et*.
2   EFGO *ac*.
3   DM add *a* (D ins. marg.).
4   G omits *et predecessore ... confirmatas*.
5   MS *nos*.
6   MS *sanycimus*.
7   MS *usiibus*.
8   FO omit *recuperare ... recuperata sunt*.
9   G *omnibus modis*.
10   F *super*.
11   F *Suttona*, O *Suthona*.
12   CEFGMO *Wicheham*, D *Wicheam*.
13   CEFO *Wicheford*, DM *Wichford*, G *Wicgeford*.
14   CM *Liteltiedford*, D *Liteltiædford*, EFG *Litlethetford*, O *Lithlethedford*.
15   CD *Winteuurtha*, EFM *Wintewrda*, G *Winteuurþa*, O *Winteword'*.
16   C *Tidbriteseia*, D *Thidbriteseia*, EG *Tidbrichteseia*, F *Tidbridteseia*, M *Tidbricteseya*, O *Tidbrigteseia*.
17   CDEF *Witleseia*, GO *Withleseia*, M *Witleseya*.
18   Hole 10 mm, MS very distorted; CDEFGO *Stunteneia*.
19   MS *necessitate*.
20   FO *ecclesiam*.
21   C *Maria*.
22   CDFGMO *Ely*, E *Hely*.

decimis et omnibus suis pertinenciis et nominatim tota decima de Beortuna[1] tua
et quicquid habebis[2] in Iselham'[3] et Heneyham[4] et Belam, septem pensas salis
in Tyrentuna,[5] quin etiam ligna in Summeresham[6] et Bluntesham, sicut melius
habuerunt[7] tempore predesessorum tuorum, et super ripam de Bluntesham una
mansura terre cum quinque acris, ubi coligantur ligna, et cum octo acris[8] praty,
unde pascantur boves, qui ligna attrahunt, vinea quoque sua in Eli[9] sicut (fo.
181v) habuerunt, priusquam episcopus esses, sex piscatores cum mansionibus
suis ad piscandum in aquis, in quibus[10] solebant; extra insulam Meldeburna,
Melretha,[11] Hauekestuna,[12] Neuetuna,[13] Warattinga,[14] Stivitheuurtha,[15] Suaham,[16] Stabilford,[17] Beorcham,[18] Stotha,[19] Meltuna,[20] Suthburna,[21] Kyngestuna,[22] sacca et socca[23] cum omnibus regalibus consuetudinibus in quinque hun-
dredis et dimidio, viginti solidos in Ryssimera,[24] Lagynca Hytha,[25] Undelea,[26]
Schepeya,[27] [Fo]testorp,[28] ad mandatum monachorum triginta milia allecium de

1 DFGMO *Bertona*, E *Bertuna*.
2 D *habebis*, *i* expunged, *a* ins. marg.; EO *habebis* corr. to *-bas*; F *habeb'*.
3 EFO *Giselham*, G *Giselam*, M *Yselham*.
4 C *Heneiham*, D *Heneieham*, EFGMO *Heneiam*.
5 CEGM *Tirentuna*, F *Tirintunia*, O *Tyrintunia*.
6 CDEFGMO *Sumeresham*.
7 CEFGO add *in*.
8 D *ubi ... acris* ins. marg.
9 CDFMO *Ely*, EG *Heli*.
10 FO omit *in quibus*, add *sicut*.
11 EFGO *Melreda*.
12 D *Haukestuna*, EFG *Hauechestuna*, M *Hauekestona*.
13 CE *Newetuna*, DM *Neutona*, FO *Newentuna*.
14 CDM *Wrattinga*, EG *Waratinga*, F *Warttinge*, O *Wartinge*.
15 C *Stivichesuurtha*, D *Stivechesuurde*, EGM *Stivecheswrda*, F *Stewechewrda*, O *Stevecheworda*.
16 CDFMO *Suafham*, E *Suuasham*, G *Swauesham*.
17 CDEFGMO *Stapelford*.
18 EG *Bercham*, FO *Berham*.
19 CEFGO *Stocha*, DM *Stoka*.
20 DM *Meltona*.
21 EFG *Sutburna*.
22 CDEFMO *Kingestuna*, G *Kynchestuna*.
23 DFMO *sacha et socha*, EG *saca et soca*.
24 CDM *Rissemera*, EGO *Rissemere*, F *Reissemere*.
25 C *Lachingahytha*, D *Lachingehytha*, EFG *Lachingehida*, M *Lachingehetha*, O *Lakinghida*.
26 EFGO *Undeleia*.
27 C *Shepeia*, DEFGM *Scepeia*, O *Schepeia*.
28 Hole 4 mm.

Duneuuico,[1] duodecym skeppe frumenti et brasii de heredibus Hardewyini[2] de Scalariis et omnes servientes suos de omnibus ministeriis suis, sive[3] ut monachi eos[4] cum mansuris suis libere possideant, hac insuper libertate eisdem monachys at te indulta et confirmata, ut tam supradicta bona ipsis[5] a tua devotione vel quorumlibet fidelium oblatione collata quam etiam inposterum rationabiliter conferenda juxta confirmationem predecessorum nostrorum supradicti, videlicet[6] (fo. 182r) Victoris et felicis memorie Innocentii Romanorum pontificum, et concessionem et scripta regum ad sustentationem liberam[7] et ab omni conditione absoluta permaneant. Terras etiam prefatis monachis, quas habent Lundonie,[8] simili sanctione firmamus. Adissimus etiam, ut juxta sacri Calcedonensis[9] consilii constitutionem decedentium episcoporum eiusdem ecclesie bona a nullo omnino homine[10] diripiantur, sed ad opus ecclesie et successoris sui inichonomi potestate illibata serventur. Decernimus ergo, ut nulli omnino hominum liceat prefatam ecclesiam temere perturbare aut eius posessiones auferre vel ablatas retinere, minuere seu aliquibus vexationibus fatigare, sed omnia integra conserventur eorum, pro quorum gubernatione et sustentatione concessa sunt, usibus omnimodis profutura, salva in omnibus apostolice sedis auctoritate. Si qua igitur inposterum ecclesiastica secularisve persona hanc nostre constitutionis paginam sciens contra eam temere venire temtaverit, secundo tertiove commonita, nisi reatum suum congrua satisfactione corexerit, potestatis honorisque sui dignitate careat reamque se divino judicio existere [de perpetrata][11] iniquitate cognoscat et a sa[cra]tissimo[12] corpore ac[13] sanguine Dei et domini redemtoris nostri Jesu Christi aliena fiat[14] atque in (fo. 182v) extremo examine districte ultione[15] subjaceat. Cunctis autem eidem loco sua jura

---

1 EFG *Dunewicho*, O *Dunewico*.
2 CEFGMO *Hardewini*, D *Hardeuuini*.
3 CDEFGMO omit.
4 FO omit.
5 M *ipsius*.
6 M *silicet*.
7 CDEFGMO *libera*.
8 O *Londonie*.
9 MS *Cacedonensis*.
10 G has slipped into the passage below *omnino hominum liceat prefatam ecclesiam temere* and reads *omnino homine liceat prefatam eccleiam et successoris*, omitting *diripiantur ... ecclesie*.
11 Hole 30 mm.
12 Hole 11 mm.
13 D *et* expunged, *ac* perhaps ins. marg. but edge of folio lacking.
14 MS *fiet*.
15 D *e* expunged, *i* ins. marg.; E *ultioni*, probably corr. from *ultione*; FGMO *ultioni*.

servantibus sit pax domini nostri Jesu Christi, quatinus et hic fructum bone actionis percipiant et aput districtum judicem premia eterne pacis inveniant. Amen.[1]

Note. Dating taken from *Liber Eliensis* ed. Blake, p. 330. The privilege of pope Victor II which confirmed the rights of the abbey of Ely was probably issued in 1055 × 1057; it is printed in *Liber Eliensis* ed. Blake, pp. 163–4, no. 93.

270 *Privilege 'Pie postulatio voluntatis' of pope Innocent II to Nigel, bishop of Ely, confirming the possessions of the church of Ely, including Chatteris abbey.*
fos. 182v–183v [At the Lateran, Rome, 5 Dec. 1138]

Cartulary copies: (A) BL Cotton MS Vesp. A. xix, fos. 44v–45r; (C) Cambridge, Trinity College MS O. 2. 41, pp. 131–3; (D) BL Cotton MS Tib. A. vi, fos. 110v–111r; (E) Cambridge, Trinity College MS O. 2. 1, fo. 135r–v; (F) Cambridge UL, EDC 1, fos. 136v–137r; (G) BL Cotton MS Titus A. i, fos. 35v–36r; (M) Cambridge UL, EDR G/3/28 'Liber M', pp. 2–3; (O) Oxford, Bodl. MS Laud. Misc. 647, fo. 85r–v.
Printed in *Papsturkunden in England* ii, pp. 155–6, no. 17 and *Liber Eliensis* ed. Blake, pp. 301–2.

Innocensius[2] episcopus servus servorum Dei venerabili[3] fratri Nigello Eliensi episcopo eiusque successoribus canonice promovendis inperpetuum. Pie postulatio voluntatis effectu debet prosequente compleri, quatinus et devotionis scynceritas[4] laudabiliter enitescat et utilitas postulata vires indubitanter assumat. Huius rei gracia, venerabilis[5] frater Nygelle episcope, tuis petitionibus clementer annuimus et Eliensem ecclesiam, cui Deo auctore[6] preesse denosceris, presentis privilegii pagina communimus. Statuentes, ut quascumque possessiones, quecumque bona eadem ecclesia in presentiarum canonice possidet aut in futurum concescione pontificum, largitione regum vel[7] principum, oblat[ione

[1] CDM add *Amen Amen*; CD continue with the subcriptions, printed in *Papsturkunden in England* ii, no. 35, pp.184–5, and CDM add the date: *Data Laterani per manum baronis sancte Romane ecclesie subdiaconi viiii kal. junii, indictione vii, incarnationis Dominice anno millesimo centesimo quadragesimo quarto, ponificatus vero domni Lucii secundi pape anno primo*; O omits *Amen* and adds an abbreviated version of the date only: *Data Laterani ix kal. junii anno Domini M°C°xliiij° pontificatus domini Lucii pape II anno primo.*
[2] Preceded by pointing hand in margin.
[3] MS *venrabili*.
[4] MS *scynceritatis*, ACDEFGMO *sinceritas*.
[5] F *venabil'r*, O *venerabil'r*.
[6] MS *autore*.
[7] AEFGO omit, CD interline.

fidelium]¹ seu aliis justis modis Deo propitio poterit adipisci, tibi tuisque successoribus firma et illibata permaneant. In qui[bus]² hec propriis nominibus (fo.
183r) duximus exprimenda: abbatiam silicet sanctimonialium de³ Chateriz,⁴
quam nimirum cum omnibus suis pertinenciis, cellis,⁵ terris, agris, pascuis,
paludibus, silvis, venationibus, aquis, piscationibus, serviciis, debitis,⁶ decimis,⁷
sensu,⁸ capitationibus, legibus, consuetudinibus, causarum discuscionibus, cor-
ectionibus, emendationibus ecclesiasticis⁹ sive secularibus nec non etiam scriptis
vel testamentis vel aliis sibi pertinentibus consuetam et diu habitam libertatem
optinere sanctimus. Nulli ergo¹⁰ hominum¹¹ liceat prefatam Eliensem ecclesiam
temere perturbare aut¹² eius possessiones¹³ auferre aut etiam alienare vel ablatas
retinere¹⁴ seu quibuslibet molestiis fatigare, sed omnia integra¹⁵ [conserv-
ent]ur¹⁶ eorum, pro quorum gubernatione¹⁷ concessa sunt, usibus profutura.
[Tua]¹⁸ itaque¹⁹ interest, ita reper[ationi²⁰ eius]dem²¹ ecclesie insudare, ita²²
magis ac magis²³ ad recuperationem eorum, que distracta vel alienata sunt, totis
viribus laborare, ut omnipotens Dominus de²⁴ tuis actibus honoretur et ecclesia
ipsa suorum²⁵ dampnorum optata solacia consequatur. Si qua sane ecclesiastica

---

1 Hole 18 mm, MS very distorted.
2 Hole 4 mm.
3 *Chaterice* marginated before *de*.
4 CEFG *Cateriz*, D *Chatriz*.
5 F repeats.
6 FO omit.
7 AEG *decimis debitis*.
8 G *censis*.
9 MS *ecclesiastibus*.
10 O adds *omnino*.
11 M *homini*.
12 A *vel*.
13 G *possessiones eius*.
14 ACDEFGMO add *minuere*.
15 A *integre*.
16 Hole 14 mm; AEGO *conservent*.
17 ACDEFGMO add *et sustentatione*.
18 Hole 3 mm.
19 *ita* interlined, *que* preceded by hole 4 mm; O adds *est*.
20 A *reparatione sustentatione*, CDEGO *reparatione*, D expunges final *e* and interlines *i*.
21 Hole 14 mm.
22 AEFGO add *ut*.
23 O omits *ac magis*.
24 D probably ins. marg., but unclear.
25 D *duorum*, *d* expunged, *s* ins. marg.

secularisve[1] persona huius nostre constitutionis paginam sciens contra eam temere venire temptaverit, secundo tertiove commonita, si non reatum suum congrua satisfactione (fo. 183v) corexerit, potestatis honorisque sui dignitate careat reamque[2] se divino judicio existere de perpetrata[3] iniquitate cognoscat[4] et a[5] sacratissimo corpore ac sanguine Dei et domini[6] redemtoris nostri[7] Jesu Christi aliena fiat atque in extremo examine districte[8] ultioni subjaceat. Cunctis autem eidem loco sua[9] jura servantibus sit pax domini nostri Jesu Christi, quatinus et hic fructum bone actionis percipiant et aput supremum judicem premia eterne pacis [invenia]nt.[10] Amen.[11]

Note. Dating taken from *Liber Eliensis* ed. Blake, p. 301.

271 *Manumission from serfdom by abbess Agnes [Ashfield] and the convent of Chatteris of John Hulot, villein of their manor of Barley (Herts.).*
fo. 183v   In the chapter-house at Chatteris abbey, 20 July 1436

O[mnibus Christi][12] fidelibus ad quos presentes littere pervenerint Agnes permisione divina abb[ati]ssa[13] de Chateriz et eiusdem loci conventus salutem in Domino sempiternam. [Noveritis nos un]animi[14] consensu perito [et][15] assensu totius capituli nostri manumisisse et ab omni jugo servitutis et villenagii liberasse Johannem Hulot nativum et vellanum nostrum pertinentem ad manerium

1 G *secularis ut.*
2 O *careat dignitate reumque.*
3 MS *perpretata.*
4 MS *connoscat.*
5 O omits.
6 G *domini et Dei nostri* for *Dei et domini.*
7 A omits.
8 O *districti.*
9 G *suo.*
10 Hole 15 mm.
11 CDEFGMO add *Amen Amen*; CDM continue with the subcriptions, printed in *Papsturkunden in England* ii, no. 17, p. 156, and the date: *Data Laterani per manum Luce presbiteri cardinalis agentis vicem domni Almerici sancte Romane ecclesie diaconi cardinalis et cancellarii nonis decembris, indictione secunda, incarnationis Dominice anno millesimo centesimo tricesimo nono, pontificatus vero domni Innocentii pape secundi anno nono*; O continues with an abbreviated version of the date only: *Data Laterani anno Domini $M^oC^oxxx^oix^o$ nonis decembris, pontificatus pape Innocentii II anno primo.*
12 Holes 7 mm and 4 mm.
13 Hole 4 mm.
14 Hole 25 mm.
15 Unclear 2 mm.

nostrum de Berle, cum omnibus suis sequelis bonis catallis suis quibuscumque, ita quod nec nos nec successores nostri aliquod jus vel clameum in dicto Johanne seu sequelis suis bonis et catallis suis in futurum habere seu vendicare poterimus, sed sumus exclusi imperpetuum per presentes. In cuius rei testimonium sigillum nostrum commune presentibus est appensum. Date apud Chateriz in domo nostra capitulari[1] vicesimo die mensis julii anno regni regis Henrici sexti post conquestum quartodesimo. (fo. 184r)[2]

272 *Grant by Isabel de Hemingford, daughter of William Ruffus, to Chatteris abbey of Peter Bonem of Hemingford with his chattels and family, and gift in free alms of the 16 acres of arable land, 2 acres of meadow and 1 messuage in Hemingford (Hunts.) which Peter Bonem held of her.*
fo. 184r–v　[1242 × s. xiii[3]]

　Transcript: Oxford, Bodl. MS Dodsworth 105, fo. 84r.

Omnibus sancte matris ecclesie filiis ad quos presens scriptum pervenerit Isabella de Hemingford' filia Willelmi Ruffi de Hemingford' salutem in Domino. Noverit universitas vestra me, caritatis intuitu et pro salute anime mee et Verengeri Monachi quondam viri mei et patris et matris mee et ...e[3] Griffin et antecessorum meorum, dedisse et concessisse Deo et ecclesie beate Marie de Chateriz et monialibus ibidem Deo servientibus Petrum Bonem de Hemingford' cum catallis s[uis],[4] cum tota sequela sua, et totum jus quod ad me [vel][5] ad heredes meos de eo possit pertinere, [cum][6] tota terra sua quam de me tenuit in villa de Hemingford', scilicet sexdecim[7] acras terre arabilis et duas acras prati cum uno mesuagio, habendas et tenendas de me et heredibus meis libere et quiete in puram et perpetuam elemosinam imperpetuum, et sicut elemosina potest liberius et quietius dari vel concedi. Et ego Isabella et heredes mei warantizabimus predictum Petrum cum tota terra sua et cum omnibus sibi pertinentibus in villa de Hemingford' dicte ecclesie de Chateriz et monialibus eiusdem loci Deo servientibus co[nt]ra[8] omnes homines et omnes feminas, et

---

1　Followed by *vise*, cancelled?
2　Heading *Hemyngford'*.
3　Hole 10 mm.
4　Hole 5 mm; *lacunae* in charter supplied from transcript in Oxford, Bodl. MS Dodsworth 105, fo. 84r.
5　Hole 6 mm.
6　Hole 6 mm.
7　Preceded by Tironian *et*.
8　Hole 2 mm.

defendemus versus dominum regem quantum pertinet de tanta [terr]a¹ in eadem villa. Et ut hec mea donatio et concessio et huius presentis (fo. 184v) carte mee confirmatio rata et inconcussa permaneat, sigilli mei appositione hanc cartam corroboravi. Hiis testibus etc.

Vide alia carta pro Hemyngford' supra folio xxj°.

> Note. Isabel and her husband occur in 2 Henry III (1217–18) in a final concord (*Hunts. Fines*, p. 5); Berenger le Moyngne was still alive in 1242–3 (*Book of Fees* ii, p. 923); William Ruffus had died by 1250 (*Book of Fees* ii, p. 1173).

273 *Presentation by Chatteris abbey of John, vicar, in an exchange of benefices with W., vicar.*
fo. 184v

Reverendo in Christo patri etc. Cum dilecti nobis in Christo Johannes et W. ecclesie de B. et A. vicarii vestre diocesis sua beneficia, certis et legittimis de causis ipsos ut asserunt in hac parte moventibus, adinvicem canonice permutare affectant, dum tamen [auc]toritas² et consensus quorum interest in hac parte intervenerint, nos dicta abbatissa et conventus, negotio permutationis huius-modi quantum in nobis est assensum prebentes et consensum, prefatum domi-num Johannem ex causa permutationis presentamus ut premittitur faciende, humiliter etc.

274 *Manumission from serfdom by abbess Agnes [Ashfield] and the convent of Chatteris of John Whiteheed', villein of their manor of Chatteris.*
fo. 184v   In the chapter-house at Chatteris abbey, 20 Sept. 1435 × 20 Aug. 1436

Omnibus Christi fidelibus ad quos presentes littere pervenerint Agnes per[mis-sione]³ divina abbatissa de Chateriz et eiusdem loci conventus salutem in Domino sempiternam. Noveritis nos unanimi assensu et voluntate manumisisse ac liberum fecisse et ab omni jugo servitutis liberasse Johannem Whiteheed' nativum et nostrum villanum pertinentem ad manerium nostrum de Chateriz predicta, ut ipse idem Johannes Whiteheed' cum tota sequela sua, tam procreata quam procreanda, et cum omnibus bonis suis et cattallis ubicumque se divertat liber et quietus ac libere conditionis permaneat in futurum, ita quod nec nos nec successores nostri nec aliquis alius nomine nostro aliquid juris seu clamei in

¹ Hole 5 mm.
² Hole 4 mm.
³ Hole 12 mm.

predicto Johanne vel sequela sua, tam procreata quam procreanda, aut eorum
bonis et catallis pretextu alicuius velenagii et servitutis in ipso Johanne prehab-
itorum de cetero exigere vel vendicare poterimus in futurum, sed ab omni
actione juris et clamei in predicto Johanne ac sequela sua tam procreata quam
procreanda sumus imperpetuum exclusi per presentes. In cuius rei testimonium
sigillum nostrum commune presentibus est appensum. Date apud Chateriz
predicta in doma nostra capitulari vicessimo [die] ... [anno]¹ regni regis Henrici
sexti post conquestum Anglie² quartodecimo. (fo. 185r)³

Note. This manumission may have been issued on 20 July 1436, together with no. 271.

275 *Grant and quitclaim by Gonnora, formerly wife of Richard, carter, to John
Vivien, her brother, of the fishery with meadow [in Chatteris] which Henry Vivien,
her father, gave to her.*
fo. 185r [s. xiii² × 1291]

Sciant⁴ presentes et futuri quod e[go Gon]nora⁵ q... ...⁶ et uxor quondam
Ricardi car[ec]tarii⁷ in legitima viduetate mea [dedi]⁸ concessi et hoc presenti
scripto [meo confirma]vi⁹ et omnino pro me et heredibus meis inposterum
quietam clamavi Johanni Vivien fratri meo totam [illam]¹⁰ piscariam quam
habui de dono predicti Henrici Vivien patris mei inter Achenewere et Horshe,
cum toto prato ad dictam piscariam pertinente et cum omnibus aliis pertinenciis
suis, tenendam et habendam predicto Johanni et heredibus suis vel suis assignatis, vel cuicumque et quandocumque dare legare vendere vel assignare voluerit,
tam in egritudine quam in sanitate, ita tamen quod nec ego predicta Gonnora
nec heredes mei nec aliquis alius nomine nostro aliquod jus vel clamium in tota
piscaria nec in toto prato de cetero exigere poterimus vel recuperare. Ut autem
hec mea donatio concessio scripti mei confirmatio et quieta clamatio robur firmitatis optineat inposterum, huic scripto sigillum meum apposui. Hiis testibus
domino Gilberto Pecche, domino Philippo de Insula, Paganno de Wyntewore,

1 Hole 24 mm; probably *mensis julii* lacking: cf. no. 271.
2 Followed by *quato*, cancelled.
3 Heading *Chat[er]iz*, in black.
4 Preceded by *nota*, marginated.
5 Hole 8 mm.
6 Hole 32 mm; followed by *piscaria*, marginated.
7 Damaged 3 mm.
8 Hole 5 mm.
9 Hole 15 mm.
10 Hole 4 mm.

Symone Pelryn de W...,[1] domino Symone capellano, Gervas' de Luton'[2] et aliis.

> Note. See also no. 83. Gilbert Pecche – the eldest son of Hamo who died in 1241 – died in 1291 (*Liber de Bernewelle* ed. Clark, pp. xxxvii, xli). Philip de Insula had a fee in Impington *c.* 1235 and occurs in 45 Henry III (1260–1) in a final concord (Ibid. p. 241; *Cambs. Fines*, p. 39). Simon Pelrim held a virgate in Over in 1279 (*Rot. Hund.* ii, p. 478). G. de Luton occurs in 1270–1 (Ault ed. *Ramsey Court Rolls*, pp. 261–2).

276 *Declaration by abbess Agnes Ashfield and the convent of Chatteris that, having examined the evidence and inquired among their tenants, there is nothing to show that John Reynold' of Dry Drayton, husbandman, nor his ancestors are or were villeins of the abbey, contrary to the slanderous assertions of his enemies.*
fo. 185r–v   In the chapter-house at Chatteris abbey, 20 July 1437

Universis Christi fidelibus presentes litteras visuris inspecturis vel audituris nos[3] Agnes Ashfeld' abbatissa monasterii sive domus monialium de Chatryz Eliensis diocesis et eiusdem loci conventus salutem in Domino sempiternam. Noverit universitas vestra quod cum nuper Johannes Reynold' de Drye Drayton' eiusdem diocesis husbondman' super ingenuitate et valibus infamatus fuerit per quosdam emulos suos, servitutis infamiam eidem irrogantes ac pristine fame natalium suorum et progenitorum eiusdem enormiter detrahentes, publice sed falso asserentes quod prefatus Johannes Reynold' ac progenitores et sequaces eiusdem fuerunt et sunt nobis monasterio et domui nostre predictis nativi et servilis conditionis, unde scrutatis evidenciis et munimentis et nostris examinatis, ac facta diligenter inquisitione inter tenentes nostros, nichil contra dictum Johannem Reynold' ac progenitores sive consanguine[os][4] suos scriptum vel probatum fuisset quod esset vel essent nati[vi] ...atim[5] nec aliqua nota servitutis vel villenagii resspersus vel ...,[6] unde quantum ad nos et monasterium nostrum sive domum d[ominarum][7] nostram pro nobis (fo. 185v) [et successoribus][8] nostris dictum Joh[annem][9] Reynold' ac filios et filias suos ac omnes progeni-

---

1 Hole 5 mm.
2 Or possibly *Litton*?
3 *Reynol[d] villanus*, marginated after *nos*.
4 Hole 4 mm.
5 Damaged 8 mm.
6 Damaged 10 mm.
7 Damaged 7 mm.
8 Damaged 25 mm, MS very distorted.
9 Hole 6 mm.

tores su[os et]¹ consanguineos suos [liber]os² esse declaram[us. In cu]ius³ rei testimonium presentibus sigillum nostrum commune apponi fecimus. Date in domo nostra capitulari vicesimo die julii anno Domini M° CCCC° tricesimo vij°.

277 *Grant by abbess Margaret Develyn and the convent of Chatteris to James [Stanley], bishop of Ely, and Walter Berkoke, gentleman, of the tithe of the church of Barley (Herts.) and the next presentation to it.*
fo. 185v [8 Nov. 1506 × 22 March 1515]

Omnibus Christi fidelibus⁴ ad quos presens scriptum pervenerit Margareta Develyn' abatissa monesterii sive domus monialium de Chateriz Eliensis diocesis et eiusdem loci conventus, vere et indubitate patrone ecclesie parochalis de Berley in comitatu ⟨Hertford' London'⟩⁵ diocesis, salutem in Domino sempiternam. Noveritis nos prefatam abbatissam et conventum nostris, unanimi assensu et consensu, dedisse concensisse et ho[c]⁶ presenti scripto nostro confirmasse reverendo in Christo patri et domino domino Jacobo Dei gracia Eliensi episcopo et Waltero Berkoke generoso decimam et proximam advocationem ac liberam dispositionem juris patronatus ecclesie parochie predicte, vel proximum jus presentandi personam quamcumque idoneam ad eandem, ita quod cum et quamcito dictam ecclesiam parochie de Berle[y]⁷ qualitercumque et quomodocumque iam proximam vacante[m]⁸ contigerit, bene licebit prefatis reverend[o]⁹ patre et domino ac Waltero communatim.¹⁰ (fo. 186r)

Note. James Stanley was bishop of Ely 8 Nov. 1506–22 March 1515; Margaret Develyn was abbess of Chatteris 13 June 1506 × 31 March 1535.

1 Unclear 5 mm.
2 Hole 5 mm.
3 Hole 15 mm, MS very distorted.
4 MS *fedilibus.*
5 Space, 22 mm.
6 Damaged 1 mm.
7 Hole 4 mm.
8 Hole 3 mm.
9 Hole 4 mm.
10 The text of the grant breaks off here at the foot of the page, showing that at least one folio has been lost between the extant fos. 185 and 186.

278 *Index of place-names compiled in the seventeenth century.*[1]
fo. 186r

Bilney, 27

Brecham, 30, 85

Barington, 34, 39, 91

Barley, 65, 94, 106, 112

Burwell', 91

Chaterice, 1, 32, 80, 90, 98, 112

Cambridge,[2] 35

Carte regum, 99

Dunstaple, 64

Dodington, 64, 95

Ditton, 31

Decime, 3[9][3]

Ely, 31, 33, 107

Elme, 33, 91

Foxton, 46, 93

Hemingford, 89, 111

Huntington, 88

Hunney, 62

Haveril', 29

Kingston, 38, 93

Kersey, 71

Lincoln, 87

Leen, 82

Madingley, 38, 92

Over, 34

Pinchbek, 87

Placita in scaccario, 103

Stuntney, 30

Sheprey, 56

Thetford, 30

Triplow, 63

Wimlington, 95

Well', 30 (fo. 186v)[4]

279 *Description of the boundaries of the common land in the marsh and of the pasture of Chatteris.*
fo. 187v[5]   ?[s. xiv × s. xv]

Cartulary copies: (K) Cambridge UL, EDR G/3/27 'Liber R' al. 'The Old Coucher Book', fo. 206r; (L) BL Add. MS 33450, fo. 3r.

Mete de communia de Chateriz ut per libros et evidencias de Chateriz et de Ramesey in marisco.[6] Communia marisci[7] de Chateriz ad falcandum scindendum et fodiendum[8] incipit ad Dribittesfen[9] et tendit infra Armytismere,[10] et

1 Written in a single column in MS.
2 MS *Cambrdge.*
3 Unclear 2 mm.
4 Fos. 186v–187r are blank.
5 Heading *Chateriz*, in black.
6 KL omit *Chateriz. Mete … marisco*, K adds *Bunde de Chateriz per terrarium abbatisse ibidem.*
7 K omits.
8 K *fodiendum sindendum et falcandum*, L interlines *ut patet per terrarium Eliensem.*
9 K *Driebitfen*, L *Driebitesfen'.*
10 K *Arnatissmere*, L *Armatysmere* with *Arnetesmere* interlined.

de[1] Armytsmere[2] usque ad Blakwell',[3] et de Blakwell'[4] usque ad[5] Biee, et de Biee[6] circa Hunney[7] usque[8] Langreche,[9] et de Langreche[10] usque ad ripam[11] de Dodyngton, et de illa ripa[12] usque[13] Bylsynges,[14] et de Bilsynges[15] usque ad Algarisfene,[16] et sic ultra mariscum usque ad Achynwerdore.[17] Pastura autem ville[18] de Chateriz tendit ad Dounham ad Wycham[19] ad Suttun'[20] ad Dodyngton' et ad Marche, ad communicandum secum cum bestiis nostris[21] et illi nobiscum[22] secum cum bestiis suis sic intercommunicandis etc.[23] (fo. 188r)[24]

Note. 'The Old Coucher Book' of Ely contains a fourteenth-century copy of a survey in 1251 of the bishop's demesne manors. The copy of the description of the Chatteris boundaries was added in a fifteenth-century hand on the last folio of the survey. The register of John Titchmarsh (BL Add. MS 33450), abbot of Ramsey, is dated 1431 × 1441.

280 *Names of those who are obliged to carry the rod [of the bishop of Ely] in Chatteris.*

fo. 188r [*c.* 1473]

Nomina eorum qui debent portare virgam ibidem quilibet post alterum imperpetuum.

1 Followed by *Arnys*, cancelled.
2 K *Arnatismere*, L *Armatysmere* with *Arnetesmere* interlined.
3 K *Blakeweld'*.
4 K *Blakeweld'*.
5 KL omit.
6 K *Bye*, and omits *et de Biee*.
7 KL *Hunneye*.
8 L adds *ad*.
9 K *Langrech'*, L *Langereche*.
10 L *Langereche*.
11 K *ripariam*.
12 K *riparia*.
13 L adds *ad*.
14 K *Belsynges*, L *Bilsyngys*.
15 K *Belsynges*, L *Bilsyngys*.
16 K *Algaresfen*, L *Algarisfen'*.
17 K *Acheneweredore*, L *Achinweredore*.
18 L *predicte*.
19 L *Wicheham*.
20 L *Sutton'*, K adds *et*.
21 Interlined above *suis*, cancelled.
22 Interlined.
23 L omits *sic ... etc.*, adds *Ista littera patet in custumarium*.
24 Heading *Chateriz*, in black.

Domina abbatissa anno xiij° regis Edwardi iiij[ti]
Thomas Rede pro Leverycchez
Johannes Berley senior
Domina abbatissa
Ricardus Webster, bovson'[1]
Johannes Berley junior
Domina abbatissa
Tenementum terre vocatum Haltons, Bysschops Yard[2]
Powres Pondez
Nicholaus Goodgrome
Nicholaus Tydde
Domina abbatissa
Johannes Clement pro tenemento Laurencii Sewter
Simon Pyper
Domina abbatissa
Johannes Beche, Vasohowffyl the[3] elder[4]
Johannes Sempole (fo. 188v)[5]

---

1 *bovson'*, in another hand.
2 *Bysschops Yard*, in another hand.
3 MS *y*[e].
4 *Vasohowffyl the elder*, in another hand.
5 Fo. 188v is blank.

Original Charter

281 *Gift by abbess Agnes and the convent of Chatteris to Geoffrey son of Eustace of ½ acre of land in Madingley, for ½ pound of pepper annually at Easter.*
Cambridge, St John's College Archives D 25. 22 [*s.* xiii[1] × 1233]

Sciant presentes et futuri quod ego Agnes dicta domina ecclesie de Chateriz et conventus eiusdem loci dedimus et concessimus et hac presenti carta confirmavimus Galfrido filio Eustachii, pro homagio suo et servicio, unam dimidiam acram terre in Madingele in crofta ipsius Galfridi versus orientem juxta terram Johannis de Litlebiri, sibi et heredibus suis tenendam de nobis in perpetuum libere et quiete, reddendo inde nobis in perpetuum annuatim unam dimidiam libram piperis ad Pascha pro omni servicio et consuetudine, salvo domini regis servicio. His testibus Simone de Insula, Ricardo de Chawelle, Michaele Pelerin, Willelmo de Burdele, Rogero Sprot, Roberto Norreis, Asketil filio Eustachii, Jordano de Berle et multis aliis.

Note. No endorsement. 54 × 125 mm. Seal: red wax pointed oval on parchment tag, 63 × 42 mm; the legend, which is completely lacking on the left hand side and only partially visible on the right, reads *[S]IGILL[UM] SAN[CTE MARIE]*; the device is the Virgin crowned, holding a book in her left hand and a flowering staff topped with a cross in her right, seated on a throne whose sides terminate in animals' heads and feet (see figure 6, p. 94).

William Burdeleys held Burdeleys manor in Madingley from *c.* 1199–*c.* 1229 and was succeeded by his son, William, who died in 1233 (*VCH Cambs.* ix, p. 167). Simon de Insula was the attorney of Simon son of Eve in a plea of land in 1194 (*R. Cur. Reg.* i, pp. 25, 75); he also occurs in 1206–18 (*Rot. Litt. Pat.*, p. 63; *CPR 1216–25*, p. 208). A Robert le Noreis occurs in Cambs. in 1235–6 and 1242–3 (*Book of Fees* i, p. 493; ii, p. 924).

Appendix 1

The Known Abbesses, Prioresses, Nuns and Lay-sister of Chatteris

CHRONOLOGICAL LIST OF THE KNOWN ABBESSES

ÆLFWEN

[*c.* 1007 × 1016]

> According to a narrative in the *Liber Eliensis*, Eadnoth, formerly abbot of Ramsey, founded Chatteris abbey after he had become bishop of Dorchester (*Liber Eliensis* ed. Blake, pp. 140–2). This narrative, which was also copied into the Chatteris cartulary, states that his sister Ælfwen became the first abbess (no. 2).

A., *see also* Agnes; Albreda; A. de Rouen

[*c.* 1191 × *c.* 1198]

> Confirmation by abbess A. and the convent of Chatteris to Adam son of Robert de Cockfield of the manor of Kersey, to be held in fee-farm for £10 annually, which manor Nigel, bishop of Ely, and Hadewisa, prioress of Chatteris, had granted and confirmed to Adam de Cockfield, grandfather of Adam (no. 186).

I. [*or* J.]

1216, before 14 June

> Remission by prior Hugh Foliot and the convent of Ramsey to I. abbess of Chatteris, following a complaint made by her to the lord treasurer, of all disputes between them until the election of an abbot, and assurance that the abbess shall have all oblations and tithes pertaining to the chapel of Honey Hill (par. Chatteris) and that, when Ramsey has an abbot, he will make any compensation necessary (no. 164).

ALBREDA, *see also* A. (above)

[*s.* xii^3 × *s.* xiii^2]

> Grant by abbess Albreda and the convent of Chatteris to William son of Hugh, reeve of Doddington, of a fishery called 'Polwere' and all the water between 'Polwere' and 'Echinewere' in Chatteris with all its fisheries, for 40 sticks of eels and 2s. annually (no. 169).

AGNES, *see also* A. (above); A. de Rouen; Agnes de Burwell; Agnes de Ely; Agnes Ashfield (below)

[*s.* xii^4 × *s.* xiii^1] *alias* A. de Rouen?

Exchange between Alan son of Alan de Shepreth and abbess Agnes and the convent of Chatteris of 2 *culture* called 'Pundefoldedole' and 'Appeltonesdole' for 1 *cultura* called 'Briggedole' in Foxton (no. 146).

[*s.* xiii^1 × 1233] *alias* A. de Rouen?

Gift by abbess Agnes and the convent of Chatteris to Geoffrey son of Eustace of ½ acre of land in Madingley, for ½ pound of pepper annually at Easter (no. 281).

[*s.* xiii^2 × 28 Sept. 1265] former abbess Agnes *alias* A. de Rouen?

Confirmation by abbess M. and the convent of Chatteris, through the intercession of Ralph de Barley, of the rent of 5s. annually in Hemingford (Hunts.) which Agnes, a former abbess, had assigned to the alms-house, namely half of the 10s. annually which Isabel de Indyngword' had given to the abbey; for which Ralph gave and quitclaimed to the abbey 10 acres of land which he held of them in Foxton and Barrington (no. 232).

[*s.* xii^4 × *s.* xiii^4] *alias* A. de Rouen, Agnes de Burwell *or* Agnes de Ely?

Lease by abbess Agnes and the convent of Chatteris to Robert son of Gorold de Shepreth, for his life, of a messuage with croft and houses, for 3½ marks and an annual rent of 12d. (no. 151).

[*c.* 1265 × 1297] *alias* Agnes de Burwell *or* Agnes de Ely?

Confirmation by abbess Agnes and the convent of Chatteris to William de la Haye, knight, of a chantry in his chapel in the manor of Shepreth, provided that Shepreth church will lose nothing and that all obventions from the chapel will be paid to it, for 1 pound of wax annually to Shepreth church (no. 162).

[*s.* xiii$^{2-4}$] *alias* Agnes de Burwell *or* Agnes de Ely?

Grant in fee-farm by abbess Agnes and the convent of Chatteris to John Marvin of Thriplow, of a messuage in Thriplow called 'Motlowe' with arable land, pasture and 'dambote', for ½ mark annually, with warranty for the life of John (no. 168).

?[*s.* xiv^4 × *s.* xv^1] *alias* Agnes Ashfield?

Release and quitclaim by John Winwick, John Cokerell and Nicholas Tyd to abbess Agnes and the convent of Chatteris of 2s. 2d. of annual rent which Richard Radewyn' of Swaffham Prior and his ancestors used to receive for various parcels of land in Chatteris (no. 80).

A. de ROUEN (*Rothomago*), *see also* A.; Agnes; Albreda (above)

[*s.* xiii$^{1-2}$]

Gift by abbess A. de Rouen and the convent of Chatteris to Alan de Ely, gardener, and Alice his wife of a messuage in Potter's Lane, Ely, for 5s. and an annual rent of 2s. 6d. (no. 93).

M.

[*s.* xiii^2 × 28 Sept. 1265] *alias* Mabel de Bancis *or* Mary de Sancto Claro (below)?

Agreement whereby abbess M. and the convent of Chatteris lease to Alice daughter of Warin de Barrington, for her life, a messuage with croft in Foxton, for 12d. annually (no. 138).

Confirmation by abbess M. and the convent of Chatteris, through the intercession of Ralph de Barley, of the rent of 5s. annually in Hemingford (Hunts.) which Agnes, a former abbess, had assigned to the alms-house, namely half of the 10s. annually which Isabel de Indyngword' had given to the abbey; for which Ralph gave and quitclaimed to the abbey 10 acres of land which he held of them in Foxton and Barrington (no. 232).

Mabel de BANCIS, *see also* M. (above)

[*s.* xiii^2, before *c.* 29 Oct. 1247]

Agreement whereby abbess Mabel de Bancis and the convent of Chatteris lease to Thomas de Bancis, for his life, a messuage and 5 acres of arable land with 5 roods of meadow in Foxton, for 3s. 6d. annually (no. 139).

[*s.* xiii^2 × 28 Sept. 1265]

Gift in free alms by Ralph de Barley to abbess Mabel de Bancis and the convent of Chatteris of a parcel of land [?in Chatteris] (no. 74).

Agreement whereby abbess Mabel de Bancis and the convent of Chatteris lease to Thomas de Bancis, for his life, a messuage and 12 acres of land in Foxton, 6 acres of which he formerly held of her at will; for 4s. annually (no. 132).

Agreement whereby abbess Mabel de Bancis and the convent of Chatteris lease to Roger, smith, and Roger his son ½ virgate of land in Foxton, which his father held of the abbey; for 40s., an annual rent of 4s. and other specified services (no. 144).

Grant by John son of Hugh de Bradehous to abbess Mabel de Bancis and the convent of Chatteris of an annual rent of 9s. 4d. owed by John son of Lambert de Bradhous for land in Pinchbeck (Lincs.), an annual rent of 6d. owed by Simon son of Joyce de Pekkesbregg' and an annual rent of 2d. owed by Reginald son of John Joyce of Fulney (Lincs.) (no. 226).

Power of attorney from abbess Mabel de Bancis and the convent of Chatteris appointing Jocelin, their serjeant, to manage and collect their rent in Lincoln (no. 228).

Mary de SANCTO CLARO (*Sancta Clara*), *see also* M. (above)

Nun or abbess

[*s.* xiii[1-2]]

An Anglo-Norman life of St Etheldreda was written in verse in the first half of the thirteenth century.[1] The author, who identifies herself as Mary, may have been a nun at Chatteris, since the nunnery's patron was the bishop of Ely and his church was founded by St Etheldreda.[2] Moreover 'La Vie Seinte Audrée', which is a re-working of sections of the Latin *Liber Eliensis*, includes a reference to Chatteris in line 317 which is absent from the Latin source.[3] M. D. Legge suggests that the author could be Mary de Sancto Claro.[4]

Abbess

[*s.* xiii[2] × 28 Sept. 1265]

Agreement whereby abbess Mary de Sancto Claro and the convent of Chatteris lease to John de Fransham, for his life, a messuage with buildings in Chatteris which Alan de Bassingbourn held of them; for 2s. annually (no. 51).

Notification and exemplification by Robert son of Robert de Lyndon' and Juliana his wife of a lease by abbess Mary de Sancto Claro and the convent of Chatteris to Robert and Juliana, for their lives, of 2 selions in Chatteris, for 20s. and an annual rent of 3s. and by providing annually 1 man for 1 day to mow their meadow and 1 man for 1 day to reap their corn (no. 69).

Release by abbess Mary de Sancto Claro and the convent of Chatteris to Eustace son of William de Barrington of villein service in a messuage and land in Barring-ton, held of Eustace by John son of Henry Broun, villein of Chatteris abbey (nos. 100/123).

Notification and exemplification by Alan le Fraunceys of the gift by abbess Mary de Sancto Claro and the convent of Chatteris to him of a messuage and 10 acres of land in Foxton, which he and his father, Robert, formerly held of them at will; for an annual rent of 4s. 2d. and 6 hens (no. 141).

Exchange between Reginald Binel of Shepreth and abbess Mary de Sancto Claro and the convent of Chatteris of 5½ acres and 1 rood of land for a *cultura* called 'Brokstrate' and 2 acres of land in Foxton (no. 145).

Notification and exemplification by Roger son of Basilia de Hemingford of the gift by abbess Mary de Sancto Claro and the convent of Chatteris to him of all their

---

1 Ö. Södergård ed. *La Vie Seinte Audrée, Poème Anglo-Normand du XIIIe Siècle* (Uppsala, 1955).

2 M. D. Legge *Anglo-Norman Literature and its Background* (Oxford, 1963) p. 264.

3 J. Wogan-Browne '"Clerc u Lai, Muïne u Dame": Women and Anglo-Norman Hagiography in the Twelfth and Thirteenth Centuries' in *Women and Literature in Britain, 1150–1500* ed. C. M. Meale (Cambridge, 1993) p. 82, n. 35.

4 Legge *Anglo-Norman Literature*, p. 264.

land in Hemingford Grey (Hunts.), for 1 mark annually and scutage of 40s. (no. 231).

Emma de SOMERSHAM (Someresham)[1]

29 Sept. 1265

Agreement whereby abbess Emma de Somersham and the convent of Chatteris lease to William de Fowlmere, carpenter, the mill called 'Mepus' in Shepreth with 1 rood of arable land, all the multure of the abbey's court in Foxton and the suit of all their tenantry within Foxton and Shepreth, for 10 years for 40s. annually (no. 163).

c. 8 July 1268

Gift in free alms by Ralph, knight, son of Ralph son of Fulk de Broadfield to abbess Emma de Somersham and the nuns of Chatteris of 3 acres and 3 roods of arable land in Barley (Herts.) and grant of the advowson of the church (no. 177).

Final concord made at Westminster between Emma de Somersham, abbess of Chatteris, querent, and Ralph son of Ralph son of Fulk de Broadfield, defendant, concerning 3 acres and 3 roods of land in Barley (Herts.) and the advowson of the church, on a plea of charter of warranty, for the reception of Ralph and his heirs into the benefits and prayers of the abbey (no. 178).

Acquittance by Ralph son of Ralph son of Fulk de Broadfield to the [unnamed] abbess of Chatteris of 40s. for the release of his claim in the advowson of the church of Barley (Herts.), at that time vacant (no. 179, dated 10 Nov. 1281, which refers to no. 178).

AMICIA, *see also* Amicia de Cambridge (below)

16 Nov. 1275

Agreement between abbess Amicia and the convent of Chatteris and Eustace de Barrington that the suit of court at Foxton which the abbey was seeking from Eustace, on account of a tenement which he held of them in Barrington, was owed by Richard March because he held a capital messuage and part of the tenement by a lease of William de Barrington, father of Eustace; and that the abbey has remitted 2 of the 8 capons which Eustace owed annually for a meadow in Barrington (no. 124).

[9 July 1268 × Jan. 1280]

Exchange between Roger de Seaton, rector of Over, and abbess Amicia and the convent of Chatteris of 2 tofts in Over, and grant by the abbess and convent to Roger of the right to close and appropriate a road in Over (no. 101).

?[9 July 1268 × Jan 1280] *or* Amicia de Cambridge?

Grant in fee-farm by abbess Amicia and the convent of Chatteris to Warin de Barrington of their half of a water-mill called 'le Estmelne' in Barrington and Foxton

1 Probably Somersham, Hunts.

and 2 pieces of meadow in Foxton towards repairing the mill, excepting 9 villeins of Foxton who were accustomed to grind there and 7 roods of meadow in Foxton; for 2s. annually (no. 119).

Agnes de ELY, *see also* Agnes (above); Agnes de Burwell (below)

Shortly before 17 Jan. 1280

Gift and quitclaim by Richard son of Richard de Myldeborn' to abbess Agnes de Ely and the convent of Chatteris of the lands, tenements, meadows and pastures formerly of John de Beauchaump in Barley (Herts.), which he recovered before the justices in eyre at Hertford; for 10 marks in advance (no. 172).

[17 Nov. 1275 × 1290]

Exchange between abbess Agnes de Ely and the convent of Chatteris and John Waryn of Barrington, clerk, of a messuage and croft in Barrington for 3 selions of land in Barrington (no. 113).

Gift by abbess Agnes de Ely and the convent of Chatteris to Alice formerly wife of William de Fowlmere, carpenter, and James her son, clerk, of a croft called 'Brondescroft' with a messuage and meadow in Barrington, for 2 marks in advance and 16d. annually (no. 120).

[17 Nov. 1275 × 13 May 1293]

Lease by abbess Agnes de Ely and the convent of Chatteris to Osbert Guthlac, Hawisia his wife and John their son of Foxton, for their lives, of a messuage with croft, 10 acres of arable land and 5 roods of meadow in Foxton, for an annual rent of 4s. and 6 capons and 2 suits of court annually (no. 128).

Grant in fee-farm by abbess Agnes de Ely and the convent of Chatteris to John de Acle of Barley, for his life, of a parcel of land with 3 roods of land in Barley (Herts.), for 18d. annually (no. 176).

Agnes de BURWELL (Borewelle),[1] *see also* Agnes; Agnes de Ely (above) [It is possible that Agnes de Burwell could be the same woman as Agnes de Ely.]

14 May 1293

Manorial court of abbess Agnes de Burwell held at Foxton (Cambridge, Trinity College Archives, Foxton 2, m. 2).

Amicia de CAMBRIDGE (Cantebr', Cantebrig'), *see also* Amicia (above)

Sacrist

[*s.* xiii[4], before 1298]

Release by Ralph son of Katherine Coveney to Amicia de Cambridge, sacrist of Chatteris abbey, of ½d. of annual rent in which she was bound to him for 1 rood of arable land which she held of him in Chatteris; for 6d (no. 47).

---

[1] Probably Burwell, Cambs.

Prioress

The prioress who was elected abbess shortly before 8 July 1298 was very probably Amicia de Cambridge (*Registrum Roberti Winchelsey Cantuariensis Archiepiscopi 1294–1313* ed. R. Graham, i (Canterbury and York Society li, 1952) pp. 262–3).

Abbess

Shortly after 29 Sept. 1300

Agreement between abbess Amicia de Cambridge and the convent of Chatteris and Alexander, butcher, of Lynn whereby they released and acquitted him from all the arrears owed for 1 mark of annual rent from a piece of land with buildings in Lynn (Norf.), and he agreed to pay the rent in future (no. 219).

[Shortly before 8 July 1298 × 27 March 1306]

Release and quitclaim by John Fithien of Chatteris to abbess Amicia de Cambridge and the nuns of Chatteris of 2½d. of annual rent [?in Chatteris] which they used to pay to him for the houses and 2 roods of land which Geoffrey le Spenser gave to the abbey (no. 38).

Gift in free alms by John Fithien (Pichiun', Pychyun') of Chatteris to abbess Amicia de Cambridge and the nuns of Chatteris of 4 selions and 1 gore of arable land with meadow in Chatteris (no. 63).

?[Shortly before 8 July 1298 × 27 March 1306] *or* Amicia?

Grant in fee-farm by abbess Amicia and the convent of Chatteris to Warin de Barrington of their half of a water-mill called 'le Estmelne' in Barrington and Foxton and 2 pieces of meadow in Foxton towards repairing the mill, excepting 9 villeins of Foxton who were accustomed to grind there and 7 roods of meadow in Foxton; for 2s. annually (no. 119).

Mary de SHOULDHAM (Schuldam, Schuldham)[1]

28 March 1306

Agreement between abbess Mary de Shouldham and the convent of Chatteris and Robert Fin of Huntingdon, following a plea before the court of common pleas, whereby Robert recognizes that he holds 3 tofts in Huntingdon of the abbey for 30d. annually, for which acknowledgement the abbey granted to him 18d. of rent from a toft in Huntingdon; Robert has paid the rent of 30d. with the arrears (no. 230).

Shortly after 29 Sept. 1317

Agreement between abbess Mary de Shouldham and the convent of Chatteris and William Wimar, burgess of Lynn, and Agnes his wife and William Chaumppaygne, burgess of Norwich, and Joan his wife whereby the abbess and convent acquitted them of the arrears of 5s. of annual rent from the lands and tenements formerly of

[1] Shouldham, Norf.

Nicholas de Bircham in Bircham (Norf.), and they agreed that they and their heirs would pay the rent perpetually to the abbess and convent (no. 225).

[30 Sept. 1300 × 1347]

Quitclaim by Agnes widow of William son of Alexander de Horseheath to abbess Mary de Shouldham and the convent of Chatteris of 3 selions of land [?in Chatteris] which the abbess acquired from Constance le Freman, but which Agnes and her heirs will warrant to the abbess (no. 66).

Lease by abbess Mary de Shouldham and the convent of Chatteris to John de Cambridge, for his life, of a messuage with close in Chatteris (no. 71).

Confirmation by abbess Mary de Shouldham and the convent of Chatteris to Richard, cobbler, of Huntingdon of the croft in Huntingdon given to him by Robert son of Hamo and held of the abbey for 6d. annually (no. 229).

Batill' de WOVETON'

The position of Batill' de Woveton' in the chronology of the abbesses of Chatteris is not certain. No. 254 contains the only known reference to her. She may have been abbess between Mary de Shouldham and Alice de Shropham, or between Matilda Bernard and Margaret Hotot. The last dated occurrence of Mary de Shouldham, who may have preceded Woveton' as abbess, is shortly after 29 Sept. 1317 (no. 225). 13 Oct. 1347 is the date of the retirement of Alice de Shropham, who may have succeeded Woveton', and the date of the election of Matilda Bernard, who may have preceded her (Cambridge UL, EDR G/1/1 de Lisle register, fos. 51r–52r). 30 Sept. 1368 × 5 Dec. 1368 is the first datable occurrence of Margaret Hotot, who may have succeeded Woveton' (no. 192).

[5 March 1329 × 1347 *or* 1347 × 1359]

Surrender and quitclaim by Ralph de Cardington, parson of Barley (Herts.), to abbess Batill' de Woveton' and the convent of Chatteris of all the lands and tenements which he had acquired in Chatteris and Doddington (no. 254).

Alice de SHROPHAM (Schropham)[1]

Abbess

[1331 × 12 Oct. 1347]

Acquittance by abbess Alice de Shropham and the convent of Chatteris to the countess of Kent of 50s. of rent from the manor of Kersey (Suff.) (no. 194).

13 Oct. 1347

Retirement as abbess and election of her successor, Matilda Bernard. Shropham was one of the seven nuns who were delegated to choose the new abbess *per viam compromissi* (Cambridge UL, EDR G/1/1 de Lisle register, fo. 51r–v).

---

[1] Shropham, Norf.

Nun, after retirement as abbess

29 Jan. 1355

Indult from pope Innocent VI to choose a confessor to give her plenary remission at her death (*Calendar of Entries in the Papal Registers Relating to Great Britain and Ireland* iii *Papal Letters 1342–62* eds W. H. Bliss and C. Johnson (PRO Texts and Calendars, 1897) p. 553).

Matilda BERNARD

13 Oct. 1347

Elected abbess following the retirement of Alice de Shropham (Cambridge UL, EDR G/1/1 de Lisle register, fos. 51r–52r).

Batill' de WOVETON', *see above*

Margaret HOTOT (Houtoft)

Nun

13 Oct. 1347

One of seven nuns delegated to choose a new abbess *per viam compromissi* on the occasion of the election of abbess Matilda Bernard (Cambridge UL, EDR G/1/1 de Lisle register, fo. 51r).

Abbess

[30 Sept. 1368 × 5 Dec. 1368]

Acquittance by Margaret Hotot, abbess of Chatteris, to Edward, prince of Wales, of 50s. of rent from the manor of Kersey (Suff.) (no. 192).

26 July 1373

Sede vacante visitation which found that certain nuns were disobedient; that the abbess did much important business concerning the convent without seeking its advice, following instead the wishes of Edward Dreng; that she had withdrawn an annual sum of 10s. intended for the nuns' clothing; and that there was insufficient bread and ale (Lambeth Palace Library, Whittlesey register, fo. 152v).

1379

Occurs in subsidy roll for clerical poll-tax (W. M. Palmer 'A List of Cambridgeshire Subsidy Rolls: The Clerical Poll Tax of 1379 in Cambridgeshire' *The East Anglian* new ser. xiii (1909–10) p. 121).

Agnes ASHFIELD (Aschefeld', Aschfeld', Ashfeld', Asshefeld)[1]

Nun

1379

Occurs in subsidy roll for clerical poll-tax (Palmer 'The Clerical Poll Tax of 1379 in Cambridgeshire', p. 122).

---

[1] Probably Ashfield, Suff.

Abbess, see also Agnes (above)

[21 July 1398 × 8 June 1413]

Acquittance by abbess Agnes Ashfield and the convent of Chatteris to William Sugge, bailiff, of 100s. of rent from the manor of Kersey (Suff.) (no. 198).

Sept. 1415

Pardon by Henry V to abbess Agnes Ashfield and the convent of Chatteris of whichever of the many offences listed they had committed (no. 259).

[9 June 1413 × 18 Jan. 1425]

Acquittance by abbess Agnes Ashfield and the convent of Chatteris to Edmund Mortimer, earl of March and Ulster, of 100s. for the fee-farm of the vill of Kersey (Suff.) (no. 197).

Shortly after 29 Sept. 1425

Acquittance by abbess Agnes Ashfield and the convent of Chatteris to the mayor and community of Lynn of 13s. 4d. (1 mark) of annual rent from their tenement in Lynn (Norf.) (no. 220).

[18 Jan. 1425 × 5 March 1427]

Acquittance by abbess Agnes Ashfield and the convent of Chatteris to Anne, countess of March, of £10 for the fee-farm of the vill of Kersey (Suff.) (no. 199).

9 May 1428

Acquittance by abbess Agnes Ashfield and the convent of Chatteris to John Holand, earl of Huntingdon, of £10 from the manor of Kersey (Suff.) (no. 203).

[20 Sept. 1435 × 20 Aug. 1436]

Manumission from serfdom by abbess Agnes Ashfield and the convent of Chatteris of John Whiteheed', villein of their manor of Chatteris (no. 274).

20 July 1436

Manumission from serfdom by abbess Agnes Ashfield and the convent of Chatteris of John Hulot, villein of their manor of Barley (Herts.) (no. 271).

20 July 1437

Declaration by abbess Agnes Ashfield and the convent of Chatteris that, having examined the evidence and inquired among their tenants, there is nothing to show that John Reynold' of Dry Drayton, husbandman, nor his ancestors are or were villeins of the abbey, contrary to the slanderous assertions of his enemies (no. 276).

After April 1456: Ashfield by then dead

Request for prayers of intercession for the souls of Agnes Ashfield, abbess of Chatteris, and Henry Buckworth, vicar of Chatteris, by the industry and at the expense of whom the book was formerly rendered into this form (no. 1).

Margery RAMSEY (Ramesey, Rameseye, Rampsey)

27 Jan. 1488

Death, recorded in the account of the election of her successor (Cambridge UL, EDR G/1/6 Alcock register, pp. 147–8).

Anne BASSET (Bassett)

4–13 Feb. 1488

Election *per inspirationem spiritus sancti* and installation of prioress Basset as abbess (Cambridge UL, EDR G/1/6 Alcock register, pp. 147–53).

18 Sept. 1492, 14 Oct. 1493, 2 Oct. 1494, 13 Oct. 1496, 12 Oct. 1497, 11 Oct. 1498

Manorial courts of abbess Anne Basset held at Foxton (CCRO L 63/17, rott. 1–3, 6–7d).

20 April 1500

Admission of Henry Walles – who had been presented by Anne Basset – as vicar of Shepreth (Cambridge UL, EDR G/1/6 Alcock register, p. 137).

12 June 1506

The manorial court held at Foxton on this date must be Basset's last, since the court held there on 21 April 1507 is Margaret Develyn's first (CCRO L 63/17, rott. 11d–12).

Margaret DEVELYN (Dulyng', Duvelyn')

Nun and prioress

4–11 Feb. 1488

Present at the election *per inspirationem spiritus sancti* of abbess Anne Basset: Develyn succeeds Basset as prioress (Cambridge UL, EDR G/1/6 Alcock register, pp. 148–50).

Abbess

21 April 1507

Manorial court of abbess Margaret Develyn held at Foxton (CCRO L 63/17, rott. 12–13).

22 April 1507, 5 June 1508

Manorial courts of abbess Margaret Develyn held at Barley (Herts.) (PRO SC 2/177/1, rott. 5–6).

[8 Nov. 1506 × 22 March 1515]

Grant by abbess Margaret Develyn and the convent of Chatteris to James Stanley, bishop of Ely, and Walter Berkoke, gentleman, of the tithe of the church of Barley (Herts.) and the next presentation to it (no. 277).

12 Oct. 1512, 14 April 1513, 6 Oct. 1513, 12 May 1514, 9 Nov. 1514, 12 Oct. 1516, 8 June 1518

> Manorial courts of abbess Margaret Develyn held at Foxton (CCRO L 63/18, rott. 4–4d, 6–7, 8, 10, 11d).

7 March 1533

> Lease of property in Barrington by abbess Margaret Develyn and the convent of Chatteris to William Totman, mentioned in a sale of former Chatteris abbey properties in 1542 (Cambridge, Trinity College Archives, Barrington 341).

22 Aug. 1533

> Grant by abbess Margaret Develyn and the convent of Chatteris to Robert Cooper, John Pory and Robert Davy of the next presentation to Shepreth vicarage (Cambridge UL, EDR G/1/7 Goodrich register, fo. 104v).

Anne GAYTON, abbess when the abbey was dissolved

1 April 1535

> Exemplification, dated 4 April 1542, of the appointment on 1 April 1535, by abbess Anne Gayton and the convent of Chatteris, of John Goderycke as the abbey's chief steward (BL Add. Ch. 15681).

3 Sept. 1538

> Signatory to the surrender of the abbey (PRO E 322/53).

> Inventory of the abbey records her reward of £3 6s. 8d. and pension of £15 (PRO E 117/11/13, fos. 5v, 8r).

17 Feb. 1539

> Warrant for pension of £15 (PRO E 315/233, fo. 129r).

24 Feb. 1556

> Still receiving pension (PRO E 164/31, fo. 12v).

CHRONOLOGICAL LIST OF THE KNOWN PRIORESSES

HADEWISA

[1 Oct. 1133 × 30 May 1169]

> Confirmation by abbess A. and the convent of Chatteris to Adam son of Robert de Cockfield of the manor of Kersey, to be held in fee-farm for £10 annually, which manor Nigel, bishop of Ely (1133–69), and Hadewisa, prioress of Chatteris, had granted and confirmed to Adam de Cockfield, grandfather of Adam (no. 186, dated *c*. 1191 × *c*. 1198).

Amicia de CAMBRIDGE, *see* list of abbesses (occurs as abbess 1298 × 1306)

Joan de DRAYTON

13 Oct. 1347

One of seven nuns delegated to choose a new abbess *per viam compromissi* on the occasion of the election of abbess Matilda Bernard (Cambridge UL, EDR G/1/1 de Lisle register, fo. 51r–v).

Agnes NORTON

1379

Occurs in subsidy roll for clerical poll-tax (Palmer 'The Clerical Poll Tax of 1379 in Cambridgeshire', p. 121).

Anne BASSET, *see* list of abbesses (occurs as abbess 1488–1506)

Margaret DEVELYN, *see* list of abbesses (occurs as abbess 1507–33)

Ellen SMYTH (Smythe), prioress when the abbey was dissolved

3 Sept. 1538

Signatory to the surrender of the abbey (PRO E 322/53).

Inventory of the abbey records her reward of 40s. and pension of £4 (PRO E 117/11/13, fos. 5v, 8r).

17 Feb. 1539

Warrant for pension of £4 (PRO E 315/233, fo. 129r).

24 Feb. 1556

Still receiving pension (PRO E 164/31, fo. 12v).

ALPHABETICAL LIST OF THE KNOWN ABBESSES, PRIORESSES, NUNS AND LAY-SISTER

A., abbess, *see* list of abbesses (occurs *c.* 1191 × *c.* 1198)

ÆLFWEN, abbess, *see* list of abbesses (occurs *c.* 1007 × 1016)

AGNES, abbess, *see* list of abbesses (first occurs *s.* xii^4 × *s.* xiii^1)

AGNES, nun

20 Sept. 1467

Bishop Grey of Ely received her profession in his chapel at Little Downham (Cambridge UL, EDR G/1/5 Grey register, fo. 69r).

ALBREDA, abbess, *see* list of abbesses (occurs *s.* xii^3 × *s.* xiii^2)

ALICE, nun

20 Sept. 1467

Bishop Grey of Ely received her profession in his chapel at Little Downham (Cambridge UL, EDR G/1/5 Grey register, fo. 69r).

AMICIA, abbess, *see* list of abbesses (occurs 1268 × 1280)

Agnes ASHFIELD, nun and abbess, *see* list of abbesses (occurs as abbess 1398 × 1437)

Elizabeth ASPLOND (Aspelond, Haspeland, Haspelond), nun

4 Feb. 1488

Present at the election *per inspirationem spiritus sancti* of abbess Anne Basset (Cambridge UL, EDR G/1/6 Alcock register, p. 148).

3 Sept. 1538

Signatory to the surrender of the abbey (PRO E 322/53).

Inventory of the abbey records her reward of 40s. and pension of £4 (PRO E 117/11/13, fos. 5v, 8r).

17 Feb. 1539

Warrant for pension of £4 (PRO E 315/233, fo. 129r–v).

Cecilia AUBYN, nun

26 July 1373

Sede vacante visitation which found that Cecilia Aubyn was not obedient to the abbess (Lambeth Palace Library, Whittlesey register, fo. 152v).

1379

Occurs in subsidy roll for clerical poll-tax (Palmer 'The Clerical Poll Tax of 1379 in Cambridgeshire', p. 122).

Mabel de BANCIS, abbess, *see* list of abbesses (occurs *s.* xiii[2] × 1265)

Anne BASSET, prioress and abbess, *see* list of abbesses (occurs as abbess 1488–1506)

Joan BATE (Bayte), nun

3 Sept. 1538

Signatory to the surrender of the abbey (PRO E 322/53).

Inventory of the abbey records her reward of 40s. and pension of 40s. (PRO E 117/11/13, fos. 5v, 8r).

17 Feb. 1539

Warrant for pension of 40s. (PRO E 315/233, fo. 131v).

Matilda BERNARD, abbess, *see* list of abbesses (occurs 1347)

Matilda de BOUGHTON (Bouton), nun

13 Oct. 1347

One of seven nuns delegated to choose a new abbess *per viam compromissi* on the occasion of the election of abbess Matilda Bernard (Cambridge UL, EDR G/1/1 de Lisle register, fo. 51r–v).

Eve BRIGHAM, nun

1379

Occurs in subsidy roll for clerical poll-tax (Palmer 'The Clerical Poll Tax of 1379 in Cambridgeshire', p. 122).

Margaret de BURGO, nun

13 Oct. 1347

Present at the election of abbess Matilda Bernard (Cambridge UL, EDR G/1/1 de Lisle register, fo. 51r).

Agnes de BURWELL, abbess, *see* list of abbesses (occurs 1293)

Joan de BURY, nun

9 June 1401

Commission by bishop Fordham of Ely to his suffragan, Thomas Barrett, bishop of Killala (*Aladensis*), to receive her profession (Cambridge UL, EDR G/1/3 Fordham register, fo. 193r).

Agnes CALDECOTE (Calcote, Caldecotte),[1] nun

4–13 Feb. 1488

Present at the election *per inspirationem spiritus sancti* of abbess Anne Basset (Cambridge UL, EDR G/1/6 Alcock register, pp. 148–9, 151–2).

Amicia de CAMBRIDGE, sacrist, prioress and abbess, *see* list of abbesses (occurs as abbess 1298 × 1306)

Katherine de CAMBRIDGE (Cantebr'), nun

13 Oct. 1347

Present at the election of abbess Matilda Bernard (Cambridge UL, EDR G/1/1 de Lisle register, fo. 51r).

---

1 Probably Caldecote, Cambs. or Hunts.

Elizabeth CHESTERTON (Chestreton'),[1] nun

12 July 1406

Commission by bishop Fordham of Ely to his suffragan, Thomas Barrett, bishop of Killala (*Aladensis*), to receive her profession (Cambridge UL, EDR G/1/3 Fordham register, fo. 203r).

Idonea de CHILHAM (Chileham, Eselynge),[2] lay-sister

18 March 1299

Notification by the archbishop of Canterbury to the abbess and convent of Chatteris that, although he had nominated Idonea de Chilham – who was illiterate and therefore ineligible to be a choir nun – for admission to the abbey as a lay-sister, this would not set a precedent for future bishops of Ely to nominate lay-sisters rather than nuns. The archbishop seems to have nominated Idonea when he confirmed the election of an abbess – probably Amicia de Cambridge – in 1298, during a vacancy in the see of Ely (*Registrum Roberti Winchelsey Cantuariensis Archiepiscopi 1294–1313* ed. R. Graham, i (Canterbury and York Society li, 1952) pp. 262–3, 324–5).

16 June 1300

Mandate from the archbishop of Canterbury to the bishop of Ely to insist that the abbess of Chatteris should feed and clothe Idonea, a lay-sister, as though she were a professed nun (*Registrum Roberti Winchelsey* ii (Canterbury and York Society lii, 1956) pp. 711–12).

Margaret daughter of Richard de COLUMBERS, nun

[*s.* xii[4] × *s.* xiii[2]]

Grant by Richard de Columbers, with the consent of Peter his heir, to Chatteris abbey, in which his daughters, Rose and Margaret, were received as nuns, of a weight of marketable cheese annually at Dunstable (Beds.) (no. 170).

Rose daughter of Richard de COLUMBERS, nun

[*s.* xii[4] × *s.* xiii[2]]

See Margaret daughter of Richard de Columbers

Margaret de CONINGTON (Conynton', Conytom'),[3] nun

13 Oct. 1347

One of seven nuns delegated to choose a new abbess *per viam compromissi* on the occasion of the election of abbess Matilda Bernard (Cambridge UL, EDR G/1/1 de Lisle register, fo. 51r–v).

---

1 Probably Chesterton, Cambs. or Hunts.
2 Chilham, Kent.
3 Probably Conington, Cambs. or Hunts.

Katherine CORONER (Coronner), nun

13 Oct. 1347

One of seven nuns delegated to choose a new abbess *per viam compromissi* on the occasion of the election of abbess Matilda Bernard (Cambridge UL, EDR G/1/1 de Lisle register, fo. 51r–v).

Adelicia daughter of Hugh de CRANWELL (*Cornewellia, Cranewellia*),[1] nun

[*s.* xii[3] × 1188]

Grant by Hugh de Cranwell to Chatteris abbey of 10s. of rent in Lincoln, from the houses held by David son of Eilsus de Lincoln, on condition that Adelicia his daughter, a nun of Chatteris, should have this rent for her life and that her prebend should not be reduced on account of it; after her death it will remain to the abbey (no. 227).

Margaret DEVELYN (Dulyng', Duvelyn'), nun, prioress and abbess, *see* list of abbesses (occurs as abbess 1507–33)

Agnes DOUSTHORP, nun

13 Oct. 1347

Present at the election of abbess Matilda Bernard (Cambridge UL, EDR G/1/1 de Lisle register, fo. 51r).

Joan de DRAYTON, prioress, *see* list of prioresses (occurs 1347)

Agnes de ELY, abbess, *see* list of abbesses (occurs 1275 × 1293)

ESELYNGE *see* **CHILHAM**

Katherine FERRERES, nun

9 June 1401

Commission by bishop Fordham of Ely to his suffragan, Thomas Barrett, bishop of Killala (*Aladensis*), to receive her profession (Cambridge UL, EDR G/1/3 Fordham register, fo. 193r).

Elinor FINCHAM (Fyncham), nun

22 Jan. 1518

Thomas Fincham (*see* A. B. Emden *A Biographical Register of the University of Cambridge to 1500* (Cambridge, 1963) p. 248) bequeathed 6s. 8d. to her in a codicil to his will (PRO PROB 11/19/5).

---

[1] Cranwell, Lincs.

Alice FISSHER, nun

4 Feb. 1488

Present at the election *per inspirationem spiritus sancti* of abbess Anne Basset (Cambridge UL, EDR G/1/6 Alcock register, p. 148).

Margaret FORDHAM,[1] nun

4–13 Feb. 1488

Present at the election *per inspirationem spiritus sancti* of abbess Anne Basset (Cambridge UL, EDR G/1/6 Alcock register, pp. 148-9, 151-2).

Anne GAYTON, abbess, *see* list of abbesses (occurs 1535–56)

Mary GRAY (Graie, Graye, Grey), nun

3 Sept. 1538

Signatory to the surrender of the abbey (PRO E 322/53).

Inventory of the abbey records her reward of 40s. and pension of 53s. 4d. (PRO E 117/11/13, fos. 5v, 8r).

17 Feb. 1539

Warrant for pension of 53s. 4d. (PRO E 315/233, fo. 130r–v).

24 Feb. 1556

Still receiving pension (PRO E 164/31, fo. 12v).

Elizabeth GYE (Gie, Gwye), nun

3 Sept. 1538

Signatory to the surrender of the abbey (PRO E 322/53).

Inventory of the abbey records her reward of 40s. and pension of 40s. (PRO E 117/11/13, fos. 5v, 8r).

17 Feb. 1539

Warrant for pension of 40s. (PRO E 315/233, fo. 131r–v).

24 Feb. 1556

Still receiving pension (PRO E 164/31, fo. 12v).

HADEWISA, prioress, *see* list of prioresses (occurs 1 Oct. 1133 × 30 May 1169)

Agnes HAREWOLD, nun

12 July 1406

Commission by bishop Fordham of Ely to his suffragan, Thomas Barrett, bishop of Killala (*Aladensis*), to receive her profession (Cambridge UL, EDR G/1/3 Fordham register, fo. 203r).

---

[1] Probably Fordham, Cambs. or Norf.

Agnes HIGDON (Hygdon), nun

3 Sept. 1538

Signatory to the surrender of the abbey (PRO E 322/53).

Inventory of the abbey records her reward of 40s. and pension of 53s. 4d. (PRO E 117/11/13, fos. 5v, 8r).

17 Feb. 1539

Warrant for pension of 53s. 4d. (PRO E 315/233, fo. 130v).

Juliana HOTOT, nun

1379

Occurs in subsidy roll for clerical poll-tax (Palmer 'The Clerical Poll Tax of 1379 in Cambridgeshire', p. 122).

Margaret HOTOT, nun and abbess, *see* list of abbesses (occurs as abbess 1368–1379)

Rose HOTOT, nun

9 June 1401

Commission by bishop Fordham of Ely to his suffragan, Thomas Barrett, bishop of Killala (*Aladensis*), to receive her profession (Cambridge UL, EDR G/1/3 Fordham register, fo. 193r).

Elinor HUTTON, nun

3 Sept. 1538

Signatory to the surrender of the abbey (PRO E 322/53).

Inventory of the abbey records her reward of 40s. and pension of 53s. 4d. (PRO E 117/11/13, fos. 5v, 8r).

17 Feb. 1539

Warrant for pension of 53s. 4d. (PRO E 315/233, fo. 131r).

24 Feb. 1556

Still receiving pension (PRO E 164/31, fo. 12v).

I. [*or* **J.**], abbess, *see* list of abbesses (occurs 1216)

Avice IPSWICH (Yepeswych), nun

1379

Occurs in subsidy roll for clerical poll-tax (Palmer 'The Clerical Poll Tax of 1379 in Cambridgeshire', p. 122).

JOAN, nun

20 Sept. 1467

Bishop Grey of Ely received her profession in his chapel at Little Downham (Cambridge UL, EDR G/1/5 Grey register, fo. 69r).

JOAN [another], nun

20 Sept. 1467

> Bishop Grey of Ely received her profession in his chapel at Little Downham (Cambridge UL, EDR G/1/5 Grey register, fo. 69r).

Alice de LYNN (*Lenna*),[1] nun

13 Oct. 1347

> Present at the election of abbess Matilda Bernard (Cambridge UL, EDR G/1/1 de Lisle register, fo. 51r).

M., abbess, *see* list of abbesses (occurs *s.* xiii[2] × 1265)

Katherine MARTYN, nun

4 Feb. 1488

> Present at the election *per inspirationem spiritus sancti* of abbess Anne Basset (Cambridge UL, EDR G/1/6 Alcock register, p. 148).

Alice daughter of Richard MOLER, nun

[*s.* xii[4] × *s.* xiii[2]]

> Grant by Robert de Insula to Chatteris abbey of 2 fisheries with specified rights and gift in free alms of the fee which Baldwin son of Augustine held of him in Upwell and Outwell (Cambs. and Norf.) for 10 sticks of eels, excepting Baldwin's tenement; with Alice, daughter of Richard Moler, his kinswoman (no. 87).

Agnes NORTON, prioress, *see* list of prioresses (occurs 1379)

Isabel NORTON, nun

1379

> Occurs in subsidy roll for clerical poll-tax (Palmer 'The Clerical Poll Tax of 1379 in Cambridgeshire', p. 122).

Agnes de OFFTON (Ofton, Ufton),[2] nun

13 Oct. 1347

> Ill and absent from the election of abbess Matilda Bernard (Cambridge UL, EDR G/1/1 de Lisle register, fo. 51r).

1379

> Occurs in subsidy roll for clerical poll-tax (Palmer 'The Clerical Poll Tax of 1379 in Cambridgeshire', p. 122).

---

1 Lynn, Norf.
2 Offton, Suff.

Lucy OVER,[1] nun

4 Feb. 1488

Present at the election *per inspirationem spiritus sancti* of abbess Anne Basset (Cambridge UL, EDR G/1/6 Alcock register, p. 148).

Anna PALFREMAN, nun

4 Feb. 1488

Present at the election *per inspirationem spiritus sancti* of abbess Anne Basset (Cambridge UL, EDR G/1/6 Alcock register, p. 148).

Tecla daughter of Henry PEREGRINUS, nun

[s. xii⁴ × s. xiii²]

Confirmation by Michael Peregrinus to Chatteris abbey of the tenement [?in Chatteris] given by his father, Henry Peregrinus, with Tecla, daughter of Henry and sister of Michael (no. 26).

Margaret POLEYN, nun

13 Oct. 1347

Present at the election of abbess Matilda Bernard (Cambridge UL, EDR G/1/1 de Lisle register, fo. 51r).

1379

Occurs in subsidy roll for clerical poll-tax (Palmer 'The Clerical Poll Tax of 1379 in Cambridgeshire', p. 122).

Elinor PYNDER, nun

4 Feb. 1488

Present at the election *per inspirationem spiritus sancti* of abbess Anne Basset (Cambridge UL, EDR G/1/6 Alcock register, p. 148).

Joan RAMSEY (Rameseye),[2] nun

1379

Occurs in subsidy roll for clerical poll-tax (Palmer 'The Clerical Poll Tax of 1379 in Cambridgeshire', p. 122).

Margery RAMSEY, abbess, *see* list of abbesses (occurs 1488)

Anne REDE (Reede, Reyde), nun

3 Sept. 1538

Signatory to the surrender of the abbey (PRO E 322/53).

---

1 Probably Over, Cambs.
2 Probably Ramsey, Hunts.

Inventory of the abbey records her reward of 40s. and pension of 53s. 4d. (PRO E 117/11/13, fos. 5v, 8r).

17 Feb. 1539

Warrant for pension of 53s. 4d. (PRO E 315/233, fos. 130v–131r).

24 Feb. 1556

Still receiving pension (PRO E 164/31, fo. 12v).

Agnes REDEWYK, nun

1379

Occurs in subsidy roll for clerical poll-tax (Palmer 'The Clerical Poll Tax of 1379 in Cambridgeshire', p. 122).

Agnes RICHARD, nun

13 Oct. 1347

Present at the election of abbess Matilda Bernard (Cambridge UL, EDR G/1/1 de Lisle register, fo. 51r).

1379

Occurs in subsidy roll for clerical poll-tax (Palmer 'The Clerical Poll Tax of 1379 in Cambridgeshire', p. 122).

A. de ROUEN, abbess, *see* list of abbesses (occurs *s.* xiii$^{1-2}$)

Mary de SANCTO CLARO, abbess, *see* list of abbesses (occurs *s.* xiii^2 × 1265)

Etheldreda de SANCTO GEORGIO, nun

13 Oct. 1347

One of seven nuns delegated to choose a new abbess *per viam compromissi* on the occasion of the election of abbess Matilda Bernard (Cambridge UL, EDR G/1/1 de Lisle register, fo. 51r–v).

Agatha daughter of Alan son of Robert de SHEPRETH (Seperey, Sephereya),[1] nun [*s.* xii^4 × *s.* xiii^2]

Gift in free alms by Alan son of Robert de Shepreth to Chatteris abbey of 15 roods and 2 acres of land in Shepreth, 5 acres in Foxton, a croft in 'Hulmo' [in Shepreth], 1 acre of meadow, and a messuage in Cambridge, with Agatha his daughter (no. 152).

Mary de SHOULDHAM, abbess, *see* list of abbesses (occurs 1300 × 1347)

Alice de SHROPHAM, abbess and nun, *see* list of abbesses (occurs as abbess 1331 × 1347)

---

[1] Shepreth, Cambs.

Margaret SKELE (Skyll), nun

3 Sept. 1538

Signatory to the surrender of the abbey (PRO E 322/53).

Inventory of the abbey records her reward of 40s. and pension of 53s. 4d. (PRO E 117/11/13, fos. 5v, 8r).

17 Feb. 1539

Warrant for pension of 53s. 4d. (PRO E 315/233, fo. 130r).

Ellen SMYTH (Smythe), prioress, *see* list of prioresses (occurs 1538–56)

Emma de SOMERSHAM, abbess, *see* list of abbesses (occurs 1265–8)

Katherine TILLY, nun

1379

Occurs in subsidy roll for clerical poll-tax (Palmer 'The Clerical Poll Tax of 1379 in Cambridgeshire', p. 122).

Katherine TYDD (Tyd),[1] nun

1379

Occurs in subsidy roll for clerical poll-tax (Palmer 'The Clerical Poll Tax of 1379 in Cambridgeshire', p. 122).

UFTON *see* **OFFTON**

Margaret VASIE (Vasy, Vasye), nun

3 Sept. 1538

Signatory to the surrender of the abbey (PRO E 322/53).

Inventory of the abbey records her reward of 40s. and pension of 53s. 4d. (PRO E 117/11/13, fos. 5v, 8r).

17 Feb. 1539

Warrant for pension of 53s. 4d. (PRO E 315/233, fo. 129v).

Juliana WESTON, nun

12 July 1406

Commission by bishop Fordham of Ely to his suffragan, Thomas Barrett, bishop of Killala (*Aladensis*), to receive her profession (Cambridge UL, EDR G/1/3 Fordham register, fo. 203r).

---

1 Tydd St Giles, Cambs., or Tydd St Mary, Lincs.

Elizabeth WIGHTON, nun

4 Feb. 1488

> Present at the election *per inspirationem spiritus sancti* of abbess Anne Basset (Cambridge UL, EDR G/1/6 Alcock register, p. 148).

Margery WILLY, nun

4 Feb. 1488

> Present at the election *per inspirationem spiritus sancti* of abbess Anne Basset (Cambridge UL, EDR G/1/6 Alcock register, p. 148).

Batill' de WOVETON', abbess, *see* list of abbesses (occurs 5 March 1329 × 1347 *or* 1347 × 1359)

YEPESWYCH *see* **IPSWICH**

Appendix 2

The Inventory of Chatteris Abbey

PRO E 117/11/13, 3 SEPTEMBER 1538

The[1] Inventory off Chaterys (fo. 1v)[2]

Chaterys[3]

The inventory of all the store and stuff of household plate, corne and catell to the late abbey off Chaterys belongyng, taken by Mr Thomas Legh and Mr Phylypp comissioners ther, vewyd and valewyd the[4] iij^de daye of September in the xxx^th yere off the reygne of owr soverayne lord kyng Henry the viij^th.

In the gret gest chamber

Item ij coverlettes, a fetherbed, a mattresse, a bolster, ij pyllowys, a payer off blanckettes, paynted clothes, a counter, a old coberd, iiij cheyres with ij coysshynns, vij formys, an old tester, whytte curtaynes off old grene saye, ij handyrons

xx s.

In the inward chamber

Item a lytyll old fetherbed, a bolster and a coverlett

v s.

In the maydens chamber

Item iiij mattres, a bolster, an olde chyst, a coverlett, ij old chystes

iiij s.

Item certain old mattres for servauntes and vj coverlettes

vjs. viij d. (fo. 2v)

---

1 *An Inventory of the Monastery of Chaterys*, added in a secretary hand, and *Co. Cambridge, Inventory of the Abbey of Chaterys, Co. Cambridge, 3rd Sept 30th Henry 8*, added in a modern hand, at top of folio.

2 Fo. 1v is blank.

3 Marginated.

4 y^e: thorn transcribed throughout as *th*.

In the hall

Item a folden table off waynscotte, ij old tables, vij formes, and old coberd, iij chayers, iij stolys, v coysshyns, vj trestylles, old paynted hangyns, a braunche off latten to set candels in, ij bankyrs

x s.

In the buttrye behynd the hall end

Item vij table clothes, v towelles, xiiij napkyns, iij latyn basons, iij pewterbasons, a candelstyke, v olde coffers

In the buttrye at the hall end

Item a bason and an euer, a garnysshe of wessell, viijth platters, xx potyngers, a salt, iij borde clothes

In the cellerers chamber

Item iij candelstykes, a chaffen dyshe with a fote, xv tabyll clothys, a dosyn and a half^1 of napkyns, vj towels, ij hedshetes, iiij payer of shetes

v li. vj s. viij d.

In the nether buttrye

Item a cownter, a long settyll, a cheyer, x wessels for ale, wyth other old bordys

ij s. (fo. 3r)

In the kyttechynne

Item vij brasse pottes off all sortes, iij pannys, a ketyll, one possenet, ij trestels, vj rackys, v spyttes, ij gredeyrons, iij fyre pannys, ij payer of hangers, a lytle trowh covered with leade, ij old brasse pottys, a collender, a brasen morter wytht a pestell, ij axes, a payer of tonges, a fyer forke, a ladell, wyth other bordys and sellys

iij li.

In the backehouse

Item crowes and tubbes and other utensiles for the same

vj s.^{2} viij d.

In the brue howse

Item iij smale leydes whereof one ys withoute a botome, a panne, a masshe fatt, ij lytle fattes, xij kyllyrs, on ale tubbe

iij li. vj s. viij d.

In the frayter

Item old bordys and formys, a lytle bell

ij s.

---

1 di'.
2 Preceded by vj li., cancelled.

In the dorter
Item certen old celles
xx s. (fo. 3v)

Catall
Item vij old horsys and geldynges, price xl s.
Item iij marys valeued at xv s.
Item v bore pygges, viij s.
Item vj sowes, vij s.
Item xvj hogges of all sortes, xiiij s.
Item ij oxen, xxvj s. viij d.
Item ij bullys, xvj s.
Item ij sterys of ij yeres age, x s.
Item vj kyen and xiij heckfordes wyth the calves on wyth an other, vj li. vj s. viij d.
Item ix old mylche kyen, iij li.
Item x yerelynges, xx s.

In the garners
Item in malte iiij quarters, x s. viij d.
Item in whete xxx quarters, vij li.

In the barne unthrasshed
Item in whete and rye xxx quartars, vj li.
Item barley xl quarters, iiij li.
Item in heye, iiij li.

Husbondrye
Item ij longe cartes and shorte cartes, ij plowys wyth ther appurtenaunces, xx s. (fo. 4r)

In the quere or chauncell
Item of the high aulter a table of alabaster, a crucifyxe and iij sayntes, ij gret candalstyckes of latten, seytes in the quere wyth certen old bookes, ij sensors of latten, ij lampes, a lytle bell, ij lectorns off iren
The north ile
Item a table of alabaster, a clocke with all the grave stonys and pavement in the quere belongyng to the nonnys
iij li.
The sowth ile gyven

In the revestre
Item ij aulter clothes of chamlett, a westement of red velvet wyth a deacon and subdeacon, a scewte of bawdkyne, iij aulter clothes of dyaper, an alter clothe of course bawdkyn, an old sute of grene bawdkyn, and old scewte of whyte bawdkyn,

a scewte of red silke saye, a scewte of old bawdkyn, ij bannert clothes of sylke, a chest of lennen clothes for lente, another chapell there, a table of alabaster, ij sayntes, an aulter clothe of grene satten

iiij li. (fo. 4v)

Pllate

Item a chaleys weying xvj ounces, the price iij li. iiij s.
Item plate of sylver taken of a woode crosse sold, ij li. xiij s. iiij d.
Item x sponnes ponderyng vij ounces at iiij s. viij d., xxv s. iiij d.
Summa viij li. ij s. viiij d.

Summa totalle lxxj li. vj s. iiij d. (fo. 5r)

Leade off the roff of the quere and ij iles wyth the steple there
Item in foders by estimacion xx^{ti}, price le foder iiij li., summa iiij^{xx} li.

Belles

Item iiij smale belles valoued by estymacion at xv li.

Summa totalle of the leade and belles by estymacion, lxxxxv li. (fo. 5v)

The namys of the nonnys

Rewardes

Domina Anne Gayton, abas	iij li. vj s. viij d.
Domina Elene Smyth, prioresse	xl s.
Domina Elizabeth Haspeland	xl s.
Domina Margarete Vasye	xl s.
Domina Margarete Skele	xl s.
Domina Mary Graye	xl s.
Domina Agnes Hygdon	xl s.
Domina Anne Reede	xl s.
Domina Elenor Hutton	xl s.
Domina Elyzabeth Gye	xl s.
Domina Johanne Bayte	xl s.
Summa of the nonnes rewardes there	xxiij li. vj s. viij d. (fo. 6r)

The namys of the servauntes wyth ther wages dewe unto them at Michelmes next

Wagis payde		Rewardes payde
Item to Sir Barnard Hartely for a quarter of a yere	xvj s. viij d.	reward v s.
Item Roberte Rede for a quarter wages	x s.	iij s. iiij d.
Item to Raff Johnson for a yere and a quarter		v s.
Item John Wylkynson for halfe a yere	xj s.	ij s.

Item to Robart Fyssher for iij quarters wages	xij s.	iiij s.
Item to Thomas Saunders for a yeres wages	xvij s.	
whereof payd[1] vij s. and so remayneth	x s.	xx d.
Item to John Tomlynson for iij quarters of a yere		
xx s. whereof payd[2] xiij s. iiij d, remayneth	v s. viij d.	iij s. iiij d.
Item to Robert Tomson for a quarter vj s. viij d.		
and for hys botes ij s. viij d.	ix s.	xx d.
Item to Robart Edge for half a yere	x s.	xx d.
Item to John Fysshe for iij quarters xx s. whereof		
paid xij d. and so remayneth xix s.	xix s.	xij d. (fo. 6v)
Item to John Netherton for iij quarters of a yere	xviij s.	xx d.
Item to Isabell Davison for iij quarters	vij s. vj d.	xx d.
Summa		

Wagys		Rewardes
Item to Alys Hall for half a yere whereof paid ix d.		
remayneth	iiij s. iiij d.	xx d.
Item Katerynne Fisshe for half a yere	v s.	xij d.
Item to Mother Conie for half a yere	iiij s.	xij d.
Item to Anne Saterd for half a yere	v s.	v s.
Item to Thomas Skoyte for half a yere	iij s. iiij d.	xx d.
Item to George Broune for half a yere	x s.	xx d.
Item to John Brache for half a yere	x s.	xx d.[3]
Item to Agnes Brune for half a yere	v s.	xij d.
Item to Harry Harrow, smythe, for half a yere	viij s.	xx d. (fo. 7r)
Item to Edmond Abraham for a quarter	ij s. vj d.	xij d.
Item to Alis Abraham for a quarter	ij s. vj d.	xij d.
Item to Ursula Hanshott		v s.
Item to the coper for iij quarters of a yere	vij s. vj d.	

Laborers in harvest payd	
Item to Mathewe	x s.
Item to Antony Gervis	
Item to Elizabeth Scotte	xx d.
Item to Agnes Walcott'	xx d.
Item to Marion Tomson	xx d.
Item to Elizabeth Monfrye[4]	ij s.

1 Interlined above *x d.*, cancelled.
2 Interlined above *x d.*, cancelled.
3 Preceded by *xx s.*, cancelled.

Item to Margaret Crathorn	iij s. iiij d.
Item to William Preson[5]	xvj d.
Item to William Skyle	ij s. x d.
Item to John Wyllekynnys	iij d.
Summa totalis	xiij li. iiij s. (fo. 7v)
Summa totalle of alle the paymentes	xxxvj li. x s. viij d.
Allso there remayneth in a spiritualtie	xxvj li. xiij s. iiij d.
And remaynethe in our handes	viij li. ij s. iiij d. (fo. 8r)

Penciones grauntede to the nonnes there

Domina Anne Gayton, abbas	xv li.
Domina Elone Smythe, priores	iiij li.
Domina Elizabeth Haspelond	iiij li.
Domina Margarete Vasie	liij s. iiij d.
Domina Margarete Skele	liij s. iiij d.
Domina Marye Graye	liij s. iiij d.
Domina Agnes Higdon	liij s. iiij d.
Domina Anne Rede	liij s. iiij d.
Domina Elenor Hutton	liij s. iiij s.
Domina Elizabeth Gye[6]	xl s.
Domina Jone Bate	xl s.
Summa of the nonnes pensions by the yere	xliij li. (fo. 8v)

Dettes that the abbas oweth

Item to master Mynnys	vij li.
Item to the parson Palfreman	xj s.
Item to John Aspelond	xl s.
Item to Antony Drynke	ix li.
Item to Mr Donhull	xlviij s.
Summa	xxj li. xix s.

The whiche dettes of the abbas remayne unpayd tyll suche tyme as the surveyer and the auditor commyth at Michelmes next to take order in all thynges and lykecase to

4 Preceded by one letter, cancelled?
5 Or possibly *Proson*.
6 Preceded by *E*, cancelled.

paye Raff Johnson, rente gatherer, iij li. vj s. viij d. dewe unto hym and to se the dyscharge of the same.

Memorandum that yt ys agreed that the sayd abbas shall receyve all mannor rentes dewe byfore the date hereof for the last hole yere past so that the receyvor shall receyve at Michelmes nexte the hole halfe yeres rente unto thuse off owr soverayn lord the kyng hys hygnes. (fo. 9r)

Item that the iijrd daye of September Mr Walter Cromewell was putt in possession of the sayd abbey off Chateries unto the use of our soverayn lord the kyng whyth wome also remayne unto hys graces use the churche wyth leade and belles, glasse and iron with all other edifyces in the howse.

Bibliography

MANUSCRIPT SOURCES

Cambridge County Record Office
  CCRO Ely consistory court probate registers, vols 1, 6–8, 10
  L 63/17–18: court rolls from Chatteris abbey's manors of Foxton with members, Barley (Herts.), Over and Chatteris, 1492–1543

Cambridge, St John's College Archives
  D 20. 130: charter
  D 25. 22: charter

Cambridge, Trinity College Library
  MSS
  O. 2. 1: 'Liber Eliensis'
  O. 2. 41: 'Liber Eliensis', cartulary and 'Libellus'
  College Archives
  Barrington 136: charter
  Barrington 341: charter
  Foxton 1–5: court rolls from Chatteris abbey's manor of Foxton with members, 1276–1325
  Foxton 6: court rolls from Chatteris abbey's manors of Foxton with members, Barley (Herts.), Over and Chatteris, 1537–42

Cambridge University Library
  Additional MS
  6394: induction book of archdeacon of Ely
  Ely Dean and Chapter MSS
  1: 'Liber Eliensis'
  1/A/2: cartulary of the almoner of Ely
  1/B/5: charter
  Ely Diocesan Registry
  C 7/28, 30–31: rolls from Witchford hundred court, 1366–90
  C 7/29, 34: rolls from sheriff's tourn exercised by bishop of Ely's steward in Witchford hundred, 1376–1464
  C 12/4/1–7: rolls from bishop of Ely's courts leet in Chatteris, 1384–1406
  C 13/1–5: rolls from Wisbech hundred court, 1303–1543
  G/1/1: register of bishops Montacute and de Lisle

G/1/2: register of bishop Arundel
G/1/3: register of bishop Fordham
G/1/4: register of bishop Bourgchier
G/1/5: register of bishop Grey
G/1/6: register of bishop Alcock
G/1/7: register of bishops West, Goodrich, Thirlby and Cox
G/3/27 'Liber R' alias 'The Old Coucher Book'
G/3/28 'Liber M': cartulary

Lambeth Palace Library
    Register of archbishop Whittlesey
    Register of archbishop Arundel
    Register of archbishops Stafford and Kempe
    Register of archbishop Warham

London, British Library (BL)
    Additional Charter
    15681
    Additional MSS
    5809: vol. viii of Cole's collections
    5819: vol. xviii of Cole's collections
    5823: vol. xxii of Cole's collections
    5846: vol. xlv of Cole's collections
    5849: vol. xlviii of Cole's collections
    5866: vol. lxv of Cole's collections
    33450: register of J. Titchmarsh, abbot of Ramsey, 1431–41
    35213: catalogue of Cotton MSS, pre-dating BL Harl. MS 6018
    36789: catalogue of Cotton MSS, c. 1635
    62576: lists of injured Cotton MSS with notes on repairs, 1837–56
    62577: repair and binding ledger of Cotton MSS, 1839–65
    62578: list of the Cottonian MSS injured or destroyed in 1731 and their present state
        of restoration, 1866.
    Cotton Charter
    xxi. 12
    Cotton MSS
    Claudius C. xi: survey (1251) of bishop's demesne manors
    Domitian A. xv: register of terriers and other documents
    Galba E. x: surveys and rentals from Ramsey abbey
    Nero C. iii: inventory of deeds belonging to the see of Ely
    Otho B. xiv: fragments of registers from Ramsey abbey
    Otho C. viii: cartulary of Nunkeeling priory (Yorks. E.)
    Tiberius A. vi: 'Liber Eliensis', cartulary
    Tiberius B. ii: survey (1222) of bishop's demesne manors

Titus A. i: 'Liber Eliensis', book II and cartulary
Vespasian A. vi: cartulary of the almoner of Ely
Vespasian A. xviii: register from Ramsey abbey
Vespasian A. xix: 'Liber Eliensis', book III and Libellus
Egerton MS
3663: register from Ramsey abbey
Harleian Charter
43 C. 11
Harleian MSS
5071: register from Ramsey abbey
6018: catalogue of Cotton MSS, 1621
Lansdowne MS
722: William Dugdale's journal of his itinerary to the fens of Ely, 1657

London, Public Record Office (PRO)
    C 66/323: patent roll 10 Richard II
    C 66/399: patent roll 4 Henry V
    C 139/140/30: inquisitions post mortem 29 Henry VI
    C 143/405/10: inquisitions *ad quod damnum* 10 Richard II
    CP 25/1/24/23, no. 29: foot of fine, Cambs., 1247
    CP 25/1/85/31, no. 594: foot of fine, Herts., 1268
    E 13/79: exchequer plea roll 27 & 28 Edward III
    E 40/10769: ancient deed
    E 40/10907: ancient deed
    E 117/11/13: inventory of Chatteris abbey in 1538
    E 164/31: cardinal Pole's certificate of pensions payable to the former religious, 1556
    E 179/23/1: clerical subsidy roll, 1379
    E 315/233: warrants for pensions to former abbess and nuns of Chatteris, 1539
    E 322/53: surrender of Chatteris abbey in 1538
    JUST 1/323-4: assize roll for Herts. eyre of 1278
    PROB 11/19/5: prerogative court of Canterbury will, 1518
    PROB 11/21/36: prerogative court of Canterbury will, 1525
    SC 2/177/1: court rolls from Chatteris abbey's manor of Minchinbury, Barley (Herts.), 1463-1508
    SC 6 HenVIII/266-74: minister's accounts for the possessions of Chatteris abbey, 1538-46
    PRO SC 11/91: rental for possessions of Ramsey abbey in Chatteris, 1472

Oxford, Bodleian Library
    MSS
    Dodsworth 78: notes from cartularies and monastic collections in the Cottonian library

Dodsworth 105: collections from chronicles and cartularies
Laud. Misc. 647: 'Liber Eliensis'
Rawl. B. 278

MAPS

Ordnance Surveyors' Drawings, 2 inch, Cambs., Hunts. and Norf.: sheet 250 (1810).

Ordnance Survey, 25 inch, 1st edn, Cambs.: sheet 20. 16 (1888).

Ordnance Survey, 1: 2500: national grid plan TL 3885–3985 (1972).

PRINTED SOURCES

St Augustine, bishop of Hippo *Enarrationes in Psalmos* (*Patrologiae Cursus Completus, Series Latina* ed. J.-P. Migne, xxxvi–xxxvii, 1845).

W. O. Ault ed. *Court Rolls of the Abbey of Ramsey and of the Honour of Clare* (New Haven, 1928).

Calendar of the Close Rolls Preserved in the Public Record Office (PRO Texts and Calendars, 1892–1963).

Calendar of Entries in the Papal Registers Relating to Great Britain and Ireland iii *Papal Letters 1342–62* eds W. H. Bliss and C. Johnson (PRO Texts and Calendars, 1897).

A Calendar of the Feet of Fines Relating to the County of Huntingdon Levied in the King's Court from the Fifth Year of Richard I to the End of the Reign of Elizabeth 1194–1603 ed. G. J. Turner (Cambridge Antiquarian Society, octavo ser. xxxvii, 1913).

Calendar of Inquisitions Post Mortem and Other Analogous Documents Preserved in the Public Record Office (PRO Texts and Calendars, 1904–).

Calendar of Memoranda Rolls (Exchequer) Preserved in the Public Record Office. Michaelmas 1326–Michaelmas 1327 (PRO Texts and Calendars, 1968).

Calendar of the Patent Rolls Preserved in the Public Record Office (PRO Texts and Calendars, 1891–).

The Cartæ Antiquæ Rolls 1–10 ed. L. Landon (Pipe Roll Society, new ser. xvii, 1939).

Cartularium Monasterii de Rameseia eds W. H. Hart and P. A. Lyons, 3 vols (Rolls Series lxxix, 1884, 1886, 1893).

Cartulary of St Mary Clerkenwell ed. W. O. Hassall (Camden 3rd ser. lxxi, 1949).

Catalogue of Additions to the Manuscripts in the British Museum in the Years 1906–10 (London, 1912).

A Catalogue of the Manuscripts in the Cottonian Library Deposited in the British Museum (London, 1802).

Charters of the Honour of Mowbray 1107–1191 ed. D. E. Greenway (British Academy, 1972).

The Chronicle of Bury St Edmunds 1212–1301 ed. A. Gransden (London, 1964).

Chronicon Abbatiæ Rameseiensis ed. W. D. Macray (Rolls Series lxxxiii, 1886).

The Complete Peerage eds V. Gibbs, H. A. Doubleday and Lord Howard de Walden, vii (London, 1929).

Curia Regis Rolls (PRO Texts and Calendars, 1922–).

Domesday Book, seu Liber Censualis Willelmi Primi 2 vols (London, 1783).

W. Dugdale *Monasticon Anglicanum* ed. J. Caley, H. Ellis and B. Bandinel, 6 vols in 8 (London, 1817–30).

Feet of Fines for the County of Norfolk for the Reign of King John 1201–1215, for the County of Suffolk for the Reign of King John 1199–1214 ed. B. Dodwell (Pipe Roll Society, new ser. xxxii, 1956).

Feet of Fines for the County of Norfolk for the Tenth Year of the Reign of King Richard the First 1189–1199 and for the First Four Years of the Reign of King John 1199–1202 ed. B. Dodwell (Pipe Roll Society, new ser. xxvii, 1950).

Final Concords of the County of Lincoln From the Feet of Fines Preserved in the Public Record Office A.D. 1244–1272 (Lincoln Record Society xvii, 1920).

Inquisitions and Assessments Relating to Feudal Aids; with Other Analagous Documents Preserved in the Public Record Office A.D. 1284–1431 6 vols (PRO Texts and Calendars, 1899–1920).

Letters and Papers, Foreign and Domestic, of the Reign of Henry VIII, Preserved in the Public Record Office, the British Museum and Elsewhere in England (PRO Texts and Calendars, 1862–1932).

Liber Eliensis ed. E.O. Blake (Camden 3rd ser. xcii, 1962).

Liber Feodorum. The Book of Fees Commonly Called Testa de Nevill 2 vols in 3 (PRO Texts and Calendars, 1920, 1923, 1931).

Liber Memorandorum Ecclesie de Bernewelle ed. J. W. Clark (Cambridge, 1907).

W. E. Lunt *The Valuation of Norwich* (Oxford, 1926).

W. M. Palmer 'A List of Cambridgeshire Subsidy Rolls: The Clerical Poll Tax of 1379 in Cambridgeshire' *The East Anglian* new ser. xiii (1909–10) pp. 90–2, 101–4, 121–4, 153–5, 173–6, 188–92, 220–4.

Papsturkunden in England ed. W. Holtzmann, 3 vols (Abhandlungen der Gesellschaft der Wissenschaften zu Göttingen, Phil.-Hist. Klasse, new series xxv, 3rd series xiv–xv, xxxiii; Berlin, 1930, 1935–6, Göttingen, 1952).

Pedes Finium: or Fines, Relating to the County of Cambridge, Levied in the King's Court from the Seventh Year of Richard I to the End of the Reign of Richard III ed. W. Rye (Cambridge Antiquarian Society, octavo ser. xxvi, 1891).

Pipe Rolls

    The Pipe Roll of 31 Henry I ed. J. Hunter (Record Commission, 1833; reprinted 1929 from 1833 edn).

    The Pipe Rolls of 2–3–4 Henry II ed. J. Hunter (Record Commission, 1844; reprinted 1930 from 1844 edn).

    The Great Roll of the Pipe, 5 Henry II– (Pipe Roll Society, 1884–).

Placita de Quo Warranto Temporibus Edw. I, II & III in Curia Receptæ Scaccarii Westm. Asservata (Record Commission, 1818).

Records of the Templars in England in the Twelfth Century ed. B. A. Lees (British Academy, 1935).

Regesta Regum Anglo-Normannorum 1066–1154 ii *Regesta Henrici Primi 1100–1135* eds C. Johnson and H. A. Cronne (Oxford, 1956).

Registrum Radulphi Baldock, Gilberti Segrave, Ricardi Newport et Stephani Gravesend, Episcoporum Londoniensium 1304–1338 ed. R. C. Fowler (Canterbury and York Society vii, 1911).

Registrum Roberti Winchelsey Cantuariensis Archiepiscopi 1294–1313 ed. R. Graham, 2 vols (Canterbury and York Society li–lii, 1952, 1956).

Rotuli Curiae Regis. Rolls and Records of the Court Held Before the King's Justiciars or Justices ed. F. Palgrave, 2 vols (Record Commission, 1835).

Rotuli Hundredorum Temp. Hen. III et Edw. I in Turr' Lond' et in Curia Receptae Scaccarii West. Asservati eds W. Illingworth and J. Caley, 2 vols (Record Commission, 1812–18).

Rotuli Litterarum Patentium in Turri Londinensi Asservati 1201–1216 ed. T. D. Hardy, i, part i (Record Commission, 1835).

Rotuli Parliamentorum; ut et Petitiones, et Placita in Parliamento 6 vols (Record Commission [1783]).

The Rule of St Benedict ed. D. O. H. Blair, 2nd edn (Fort-Augustus, 1906).

Ö. Södergård ed. *La Vie Seinte Audrée, Poème Anglo-Normand du XIIIe Siècle* (Uppsala, 1955).

Taxatio Ecclesiastica Angliae et Walliae Auctoritate Nicholai IV circa A.D. 1291 [ed. T. Astle et al.] (Record Commission, 1802).

Valor Ecclesiasticus Temp. Henr. VIII Auctoritate Regia Institutus ed. J. Caley, 6 vols (Record Commission, 1810–34).

Visitations of Religious Houses in the Diocese of Lincoln ed. A. H. Thompson, 3 vols (Canterbury and York Society xvii, xxiv, xxxiii; 1915, 1919, 1927).

SECONDARY WORKS

The Agrarian History of England and Wales iii *1348–1500* ed. E. Miller (Cambridge, 1991).

M. Bailey 'The Prior and Convent of Ely and their Management of the Manor of Lakenheath in the Fourteenth Century' in *Medieval Ecclesiastical Studies in Honour of Dorothy M. Owen* eds M. J. Franklin and C. Harper-Bill (Woodbridge, 1995) pp. 1–19.

British Heraldry, from its Origins to c. 1800 comp. and ed. R. Marks and A. Payne (London, 1978).

C. N. L. Brooke *A History of Gonville and Caius College* (Woodbridge, 1985).

C. Brown and R. H. Robbins *The Index of Middle English Verse* (New York, 1943).

J. Burton *Monastic and Religious Orders in Britain 1000–1300* (Cambridge, 1994).

— *The Yorkshire Nunneries in the Twelfth and Thirteenth Centuries* (Borthwick Paper no. 56; York, 1979).

W. Camden *Britannia* 2nd edn, 4 vols (London, 1806).

C. T. Clay 'Notes on the Early Archdeacons in the Church of York' *Yorkshire Archaeological Journal* xxxvi (1947) parts 143–4, pp. 269–87, 409–34.

— 'The Seals of the Religious Houses of Yorkshire' *Archaeologia* lxxviii (1928) pp. 1–36.

D. K. Coldicott *Hampshire Nunneries* (Chichester, 1989).

K. Cooke 'Donors and Daughters: Shaftesbury Abbey's Benefactors, Endowments and Nuns *c.* 1086–1130' in *Anglo-Norman Studies* xii *Proceedings of the Battle Conference 1989* (Woodbridge, 1990) pp. 29–45.

— 'The English Nuns and the Dissolution' in *The Cloister and the World: Essays in Medieval History in Honour of Barbara Harvey* eds J. Blair and B. Golding (Oxford, 1996) pp. 287–301.

C. Cross 'The Religious Life of Women in Sixteenth-century Yorkshire' in *Women in the Church* eds W. J. Sheils and D. Wood (Studies in Church History xxvii; Oxford, 1990) pp. 307–24.

H. C. Darby *The Changing Fenland* (Cambridge, 1983).

— *The Medieval Fenland* (Cambridge, 1940).

G. R. C. Davis *Medieval Cartularies of Great Britain. A Short Catalogue* (London, 1958).

P. G. M. Dickinson *A Little History of the Abbey of St Mary and the Parish Church of S. Peter and S. Paul, Chatteris, Cambridgeshire* (Chatteris, 1954).

R. B. Dobson and S. Donaghey *The History of Clementhorpe Nunnery* (The Archaeology of York ii, fasc. i, 1984).

S. B. Edgington *The Life and Miracles of St Ivo* (St Ives, Cambs., 1985).

S. K. Elkins 'The Emergence of a Gilbertine Identity' in *Distant Echoes. Medieval Religious Women* i, eds J. A. Nichols and L. T. Shank (Kalamazoo, Michigan, 1984) pp. 131–50.

— *Holy Women of Twelfth-Century England* (Chapel Hill, North Carolina, 1988).

R. H. Ellis *Catalogue of Seals in the Public Record Office. Monastic Seals* i (London, 1986).

A. B. Emden *A Biographical Register of the University of Cambridge to 1500* (Cambridge, 1963).

W. Farrer *Feudal Cambridgeshire* (Cambridge, 1920).

— *Honors and Knights' Fees* 3 vols (London, 1923–5).

T. Foulds 'Medieval Cartularies' *Archives* xviii, no. 77 (1987) pp. 3–35.

J.-P. Genet 'Cartulaires, Registres et Histoire: l'Exemple Anglais' in *Le Métier d'Histoire au Moyen Age* ed. B. Guenée (Publications de la Sorbonne, série 'Études' xiii, 1977) pp. 95–142.

A. Gibbons *Ely Episcopal Records. A Calendar and Concise View of the Episcopal Records Preserved in the Muniment Room of the Palace at Ely* (Lincoln, 1891).

J. S. W. Gibson *Wills and Where to Find Them* (Chichester, 1974).

R. Gilchrist 'The Archaeology of Medieval Nunneries: a Research Design' in *The Archaeology of Rural Monasteries in England and Wales* eds R. Gilchrist and H. Mytum (BAR British series 203; Oxford, 1989) pp. 251–260.

— *Gender and Material Culture: the Archaeology of Religious Women* (London, 1994).

R. Gilchrist and M. Oliva *Religious Women in Medieval East Anglia: History and Archaeology c. 1100–1540* (Studies in East Anglian History i; Norwich, 1993).

B. Golding *Gilbert of Sempringham and the Gilbertine Order c. 1130–c. 1300* (Oxford, 1995).

M. Goodrich 'The White Ladies of Worcester: their Place in Contemporary Medieval Life' *Transactions of the Worcestershire Archaeological Society* 3rd ser. xiv (1994) pp. 129–47.

C. V. Graves 'Stixwould in the Market-Place' in *Distant Echoes. Medieval Religious Women* i, eds J. A. Nichols and L. T. Shank (Kalamazoo, Michigan, 1984) pp. 213–35.

A. Gray *The Priory of St Radegund* (Cambridge Antiquarian Society, octavo ser. xxxi, 1898).

D. Haigh *The Religious Houses of Cambridgeshire* (Cambridge, 1988).

Handbook of British Chronology eds E. B. Fryde, D. E. Greenway, S. Porter and I. Roy, 3rd edn (London, 1986).

C. Hart 'Eadnoth, First Abbot of Ramsey, and the Foundation of Chatteris and St Ives' *Proceedings of the Cambridge Antiquarian Society* lvi–lvii (1964) pp. 61–7.

B. Harvey *Westminster Abbey and its Estates in the Middle Ages* (Oxford, 1977).

T. A. Heslop 'Seals' in *English Romanesque Art 1066–1200* eds G. Zarnecki, J. Holt and T. Holland (London, 1984) pp. 298–319.

R. F. Hunnisett *Editing Records for Publication* (British Records Association, Archives and the User series, iv; London, 1977).

Kelly's Directory of Cambridgeshire 1937 (London, 1937).

E. W. Kemp 'The Archbishop in Convocation' in *Medieval Records of the Archbishops of Canterbury* [usually catalogued under I. J. Churchill, author of the first lecture] (London, 1962).

D. Knowles *The Monastic Order in England. A History of its Development from the Times of St Dunstan to the Fourth Lateran Council 940–1216* 2nd edn (Cambridge, 1963).

— *The Religious Orders in England* 3 vols (Cambridge, 1948–59).

D. Knowles, C. N. L. Brooke and V. C. M. London eds *The Heads of Religious Houses England and Wales 940–1216* (Cambridge, 1972).

D. Knowles and R. N. Hadcock *Medieval Religious Houses: England and Wales* 2nd edn (London, 1971).

D. Knowles and J. K. S. St Joseph *Monastic Sites from the Air* (Cambridge, 1952).

L. Landon *The Itinerary of King Richard I* (Pipe Roll Society, new ser. xiii, 1935).

M. D. Legge *Anglo-Norman Literature and its Background* (Oxford, 1963).

J. H. Lynch *Simoniacal Entry into Religious Life from 1000–1260: a Social, Economic and Legal Study* (Columbus, Ohio, 1976).

F. Martin 'Origin of the Tressure of Scotland' *Archaeologia* xxiii (1831) pp. 387–92.

M. A. Meyer 'Patronage of the West Saxon Royal Nunneries in Late Anglo-Saxon England' *Revue Bénédictine* xci (1981) pp. 332–58.

E. Miller *The Abbey and Bishopric of Ely: The Social History of an Ecclesiastical Estate from the Tenth Century to the Early Fourteenth Century* (Cambridge, 1951).

E. Miller and J. Hatcher *Medieval England – Rural Society and Economic Change 1086–1348* (London, 1978).

J. Mountain 'Nunnery Finances in the Early Fifteenth Century' in *Monastic Studies* ii *The Continuity of Tradition* ed. J. Loades (Bangor, 1991) pp. 263–72.

J. le Neve *Fasti Ecclesiae Anglicanae 1066–1300* i *St Paul's, London* comp. D. E. Greenway (London, 1968).

— *Fasti Ecclesiae Anglicanae 1066–1300* ii *Monastic Cathedrals* (Northern and Southern Provinces) comp. D. E. Greenway (London, 1971).

— *Fasti Ecclesiae Anglicanae 1066–1300* iii *Lincoln* comp. D. E. Greenway (London, 1977).

— *Fasti Ecclesiae Anglicanae 1300–1541* iv *Monastic Cathedrals* (Southern Province) comp. B. Jones (London, 1963).

— *Fasti Ecclesiae Anglicanae 1300–1541* v *St Paul's, London* comp. J. M. Horn (London, 1963).

J. A. Nichols 'Medieval Cistercian Nunneries and English Bishops' in *Distant Echoes. Medieval Religious Women* i, eds J. A. Nichols and L. T. Shank (Kalamazoo, Michigan, 1984) pp. 237–49.

— 'The Internal Organization of English Cistercian Nunneries' *Citeaux* xxx (1979) pp. 23–40.

M. Oliva 'Aristocracy or Meritocracy? Office-holding Patterns in Late Medieval English Nunneries' in *Women in the Church* eds W. J. Sheils and D. Wood (Studies in Church History xxvii; Oxford, 1990) pp. 197–208.

— *The Convent and the Community in Late Medieval England: Female Monasteries in the Diocese of Norwich, 1350–1540* (Woodbridge, 1998).

— 'Counting Nuns: a Prosopography of Late Medieval English Nuns in the Diocese of Norwich' *Medieval Prosopography* xvi, no. 1 (1995) pp. 27–55.

D. M. Owen *A Catalogue of the Records of the Bishop and Archdeacon of Ely* (Cambridge, 1971).

— ed. *The Making of King's Lynn. A Documentary Survey* (London, 1981).

W. M. Palmer *John Layer (1586–1640) of Shepreth, Cambridgeshire. A Seventeenth-century Local Historian* (Cambridge Antiquarian Society, octavo ser. liii, 1935).

E. Power *Medieval English Nunneries c. 1275–1535* (Cambridge, 1922).

S. Raban 'The Church in the 1279 Hundred Rolls' in *Medieval Ecclesiastical Studies in Honour of Dorothy M. Owen* eds M. J. Franklin and C. Harper-Bill (Woodbridge, 1995) pp. 185–200.

— 'The Land Market and the Aristocracy in the Thirteenth Century' in *Tradition and Change. Essays in Honour of Marjorie Chibnall Presented by her Friends on the Occasion of her Seventieth Birthday* eds D. E. Greenway, C. Holdsworth and J. Sayers (Cambridge, 1985) pp. 239–61.

— *Mortmain Legislation and the English Church 1279–1500* (Cambridge, 1982).

R. H. Robbins and J. L. Cutler *Supplement to the Index of Middle English Verse* (Lexington, 1965).

J. H. Round *Studies in Peerage and Family History* (Westminster, 1901).

M. Rubin *Charity and Community in Medieval Cambridge* (Cambridge, 1987).

I. J. Sanders *English Baronies. A Study of their Origin and Descent* (Oxford, 1960).

T. Tanner *Notitia Monastica* (London, 1744).

S. Thompson 'Why English Nunneries Had No History: a Study of the Problems of the English Nunneries Founded After the Conquest' in *Distant Echoes. Medieval Religious Women* i, eds J. A. Nichols and L. T. Shank (Kalamazoo, Michigan, 1984) pp. 131–50.

— *Women Religious: the Founding of English Nunneries after the Norman Conquest* (Oxford, 1991).

J. H. Tillotson *Marrick Priory: a Nunnery in Late Medieval Yorkshire* (Borthwick Paper no. 75; York, 1989).

— 'Visitation and Reform of the Yorkshire Nunneries in the Fourteenth Century' *Northern History* xxx (1994) pp. 1–21.

E. Van Houts 'Nuns and Goldsmiths: the Foundation and Early Benefactors of St Radegund's Priory at Cambridge' in *Church and City 1000–1500: Essays in Honour of Christopher Brooke* eds D. Abulafia, M. Franklin and M. Rubin (Cambridge, 1992) pp. 59–79.

N. Vickers 'The Social Class of Yorkshire Medieval Nuns' *Yorkshire Archaeological Journal* lxvii (1995) pp. 127–32.

The Victoria History of the Counties of England. Cambridge and the Isle of Ely 9 vols, ii ed. L. F. Saltzman, iv ed. R. B. Pugh, v ed. C. R. Elrington, viii ed. A. P. M. Wright, ix eds A. P. M. Wright and C. P. Lewis (London, 1948–89).

The Victoria History of the Counties of England. Hertfordshire 4 vols, iii–iv ed. W. Page (London, 1912–14).

The Victoria History of the Counties of England. Huntingdonshire 3 vols, ii eds W. Page, G. Proby and S. I. Ladds (London, 1932).

The Victoria History of the Counties of England. Shropshire 11 vols, i ed. W. Page, ii ed. A. T. Gaydon (London, 1908, 1973).

The Victoria History of the Counties of England. Wiltshire 15 vols, iii eds R. B. Pugh and E. Crittall (London, 1956).

J. Wake and W. A. Pantin 'Delapré Abbey, its History and Architecture' *Northamptonshire Past and Present* ii (1958) pp. 225–41.

D. Walker 'The Organization of Material in Medieval Cartularies' in *The Study of Medieval Records: Essays in Honour of Kathleen Major* eds D. A. Bullough and R. L. Storey (Oxford, 1971) pp. 132–50.

J. Wogan-Browne '"Clerc u Lai, Muïne u Dame": Women and Anglo-Norman Hagiography in the Twelfth and Thirteenth Centuries' in *Women and Literature in Britain, 1150–1500* ed. C. M. Meale (Cambridge, 1993) pp. 61–85.

S. Wood *English Monasteries and their Patrons in the Thirteenth Century* (Oxford, 1955).

A. B. and A. Wyon *The Great Seals of England from the Earliest Period to the Present Time* (London, 1887).

B. Yorke '"Sisters Under the Skin?" Anglo-Saxon Nuns and Nunneries in Southern England' in *Medieval Women in Southern England* (Reading Medieval Studies xv, 1989) pp. 95–117.

THESES

B. Golding 'The Gilbertine Priories of Alvingham and Bullington: their Endowments and Benefactors', D.Phil. thesis (University of Oxford, 1979).

J. A. Nichols 'The History and Cartulary of the Cistercian Nuns of Marham Abbey, 1249–1536', Ph.D. thesis (Kent State University, 1974).

M. Oliva 'The Convent and the Community in the Diocese of Norwich from 1350 to 1540', Ph.D. thesis (Fordham University, 1991).

C. Paxton 'The Nunneries of London and its Environs in the Later Middle Ages', D.Phil. thesis (University of Oxford, 1992).

A. Rumble 'The Structure and Reliability of the Codex Wintoniensis (B.M. Add. MS 15350; the Cartulary of Winchester Cathedral Priory)', Ph.D. thesis, 2 vols (University of London, 1979).

W. M. Sturman 'Barking Abbey. A Study in its Internal and External Administration from the Conquest to the Dissolution', Ph.D. thesis (University of London, 1961).

— 'The History of the Nunnery of St Mary and St Michael Outside Stamford', M.A. thesis (University of London, 1946).

Index

References in roman type are to page numbers in the introduction and appendices; references in bold type are to entry numbers in the edition of the cartulary. References to items occurring in long entries in the cartulary are followed by the relevant folio number.

Personal and place-names are given in their modern form, where possible. Patronymics and matronymics are indexed under the name of the parent. Peers are indexed under their surname or – as in the case of John, duke of Bedford, and some countesses – under their forename, where no surname is evident. For the sake of consistency, and because it is impossible to date many documents precisely, occupations are not treated as surnames. An exception has been made in the case of fifteenth-century documents where it seems clear that the occupations given are true surnames. Place-names have been standardized, where possible, and indexed by parish-unit. All places are in Cambridgeshire, unless otherwise stated; pre-1974 counties are given for places not in Cambridgeshire.

The following abbreviations are used in the index:

adcn	archdeacon	n	note
abp	archbishop	par.	parish
bp	bishop	rel.	relating
dau.	daughter	W	witness to a charter
M	*magister*		

A., abbess of Chatteris, 391; **186**

Absolon, John son of, *see* Cambridge, John son of Absolon de

account (*compotus*) of escheator of Suff., 212

Ace, Philip son of William, of Doddington, **248–52**

acknowledgement (*recognitio*), **230**

Acle, John de, of Barley, Herts., **176**

Aconbury priory, Herefords., 95

acquittance, of payment for procuration, **263**

— of payment for release of claim in advowson, **179**

— of rent, **7, 192, 194, 197–9, 202–3, 205, 219–20, 225**

— of subsidy of ninth, **260** (fo. 177v), **261** (fo. 178v)

action (*actio, assisa*), 80, **171–2, 189, 256** (fo. 173r), **257** (fo. 174r), **259** (fo. 176r), **274**

Adam, land of [in Shepreth], **149** (fo. 129r)

— reap-reeve (*messor*), **177**

admission to benefice, **266–7**

Ado (*Adon'*), Philip son of, W **243**

advowson, of Barley, Herts., 33, 36, 76; **177–9, 242, 277**

— of Chatteris, 14, 34; **10, 76**

— of Foxton, 34

— of Shepreth, 32, 35; **160**n

Ælfegus, see Ælfheah

Ælfgar (*Alfgarus*), bp of Elmham, 2

Ælfheah (*Ælfegus, Alphegus*), St, martyr and abp of Canterbury, 2

Ælfwaru, dau. of Æthelstan Mannessune, **25–7**

Ælfwen (*Alfwenna*), abbess of Chatteris,
  8–9, 26, 96, 100, 391; **2**
Æthelwine (*Egelwinus*), ealdorman of
  East Anglia, **2**
affidation *see* oath, swearing of; pledge
Agnes, abbess of Chatteris, 50, 93, 392;
  80, 146, 151, 162, 168, 232, 281; *see
  also* Ashfield, Agnes; Ely, Agnes de
— nun of Chatteris, 403
— William son of, cook (*cocus*), **55**
agreement, rel. to land in Foxton, 130–1,
  136
— rel. to pasturing cattle in Foxton, **147**
— rel. to rent in Bircham, Norf., **225**
— rel. to rent in Lynn, Norf., **219**
— rel. to suit of court in Foxton, **124**
— rel. to tofts in Huntingdon, **230**
— to lease, **51, 60, 75, 118, 132, 137–9,
  144, 163**
aid (*auxilium*), 4, 91, 109, 148, 221, 223,
  231, **256** (fo. 173r), **257** (fo. 174r)
Alan [of Shepreth], **150, 156**
— chaplain, 105; W **110**
— clerk, vicar of Chatteris, 34; **79**
— Margery formerly wife of Andrew son
  of, **132**
— Norman son of, **121**
— Robert brother of, *see* Folcold, Robert
  son of
— Robert son (*recte* brother) of, *see*
  Folcold, Robert son of
Alb[*eneio*], William de, *see* Aubigny,
  William d'
Alberd', Stephen, **74**
— Thomas, of Chatteris, 44, 77; **81**
Albreda, abbess of Chatteris, 391; **169**
Alcock, John, bp of Ely, 20
Alexander III, pope, 29–30; **3** (fo. 73v)
— butler (le boteler'), **245, 248, 251**
— butcher (*carnifex*) of Lynn, Norf., **219**
— chaplain of adcn of Norwich, W **204**
— 'esturesman', *see* Ingelram, Alexander
  son of
— Pain son of, clerk, of Ely, *alias*
  Muschet, Pain uncle of Richard, 92,
  93, 99
Aleyn, John, **210**
Alfgarus, see Ælfgar

Alfwenna, see Ælfwen
Alice (*Aelicia*), *amica* of William of Ely,
  alias Edelyna, *see* Ely, Ralph of
— nun of Chatteris, 404
— wife of Hingenolf, *see* Hingenolf
— wife of Humphrey, **116, 122**
— formerly wife of William, carpenter,
  of Fowlmere, *see* Fowlmere, William
  de
allowance in accounts, 7, **202**
Alphegus, see Ælfheah
altar-dues, 34–5; **11–12, 78**
altilia, see hens
Alveyne (Halwyne), William, **113**
Alvingham priory, Lincs., 46
Alwin, cordwainer, *see* Elwin,
  cordwainer
Ambrose, Richard, W **210**
amercement, 189, **256** (fo. 173r), **257** (fo.
  174r), **259** (fo. 176r)
Amesbury priory, Wilts., 3, 37
Amianus, clerk, W **204**
Amicia, abbess of Chatteris, 395–6; **101–
  3, 119, 124**; *see also* Cambridge,
  Amicia de
Amphelisa [of Shepreth], **149** (fo. 128v)
Andrew, Alan son of, widow of, **135**
Anglesey (Angleseye) priory, **261** (fo.
  178v)
— prior of, 23; **260–1**
— — attorney of, **260** (fo. 176v), **261** (fo.
  178r); *see also* Bernard', Gilbert de;
  Charwelton, Simon de
animals (*bestie*), 417; **279**; *see also* cattle;
  sheep
Ankerwyke priory, Bucks., 18–19, 85
Anne, countess of Huntingdon, formerly
  countess of March, 199, **202**
annuity, grant of, **72**; *see also* prebend;
  rent
Ansty, John, senior, **210**
appropriation *see* churches
arable (*terra arabilis, frugifera, lucrabilis*),
  34–6, 39, 43, 47, 62–3, 121, 128, 139,
  161, 163, 168, 177, **181** (fo. 143r),
  191, 248, 272
Arches, William de, **15**

Arenis, Henry de, knight templar, W 227

Arnald, Simon son of, 213–15, 217

Arnold, miller (*molendini*), 155

Arques, Emma dau. of William de, 12

arrears *see* rent

Aryng', Margery, 230

Ashfield (Aschefeld', Aschfeld', Ashfeld'), Agnes, abbess of Chatteris, 56, 98, 108, 110, 120, 399–400; 1, 197–9, 203, 220, 259 (fo. 175r), 271, 274, 276

Asplond (Aspelond, Haspeland, Haspelond), Elizabeth, nun of Chatteris, 98, 101, 103, 404, 418, 420

— John, 101

Assandun, Essex, battle of, 8, 25; 2

assarts, 180

assent, of heir, 49; 25, 27, 40–1, 90, 170

— of lord, 19, 23

— of wife, 49; 25, 41, 92

assessors and vendors of the ninth, 260n

assize of bread and ale, 16

— of mort d'ancestor, 142

Astyn, Thomas, 219

Atteaplue, Thomas son of Alexander, of Barrington, 119

attorney (*attornatus*), power of, 228

— of Chatteris abbey, *see* Chatteris abbey

— of prior of Anglesey and abbess of Chatteris, *see* Bernard', Gilbert de; Charwelton, Simon de

Aubigny (*Alb[eneio]*), Nigel d', 14

— William d', butler (*pincerna*), W 5, 6n

Aubyn, Cecilia, nun of Chatteris, 18, 404

Auger, Robert son of, 185

— Robert son of Bartholomew son of, 153

— — William son of (?*alias* Shepreth, William son of Robert de), 153

augmentation of vicarage, 161

Augustine, St, bp of Hippo, 99; 206n

— Baldwin, priest of Scopwick (Scapewic), Lincs., W 227

— Baldwin son of, 87

— Henry son of, 243

aureus, *see* gold coin

Austyn, Adam, 245

Aveline, Henry son of, 53; 114–15

averia, *see* cattle

Aylmer, William son of, 111

Azo *see* Noreis, Azo le

— Emma dau. of, *see* Noreis, Emma

Babbe, Guy, 133, 139

— — Edith wife of, 139

Babenton' *see* Barrington

bachelor of canon law *see* Buckworth, Henry

bag for accounts, 212

Bagnaria, Manuel (Gamyelis) de, rector of Foxton, 34; 147

bailiffs, accounts of, 202

— of bishop of Ely, 94–7

— of Chatteris abbey, 76–7; 51, 124, 161, 231

— royal, 258 (fo. 175r)

— *see also* Kersey; Skeet, John; Sugge, William

Baldewyn *see* Baldwelle

Baldock (Baldok, Baldolk), Ralph, bp of London, 23, 71, 92

— Robert, of Chatteris, 234

— — Alicia wife of, 234

Baldwelle (Baldewyn'), William, of Swaffham, 43

Baldwin, reeve, 244

Balsham (Balesham), document dated at, 112

— Hugh de, bp of Ely, 34–5, 72; 16, 77, 95–7, 103, 161

— Humfrey de, 246

— John, of Wimblington, 245

— *see also* More, Thomas, of

Baltewene, John, junior, 245

Bancis (Banns, Bannz), Eustace de, W 240

— — (*another*), 48

— G. de, 139

— Mabel de, abbess of Chatteris, 48, 53, 69, 77–8, 101–2, 393; 74, 132, 139, 144, 226

— Roger de, 48

— Thomas de, of Foxton, serjeant (*serviens*) of Chatteris abbey, 45, 48, 53, 69, 78, 102, 104; 114–15, 117, 125–6, 132–134, 139, 142, 148, W 240
— — Juliana wife of, 114–15
— William de, 111
— — (?*same*), 146
— — (?*same*), 48
— — (?*another*), 129
— — Beatrice sister of, 111
bank (*ripa*), 243, 269 (fo. 181r), 279
Barantun' *see* Barrington
Bardolf, Hugh, W 9
Barengton', Barenton', *see* Barrington
Barham (Beorcham, Bercham, Berham), Suff., 269 (fo. 181v)
Barington *see* Barrington
Barking abbey, Essex, 3–4, 20, 22, 37, 89, 95, 100, 102
Barkway (Berkwey, Berqweweye), Herts., inquisition held at, 260 (fo. 177v)
Barley (Berele, Berle, Berlee, *Berleia*, Berley, *Berleya*, Berleye), Herts., 278
— church, 38; 180–2
— — advowson of, 33, 36, 76; 177–9, 242, 277
— — patrons of, 277
— — rector of, *see* Cardington, Ralph; Herbert; Osbert; Passelewe, Robert; Richard
— — — presentation of, 266, 277
— court of Chatteris abbey at, 16, 74–5
— demesne of Chatteris abbey in, 180, 182
— document dated at, 171
— land in, 12–69 *passim*; 3 (fo. 74r), 171–8, 180–2, 242
— ninth in, 260, 262
— spiritualities and temporalities in, 260
— tithes in, 33, 36, 64, 76; 180–2, 277
— villein of, *see* Hulot, John
— 'Blerestrate', 177
— 'Bradehepedelle', 177
— 'Chalkyhil', 176
— 'le Eldebery', 176
— 'Holecroft', 175
— 'Wycheney', 175
— 'Wydiheya', 180
— Alexander de, 233
— — Hamo brother of, 233
— Castayna de, 177
— Ebrard de, 129
— John, junior, 280
— John, senior, 280
— Jordan de, W 281
— Matilda de, 35; 11–12, 78
— Ralph de, 17, 59
— — (?*same*), 18
— — (?*same*), 21, 70
— — (?*same*), 61; 30
— — (?*same*), 74
— — (?*same*), 174
— — (?*same*), 175
— — (?*same*), 51; 232
— — (?*same*), 233
— — (?*same*), W 240
— — Adelicia wife of, 21, 70
— — Cistillia wife of, 233
— — Godfrey uncle of, 174
— — Ralph son of, W 240
— Richard de, W 110
— — father of Ralph (?*same*), 174
— *see also* Acle, John de, of; Myldebourn', Richard de, of; Pompun, John, of
Barnard', William, W 110
Barnwell (Bernewelle) priory, prior of, 23; *see also* Domesman, Hugh
— — land of, 238–9
— Geoffrey de, cook, 50; 35, 56, 62
barons of exchequer, 7, 260 (fo. 176v), 261 (fo. 178r), 262
Barrett, Thomas, bp of Killala (*Aladensis*), 17
Barrington (Babenton', Barantun', Barengton', Barenton', Barington, Baryngton', Barynton'), 278
— church, 112
— — rector of, *stodum* of, 113
— homage and rent for tenements in, 114
— homage and service for land in, 115
— manorial court for, 16, 33, 67, 73–5
— mill in, 27, 37, 59, 71–3; 3 (fo. 74r), 112, 118–19

— ninth in, **261-2**
— property in, 12-73 *passim*, **131**; 3 (fo. 74r), **100**, **113**, **116-18**, **120-4**, **185**, **232**, **237**, **261** (fo. 178v)
— revenue from temporalities in, **264**
— road to Foxton, **119**, **135**, **146**
— tithes in, 33, 36-7, 64, 71; **112**
— villein of, *see* Broun, John son of Henry
— 'Blakewelle', well (*fons*) called, **121**
— 'Brondescroft', **120**
— 'le Cumbes', **121**
— east field, **113**, **121**
— 'le Estmelne', **119**
— 'le Fordexis', **113**
— 'le Hakk'', **113**, **121**
— 'le Holm', **124**
— 'Longeweye', **121**
— 'le Madwerescroft', **121**
— 'Mamereswelle, **121**
— 'le Mersh', **121**
— 'le Mylnestede', **121**
— 'le Sik'', **121**
— 'Storkesdene', **113**
— 'Theford', **118**
— 'Voxhelledon'', **121**
— 'Whithakkis', **121**
— 'Wlmaresdong', **121**
— west field, **113**, **121**
— Agnes de, **120**
— Alice dau. of Warin de, **138**
— — William brother of, **138**
— Eustace de, **129**
— — Richard brother of, **129**
— Eustace son of William de, **100**, **123-4**
— Henry son of John de, **117**, **121**
— Henry son of Walter de, **237**
— — Warin brother of, **237**
— John son of Adam de, **116**, **122**
— Nicholas son of Robert de, **149** (fo. 129v)
— Roger son of Osbert de, **129**
— Warin de, W **239**
— — (*another*), 71; **119**, W **162n**
— — miller (?*same*), 71; **118**
— William de, father of Eustace, **124**
— William son of Eustace de (?*same*), **114**, **116-17**, **121-2**

— — Agatha wife of, **116**, **122**
— *see also* Atteaplue, Thomas, of; Waryn, John, of
Bartholomew, clerk, *see* Shepreth, Bartholomew father of Basilia
Barton *see* Ely
Barway (Bereweye, Berquee), Margaret dau. of Walter de, **90** (fo. 101v), **91** (fo. 102v)
Baryngton', Barynton', *see* Barrington
Basilia, widow, **111**
Basset (Bassett), Anne, abbess of Chatteris, 20-1, 23, 85, 98, 401
— Michael, of Impington, W **231**
— Philip, **187**, **189**
— Ralph, W 6n
— Robert, **260** (fo. 177v)
Bassingbourn (Bassingbourne), Alan de, **51**
Bate (Bayte), Joan, nun of Chatteris, 98, 101, 103, 404, 418, 420
Batesford' *see* Battisford
Bath (*Bathon'*), Henry de, justice in eyre, 142
Battisford (Batesford', Batysford'), H. de, 189
— John, **210**
battle of *Assandun*, Essex, 2
baxter (baxstere), *see* Dreng, John
Baysdale priory, Yorks. N., 93
Bayte *see* Bate
Beatrice, William son of, 75, 137
Beauchaump (Beauchaunp'), John de, 58; 171-3
— — Eldreda dau. of, 173
Beche, John, **280**
Bedford (Bedeford'), county of, *see* Cranfield; Dunstable
— duke of, *see* John
— *see also* Hugh, clerk, of
beggars, feeding of, 53, 67
Beigate *see* Reigate
Bek, William de, 73; **82**
'Belam' (*unidentified*), **269** (fo. 181r)
Belsynges, Bilsingges, Bilsynges, *see* Doddington, Beezling fen
Bene, Hugh, 56

Benedict, St, rule of, 51, 85; **3, 269** (fo. 180v)

Benwick, fishery in, 31

— property in, 39

Beorcham *see* Barham

Beortuna, see Ely, Barton

Bercham *see* Barham

Bercok (Berkoke), Walter, 36, 76; **277**

Berele *see* Barley

Bereweye *see* Barway

Bergham, Roger de, prior of Ely, **12, 78**

Berham *see* Barham

Berkhamsted (Berkehamsted'), Herts., document dated at, **193**

Berkoke *see* Bercok

Berkwey *see* Barkway

Berlay, Berle, Berlee, *Berleia,* Berley, *Berleya,* Berleye, *see* Barley

Bernard', Gilbert, **241**

— — attorney of the prior of Anglesey and the abbess of Chatteris (*?same*), 260n

— Matilda, abbess of Chatteris, 20-1, 23, 96, 98, **399**

Bernewelle *see* Barnwell

Berquee *see* Barway

Berqweweye *see* Barkway

Bertona, Bertuna, see Ely, Barton

bestie, see animals

Betekesham *see* Bottisham

Bettys, William, 32

Beyvin, Osbert, **118**

Bilney (Bylneye), Norf., **278**

— part of mill in, 30, 72-3; **82**

binding sheaves, 144

Binel (Bynel), Reginald, of Shepreth, 62; **132, 145**

Bircham (Brccham, Briccham), Norf., **278**

— land in, 29-30, 39, 129; **91** (fo. 102v), **221-4**

— rent in, 63; **225**

— Nicholas de, **225**

— Ralph de, **222**

— — **224** (*?same*)

— — merchant, son of Agnes (*?another*), **221**

— Richard de, 29, 124, 129; **91, 223**

birds *see* capons, hens

Bishop's Lynn *see* Lynn

Black *see* Niger

Blackborough priory, Norf., 47

Blankpayn (Elankpayn), Henry, **257** (fo. 173r)

Bleysie, Constance, **233**

Blois, Mary of, abbess of Romsey, 100

Blomvyll', John, prior of Little Dunmow (Donemawe), Essex, 260n

Blower, Reginald le, **56**

Bluntisham (Bluntesham), Hunts., **269** (fo. 181r)

Boggari, Walter, **180**

Bokeland, William, of Swaffham Prior, 80

— — Katherine wife of, 80

Bokesham *see* Bottisham

Bollonde, Robert, 50, 55-7

— — Olliff wife of, 55-7, 87

bond to warrant, 171

Bonegent, Adam, 121

Bonem, Peter, of Hemingford, Hunts., villein, 42, 49; **272**

Bonyard (Boneyerd), John, **210**

— Richard, 54-5

book *see* cartulary; *see also* evidence

boon-works, 144; *see also* carrying-service; labour-services; plough-service

Boreston *see* Briston

Borewelle *see* Burwell

Boseby *see* Roseby

boteler' *see* Alexander

Bottisham (Betekesham, Bokesham, Botkysham), Anglesey priory in par. of, **261** (fo. 178v)

— ninth in, **261**

Boughton (Bouton), Matilda de, nun of Chatteris, **405**

Boulogne, fee of, 13

boundaries, **168, 279**

Bouton *see* Boughton

Boydon' (Eoydon'), John, **257** (fo. 173r)

Bradefeld' *see* Broadfield

Bradehous (Bradeho, Bradehowes, Bradehouus), John son of Hugh de, **226**

— John son of Lambert de, **226**

— Jolanus de, **111**

— — Beatrice wife of, 49; **111, 240**

'Bradewere', fishery, *see* Upwell and Outwell

Bradwey, Richard, 54

Braughing (Brakkyng'), deanery of, taxation in, **260** (fo. 177r)

Braxton *see* Briston

Bray, Margaret wife of Stephen le, 48

— William, vicar of Chatteris, 54, 56, 93, 101

Brecham *see* Bircham

Breng', Brenge, *see* Dreng

Brewood Black Ladies priory, Staffs., 6, 12n

Briccham *see* Bircham

Brickeston', Bricston', *see* Briston

Bricstan, 47

Bridge (*ad Pontem*), Walter, **149** (fo. 129r)

bridges, **119, 149** (fo. 128v), **209–10, 230**

Brigham, Eve, nun of Chatteris, 405

Brigston' *see* Briston

Brine, Robert, **129**

Briston (Boreston, Braxton, Brickeston', Bricston', Brigston', Brixston', Brixton', Brustin, Bruston, Bryghston', Brygston', Bryston'), land of, **35, 62**

— Alexander, **58**

— Alexander son of Ralph (?*another*), **85**

— Alice, of Chatteris, 46

— — (*Elicia*), (?*another*), **65**

— — dau. of Ralph, *see* Henry, priest

— Aveline, formerly wife of Henry, of Chatteris, 44; **44**

— Ebrard, son of Robert, chaplain of Chatteris, *see* Ebrard, chaplain of Chatteris

— Henry, **32, 37, 53**

— Ismaena dau. of Ralph, *alias* Merchyt, Ismaena wife of Henry de, 47–9; **20–2, 24, 45, 64, 70, 84**

— Ralph, **19, 23**

— — (?*same*), *see* Henry, priest

— — (*another*), **211**

Britanny, fee of [duke of], **145**

Brixston', Brixton', *see* Briston

Broadfield (Bradefeld'), Ralph son of Fulk de, knight, *alias* Fulk, Ralph son of, **155, 177**

— — Ralph son of, knight, *alias* Fulk, Ralph son of Ralph son of, *alias* Shepreth, Ralph son of Ralph son of Fulk de, 36, 45; **153, 159**, W 162n, **177–9**

— — — Petronella mother of, 177

Broel, Theobald de, 177

Broun, John, W 233

— — (?*another*), **252**

— — son of Henry, villein of Barrington, 100, 123

Bruisyard abbey, Suff., 102

Brustin, Bruston, Bryghston', Brygston', Bryston', *see* Briston

Brye, Margaret, 55

— Thomas, 55

Buckworth (Bucworth, Bukworth), Henry, bachelor of canon law, vicar of Chatteris, 54, 56, 108, 110, 120; 1, 200

building of churches, 2

buildings, in Barrington, 117–18

— in Cambridge, 104–6

— in Chatteris, 51, 69

— in Doddington, 249

— in Foxton, 132, 138

— in Kersey, Suff., 210

— in Lynn, Norf., 216–17, 219

— *see also* house; messuage

bull *see* privilege

Bullingham priory, Lincs., 46

Burdele, William de, W 281

Burel, Reginald, 149

— — (*another*), W 241

Burewelle *see* Burwell

Burgo, Geoffrey de, bp of Ely, 34; 129–30

— Margaret de, nun of Chatteris, 405

— Thomas son of Henry de, 204

burial, of benefactor at Chatteris abbey, 62

— of St Ælfheah and Eadnoth, bishop of Dorchester, 2

Burton [royal scribe], **256n**

Burwell (Borewelle, Burewelle, Burwelle), **278**
— land in, 12, 26–7, 37, 39; 3 (fo. 74r), **236**
— men and rights in, **236**
— parson of, *see* Thomas
— Agnes de, abbess of Chatteris, 100, 396
Bury, Joan de, nun of Chatteris, 405
Bury St Edmunds, chronicle of, 107
But, John, 179
butcher (*carnifex*), *see* Alexander, Peter
butler (le boteler, *pincerna*), *see* Alexander; Aubigny, William de
Bylneye *see* Bilney
Bylsynges *see* Doddington, Beezling fen
Bynel *see* Binel

Cade, Guinora, 32, 37, 53
— John, 20
Calcedonensis, *see* Chalcedon
Caldecote (Calcote, Caldecotte), Agnes, nun of Chatteris, 101, 405
Cambridge (Cambrdge, Cant', Cantabr', Cantabr'g', Cantabrig', Cantabrigg', Cantebr', Cantebrig'), **278**
— county of, escheator in, *see* More, Thomas
— — exannual roll for, **262**
— — exchequer plea rel. to, **261**
— — pipe roll for, **261** (fo. 178r)
— — sheriff of, **261** (fo. 178r)
— custom of, 104, 106
— document dated at, **257** (fo. 174r)
— final concord made at, 133, 142
— grain-store of Chatteris abbey in, 70
— harbour (*portus*) in, 27; 3 (fo. 74r)
— hospital of St John the Evangelist, 58, 60, 70
— inquisition held at, **257** (fo. 173r), **261** (fo. 178v)
— justices at, **148**
— par. of Holy Trinity, 108
— par. of St John Zachary, 49; 105, 107
— property in, 27, 49, 52, 70, 76, 101; 3 (fo. 74r), 105, 107, 152
— rent in, 43, 70; 104, 106, 108

— St Radegund's priory, 23, 40, 47, 89
— university of, Michaelhouse, 32
— — St John's College, 7, 60, 70, 73
— — Trinity College, 32
— 'Heneye', 107
— 'Myllestrete' (Mylnestrete, Mylnestrate), 105, 107
— Amicia de, abbess and sacrist of Chatteris, 44, 100, 103, 396–7; **38, 47, 63, 219**
— John de, 122; **32, 37, 53, 67**
— (*another*), 76; **71**
— (?*same*), 190 (fo. 146r)
— John son of Absolon de, chaplain, *alias* Absolon, John son of, 45; **104–6**
— — Amicia sister of, *alias* Godsho, Amicia sister of Cecilia, 49; **104–6**
— — Cecilia Godsho sister of, 49; **105–6**
— Katherine de, nun of Chatteris, 101, 405
— Nicholas de, 190 (fo. 146r)
— Yvo de, **239**
— *see also* Percy, John
Campsey Ash priory, Suff., 5–6, 104
candle (*cereus*), *see* Chatteris abbey, light
canon law, bachelor of, *see* Buckworth, Henry
Canterbury, Kent, abp of, *see* Ælfheah; Corbeil, William de; Kempe, John; Whittlesey, William; Winchelsey, Robert
— cathedral priory, prior of, **191**
— St Sepulchre priory, 6, 12n, 96
Canute *see* Cnut
Capella, *see* Chapel
capellanus, *see* chaplain
capons, as rent, 124, 128
— — grant of, **99**
cardinal, procuration for, **263**
Cardington (Carleton', Kerdington), Ralph de, rector of Barley, Herts., 45; **241, 252, 254**
carectarius, *see* carter
Carleton' *see* Cardington
carnifex, *see* butcher
carpenter (*carpentarius*), *see* Fowlmere, William de; Gilbert

carrying-service ('petit cariante'), 144, 189; *see also* boon-work; labour-services; plough-service

carter (*carectarius*), *see* John; Vivien, John

cartulary, 1, 183-4; *see also* evidence

— damage to, 3

— production and arrangement of, 107-31

— scribe of, 108-12, 115-17, 120-34, 136

Carwelton' *see* Charwelton

Cassandra [of Shepreth], 149

Cateline, Henry, 149 (fo. 129v)

Cateric, Caterit, Cateriz, Catheriz, *Catricia*, Catriz, *see* Chatteris

Catesby priory, Northants., 62

cattle (*averia*, *boves*), 144, 147, 231, 269 (fo. 181r); *see also* animals

cause, 259 (fo. 176v)

cells, 270 (fo. 183r)

Chalcedon (*Calcedonensis*), council of, 269 (fo. 182r)

chancellor, royal, 259 (fo. 176v); *see also* Longchamp, William; Rufus, Geoffrey

chancery, royal, 7-8, 255, 256 (fo. 173r), 258 (fo. 174v)

— — rolls of, 260n

chantry, 35; 162

Chapel, Aubrey, 148

— — Alice wife of, *alias* Martin, Alice sister of Matilda wife of Hugh son of, 133, 142, 148

chapels *see* Chatteris, Honey Hill; Lindsey, Suff.; Shepreth

chaplain (*capellanus*), 11-12, 78, 266; *see also* Alan; Cambridge, John de; Childerley, Alexander de; Foxton, Roger de; Frauncéys, Roger le; Hoor, Richard; John, Robert; Lansill', Thomas de; Neve, Henry; Nicholas; Percy, John; Simon; Taillour, John

— of adcn of Norwich, *see* Alexander

— of Chatteris, *see* Ebrard, *alias* Briston, Ebrard; Ralph; Roger; Thomas

— of the cross, *see* Nicholas

— of St Mary, *see* Chatteris abbey, chaplain of St Mary; William

— of Shepreth chapel, *see* Shepreth

charge (*oneratio*), of freehold, 259 (fo. 176r)

charter of warranty, plea of, 178

Charwelton (Carwelton', Chirwelton'), Robert de, clerk of exchequer pleas, 260 (fo. 177v), 261 (fo. 178v)

— Simon de, attorney of the prior of Anglesey and the abbess of Chatteris, 260n

chattels, of Chatteris abbey and Anglesey priory, 260 (fo. 177v)

— of felons, 189

— of serfs, 75, 271-2, 274

Chatteris (Cateric, Caterit, Cateriz, Catheriz, *Catricia*, Catriz, Chaterhit, Chateric', Chaterice, Chaterich, Chatericht, Chateriht, Chateris, Chaterise, Chateriz, Chatrich, Chateryz, Chatrix, Chatriz), 278

— abbey, abbess of, *see* A.; Ælfwen; Agnes; Albreda; Amicia; Ashfield, Agnes; Bancis, Mabel de; Basset, Anne; Bernard, Matilda; Burwell, Agnes de; Cambridge, Amicia de; Develyn, Margaret; Ely, Agnes de; Gayton, Anne; Hotot, Margaret; I.; M.; Ramsey, Margery; Rouen, A. de; Sancto Claro, Mary de; Shouldham, Mary de; Shropham, Alice de; Somersham, Emma de; Woveton', Batill' de; *see also* appendix 1

— — — carrying rod in Chatteris, 280

— — — chamber of, 85

— — — debts of, 420

— — — election of, 20-3, 86, 106

— — — income of, *see* Ely; Norwich

— — — land of, in Barley, Herts., 175

— — — — in Barrington, 121

— — — — in Chatteris, 34-6, 49, 62-3

— — — — in Shepreth, 149 (fo. 129r)

— — — land, messuages and rent in Chatteris held of, 257 (fo. 173v)

— — — maid (*ancilla*) of, *see* Elsworth, Matilda de

— — — meadow in Chatteris of, 234

— — — permission (*licencia*) of, 3 (fo. 74v)

— — — vacancies, 21-3

— — — windmill in Chatteris of, 72–3;
  28
— — almonry (*almaneria, domus
  elimosinaria, elemosinaria,
  elimosinaria*) of, 49–50, 103; **21, 49,
  58, 62, 67, 70, 232**
— — alms of, **33, 53**
— — attorney of, **104, 106, 136, 178,
  218–19, 260** (fo. 176v), **261** (fo. 178r);
  see also Bernard', Gilbert de;
  Charwelton, Simon de; Jocelin
— — bailiffs of, 76–7; **51, 124, 161, 231**
— — benefactors of, 45–57
— — bequests to, 54–7, 87
— — boarders at, 84
— — boat of, 70, 73
— — books and evidence of, 99, 130–1,
  417; **279**
— — buildings of, 69, 71, 80, 82, 84–93,
  103, 415–18, 421
— — burials at, 50, 55, 86, 417
— — cartulary of, *see* cartulary
— — cattle in Foxton of, **147**
— — chaplains of, 17, 104–5
— — chaplain of St Mary at, 50, 102, 105;
  115; *see also* William, chaplain of St
  Mary
— — chapter-house of, 86
— — — documents dated at, **266, 271,
  274, 276**
— — churchyard of, 56
— — clock of, 55, 417
— — cloister of, 88–91
— — confessors at, 17
— — conventual church of, 49, 55–6, 71,
  86–93, 417–18, 421
— — — chapel of St Mary, 54, 93
— — court of, **75, 137**
— — — in Foxton, **124, 143, 163**
— — — demesne of, 62–71, 73
— — — in Barley, Herts., **180, 181** (fo.
  142v), **182**
— — — in Barrington, **100, 123**
— — — in Foxton, **129–30**
— — — in Kersey, Suff., **208**
— — dispenser of, 77; *see also* Thomas
— — disputes with Ramsey abbey,
  Hunts., **164**

— — dissolution of, 32, 87, 131
— — evidence and muniments of, **276**
— — fee of, **8, 255, 256** (fo. 172v), **258**
  (fo. 174v)
— — — in Barrington, **237**
— — — in Hemingford, Hunts., **231**
— — — in Huntingdon, **230**
— — — in Kersey, Suff., **186, 208**
— — fire at, 23, 71, 92, 121
— — foundation of, 8–9, 25–7, 79–80,
  120–1; **2**
— — grain-stores of, 70, 73, 80, 417
— — guest-house (*hospitium*) of, 69, 82,
  84, 415
— — income of, from spiritualities, **265**
— — — from temporalities, **264**
— — infirmary of, 49, 60, 86, 103; **72,
  91–2, 223**
— — inventory of, 55, 69, 82, 84–7, 91,
  99, 103, 105, appendix 2
— — lay-sister of, *see* Chilham, Idonea de
— — light (*lumen, luminare*), of high altar
  at, 49; **65**
— — — of St Katherine at, 49, 86, 129; **54**
— — — of St Mary at, 49–50, 86, 102,
  104; **57, 62, 115**; (*cereus*) **240**
— — mass at, 54
— — mass of St Mary at, 50, 86, 102,
  104–5; **115, 240**
— — men of, **182**
— — messengers of, **95, 170**
— — messuage in Doddington of, **253**
— — nuns of, 96–104, 418, 420; **2, 4**; *see
  also* appendix 1
— — obedientiaries at, 103
— — patronage of, 8–24, 38, 120, 127; **4–
  6**
— — prebend in, **227**
— — prioress of, *see* Drayton, Joan de;
  Hadewisa; Norton, Agnes; Smyth,
  Ellen; *see also* appendix 1
— — proctor of, **112, 181** (fo. 143v); *see
  also* Jocelin
— — reeve of, 77
— — right (*jus*) of, **190, 195, 198, 200,
  205, 208, 230**
— — rights confirmed to bp of Ely over,
  9, **269** (fo. 180v), **270** (fo. 183r)

— — rights given to bp of Ely over, *see* Chatteris abbey, patronage
— — sacrist of, *see* Cambridge, Amicia de
— — seal of, 93–5; **281n**
— — serjeant (*serviens*) of, *see* Bancis, Thomas de; Jocelin
— — servants of, 105, 418–20
— — site of, 69, 79–83; **3** (fo. 74r)
— — stewards of, 74–7; **161**; *see also* Impington, Hugh de
— — value of temporalities and spiritualities, 37–40
— — villeins of, 75, 100, 119, 123, 137, 161, 271–2, 274
— — visitations of, 17–20, 22
— — ward-penny of, 10, 126–7; **6, 269** (fo. 180v)
— — women under authority of, 50; **49**
— carrying rod of bp of Ely in, **257**, 280
— chaplain of, *see* Ebrard; Hoor, Richard; Neve, Henry; Ralph; Roger; Taillour, John; Thomas
— church of St Peter, 24, 29, 33–5, 38–9, 87, 92–3; **3** (fo. 74r), **11–12, 15n, 16, 77–9, 265**
— — bequests to, 55–6, 93
— — burials at, 55–6
— — lordship and advowson of, 14, 34, 124; **10, 76**
— — parsons before appropriation of, *see* Crochem, Roger; Phil', Walter
— — rectory of, 32
— — vicar of, *see* Alan, clerk; Buckworth, Henry; Ralph; West, Warin
— — — presentation of, **267**
— — vicarage of, 34–5, 38; **11–12, 78–9, 267**
— common land, boundaries of, **279**
— dispenser of, *see* Thomas
— documents dated at, **192, 203, 205, 225, 230**; *see also* Chatteris abbey, chapter-house of
— dower of Aveline Briston in, 44; **44**
— fisheries in, 43, 47–8, 62, 105; **13–14, 83–6, 88–9, 211, 275**
— manorial courts held in, 16, 74–5
— property in, 14–122 *passim*; **3** (fo. 74r), **13–15, 17–19, 22–37, 39–43, 45–6,**

48–69, 71, 74, 80–1, 234, 254, 256 (fo. 172v), **257, 258** (fo. 174v), **279**
— rents in, 27, 43–4, 47–8, 50, 103; **3** (fo. 74r), **13–14, 20–1, 38, 47, 65, 70, 80, 256** (fo. 172v), **257, 258** (fo. 174v)
— road to 'Elmeneford', 67
— road to 'Elmenswrth'' (Elmenestirch'), 32, 37
— revenue from temporalities in, **264**
— settlement at, 79–83
— stone buildings in, 91–2
— tithes in, 33–6, 55; **79**
— villein of, *see* Whiteheed', John
— 'Achenewere' (Achenwere, Echinewere, Ethenewere, Ethneswere, Hachenewere), fishery, 83, 85–6, 88, 169, **275**
— 'Acheneweredore' (Achinweredore, Achynwerdore), **279**
— 'Algarisfen'' (Algaresfen, Algarisfene), **279**
— 'Armatysmere' (Armytsmere, Arnatismere, Arnatissmere, Arnetesmere), **279**
— 'Biee' (Bye), **279**
— 'Blakwell'' (Blakeweld'), **279**
— 'Burtefen' (Bourtefen), 34
— 'Bysschops yard', **280**
— church, field below (*subtus*), 31, 34
— 'Commannelond'', 34
— 'Cotestede', **234**
— 'Dribittesfen' (Driebitesfen, Driebitfen), **279**
— 'Egeswera', fishery, 89
— 'Elmene' (Ellemannesfeld, Elmenefeld', Elmenesfeld', Elmethe), 28–9, 32, 34, 37, 67, **233**
— 'Elmeneford', road to, 67
— 'Elmenswrth'' (Elmenestirch'), road to, 32, 37
— 'Erche', 33
— 'Fligellis' (Fliggele), 25, 41
— 'Frankewode' (Frangkwode), 25, 41
— 'Gravesten'', 30
— 'Haltons', **280**
— 'Herberhovedlond'' (Herberd' Hoved' Lond'), 35, 62

— Honey Hill (Honezeh', Honneye, Hunney, Hunneye), 278-9
— — chapel of, 29, 33, 35-6, 129-30; 3 (fo. 74v), 81, 164
— Horseway (Horesethe, Horse, Horseche, Horsedefeld', Horsethe, Horsethefeld', Horshee, Horshethe, Horsidefeld', Horsideweye), 18, 24, 28, 35-6, 45, 62, 234
— Horseway weir (Horse, Horsethewere, Horsewere, Horshe, Horswere), fishery, 35, 83-6, 88, 275
— Horseway wood (Horsechewode), 36
— Horslode (Horinglade Feld, Horingslade, Horinslade, Hornyngsladefeld', Horyngslade, Horyngsladefeld', Horyngsladefen, Horynngsladefeld', Horynsslade), 24, 32-3, 35, 37, 45-6, 49, 52-4, 61-3, 81, 234
— 'Ipyslake', 211
— 'Langreche' (Langereche, Langrech'), 279
— 'Markis...', 45
— 'Myle Water', fishery, 211
— 'Newewere' (Newere), fishery, 85-6, 88
— 'Northstrete', 56
— 'Northtdelf', fishery, 89
— 'Pamplake', 211
— Park House, 80, 82, 89-92
— 'Polwere', fishery, 62; 89, 169
— Restages (Redesteche, Rodesteche), fishery, 84-6, 88
— 'Segwere', fishery, 89
— Several water (*Aqua Severilla*, Severyll Water), 211
— Sheep Horn fen (Schipchirnefen), 35
— 'Sichich' (Sicheis), 69
— Slade (le Slade, Sladefeld', Sladeford'), 42, 47, 50, 57-8, 71
— 'Southwode', 34
— Stocking (le Stokking', le Stokkyng'), 44; 28-9, 34
— 'Toft'', 233
— 'Tomesdych'' (Comesdich'), 31, 34
— 'le Wellestolt'', 72; 28

— 'le Welsteche' (le Wellesteche, le Welstecche), 34, 36
— Wenny (Wenneye), 234
— 'Westfen', 89
— Willystub (Wylystub), 48
— windmill, field of abbess's, 72; 28
— 'Wodecroft', 27, 40
— *see also* Alberd, Thomas, of; Baldock, Robert, of; Briston, Alice and Henry, of; Cockerell, John, of; Fithien, Henry and John, of; Freman, Margaret le, of; Gaugi, Richard, of; Horseheath, Alexander de, of; Kersey, Ralph de, of; Litton, Gilbert son of Gilbert de, of; Noreis, Azo le, of; Pichinn, John, of; Tyd, Nicholas, of; Vivien, John, of; Winwick, John, of
Chaumppayne, William, burgess of Norwich, 225
— — Joan wife of, 225
Chawelle, Richard de, W 281
cheese, 52-3, 101; 170
Chesterton (Chestreton'), Elizabeth, nun of Chatteris, 101, 406
Chettisham (Chedesham), Stephen de, ?*alias* Stephen, 52, 54-5, 61, 81
chief, land held of king in, 8, 255, 256 (fo. 172v), 257 (fo. 173v), 258 (fo. 174v)
Childerley (Childerlegh', Chyrdyrleye), Alexander de, chaplain, 105; 178
Chilham (Chileham, Eselynge), Idonea de, lay-sister of Chatteris, 21, 105-6, 406
'Chinnora', 25-6
Chipman, Edmund, 252
chirograph (*carta indentata, cyrographum, scriptum cyrographatum, scriptum indentatum*), 51, 60, 71, 101-3, 113, 118, 124, 128, 132-3, 144, 147, 162, 168, 210, 219, 225, 230
Chirwelton' *see* Charwelton
Christian (*Christiani*), Matthew, W 235
christians, 83, 114, 211
chronicle, 8-9, 25-6, 79, 120-2; 2, 4, 183
Church (*ad Ecclesiam*), Richard, of Harleston, W 162n

churches, appropriation of, 24, 29–30, 33–5; 10–12, 76, 78, 160, 161 (fo. 133v), 261 (fo. 178v)
— building of, 2
— rent from, 73, 188, 204
— *see also* Barley, Herts; Barrington; Chatteris; Ely; Foxton; Kersey, Suff.; Lynn, Norf.; Over; St Ives, Hunts.; Shepreth; Stok'
Chyrdyrleye *see* Childerley
cissor, *see* tailor
cithara, *see* harp
Clement, John, 280
Clementhorpe *see* York
clerk (*clericus*), *see* Alan; Alexander; *Amianus*; Fowlmere, James son of Alice formerly wife of William de; Freman, Edmund; Harpswell, Robert de; Henry; Hugh; Lovetopp, John; Ousthorp, John de; Shelford, Peter de; Shepreth, Bartholomew father of Basilia de; Simon; Stuntney, Richard de; Thomas; Thurstan; Waryn, John
— of exchequer pleas, *see* Charwelton, Robert
Clerkenwell priory, Middx, 48, 57
Cleveland (Clevelandye, Cleveland', Clyveland'), adcn of, *see* Ely, William of
Clinton (Clint', Clintune), Edward, lord Clinton and Saye, 32
— [of Glympton], Geoffrey de, W 5, W 6n
Cliveland' *see* Cleveland
cloak, 214
Clopton, John, 210
close (*claustura*), 27, 40, 71
clove, as rent, 156, 244
Clyveland' *see* Cleveland
Cnut, king of England, 2
Cobbeham *see* Cobham
cobbler (le cobeler'), *see* Richard
Cobham (Cobbeham, Cobeham), John de, justice of common pleas, 178
— Reginald, justice in eyre, 142
Cockfield (Cokefeld', Kokefeld'), Adam son of Robert de, 13, 43, 45, 61; 73, 186, 188, 204

— — Adam grandfather of, 13–14, 33, 61; 186
— Nesta de, 13, 33; 189
cocus, *see* cook
Codygton' *see* Doddington
Cokefeld' *see* Cockfield
Cokerell (Cokerel), John, of Chatteris, 44; 80
Colman, John, of Offton, 209–10
Colne, Hunts., land in, 31
coloni, *see* villeins
Columbers, Richard de, 52, 101; 170
— — Margaret dau. of, nun of Chatteris, 52, 100–1, 406; 170
— — Rose dau. of, nun of Chatteris, 52, 100–1, 406; 170
commission to hold an inquisition, 190
common land, 116, 122, 147, 211, 279
complaint, 164
confirmation, 90–1, 100, 123
— of appropriation of Chatteris church, 11–12, 78
— of chantry in Shepreth, 162
— of exchange of tofts in Over, 102–3
— of prebend, 95–7
— of property, in Barley, Herts., 242
— — in Barrington, 117
— — in Bircham, Norf., 221
— — in Chatteris, 13–15, 26, 32, 37, 42
— — in Elm, 98
— — in Foxton, 126, 129
— — in Hemingford, Hunts., 232
— — in Huntingdon, 229
— — in Kersey, Suff., 186
— — in Lynn, Norf., 213, 215–16
— — in Madingley, 109
— — in Shepreth, 158
— — in Thriplow, 165, 167
— — of Chatteris abbey, 3
— — of church of Ely, 269–70
— of quitclaim, 174
— of quitrent, 106
— of remission of ward-penny, 9
— of rent from church, 204
— of tithe settlement, 79, 181–2
— *see also* inspeximus
congregations, enlargement of, 2

Conington (Conynton', Conytom'),
   Margaret de, nun of Chatteris, 101,
   406
consent *see* assent
Contennham *see* Cottenham
contributions, 256 (fo. 173r), 257 (fo.
   174r)
controversia, see dispute
convocation of 1453, 23
Conynton', Conytom', *see* Conington
Cook, Robert, W 210
— (*cocus*), *see* Agnes, William son of;
   Barnwell, Geoffrey de; Joecus; John
Copnote (Kopnote), John, burgess of
   Lynn, Norf., 220
Corbeil, William de, abp of Canterbury,
   12
cordwainer (cordewaner, *cordewanerius,
   cordewarnerius*, cordwaner), *see* Elwin
Coresford *see* Cosford
corn, 69, 136, 144, 269 (fo. 181v)
— ninth of, 260 (fo. 177r), 261 (fo. 178r)
— tithes of, 112, 161
Cornewellia, see Cranwell
Coroner (Coronner), Katherine, nun of
   Chatteris, 407
coroners, 259 (fo. 176r)
Corwersham, W 243
Cosford (Coresford), Suff., half-hundred
   of, 189
Cottenham (Contennham, Cotenham),
   Henry de, 234
Cotton, Sir Robert, 107–8
court, hundred, 15; 15, 66, 243, 257 (fo.
   173v)
— manorial, 75, 137
— — perquisities of, 39, 75
— — in Barley, Herts., 16, 74–5
— — in Barrington, 16, 33, 67, 73–5
— — in Chatteris, 16, 74–5
— — in Foxton, 16, 33, 66–7, 73–6; 124,
   143, 163
— — in Kersey, Suff., 191, 201, 210
— — in Madingley, 16, 74
— — in Over, 16–17, 74–5
— — in Shepreth, 16, 33, 67, 74–5
— royal, 259 (fo. 175v)
— — of common pleas, 142, 178, 230
— of bishop of Ely, 185
— of palace of Ely, 15; 257 (fo. 173v)
— *see also* suit of court
courtyard of rector of Over, 101–3
Coveney (Coveneye, Covenye, Coveye,
   Covneya), Geoffrey de, 25, 41
— Henry son of Robert de, 249–53
— — Matilda wife of, 250
— Katherine de, 24, 45, 233
— — Ralph son of, 44, 103; 47
Crabhouse priory, Norf., 47, 89, 91, 104
Cranfield (Cramfeud'), Beds., *see* Simon,
   parson of
Cranwell (*Cornewellia, Cranewellia*),
   Hugh de, 29, 53, 101, 130; 227
— — Adelicia (Idelicia), dau. of, nun of
   Chatteris, 53, 102, 407; 227
Crawedane, Agnes wife of William de,
   132
crimes pardoned, 259
Crochem, Roger, parson of church of St
   Peter, Chatteris, 10, 76
croft, in Barley, Herts., 180
— in Barrington, 113, 117, 120–1
— in Bircham, Norf., 221
— in Chatteris, 18–19, 30, 60, 65
— in Doddington, 246–7, 251–2
— in Foxton, 128, 138, 140, 145
— in Huntingdon, 229
— in Kingston, 111
— in Madingley, 239, 281
— in Shepreth, 149–52, 156, 159, 161
Cromwell, Sir Oliver, 32
— Thomas, 87
cross, chaplain of the, *see* Nicholas
Cruce Roesia, Cruce Rois, see Royston
Cruser, Godard le, 145
culture, 27–9, 34, 40, 145–6, 180
cure of souls, 11–12, 78
customary services *see* boon-works;
   carrying-service; labour-services;
   plough-service
customary tenant, 144
Cuthbert, Adam son of, *alias* Cuberd',
   Adam, 121

damages, 8, 51, 112, 147, 161–2, 171, 255, 259, 270 (fo. 183r); *see also* inquisition *ad quod damnum*

'dambote', 168

danegeld, 109, 167

Danes, Ælfheah stoned by, 2

Davington priory, Kent, 88

death-bed, 114

declaration that tenant is not villein, 276; *see also* manumission

deductions (*reprise*), 191, 212, 257 (fo. 174r)

demesne of Chatteris abbey *see* Chatteris abbey

Denny abbey, 23, 40, 47, 89, 95

Denston, John, 210

Derislee, Rose de, 108

Dery (Dony), Henry, 243–4

— — Eleanor wife of, 243–4

Despenser (Spenser), Hugh le, earl of Winchester, 61; 191

— — junior, 61, 72; 190–1

Develyn' (Dulyng', Duvelyn'), Margaret, abbess of Chatteris, 401–2; 277

digging in marsh, 279

dike (*fossa, fossatum, fovea*), 19, 25, 27, 34, 36, 40–1, 149 (fo. 129v), 233

discovery of body of St Ivo, 2

dispenser (*dispensarius*), *see* Thomas

dispute (*controversia, lis, querela*), 112, 129–31, 147, 161, 164, 180–2

distraint, 104, 106, 124, 189, 208, 218–19, 225, 230–1, 260 (fo. 176v), 261 (fo. 178r)

Ditton *see* Fen Ditton

Doddington (Codygton', Dodington, Dodygton', Dodyngton', Dodynton', Dudyngton', Dudyngtone, Dudyngtun', Dundyton'), 278

— bank (*ripa*) of, 279

— common marsh of, 243–4, 248–9, 251

— document dated at, 245

— manor of bp of Ely in, 257 (fo. 173v)

— pasture of Chatteris extends to, 279

— property in, 15, 39, 42–3; 243–4, 246–54, 256 (fo. 172v), 257 (fo. 173v), 258 (fo. 174v)

— stone buildings in, 91–2

— Beezling fen (Belsynges, Bilsynges, Bilsyngys, Bylsynges, Hilsingges), 243, 279

— 'le Fenhous', 252

— 'le Hil' (le Hyl), 244, 248, 250, 253

— 'Suthfen', 249

— Walter son of Richard de, 244

— — Joan wife of, 244

— William son of Hugh, reeve, de, 169

— *see also* Ace, Philip son of William of; Geoffrey, potter, of; Penw..., Robert, of; Polwere, Alexander de, of

Domesday book, 3, 16, 25–7, 31, 33, 37–8, 41, 71, 79–80

Domesman, Hugh, prior of Barnwell, 109

domus, see house

Donemawe *see* Blomvyll', John, prior of Little Dunmow

Donolt, Thomas, 77

Dony *see* Dery

Dorchester, Oxon., bps of, 11; *see also* Eadnoth I; Eadnoth II

'dormant' documents, 202, 208

Dousthorp, Agnes, nun of Chatteris, 407

dower, 44; 29, 44, 249–50, 252; *see also* marriage-portion

Downham, Little (Dounham, Douunham), 279

— documents dated at, 16, 77

— Thomas, monk of Ely, 17

dowry-grants, 51–4, 101–2; 26, 87, 152, 170, 227

Drayton, Joan de, prioress of Chatteris, 101, 403

Dreng' (Breng', Brenge), Edmund, 241

— Edward, 18

— John, baxter, 14, 42; 256 (fo. 172v), 257 (fo. 173r), 258 (fo. 174v)

Dry Drayton (Drye Drayton'), *see* Reynold, John

Dudyngton', Dudyngtone, Dudyngtun', *see* Doddington

Dugdale, William, 80

Duluestre *see* Ulster

Dundyton' *see* Doddington

Duneuuicum, Dunewichum, Dunewicum, see Dunwich

Dunmow, Essex, *see* Blomvyll', John,
　　prior of Little Dunmow
Dunstable (Dunstaple, Dunstapyl) Beds.,
　　278
— weight of cheese payable at, 101; 170
Dunwich (*Duneuuicum, Dunewichum,
　　Dunewicum*), Suff., 269 (fo. 181v)
Durham, bp of, *see* Puiset, Hugh du

Eadnoth I (*Ednodus*), monk of
　　Worcester, abbot of Ramsey and bp
　　of Dorchester, 4, 8–9, 11, 25–7, 120;
　　2, **183**
Eadnoth II, bp of Dorchester, 26
Ebrard (*Eborardus, Ewarardus*), chaplain
　　of Chatteris, *alias* Briston, Ebrard, 45,
　　105; **88**, W **110**, W **238**
Ecclesia, see Church
Edelmus, William son of, 127
Edelyna, *amica* of William of Ely, *alias*
　　Alice, *see* Ely, Ralph of
Edgar I, king of England, 26, 79
Edith, widow, 39, 42–3
Edmund II Ironside, king of England, 2
— earl of March and Ulster, *see*
　　Mortimer, Edmund
Ednodus, see Eadnoth
Edward I, king of England, 22; **7**, **260** (fo.
　　177r), **261** (fo. 178r)
— II, king of England, 22; **7**
— III, king of England, 22, 124–5, 135; **7–
　　8**, **190** (fo. 146r), **255**, **256** (fo. 172v),
　　258 (fo. 174r), **260–1**
— prince of Wales (the Black Prince), **192**
eels, 80; **269** (fo. 181r)
— as rent, **87**, **169**
— exchange and grant of, 62; **89**
Egelwinus, see Æthelwine
eggs, 144
Elankpayn *see* Blankpayn
Eleswith *see* Elsworth
Eli *see* Ely
Eling (Hellingas), Hants., document
　　dated at, 6n
Elm (Elme), **278**
— land in, 42, 122; **98**, **235**

— 'Pepyrfeld' (Pepirfyld), **98**, **235**
'Elmene' *see* Chatteris
Elmham (*Helmanensis*), bp of, *see* Ælfgar
Elrington, Edward, 32
Elstow abbey, Beds., 12, 18–19, 52, 84
Elsworth (Eleswith, Esewyth), Matilda
　　de, maid (*ancilla*) of abbess of
　　Chatteris, 105; **60**
Elwin (Alwin, Elwyn), cordwainer
　　(*cordewaner, cordewanerius,
　　cordewarnerius, cordwaner*), of Lynn,
　　Norf., **213–17**
— — Alice wife of, **214**
— — Walter, cordwainer, son of, of
　　Lynn, **215**
— — William, cordwainer, son of, of
　　Lynn, **213–16**
— — — Laurence, son of, **216**
Ely (Eli, Heli, Hely), **278**
— abbey (*ecclesia*), abbot of, 14, 16, 25,
　　27, 38, 79–80
— — body of Eadnoth brought to, **2**
— — income of, 38
— adcn of, *see* FitzNeal, Richard;
　　Lavington, William de
— bp of, 70; **162**, **181** (fo. 143v), **189**; *see
　　also* Alcock, John; Balsham, Hugh de;
　　Burgo, Geoffrey de; Eustace;
　　Fordham, John; Fountains, John of;
　　Grey, William; Hervey; Lisle,
　　Thomas de; Longchamp, William;
　　Montacute, Simon; Morgan, Philip;
　　Nigel; Northwold, Hugh de; Orford,
　　Robert; Ridel, Geoffrey; Stanley,
　　James; Walpole, Ralph de
— — bailiffs of, **94–7**
— — carrying of rod of, **257**, **280**
— — court of, **185**
— — court of palace of, 15; **257** (fo. 173v)
— — exchequer of, **7**, **95–7**
— — farmers of, **94**, **96–7**
— — fee of, **13–14**, **104**, **106**, **145**
— — hundred of Ely of, 15
— — land of, **168**, **248**, **251**
— — land held of, **253**, **257**
— — manor in Doddington of, **257** (fo.
　　173v)
— — marshall of, *see* Stockton, John de

— — papal privilege to, 269–70
— — register of, 109
— — rights over Chatteris abbey
  confirmed to, 10; 9, 269 (fo. 180v),
  270 (fo. 183r)
— — rights over Chatteris abbey given
  to, 9–24, 38, 120; 4 (fo. 75v), 5–6
— — stewards of, 95
— — *sturesmannus* (esturesman) of, *see*
  Ingelram, Alexander son of
— cathedral priory (*ecclesia*), almonry of,
  34
— — men of, 269 (fo. 180v)
— — monks of, 269
— — — fee in Stuntney of, 99
— — prior of, 23, 70; *see also* Bergham,
  Roger de; Hemmingestone, John de;
  Solomon
— — prior and convent of, 34, 128; 12,
  78, 97, 147
— — records of, 9, 11
— — ward-penny of, 269 (fo. 180v)
— church of St Mary, 269 (fo. 181r)
— clerk of, *see* Alexander
— diocese of, 9–10, 12
— — clergy of, 76
— — income of abbess of Chatteris in,
  263
— — taxation in, 261 (fo. 178r)
— document dated at, 97
— Isle of, 4, 269 (fo. 181r–v)
— liberty of, 13, 16
— messuage in, 30, 42, 49, 59–60; 92
— rent from tenement in, 30, 43; 99
— see of, 5, 9
— — knight-service of, 269 (fo. 180v)
— — temporalities of, 7
— — vacancy in, 7
— vineyard in, 269 (fo. 181r)
— Barton (*Beortuna, Bertona, Bertuna*),
  269 (fo. 181r)
— Potter's Lane (Potterislane,
  Potterysslane), 49, 59–60; 92–3, 99
— Turbutsey (*Thidbriteseia,
  Tidbrichteseia, Tidbricteseya,
  Tidbridteseia, Tidbrigteseia,
  Tidbriteseia, Tydbrytesya*), 269 (fo.
  181r)

— Agnes de, abbess of Chatteris, 100,
  396; 113, 120, 128, 172, 176
— Alan de, gardener, 60; 93
— — Alice wife of, 60; 93
— Ralph of, son of William of Ely and
  Alice, *alias* Edelyna, *amica* of
  William, 43, 86; 72, 90 (fo. 102r), 91
— William of, adcn of Cleveland and
  treasurer, 29, 45, 86, 124, 129; 90–1,
  223–4, W 239
— — Peter, M, uncle of, 91 (fo. 102v)
— *see also* Hildersham, Richard, of; *Liber
  Eliensis*
Emma, abbess of Chatteris, *see*
  Somersham, Emma de
— dau. of William de Arques, *see* Arques
Empigton' *see* Impington
Enarratio in Psalmum, 206
England, king of, *see* Cnut; Edgar I;
  Edmund II Ironside; Edward I;
  Edward II; Edward III; Henry I;
  Henry II; Henry III; Henry V; John;
  Richard I; Richard II; Stephen
English, poem written in, 207
Eoydon' *see* Boydon'
episcopal documents, 10–11, 13–16, 76–
  7, 79, 89, 94–6, 103, 129–30, 160–1,
  165–7, 185, 224, 246
escheators 258 (fo. 175r), 259 (fo. 176r);
  see also Fox, John; More, Thomas;
  Suffolk
escheats, 65, 115, 155, 240, 246
Eselynge *see* Chilham
Esewyth *see* Elsworth
Essex, exannual roll for, 262
— *see also, Assandun*; Dunmow
Esthemnygford', Estmingford', *see*
  Hemingford
Estrild', wife of Hugh, 116, 122
'esturesman' *see* Ingelram
Etheldreda, St, honour of, 6, 89, 165–7,
  185
— — life of, 99–100
— — miracle of, 47
Eustace, bp of Ely, 24, 35, 45; 160
— Alan, 143
— Asketil son of, W 281
— Geoffrey son of, 93; 281

Eversden (Everisdone, Eversdon'), rent in, 111

evidence, books and, 279

— muniments and, 276

— *see also* cartulary

exannual roll, 262

exchanges, 164

— of benefices, 273

— of eels, 62; 89

— of lands, in Barrington, 62; 113

— — in Chatteris, 61; 30, 233

— — in Foxton, 62; 136, 145–6

— — in Over, 62; 101–3

— of rent in Ely and land in Stuntney, 99

— of tithes in Barley, Herts., 180

exchequer, of bishop of Ely, 7, 95–7

— of king of England, 7, 191

— — barons of, 7, 260 (fo. 176v), 261 (fo. 178r), 262

— — *see also* treasurer

— pleas, 135; 260–1, 278

exemplification, 69, 141, 231

exitus, see revenue

expedition abroad, royal, 260n

expenses, 112, 161, 170, 263

extent, of manor of Kersey, Suff., 191

— and value of lands in Barley, Herts., 171–3

faber, see smith

Fader, Richard, 30

fallow-land, 136

family (*sequela*), 75, 118, 271–2, 274

farmers, of temporalities of Ely, 7

— of mill of Barrington, 118

— of Fen Ditton, 94, 96–7

Fechien, Fechyon', *see* Fithien

fee, chief lord of, 224, 244–5, 248, 253

— chief lords of, 119, 209–10, 234, 241, 247, 249–52, 258

— and heredity, 121, 141, 214, 234, 245, 252–3; *see also* inheritance; hereditary right

— knight's, 189

— lord of, 17, 55, 59, 62, 91, 223

— *see also* Alexander, Pain son of; Augustine, Baldwin son of; Britanny, duke of; Chatteris abbey; Ely, bp of; Ely cathedral priory; Gilbert, carpenter; king of England; Mandeville; Martin, Robert; Mepal, lady of; Mora, Michael de; Noreis, Azo le; Over church

fee-farm, 33, 59, 61, 63–4, 71–3; 119, 168, 176, 186–7, 189–203, 205, 208, 212

felling, 279; *see also* timber; woods

Fen Ditton (Ditton), 278

— 20s. in, 30, 43; 94–7

Ferreres, Katherine, nun of Chatteris, 407

Fichien, Fichyen, *see* Fithien

Fieschi, Ottobuono, cardinal deacon of St Adrian and former papal legate, 161

Fin (Fyn'), Matilda, 229

— Robert, of Huntingdon, 230

final concord, 133, 142, 178–9

Fincham (Fyncham), Elinor, nun of Chatteris, 407

fire, 51

fisheries, 31; 13–14, 26, 119, 270 (fo. 183r)

— eels from, 62; 89

— grant of, 43, 52, 101, 105; 55, 83–8, 90–1, 169, 211, 275

— sale and quitclaim of, 90

fishermen, 269 (fo. 181v)

Fissher, Alice, nun of Chatteris, 408

Fithien (Fechien, Fechyon, Fichien, Fichyen, Phichien, Pichiun, Pychyun'), Henry, of Chatteris, 29

— John, of Chatteris, 44, 72; 28, 35, 38, 63

— — (?*same*), 211

— — (*another*), 252

— Juliana, formerly wife of Henry, of Chatteris, 44; 29

FitzNeal, Richard, adcn of Ely, bp of London and treasurer, 29; W 9, 76, 91 (fo. 102v), 109, 222–4

— — Robert brother of, 29, 42; 109

FitzSimond', Hugh, 260n

fleeces, ninth of, 260 (fo. 177r)

Fleg', William de, W 110

Flocthorp, John de, 108

Folcold, Robert son of, *alias* Alan,
    Robert brother of, *alias* Alan, Robert
    son (*recte* brother) of, 165–7

foldage, 221

Foliot, Hugh, prior of Ramsey, 164

Folkard, Hugh, 220

food, **69**, 144

Fordham, John, bp of Ely, 17

— Margaret, nun of Chatteris, 101, 408

Forest (*de Foresta*), William, W 240

forfeiture, **259** (fo. 176r)

— of manor of Kersey, Suff., 190

forgery, 90n

'Fotestorp', Norf., **269** (fo. 181v)

Foulmere *see* Fowlmere

Fountains, John of, bp of Ely, 29, 34,
    124; **11–14**, 78

Fowlmere (Foulmere, Fulmere), land of,
    143

— mill of, 163

— road, 145, **149** (fo. 128v)

— Philip de, 129

— Thomas de, 142

— William de, M, carpenter, 72; **163**

— — Alice formerly wife of, 120

— — — James son of, clerk, 120

Fox, John, escheator, 212

Foxton (*Foxtona*, Foxtone, Foxtun'), 278

— bailiff of, 161

— bridge, 119, **149** (fo. 128v)

— capons rendered at, **124**

— cattle in, 128; **147**

— church, 33–4

— — land of, 33–4; **128–131**, 147

— — rector of, *see* Bagnaria, Manuel de;
    Ilbert, Richard son of; Shelford, Peter
    de; Simon

— — — land of, 127, 135, **145–6**

— — — messuage of, **141**

— court of Chatteris abbey at, 16, 33, 66–
    7, 73–6; **124**, 143, 163

— demesne of Chatteris abbey in, 129–30

— documents dated at, **124**, 241

— homage and service for land in, 115

— mill in, 27, 37, 59, 71–3; **3** (fo. 74r),
    119, 143

— ninth in, 261–2

— property in, 12–78 *passim*, 101–2; **3**
    (fo. 74r), 119, **125–36**, **138–46**, 148,
    152, 185, 232, 241, 261 (fo. 178v)

— revenue from temporalities in, 264

— road from Barrington, 119, 127, 135,
    146

— road from Fowlmere, 145

— road from 'Lythlowe', 127

— steward of, 161

— stream (*rivulus*) between Shepreth and,
    146

— tenantry of Chatteris abbey in, 163

— villeins of, 119

— 'Appeltonesdole', 146

— 'Bradeweye', 143

— 'Briggedole', 146

— 'le Brokis', 145

— 'Brokstrate', 145

— Chadwell field (Caldewelle,
    Calldewellefeld', Cheldewellefeld'),
    132, 135, 143, 145

— 'Collande', 135

— Down field (Denefeld', Donefeld,
    Douunfeld', Drunefeld', Dunefeld',
    Dune Feld), 132, 135, 143, 145, 152

— Draymer's (Dreymere), 127

— 'Edeswelle', 143

— 'le Estmelne', 119

— Ham, 127

— Hayditch (Heydik, Heydych,
    Heydyk, Hoydych), 127, 132, 144,
    147, 152

— 'Horsecroft', 135

— 'Jewedich'', 135

— 'Lythlowe', road from, 127

— Mare Way (Marewye, Mereweye), 145

— 'Pundefoldedole', 146

— 'Sik', 143

— 'Wodegate Herne', 145

— 'Wodegate Howe', 135

— 'Wodeweye' (Wodeweyeherne), 145

— Isabel dau. of Hervy de, *alias* Hervy,
    Isabel, 44, 77; **52**, 54

— Roger de, chaplain, 65; **136**

— *see also* Bancis, Thomas de, of;
    Fraunceys, Alan le, John and Roger

le, of; Guthlac, Osbert, of; J., smith,
　　of; Lowe, Richard, of
France *see* Lyons; St-Pierre-sur-Dives
frank-pledge *see* view
Fransham (Franesham), John de, M, 51
Fraunceys, Alan le, of Foxton, 135
— — (?*same*), 141, 145
— — (?*same*), W 240
— — Christiana sister of, 132
— — Nicholas son of, 135
— — Robert father of, 141
— John, of Foxton, 128
— Roger le, of Foxton, chaplain, 45; 140
Fraunkelein (Fraunkeleyn), Henry le,
　　121
— Reginald le, 138
freehold (*liberum tenementum*), 100, 259
　　(fo. 176r)
Freman, Constance le, 66
— Edmund, clerk, W 210
— Margaret le, of Chatteris, 49
French, Anglo-Norman, documents
　　written in, 193, 196, 202
Frere, John, 257 (fo. 173r)
Fressingfield (Fresingefeld'), Richard de,
　　W 204
Frie, Robert le, 132
Friso, 152
Fulk, Ralph son of, knight, *see*
　　Broadfield, Ralph son of Fulk de
— — Ralph son of, *see* Broadfield, Ralph
　　son of Ralph son of Fulk de
— Theobald son of, 242
— — Alan son of, 242
— — — Theobald brother of, 242
— — Fulk son of, 242
Fulmere *see* Fowlmere
Fulney (Fulneyne), Lincs., *see* Joyce,
　　Reginald, of
furca (a liberty), 189
Fyn' *see* Fin
Fyncham *see* Fincham

gallina, see hens
gardener (*gardinarius*), *see* Ely, Alan de
gardens, 191

Gascoyne family, 80, 91
gathering corn, 136
Gaugi (*dictus* Gaugi), Roger, of Chatteris,
　　45; 55, 60
Gayton, Anne, abbess of Chatteris, 103,
　　402, 418, 420
Geddeworth, Robert de, 260n
Geoffrey, bp of Ely, *see* Burgo, Geoffrey
　　de; Ridel, Geoffrey
— chancellor, *see* Rufus, Geoffrey
— potter (le pottere), of Doddington,
　　248-9, 251
Gerard, John, 34
Gibbes (Gybbes), John, of Kersey, Suff.,
　　209-10
Gie *see* Gye
gift, in Barley, Herts., 172, 175
— in Barrington, 116, 120-2, 232, 237
— in Bircham, Norf., 222, 224
— in Chatteris, 35, 50, 52, 54, 56-7, 61,
　　81, 234
— in Doddington, 243-4, 246-53
— in Ely, 93
— in Foxton, 134, 141, 232, 241
— in Hemingford, Hunts., 231
— in Lynn, Norf., 214
— in Madingley, 281
— in Shepreth, 155-6, 241
— in Wimblington, 245
— in alms, in Cambridge, 105
— — of Chatteris abbey, 5
— — in Lynn, Norf., 217
— — in Thriplow, 166
— in free alms, in Barley, Herts., 177
— — in Bilney, Norf., 82
— — in Bircham, Norf., 91, 223
— — in Cambridge, 152
— — in Chatteris, 17-19, 23-5, 27-8, 31,
　　33-4, 36, 39-41, 45-6, 48-9, 53, 55,
　　58-9, 62-3, 65, 67-8, 74, 256-8
— — in Doddington, 256-8
— — in Elm, 235
— — in Ely, 92
— — in Foxton, 125, 127, 140, 143, 152
— — in Hemingford, Hunts., 272
— — in Madingley, 110, 238-9
— — in Shepreth, 149-50, 152, 157
— — in Stuntney, 91

— — in Wimblington, 256–8

— — in Upwell and Outwell, Cambs. and Norf., 87

Gilbert, carpenter (*carpentarius*), fee of, 92–3, 99

— Herbert son of, 23

— John son of, 219

— Robert son of, 17, 59

Gilbertine order, 59, 70, 88

Giselam, Giselham, *see* Isleham

Glastonbury abbey, Somerset, 38

Gledeseye, John de, 177

Glenman (le Glenman), John, 53; 114–15

gloves, as rent, 155

Gocelin *see* Jocelin

Godmanchester, William of, abbot of Ramsey, 102

Godsho, Cecilia, *see* Cambridge, John

— — Amicia sister of, *see* Cambridge, John

Godstow abbey, Oxon., 19, 51, 85–6

Godyng', Walter, 48, 50, 57

— William, 60

Gold', John, 139

gold coin (*aureus, talentum, talentum auri*), 116, 122, 130–1, 216, 222

Gonnora, former wife of Richard, carter (*carectarius*), *see* Vivien, John

Goodgrome, Nicholas, 280

Goodryke, John, 76–7

Goodwen, William, W 209

Gorold, 152

Goudlok, J., W 241

— W., W 241

Graie *see* Gray

grant, of advowson of Barley, Herts., 177

— of annuity, 72

— of Chatteris church, 10, 76; *see also* appropriation

— of cheese, 170

— of claim in dower-land, 250

— of eels, 89

— of fisheries, 55, 83–8, 90–1, 169, 211, 275

— of freedom from secular service in confirmation, 167

— of homage and rent, 20, 114

— of homage and service, 115

— of increase of quitrent, 106

— of licence to acquire property in mortmain, 8, 255

— of man, 91, 222–4, 272

— of power to cleanse and extend mill-pond, 159

— of prebend, 94

— of quitrent, 104

— of remission of ward-penny, 6

— of rent, fom church, 73, 188

— — in Cambridge, 108

— — in Chatteris, 21, 65, 70

— — in Ely, 99

— — in Huntingdon, 230

— — in Kingston, 240

— — in Kingston, Eversdon and Wimpole, 111

— — in Lincoln, 227

— — in Pinchbeck, Lincs., 226

— — in Shepreth, 155

— — in Stuntney, 90–1

— — in Thetford, Little, 90–1

— — in Thriplow, 95

— of right to claim title to land, 173

— of right to close road, 101

— of right to have sheep-fold, 167

— of tithe of and presentation to Barley, Herts., 277

— in fee-farm, 119, 168, 176

Graveney, Alard de, 189

Gray (Graie, Graye, Grey), Henry, knight, earl of Tankerville (*Tancarvill'*), lord of Kersey, Suff., 208, 212

— — Richard son of, 212

— Mary, nun of Chatteris, 98, 104, 408, 418, 420

— *see also* Grey

Greenwich (*Grenewicum*), Kent, St Ælfheah stoned at, 2

Gregory, croft of [in Shepreth], 150, 156

Grenewicum, see Greenwich

Grey, William, bp of Ely, 17

— *see also* Gray

Griffin, 272

Grimbald' (Grymbaud'), William, 260 (fo. 177v)

Guchmund', Juliana dau. of Robert, 156

Gunwara, 239
Guthlac, Osbert, of Foxton, 128
— — Hawisia wife of, 128
— — John son of, 128
Gwye *see* Gye
Gybbes *see* Gibbes
Gye (Gie, Gwye), Elizabeth, nun of
    Chatteris, 103–4, 408, 418, 420
Gykeles, Alice, 118
Gypwicum, *see* Ipswich

habit, of nun, 26, 87; *see also* veil
Hadelegh' *see* Hadleigh
Hadewisa, prioress of Chatteris, 13–14,
    61, 402; 186
Hadfield (Hadfeld'), John de, 143
Hadham, document dated at, 161
Hadleigh (Hadlegh), manor of, 191
— *see also* Illary, Robert, of; Ston', Hamo
    atte, of; Sugge, William, of; Talbot,
    John, of
Hainey Hill *see* Soham
Haked, Richard, 239
Halden', Richard, of Kersey, Suff., 209
Halsteyn, William, 257 (fo. 173r)
Halwyne *see* Alveyne
Hamo, Robert son of, 229
Hampshire *see* Eling
hand, amputated, 2
harbour (*portus*), in Cambridge, 27; 3 (fo.
    74r)
Hardewyne *see* Hardwin
Hardlestune *see* Harleston
Hardwin (Hardewyne, Hardwyne),
    house of [in Shepreth], 152
— Robert, 150, 156
Harewold, Agnes, nun of Chatteris, 408
Harleston (Hardlestune), Gilbert de, W
    240
— *see also* Church, Richard, of
harp (*cithara*), 206
Harpswell (Harpeswelle), Robert de,
    clerk, 247
Hartely, Sir Barnard, 105

Haslingfield (Haselinfeld', Haselingefeld',
    Haselyngfeld', Haslyngfeld'), ninth
    in, 261 (fo. 178r)
— parson of, *see* Walter
Haspeland, Haspelond, *see* Asplond
Hauxton (*Hauechestuna, Hauekestona,
    Hauekestuna, Haukestuna*), 269 (fo.
    181v)
'Haveril" *see* Stuntney
Hawarden, John, 212n
hay, carrying of, 144
— tithes of, 112
Haye, William de la, 35, 131; 132, 135,
    149
— — (?*same*), 150, 156
— — knight, 147, 162
— — Ralph son of, 149 (fo. 129r)
Haylston', Robert, 163
Heacham (Hecham), *see* Homo Dei,
    Adam
heirs (not *sui et heredibus suis*), 25, 27,
    40–1, 93, 170–1, 189, 212, 222, 242
Heli *see* Ely
Hellingas *see* Eling
Helmanensis, *see* Elmham
Hely *see* Ely
Hemingford (Esthemnygford',
    Estmingford', Hemmyngford',
    Hemyngford'), Hunts., 278
— fee of Chatteris abbey in (Hemingford
    Grey), 231
— land in, 42, 49, 59; 231 (Hemingford
    Grey), 272
— rent in, 43, 49–50; 232
— Isabel de, dau. of William Ruffus, 49;
    272
— — Verenger Monachus, formerly
    husband of, 272
— Roger son of Basilia de, 231
— *see also* Bonem, Peter, of
Hemmingestone, John de, prior of Ely,
    97
Hemmyngford', Hemyngford', *see*
    Hemingford
Heneiam, Heneieham, Heneiham,
    Heneyham *see* Soham, Hainey Hill
Hengham, Ralph de, chief justice of
    court of common pleas, 230

— Robert de, 222

Henry I, king of England, 8–12, 14, 27, 38, 45, 126–8; **5–6, 9, 269** (fo. 180v)

— II, king of England, 9

— III, king of England, 7, **189**

— V, king of England, 259 (fo. 175r)

— clerk, W **221**

— *dominus*, **253**

— knight [of Barrington], 121

— miller, 163

— priest (*sacerdos*), Andrew son of, 48; **86**

— — — Alice wife of, dau. of Ralph Briston, 48; **86**

hens (*altilia, gallina*), 144

— as rent, 141

Herbert, rector of Barley, Herts., 36, 64; **181** (fo. 142r), **182**

hereditary right, 155, 172–3, 222, 224, **269** (fo. 181r); *see also* fee and heredity; inheritance

Herewen, anchoress, 9

heriot, 144

herrings, **269** (fo. 181v)

Hert, William, of Norfolk, W **80**

Hertford (Hertf'), justices in eyre at, 172–3

— county of, *see* Barkway; Barley; Berkhamsted

— — exchequer plea rel. to, 260, 261 (fo. 178v)

— — pipe roll for, 260 (fo. 177r)

— — sheriff of, 260

Hervey (*Herveus*), bp of Ely, 10–12, 25, 38, 41, 45, 120, 127–8; **4–6, 9**

Hervy, Isabel, of Foxton, *see* Foxton, Isabel

'Hevereshille', 'Heverhille', *see* Stuntney

hide, 109, 131, **185**

Higdon (Hygdon), Agnes, nun of Chatteris, 98, 409, 418, 420

Higham priory, Kent, 88

Hildersham (Hyldresham), Richard, of Ely, W **80**

Hinchingbrooke priory, Hunts., 40, 47, 89, 96

Hingenolf, 42

— Alice wife of, 42

Holand (Holond), John, earl of Huntingdon, 200–3

— — — court of, 201

Holbroke, John, 212n

— Thomas, 212n

'Holmo' *see* Shepreth

Holond *see* Holand

Holy Trinity priory, prior of, *see* London

homage (feudal allegiance), 65, 100, 123, 214, 240, 242; (tenantry) 163

— and rent, grant of, 20, 114

— and service, 42, 56, 90, 93, 116–17, 120–22, 134, 141, 155, 224, 231, 237, 242–3, 281

— — grant of, **115**

Homo Dei, Adam de, of Heacham, 127

Honey (Honezeh', Honneye, Hunney, Hunneye), William de, 65

— *see also* Chatteris, Honey Hill

honour *see* Etheldreda, St

Hoor, Richard, chaplain, 105

Horseheath (Horesethe, Horseheth', Horsethe), Agnes widow of William son of Alexander de, 66

— Alexander de, of Chatteris, W **234**

— Quena dau. of Codewin de, 61

hospitality, **269** (fo. 180v)

Hotot (Houtoft), Juliana, nun of Chatteris, 100, 409

— Margaret, abbess of Chatteris, 18, 98, 100, 399; **192**

— Rose, nun of Chatteris, 100, 409

Hotte, Robert, *see* Vite, Robert le

house (*domus*, not religious; *mansio, mansura, mansus*), 11–12, 38, 51, 78, 139, 151, 161, 166, 180, 219, 227, 230; *see also* buildings; messuage

Houtoft *see* Hotot

Hovere *see* Over

Howardyn, John, W **210**

Huberd', Robert, 107

Hugh, bp of Durham, *see* Puiset, Hugh du

— bp of Ely, *see* Balsham, Hugh de; Northwold, Hugh de

— clerk of Bedford, W **110**

— earl of Winchester, *see* Despenser,
  Hugh le
— prior of Barnwell, *see* Domesman,
  Hugh
— prior of Ramsey, *see* Foliot, Hugh
— reeve, 180; *see also* Doddington,
  William son of Hugh
— *see also* Estrild'
'Hulmo' *see* Shepreth
Hulot, John, villein of Barley, Herts., 68;
  271
Humphrey *see* Alice
— Thomas of, 121
hundred, 189, 269 (fo. 181v)
— court, 15; 15, 66, 243, 257 (fo. 173v)
— rolls, 7, 12–13, 16, 30–1, 60, 65–7
Hunney, Hunneye, *see* Chatteris, Honey
  Hill
hunting, 270 (fo. 183r)
Huntingdon (Huntedon', *Huntidonia*,
  Huntyndon', Huntyngdon'), 278
— countess of, *see* Anne
— county of, *see* Bluntisham;
  Hemingford; Ramsey; St Ives (*Slepa*);
  Somersham
— croft in par. of St Andrew, 229
— earl of, *see* Holand, John
— fee of Chatteris abbey in, 230
— prison in, 230
— property in, 27, 29, 39, 63; 3 (fo. 74r)
— rent in, 230
— small bridge in, 230
— tofts in, 230
— Bridge Street (*vico pontis*), 230
— Tiled House (*Aula Teculata*), 230
— *see also* Fin, Robert, of; Richard,
  cobbler, of;
Hutton, Elinor, nun of Chatteris, 104,
  409, 418, 420
— James, commissary of the bp of Ely,
  21
Hyldemere, Alan, 143
Hyldresham *see* Hildersham

I., abbess of Chatteris [*?or* J.], 391; 164
I..., John de, 93

Ickleton priory, 20, 23, 40, 47, 88–9, 96
Ide, Andrew, 48
Ilbert, Richard son of, rector of Foxton,
  alias Robert, Richard son of, 33; 129,
  131
Illary, Robert, of Hadleigh, 209–10
Impington (Empigton', Impetun'), land
  in, 31
— Hugh de, W 231
— — steward of Chatteris abbey (*?same*),
  76; W 240
— *see also* Basset, Michael, of
imprisonment, 259 (fo. 175r)
index of place-names, 278
Indyngword' [*?or* Judyngword'], Isabel
  de, 49–50; 232
infangthief, 5, 9
Ingelond', Richard, W 241
Ingleram, steersman (*sturesmannus*) of bp
  of Ely, Alexander son of, *alias*
  Alexander 'esturesman' of bp of Ely,
  90–1
— — — John son of, 90 (fo. 101v)
ingress and egress, of water at mills, 119,
  163
Ingreth', Richard, 38
inheritance, 149 (fo. 129v), 250, 259 (fo.
  176r); *see also* fee and heredity;
  hereditary right
Innocent II, pope, 10; 269 (fo. 182r), 270
  (fo. 182v)
— IV, pope, 27, 29–30, 36, 72–3, 120–1; 3
  (fo. 73v), 112, 181 (fo. 142r), 184
inquisition, 72; 161, 191, 260 (fo. 177v),
  261 (fo. 178v), 276
— *ad quod damnum*, 14–15; 8, 255–8
— commission to hold, 190
— post mortem, 212
inspection of documents, 126, 174, 181
  (fo. 143r), 182, 229, 276
inspeximus, 96–7, 102–3
institution to benefice, 266–7
Insula, Philip de, 150, 156, W 275
— Robert de, 52, 101; 87; *see also* Moler,
  Alice
— — Cassandra mother of, 87
— — Ralph father of, 87
— Simon de, 45; 68, W 281

— — Amicia wife of, **68**

— Warin de, **234**

inter-commoning, **279**

Ipswich (*Gypwicum, Yepeswych*), Suff., priory of Holy Trinity, prior of, **161**

— Avice, nun of Chatteris, **409**

Isabel, William son of, **129**

Isleham (*Giselam, Giselham, Iselham', Yselham*), **269** (fo. 181r)

Ivinghoe, Herts., St Margaret's priory, **6**, 12n

Ivo (*Yvo*), St, **8**, 120; **2**

J. abbess of Chatteris, *see* I.

J. smith (*le smyth'*), of Foxton, **241**

James, bp of Ely, *see* Stanley, James

James, clerk, *see* Fowlmere, William de

— — of Kersey, Suff., **189**

janitor, *see* porter

Jerusalem (*Jerosolimitanus*), pilgrimage to, 42, 58; **110**

jews, **83**, 114, 120, 211, 237

Jhoneson, Ralph, **77**

Joan, countess of Kent, **193**

— nun of Chatteris, **409**

— — (*another*), **410**

Joce, Gilbert, **71**

Jocelin (*Gocelin*), serjeant (*serviens*), proctor and attorney of Chatteris abbey, 77–8; **228**, W 240

Joecus, cook (*cocus*), **68**

John, bp of Ely, *see* Fountains, John of

— bp of London, *see* Kempe, John

— carter (*carectarius*), 75, 137

— — Goditha wife of, 75, 137

— cook (*cocus*), **17**, 59

— — (?*same*), **18**

— duke of Bedford, **259** (fo. 176v)

— king of England, **10**; 189

— prior of Ely, *see* Hemmingestone, John

— reeve (*prepositus*), **132**

— scribe (*scriptor*), **23**

— — Robert son of, **19**, 23

— smith (*faber*), **149** (fo. 128v)

— tailor (*talliour, taylour*), **257** (fo. 173r)

— vicar, **273**

— Pain son of, W 5

— Reginald son of, **158**

— Robert, chaplain, **252**

— Robert son of, **25**, 41

Jordan, W 110

— John son of, **240**

Joyce (*Joceus*), Reginald son of John, of Fulney, Lincs., **226**

judgement, 112, 129, 161, 171–3

Judith, niece of William I, **12**

Judyngword' *see* Indyngword'

jury, 129, 190–1, 201, 212, 256 (fo. 172r), 257 (fo. 173r), 260 (fo. 177v), 261 (fo. 178v)

justices, 178, 258, 259 (fo. 176v)

— in eyre, 133, 142, 148, 172–3, 189

Kant' *see* Kent

Kareseya, Kareseye, Kareshe, Karesheia, Karysseye, see Kersey

Katherine, St, light of, *see* Chatteris abbey

Keche (*Kithe*), John, 132, 139

Kelleshull', Richard de, 260n

Kempe, John, bp of London and abp of Canterbury, **23**; 266

Kent (*Kant'*), *see* Greenwich

— countess of, *see* Joan; Margaret

— earl of, *see* Edward, prince of Wales

Kerdington *see* Cardington

Kersey (*Kareseya, Kareseye, Kareshe, Karesheia, Karysseye, Keresey, Kereseye, Kerisey, Kerseie, Kerseye*), Suff., **278**

— bailiff of, 205; *see also* Skeet, John; Sugge, William

— — of countess of Kent, **193**

— — of countess of March, **199**

— — of earl of Huntingdon, 200, 202–3

— — of earl of March and Ulster, 195–7

— bridge (Kersey brigge), road from, 209–10

— church, 27, 33, 37, 43; **73**, 188, 204

— — road to, 209–10

— clerk of, *see* James

— court held at, 201, 210

— documents dated at, 209–10
— extent of manor of, 191
— fee of St Mary in, 186
— inquisition held at, 212
— land in, 185
— lord of, *see* Gray, Henry
— manor of, 12–14, 27, 33, 37, 39, 61, 64, 72, 77, 131; **186–7, 189–96, 198, 203, 205, 208, 212;** *see also* Kersey, vill of
— mill in, 27, 37, 71–2; **191**
— priory, 33
— — prior and convent of, 209–10
— section of cartulary rel. to, 121–2
— steward of earl of Huntingdon, *see* Wynter, Edmund
— tenants of, 187, 201
— tenement in, 209–10
— vill of, 3 (fo. 74r), 197, 199–202; *see also* Kersey, manor of
— Ralph de, 135
— — (*?same*), 145
— — (*?same*), W 233
— — of Chatteris (*?same*), W 234
— *see also* Gibbes, John, of; Halden, Richard, of; Meller, Thomas, of; Pery, Robert, of; Pusk, John, of; Skeet, John, of; Waleys, Adam de, of; Waryn, John, of; Webbe, Nicholas, of
Ketton (Keten', Ketene), Juliana de, 101–3
Killala (*Aladensis*), bp of, *see* Barrett, Thomas
Kille (Kylle), William, 244
king of England, 269 (fo. 180v); *see also* Cnut; Edmund II Ironside; Edward I; Edward II; Edward III; Henry I; Henry II; Henry III; Henry V; John; Richard I; Richard II; Stephen
— fee of, 104, 106
Kingestuna, *see* Kingston
King's Lynn *see* Lynn
Kingston (*Kingestuna, Kynchestuna*, Kyngeston', Kyngestun', *Kyngestuna*, Kynggeston, Kynggestone, Kyngston'), 269 (fo. 181v), 278
— property in, 48
— rents in, 43, 49; 111, 240
— revenue from temporalities in, 39; 264

— *see also* Sprotford, Richard de, of
Kithe *see* Keche
knight *see* Broadfield, Ralph; Gray, Henry; Haye, William de la; Henry; Mortimer, William de; Swythesthorp, Richard de
knight-service, 37; **212, 242, 269** (fo. 180v)
knight's fee, 189
knights templar, 227
— clerk of the Temple, *see* Thurstan
Knyth (Knygth), Hemerus le, 141
— Henry le, **128**
— Hugh le, 149 (fo. 129r)
Kokefeld' *see* Cockfield
Koo (Kos, Ku), John, 209–10
— William, 257 (fo. 173r)
Kopnote *see* Copnote
Kos *see* Koo
Ku *see* Koo
Kylle *see* Kille
Kynchestuna, Kyngeston', Kyngestun', *Kyngestuna*, Kynggeston, Kynggestone, Kyngston', *see* Kingston

labour-services 62, 65–8; **69, 191;** *see also* boon-work; carrying-service; plough-service
Lachingahytha, Lachingehetha, Lachingehida, Lachingehytha, see Lakenheath
Ladman, James son of William le, **18**
lake, 211
Lakenheath (*Lachingahytha, Lachingehetha, Lachingehida, Lachingehytha, Lagynca Hytha, Lakinghida*), Suff., **269** (fo. 181v)
lambs, ninth of, 260 (fo. 177r); *see also* sheep
Langley priory, Leics., 19, 84–5
Lansill', Thomas de, chaplain, 252
Lateran *see* Rome
Lavington (Laventon'), William de, adcn of Ely, 72; 165–7
— clerk of, *see* Stuntney, Richard de
Lawe, croft 'de la', 145

— wall 'de la', 145
— Elloria de la, 53; 115, 145
Laxton, Sir William, 32
Layer, John, 32, 75, 131
Layham (Leyham), Suff., manor of, 212
— Matthew de, 189
lay-sister of Chatteris abbey, *see*
  Chilham, Idonea de
leases, 62–4, 69–73, 76, 78, 102, 105
— in Barrington, 124
— in Foxton, 144
— for life, in Barrington, 118
— — in Chatteris, 51, 60, 71
— — in Foxton, 132, 138–9
— — in Kersey, Suff., 210
— — in Shepreth, 151
— for lives, 75, 137
— — in Chatteris, 69
— — in Foxton, 128
— — in Kersey, Suff., 209
— for ten years, in Shepreth, 163
leased lands in Kersey, Suff., 191
Leen *see* Lynn
Lega, see Leighs
Legat', Roger, 135
legate *see* Fieschi, Ottobuono;
  Longchamp, William
Legbourne priory, Lincs., 18–19
Leger', John, 145
Leigh, Dr Thomas, 87
Leighs (*Lega*), priory, prior of, 181 (fo.
  142r)
Leleseya, Lelseia, see Lindsey
Lenna, Lenn' Episcopi, Lennia, see Lynn
Lepham, Arnulph de, 189
Lesseya, see Lindsey
Lestere, Roger le, 230
letters of attorney, 228
letters patent, 95, 171, 182
— royal, 8, 190, 255, 256 (fo. 172v), 258–
  9, 260n
'Leverycchez' (?tenement in Chatteris),
  280
Lewis, adcn of, *see* Passelewe, Robert
Leyham *see* Layham
leyrwite, 68
Liber Eliensis, 8, 10–11, 25–6, 79, 99, 120,
  126–8; 2n, 4n, 5n, 6n, 269n, 270n

liberties, 3, 5, 9, 17, 55, 59, 89, 116–17,
  119, 122, 189, 213, 215–16, 218, 242,
  269 (fo. 180v), 270 (fo. 183r)
liberum servicium, see service, of
  freeholder
licence to acquire property in mortmain,
  8, 255, 256 (fo. 172v), 258, 259 (fo.
  176r)
life tenure, 51, 60, 69, 71, 75, 118, 128,
  131–2, 137–9, 151, 176, 185, 209n,
  210, 227
light (*lumen, luminare*), *see* Chatteris
  abbey, light
Lincoln (*Lincolnia*), 278
— bps of, 11–12; *see also* Eadnoth, bp of
  Dorchester
— county of, *see* Fulney; Pinchbeck;
  Scopwick
— diocese of, 9, 12, 18
— land in, 27; 3 (fo. 74r)
— rent in, 29, 43, 53, 63, 78, 101–2; 227–
  8
— David son of *Eilsus* de, 227
Lindsey (*Leleseya, Lelseia, Lesseya*), Suff.,
  chapel of, 43; 73, 188, 204
Linton (*Lynton'*), Geoffrey de, 65
— Gilbert de, W 233
Lisle, Thomas de, bp of Ely, 17, 22, 87–8,
  92
Litelmold' (*Lytelmold'*), William, 61
Liteltiædford, Liteltiedford,
  Lithlethedford, *see* Thetford, Little
Litlebir', Litlebiri', *see* Littlebury
Litlethetford *see* Thetford, Little
Litlington (*Littyngton'*), ninth in, 261
  (fo. 178r)
Littlebury (Litlebir', Litlebiri',
  Lytlebur'), John de, 281
— Martin de, justice of common pleas,
  178
Littlemore priory, Oxon., 85
Little Thetford *see* Thetford, Little
Litton (*Littone, Luyton'*), Geoffrey de,
  35, 62
— Gilbert son of Gilbert de, of Chatteris,
  234
— — Agnes wife of, 234
Littyngton' *see* Litlington

loaves, 144

Lolworth (Lolleworth', Lolleworthe), John, 257 (fo. 173r)

London (*Londonia, Londonie*, Londres, *Lundonia*), Ælfheah buried at, 2
— adcn of, 181 (fo. 142r-v)
— bp of, *see* Baldock, Ralph; FitzNeal, Richard; Kempe, John; Niger, Roger
— cathedral of St Paul, chapter of, 36, 64; 181
— — dean of, *see* Lucy, Geoffrey de
— diocese of, taxation in, 260 (fo. 177r)
— document dated at, 196
— Holy Trinity priory, Aldgate, prior of, 112
— lands of monks of Ely in, 269 (fo. 182r)
— men of city and diocese of, 112
— St Bartholomew's priory, prior of, 112
— St Helen's priory, Bishopgate, 57, 88

Longchamp, William, bp of Ely, papal legate and chancellor, 34; 9, 79

lord of the fee *see* fee

Lovell (Luvel), Maurice, 212n
— Roger, W 240

Lovetopp, John, clerk, W 210
— William, W 210

Lowe, Richard son of John de la, of Foxton, 125–6, 134

Lucius II, pope, 10; 269 (fo. 180r)

Lucy, Geoffrey de, dean of St Paul's cathedral, London, 64; 182

Lugd', *see* Lyons

Lundonia, see London

Luton', Gervase de, W 275

Luvel *see* Lovell

Luyton' *see* Litton

Lyminster priory, Sussex, 12

Lyndon' (Lyadon'), Robert son of Robert de, 69
— — Juliana wife of, 69

Lynn (Leen, *Lenna, Lenn' Episcopi, Lennia*), later King's Lynn, Norf., 278
— burgess of, *see* Copnote, John; Wimar, William
— church of St Margaret, 218–19
— — cemetery of, 213–17
— land in, 30, 63–4, 122; 213–17, 219

— mayor and corporation of, 220
— — tenement of, 220
— messuages in, 218
— Alice de, nun of Chatteris, 410
— Warin son of Gilbert de, 218
— *see also* Alexander, butcher, of; Elwin, cordwainer, of

Lynton' *see* Linton

Lyons (*Lugd'*), France, documents dated at, 112 (fo. 111v), 181 (fo. 142v)

Lytelmold' *see* Litelmold'

Lyteltieford *see* Thetford, Little

Lytlebur' *see* Littlebury

M., abbess of Chatteris, 50, 393; 138, 228, 232

Ma..., John, 212n

Mabel, abbess of Chatteris, *see* Bancis, Mabel de
— Richard son of, 143

Madingley (Madingele, Maddyngel', Maddynggel', Maddyngl', Maddyngle, Maddynglee, Madynglee), 278
— manorial court for, 16, 74
— property in, 29–30, 39, 42, 58, 60, 68–9, 93, 105; 109–10, 238–9, 281
— revenue from temporalities in, 264
— 'Aschwieshevvedland', 239
— 'Bernewelledych', 'Bernoluesdychs', 110, 239
— 'Clynt', 239
— 'F. Pockedeha...ke', 239
— 'Litlebureshenet', 238
— 'Litlewellebrot'', 239
— 'Sigares Broke', 238
— 'Mersse', 239
— 'Morolwesdale', 239
— 'Musemere', 239
— Aubrey son of Eustace de, 29, 58, 105; 110, 238

Malketon', Avice de, 149 (fo. 129r)

Malling abbey, Kent, 6, 12n

malt, 269 (fo. 181v)

man in Bircham, Norf., grant of, 91, 222–4; *see also* men

mandate, papal, 112, 181

Mandeville (Maundevyle), fee of, **65**
Mannessune, Æthelstan, 25, 79, 100
manor, of Barley, Herts., **271**
— of Chatteris, **274**
— of Doddington, **257** (fo. 173v)
— of Kersey, Suff., **186-7, 189-96, 198,
    205, 208, 212**
— of Shepreth, **162**
— of Stuntney, **269** (fo. 181r)
— of Thriplow, **165**
— *see also* court, manorial
Manton', William, **127**
manumission, 68-9; **271, 274**; *see also*
    declaration
manuring, **136**
March (Marc', Marche, la Marche,
    Marchia), **279**
— countess of, *see* Anne
— earl of, *see* Mortimer, Edmund
— Richard, **124**
Marchaunt, Alexander, **212**n
Marche, la Marche, *Marchia, see* March
marescallus, mareschallus, see marshall
Margaret, 30
— countess of Kent, **194**
Margery formerly wife of Andrew son of
    Alan *see* Alan
Marham abbey, Norf., 47
market-day, **191**
Markyate priory, Beds., 93
marriage-portion, 49; **83, 111**; *see also*
    dower
Marrick priory, Yorks. N., 62, 88, 102
marsh, in Chatteris, **19, 27, 40, 211, 279**
— in Doddington, **243-4, 248-9, 251**
Marsh (*de Marisco*), Stephen, W **235**
marshall (*marescallus, mareschallus*), *see*
    Reynold; Stockton, John de
Martin, Hugh, **156**
— Hugh son of (?same), *alias* Shepreth,
    Hugh son of Martin de, **133, 142, 148**
— — Matilda wife of, **133, 142, 148**
— — — Alice sister of, *alias*, Chapel,
    Alice wife of Aubrey, **133, 142, 148**
— Robert, 35; **155**
— Simon son of Walter, of Shepreth, 42,
    45; **149, 156**
— Walter, of Shepreth, W **162**n

Martyn, Katherine, nun of Chatteris, 410
martyrs, **2**
Marvin (Martyn), John, of Thriplow,
    168
Mary, half-sister of Henry II, abbess of
    Shaftesbury, 100
— St, chaplain of, *see* William
— — fee of, **186**
— — light of, *see* Chatteris abbey
— — mass of, *see* Chatteris abbey
mass, 50, 54, 86, 102, 104-5; **2, 115, 240**
Mathewe, John, 54
Matilda, empress, seal of, 95
Maud, sister of Henry III, abbess of
    Barking, 101
Maurice, porter (*janitor*), W **204**
Mayseynt, Alice, **18**
meadow, **3** (fo. 74v)
— in Barley, Herts., **172**
— in Barrington, **113, 116-17, 120-2,
    124**
— in Bluntisham, Hunts., **269** (fo. 181r)
— in Chatteris, **13-14, 17, 19, 28, 34, 55,
    59, 63, 69, 80, 83, 211, 233-4, 256-8,
    275**
— in Doddington, **243, 247, 256-8**
— in Foxton, **119, 128-30, 132, 139-40,
    143, 147**
— in Hemingford, Hunts., **272**
— in Kersey, Suff., **186**
— in Madingley, **238-9**
— in Shepreth, **152, 155, 159**
— in Stuntney, **90-1**
— in Wimblington, **256-8**
Measse, Margaret, 55, 57
Mech, Meche, *see* Merchyt
Melbourn (*Meldeburna*), **269** (fo. 181v)
Meldreth (*Melreda, Melretha*), **269** (fo.
    181v)
Melksham (Melkesham), Richard de, W
    235
Meller *see* Millere
Melreda, Melretha, see Meldreth
Melton (*Meltona, Meltuna*), Suff., **269** (fo.
    181v)
memoranda rolls, **191, 262**
memorandum, **263**

men in Burwell, surrender of, **236**; *see also* man

Mepal (Mephale), lady of, fee of, 60

— — land of, **34**

'Mepus' *see* Shepreth

merchant (*mercator*), *see* Brecham, Ralph

merchet (*guersumma pro filia sua*), 65, 68; **144**

Merchyt (Mech, Meche, Merthyt), Henry de, 49; **22, 64**

— — Ismaena wife of, *see* Briston, Ismaena dau. of Ralph

messenger (*nuncius*), 95, 170

messor (reap-reeve), *see* Adam

messuage, in Barrington, 100, 113, 116–18, 120–4, 237

— in Bluntisham, Hunts., 269 (fo. 181r)

— in Cambridge, 104, 106–8, 152

— in Chatteris, 17–18, 23, 51, 55–6, 59–60, 68–9, 71, 256–8

— in Doddington, 246–9, 251–3, 256–8

— in Ely, 92–3

— in Foxton, 128–30, 132–3, 138–42, 145

— in Hemingford, Hunts., 272

— in Kersey, Suff., 191, 209–10

— in Kingston, 111

— in Lynn, Norf., 218

— in Shepreth, 150–1, 153, 155–7, 185

— in Thriplow, 168

— in Wimblington, 256–8

— *see also* buildings; house

Middlesex (Midd'), archdeaconry of, taxation in, 260 (fo. 177r)

mill-door, 149 (fo. 129r)

miller (*molendini, molendinarius*), *see* Arnold; Barrington, Warin de; Henry

Millere (Meller), John, **201**

— — (?*same*), W **209**

— Thomas, of Kersey, Suff., 209

mill-pond, 119, 149 (fo. 129v), **159, 163**

mills, 71–3; **3** (fo. 74v)

— in Barrington, 27, 37, 59, 71–3; **3** (fo. 74r), **118**

— — tithes of, 71; **112**

— in Bilney, Norf., 30, 72–3; **82**

— in Chatteris, 72–3; **28**

— in Foxton, 27, 37, 59, 71–3; **3** (fo. 74r), **119**

— in Kersey, Suff., 27, 37, 71–2; **191**

— in Shepreth, 27, 37, 71–3; **3** (fo. 74r), **149** (fo. 129r), **163**

— in Thriplow, 27, 43–4, 59, 72; **3** (fo. 74r), 7, **95**, 165–7

millstones, **163**

ministers, 258, 269 (fo. 181v)

minister's accounts, 30–1, 36, 38–40, 60–1, 69–70, 72, 75–7

Minster in Sheppey priory, Kent, 6, 12, 88

'The Mirror of Simple Souls', quotation from, 99; **207**

Mody, William son of Adam, **245**

molendini, molendinarius, *see* miller

Moler, Alice daughter of Richard, kinswoman (*consanguinea*) of Robert de Insula, nun of Chatteris, 52, 101, 410; **87**

Monacus, *see* Moyngne

Montacute, Simon, bp of Ely, 84

Montgomery, Roger de, earl of Shrewsbury, 12, 13n

Moor, Mor, Mor', *see* More

Mora, Michael de, fee of, **127**

More (Moor, Mor, Mor'), Thomas, of Balsham, escheator in Cambs., 256 (fo. 172r), 257 (fo. 173r), 258 (fo. 174v)

Morgan, Philip, bp of Ely, **267**

mort d'ancestor, 142

Mortimer (*Mortuo Mari*), Edmund, earl of March and Ulster, 195–7

— Robert de, **135**

— William de, knight, W **162n**

mortmain, 259 (fo. 176r)

— statute of, 41; **8**, 255–8

mother-church, Shepreth, **162**

Mountfitchet, barony of, 13

mowing, 69, 144, 279

Moyngne (*Monachus*), Alice formerly wife of Geoffrey le, *see* Thomas, chaplain, Alice niece of

— Berenger le, **56**

— Verenger, husband of Isabel de Hemingford (?*same*), **272**

multure, 71–3; **163**
muniments *see* evidence
murder-fine, **109**, **167**
Muschet, Richard, 45, 49, 60; **92**
— — Pain uncle of, *see* Alexander, Pain
son of
Myldebourn' (Myldeborn', Myldeburn'),
Richard de, of Barley, Herts., 171
— — Richard son of, 58; **171–2**

nativi, *see* villeins
*Neuetuna, Neutona, Newentuna,
Newetuna, see* Newton
'Neustale', fishery, *see* Upwell and
Outwell
Neve, Henry, chaplain, 105
Newmarket (*Novo Foro*), Peter de, W
234
Newton (*Neuetuna, Neutona, Newentuna,
Newetuna*), **269** (fo. 181v)
Nicholas IV, pope, *see* taxation
— chaplain, M, W **204**
— chaplain of the cross, W **204**
Nigel, bp of Ely, 10, 13–14, 24–5, 29, 34–
5, 41, 45, 47, 61–2, 72, 123–4, 128; **10,
76, 89, 109, 165–7, 185–6**, **269** (fo.
180r), **270** (fo. 182v)
Niger, Roger, 94, 96–7
— — bp of London, **181–2**
night, in fishery, 87, 89
ninth, subsidy of, **260–2**
Noreis (Nores, Noreys, Norreis), Agnes
formerly wife of Azo le, of Chatteris,
39
— Azo le, son of Robert, 49; **25, 27, 32–
3, 37, 40–1, 43, 67**
— — (*another*), 211
— — father of Robert le, 42
— Emma daughter of Azo, 52, 54, 61, 81
— Robert le, son of Azo, 49; **19, 25, 41–
2**, W **281**
— — (?*another*), 234
— — Margaret wife of, 49; **25, 41**
Norfolk *see* Bilney; Bircham; 'Fotestorp';
Lynn; Terrington; Upwell and
Outwell; Hert, William, of

Norreis *see* Noreis
Northwold, Hugh de, bp of Ely, 37, 64,
72; **15, 95, 112**
Norton, Agnes, prioress of Chatteris,
100, 403
— Isabel, nun of Chatteris, 100, 410
Norwich (Northwic, *Northwicum*,
Northwyc, Nortwic, Norwic,
Norwycum), adcn of, *see* Alexander,
chaplain
— burgess of, *see* Chaumppayne, William
— castle of, **269** (fo. 180v)
— diocese of, income of abbess of
Chatteris in, 263
— men of city and diocese of, **112**
notification, of agreement, 130
— of bond to warrant, 171
— of gift, 141, 231
— of grant, **95**
— of lease, 69
— of quitclaim, 185
— of rent owed, **218**
— of settlement, 161
Novo Foro, see Newmarket
Nun Appleton priory, Yorks. W., 93
Nun Cotham priory, Lincs., 52
Nuneaton priory, Warwicks., 95
Nunkeeling priory, Yorks. E., 88, 95
Nunminster *see* Winchester
Nun Monkton priory, Yorks. E., 88

oath, 162, 190, 201, 212, **256** (fo. 172r),
257 (fo. 173r), **260** (fo. 177v), **261** (fo.
178v); *see also* pledge
— swearing of, 22, 51, 64, 90, 143, 162,
169, **181** (fo. 143v), **185, 222**
oats, 144
oblations, 36; **164, 269** (fo. 181r)
obventions, 35; **79, 162**
Oen, Oeyn, *see* Owen
offences pardoned, 259
Offton (Ofton, Ufton), Agnes de, nun of
Chatteris, 98, 410
— *see also* Colman, John, of
Oggerston (Ogerestan), Gilbert de,
knight templar, W **227**

oratory, 162
order to pay rent, 7, 193, 196, 202, 208
Ordgarus, 180
Oressy, Hugh, 261 (fo. 178v)
Orford, Robert, bp of Ely, 23, 71, 92
Orwell, property in, 12, 27, 30-1, 37, 60
Osbert, rector (*persona*) of Barley, Herts.,
    36; 180
— Reginald son of, 152
— William son of, 111
Oswald, St, abp of York, 26; 2
Ottobuono, cardinal deacon of St
    Adrian, *see* Fieschi
Ousthorp, John de, clerk, 247
Outwell *see* Upwell
Over (Hovere, Overe), 278
— church, fee of, 101-3
— — patrons of, 102
— — rector of, *see* Seaton, Roger de
— land in, 3 (fo. 74r)
— manorial court for, 16-17, 74-5
— property in, 12-14, 25-7, 30, 37, 39,
    67-9
— revenue from temporalities in, 264
— road in, 101-3
— tofts exchanged in, 62; 101-3
— Lucy, nun of Chatteris, 101, 411
Owen (Oen, Oeyn, Owe', Owein,
    Owyn'), William, *alias* Owen,
    William son of, 15, 17-18, 59

Palavicino, Henry, 32
Palfreman, Anna, nun of Chatteris, 411
papal judges delegate, 36, 64, 71; 112,
    181-2
parceners, 172
pardon, 259
parliament, 259 (fo. 175r), 260n
parson (*persona*), *see* Crochem, Roger;
    Osbert; Phil', Walter; Simon;
    Thomas; Walter
Parva Thetford, Parva Thetforth', *see*
    Thetford, Little
Passelewe, Robert, adcn of Lewes, [rector
    of Barley, Herts.], 36-7, 64, 71; 112
pasture, 3 (fo. 74v), 270 (fo. 183r)

— in Barley, Herts., 172
— in Barrington, 116, 119, 122
— in Chatteris, 13-14, 55, 80, 279
— in Doddington, 246-7
— in Foxton, 119, 147
— in Kersey, Suff., 186, 191
— in Shepreth, 155
— in Thriplow, 168
path (*semita*), 3 (fo. 74v), 116, 119, 122,
    149 (fo. 128v), 155; *see also* road
patronage of Chatteris abbey, 4
patrons, of Barley church, Herts., 277
— of Over church, 102
Pecche, Gilbert, W 275
Peit (Peyte), Jordan, 35, 62
Pekkesbregg', Simon son of Joyce
    (*Joeceus*) de, 226
Pelryn (Pelerin), Michael, W 281
— Simon, W 275
Pemberton, Richard, 212
pension, 161
Penw..., Robert, of Doddington, 245
pepper, as rent, 281
Percy, John, chaplain, son of the late
    Thomas Percy of Cambridge, 45; 108
Peregrinus, Michael, 52; 26
— — Henry father of, 52, 101; 26
— — Tecla sister of, nun of Chatteris, 52,
    101, 411; 26
perquisites *see* court, manorial
Persun, William, 149, fo. 128v
Pery (Perye, Pyrye), Robert, of Kersey,
    Suff., 209-10, 212n
— — Agnes, wife of, 209-10
— — Meliora, formerly wife of, 210
Peter, butcher (*carnifex*), 219
— M, uncle of William of Ely, *see*
    Stuntney, Peter de
— Geoffrey son of, W 9
'petit cariante' *see* carrying-service
petition, 22, 64, 87, 166-7
— for rent owed, 190, 195, 200
— to king, 6, 260n
— to pope, 181, 270 (fo. 182v)
— to prior and convent of Ramsey, 164
Peverel, Elizabeth, 84
Peyte *see* Peit
Phichien *see* Fithien

Phil' (Pil'), Walter, parson of church of
  St Peter, Chatteris, 10, 76
Philip, W 231
— bp of Ely, *see* Morgan, Philip
— Alan son of, 116, 122
Philippa, abbess of Romsey, 22
Pichiun' (Pychyun'), John, of Chatteris,
  see Fithien, John
Picot, Ernald, 42
Pil' *see* Phil'
pilgrimage to Jerusalem, 110
Pincebec *see* Pinchbeck
pincerna, see Aubigny, William de
Pinchbeck (Pincebec, Pinchbek,
  Pynchebec), Lincs., 278
— rent in, 43; 226
pipe roll, 10; 260 (fo. 177r), 261 (fo. 178r)
Pipewell abbey, Northants., 108
Pirun (Piron', Pyrun), Peter, 101–3
Piteman [land in Shepreth], 149 (fo.
  128v)
place-dates, at Balsham, 112
— at Barley, Herts., 171
— at Berkhamsted, Herts., 193
— at Cambridge, 257
— at Chatteris, 192, 203, 205, 225, 230
— at Chatteris abbey chapter-house, 266,
  271, 274, 276
— at Doddington, 245
— at Downham, Little, 16, 77
— at Eling, Hants., 6n
— at Ely, 97
— at Foxton, 124, 241
— at Hadham, 161
— at Kersey, Suff., 209–10
— at London, 196
— at Lyons, France, 112 (fo. 111v), 181
  (fo. 142v)
— at Rome, 269–70
— at St-Pierre-sur-Dives, France, 5
— at Westminster, 7–9, 190 (fo. 147r),
  255, 256 (fo. 173r), 258 (fo. 175r), 259
  (fo. 176v)
plain, 3 (fo. 74v), 116, 122, 186
plea, of charter of warranty, 178
pledge, 225; *see also* oath
plough-service, 144; *see also* boon-work;
  carrying-service; labour-services

plough-team (*caruca*), 144, 147
poem, quotation from, 207
Polesworth abbey, Warwicks., 4, 88
Poleyn, Margaret, nun of Chatteris, 98,
  411
Polstead (Polsted'), William, W 209
Polwere, Alexander, of Doddington, 243
Pompun, John son of John, of Barley,
  Herts., 58; 175
Pondez, Powers, 280
Ponte Largo (Pont de l'Arche), William
  de, W 6n
Pontem, Walter *ad, see* Bridge
poor, the, 11, 33, 49, 53, 67
pope *see* Alexander III, Innocent II,
  Innocent IV, Lucius II, Nicholas IV,
  Victor II
— letters of, 112, 181–2
— mandate of, 112, 181
— privilege of, 3, 269–70
— *see also* papal judges delegate
porter (*janitor*), *see* Maurice; Simon
portus, see harbour
potter (le pottere), *see* Geoffrey; William
power of attorney, 228
prayers, 149 (fo. 129v), 177–8
— of intercession, 1
prebend, 53; 94–7, 227; *see also* annuity;
  rent
prepositus, see reeve
presentation, in exchange of benefices,
  273
— to vicarage of Chatteris, 11–12, 78–9,
  267
— to vicarage of Shepreth, 268
— to rectory of Barley, Herts., 266, 277
presentment, 189
Prestwick (Prestwik), [royal scribe], 259
  (fo. 176v)
priest (*sacerdos*), *see* Augustine, Baldwin;
  Henry, Andrew son of; William
privilege, papal, 27, 29–30, 36, 72–3, 120–
  1, 123, 128; 3, 184, 269–70
proctor *see* Chatteris abbey; Ely, prior
  and convent of
procuration, 263
profession of nuns, 17; 3 (fo. 74v)
promise, 147

Prykke, John, 257 (fo. 173r)
Prylle, Robert, 212n
psalm, 206
Puiset, Hugh du, bp of Durham, W 9
punishment, 259 (fo. 176v)
Pusk (Puske), James, W 209
— John, of Kersey, Suff., 209–10, 212n
Pychynn' *see* Pichinn'
Pynchebec *see* Pinchbeck
Pynder, Elinor, nun of Chatteris, 411
Pyper, Simon, 280
Pyrun *see* Pirun
Pyrye *see* Pery

querela, *see* dispute
Queye *see* Stow cum Quy
quitclaim, in Barley, Herts., 171–4
— in Barrington, 185
— in Cambridge, 107
— in Chatteris, 29, 38, 43–4, 66, 80, 83, 233, 254, 275
— in Doddington, 254
— in Foxton, 133, 135, 142, 148, 185
— in Kersey, Suff., 185
— in Shepreth, 153–4, 185
— in Stuntney, 90
— in Thetford, Little, 90
— in Thriplow, 95
— in Upwell and Outwell, Cambs. and Norf., 90
quitrent, *passim*
— confirmation of, in Cambridge, 106
— grant of, in Cambridge, 104

R. [benefactor in Madingley], 239
Radewyn', Richard, of Swaffham Prior, 44; 80
Ragenhulle, Robert de, 105
Rakeh', John de, 135
Ralph, bp of Ely, *see* Walpole, Ralph de
— chaplain of Chatteris, 105; W 238
— rector of Barley, Herts., *see* Cardingon, Ralph de
— tailor (le taillur'), 121
— — (*cissor*) (?*same*), 143

— vicar [of Chatteris], W 233
— Ralph son of, 149
Ramsey abbey (Rames', Ramesch', *Rameseia*, *Rameseya*, Ramesey, Rameseye, Ramesh', Rameys', *Ramisiensem*, Rampsey, Ramsye, *Remeseia*), Hunts., 25–6, 70, 79
— abbot of, 14, 27, 38, 70, 79–80; *see also* Eadnoth; Godmanchester, William of; Wulfsige
— — election of, 164
— — land of, 32, 34, 37, 58, 63, 67
— — land held of, 33
— — meadow of, 234
— abbot and convent of, patrons of Over church, 102
— bodies of St Ivo and Eadnoth brought to, 8; 2
— books and evidence of, 130; 279
— disputes with Chatteris abbey, 35–6; 164
— monks of, 164
— prior of, *see* Foliot, Hugh
— Joan, nun of Chatteris, 411
— Margery, abbess of Chatteris, 21, 23, 96, 100, 401
Ranulf, Walter son of, W 243
Rasen [royal scribe], 125; 255
Ray, Richard le, 30
Rayment, Richard, vicar of Shepreth, 35
reaping, 69, 136, 144
reap-reeve (*messor*), *see* Adam
recognitio, *see* acknowledgement
recovery, of damages, 171
— of lands, 172, 269 (fo. 181r), 270 (fo. 183r)
rector, of Barley, Herts., *see* Cardington, Ralph; Herbert; Osbert; Richard
— of Foxton, *see* Bagnaria, Manuel de; Ilbert, Richard son of; Shelford, Peter de; Simon
— of Over, *see* Seaton, Roger de
— of Stok', *see* Stok'
rectory of Barley, Herts., 266
redditus assisus, *see* rent, fixed
Rede (Reede, Reyde), Agnes formerly wife of William le, 49

— Anne, nun of Chatteris, 104, 411–12, 418, 420

— Thomas, 280

Redewyk, Agnes, nun of Chatteris, 412

Redlingfield priory, Suff., 12

Reede *see* Rede

reeve (*prepositus*), 77; *see also* Baldwin; Doddington, William son of Hugh de; Hugh; John

register of bishop of Ely, 109

Reigate (Beigate), John de, justice in eyre, 172

Reinaldus, see Reynold

Reissemere *see* Rushmere

release, of claim in advowson, 179

— of rent, 44; 38, 47, 80

— of villein-service, 100, 123

relief (*redemptio, relevium*), 65, 100, 123, 240, 256 (fo. 173r), 257 (fo. 174r), 259

remainder-clause, 139, 210, 227

remembrancer, king's, 212

Remeseia, see Ramsey

remission, of disputes, 164

— of ward-penny, 6

— — confirmation of, 9

rent, fixed (*redditus assisus*), 191

— held of king, 8, 255

— in Chatteris, 3 (fo. 74r), 13–14

— in kind, *see* capons, clove, eels, gloves, hens, pepper, spurs, wax

— money, *passim*

— — acknowledgement of, in Kersey, Suff., 187

— — acquittance of, 7, 192, 194, 197–9, 202–3, 205, 219–20, 225

— — arrears of, 259 (fo. 176r)

— — — in Bircham, Norf., 225

— — — in Hemingford Grey, Hunts., 231

— — — in Huntingdon, 230

— — — in Kersey, Suff., 189–90, 192– 200, 202–3, 205, 208

— — — in Lynn, Norf., 218–19

— — — in Thriplow, 7

— — collection of, in Lincoln, 228

— — confirmation of, in Foxton, 126

— — — in Hemingford, Hunts., 232

— — — in Rushmere, Suff., 269 (fo. 181v)

— — from church, 73, 188, 204

— — grant of, 29–30, 43, 49, 101–2

— — — in Barrington, 114

— — — in Cambridge, 105, 108

— — — in Chatteris, 20–21, 55, 65, 70, 256–8

— — — in Doddington, 256–8

— — — in Ely, 99

— — — in Kingston, 240

— — — in Huntingdon, 230

— — — in Lincoln, 227

— — — in Pinchbeck, Lincs., 226

— — — in Shepreth, 155

— — — in Stuntney, 90–1

— — — in Thetford, Little, 90–1

— — — in Upwell and Outwell, Cambs. and Norf., 90

— — — in Wimblington, 256–8

— — notification of, in Lynn, Norf., 218

— — order to pay, 7, 193, 196, 202, 208

— — release of, in Chatteris, 44, 103; 38, 47, 80

— — reserved in charters, 43–4

— *see also* annuity; fee-farm; prebend; quitrent

rent-seck ('rentt seke'), 189

repairs (*emendationes*), 139

reservation (*retenementum*), 32, 84–8, 115, 119, 125, 127, 134, 154–5, 157, 240

restitution of lands and liberties, 269 (fo. 180v)

revelation of body of St Ivo, 2

revenue (*exitus*), 190, 212, 256 (fo. 172v), 257 (fo. 173v), 258, 259 (fo. 176r)

reversion, 51, 60, 69, 118, 130, 132, 163, 176, 252; *see also* surrender

Reyde *see* Rede

Reynold (*Reinaldus*), marshal (*mareschallus*), W 204

Reynold', John, of Dry Drayton, 130; 276

Ria, see Rye

Richard I, king of England, 95; 6n, 9

— II, king of England, 22; 256 (fo. 172r), 258 (fo. 174r)

— adcn of Ely and treasurer, *see* FitzNeal, Richard

— bp of London, *see* FitzNeal, Richard
— clerk of William de Lavington, *see* Stuntney, Richard de
— cobbler (le cobeler'), of Huntingdon, 229–30
— rector of Barley, Herts., 36; 181 (fo. 142)
— Agnes, nun of Chatteris, 98, 412
— Gilbert son of, 239
— Robert son of, 121
— — knight templar, W 227
Ridel (Rydel), Geoffrey, bp of Ely, 45, 100; 94–7, 129n, 130n
right, episcopal, 160
— episcopal and parochial, 11–12, 78
ring, hand amputated for, 2
Rissemera, Rissemere, *see* Rushmere
road, 3 (fo. 74v), 19, 24, 32, 34, 36–7, 45, 56, 67, 107, 116, 119, 122, 127, 135, 145–6, 149, 155, 163, 176, 209–10, 219; *see also* path
— closure of, 101–3
Robert, servant *see* Stuntney, Richard de
— J. son of, 239
— Richard son of, rector of Foxton, *see* Ilbert, Richard son of
rod (*virga*) of bishop, carrying of, 257 (fo. 173v), 280
Roger, bp of London, *see* Niger, Roger
— bp of Salisbury, W 6n
— chaplain of Chatteris, 105; W 110, W 238
— prior of Ely, *see* Bergham, Roger de
— smith (*faber*), 135
— — (?*same*), 163
— — (?*same*), 144
— — Roger son of, 65; 144
— steward, 238
— — Alice daughter of, 238
— Hugh son of, 239
Roland, Richard son of, 82
Rome, the Lateran, documents dated at, 269–70
— pope of, *see* Alexander III; Innocent II; Innocent IV; Lucius II; Victor II
Romsey abbey, Hants., 3–4, 22, 37, 62, 96

Roseby (Boseby, Rosbery, Rosebi), Robert de, 122; 98, 235
— — Agnes daughter of, 122; 98
— — Chastanea wife of, 235
Rouen (*Rothomago*), A. de, abbess of Chatteris, 393; 93
Rowe, Thomas, 32
Rowlatt, Ralph, 32
royal charters, 5–9, 190, 255–6, 258–9, 278
Royston (*de Cruce Roesia, de Cruce Rois*), priory, prior of, 181 (fo. 142r)
Ruffe, Margery, 135
Ruffus, William, *see* Hemingford, Isabel de
Rufus, Geoffrey, chancellor, W 5, W 6n
Rule of St Benedict, 3 (fos. 74r, 75r), 269 (fo. 180v)
Ruly, Hubert de, 189
Rushmere (Reissemere, *Rissemera*, Rissemere, *Ryssimera*), Suff., 269 (fo. 181v)
Rya, *see* Rye
Rydel *see* Ridel
Rye (*Ria, Rya*), Hubert de, 221–2, 224
— — Henry father of, 221
Ryssimera, *see* Rushmere

sac and soc, 5, 9, 269 (fo. 181v)
sacerdos, *see* priest
Saham *see* Soham
St Bartholomew, priory of, prior of, *see* London
St Ives (*Slepa*), Hunts., church at, 2
— discovery of St Ivo at, 8, 120; 2
St Ivo *see* Ivo
St-Pierre-sur-Dives (*Sanctus Petrus desuper Divam*), France, document dated at, 5
St Radegund's priory, *see* Cambridge
St Sepulchre priory, *see* Canterbury
sale and quitclaim, 90
Sales, Alice de, 177
Salisbury, bp of, *see* Roger
Salman, John, 257 (fo. 173r)
salt, 269 (fo. 181r)

Sancto Claro (*Sancta Clara*), Mary de, abbess of Chatteris, 59, 99–100, 394–5; **51, 69, 100, 123, 141, 145, 231**
— Philip de, W **162n**
Sancto Georgio, Etheldreda de, nun of Chatteris, 101, 412
Sanctus Petrus desuper Divam, see St-Pierre-sur-Dives
Sarle (Serle), Roger, **33**
— Stephen son of Hugh, **34, 36**
Sauser, John le, M, **120**
Scalers (*Scalariis*), Hardwin de, **269** (fo. 181v)
Scapewic see Augustine, Baldwin
Scepeia, Scepere, *Scepereya*, *Scepereye*, Sceph', see Shepreth
Schelford' see Shelford
Schepeia, Scheper', Schepere, Scheperech', Schepereche, Scheperede, Scheperethe, Scheperey, *Schepereya*, Schepereye, Scheperheye, *Schepeya*, see Shepreth
Schuldam, Schuldham, see Shouldham
Scolicia, Geoffrey son of Walter son of, 70
Scopwick (Scapewic), Lincs., priest of, see Augustine, Baldwin
scot and lot, 144
scribe (*scriptor*), see John; see also Burton, Prestwick and Rasen, royal scribes, and Thurstan, clerk of the Temple
Sculham, William de, W **235**
scutage, **231, 259** (fo. 176r), **269** (fo. 180v)
seal, *passim*
— great, **260** (fo. 176v)
— privy, 8n, **255**
Seaton (Seyton), Roger de, M, rector of Over, justice of common pleas, 62; **101–3, 178**
Seemode (Seemod), land in Shepreth of, **149** (fo. 129r)
Self', Peter de, see Shelford, Peter de
selions, 25, 32–3, 37, 41, 53, 58, 63, 66–7, 69, 113, 234, 238
Sempole, John, **280**
senescallus, see steward

Seperch', Sepere, *Sepereia*, Seperey, *Sepereya*, Sepereye, *Sepereyha*, Seperheye, Seph', Sepherede, *Sephereya*, *Sepprea*, Seppree, see Shepreth
sequela, see family
serfdom, 271, 274, 276
serjeant (*serviens*), see Bancis, Thomas de; Jocelin
Serle see Sarle
servant (*serviens*), see Stuntney, Robert servant of Richard de
service, of carrying rod, 257, 280
— foreign, 43, 69, 111, 141
— of freeholder (*liberum servicium*), 221
— grant of, 115
— of king, 43, 116–17, 121–2, 231, 237, 281
— labour, 69, 144, 189, 191
— see also homage; knight-service
settlement of dispute, 79, 161, 180–2
Sewale (Suale), William, **149** (fo. 128v)
Sewardsley priory, Northants., 19
Sewter, Laurence, **280**
Seyton see Seaton
Shaftesbury abbey, Dorset, 3–4, 20, 22, 37, 40, 51, 96
sheep, 144, 167; see also animals; lambs
Shelford (Schelford', Self', Siolf'), Peter de, clerk, rector of Foxton, 33; **129–30**
Shepreth (*Scepeia*, Scepere, *Scepereya*, *Scepereye*, Sceph', *Schepeia*, Scheper', Schepere, Scheperech', Schepereche, Scheperede, Scheperethe, Scheperey, *Schepereya*, Schepereye, Scheperheye, *Schepeya*, Seperch', Sepere, *Sepereia*, Seperey, *Sepereya*, Sepereye, *Sepereyha*, Seperheye, Seph', Sepherede, *Sephereya*, *Sepprea*, Seppree, Shepe', *Shepeia*, Shepere, Sheprey), 278
— bailiff of, **161** (fo. 134r)
— bridge from Foxton, **149** (fo. 128v)
— chapel of William de la Haye in, 35, 131; **162**
— — chaplain of, **162**

— church, 24, 29–30, 33–5, 38–9; **3** (fo. 74r), **15n**, **16**, **77**, **160–2**, **261** (fo. 178v), **265**
— — advowson of, 32, 35; 160n
— — land of, **161**
— — vicar of, 35; **161**
— — — presentation of, **268**
— manorial court for, 16, 33, 67, 74–5
— mill in, 27, 37, 71–3; **3** (fo. 74r), **163**
— mill-pond in, **159**
— ninth in, **261–2**
— property in, 12–69 *passim*, 101; **3** (fo. 74r), **149–58**, **185**, **241**, **261** (fo. 178v)
— rent of bp of Ely in, **269** (fo. 181v)
— road to 'Archesford'', **149** (fo. 129r)
— road to Fowlmere, **149** (fo. 128v)
— steward of, **161** (fo. 134r)
— stream (*rivulus*) between Foxton and, **146**
— tenantry of Chatteris abbey in, **163**
— tithes in, 35; **161**
— villein of, 35; **161**
— 'Archesford'', road to, **149** (fo. 129r)
— 'Babbyngeshaveden', **149** (fo. 129r)
— 'le Banches', **149** (fo. 129r)
— Barrington, field towards, **149** (fo. 129r)
— 'le Blakelond', **149** (fo. 129r)
— 'le Brembaker', **149** (fo. 129r)
— Carver (Caleberwe), **149** (fo. 128v)
— 'le Crouch madwe', **149** (fo. 128v)
— Fowlmere, field towards, **149** (fo. 128v)
— 'le Fyshowes', **149** (fo. 129r)
— 'le Hale', **149** (fo. 129r)
— the Headland (*Forera*), **149** (fo. 128v)
— 'Heyhaveden', **149** (fo. 129r)
— 'Holmo' (Hulmo), **150**, **152**, **156**
— How (la Howe), **156**
— 'Irechemesaker', **149** (fo. 129r)
— 'Litlehowe', **149** (fo. 129v)
— 'Longelond'', **149** (fo. 128v)
— 'Melie', **158**
— 'Mepus', **149** (fo. 128v)
— — mill called, **163**
— 'le Mere', **149** (fo. 129r)
— 'Methlehowe', **149** (fo. 129r)
— 'Milleree' (Mylleree), **149** (fo. 128v)

— 'Niwemade', **159**
— Oslocks (Oslacunlue...), **152**
— 'le Peselond', **149** (fo. 129r)
— 'le Peth', **149** (fo. 129r)
— 'del Reydole', **149** (fo. 128v)
— 'le Sladeweye', **149** (fo. 128v)
— 'Smalemadwe', **149** (fo. 129r)
— 'Watelond'', **149** (fo. 129v)
— 'Westfeld'', **152**
— 'Wodesmanneshaveden'', **149** (fo. 129r)
— 'Wymundeshoga', **152**
— Alan de, **129**
— — (?*same*), W **239**
— Alan son of Alan de, 62; **146**
— Alan son of Robert de, 52, 101; **152**
— — Agatha dau. of, nun of Chatteris, 52, 101, 412; **152**
— Basilia de, **155**, **158**
— — Bartholomew, clerk, father of, **155**
— — Helen (Elloria), sister of, **155**, **158**
— — Isolda (Isodia), sister of, **155**, **158**
— — Robert brother of, **158**
— Hugh son of Martin de, *see* Martin, Hugh son of
— Osbert son of Beatrice de, **129**
— Ralph son of Ralph son of Fulk de, *see* Broadfield, Ralph son of Ralph son of Fulk de
— Richard son of Stamard de, **129**
— Robert son of Gorold de, **151**
— Walter de, **149**
— William son of Robert de (?*alias* Auger, William son of Robert son of Bartholomew son of), 58; **154**
— — (?*same*), **157**
— *see also* Binel, Reginald, of; Martin, Simon son of Walter, of; Martin, Walter, of
Sherborne abbey, Dorset, 117
sheriff, 258, **259** (fo. 176r); *see also* Cambridge, county of; Hertford, county of; Suffolk
— aid of, 109
— tourn of, 15; **231**
Shouldham (Schuldam, Schuldham) Norf., priory, 5–6, 47, 89

— Mary de, abbess of Chatteris, 76, 100, 397–8; **66, 71, 225, 229–30**
Shropham, Alice de, abbess of Chatteris, 20–1, 23, 84, 96, 100, 398–9; **194**
Sigillo, Robert de, W 6n
Simon (Symon), 107
— *(another)*, **150**
— chaplain, W **275**
— clerk, W **204**
— parson of Cranfield, Beds., 45; **236**
— porter *(janitor)*, **111**
— rector *(persona)* of Foxton, 34; W **110**
— — *(?same)*, **129**
— William brother of, **107**
sineschallus, see steward
sins, redemption of, **6, 227**
Siolf' *see* Shelford
Skeet (Skete), John, of Kersey, Suff., bailiff of earls of Huntingdon and March at Kersey, **197, 201, 203, 209–10**
Skele (Skyll), Margaret, nun of Chatteris, **413, 418, 420**
Skoyte, Thomas, **105**
Skyll *see* Skele
slander, **276**
Slepa, see St Ives
sluice *(exclusa)*, **119**
smith *(faber,* le smyth'), **2** (fo. 73r); *see also* J.; John; Roger; William
Smyth (Smythe), Ellen, prioress of Chatteris, **103, 403, 418, 420**
— Thomas, 212n
socage, **26, 189**
Soham (Saham), Hainey Hill (Heneiam, Heneieham, Heneiham, Heneyham), **269** (fo. 181r)
— Basilia de, **28**
— Mabilia de, **58**
— Warin de, **24, 32, 37, 45, 53**
Solomon, prior of Ely, **109**
Somersham (Someresham, Sumeresham, Summeresham), Hunts., wood in, **269** (fo. 181r)
— Emma de, abbess of Chatteris, 100, 395; **163, 177–9**
song, **206**
sowing, **136**

Speed (Sped'), Richard, **257** (fo. 173r)
Spenser, Geoffrey le, 44; **38**
— *see also* Despenser
spiritualities, of Chatteris abbey, valuation of, **265**
— of Chatteris abbey and Anglesey priory, in Barley, Herts., **260**
— — in Cambs., **261**
Sprot, Roger, W **281**
Sprotford, Richard de, of Kingston, **241**
spurs, gilded, as rent, **91, 189, 222–4**
Stabilford *see* Stapleford
Stacy, J., W **241**
Stamford priory, Northants., 47, 98
Stanley, James, bp of Ely, 36, 76; **277**
Stapleford (Stabilford, Stapelford), **269** (fo. 181v)
statute, of liveries, **259** (fo. 175r)
— of mortmain, 8, 255–8
Stephen, king of England, **269** (fo. 180v)
— Andrew, **129**
— Richard son of, **52, 54, 81**
— Robert son of, **24, 45**
— *see also* Chettisham, Stephen de
Stertlowe, John, **229**
Stetchworth (Steveceworda, Stewechewrda, Stivechesuurde, Stivecheswrda, Stivichesuurtha, Stivitheuurtha), **269** (fo. 181v)
steward *(senescallus, sineschallus), see* Roger
— of bishop of Ely, **95**
— of Chatteris abbey, 74–7; **161**; *see also* Impington, Hugh de
— of earl of Huntingdon, *see* Wynter, Edmund
Stixwould priory, Lincs., 19
Stocha, see Stoke
Stockton (Stokston, Stokton'), John de, marshall of bp of Ely, **246**
Stok' *(unidentifed)*, rector of church of, **112**
Stoke *(Stocha, Stoka, Stotha),* Suff., **269** (fo. 181v)
— dean of college of, *see* Wolflete, William
Stokston, Stokton', *see* Stockton
Ston', Hamo atte, of Hadleigh, **209**

Stotha, see Stoke

Stow cum Quy (Stowe, Stowe cum Qweia), ninth in, 261 (fo. 178r)

Stratford-at-Bow priory, Middx, 6, 12n, 57

stream (*filum aque, rivulus*), 146, 168; *see also* watercourse

Studley priory, Oxon., 93

Stukeley (Stivecle), John, 8, 11

Stuntney (*Stunteneia, Stunteneya, Stunteneye, Tunteneya*), 269 (fo. 181r), 278

— land in, 30, 42; 90 (fo. 101v), 91 (fo. 102v), 99

— rent in, 43; 90 (fo. 101v), 91 (fo. 102v)

— 'Haveril'' (Hevereshille, Heverhille), 90 (fo. 101v), 91 (fo. 102v), 278

— Peter de, M, uncle of William of Ely, 90 (fo. 101v), 91 (fo. 102v)

— Richard de, clerk of William de Lavington, *alias* Richard, clerk, 72; 165-7

— — Robert servant of, 166

sturesmannus, see Ingelram

Suafham, Suaham, *see* Swaffham Prior

Suale *see* Sewale

Sudbourne (*Sutburna, Suthburna*), Suff., 269 (fo. 181v)

Suffolk, escheator of, 191

— sheriff of, 190

— *see also* Barham; Cosford; Dunwich; Kersey; Lakenheath; Layham; Lindsey; Melton; Rushmere; Stoke; Sudbourne; Undley; Wratting, West

Sugge (Sug), William, of Hadleigh, bailiff of Kersey, Suff., 198-9, 209-10

suit, of court (not *pro omnibus serviciis sectis*), 231, 256 (fo. 173r), 257 (fo. 174r)

— — owed at Foxton, 124, 128

— — of palace of Ely, 257 (fo. 173v)

— of hundred, 66, 243, 257 (fo. 173v)

— of mill, 72; 163

Sumeresham, Summeresham, *see* Somersham

sureties (*fidejussores*), 118

surrender, 75, 137

— in Barley, Herts., 173

— in Burwell, 236

— in Chatteris, 22, 64, 254

— in Doddington, 254

— in Foxton, 133, 135, 138, 148

— in Shepreth, 153-4

— *see also* release; reversion

suspension from celebration of divine service, 162

Sutburna, Suthburna, see Sudbourne

Sutton (*Suthona,* Sutton', *Suttona,* Suttun', *Suttuna*), 269 (fo. 181r), 279

Swaffham Bulbeck priory, 20, 23, 40, 47

Swaffham Prior (Suafham, Suaham, Suuasham, Swafham Prioris, Swafham Priour, Swauesham), 269 (fo. 181v)

— ninth in, 261 (fo. 178r)

— *see* Bokeland, William, of; Radewyn, Richard, of

Sweyn, Warin son of, 121

Swine priory, Yorks. E., 93, 95

Swythesthorp, Richard de, knight, 112

Sybry, John, W 209

Symon *see* Simon

Syon abbey, Middx, 40

tailor (*cissor,* le taillur', talliour, taylour), *see* John; Ralph

Taillour, John, chaplain, 105

Talbot, John, of Hadleigh, Suff., 209-10

talentum, talentum auri, see gold coin

tallage, 65; 144, 256 (fo. 173r), 257 (fo. 174r)

Tankerville (*Tancarvill', Tancarvilla*), earl of, *see* Gray, Henry

— William de, W 6n

taxation of pope Nicholas IV, 30-1, 38-9, 60, 123; 260 (fo. 177r), 261 (fo. 178r), 264-5

taylour *see* tailor

Temple *see* knights templar

temporalities, of Chatteris abbey, valuation of, 264

— of Chatteris abbey and Anglesey priory, in Barley, Herts., 260

— — in Cambs., 261

— of see of Ely, 7

tenants, 147, 187, 189, 201, 259 (fo. 176r)
— of Chatteris abbey, 163, 182, 230, 276
tenements, 8, 90, 212, 255, 256 (fo. 172v), 257 (fo. 174r), 258 (fo. 174v), 259 (fo. 176r), 280
— in Barley, Herts., 171–4, 260
— in Barrington, 100, 114–15, 119, 123–4
— in Bircham, Norf., 91, 222–5
— in Cambridge, 105, 108
— in Chatteris, 13, 19, 26, 80, 254
— in Doddington, 254
— in Ely, 99
— in Foxton, 115, 119, 126, 130, 143–4, 148, 241
— in Kersey, Suff., 209–10
— in Kingston, 111
— in Lynn, Norf., 214, 219–20
— in Shepreth, 154–5, 241, 261 (fo. 178v)
— in Thriplow, 168
— in Upwell and Outwell, Cambs. and Norf., 87
tenth, clerical subsidy of, 260
Terrington (*Tirentuna, Tirintunia, Tyrentuna, Tyrintunia*), Norf., 269 (fo. 181r)
Tey (Teye), William de, 260n
Thecesham, Stephen de, 60
Thetford, Little (Liteltiædford, Liteltiedford, Lithlethedford, Litlethetford, Lyteltieford, Parva Thetford, Parva Thetforth', Thetford), 269 (fo. 181r), 278
— rent in, 30, 43; 90 (fo. 102r), 91 (fo. 103r)
Thidbriteseia, see Ely, Turbutsey farm
Thomas [of Barrington], 121
— chaplain of Chatteris, 105; 50
— — Alice niece of, *alias* Moyngne, Alice formerly wife of Geoffrey le, 105; 50, 57
— clerk (le clerk), 249
— dispenser (*dispensarius*), of Chatteris, 44, 77; 52, 81
— parson of Burwell, W 110, W 238
— William son of, 168
Thorington (Thorinton, Thorunton), Roger de, W 162n

— — (?*same*), 30–1
Thornborough (Thornbrowgh), William, 54
Thorney abbey, 10
— abbot of, 23
Thriplow (Treplowe, Triplow, Trippelawe, Trippelowe, Tryppelowe), 278
— land in, 27, 30, 43–4, 72; 3 (fo. 74r), 165–8
— messuage in, 168
— mill in, 27, 43–4, 59, 72; 3 (fo. 74r), 7, 95, 165–7
— sheep-fold in, 167
— stream (*filum aque*) between Whittlesford and, 168
— Guy son of Felka de, 143
— Henry son of William son of Alexander de, 129
— *see also* Marvin, John, of
Thurstan (*Turstanus*), clerk of the Temple and scribe, 130; W 227
Tidbrichteseia, Tidbricteseya, Tidbridteseia, Tidbrigteseia, Tidbriteseia, see Ely, Turbutsey farm
Tilly, Katherine, nun of Chatteris, 413
Tilney (*Tilneia*), William de, M, W 204
timber (*arbor, ligna, meremium*), 51, 163, 269 (fo. 181r); *see also* felling; woods
Tirentuna, Tirintunia, see Terrington
Tison, Gilbert, 15
tithes, 23, 33, 71, 92; 3, 269 (fo. 181r), 270 (fo. 183r)
— in Barley, Herts., 33, 36, 64, 76; 180–2, 277
— in Barrington, 33, 36–7, 64, 71; 112
— in Barton, Ely, 269 (fo. 181r)
— in Chatteris, 34; 79
— in Honey Hill, 33, 35–6; 3 (fo. 74v), 164
— in Shepreth, 35; 161
tithe-suit, 36–7, 64, 71; 112, 181
Toft (Toftes), Reginald de, W 221
tofts, 30, 101–3, 230, 256–8
toll and team, 5, 9
treasurer, royal, 7, 164, 259 (fo. 176v), 260n; *see also* Ely, William of; FitzNeal, Richard

trees *see* felling; timber; woods
Treplowe, Triplow, Trippelawe,
    Trippelowe, Tryppelowe, *see*
    Thriplow
'tripechett'', 189
tumbrel, 189
Tunteneya, see Stuntney
turfs, 43
Turnour', William, 212n
Turstanus, see Thurstan
Tydbrytesya, see Ely, Turbutsey farm
Tydd (Tyd, Tydde), Katherine, nun of
    Chatteris, 413
— Nicholas, 44; 280
— — of Chatteris, 80
Tyrentuna, Tyrintunia, see Terrington

Ufton *see* Offton
Ulster (Duluestre, *Ulton', Ultonia*), earl
    of, *see* Mortimer, Edmund
Undley (*Undelea, Undeleia*), Suff., 269
    (fo. 181v)
Uprey, Walter, 149 (fo. 129v)
Upwell and Outwell (Well', Welles),
    Cambs. and Norf., 278
— fee in, 52; 87
— 'Bradewere', fishery, ?in, 43, 52, 101;
    87
— 'Neustale', fishery, ?in, 43, 52, 101; 87
— 'Tryllinge' (Tryllynge), fishery, 30, 43;
    90 (fo. 102r), 91 (fo. 102v)
uses, 3 (fo. 74v), 10, 76, 260 (fo. 177v),
    269; *see also* appropriation

vacancy, at Chatteris abbey, 21–3
— in see of Ely, 7
Valor Ecclesiasticus, 38, 40
valuation, of mill, 163
— of Norwich, 38
Vasie (Vasy, Vasye), Margaret, nun of
    Chatteris, 413, 418, 420
Vasohowffyl the elder, 280
Vasy, Vasye, *see* Vasie
Vavasour, Alan le, 149 (fo. 129r)
veil, of nun, 170; *see also* habit

Veirus, Alice, 135
— William son of, 129
Vevien *see* Vivien
vicar *see* John
— of Chatteris, *see* Alan; Buckworth,
    Henry; Ralph
— of Shepreth, *see* Shepreth
vicarage *see* Chatteris church; Shepreth
    church
Victor II, pope, 269
view of frank-pledge, 15–17; 189, 256 (fo.
    173r), 257 (fo. 174r)
vigilia, see watch
villeinage, 63, 67; 100, 121, 123, 271, 274
villeins (*coloni, nativi, villani*), 62, 65–9,
    77, 80, 130; 75, 100, 119, 123, 137,
    161, 180, 271–2, 274
vineyard, 3 (fo. 74v), 269 (fo. 181r)
virgate, 75, 111, 129–30, 137, 144, 180,
    185
visitations, 17–20, 22, 52, 84–8, 98–9
Vite, Robert le, *alias* Hotte, Robert, 17,
    59
Vivien (Vevien, Viven, Vivian), John, of
    Chatteris, 47, 123; 31–4, 36–7, 83,
    233, 275
— — Gonnora, former wife of Richard,
    carter, and sister of, 83, 275
— — Henry, father of, 83, 233, 275
Vycary, John, 257 (fo. 173r)

Wadsand *see* Watsand
Waldingfield (Waldyngefeld'), William
    de, W 204
Wales, prince of, *see* Edward
Waleys, Adam de, of Kersey, Suff., 189
Walpole (Walpol), Henry de, W 235
Walpole, Ralph de, bp of Ely, 246
Walter, cordwainer, *see* Elwin,
    cordwainer
— parson of Haslingfield, W 110, W 238
— son, W 243
— Robert son of, 121
— Walter son of, 104, 106
Walton, Alfred de, 213–15, 217
— — Henry brother of, 213–15, 217

— — William brother of, 213–15, 217

war, in reign of Stephen, 180

Waratinga, Warattinga, see Wratting, West

Warde, Hugh, 257 (fo. 173r)

ward-penny, 6, 9, 269 (fo. 180v)

wardship, 65, 100, 115, 123, 240

warranty, default of, 99, 171

— vouched, 171–2

warren, 189

Warren, Sir Ralph, 32

Wartinge, Warttinge, see Wratting, West

Waryn, John, of Barrington, clerk, 62; 113

— — of Kersey, Suff., 209–10

watch (*vigilia*), 256 (fo. 173r), 257 (fo. 174r), 269 (fo. 180v)

watercourse (*cursu aque*), 119; *see also* stream

Watesford', Ralph de, 189

Watsand (Wadsand, Wydgand'), Alan de, justice in eyre, 142

Wattisham (Wechesham), Gerard de, 61; 222

wax, as rent, 162

Waylond, Simon, 212n

Weasenham (Wesenham), John de, farmer of temporalities of bishopric of Ely, 7

Webbe, Nicholas, of Kersey, Suff., 209

Webster, Richard, 280

Wechesham *see* Wattisham

weir (*gordus, gurges, paludes*), 84–6, 119, 269 (fo. 181r), 270 (fo. 183r)

well, 121

Well', Welle, Welles, see Upwell and Outwell

Wenlock minster, Shrops., 13n

Wentworth (*Winteuurþa, Winteuurtha,* Winteword', *Wintewrda,* Wyntewore, Wyntewrth', *Wyntwortha*), 269 (fo. 181r)

— Pain de, 65, W 275

Werry, wife, 163

Wesenham *see* Weasenham

West', Simon, 118

— Warin, vicar of Chatteris, 105

Westminster (Westm', Westmon'), abbey, monks of, 61

— adcn of, 112

— documents dated at, 7–9, 190 (fo. 147r), 255, 256 (fo. 173r), 258 (fo. 175r), 259 (fo. 176v)

— final concord made at, 178

— hall of, 179

Weston, Juliana, nun of Chatteris, 413

Wherwell abbey, Hants., 3, 20, 22, 37, 40

Whitefield (Whitefeld'), Robert de, W 9

Whiteheed', John, villein of Chatteris, 68; 274

White Ladies priory, *see* Worcester

Whittlesey (*Withleseia, Witleseia, Witleseya, Wytleseya*), 269 (fo. 181r)

— William, abp of Canterbury, 18

Whittlesford (Witlesford), stream (*filum aque*) between Thriplow and, 168

Wicgeford, Wich', Wicheford, *see* Witchford

Wicheam, Wicheham, *see* Witcham

Wichford *see* Witchford

widow *see* Andrew, Alan son of; Basilia; Edith; Horseheath, Agnes

widowhood, 29, 44, 49, 57–8, 61, 66, 106, 240, 275

Wighton (Wyghton), Elizabeth, nun of Chatteris, 414

— William, 210

Wilberfoss priory, Yorks. E., 91

Wilberton' *see* Wilburton

Wilbraham, Little (Wylberam Parva, Wylberham Parva), ninth in, 261 (fo. 178r)

Wilburton (Wilberton'), property in, 31, 39

— revenue from temporalities in, 264

Wilford (Wylford), William, W 210

will, land held at, 132, 135, 141

William, abbot of Ramsey, *see* Godmanchester, William de

— adcn of Cleveland, *see* Ely, William of

— adcn of Ely, *see* Lavington, William de

— bp of Ely, *see* Longchamp, William

— carpenter, of Fowlmere, *see* Alice, former wife of

— chaplain of St Mary, W 204

— cordwainer, *see* Elwin, cordwainer
— potter (le pottere), Walter son of, **253**
— — Agnes wife of, **253**
— priest (*sacerdos*), **151**
— smith (*faber*), **50, 57**
— treasurer, *see* Ely, William of
— Eustace son of, **239**
Willingham, 17
Willy, Margery, nun of Chatteris, 414
Wilmyngton *see* Wimblington
Wilton (Wylton'), Wilts., abbey, 3–4, 20, 37, 40, 96, 117
— William de, justice in eyre, 142
Wimar, William, burgess of Lynn, Norf., **225**
— — Agnes wife of, **225**
Wimblington (Wilmyngton, Wimlington, Wyllmyngton', Wylmyngton', Wymlygton', Wymlyngton'), **278**
— property in, 15, 31, 39, 42–3; **245, 256** (fo. 172v), **257** (fo. 173v), **258** (fo. 174v)
— 'Bradforlong" in, **245**
— Coneywood (Coniwode) in, **245**
— *see also* Balsham, John, of
Wimpole (Wympol, Wynepol), property in, 48
— rent in, 111
Winchelsey, Robert, abp of Canterbury, 21, 106
Winchester (*Wyntonia*), Hants., cathedral priory, cartulary of, 117
— Nunminster in, 3, 37, 95–6
— earl of, *see* Despenser, Hugh le
Wingfield (Wingefeld), Robert, 77
Winteuurþa, Winteuurtha, Winteword', *Wintewrda, see* Wentworth
Winwick (Wynewyk), John, of Chatteris, 44; **80**
Wisbech, hundred court of, 15
Witcham (Wicheam, Wicheham, Wycheham, Wycham), **269** (fo. 181r), **279**
— John de, W **233**
Witchford (Wicgeford, Wich', Wicheford, Wichford, Wych', Wycheford), **269** (fo. 181r)

— hundred, court of, 15; **257** (fo. 173v)
— — courts leet in, 16
Withleseia, Witleseia, Witleseya, *see* Whittlesey
Witlesford *see* Whittlesford
witnesses, 112, 180–1
witness-lists, 41, 46; **5, 6n, 9, 80, 109–10,** 162n, 204, 221, 227, 231, 233–5, 238–41, 243, 259, 275, 281
Wittham *see* Witham
Wlfrith (Wlfrich), John, **39, 42–3**
Wlsius *see* Wulfsige
Wlwina (Wluina), Osbert son of, **129**
— William son of, **129**
Wolflete, William, dean of college of Stoke, 210
Wolmar, William, **149** (fo. 129r)
women benefactors, 48–9
woods (*boscum, nemus, silva*), 3 (fo. 74v), 26–7, 40, 186, 270 (fo. 183r); *see also* felling; timber
Wootton (Wotton'), William son of Wluric de, 30, 63; **213–17**
Worcester, monk of, *see* Eadnoth
— White Ladies priory, 102
works *see* boon-work; carrying-service; labour-services; plough-service
Wotton' *see* Wootton
Woveton', Batill' de, abbess of Chatteris, 398; **254**
Wratting, West (*Waratinga, Warattinga,* Wartinge, Warttinge, *Wrattinga*), Suff., **269** (fo. 181v)
writ, 7, 8n, 190, 212, 230, 255, **256** (fo. 173r), **257** (fo. 173r), **260** (fo. 176v), **261** (fo. 178r), **262**
Wroh, Matilda de, 30
Wroxall priory, Warwicks., 88
Wulfsige (Wlsius), abbot of Ramsey, 2
Wych' *see* Witchford
Wycham *see* Witcham
Wycheford *see* Witchford
Wycheham *see* Witcham
Wydgand' *see* Watsand
Wyghton *see* Wighton
Wylberam Parva, Wylberham Parva, *see* Wilbraham, Little
Wyld', Walter le, **156**

Wylford *see* Wilford

Wyllmyngton', Wylmyngton',
    Wymlygton', Wymlyngton', *see*
    Wimblington

Wylton' *see* Wilton

Wymar, John son of, 111

Wymart (Wymar'), land of, 149 (fo.
    129v)

— Richard, 149 (fo. 128v)

Wympol, Wynepol *see* Wimpole

Wymund', Robert, 107

— Walter, 105

Wynewyk *see* Winwick

Wynter (Wynt'), Andrew, 135, 138

— Edmund, steward of earl of
    Huntingdon, 201

Wyntewore, Wyntewrth', *Wyntwortha,*
    see Wentworth

Wyntonia, see Winchester

Wytereshulle, Isabella de, 22

Wytleseya, see Whittlesey

yard (*curtilagium*), 60, 248

Yedingham priory, Yorks. N., 93

Yepeswych *see* Ipswich

York, abp of, *see* Oswald

— Clementhorpe priory, 6, 12n, 57

— men of city and diocese of, 112

Yselham *see* Isleham

Yvo *see* Ivo